Human Rights and the Private Sphere

A Comparative Study

Human Rights and the Private Sphere: A Comparative Study analyses the interplay between constitutional rights and freedoms on the one hand and private law on the other, and the extent to which human rights are protected in the private sphere in fifteen jurisdictions. Focusing on civil and political rights, the book is composed of contributions by constitutional and private law experts covering Canada, Denmark, France, Germany, Greece, India, Ireland, Israel, Italy, New Zealand, South Africa, Spain, England and Wales, the United States, and the European Convention for the Protection of Human Rights and Fundamental Freedoms. The book concludes with a comparative essay, which sets out the common features and differences in the jurisdictions under review and attempts to identify common trends in this important area of the law, and a chart which summarises the position in each jurisdiction in the study, designed to guide readers to particular points of comparison.

References to the most important cases in the various jurisdictions and a detailed index make *Human Rights and the Private Sphere* a valuable resource both for academics and practitioners.

Dawn Oliver is Professor of Constitutional Law at University College London. She is particularly interested in constitutional reform, the UK Human Rights Act 1998, and the public law/private law divide. She is the author of *Constitutional Reform in the United Kingdom* (OUP, 2003) and co-editor of *The Changing Constitution* (OUP, 6th edn, 2007). In 2005 she was elected a Fellow of the British Academy.

Jörg Fedtke is Reader in Comparative Law at University College London, where he is Director of the Institute of Global Law. He also holds a post as Visiting Professor at the University of Texas at Austin, where he teaches European Union and comparative constitutional law. In 2005 he was invited by the United Nations to act as an external advisor to the constitutional negotiations in Iraq. His research interests are in constitutional law, administrative law, comparative methodology and tort law.

The University of Texas at Austin, Studies in Foreign and Transnational Law
General Editors: Sir Basil Markesinis and Dr Jörg Fedtke

The *UT Studies in Foreign and Transnational Law* series aims to publish books covering various aspects of foreign, private, criminal, and public law as well as transnational law. This broad ambit of the series underlines the editors' belief that in a shrinking world there is a growing need to expand our knowledge of other legal orders – national or supranational – and to publish books discussing comparative methodology and not merely describing foreign systems.

Titles in the series:
The French Civil Code, J.-L. Halpérin, transl. T. Weir
Judicial Recourse to Foreign Law, B. Markesinis and J. Fedtke
International Negotiation in the Twenty-First Century, A. Plantey, transl. F. Meadows
Italian Private Law, G. Alpa and V. Zeno-Zencovich

Forthcoming titles
Civil Disobedience and the German Court: The Pershing Missile Protests in Comparative Perspective, P.E. Quint (2007)
The Protection of Human Rights in German and English Law, J. Fedtke and M. O'Cinneide (2008)

HUMAN RIGHTS AND THE PRIVATE SPHERE

A Comparative Study

Edited by Dawn Oliver and Jörg Fedtke

First published 2007
by Routledge-Cavendish
2 Park Square, Milton Park, Abingdon, Oxon, OX14 4RN

Simultaneously published in the USA and Canada
by Routledge-Cavendish
270 Madison Ave, New York NY 10016

Routledge-Cavendish is an imprint of the Taylor & Francis Group, an informa business

Transferred to Digital Printing 2007

Typeset in Sabon by Exeter Premedia Services Private Ltd, Chennai, India

British Library Cataloguing in Publication Data
A catalogue record for this book is available from the British Library

Library of Congress Cataloging in Publication Data
A catalog record for this book has been requested

ISBN10: 0–415–42301–5 (hbk)
ISBN10: 0–415–44351–2 (pbk)

ISBN13: 978–0–415–42301–4 (hbk)
ISBN13: 978–0–415–44351–7 (pbk)

Contents

Preface ix

PART I: INTRODUCTION

Human Rights and the Private Sphere – the Scope of the Project 3
Dawn Oliver and *Jörg Fedtke*

PART II: NATIONAL JURISDICTIONS

European Convention on Human Rights

Chapter 1: Denmark 27
Drittwirkung and Conflicting Rights – Viewed from National and International Perspectives
Jonas Christoffersen

Chapter 2: England and Wales 63
The Human Rights Act and the Private Sphere
Dawn Oliver

Chapter 3: France 98
Horizontal Application and the Triumph of the European Convention on Human Rights
Myriam Hunter-Henin

Chapter 4: Germany 125
Drittwirkung in Germany
Jörg Fedtke

Chapter 5: Greece 157
Taking Private Law Seriously in the Application of Constitutional Rights
Christina Akrivopoulou

Chapter 6: India 180
Protection of Human Rights against State and Non-State Action
Mahendra P. Singh

Chapter 7: Ireland 213
Irish Constitutional Law and Direct Horizontal Effect – A Successful Experiment?
Colm O'Cinneide

Chapter 8: Israel 252
Human Rights in Private Law – The Israeli Case
Daphne Barak-Erez and *Israel Gilead*

Chapter 9: Italy 276
The Protection of Constitutional Rights in the Private Sphere
Chiara Favilli and *Carlo Fusaro*

Chapter 10: New Zealand 312
Taking Human Rights into the Private Sphere
Paul Rishworth

Chapter 11: South Africa 351
From Indirect to Direct Effect in South Africa: A System in Transition
Jörg Fedtke

Chapter 12: Spain 378
A Jurisdiction Recognising the Direct Horizontal Application of Human Rights
Andrea Rodríguez Liboreiro

Chapter 13: The United States and Canada 399
State Action, Constitutional Rights and Private Actors
Eric Barendt

Chapter 14: The European Convention on Human Rights 427
The European Court of Human Rights
Dean Spielmann

PART III: COMPARATIVE ANALYSIS

Comparative Analysis 467
Dawn Oliver and *Jörg Fedtke*

Country by Country Chart 520

Further Reading 558
The Authors of this Book 568
Index 571

Preface

The interplay between private law and human rights guarantees is becoming increasingly topical and often problematic in a number of democracies around the world. Whereas at one time it was assumed that human rights protection could bind only states in their relationships with citizens, nowadays it is widely accepted that citizens may also require legal protection against the abuse of power by private bodies. Much of this protection is provided by ordinary legislation; most countries make provision for the protection of constitutional interests such as privacy or the security of tenure for tenants (to take just two examples from the many areas of the law discussed in this collection). But in some jurisdictions the protection has a more 'fundamental' or 'entrenched' legal status than ordinary legislation. It is this kind of special protection that is the subject matter of our study.

Our focus is on what are generally considered to be 'first generation' rights, namely the range of civil and political rights that find expression in national constitutions such as those of the United States or Germany, and international instruments such as the European Convention on Human Rights or the International Covenant on Civil and Political Rights. This focus on civil and political rights is not to suggest that second generation social and economic rights or third generation environmental and cultural rights are any less important; the fact of the matter is, however, that civil and political rights find expression in constitutional documents more commonly than second or third generation rights, and their protection in the private sphere is more developed in most systems. It may very well be that the next project should be a study of the protection offered to second and third generation rights in the private sphere.

The list of colleagues who have contributed to this collection of essays spans the globe. It was a fruitful collaboration, for which we are most grateful.

13 December 2006
Bentham House
University College London

Dawn Oliver
Jörg Fedtke

Part I: Introduction

Human Rights and the Private Sphere – the Scope of the Project

Dawn Oliver and Jörg Fedtke

This book is about some of the ways in which private individuals and bodies are required by law to respect the civil and political rights of others. It is a question of considerable practical importance and, in many systems, political relevance. Some of the countries considered in this collection have moved fairly recently towards new forms of human rights protection and are now considering how – if at all – these changes impact on the private sphere. South Africa (with its new constitutional settlements of 1993 and 1996) and the United Kingdom (with the introduction of the Human Rights Act 1998) fall into this category. Others have been grappling with the issue of private sphere protection for decades: in these jurisdictions outbursts of debate and discussion still take place when new legislation is passed or when court decisions are made on the subject. Germany is a good example. We shall be considering how human rights have affected private relationships in these and a range of other jurisdictions, and seeking to draw lessons from comparisons between them. The application of human rights protections such as are found in constitutional documents, case law or international instruments in the private sphere is, as we shall see, conceptualised in different ways in different jurisdictions. In Germany the fairly well-know term *Drittwirkung* (or 'third party effect') is used but, as we shall see, there are a number of other ways in which the effect or function of private sphere protection is expressed. We have chosen the phrase 'human rights and the private sphere' as the title for this collection in order to be able to generalise about these issues and avoid assuming any particular model or conceptualisation of the phenomenon.

In this introductory chapter we consider a number of general issues before moving on to the jurisdiction-based chapters in Part II.

With what senses of human *rights* is this project concerned? Why have we focused on civil and political rights rather than social, economic, cultural or environmental rights? What rationales or reasons might be offered for civil and political rights to apply in the private sphere? What are the sources of private sphere rights? What are the positive and negative implications of extending rights protection to the private sphere, and how does private sphere protection affect public-private divides? We now turn to these.

A. Human 'rights'

A question that is bound to arise in what follows is: what is implied by the fact that our inquiry is into whether and how human *rights* are protected in the private sphere? All democratic legal systems provide substantial private sphere protections, though of varying degrees, for life, liberty, privacy, freedom of association, property, speech, conscience and so on against intrusion by individuals or private bodies, even in the absence of a bill of rights or equivalent domestic law instrument. Criminal law punishes murder, manslaughter, assault, false imprisonment, damage to property and, commonly, speech that causes disturbances or breaches of the peace. Civil law or the law of tort also protects these interests, plus reputation, and, in various ways, privacy. In every country rights to marry and divorce and the upbringing of children are regulated. But the concept of 'human *rights*' with which we are concerned here entails that the rights or freedoms in question enjoy *enhanced* or *special* legal status and protection, over and above that provided by the ordinary domestic criminal or civil law. That said, it is also important to note that the content of particular rights such as freedom, property, or privacy may differ within a single legal system. Even 'life' is sometimes defined differently depending on whether the notion is used in the constitutional, criminal or private law context. This in turn begs the question whether these various sub-systems exist side by side or, alternatively, whether a right or freedom with enhanced or special (typically constitutional) status should override or in some other way affect the way particular interests are protected in other parts of a legal system.

In the absence of special legal protection, it is generally considered to be lawful for the legislature to authorise interference with these rights or freedoms by the passage of legislation according to normal procedures – commonly simple majorities in the chambers of an elected parliament – just as it can normally change the law relating to, for example, traffic regulation. It does not follow from the fact, if it is the case, that human 'rights' do not receive *special* legal protection in the private sphere, that they receive *no* protection at all. The extent to which the protection of the ordinary law in practice secures that these rights are not infringed depends in large part on what private law actually lays down, on whether and to what extent private sphere relationships are regulated by statutory provisions (e.g. in relation to employment), on the political culture (i.e. whether the legislature and the executive do in fact take steps to secure that these 'rights' are legally protected, even without any 'special' legal status), and the civic culture (the extent to which in practice private bodies such as the press, employers, landlords etc. feel it to be legitimate for them to interfere with the 'rights' of those with whom they have dealings). This calls for two additional observations. Private interests can, first, be at risk not only through legislative or judicial *inactivity* – where the outcome of disputes is left to the free competition of social or market forces – but also through legislative or judicial *activity* which favours one particular private interest over another. When it comes to the protection of individual rights, state intervention in private relationships can thus be as relevant as regulatory restraint. It is, second, sometimes difficult or even impossible to determine who actually 'interferes' with a right in a particular situation. To take two examples which have reached the courts in Germany: is the tenant who uses the façade of his rented apartment to display political placards or attach a television antenna 'interfering' with the property rights of the landlord, or is the landlord, in turn, 'interfering' with the rights of the tenant to free speech or unrestricted access to generally available information if he prohibits such use of his property? As will be discussed in more detail below, conflicts in the private sphere are characterised by the fact that both sides to the dispute can invoke rights, whereas only one – the citizen – will be able to do so in 'vertical' relationships with public authorities.

Special and institutionalised legal or political protection for human rights, where it exists, is generally designed primarily to give protection to rights vertically – against state bodies – rather than in the private sphere. But there are significant exceptions to this rule of the thumb, at least on the surface of things. In Europe, Greece is such an exception with its constitutional provision that constitutional rights 'apply to the relations between individuals to which they are appropriate'. In Southern Africa, Namibia and, since 1996, South Africa have expressly made their bills of rights binding on natural or juristic persons, though the effect of these rules remains ambiguous in constitutional practice. In India it has long been recognised that rights are commonly threatened by powerful private bodies rather than the state and thus human rights protection extends naturally to the private sphere. Finally, even systems which, *in principle*, take the view that constitutional rights should regulate only disputes between the state and its citizens often contain expressly codified exceptions. Germany's Basic Law of 1949 thus determines in Article 9(3) BL that private activities are directly subject to the right to form associations aimed at safeguarding and improving working conditions and, more generally, the economic environment of the country. The image of a general rule (vertical application) which is confirmed by single exceptions (horizontal application) is, however, dangerously deceptive. As we shall see, in a number of jurisdictions the courts have built on and developed existing constitutional rights so as to provide varying degrees of private sphere protection. But in other jurisdictions the declaration of a binding effect of human rights in the private sphere in the text of a constitution may have to be taken with a pinch of salt: in practical terms the relevant provision of the South African Constitution of 1996 on this is currently dead letter law.

Special protection can take a number of forms, as the chapters that follow will demonstrate. Weak protections include pre-legislative scrutiny of measures that would interfere with rights, with a view to deterring but not preventing the legislature from passing legislation that breaches rights. The United Kingdom is an example, as is New Zealand. The strongest protection exists where a Supreme Court or equivalent has the power to 'strike down' legislation or official action that interferes with rights, as in Germany and the United States. Between those two extremes of 'weak' and 'strong' protection are requirements that laws that may interfere with rights be 'read down' or interpreted compatibly with those rights, as in many of the jurisdictions in this study, or the practice of the courts in developing the law so as to give effect to human rights, as in Canada, Denmark, England and Wales, France, Greece, India, Ireland, Israel and New Zealand. Other techniques include: the recognition either in a constitutional text or by the judiciary of the importance of particular *values* (on which see below) that underlie rights (as in the United Kingdom, Greece and Israel); special powers for the executive to introduce amending legislation removing incompatibilities with human rights (as in the United Kingdom); special legislative majorities (as in the United States); and delaying powers (as, again, in the United Kingdom). These various mechanisms can exist side by side in single systems, which will often seek to combine their effects not only with a view to enhancing human rights protection but also to uphold other constitutional principles. In Germany, the exceptional power wielded by the Federal Constitutional Court is thus tempered by the use of interpretative techniques which seek, as far as possible, to uphold statutes (*verfassungskonforme Auslegung*) in order to maintain the division of powers between the legislature and the judiciary.

In common parlance the word 'right' in a human rights context refers to specific rights to, for instance, life, freedom of expression and association, privacy and so on. These rights are in practice concrete expressions of deeper and often overlapping values such as autonomy, dignity, respect, or equality. In some jurisdictions these deeper values are expressed as rights; an Israeli Basic Law, for example, refers to a right to human dignity. But in many jurisdictions these values underlie rights, and recognition of their existence and importance influences the courts when deciding particular cases which have to do with rights.

B. Civil and political rights

Our concerns in this book are with private sphere protection of civil and political rights. These commonly find expression in domestic instruments – written constitutions – either self-executing or not self-executing, basic laws, bills or charters of rights, and laws incorporating international human rights provisions into domestic law. This is true for all of the jurisdictions covered by our study. They are also included in many international instruments such as the European Convention on Human Rights (ECHR), the International Covenant on Civil and Political Rights (ICCPR), and the Harare Declaration of Human Rights. Many of the jurisdictions in our study are parties to the ECHR, whose protections are broadly typical of the rights set out in many constitutions or human rights instruments. They include the right to life (Article 2), freedom from torture or inhuman and degrading treatment (Article 3), freedom from slavery (Article 4), the rights to liberty and security (Article 5), a fair trial (Article 6), respect for private and family life (Article 8), freedom of thought, conscience and religion (Article 9), freedom of expression (Article 10), freedom of assembly and association (Article 11), the rights to marry and found a family (Article 12), freedom from discrimination of various kinds (Article 14), rights to peaceful enjoyment of possessions (First Protocol, Article 1), to education (First Protocol, Article 2), and to vote and participate in free elections (First Protocol, Article 3).

But there are many more rights that could be covered in a discussion of the protection of human rights in the private sphere – social and economic rights, environmental and cultural ones' for instance. Our focus on civil and political rights is not intended to suggest that second generation social and economic rights, or third generation environmental or cultural rights, are any less important. The fact of the matter is that there is a greater degree of comparability between the protection of first generation rights, and there is a more developed system for their protection in private law than there is in relation to second and third generation rights. Perhaps because civil and political rights find expression more commonly than second or third generation rights in constitutional documents, they are starting to penetrate the private sphere more recognisably than are second and third generation rights. Significantly, in some jurisdictions – India is a strong example – environmental rights are protected via civil rights as the courts develop the idea that a right to a healthy environment is embraced in the right to life, for instance. Another example is Greece, where the constitutional rights to respect for the natural and cultural environment and personality have enabled the judges to hold that the right to personality enshrined in the Greek Civil Code protects those constitutional rights. Our decision to focus on civil and political rights is thus largely pragmatic, influenced by the availability of material and considerations of space – a book that covered all rights would be enormous. We also feel that socio-economic rights are, in the vast majority of cases, directed more against the state than single fellow citizens, though even classical-liberal constitutions can include some very specific socio-economic rights and obligations such as the duty of parents to care for the wellbeing of their children.[1] Finally, the vast differences between most systems when it comes to environmental regulation, health care, education and social security protection would render a more comprehensive study difficult, if not impossible.

At this point we need to address a number of fundamental questions about the application of human rights in the private sphere which we anticipate will recur in many of the jurisdictions that will be explored in Part II of the book. Since this is a comparative study and one of our objectives is to bring the similarities and differences between the legal systems under consideration, we shall not seek definitive answers to these questions. To do so would constrain unduly the contributions in Part II of the study. But it will be useful at least to articulate the principal issues that arise. In the comparative section of the book (Part III), we shall try to draw together the threads from the chapters in Part II.

C. Rationales for human rights protection

The first and perhaps most fundamental question is: what are the rationales for the protection of civil and political rights, whether against state or private interference? And, given the rationales that lie behind each jurisdiction's approach to this matter, what are the arguments for and against extending human rights protections against the state to the private sphere?

The rationales for the protection of civil and political rights vary from country to country. They reflect the different cultures and histories that have given rise to constitutionalised human rights protection, and they affect the forms such protections take. The United States was the first country to adopt a bill of rights in 1791. A number of former British colonies and dominions had bills or charters of rights included in their constitutions on achieving independence, often at the initiative of the United Kingdom, the colonial power. As we shall see, some bills of rights explicitly limit protection to state action (as in the United States and Canada) while others are silent on the reach of protection so that it has been left to the courts to respond to claims that protection does indeed extend to the private sphere. The reasons for these differences have varied. Liberal economic theory has been

[1] See Article 6(2) of the German Basic Law.

one – acceptance of a need to protect private economic actors not only from state interference but from non-contractual liabilities to other private parties, including employees and customers, with whom they deal. Mistrust of the executive is another strong theme. Expressed more openly in recently drafted bills of rights such as the South African, which has established a right to just administrative action, the idea that the individual may need special rights as a protection against powerful public administrations has spurred human rights thinking in many systems. Access to information held by public authorities, data protection, and the special rights of arrested, detained or accused persons are other examples of rights closely linked to the need to make public authorities more accountable. The principle of proportionality, finally, to which we shall return shortly, also reflects this concern in that it requires the state to show that a particular measure was indeed suitable to reach a certain public aim, necessary for lack of less onerous alternatives, and reasonable with respect to the burden placed on the individual citizen.

Human rights protections became a particular concern of international bodies in the aftermath of the Second World War experiences of abuse by state bodies, and this is reflected in human rights instruments adopted in that post-war period such as the International Covenant on Civil and Political Rights and the European Convention on Human Rights. Consciousness of the dangers of abuses by the state was higher than that of abuse by powerful private bodies at that time, though the human rights infringements by professional bodies, schools and universities, commercial and industrial enterprises, and scientific and cultural institutions in Hitler's Germany and Mussolini's Italy had already shown the significant dangers that human rights are exposed to in the private sphere. States are, however, the parties to international instruments, individuals are not. States would be directly responsible under these instruments for their own interferences with human rights, whereas their responsibility for interferences by private bodies would be less direct – though they may exist nonetheless, as under the doctrine of positive obligation developed by the European Court of Human Rights.

The lessons of the Second World War thus included the need to protect individuals against state power, expressed in the European Convention. The United Kingdom then found itself committed to the protection of civil and political rights. But its own view was that the common law and the United Kingdom's national constitutional arrangements provided perfectly satisfactory protection, and there was no need for the country itself to incorporate the Convention into domestic law.[2] However, the United Kingdom was less confident of the commitment of some of its former colonies and dominions to the protection of these rights, and therefore included bills or charters of rights in the constitutions which the British government was normally very active in drafting and approving for them. The point brings out a factor that will be influential both in the decisions in particular jurisdictions as to whether human rights protections are required, and also as to the democratic theories that underlie such decisions. For instance, in Anglo-American jurisprudence there is a strong pro-majoritarian theme, to the effect that it would be wrong and undemocratic to restrict the ability of the majority to pass whatever laws it desires.[3] But this approach is explicitly limited, for instance by Waldron,[4] to systems where democratic institutions are in reasonably good working order; where a set of independent judicial institutions upholds the Rule of Law; where there is a general social commitment to the idea of individual and minority rights; and where there is persistent, substantial and good-faith disagreement about rights. If constitutional protections for human rights that limit the powers of the majority are included in a constitution, one explanation may be that the makers of the constitution were not confident that the society and its culture possessed these qualities.

Many mainland European countries which had experienced defeat or occupation in the Second World War came to accept that reliance on international law, politics, parliamentary sovereignty and a majoritarian system exposed them to the risk of abuse of power of the kind they were just recovering from at the time that the ECHR was drafted and they were adopting their own new constitutions. Thus it was considered right for Germany, for instance, and some other European constitutions to include entrenched

---

2 See E. Wicks, '"Declaratory of existing rights" – the UK's role in drafting a European Bill of Rights, Mark II' [2001] *Public Law* 527.

3 See, e.g., J. Goldsworthy, *The Sovereignty of Parliament. History and Philosophy* (1999); J. Waldron, *Law and Disagreement* (1999).

4 See, e.g., J. Waldron, op. cit. note 3, and 'Some models of dialogue between judges and legislators', *Supreme Court Law Review* (2d), 23 (2004) 7.

human rights protections where their pre-war arrangements had not done so. This trend formed part of the move towards constitutionalism, the idea that governments, parliaments and the judiciary should be subject to some formal constraints in the exercise of their powers, not only in the interests of individuals who might be damaged by their activity, but also in the name of keeping the political system and its processes open and in that sense democratic.[5] The German counterpart to the English Rule of Law, the *Rechtsstaatsprinzip* or constitutional state principle, symbolises this shift in that it demands not only formal adherence to established procedures but also respect for substantive values as expressed in human rights provisions, the principle of proportionality, and, more generally, the idea of justice (*ein auf Gerechtigkeit bezogener Staat*). This wider notion of the Rule of Law in many ways supports democratic rule by safeguarding core freedoms such as free speech, freedom of association, and freedom of assembly, which democracy inherently depends on. At the same time, however, the principle limits the will of the democratically elected majority by protecting these rights against undue limitation. Despite this general 'Continental' trend, however, we still find interesting differences in the effect or enforceability of constitutional human rights protections. In Denmark and France, for instance, the constitutional provisions for human rights are not enforceable in the ordinary courts and are largely politically respected rather than judicially enforceable. In both jurisdictions the courts have, interestingly, turned to the ECHR as a source of rights that they may enforce, giving to the Convention a practical importance similar to the one it enjoys in the United Kingdom. To some extent, recourse to the Strasbourg Court thereby performs the function of a back door, which allows judges to put in question legislation duly enacted by parliament – a function which their national systems traditionally would not allow them to perform. By contrast, in Spain and Ireland constitutional rights may give rise to directly enforceable private (and public) sphere protection.

Most recently, the commitment of South Africa to a strongly entrenched bill of rights and explicit provision for its application in the private sphere reflects the history of apartheid and is the fruit of a conscious effort on the part of the drafters of the two

---

[5] See J. Hart Ely, *Democracy and Distrust* (1981).

constitutional arrangements of 1993 and 1996 to draw lessons from other successful democracies. Not surprisingly, Germany and its own transition from the Third Reich to the Basic Law of 1949 was of particular interest in this respect – while differences in court structure and, more importantly, the overall approach of a system strongly influenced by the common law made legal transplants difficult.

There is a vast academic literature, both Anglo-American and Continental European, on the rationales for the protection of civil and political rights, and it is beyond the scope of this book to go into them in any detail.[6] But they may be broadly categorised for our purposes as those that are designed to protect human dignity (including autonomy),[7] and those that are designed to promote open democratic processes.[8] These justifications broadly cover, respectively, civil and political rights. Many rights are protected for both purposes – free speech, for instance, enables individuals to express their own personalities and contribute to the democratic and political discourse.[9]

D. The private sphere

Partly for reasons of space, we have tried to focus on 'pure' private sphere protection. If we were to include consideration of 'quasi-public' protection, for instance against bodies that may form part of the state or are closely related to it or perform 'public' functions, the book would again be far too long. In countries where human rights protections are only available against state bodies or in respect of public functions there is a rich case law on the reach of 'the state' and the characteristics of 'public functions'. In Germany, the limitation of human rights, in principle, to vertical relationships has even led to discussions if and to what extent the state may 'escape' the restrictions established by the Basic Law by privatising certain public functions (so-called *Flucht ins Privatrecht*).

---

6 For a succinct summary of the Anglo-American literature, see D. Feldman, *Civil Liberties and Human Rights in England and Wales* (2nd edn, 2002), ch 1.

7 See D. Feldman, 'Human Dignity as a Legal Value' [1999] *Public Law* 682 and [2000] *Public Law* 61.

8 See J. H. Ely, *Democracy and Distrust* (1981); A. Clapham, *Human Rights in the Private Sphere* (1993).

9 See E. Barendt, *Freedom of Speech* (2nd edn, 2005).

In some of the jurisdictions covered by our study these matters are considered, since they are central to the understanding of the position in the 'pure' private sphere. For instance, the position in the United States and Canada is grounded in the 'state action' doctrine in their respective Constitutions, and consideration of private sphere protection is impossible without dealing with that doctrine. And the jurisprudence of the European Court of Human Rights on the subjects of state responsibility for human rights breaches by 'state' bodies and positive obligations of states to secure protection as between private parties has been influential in the development of private sphere protection in countries that are parties to the European Convention on Human Rights. However, for the most part our project has been limited to the purely private sphere. This is a subject which deserves consideration in its own right, and without going too deeply into how the private and public spheres may be distinguished from one another. *We shall work according to how each of the jurisdictions in our project themselves define or deal with the private sphere.*

The application of human rights protections in the private sphere may be 'direct' (as in India and Ireland, among our examples) or 'indirect' (as in most of the jurisdictions in our study, notably Canada, Denmark, Germany, Israel, New Zealand and the United Kingdom). Broadly speaking, the effect of human rights protections in the private sphere will be 'direct' if parties can rely explicitly on human rights protections in their litigation; it will be 'indirect' if they may not do so, but may press the courts to interpret, apply or develop the rest of the law so as to protect the interests in question in the light of constitutional rights or values. In all systems, there is also an overall 'indirect' effect on the private sphere via the continuous enactment and revision of legislation which pertains to private or labour law issues and is bound by human rights considerations contained in a constitution, higher ranking laws as in Israel or, as in the United Kingdom, special legislation establishing human rights standards and international human rights instruments. As indicated above, this effect will again be stronger or weaker depending on the ability of affected citizens to question the validity of legislation (as in Germany by means of an individual constitutional complaint), the authority of courts to strike down unconstitutional statutes if approached by those involved in the law-making process (as the *Conseil constitutionnel* in France), or by political pressure exerted by courts and legislative bodies (as in the

United Kingdom through a judicial declaration of incompatibility or political intervention by the House of Lords), administrative watchdogs (as, for example, in Germany through ombudsmen for data protection and consumer interests) or the general public.

E. Sources of private sphere protection

The obligation or power (if any) of the courts to give either direct or indirect effect to human rights protections whether 'vertically' against state bodies or 'horizontally' in the private sphere may flow from one or more of a number of sources:

- human rights provisions in *constitutions* or *basic laws*, as in most of the jurisdictions in our study (notable exceptions being England and Wales, France, Denmark and New Zealand);
- specific *statutory provisions* either alone or in combination with the ordinary law (as in the United Kingdom since the coming into effect of the Human Rights Act 1998, and in Denmark and Ireland, both of which have Acts incorporating the European Convention on Human Rights into domestic law);
- the fact that a state is party to *international instruments* – the European Convention on Human Rights being the one most cited in the countries considered in this project – and the willingness of the courts to take this into account either in their interpretation of domestic law (as in Denmark, England and Wales, France, Germany, India, Italy and New Zealand) or in order to develop the law (as in India);
- the *values* that underlie a bill or charter of rights, a constitution, international instruments, or the ordinary law, when they are recognised to have broad effect across a legal system, so that these values, for instance dignity, are taken into account by judges when applying or developing the law from case to case. This is the position in Canada, England and Wales, France, Ireland, Israel, Spain and Germany.

F. Extending civil and political rights protection to the private sphere – some issues

There would have been reservations on the part of those drafting the major international human rights instruments after the Second

World War, and those drafting constitutions that included bills of rights or their equivalents, about extending human rights protection to the *private* sphere. First, in practical terms there is a far greater imbalance of power between the state and individuals than there is between individuals or other non-state bodies. This may be changing today with the emergence of companies which operate on a global scale. To give but one example – Google and other internet service providers probably already accumulate more information about single individuals than most national public administrations have on file about their citizens. To the extent that human rights protections are designed to control abuses of power, the state, however, with its legally recognised powers of physical coercion, expropriation, censorship and so on, was the obvious target for human rights protections. Further, an assumption in favour of imposing such duties on the state but not on private bodies, which finds expression in the legal systems of some democracies including that of the United Kingdom, is that to impose upon state bodies duties to respect the rights of citizens would not be regarded as inappropriate interference with their own autonomy or freedom of action, since state bodies and officials are under duties of selflessness and public service alongside general duties to promote the public interest and general good in what they do, and have no interests or rights of their own or exercisable in their own interests.[10] By contrast, the imposition of such duties in private relationships could amount to a potentially unjustifiable interference with the rights of private parties to autonomy and to promote their own interests, since they do have the right in principle to promote their own interests and exercise their own autonomy. This approach is reflected, for example, in arrangements and debates in Denmark, the United States and Canada.

However, this approach to the interests and autonomy of the state is not universal. It implies that the state can be expected to abuse its power for its own ends and treats the protection of the individual against the state as a primary purpose of constitutional law. In Germany, this idea was expressed in a draft version of Article 1(1) of the Basic Law as proposed by the Herrenchiemsee

---

[10] In relation to the United Kingdom see, e.g., *Padfield v Minister of Agriculture* [1968] AC 997; *Derbyshire County Council v Times Newspapers* [1993] AC 534; *R v Somerset County Council, ex p Fewings* [1995] 3 All ER 20.

Conference of 1948, which declared unequivocally that: '[T]he state exists for the sake of the human being, not the human being for the sake of the state.' In France, by contrast, the Constitution of 1958, including any protections it gives to civil and political rights, is regarded as a social contract, and there is not the same mistrust of the state as exists in Germany or the United Kingdom.

Such a view of the position of the state, as lacking its own interests, would be inconsistent with the majoritarian theory of democracy which prevails in some jurisdictions and is supported by a number of influential academic commentators.[11] According to this approach, the majority should be free to make what laws it chooses, even laws that interfere with the 'rights', interests and liberties of some citizens. This very theory of democracy had been invoked to legitimise human rights abuses before the Second World War, and the adoption of international human rights instruments and of constitutions containing indefeasible human rights protections represented a deliberate rejection by the international community and some countries (but not the United Kingdom) of majoritarianism and a preference for systems limited by legally underpinned responsibilities for human rights.

However, the extension of duties to respect the human rights of individuals to private actors would have been objectionable in the post-war era on other grounds, some principled and others pragmatic. Although these objections have weakened in recent years, the starting point – that human rights obligations bind only the state – has still not been abandoned.

One principled objection to binding private actors to respect the human rights of others rests on liberal economic theory. Hayek[12] regarded all state intervention in the market (other than that which is designed to promote the efficient operation of the market) as an unjustifiable interference in the private sphere, the assumption being that, as a matter of democratic principle, no state regulation of the private sphere is acceptable.

Another objection to extending the duty to respect human rights to the private sphere is more pragmatic. Human rights are commonly in conflict with one another, and it is impossible to

---

[11] See, e.g., J. Waldron, *Law and Disagreement* (1999).

[12] See F. A. von Hayek, *The Constitution of Liberty* (1960) and *Law, Legislation and Liberty* (1981).

resolve these conflicts by simple application of the provisions of a bill of rights or an international instrument such as the ECHR, which were not written with application in the private sphere in mind. A balancing exercise has to be undertaken.[13] This concern is reflected in a number of our chapters, but it has not prevented or inhibited the development of private sphere protection in any of them except the United States and Canada. Of course, similar conflicts or even more problematic ones arise where the parties are the individual and the state. But the ECHR does give some guidance about the balancing of public and private interests in the articles that allow for exceptions in the name of public health, public morals and the like. Such exceptions may not be applicable in relationships between private individuals and corporations. Specific legislative regulation or guidance may be required if the courts are to adjudicate on such conflicts. For instance, there is clear scope for conflict between the freedom of the press and the right of individuals to respect for their private lives. Such conflicts arise even where there is no constitutional human rights protection, as was the case in the United Kingdom before the coming into effect of the Human Rights Act 1998. But, it could be argued, resolution of such conflicts is made more difficult when the two conflicting 'rights' each enjoy 'constitutional' protection and the terms of the human rights provisions do not indicate how conflicts can be resolved. While a doctrine of proportionality may assist the courts in making the appropriate balance,[14] and is being developed in some of the jurisdictions in our study (for instance, in Germany, England and Wales, France, New Zealand and by the European Court of Human Rights), commonly specific legislation, for instance on the right to privacy, may be required to guide the courts in these matters. One should also bear in mind, however, that the legislator, when creating rules of private, labour, criminal or even administrative law, is constantly balancing private interests (for example, those of landlord and tenant, producer and consumer, celebrity and the press, or land owner and new developer), and may have to defend the choice of a particular solution on constitutional grounds if challenged in court. The validity of a law which makes intrusions of

---

[13] See A. Barak in D. Friedmann and D. Barak-Erez (eds), *Human Rights in Private Law* (2001).

[14] See, e.g., C. Starck in D. Friedmann and D. Barak-Erez (eds), op. cit.

paparazzi into the private sphere of individuals with the help of long-lens cameras and the like a criminal offence (as done by § 301a of the German Criminal Code) would, if questioned in court, thus be tested by establishing whether the legislator has struck an appropriate balance between the privacy rights of the victim and the freedom or even duty of the press to report on or investigate the lives and activities of certain individuals. Conflicting constitutional rights again appear on both sides of the equation, the only difference to a 'direct' application of rights in the private sphere being that the so-called 'balancing exercise' is applied to legislation which impacts on private relationships.

There may also be conflict between the *rights* of one party and the *vital interests* of another, not necessarily falling within the category of rights. An employer may have a right to freedom of contract and enjoyment of his property which he wishes to exercise against the interests of an employee, whose livelihood, but not human rights, may be affected. This, of course, depends on the scope of a bill of rights, for some systems might actually offer constitutional protection for all forms of activity aimed at securing a livelihood, including employed positions (as do Article 12 of the German Basic Law, section 22 of the Final South African Constitution, and Article 15 of the EU Charter of Fundamental Rights and Freedoms). Or the employer may have interests in his business which come into conflict with his employee's right to privacy. In the absence of specific legislation in such cases, a heavy burden lies on the judges charged with resolving these conflicts. This in turn raises issues to do with the appropriateness of the courtroom and adversarial procedures for the resolution of such disputes (in those jurisdictions in which the adversarial process applies in private disputes), and with the accountability of judges for what may be politically controversial decisions – the very same issues that are raised in relation to the application of human rights protections in disputes between the individual and the state.

A response to such questions that is adopted in many of the jurisdictions with which we are concerned in this volume is for the legislature to enact specific legislation which lays down how conflicting interests are to be resolved. Examples of such legislation include the statutory regulation in the United Kingdom of the right of a landlord to obtain possession of residential accommodation let to a tenant, where the landlord's right to property conflicts with the tenant's right to respect for his home. Employment protection legislation regulates the employer's right to property and freedom of contract as it affects the employee's interest in his status and security derived from the employment. In the absence of such specific regulation the courts would have to exercise a very wide and rather unstructured discretion, as is the case in the United Kingdom with the resolution of conflicts between the freedom of the press and the individual's right to respect for his private and family life, his home and correspondence. Such wide discretion could result in the courts making unworkable decisions, and in their legitimacy being called in question, attracting allegations of bias or incompetence. Further, it could undermine the stability and legal certainty provided by the ordinary law. We can see concerns about this in, for example, Ireland, where the earlier enthusiasm for a 'constitutional tort' has waned in recent years. It would also raise separation of powers issues – especially in countries such as France, where a separation of powers is historically quite strongly embedded in the constitution or legal culture – if judges were, in effect, in the position of legislators rather than adjudicators. Despite a considerable degree of convergence between the two legal families when it comes to the role of the judge in the development of the law, this may still be less intellectually troublesome for common law jurisdictions than it is for many civil law systems.

Returning to the principal rationales for human rights protection that we have identified – broadly the promotion of human dignity, freedom and democratic political processes – a point for our purposes is that it has come to be recognised that a person's dignity and ability to participate effectively in the political process may be threatened by their private relationships – with employers, spouses, parents, banks and insurers, professional or trade associations, and political parties – just as much as, and perhaps even more often than, it would be threatened in relationships with state bodies. As already mentioned above, the power of private bodies over individuals has increased over the last few decades with globalisation, concentrations of monopolistic power locally, nationally or internationally, technology, and the increasing dependence of individuals on bodies such as banks, building societies and insurers for their security, which has grown as state bodies have shifted some of the responsibilities they took on in the second half of the twentieth century (for providing housing, health services, education and so on) to the private sphere. Appreciation of the vulnerability of people in private relationships is one of the factors that has contributed to the interest in the protection of human rights in the private sphere in some of the jurisdictions in our study. The imposition of duties to respect the rights of individuals in private relationships may therefore be regarded as a technique for reducing inequality.

Similarly, it has come to be recognised that much activity in the private sphere positively contributes to the democratic and political process and thus deserves protection from politically motivated interference. Membership of trade unions, pressure groups, professional bodies, community associations, mutual support organisations and religious bodies, may, for instance, enable people to influence public bodies and their policy. Indeed, without opportunities for collective involvement in politics, the influence of citizens on politics and the activity of the state is bound to be small, reduced even to voting in elections only every four or five years. But private organisations such as these and their leaders may also interfere with the dignity of their members and others, or abuse the political influence which the fact of membership gives them. We shall see that this has been a problem in relation to trade union power in Canada, England and Wales, and Ireland, and religious organisations in India. Again, appreciation of these factors may underlie some of the concern that human rights protection should extend to these relationships, and it comes as no surprise that particular systems sometimes make rights pertaining to, for example, trade unions directly applicable to private relationships or put particular entities such as political parties under special constitutional obligations when it comes to their internal organisational structures (i.e. the ability of members to influence in a meaningful way the decisions taken by the party leadership).

A further objection to treating the private sphere differently from the public sphere when human rights are at stake is that, in reality, the state itself as the fountain of law constitutes relationships in the private sphere just as much as in the public sphere. If the state's law does not require private actors to comply with human rights norms, that is as much the product of the state's intervention as the opposite position would be.[15] This approach is

[15] See A. Clapham, *Human Rights in the Private Sphere* (1993); C. Sunstein, *The Partial Constitution* (1993); M. Hunt, 'The "Horizontal Effect" of the Human Rights Act' [1998] *Public Law* 423.

reflected in the jurisprudence of the European Court of Human Rights on positive obligations and state responsibility and can also be found in more recent attempts to conceptualise the notion of indirect *Drittwirkung* in Germany.

G. Public–private law divides

Where civil and political rights do have some effect in the private sphere, whether directly or indirectly, issues arise as to whether this involves, for instance, the constitutionalisation[16] or 'publicisation'[17] of private law, or the privatisation of human rights.[18] Each of these interpretations of the process assumes a public–private divide or distinction of some sort. Such divides operate in many jurisdictions, especially in civil law systems. Indeed, they may be seen as essential and fundamental to the whole constitutional set-up. However, it is not inevitable that a broadly democratic legal system will be 'dis-integrated' in this way. Public–private divides of various kinds are of relatively recent invention in some common law systems, notably England and Wales, India, Ireland and New Zealand in our study, which have been far less category-based than civilian legal systems tend to be. Spain is, however, an exception in that public–private divides are relatively unimportant in this area.

In the conditions of the twenty-first century there is by no means universal agreement that strict public–private divides are possible or even desirable. In an era in which many democracies are privatising formerly state-owned industries in various ways, and state bodies are entering into 'partnerships' with non-state bodies for the delivery of services (a process often known as a shift from 'government' to 'governance'[19]), divisions between state and other bodies, or state and other functions become increasingly problematic. That said, we also note that traditional distinctions between 'public' and 'private' law still affect the thinking about the application of human rights in the private sphere in many systems and, more importantly, lead to real practical difficulties if reproduced

---

[16] B. Markesinis, *Always on the Same Path* (2001).

[17] A. Clapham, *Human Rights in the Private Sphere* (1993), p 352.

[18] See A. Clapham, op. cit., p 356 and A. Barak in D. Friedmann and D. Barak-Erez (eds), op. cit., p 13.

[19] See J. Newman, *Modernising Governance. New Labour, Policy and Society* (2001); N. D. Lewis, *Law and Governance* (2001).

in specialised court structures. The latter is the case in countries like Germany (where conflicts have arisen between courts with private or labour law jurisdiction and the specialised Federal Constitutional Court) and, to a lesser extent, South Africa (which introduced in 1993 disputes of a constitutional nature as a special category of cases and assigned these to the final jurisdiction of a newly established specialised constitutional court).

But given that our focus in this book is explicitly on human rights in the private sphere and that that, too, assumes a separate and identifiable private sphere which may be hard to delineate, we recognise that in practice there are sliding scales of 'publicness' or 'privateness' of institutions or functions in many democracies, and that a categorical approach is perhaps artificial and difficult to sustain. The scale may operate differently in different jurisdictions. Despite the difficulties in making such distinctions, our focus will be on situations in which the legal system in question operates on the basis that there is no case for suggesting that an institution or a function is 'public'. While those situations might vary from jurisdiction to jurisdiction, and while that might be one of the most interesting points to emerge from what follows, as indicated earlier *our focus will be on the 'private sphere' as defined by the jurisdictions with which this collection is concerned*. Thus we shall not be concerned with disputes that are conceived in the jurisdiction in question as being between individuals (or private corporations) and state bodies, nor with disputes between parties the legal position of one of which depends upon whether they are performing a public function or a function of a public nature, to adopt the phrases used in English law. We shall be primarily concerned with relationships such as those between individuals on the one hand, and employers, insurers, bankers, landlords, property owners, the press and other media, and even more powerful family members, on the other. We shall note in due course that, frequently, human rights issues arise in relationships where there are inequalities or imbalances of power or market or economic pressures which militate against one party respecting the interests of another, often dependent, party.

H. The line of inquiry

The jurisdiction based chapters in this collection will stand on their own as accounts of the position in relation to private sphere protection. In Part II there are 14 chapters. Of these, 13 outline the approach to private sphere protection in the country (or, in Chapter 14, two countries – the United States and Canada) and give examples of issues and leading cases of particular interest in the jurisdiction. The remaining chapter is concerned with the case law of the European Court of Human Rights.

We have chosen democratic jurisdictions that reflect a broad range of approaches, including systems based on civil law, common law, Roman Dutch law and Nordic law, members of the European Community and others, states which are parties to the European Convention on Human Rights and some which are not, developed and developing countries, and countries giving strong and weak private sphere protection. Our hope is that the range of countries within the study will make for illuminating comparisons.

The chapters in Part II are supplemented in Part III by a chart summarising the position in each of the jurisdictions under consideration, and this may be used, together with the index, to find the material referred to in the chapters in Part II, rather than via footnoted cross-references.

I. Comparing jurisdictions

In our comparative analysis in Part III we apply comparative methodology to the material, identifying, analysing and drawing lessons from the similarities and differences between jurisdictions, considering how these are affected by matters such as the type of legal system – common law, civil or other, monist or dualist – and the political, historical and cultural background or philosophical and theoretical approaches that are influential in each jurisdiction. This final section of the book seeks to draw some conclusions from this wealth of material.

Part II: National Jurisdictions European Convention on Human Rights

Chapter 1: Denmark
Drittwirkung and Conflicting Rights – Viewed from National and International Perspectives

Jonas Christoffersen

A. Introduction

The horizontal effect of human rights (*Drittwirkung*) is subject to dispute in Danish law as in other jurisdictions.[1] The implementation of human rights in relations between individuals has been met with scepticism in legal doctrine, although neither legislation nor judicial practice has rejected the horizontal effect of human rights.

I will argue in the following that scepticism about the horizontal effect of human rights is based on illogical arguments that do not survive close scrutiny. The principle of the binding force of human rights can be invoked both to justify the recognition of

---

[1] In Denmark, the words 'mittelbare/unmittelbare Drittwirkung' are used regularly and synonymously with indirect/direct effect. The terminology can produce confusion. E.g., Professor Werlauff uses the term Drittwirkung to denote the obligation to give internal effect to international human rights and the term indirect (mittelbare) Drittwirkung to denote horizontal effect regardless of the direct or indirect nature of this effect, i.e. irrespective of the presence or absence of a domestic legal basis regulating the relations between individuals: see E. Werlauff, *Europæiske Menneskerettigheder – en praktisk indføring* (2006) pp 80 and 82. See M. Nørregaard, *Den europæiske menneskerettighedskonventions anvendelse ved afgørelser af retlige konflikter mellem private i dansk ret* (2003) pp 293–9. I will use the phrase 'horizontal effect' to denote the application of human rights in relations between individuals as opposed to vertical application in relations between individuals and the state. The state in this context comprises all physical and legal persons, including in particular public authorities, for whose acts and omissions the state is responsible, i.e. whose acts and omissions are imputable to the state. A distinction will, however, be drawn between direct and indirect effect. The application is indirect if domestic law is interpreted in conformity with international law, whereas the effect would be direct if there were no legal basis in domestic law on which the application of international law can (indirectly) be based and yet the rights in question receive legal protection.

horizontal effect and to reject it. The argument in favour of horizontal effect is based in Danish law on the need to protect individuals against violations of their rights in their relations with other individuals. The argument against horizontal effect is ironically likewise based on that very argument, namely that the legal position or interests of one individual should not be interfered with for the purpose of protecting another individual. The controversy surrounding the horizontal effect of human rights thus in essence reflects a conflict of rights leading to an inevitable need to resolve or delimit conflicting rights, normally by means of a process of weighing and balancing.

This insight, moreover, raises new issues concerning the delimitation of the doctrine of horizontal effect. I will argue that the delimitation should be based on substantive considerations of the existence, directly or indirectly, of conflicting individual rights rather than on formal considerations concerning the positive or negative nature of the state's obligations, or the individual's opponent in specific proceedings, let alone the private or public character of the applicable domestic law.

My examination will first briefly introduce the protection of human rights in Danish law (part B), before I turn to focus on the Danish perspective on horizontal effect (part C) as well as the judicial enforcement of human rights in relations between individuals (part D) in order to summarise and conclude the examination (part E).

B. Human rights in Danish law

On a general note, it may be observed that the Danish legal system shares many features with the other Nordic countries and is best viewed as a mix between a civil law and a common law system. In private law, no civil code has ever been adopted and wide areas of law – the law of obligations, civil liability law, company law, property law etc. – have thus been subject to development through judicial practice. The (post-)modern state's increasingly close legislative regulation of many areas of society has, however, also impinged on these legal fields, which are thus subjected to legislative regulation to higher or lesser degree.

In the present context, the main characteristics of the Nordic countries may be a very low level of constitutional protection due to traditionally very formal perceptions of the notion of democracy, calling for considerable judicial restraint in the interpretation of constitutional rights. Over the last 15 years, all Nordic countries have, however, witnessed an increasing focus on international human rights and, accordingly, an increasing awareness of the tension inherent in the traditional perception of wide parliamentary sovereignty and the current balance of powers between the highest organs of the state.

Human rights are thus a relatively new thing in Danish law. While the *constitutional* protection of rights is largely considered a political task, the *international* protection of human rights has traditionally been viewed as a foreign policy matter of little, if any, relevance to the everyday life of Danish lawyers. This is because Denmark is regarded as a dualist legal system, generally requiring incorporation of international obligations if they are to be enforceable in domestic law.

Things have changed, however, over the last 15 years. Denmark incorporated the European Convention on Human Rights and Fundamental Freedom (ECHR) into domestic law in 1991, and increased awareness and application of international human rights followed. The use of national or international human rights in the sphere of relations between individuals has only very recently been made the subject of scholarly interest. The horizontal effect of human rights is thus far from settled in Danish law.

The Danish Constitution of 1849, as amended in 1953, protects a limited number of individual rights such as the independence of judges (Article 64), the right to a public trial (Article 65), the freedom of religion (Article 67), non-discrimination on the basis of faith or descent in the enjoyment of civil and political rights (Article 70), the right to personal liberty (Article 71), freedom of home and correspondence (Article 72), protection of property (Article 73), right of access to occupation (Article 74), access to work (Article 75), right to education (Article 76), freedom of expression (Article 77), freedom of association (Article 78) and freedom of assembly (Articles 79–80).

The interpretation of the constitutional protection of human rights has traditionally been very restrictive and the Danish courts have only once struck down legislation by reason of non-constitutionality.[2] Danish courts have generally resorted to international

2 Ugeskrift for Retsvæsen (Weekly Law Review, WLR) 1999.841 H. See e.g. T. Melchior, 'Maastricht, Tvind ... og hvad så?' in T. Iversen, L. Hedegaard Kristensen and E. Werlauff (eds) *Hyldestskrift til Jørgen Nørgaard* (2003).

human rights in the interpretation of legislative and other measures. The Danish Supreme Court has indicated its willingness to interpret the constitution in the light of the ECHR, but the scope of the interpretative impact of the ECHR is disputed and not likely to be wide.[3]

As a result of the absence of effective constitutional protection in Danish law, due to very considerable judicial restraint, the *horizontal effect of constitutional rights* has not been widely discussed. Constitutionally protected rights have, however, largely been approached on the basis of the assumption that the provisions provide protection against state interferences,[4] but case law from the beginning of the twentieth century has applied the constitutional protection of property in relations between individuals.[5] More recent case law, e.g. on the protection of property,[6] and the freedom of expression[7] and assembly,[8] has implicitly recognised the indirect

---

[3] J. Christoffersen: 'Folkeretskonform grundlovsfortolkning' in H. Koch (ed), *Jura og Politik – Festskrift til Ole Espersen* (2004); P. Lorenzen, 'Den Europæiske Menneskerettighedskonventions retlige stilling i Danmark' in H. Zahle (ed), *Danmarks Riges Grundlov med kommentarer* (2006); J.E. Rytter, 'Grundlovsfortolkning' in H. Zahle (ed), *Danmarks Riges Grundlov med kommentarer* (2006). A more radical view is taken by J.E. Rytter, *Den Europæiske Menneskerettighedskonvention – og dansk ret* (2003).

[4] H. Zahle, *Dansk forfatningsret bd. 3* (2003) pp 23–25.

[5] H. Zahle, 'Ytringsfrihed for privat ansatte', *WLR* 1995 B.361 p 365 and WLR 1921.148, WLR 1921.153, WLR 1921.168, WLR 1921.169 and WLR 1921.664.

[6] WLR 1966.385 H (easement registered on property replaced by agreement and thus enforced after the sale of property in violation of the agreement (easement) not in violation of provision prohibiting entailed estate).

[7] T. Jensen, 'Ytringsfrihed contra Erhvervsinteresser', *WLR* 1981 B.25; and M. Munch, 'Trykkefrihed og Forbud', WLR 1982 B.61 and WLR 1980.1037 H (artist's expression accusing, in a satiric note, the food industry of administering hormones to industrially raised pigs justified; no express reference to the Constitution); WLR 1988.411 V (journalist's poster aimed at chairmen of bank not protected by the freedom of expression); WLR 1999.449 V (advocate's criticism of a colleague not protected by freedom of expression); WLR 2003.2438 V (restaurant owner's refusal to serve French and German tourists due to France and Germany's lack of support for the war in Iraq discriminatory and not protected by freedom of expression); WLR 2005.2436 H (restriction on journalist's means of reporting on a public trial in the light of death threats made against the defendant justified; no express citation of the Constitutional right to a public trial and freedom of expression).

[8] WLR 1979.210 H and WLR 1980.896 H (trade union's blockade sanctioned by a fine not in violation of freedom of assembly); WLR 1999.1798 H (prohibition

applicability of constitutional provisions in the sphere between individuals. In the light of the scarce case law and academic literature on the horizontal effect of rights under constitutional law, I will focus in the following primarily on the interpretation and application of international human rights in Danish law, which – apart from the introduction of ordinary legislation – has been the primary technique for introducing human rights protection in the private sphere in Denmark.

Denmark is a Contracting Party to *all major international human rights instruments*, except Protocol No. 12 to the ECHR, but the international human rights treaties have not been incorporated into Danish law, except for the ECHR and attached Protocols.[9]

Danish law is dualistic, but the lack of incorporation is generally assumed not to bar the application of international treaties in Danish law, to the extent that Danish law can be interpreted in conformity with Denmark's international obligations. The difference between the internal effect of incorporated and non-incorporated treaties is thus minor in practice. The internal effect of the incorporated ECHR is, however, somewhat wider than that of the various non-incorporated treaties, as non-incorporated treaties may not be given primacy over national legislation.[10] It has been argued that non-incorporated treaties might be given direct effect, but the issue remains unsettled in practice.[11] I will further address the distinction between incorporated and non-incorporated treaties below.

The Danish *judicial system of enforcement* of constitutional and international human rights is not divided into specialised courts. The courts are thus competent to adjudicate on disputes of all kinds, including criminal law, private law, administrative law, constitutional law, etc. All courts have the right and duty to enforce constitutional and international human rights. The courts are

---

of gang member's stay at designated properties in the interest of the safety of passers by not in violation of freedom of assembly); WLR 2001.1057 H (prohibition of gang member's stay at designated properties not subject to monetary compensation).

9 Act No. 285 of 29 April 1992 on the European Convention on Human Rights.

10 WLR 2006.770 H; O. Spiermann, 'Lovgivnings tilsidesættelse og det retlige grundlag herfor: grundlov – menneskerettighedskonvention – traktat', *WLR* 2006 B.187; J. Christoffersen, 'Internationale Menneskerettigheder i dansk ret' in H. Zahle (ed), *Danmarks Riges Grundlov med kommentarer* (2006).

11 J. Christoffersen, 'Folkerettens virkning i dansk ret', *WLR* 2001 B. 143; Commission report No. 1407/2001 on the Incorporation of the Human Rights Conventions in Danish Law (with a Summary in English) p 27.

hierarchically organised, comprising one Supreme Court, two High Courts (Eastern and Western), and 24 municipal courts.[12]

The parliamentary scrutiny of the conformity of proposed legislation with constitutional and international human rights is informal. Governmental bills must be accompanied by comments on the issue where relevant, and parliamentary committees may discuss any issue brought up during the legislative process and decide not to pass the bill as presented by the government.[13]

C. The Danish perspective on the doctrine of horizontal effect

The perception of the horizontal effect of international human rights in domestic law is decisively dependent on whether one views the issue from the perspective of national or international law.

The *international law* perspective is addressed in the chapter on the European Convention on Human Rights (Chapter 14) so I shall leave it aside here. It should, however, be reiterated that, from the point of view of international law, the Contracting Parties are granted a wide measure of implementation freedom in the choice of means adopted to bring national law into line with international standards. From the perspective of *internal Danish law*, the issue is thus whether national law should be brought into conformity with international standards by means of legislation or by way of administrative or judicial practice.

Legislative implementation of international human rights has, as far as I am aware, never been discussed from the perspective of horizontal effect. Danish legislation will thus regularly have horizontal effect and no provision is made for or against horizontal effect in the Constitution or in legislative practice.

The most important argument made against the horizontal effect of international human rights is based on the conflicting rights or interests of the individual affected directly or indirectly by the

---

[12] The number of municipal courts was reduced from 82 to 24 as of 1 January 2007.

[13] P.B. Koch, *Forfatningskontrol – fremtidige perspektiver og udfordringer* (2002) and P.B. Koch, 'Forfatningskontrol' in H. Zahle (ed), *Danmarks Riges Grundlov med kommentarer* (2006).

application of another individual's human rights.[14] It is widely ignored that horizontal effect is unproblematic in so far as the state has properly implemented its international obligations. The introduction of domestic legislation providing adequate legal protection of individual rights in the relations between individuals will not give rise to concern, as long as the legal protection does not in itself violate the rights of other individuals.[15] Judicial implementation can thus be the main centre of our attention.

The impact of *judicial implementation* of international obligations in relations between individuals has been discussed in Danish legal doctrine since the 1960s. A distinction is drawn between public and private bodies, but the nature of the regulation – i.e. the public–private law divide – has not played any role. It has been argued that contract law should not be subject to the direct application of international human rights law, but a general distinction between different types of relationship between private parties is not generally drawn.[16]

The basic assumption since the 1960s has been that international human rights place merely negative obligations on the Contracting Parties not to interfere with individuals' rights.[17] The argument is often made that the judicial implementation of international human rights in relations between individuals would subject individuals to international obligations. The focus on positive and negative obligations would appear to flow from the view that negative obligations do not affect other individuals and are thus unproblematic, whereas positive obligations will affect individuals negatively. As I shall show below, the assumption is flawed.

The issue of horizontal effect was discussed at a meeting of Nordic lawyers in 1978. The Danish member of the Strasbourg Court, Mrs. Helga Pedersen, avoided the issue, arguing that it was not a

---

[14] The underlying conflicting rights are rarely made explicit, though hinted at by P. Mortensen, 'Har grundrettigheder direkte virkning mellem private kontraktsparter i dansk ret?', *Juristen* vol 84 (2002) 201–16 at 205 and 215.

[15] See further at note 46 below.

[16] P. Mortensen, 'Har grundrettigheder direkte virkning mellem private kontraktsparter i dansk ret?', *Juristen* vol 84 (2002) 201–16; H. Zahle, 'Ytringsfrihed for privat ansatte', *WLR* (1995) B.361.

[17] O. Espersen, 'Den europæiske menneskerettighedskonventions forhold til dansk ret', *Juristen* (1966) 401–13.

pressing practical issue.[18] But the Court in Strasbourg had at the time delivered several judgments recognising the horizontal effect of the ECHR[19] and more cases were in the pipeline.[20] Hence, the doctrine of positive obligations was at the time firmly established under the ECHR. The Court's judgment in *Young, James and Webster v United Kingdom* called for the introduction in Denmark of legislation protective of the right not to be forced to become – or remain – a member of a trade union in order to obtain – or maintain – employment (negative freedom of association). The government did not hesitate to introduce new legislation in Parliament recognising Denmark's international obligation to implement the ECHR as interpreted in Strasbourg.[21] Concurrently, the Danish Supreme Court implicitly recognised the indirect horizontal effect of the constitutional protection of freedom of expression and assembly,[22] but the horizontal effect of the ECHR in Danish law remained subject to dispute.

Prior to the incorporation of the ECHR in 1991, the Danish Supreme Court stated in 1986 – in a case concerning the dismissal of bus drivers who had renounced their membership of a trade union, which membership was required under a closed shop agreement – that ECHR Article 11 could not be applied directly and that the

---

[18] H. Pedersen, Oral intervention in *Forhandlingerne ved det 28. Nordiske Juristmøde i København (del 2)* (1978), Den danske styrelse (ed), p 351.

[19] See *Ringeisen v Austria (Article 50)* (22 June 1972, Series A no. 15) § 27; *National Union of Belgian Police v Belgium* [PL] (27 October 1975, Series A no. 19) § 39; *Swedish Engine Drivers Union v Sweden* [PL] (27 May 1974, Series B no. 18) § 40; *Schmidt and Dahlström v Sweden* (6 February 1976, Series A no. 21) § 36; *Marckx v Belgium* [PL] (13 June 1979, Series A no. 31) § 31; and *Golder v United Kingdom* (21 February 1975, Series A no. 18) § 26 and §§ 35–36.

[20] *Airey v Ireland* (9 October 1979, Series A no. 32) § 25; *Young, James and Webster v United Kingdom* [PL] (22 June 1981, Series A no. 44) § 49.

[21] Act No. 285 of 9 June 1982 on the protection against dismissal due to union affiliation (Freedom of Association Act); cf. Parliamentary Journal (Folketingstidende) 1981–82 Addendum A column 1604 ('en selvfølge at Danmark skal overholde sine forpligtelser efter Menneskerettighedskonventionen'). The Act was subsequently the object of several judgments of the Danish Supreme Court, which interpreted the Act in the light of subsequent Strasbourg practice, see note 83 below. In *Sørensen and Rasmussen v Denmark* [GC] (11 January 2006, Appl. no. 52562/99 and 52560/99) the Strasbourg Court amended the interpretation of Art 11, and the Freedom of Association Act was amended by Act no. 359 of 26 April 2006.

[22] See notes 7 and 8 above.

assessment of the legality of the dismissal had to be based on the Danish Freedom of Association Act.[23] The Supreme Court at the same time sent the signal that the Freedom of Association Act, adopted in the light of the Strasbourg judgment in *Young, James and Webster v United Kingdom*, did not leave interpretative doubt, which Article 11 could clarify.[24] It was fairly clear that a right to re-employment could not be based on Article 11,[25] but the Supreme Court's judgment could be taken to imply that the impact of the non-incorporated ECHR in Danish law would be limited to informing the interpretation of national law. The Supreme Court confirmed the interpretative impact – despite the absence of incorporation – of the ECHR in four cases delivered in 1989 and 1990.[26] In one of the cases, the Supreme Court indicated that Danish law on the public care of children, which concerns the sphere between individuals, should be interpreted in the light of the ECHR.[27]

The incorporation of the ECHR in 1991 could thereafter be based on the view that the ECHR was applicable in Danish law and that incorporation would merely provide a more solid legal basis for the application of the ECHR in Danish law.[28] However, since the Incorporation Act has the same hierarchical status as other ordinary legislation, it is in practice considered to have quasi-constitutional status in the sense that it takes supremacy over other legislation also beyond the scope of permissible interpretation.

The Commission Report preparing the incorporation of the ECHR took the view that the horizontal application of the ECHR would not give rise to significant problems in practice.[29] The Commission Report noted, moreover, that the judgments delivered by the Strasbourg Court concerned only the responsibility of the state and, unlike the preliminary rulings of the Court of Justice of

---

[23] WLR 1986.898 H.

[24] E. Riis, 'UfR 1986 s. 898 – Højesterets dom af 24. oktober 1986, Offentlige myndigheders afskedigelse af uorganiserede chauffører', *WLR* (1987) B. 50.

[25] *Steen Bille Frederiksen and others v Denmark (dec.)* (3 May 1988).

[26] WLR 1989.928 H, WLR 1990.13 H, WLR 1990.181 H and WLR 1990.903 H.

[27] WLR 1989.928 H; cf. WLR 1988.404 V.

[28] Commission Report No. 1220/1991 on the Incorporation of the European Convention for the Protection of Human Rights and Fundamental Freedoms in Danish Law (with a Summary in English); J. Christoffersen, 'Højesteret og Den Europæiske Menneskerettighedskonvention', *WLR* (2000) B. 593.

[29] Commission Report No. 1220/1991, pp 151–2.

the European Communities, are not binding in a pending case. The Commission Report stated:

> An interpretation from the European Court of Human Rights, which is unexpected, or which shows that domestic legislation cannot be given effect, will thus not retroactively affect the legal position of the involved, private parties. If the legislature responds swiftly to such judgment and enacts the necessary legislative changes, such judgment will not in itself affect the legal position of individuals ... In any event, the courts should be mindful of the fact that the State, and not the private parties, are responsible for the fulfilment of the Convention obligations.

The scope of the caveat is unclear, as the Commission mentioned three factors limiting the horizontal effect of incorporation on the legal position of individuals: (i) an unexpected interpretation; (ii) the non-applicability of legislation (i.e. a finding by the Strasbourg Court that the domestic legislation should not be given effect); and (iii) the state's responsibility. The state, of course, has sole international responsibility and the application of the Incorporation Act emerges only if otherwise applicable legislation cannot be interpreted in accordance with the ECHR. The caveat thus hinges on the unexpected or unforeseeable nature of the development in the Strasbourg Court's practice.

The Commission referred, moreover, to general considerations concerning the balance between the legislature and the judiciary, and the statement can thus be taken to imply that the horizontal effect of the ECHR cannot be excluded, although the interest in legal certainty and foreseeability perhaps calls for a particularly cautious interpretation of the ECHR in case of a potential horizontal application of the ECHR.[30] The chief prosecutor at the time, Asbjørn Jensen, now member of the Supreme Court, questioned the horizontal effect of the ECHR, but the Bill presented to Parliament was based on the position of the preparatory report and did not address the issue directly.[31]

The question whether to incorporate further international human rights treaties, in addition to the ECHR, was considered in 2001. The Commission Report recommended the incorporation of three human rights treaties, but the government subsequently considered it undesirable to incorporate more human rights treaties

---

30 Commission Report No. 1220/1991, pp 151–2; cf. p 149.

31 M. Nørregaard, *Den europæiske menneskerettighedskonventions anvendelse ved afgørelser af retlige konflikter mellem private i dansk ret* (2003), pp 286–7.

arguing, inter alia, that an act of incorporation is unnecessary due to the domestic applicability of international law in Danish law through the duty of interpretation.

The Commission Report remains important, however, as it is widely considered to reflect the current state of Danish law. The Commission Report was based, like its 1991 predecessor, on the view that the incorporation of further human rights treaties would primarily clarify the legal basis of the domestic application of international law recognised in judicial and administrative practice. In respect of horizontal effect, the Commission Report delimited the horizontal effect on the basis of considerations of foreseeability:

> When a treaty is incorporated by means of legislation, the treaty becomes a part of Danish legislation and will as such be invokable by the citizens – also in respect of other citizens. The application of a treaty in the sphere between individuals will rarely cause problems to the extent that Danish legislation is unclear or leaves room for interpretation, as it will be possible to interpret Danish law in the light of and in conformity with the international obligations. The citizens may as a result of such an interpretation be subject to obligations in the relationship with other citizens. This shall be seen in the light of the member States' possible positive obligations to ensure that their legislation does not allow private parties to violate other private parties' rights under the treaties …
>
> In the view of the Commission, however, there may be special circumstances justifying a departure from the starting point that one citizen can invoke an incorporated treaty also in respect of relations with other citizens. This could be the case if Danish legislation is not in conformity with a treaty, without it being possible to remove the conflict by means of interpretation. Such a situation could for example emerge, if the treaty has been given a different content than assumed due to new or changed practice of the treaty bodies. The responsibility for the inconsistency should in the first place rest on the Government and the legislature. It would be cause for concern from the point of view of legal certainty if a citizen has relied in good faith on clear Danish law but had to bear the risk of this law not being in conformity with the treaty … It accordingly ought to be a judicial consideration of considerable weight whether disregard of such a legal position would entail that one citizen vis-à-vis another citizen is subjected to a legal obligation, which he has had no reasonable possibility of adjusting to. Cause for concern is not present, however, if clear and commonly familiar practice from the international treaty body exists, and has made it possible to adjust to practice before acting in a manner that is in violation of other individuals' rights under the treaties.[32]

[32] Commission Report No. 1407/2001, pp 304–5.

While the 2001 Commission distinguished indirect effect ('possible to interpret Danish law in the light of and in conformity with the international obligations') from the application of the Incorporation Act ('the treaty becomes a part of Danish legislation and will as such be invokable'), it kept focus on foreseeability by emphasising the interest of an individual, who has 'relied in good faith on clear Danish law', and the presence or absence of a 'reasonable possibility of adjusting' to the state's international obligations. It has similarly been argued that the interest in legal certainty prevents the horizontal effect of international human rights irrespective of the incorporated or non-incorporated nature of the treaty in issue.[33]

At this juncture it should be said that the distinction between *indirect and direct effect* generally plays a very prominent role in Danish law, as judicial implementation is generally considered limited to interpreting Danish legislation and other sources of law in conformity with international law. The reason is that the justification or legal basis for the horizontal – as well as vertical – application of international human rights in Danish law is not generally thought to be the binding effect of international law. Rather, the legal basis is generally considered to be either the Incorporation Act or the duty of all public authorities to interpret national law in conformity with international law.

The Incorporation Act, as well as the rule of interpretation, are, however, both based on the acceptance of the binding effect of international law and Denmark's ensuing obligation to secure that domestic law is in conformity with the international obligations.

The theoretical underpinning of the domestic application of international human rights is not immaterial, but the issue is not widely considered by Danish lawyers. If the domestic effect of international law – be it vertical or horizontal – is based on the rule of interpretation, the direct effect of international human rights law will generally be excluded as the issue of direct effect emerges only in the absence of a domestic legal basis that can be interpreted in line

---

[33] See, e.g., T. Jensen, 'Incorporation of the European Convention Seen From a Danish Point of View' in C. Gulmann and L.A. Rehof (eds), *Human Rights in Domestic Law and Development Assistance Policies of the Nordic Countries* (1989), p 161; S. Stenderup Jensen, 'Folkeretten som retskilde i dansk ret', *WLR* (1990) B 1-11 p 10; J. Christoffersen, 'Folkerettens virkning i dansk ret', *WLR* (2001) B. 143 p 148; M. Ahsan and S. Skibsted, 'Menneskerettighedskonventioners retskildemæssige status i dansk ret', *Juristen* (2002) 92–104 pp 96–97.

with Denmark's international obligations. If, however, the internal effect is based on the binding effect of international law, the direct effect of international law will be recognised, save to the extent that the direct or indirect effect of one individual's human rights under international law violates another individual's human rights under international law.

The prima facie conflicting right may be derived from different international instruments, thus giving rise to difficult issues of resolving conflicts of norms, which need not be addressed here.[34]

The point is merely that the internal effect of international law should be excluded only if and to the extent that conflicting rights are violated. The scope of the horizontal implementation of human rights is, in other words, a pragmatic, fact-sensitive matter and depends on all the circumstances of the particular case. The rule of law's protection of the interests of one individual relying on domestic legislation is particularly important, but not decisive, consideration in this context.[35]

In the light of the distinction between direct and indirect effect, it is important to observe that the 2001 Commission Report seems at first sight to suggest that the Incorporation Act can be interpreted in the light of international human rights and provide a sufficient legal basis for indirect horizontal effect, thus making the distinction between direct and indirect horizontal effect immaterial in respect of incorporated treaties. In that case, it will always be possible to resolve the conflict by granting the Incorporation Act priority over the clear but conflicting legislation which the other individual relies on.

The Commission Report, however, at the same time focused on the possibility of avoiding the lack of conformity of Danish legislation with a treaty by means of interpretation. The Commission Report's focus on legal certainty should thus, in my view, be taken to mean that the distinction between direct and indirect horizontal effect should be drawn without taking account of the

---

34 The conflict should be resolved as far as possible by interpreting each of the various international instruments in the light of international law; see the Vienna Convention on the Law of Treaties Article 31 § 3(c).

35 J. Christoffersen, 'Folkerettens virkning i dansk ret', *WLR* (2001) B. 143; J. Christoffersen, 'Folkeretskonform grundlovsfortolkning' in H. Koch (ed), *Jura og Politik – Festskrift til Ole Espersen* (2004).

Incorporation Act.[36] The legislation relied on by one individual must thus be amenable to interpretation in the light of international human rights law in order to grant international human rights indirect horizontal effect. Yet the Commission Report described interpretation as an exception to a starting point recognising full horizontal effect of implemented treaties. This means that the scope of the permissible horizontal effect is left open for judicial development.

Danish courts have apparently never been required to apply international human rights law directly, although they have stretched the notion of interpretation very far in order to achieve the result required by international human rights law.[37] In WLR 1995.249, concerning a father's right pursuant to ECHR Article 8 to seek to have his paternity established, the Western High Court accepted jurisdiction in a paternity case despite firm administrative and judicial practice to the contrary. The most wide-ranging decision may be WLR 2000.1260, concerning the enforcement of the obligation of a parent to hand a 13-year-old child over to the other parent, who had parental authority over the child. The Western High Court decided that the magistrate court had the obligation to hear the child, although such an obligation did not follow from the applicable provisions in the Administration of Justice Act.[38] The Western High Court established an obligation to hear the child on the basis of the UN Convention on the Rights of Children Article 12 and the principle inherent in a provision of the Act on Parental Authority and Access. The Western High Court thus went beyond extensive interpretation or analogous application of the Act on Parental Authority and Access, which does not govern the enforcement of decisions. The decision illustrates how far the Danish Courts are willing to go if it is considered necessary to respect individual rights even in the private sphere.[39]

---

[36] Professor Mortensen finds that the Incorporation Act does not provide a legal basis for the horizontal effect of the ECHR in contract law. The recognition of the indirect effect of the ECHR thus presupposes the existence of another domestic legal basis for the application of the ECHR than the Incorporation Act; see P. Mortensen, 'Har grundrettigheder direkte virkning mellem private kontraktsparter i dansk ret?', *Juristen* vol. 84 (2002) 201–16 at 203, 205 and 210.

[37] J. Christoffersen, 'Folkerettens virkning i dansk ret', *WLR* (2001) B. 143 p 146; Commision Report No. 1407/2001, pp 57–58.

[38] Commision Report No. 1407/2001, p 61.

[39] It may be noted that the High Court's interpretation of international human rights law was hardly called for as it cannot be the responsibility of the magistrate

The non-applicability of international human rights treaties in the relations between individuals is in any event largely a theoretical issue in Danish law, because of the general existence of domestic law governing the relationship between individuals and thus providing a basis for the widely recognised indirect horizontal effect of international human rights treaties. Hence even professor Mortensen, who has voiced the strongest opposition against direct, horizontal effect in contractual relations, recognised a very wide-ranging scope for indirect horizontal effect on the basis of, for example, the general reasonableness clause in the Act on Contracts.[40]

In conclusion, the prevailing view seems to recognise the indirect horizontal application of international human rights, i.e. implementation in the sphere between individuals insofar as this is possible by means of interpretation. A few commentators appear to exclude in principle direct horizontal effect beyond the scope of what is possible by means of interpretation,[41] but the majority is not ready to exclude some measure of direct effect altogether and accordingly leave open a minor loophole, provided very weighty reasons justify the interference in the legal position of the interests of another individual.[42] The scope of the horizontal effect

---

court to review the legitimacy or appropriateness of the decisions on the holder of parental authority, let alone the distribution of parental authority. These matters must be considered by the competent authorities and challenged via the ordinary channels of review. The enforcement proceedings ought not normally to be delayed or impaired by further considerations in the magistrate courts of the merits of decisions made by other authorities.

40 P. Mortensen, 'Har grundrettigheder direkte virkning mellem private kontraktsparter i dansk ret?', *Juristen* vol. 84 (2002) 201–16 at 204–5. The general clause in the Act on Contracts no. 781 of 26 August 1996 (consolidated) s 36 authorises the full or partial invalidity of a contract or other legal transaction if it would be unreasonable or against honest course of conduct to invoke it.

41 N. Holst-Christensen, 'Gælder menneskerettighederne i Danmark', *Juristen* (1989) 48–57; P. Mortensen, 'Har grundrettigheder direkte virkning mellem private kontraktsparter i dansk ret?', *Juristen* vol. 84 (2002) 201–16 (deals only with contracts). The direct, horizontal effect may be recognised by some authors, who apparently do not draw any distinction between the direct and indirect effect of human rights in relations between individuals; see E. Werlauff, 'Frihedsrettigheders virkning mellem private', *WLR* (2001) B. 261 and note 1.

42 C. Gulmann, 'The position of international law within the Danish legal order' in *Nordisk tidskrift for international ret (Acta scandinavia juris gentium)* vol 52 (1983) 45–52, p 50 ('one should not altogether exclude the possibility that there may be cases where also positive rights can be invoked successfully without any

of international human rights law is in Denmark left to judicial development.

As we shall see in what follows, judicial practice has – apparently without exception – been able to take sufficient account of international human rights and avoid violations of international human rights law also in the private sphere.

D. Substantive protection in judicial practice

Before reviewing judicial practice, it should be noted that it is impossible to assess the impact of constitutional or human rights values in the private sphere via legislation as a broad range of legislative measures are directly or indirectly, implicitly or expressly, based on human rights and similar considerations. It is thus a requirement that government's Bills presented to Parliament be accompanied by consideration of the effect on constitutional and human rights norms. In the light of the wide variety of different considerations that support most legislative measures, it is impossible – within the scope of this chapter – to elaborate on the impact of a particular kind of consideration, which is, moreover, hardly distinguishable from general considerations of policy and expediency.

It may, however, be noted that Denmark – apart from a fairly limited number of judgments and friendly settlements in respect of the reasonable time requirement in ECHR Article 6 – has been found in violation of the ECHR in a mere six judgments.[43] The human rights standards of Danish legislation are generally higher than international standards. If Danish legislation will affect international standards, Bills have generally included fairly elaborate considerations

---

positive basis in Danish law'); J. Lundum, 'De danske domstoles anvendelse af Den Europæiske Menneskerettighedskonvention ved afgørelsen af retssager mellem to private parter efter inkorporationen i dansk ret (indirekte Drittwirkung)' in K. Slavensky (ed), *Grundloven og Menneskerettigheder* (1997), p 404; J. Christoffersen, 'Folkerettens virkning i dansk ret', *WLR* (2001) B. 143 p 148; J.E. Rytter, 'Grundrettigheder som almene retsprincipper', *Juristen* vol. 83 (2001) 121–33 at 131–2; M. Ahsan and S. Skibsted, 'Menneskerettighedskonventioners retskildemæssige status i dansk ret', *Juristen* (2002) 92–104 at 97.

[43] *Hauschildt v Denmark* [PL] (24 May 1989, Series A no. 154); *Jersild v Denmark* [GC] (23 September 1994, Series A no. 298); *A. and others v Denmark* (8 February 1996, Reports 1996-I); *Amrollahi v. Denmark* (11 July 2002, Appl. no. 56811/00); *Vasileva v Denmark* (25 September 2003, Appl. no. 52792/99); *Sørensen and Rasmussen v Denmark* [GC] (11 January 2006, Appl. no. 52562/99 and 52560/99).

as to the effect on international human rights standards.[44] Moreover, Danish courts have taken a very flexible position on the judicial enforcement of international human rights.

The Weekly Law Review has, as of June 2005, reported approximately 300 judgments and decisions by Danish courts since 1986 referring to international human rights treaties, of which approximately 94% concerned the ECHR and 6% other human rights treaties.[45]

In the present context, it is, of course, particularly important to distinguish horizontal effect from vertical effect. This is, however, not an easy task, because the very concept of horizontal effect is surrounded by some lack of clarity. It is necessary, therefore, to address the very concept of horizontal effect (section 1 below), before an analysis of the Danish case law can be made (section 2 below).

1. Delimitation of the doctrine of horizontal effect

In my view, the doctrine of horizontal effect can be defined and delimited on the basis of a range of different criteria. As mentioned above, the division between private law and public law has not played any role in Danish law, perhaps due to the single-stranded judicial system, and the distinction is, of course, immaterial from the perspective of international law. If an individual has an internationally protected human right, the right must be protected regardless of national law distinctions between private and public law.

In a Danish context, the main controversy emerging in the context of horizontal effect is based on the argument that the implementation of one individual's human rights should not impair the legal position or interests of another individual. It is, in other words, the other individual's rights or interests that define the scope of the

---

44 Some development may be seen in this respect as various immigration and expulsion measures adopted 1996–2001 failed to elaborate on the protection of human rights, but the legislative loopholes seem generally to have been sufficiently remedied, see J. Christoffersen, 'Den danske debat om den internationale menneskeret', *Nordisk Tidsskrift for Menneskeret* vol. 24 (2006) 97–114.

45 Commission Report No. 1407/2001 (Appendix 1); K. Ravn, 'Oversigt over trykte afgørelse afsagt af danske domstole, hvor internationale konventioner om menneskerettigheder er blevet påberåbt eller anvendt', *Rettid* (2005) 59–124. From 1989 to 2001 the numbers are 158 concerning the ECHR and 12 concerning other treaties and for 2001–05 the count is 125 and 5 respectively.

doctrine of horizontal obligations. This should be explained a bit more thoroughly before addressing Danish case law.

As indicated above,[46] the argument against the horizontal effect of international human rights is in essence based on conflicting rights, i.e. on the obligation to protect, on the one hand, the international human right of one individual (A) and, on the other hand, the legal position of another individual (B) which legal position may of course itself be protected by international human rights law.

The question emerges, in other words, what kind of substantive interests individual B may invoke before the problem of horizontal effect emerges? The wide or narrow delimitation of the relevant interests of individual B defines the wide or narrow nature of the doctrine of horizontal effect.

The widest delimitation of the doctrine of horizontal effect is based on the widest perception of the interests of B. It may thus be said that *any interest* of B should remain unaffected by the human rights of A.

The narrowest delimitation of the doctrine of horizontal effect is based, on the other hand, on the narrowest comprehension of the interests of B. It may thus be said that *only a violation of human rights* of B should impair the implementation of the human rights in the relations with A.

A more moderate delimitation might be based on the view that the legally protected interests of one individual should not be impaired by the implementation of another individual's rights. This is where the argument against *direct horizontal effect* comes into play. The argument is, in essence, an argument in favour of upholding the rule of law in the relations between individuals, the rule of law at the same time being implicitly defined narrowly without reference to the human rights of other individuals and without inclusion of the Incorporation Act.

A strict doctrine of non-recognition of direct horizontal effect thus gives precedence in a conflict between individuals to the resolution adopted in the immediately applicable domestic law. Under a doctrine of non-recognition of direct horizontal effect, substantive arguments concerning the merits of the interests invoked by individual A (under human rights law) automatically give way to formal arguments concerning the legal position of individual B (under domestic law).

---

[46] See the text at note 15 above.

The argument against horizontal effect thus ironically turns against the position it is meant to protect, because the horizontal effect might as well be addressed from the perspective of B. Regardless of the point of view, the argument for and against horizontal effect presupposes an obligation to protect A against B's interference with A's enjoyment of his or her rights.

Let us use the Strasbourg judgment in the *von Hannover* case as an example.[47] A, a tabloid paper, claimed that its right to freedom of expression comprised a right protected by domestic law to publish pictures of a prima facie public person, and B, the alleged prima facie public person, claimed that her right to private life entailed a freedom from the press' interference in her everyday life. The issue of horizontal effect emerges regardless of whether the case is considered from the point of view of A (the press) or B (the public figure).

The Strasbourg Court resolved the conflicting rights in favour of B (the public figure) and found a violation of Article 8, but the result might have to be different in a domestic law context as A (the press) might have a legally protected right to non-interference with its freedom of expression without due basis in domestic law. Hence, if it were too unforeseeable under domestic law that a domestic court would resolve the conflict in favour of B (the public figure), the interference in A's freedom of expression would not be prescribed by law.

If we turn to consider the argument against *indirect horizontal effect*, it will be seen that Danish law is preoccupied with the issue of foreseeability. Yet the doctrine is not clearly delimited, because the nature of the interests that are assumed to stand in the way of the horizontal application of A's rights is not clearly defined.

It is, in my view, necessary to address the interaction between individual and general public interests in order to understand the issue of horizontal effect and to reconsider the distinction between the doctrines of vertical and horizontal effect.

If A claims a human right vis-à-vis a public authority, the right will commonly be addressed on the basis of a distinction between the state's positive and negative obligations. The *von Hannover* case mentioned above, however, shows that the resolution of conflicting rights involves both positive obligations (to protect B from A) and

---

47 *von Hannover v Germany* (24 June 2004, Appl. no. 59320/00).

negative obligations (to protect A from the unforeseeable implementation of Bs rights).

A distinction between the positive obligation to protect one right (the right to private and family life of B) and the negative obligation to protect another right (the freedom of expression of A) does not really make sense, as the two kinds of obligations are in play at the same time. The interference in the rights of B may be based on the obligation to protect A and we should appreciate the necessary link between the conflicting rights or interests and the doctrine of horizontal effect.

The proper delimitation of the doctrine of horizontal effect cannot be based on all or any, however unimportant, interests of B. If any interest of B could bar the implementation of the human rights of A, the state would be obliged also to protect all or any interests of B. This is a logical consequence of the conflicting nature of the interests of A and B.

Hence from *the perspective of international human rights law*, the scope of horizontal effect can only be determined by reference to the scope of the rights of A and B under international human rights law. If the implementation of A's rights under international law is hindered by the protection of B's rights or interests under national law, national law will have to give way in accordance with the principle that domestic law cannot be invoked to excuse the non-observance of international law.

From the perspective of national law, with which we are primarily concerned here, the scope of the doctrine of horizontal effect should likewise focus on the substantive interests protected by international human rights law and domestic law. The distinction between direct and indirect effect should thus be viewed as a consequence of the right – under domestic law and perhaps under international law – to respect for one individual's legally protected interests. The rule of law, including legal certainty, is a consideration of weight, but it cannot be given priority over any, however weighty, substantive interest of another individual. The Strasbourg Court's judgments on the criminal liability of the German border guards provide an extraordinary example of the legal position of the border guards giving way to the legal protection of the victims.[48] The Strasbourg Court's acceptance of the gradual

48 *K-H W v Germany* [GC] (22 March 2001, ECHR 2001-II) and *Streletz, Kessler and Krenz v Germany* [GC] (22 March 2001, ECHR 2001-II).

development of criminal law to prohibit spousal rape is another example.[49]

The distinction between vertical and horizontal effect cannot therefore be based on formal considerations of the nature of an individual's opponent in particular proceeding, let alone the public or private nature of the applicable domestic law. The distinction can be properly made only on the basis of substantive considerations of the existence, directly or indirectly, of conflicting individual rights.[50]

Distinguishing between the doctrines of horizontal and vertical effect is, however, made difficult by the fact that the protection of individual rights or interests may be implemented in the shape of the enforcement of public or societal interests. Individual interests may lie behind public interests.[51] The countervailing interests that need to be weighed and balanced can rarely be strictly delimited on the basis of a distinction between individual and societal interests.[52]

For instance, a wide range of criminal charges are pursued by the public prosecutor, even when there may have been a violation by the perpetrator of the victim's rights or interests. The victim's interest in the outcome of the criminal trial may be procedurally recognised where the victim has lodged a civil liability claim which may be determined in the course of the criminal proceedings, parasitically upon them. In Danish law, the link between criminal and civil liability is particularly strict, as a decision on civil liability must follow the decision on criminal liability.[53] The delimitation of the scope of criminal law in the light of international human rights law will thus entail giving horizontal effect or protection to international human rights. This is quite clear where criminal liability is pursued by the victim, such as in defamation cases, but it is likewise

---

[49] *CR v United Kingdom* (22 November 1995, Series A no. 335-C) and *S W v United Kingdom* (22 November 1995, Series A no. 335-B).

[50] See further note 88 below.

[51] J. Nørregaard, *Den europæiske menneskerettighedskonventions anvendelse ved afgørelser af retlige konflikter mellem private i dansk ret* (2003), pp 301–6.

[52] R. Alexy, *A Theory of Constitutional Rights* (2002), p 311 talks of a 'triadic structure' of constitutional rights (individual right, common interest, individual right).

[53] Administration of Justice Act, s 992. It has been argued that this provision entails a disproportionate restriction on the victim's access to court in respect of the civil liability claim; see, e.g., P. Garde: 'Adhæsionsprocessens brister', *WLR* (1998) B.31. It is not necessary to deny the victim access to court as the acquitted person's right to the presumption of innocence can be respected in the determination of the civil claim; see J. Christoffersen, 'Erstatning m.v. efter frifindelse', *Juristen* (2004) 16–21.

the case where one or more victims of a criminal offence are identifiable. Also, a broad variety of public law regulation protects individual interests despite being enacted in the public interest.[54] One example is legislation prohibiting racially discriminatory speech, which protects a part of the population against discriminatory statements, and which – seen from the perspective of ECHR Article 17 – prohibits the use of the freedom of expression to destroy the rights and freedoms of others.[55]

In Danish law, the doctrine of horizontal effect is construed broadly and normally seen to emerge if the interests of an individual is affected by the implementation of human rights, irrespective of whether the interests are at the same time protected by international human rights.[56]

2. *Analysis of Danish case law*

Despite the difficulty inherent in distinguishing vertical from horizontal effect, which difficulty is an independent argument for not drawing the distinction too rigidly, horizontal effect has been subjected to some scepticism also in Danish judicial practice. The High Courts of Denmark thus rejected the horizontal effect of the ECHR in 1998–99.[57]

The Eastern High Court stated that the ECHR could not apply to a conflict between a real estate creditor and a debtor concerning the time-bar on the creditor's debt recovery.[58] It is, however, clear that the ECHR could not be interpreted to support the claim made by the creditor, and the precedent value of the judgment was thus very limited.[59] The Western High Court made similar remarks in a

[54] See, e.g., WLR 1999.1728 H and WLR 2000.1057 H (prohibition on remaining at certain designated properties in the interest, inter alia, of the safety of passers by) and WLR 2004.2149 H (prohibition on the erection of an antenna in the interest, inter alia, of neighbours).

[55] WLR 1999.1113 Ø (Muslims in general); WLR 2000.2234 H (Muslims in general); WLR 2003.1411 Ø (Muslims in general, Art 17 cited); WLR 2003.1428 Ø (Jews in general); WLR 2004.734 H (Muslims in general, Art 17 cited).

[56] See implicitly, e.g., M. Nørregaard, *Den europæiske menneskerettighedskonventions anvendelse ved afgørelser af retlige konflikter mellem private i dansk ret* (2003), chs 10 and 11.

[57] See also the municipal court's judgment in WLR 1999.656 V.

[58] WLR 1999.2102 Ø.

[59] M. Nørregaard: *Den europæiske menneskerettighedskonventions anvendelse ved afgørelser af retlige konflikter mellem private i dansk ret* (2003) pp 324–5.

case concerning the negative freedom of association, but the Supreme Court did not repeat them and interpreted the Freedom of Association Act extensively so as to provide effective protection of the negative freedom of association as required by the Strasbourg Court at the time.[60] The Eastern High Court has recently expressly recognised the horizontal effect of ECHR Article 11 in a case concerning the right of an individual to renounce his membership of a trade union with appropriate notice.[61]

Apart from these few judgments, very firm case law implicitly or expressly recognises the horizontal effect of the ECHR and other international treaties to the extent necessary to secure the proper protection of international human rights in the sphere between individuals. Horizontal effect has been recognised in respect of the incorporated ECHR as well as non-incorporated treaties.[62]

Of course, it falls far beyond the scope of this chapter to account extensively of Danish case law on horizontal effect, but it can be briefly mentioned that case law concerns, inter alia:

- the right of access to court of employees, despite valid arbitration clauses, provided the trade union does not pursue the claim before the relevant arbitration court (ECHR Article 6);[63]
- the right of access to court in a case concerning the dissolution of a marriage vis-à-vis the spouse's diplomatic immunity (ECHR Article 6);[64]
- right to custody (ECHR Article 8);[65]
- parental access (ECHR Article 8);[66]

---

60 WLR 1999.1316; WLR 1999.1496; WLR 2000.1728 H.

61 WLR 2005.1677 Ø.

62 The leading case on the non-incorporated treaties is WLR 1989.399 H, concerning the interpretation of criminal law in the light of CERD; cf. J. Hermann, 'U.f.R. 1989 s. 399, Højesterets dom af 13. februar 1989: Presse og radio – ansvar for medvirken til offentlig fremsættelse af raceforhånende udtalelser', *WLR* (1990) B.25. The judgment was found in violation of ECHR Article 10 in *Jersild v Denmark* [GC] (23 September 1994, Series A no. 298). See also WLR 1999.920 V (interpretation of tort law in the light of ICERD); WLR 1999.1113 Ø (interpretation of criminal law in the light of ICERD); WLR 2000.1260 V (hearing of child at enforcement of parental rights in the light of CRC).

63 WLR 1994.953 H (salary); WLR 2002.18 H (dismissal); WLR 2002.2060 (salary); WLR 2003.787 Ø (dismissal); WLR 2004.1378 V (dismissal).

64 WLR 2003.1136 Ø.

65 WLR 1999.321 Ø.

66 WLR 2004.2764 H.

- transfer of custody to a parent, who was a Jehovah's witness (ECHR Article 8 or 9);[67]
- restrictions on daughters' visits to their senile mother (ECHR Article 8);[68]
- daughter's access to special judicial review proceedings of an administrative decision to discontinue, on the basis of the parents' desire, public care of the daughter (ECHR Articles 6 and 8);[69]
- resumption of paternity dispute despite firm administrative and judicial practice (ECHR Article 8);[70]
- employees' right to wear religiously motivated headdress (ECHR Article 9);[71]
- restrictions on employees' place of prayer (ECHR Article 9);[72]
- tenants' right to mount satellite dishes in apartment buildings (ECHR Article 10);[73]
- right to erect an antenna in open land (ECHR Article 10);[74]
- press' extensive quotation from book,[75] defamatory statements,[76] allegations of the committal of criminal offences,[77] violation of domestic peace[78] (ECHR Article 10);[79]
- non-press freedom of expression (ECHR Article 10);[80]
- restaurant owner's discriminatory refusal to serve French and German tourists due to the non-participation of France and Germany in the invasion of Iraq (Article 10);[81]

---

[67] WLR 2004.2764 H (ECHR was not cited, but relevant academic literature is mentioned in a footnote to the judgment).

[68] WLR 2001.464 V.

[69] WLR 1997.668 Ø.

[70] WLR 1995.249 V.

[71] WLR 2003.2350 Ø and WLR 2005.1265 H.

[72] WLR 2001.83 H.

[73] WLR 1997.490 V; WLR 1997.1087 V; and WLR 1999.656 V.

[74] WLR 2004.2149 H.

[75] WLR 1999.1462 Ø.

[76] WLR 1989.399 H (CERD); WLR 1997.259 H; WLR 1999.122 H; WLR 2004.698 Ø; WLR 2004.1773 H; WLR 2005.123 Ø.

[77] WLR 1999.509 Ø; WLR 1999.560 H; WLR 2000.2492 V; WLR 2002.2398 H; WLR 2003.624 H (presumption of innocence cited).

[78] WLR 11994.988 H.

[79] For the interpretation of Danish law in the light of ECHR Article 10, see, e.g., J.E. Rytter, 'Legal Integration British Style – The Impact of the ECHR on UK Law in a Danish Comparison' in A.W. Bentzon, B. Bjørst and H. Koch (eds), *Retskulturer* (2002).

[80] WLR 1999.1910 Ø; WLR 2001.2134 Ø; WLR 2003.2044 H.

[81] WLR 2003.2438 V.

- seizure or provision of unedited tapes of the press (ECHR Article 10);[82]
- obligation to enter collective bargaining agreement (ECHR Article 11);[83]
- non-observance of closed shop agreement sanctioned by a fine issued by a trade union under membership agreement (ECHR Article 11);[84]
- right to renounce membership of a trade union with appropriate notice (ECHR Article 11);[85]
- retrospective effect of new trademark legislation (ECHR Protocol 1, Article 1).[86]

The complexity of the distinction between vertical and horizontal rights and obligations can be illustrated by a case decided by the Western High Court in 2002. A member of a regional council was charged with a violation of his duty of professional secrecy by having disclosed confidential and personal information about two young boys, who were in the process of being placed in public care. Although criminal liability rested on the member of the city council personally, the case concerned the regional council's negative obligation not to violate the young boys' right to personal life by disclosing confidential, personal information. A journalist claimed that he had received the confidential information from one or more members of the regional council, but declined to disclose the source of information. The implementation of the right of the journalist not to disclose the source of information thus indirectly conflicted with the effective protection of the right to private life, which took the form of the effective enforcement of criminal law protection against the non-disclosure of confidential information. The High Court found that Danish law did not require a balancing of the

---

82 WLR 1980.907 H (seizure; no reference to human rights); WLR 1992.48 Ø (provide with a view to police's inspection); WLR 1995.402 Ø (provide); WLR 1998.410 H (seizure); WLR 1999.336 Ø (provide); WLR 2002.2503 H (obligation to provide unedited tapes limited by means of the principle of proportionally in the light of the seriousness of the criminal charge, the significance of the documentation to the investigation and the working methods of the press).

83 WLR 1999.1316 H; WLR 1999.1496; WLR 2000.1728 H (negative freedom of association).

84 WLR 2004.241 Ø.

85 WLR 2005.1677 Ø.

86 WLR 1999.1621 SH.

right of journalists against the public interest in the detection of a crime, and the journalist was not obliged to disclose the source of the information.[87]

It is, in my view, clear that this case represents a grey zone between vertical and horizontal effect, but it is nonetheless essential to reflect on the nature of such a case as it challenges, I think, the general assumption that the case concerns a vertical conflict between the journalist and the police. Despite the procedural setting (journalist–police) and the nature of domestic law (public regulation protecting journalists' sources), a horizontal conflict was at the bottom of the case. The journalist's obligation to provide information was merely a procedural step towards the implementation against the council member of criminal law protection of the young boys' right to private life (boys-council member).

The duty to provide information is a particularly good demonstration of the unclear boundaries of the doctrine of horizontal effect. The lack of clarity derives from the uncertainty attached to the rationale behind the very distinction between vertical and horizontal obligations and, ultimately, between negative and positive obligations.

Since Danish courts have faced particularly challenging issues of conflicting rights and horizontal effect in the field of the duty to provide information, I have chosen as my main examples the protection against self-incrimination (section (a) below) and defendants' right to hear underage witnesses in criminal cases (section (b) below). These areas of case law are also useful illustrations of the interaction between judicial and legislative implementation of international human rights law. My analysis below thus emphasises the importance of delimiting the concept of horizontal effect on the basis of substantive rather than formal considerations.[88]

(a) The right of access to information versus the privilege against self-incrimination

The Danish legislature and judiciary have recently been required to reconsider the scope of the protection against self-incrimination, which has traditionally held a very prominent place in Danish law.

---

[87] WLR 2002.1586 V.

[88] See the text at note 50 above.

In Danish law, the right to remain silent is generally considered absolute if the duty to give a witness statement or otherwise provide information to the authorities might tend to incriminate that individual,[89] and if the authorities had reason to assume at the time that a criminal offence might have been committed.[90] The right to remain silent is a fundamental principle of criminal procedural law[91] and the Administration of Justice Act does not authorise the courts to set aside the right to remain silent in the circumstance of particular cases.[92]

An individual's right to remain silent may, however, interfere with another individual's right of access to the information under domestic law. The right to information may be essential to the effective enforcement of both human rights protected by international or national law and other interests protected by the domestic legal order. The need to balance the interests at stake has emerged in judicial practice in different situations that have not been resolved in the same manner.

(i) An absolute right to remain silent

In 1999 the defendants in a criminal case concerning very serious economic crime called their former accountant as a witness. The accountant had, however, been brought before the competent disciplinary body and faced serious sanction in the form of a very substantial fine as well as the risk of losing his authorisation as a chartered accountant. The Eastern High Court of Denmark found that the accountant faced criminal charges and could invoke the right to remain silent, as the Act on Chartered Accountants had not imposed on accountants special duties to provide information overriding the right to remain silent. The Supreme Court concurred and added that the enforcement of the accountant's right to remain silent did not entail a violation of the defendants' rights under ECHR Article 6, i.e. the right to examine witnesses pursuant to Article 6 § 3(d).[93] The opposite result might have violated the accountant's right to protection against self-incrimination. The horizontal effect

89 WLR 2002.2729 V.

90 WLR 2002.1931 Ø.

91 WLR 2000.1201 H.

92 Administration of Justice Act no. 910 of 27 September 2005 (consolidated) s 752, s 754 and s 171, sub-s 2(1) and sub-s 3.

93 WLR 1999.1015 H.

thus emerged beyond the scope of what might normally be considered the private sphere, but the enforcement of the accountant's rights certainly impinged, though proportionately, on the rights of the defendants.

The Supreme Court reached a similar result the following year in a case concerning the duty to provide information to the trustee of a bankrupt estate. A former board member had been charged with a serious criminal offence of fraud against agents and creditors but was nonetheless summoned to provide the potentially self-incriminating information to the bankruptcy estate. The Supreme Court found that the duty pursuant to the Bankruptcy Act to provide all information necessary to wind up the estate was not restricted by witnesses' right to remain silent, but that a fundamental right to remain silent flowed from a general principle in the Administration of Justice Act and the privilege against self-incrimination in ECHR Article 6.[94]

The horizontal conflict thus emerging might not fall within my narrow delimitation of the scope of horizontal effect, as the creditors' right to information for the purpose of winding up the estate – and in this connection to enforce their claims either against the estate or those responsible for the bankruptcy – might not be covered by the protection of property in, for example, ECHR Protocol 1, Article 1. The non-enforcement of the access to information protected by Danish law – due to the restrictive interpretation of the Bankruptcy Act – however, clearly detrimentally affected the legal position of the bankruptcy estate and the creditors.

(ii) Restrictions on the right to remain silent

Despite the very strong protection of the right to remain silent in Danish law, the Danish Supreme Court accepted in 2003 the wide duties to provide information imposed during EU competition law proceedings.[95] The Supreme Court accepted the narrow interpretation of the protection against self-incrimination adopted by the European Court of Justice (ECJ) in *Orkem*:

> ... whilst the Commission is entitled ... to compel an undertaking to provide all necessary information concerning such facts as may be known

---

[94] WLR 2000.1201 H.

[95] Regulation No. 17 of 6 February 1962 and Regulation no. 1/2003 of 16 December 2002.

> to it and to disclose to it, if necessary, such documents relating thereto as are in its possession, even if the latter may be used to establish, against it or another undertaking, the existence of anti-competitive conduct, it may not, by means of a decision calling for information, undermine the rights of defence of the undertaking concerned.
>
> Thus, the Commission may not compel an undertaking to provide it with answers which might involve an admission on its part of the existence of an infringement which it is incumbent upon the Commission to prove.[96]

The Supreme Court did not consider the duty to provide information unlawful in this case and thus accepted a wide inroad on the right to remain silent.[97]

A general Act concerning, inter alia, the right not to comply with duties imposed under administrative law to provide information that might tend to incriminate the individual was passed in 2004.[98] The obligation in national competition law proceedings to provide information was, however, intended to override the right to remain silent as the national competition law obligations are interpreted as widely as the EU competition law obligations.[99]

The duty to provide information clearly impinged on the interests of the company under scrutiny in the interests of others. Those other interests are, in the first place, the competition authorities and it would not be unreasonable to consider the conflict vertical, but the

---

[96] Case 374/87, *Orkem SA v Commission* (ECR 1989 3283) §§ 34-35.

[97] WLR 2003.1328 H. In spite of the Supreme Court's acceptance of the non-applicability of the right to remain silent vis-à-vis EU competition law duties to provide information, it was widely assumed in Danish law at the time than the protection against self-incrimination entailed a right to remain silent rather that a measure of protection against the subsequent use of the information as evidence in a criminal case. Commission Report No. 1428/2003 of the Commission on Legal Certainty pp 65 and 75. See, however, J. Christoffersen, 'Forslag til lov om retssikkerhed ved forvaltningens anvendelse af tvangsindgreb og oplysningspligter', *EU-ret & Menneskeret* (2003) 272–300 at 283 ff.

[98] Act no. 442 of 9 June 2004 on Legal Certainty in respect of the Administrative Use of Force and Duties of Information; cf. A.O. Hasselgaard, J. Møller and J.S. Sørensen, *Retssikkerhedsloven med kommentarer* (2005).

[99] Hasselgaard, Møller and Sørensen, op. cit., pp 186–7; L 96/2004 bilag 34 p 8; Parliamentary Journal 2001-02 Addendum A, p 4450. See also K. Lundgaard Hansen, L. Kjølbye and H. Saugmandsgaard Øe, *EU-konkurrenceretten* (1998), s. 503–9, A. Christensen, *Konkurrenceretten i EU* (2005), pp 870–80, and J. Christoffersen, 'Retlig kreolisering – om selvinkriminering i dansk, europæisk og amerikansk menneskeret' in H. Koch and A.L. Kjær (eds), *Europæisk retskultur – på dansk* (2004), s. 249–87.

competitors that might have suffered losses as a result of the violation of EU competition law would likewise benefit from the duty of the company to submit the relevant information to the authorities. The right to remain silent thus affects the competitors' legal position.

(iii) Unlawful restrictions on the right to information

The conflict between the right to remain silent and the right to receive information was played out most recently in the context of the implementation of the EU directive on the enforcement of intellectual property rights (the Enforcement Directive).[100] The purpose of the Enforcement Directive is, inter alia, to harmonise the procedural rules applicable in the Member States in the enforcement of intellectual property rights. The Directive aims at approximating domestic systems in order to ensure a high, equivalent and homogeneous level of protection in the internal market.

The Enforcement Directive grants the holder of intellectual property rights a wide right to information concerning, for example, (a) the names and addresses of the producers, manufacturers, distributors, suppliers and other previous holders of the goods or services, as well as the intended wholesalers and retailers, and (b) information on the quantities produced, manufactured, delivered, received or ordered, as well as the price obtained for the goods or services in question.

The duty to provide information to the holder of (violated) intellectual property rights rests on the infringer of intellectual property rights and/or any other person who: (a) was found in possession of the infringing goods on a commercial scale; (b) was found to be using the infringing services on a commercial scale; (c) was found to be providing on a commercial scale services used in infringing activities; or (d) was indicated by the person referred to as being involved in the production, manufacture or distribution of the goods or the provision of the services (Article 8 §§ 1-2).

The right to information may of course conflict with the right to remain silent of the infringer or any other of the designated persons. The conflict is clear: the right to information must be limited when

---

[100] Directive 2004/48/EC of the European Parliament and of the Council of 29 April 2004; cf. Official Journal 2004 L 157 p 45 and Act no. 279 of 5 April 2006 on the amendment of the Administration of Justice Act (implementation of EU rules on the enforcement of intellectual property rights).

in conflict with the right to remain silent or the right to remain silent must be limited when in conflict with the right to information. A choice will inevitably have to be made between the rights protected under ECHR Article 6 (self-incrimination) vis-à-vis ECHR Protocol 1, Article 1 (protection of property).

The preamble declares respect for 'the fundamental rights and observes the principles recognised in particular by the Charter of Fundamental Rights of the European Union' (no. 32), but it is not clear which of the conflicting rights should be given priority. On the one hand, the Directive states that enforcement proceedings 'should have regard to the rights of the defence and provide the necessary guarantees, including the protection of confidential information' (no. 20). But, on the other hand, the Directive seeks '[i]n particular ... to ensure full respect for intellectual property, in accordance with Article 17(2) of that Charter' (no. 32).

The preamble is thus not particularly clear, but Article 8 § 3(d) of the Enforcement Directive provides that the right of information shall apply without prejudice to other statutory provisions which, inter alia: 'afford an opportunity for refusing to provide information which would force the person referred to in paragraph 1 to admit to his/her own participation or that of his/her close relatives in an infringement of an intellectual property right.'

The scope of Article 8 § 3(d) may be subject to doubt, but it does not seem unreasonable to interpret the words 'force the person ... to admit' in accordance with the wide duty of information known from EU competition law.[101] The wide duty of information is based on the need to secure the effective implementation of EU competition law.[102] The effective enforcement of intellectual property rights likewise plays a significant role in the Enforcement Directive's emphasis on the need to secure the effective application of substantive law on intellectual property (preamble no. 3), the objective of a high level of protection in the internal market (no. 10), the paramount importance of evidence for establishing the infringement of intellectual property rights (no. 20), and the existence in certain Member States of measures designed to ensure a high level of protection, including 'the right to information, which allows precise information to be obtained on the origin of the

101 Case 374/87, *Orkem SA v Commission* (ECR 1989 3283) § 34.
102 Ibid, § 34.

infringing goods or services, the distribution channels and the identity of any third parties involved in the infringement' (no. 21).

The right to effective enforcement of intellectual property rights may thus be assumed to have been granted priority over the right to remain silent. It is clear, however, that the unrestricted duties to provide information on one's own violation of intellectual property rights may subject one to criminal liability and thus violate the privilege against self-incrimination. But the Enforcement Directive provides for domestic authorities to place restrictions on the use in criminal proceedings of the information communicated under the right to information (Article 8 § 3(b)).

Danish implementation of the Enforcement Directive resolved the conflict to the detriment of the holder of intellectual property rights by prescribing that the right to information yields to the ordinary rules on, inter alia, self-incrimination in the Administration of Justice Act.[103] The Ministry of Justice noted in the Bill presented to Parliament that the protection against self-incrimination may entail a significant restriction on the application of the right to information.[104] The Danish Legislature thus resolved the conflict in favour of Article 6 and to the detriment of Article 1 of Protocol 1. The horizontal effect of the privilege against self-incrimination is readily identifiable and clearly recognised due to the procedural relationship between the holder of intellectual property rights and infringer of those rights.

(b) The right to hear underage witnesses v the right of underage witnesses to private life

The examination of underage witnesses likewise gives rise to clear issues of conflicting rights and thus horizontal effect. In a case decided by the Supreme Court in 2004, the mother of two boys aged 5 and 9 and her boyfriend were charged with the offence of serious violence against the boyfriend's child aged 1½ years. The defendants had given contradictory statements to the police, who then called the older boys as witnesses as they were thought to have been present when the alleged crime had been committed.

---

103 The Administration of Justice Act, s 306, sub-s 4; cf. ss 169–172.

104 Parliamentary Journal (Folketingstidende) 2005-6 Addendum A, p 2008 ff (L 67 p 18 (general comments section 4.3.1) and p 22 (special comments to s 306, sub-s 4).

The rights of the children to not give testimony against their mother obviously concerns the relations between parent and children, but the protection of that relationship obviously impinges on the criminal law protection of the youngest child, a right clearly recognised under international human rights law.[105] The Supreme Court considered the children's witness statements of decisive importance to the detection of the alleged crime and compelled the boys to give evidence in the criminal trial against their mother, observing that such an obligation violated the children's rights under neither ECHR Article 8, nor CRC Article 3.[106]

In order not to expose children to the trauma of reliving the abuse several times and in order to secure the evidence given by children, Denmark, like many other countries, has followed a practice of interviewing underage witnesses prior to the criminal trial and recording their statements on videotape, which is then used as evidence during the trial. The regulation, in other words, affects several individuals, namely the defendant in the criminal trial (ECHR Article 6), the child (ECHR Article 8) and the person subjected to violence or abuse (ECHR Article 8 or Article 3).

The Supreme Court decided in March 2000 that the defendant and his or her defence lawyer had the right to watch such interviews via a TV screen placed in a different room and pose questions to the child through the police officer conducting the interview.[107] The interpretation was not based on domestic legislation but on the view that the defendant should be placed as far as possible in a situation equivalent to the hearing of the child during a trial. The Supreme Court did not refer to the ECHR, which does not include a similar right of the defendant.[108]

Prior to 2000 only the defence lawyer had had the right to watch the interview and a violation of that right might lead to the exclusion

---

105 See, e.g., *A v United Kingdom* (17 December 1998, Reports 1998-VI) (lack of criminal law against parental violence violated Article 3) and, similarly, *X and Y v The Netherlands* (26 March 1985, Series A no. 91) (lack of criminal law protection against sexual abuse violated Article 8).

106 WLR 2004.1047 H.

107 WLR 2000.1326 H and, e.g., J. Jochimsen, 'Dokumentation af forklaringer i straffesager' in *Tidsskrift for Kriminalret* (2001), p 197.

108 J. Christoffersen, 'Højesteret og Den Europæiske Menneskerettighedskonvention', *WLR* (2000) B. 593 p 600; O. Spiermann, 'Tilbageholdenhed i anvendelsen af internationale menneskerettighedskonventioner', *WLR* (2002) B.412 p 418; J.E. Rytter, *Den Europæiske Menneskerettighedskonvention – og dansk ret* (2003), pp 121–2.

of the video recording as evidence during the criminal trial.[109] In an April 2000 decision, the Eastern High Court excluded as evidence a video recording and acquitted the defendant charged with having sexually abused a 6-year-old boy. The Supreme Court, however, defined the temporal effect of the March decision by stating in May 2000 that the March decision could apply to recordings conducted prior to the March decision.[110]

On the basis of a Commission Report,[111] the Danish Parliament in 2003 enacted an amendment to the Administration of Justice Act overriding the Supreme Court's interpretation of March 2000, while maintaining the right of the defence lawyer to watch the interview via a TV screen and pose questions to the child via the person conducting the interview.[112] The video interview may be used as evidence, provided the rules governing the recording have been followed.

The horizontal effect emerges from a recent decision delivered by the Eastern High Court in 2005. A person was convicted of indecent exposure against seven girls aged 6–10 years and sentenced to six months' imprisonment. The Eastern High Court held that the video interview of the victims should be excluded as evidence[113] and the case was remitted to the municipal court for re-examination.[114] Despite the immediate vertical appearance of the conflict between the defendant and the prosecutor, the horizontal aspect is very weighty indeed as the victim's interests were at stake.

E. Summary and conclusions

In Denmark, the doctrine of indirect horizontal effect is widely recognised in judicial practice, legislative practice and academic literature. Most commentators are ready to accept some limited

---

109 WLR 1989.748 H (playback denied); WLR 1995.346 Ø (playback denied); WLR 1996.992 Ø (playback permitted). See also WLR 1998.811 V (playback permitted, defendant present).

110 WLR 2000.1751 H. See also WLR 2000.2383 Ø (evidence excluded, defendant acquitted) and WLR 2002.551 H (evidence admitted).

111 Commission Report No. 1420/2002 on criminal procedure in cases concerning sexual abuse of children.

112 Administration of Justice Act s. 745 a.

113 WLR 2005.474 Ø (playback rejected as the defendant had not been informed of the possible use of the recording as evidence and the loss of the right to re-examination if that was not requested within reasonable time).

114 WLR 2005.1424 Ø.

measure of direct horizontal effect and the scope of the horizontal effect of international human rights law is in Denmark left to judicial development.

Legislative implementation of international human rights has, as far as I am aware, never been discussed from the perspective of horizontal effect. The introduction of domestic legislation providing adequate legal protection of individual rights in the relations between individuals will not give rise to concern, as long as the legal protection does not in itself violate the rights of other individuals. Danish legislation will thus regularly have horizontal effect and no provision is made for or against horizontal effect in the Constitution, legislative practice or otherwise.

As regards *judicial implementation*, the most important argument made against the horizontal effect of international human rights is the conflicting rights or interests of the individual affected directly or indirectly by the application of another individual's human rights. The scepticism against positive, horizontal obligations appears to flow from the view that negative obligations and vertical positive obligations do not affect other individuals and are thus unproblematic, whereas horizontal positive obligations will affect other individuals negatively. The public–private law divide has not played a noticeable role.

The distinction between *indirect and direct effect*, however, generally plays a very prominent role in Danish law as judicial implementation is generally considered to be limited to interpreting Danish legislation and other sources of law in conformity with international law. The reason is that the justification or legal basis for horizontal – as well as vertical – application of international human rights in Danish law is not generally thought to be the binding effect of international law. Rather, the legal basis is generally considered to be either the Incorporation Act or the duty of all public authorities to interpret national law in conformity with international law.

The non-applicability of international human rights treaties in the relations between individuals is, in any event, largely a theoretical issue in Danish law, because of the general existence of domestic law governing the relationship between individuals and thus providing a basis for the widely recognised indirect horizontal effect of international human rights treaties.

In a Danish context, the main controversy emerging in the context of horizontal effect is based on the argument that the implementation of one individual's human rights should not impair the legal position or interest of another individual. It is, in other words, the nature of the other individual's rights or interests that defines the scope of the doctrine of horizontal obligations. It is accordingly essential to distinguish horizontal effect from vertical effect, but this is not an easy task, because the very concept of horizontal effect is surrounded by some lack of clarity.

The proper delimitation of horizontal vis-à-vis vertical effect can be based only on the nature of the interests of individuals. If any interest of individuals could bar the implementation of human rights, the state would be obligated to protect all interests. This is a logical consequence of the conflicting nature of the interests of individuals.

Hence from the perspective of international human rights law, the scope of horizontal effect can only be determined by reference to the scope of the rights of individuals under international human rights law. From the perspective of national law, the scope of the doctrine of horizontal effect should likewise focus on the substantive interests protected by international human rights law as well as by domestic law, including the rule of law's protection of legal certainty and foreseeability.

The distinction between direct and indirect effect should thus be viewed as a consequence of the right – under domestic law and perhaps under international law – to respect for one's legally protected interests. The rule of law is a consideration of weight, but it cannot be given priority over any, however weighty, substantive interest of another individual. The delimitation can be properly made only on substantive considerations of the existence, directly or indirectly, of conflicting individual rights.

The distinction between the doctrines of horizontal and vertical effect is, however, made difficult by the fact that the protection of individual rights or interests may be implemented in the name of the enforcement of public or societal interest.

Chapter 2: England and Wales The Human Rights Act and the Private Sphere

Dawn Oliver

A. The constitutional background to human rights protection

A peculiarity of the context in which English law has come to give human rights protection in the private sphere is the absence in the United Kingdom of a written constitution – a peculiarity shared with New Zealand and Israel only (the subjects of Chapters 10 and 8 respectively). In one sense, then, there is no 'constitutional' background to the protection of human rights in the private sphere in England. England's[1] is a legal system in which areas where Parliament has not occupied the field (and where European Community law does not apply), including much of the private sphere, are regulated – or not regulated – by the common law and equity. At least in the private sphere everyone enjoys freedom to do as they will unless there is a positive law to the contrary.

As in New Zealand, the basic principle of the UK constitution is the courts' acceptance of the legislative supremacy of Parliament.[2] These two principles – the reliance on common law and equity for the protection of residual liberties and the legislative supremacy of Parliament – form the core of the 'constitutional' background to

---

[1] There are three separate legal systems in the United Kingdom, those of England and Wales (normally referred to as English law), Scotland and Northern Ireland. There is also a considerable body of law, mostly statute based, that applies to all of Great Britain, or to the whole of the United Kingdom. This chapter focuses on the law that applies in England and Wales.

[2] See A. W. Bradley and K. Ewing, *Constitutional and Administrative Law* (13th edn, 2003), ch 4; A. W. Bradley in J. Jowell and D. Oliver (eds), *The Changing Constitution* (5th edn, 2004).

the protection of rights in the private sphere. Thus Parliament may legislate contrary to human rights, and the courts will give effect to that legislation. But it may also legislate to protect human rights, and has done so in the Human Rights Act 1998, discussed below. Parliament may also repeal human rights legislation.

It does not follow, however, that there is no 'special status' protection for civil and political rights in the United Kingdom. To the extent that the term 'rights' implies special legal protection beyond that provided by the ordinary law of contract, tort, property and crime, for instance, civil and political rights are protected in both the public and the private spheres in various ways in the United Kingdom.

Here we shall first summarise the ways in which the protection of civil and political rights had developed in English law, through a combination of statutory provisions and case law, prior to the coming into force of the Human Rights Act 1998, and the impact of the doctrine of parliamentary sovereignty on the protection of rights, focusing so far as possible on the private sphere. In the following section the provisions of the Human Rights Act will be summarised. Its operation in the private sphere will be illustrated through two case studies, both on the development of the right to privacy, one in relation to press intrusions on private life, the other on discrimination on grounds of sexual orientation in relation to housing. Finally, some conclusions about the protection of human rights in the private sphere in English law will be drawn from the earlier discussion.

B. Pre-Human Rights Act human rights protection in the private sphere: statutes and the common law

Over the last century or so in England, Acts of Parliament and the common law have combined to afford extensive protections to the human 'rights' – until recently the words 'freedom' or 'liberties' would have been preferred[3] – of individuals and private bodies, both as against the state and as against one another. These liberties did not, however, enjoy a specially protected legal status

[3] See, e.g., per Brooke LJ at para 64 *in Douglas v Hello! Ltd* [2001] QB 967.

until relatively recently. In the last decade or so principles of statutory interpretation have been developed so as to protect internationally recognised civil and political rights, and the courts have allowed their awareness of international standards to influence their development of the common law and equity.[4] The coming into effect of the Human Rights Act, discussed in the next section, has enhanced this special legal protection in various ways.

The development of substantive protection for civil and political rights in the private sphere in English law is particularly remarkable given that many ancient common law rules were antithetical to such protection. When Blackstone wrote of the law of persons[5] in the late eighteenth century, he showed (with no trace of irony or criticism) how certain 'great relationships' of sovereign and subject, master and servant, husband and wife, and parent and child were woven through with a sense that there needed to be authority – male authority – in relationships, and that without it a Hobbesian world of disorder and brutality would flourish.[6] Thus the sovereign was entitled to the loyalty of subjects and their military service; masters had control of their servants; husbands had control over their wives' bodies and their property and over their children; mothers had no rights over their children, and so on.[7] The more vulnerable parties in these relationships therefore lacked protection for what would now be regarded as important civil rights, for instance to personal security or privacy. It was largely as a result of Acts passed by the UK Parliament from the mid-nineteenth century that the vulnerable parties in such private relationships acquired substantial protection for their autonomy and dignity – their liberties and rights. Employment statutes have provided considerable security for employees.[8] Statutes on family law, and especially on the law of marriage, have granted married women the right to own property which the common law had denied them, and the right to equal treatment on divorce.[9] Children's legislation

---

[4] See, e.g., M. Hunt, 'The "horizontal effect" of the Human Rights Act' [1998] *Public Law* 423, at 435–6.

[5] *Commentaries on the Law of England*, vol I.

[6] See T. Hobbes, *Leviathan* (1640, 1968 edn, Penguin, London).

[7] See Blackstone's *Commentaries on the Laws of England*, vol I.

[8] See S. Deakin and G. Morris, *Labour Law* (3rd edn, 2001).

[9] See, e.g., Married Women's Property Act 1885; Law Reform (Married Women and Tortfeasors) Act 1935. See generally S. Cretney, J. Masson and R. Bailey-Harris, *Principles of Family Law* (7th edn, 2002).

has granted parents equal authority over their children and provided that the best interests of the child were to prevail over parental interests in disputes about the upbringing of children.[10]

The courts have responded to this protective legislation by developing the common law and equity in line with the spirit of statutory provisions. In the employment relationship the employer is now subject to 'duties to care for the physical, financial and even psychological welfare of the employee'.[11] In 1991 the Appellate Committee of the House of Lords (the highest court of appeal for English law, to be transformed into a Supreme Court in about 2008) decided that the old common law rule that a husband who forced himself on his wife could not be guilty of rape because she was presumed to have consented was no longer applicable and the normal rules as to consent applied: the marital rape exemption, as it had been called, was no longer acceptable.[12] As Lord Keith of Kinkel put it in *R v R*: '[T]he common law is ... capable of evolving in the light of changing social, economic and cultural developments ... . [M]arriage is in modern times regarded as a partnership of equals, and no longer one in which the wife must be the subservient chattel of the husband.' In relation to children, in *Gillick v West Norfolk and Wisbech Area Health Authority*[13] the Appellate Committee of the House of Lords held that parental rights over children were exercisable for the benefit of the children and not at the whim of parents, and that, as children developed and matured, they acquired the right to make decisions for themselves, in that case about contraception.

Such cases did not, however, conceptualise the function of the courts as upholding 'rights' or even liberties in the private sphere, but rather as protecting the autonomy and dignity of individuals against abuses of private power.[14] Given that these are the values underlying contemporary recognition of the importance of rights,

---

[10] Guardianship of Infants Act 1925; Children Act 1989. See generally D. Oliver, *Common Values and the Public Private Divide*, chs 6 and 7.

[11] Per Lord Slynn in *Spring v Guardian Assurance plc* [1995] 2 AC 296 at 335.

[12] *R v R* [1992] AC 599. This decision was upheld by the European Court of Human Rights in *SW v United Kingdom* (1995) 21 EHHR 363.

[13] [1986] AC 112.

[14] See, e.g., Sedley LJ in *Douglas v Hello! Ltd* [2001] CB 967 at para 126; S. Sedley, 'Public power and private power' in S. Sedley, *Freedom, Law and Justice* (Hamlyn lectures, 1999); T. Honore, *The Quest for Security: Employees, Tenants, Wives* (Hamlyn lectures, 1982).

these legal developments may be seen as early insights about the often unarticulated rationale for rights in the private sphere, the need to protect weaker parties in situations where there is an imbalance of power. There has, in the last 100-odd years, been an increasing awareness that private bodies exercise power that can undermine the dignity, autonomy, status and security of individuals in ways that may be as objectionable as, or more so than, state interference.

C. The changing doctrine of parliamentary sovereignty

Parliamentary sovereignty, a central principle of English law, is currently undergoing a number of modifications which affect the ways in which human rights provisions may be protected in the private sphere. First, the courts accept that European Community law prevails over other provisions of English law, including statutes, basing this acceptance on the requirements of the UK Parliament's European Communities Act 1972, and, according to at least one judge, on the common law itself.[15] Thus, to the extent that European law protects civil and political rights in the private sphere, as for example in its laws on discrimination in employment, the English courts will give effect to European law in preference to any Act of the UK Parliament – or to English common law. In this respect European Community law rights have a specially protected legal status. This is subject to the possible exception that the courts would give effect to UK statutory provisions that are incompatible with European law if Parliament has deliberately passed them, knowing and intending that they override European law.[16] This point has not, however, been tested in the courts and is unlikely to be.

Second, a distinction seems to be emerging in the case law between 'constitutional statutes' and other statutes, the former being protected at common law against implied repeal.[17] The issue in the

15 Laws LJ in *Thoburn v Sunderland City Council* [2003] QB 151, CA, paras 59–70.

16 See *Garland v British Rail Engineering Ltd* [1983] 2 AC 751; *Macarthys v Smith* [1981] QB 180.

17 See per Laws LJ, *Thoburn* paras 59–70.

Thoburn case was rather technical and complex but, briefly, Laws LJ held that there was a category of 'constitutional statute' – of which the European Communities Act 1972 was one and the Human Rights Act 1998 another – which could not be impliedly repealed by a later Act. A constitutional statute would be one 'conditioning the legal relationship between the citizen and state in some overarching manner', or 'which dealt with fundamental constitutional rights'.[18] While ordinary, non-constitutional statutes are subject to the doctrine of implied repeal,[19] constitutional statutes may be treated by the courts as having been repealed by a later inconsistent Act only if Parliament has used express words, or words 'so specific that the inference of an actual determination to effect the result contended for [i.e. repeal of earlier legislation] was irresistible'.[20] The other two judges in the case decided the case on other grounds and the approach of Laws LJ has not been approved or followed in subsequent cases. Laws LJ included the Human Rights Act 1998 in the category of constitutional statutes, and as we shall see, that Act does create some rights in the private sphere. If it does, indeed, become an established doctrine of English common law that 'constitutional statutes' are not subject to the doctrine of implied repeal, it follows that if Parliament wishes to amend or repeal the Human Rights Act so as to undermine the protection of Convention rights, whether in the private or public sphere, it must do so deliberately and expressly and may not rely on the doctrine of implied repeal.

Third, the courts have for long adopted as a principle of interpretation, that English statutes should so far as possible be interpreted compatibly with our international obligations.[21] As far back as 1979, this principle of compatible interpretation was being applied to check the compatibility of English law with the European Convention on Human Rights.[22] The United Kingdom is party to an increasing number of international instruments that protect civil and political rights in the private sphere (as, for example, the International Labour Organization and the International

---

[18] Ibid, at para 62.

[19] See *Ellen Street Estates v Minister of Health* [1934] 1 KB 590.

[20] *Thoburn*, para 63.

[21] *Salomon v Commissioners of Customs and Excise* [1967] 2 QB 116; *Garland v British Rail Engineering* [1983] 2 AC 75.

[22] See M. Hunt, op. cit., at pp 436–7.

Convention on the Rights of the Child) or impose positive obligations on the state to protect rights in the private sphere. It follows that domestic legislation across a growing range of subject matter will be interpreted by the courts so as to give effect to those rights.

These then are the ways in which the doctrine of parliamentary sovereignty, which on its face validates statutory provisions that might interfere with human rights in the private sphere, has come to be modified so as to mitigate its potential to authorise interferences with these rights. Such rights have come to enjoy a degree of special legal status and protection against Parliament legislating, save expressly, in breach of them.

D. The Human Rights Act 1998

The Human Rights Act 1998 (HRA) enhances the legal status of civil and political rights in the United Kingdom, in both the public and the private spheres, in subtle and important ways. The central provision of the Act is that the principal substantive provisions of the European Convention on Human Rights (ECHR), Articles 2–12 and Article 14 (but not Article 13, on remedies) shall 'have effect'[23] in various ways. These provisions are known as 'Convention rights'. The Act is primarily concerned to give the Convention rights effect against 'public authorities' and private bodies exercising functions of a public nature.[24] But the Act also produces some of what is being understood in the United Kingdom as 'horizontal' effect.[25] It is worth pausing here to note that the discussion in English law and legal literature of human rights in the private sphere tends not to be in terms of the constitutionalisation (as in Germany), of conventionalisation (as in France) or privatisation[26] of human rights, as in some other jurisdictions

---

23 Human Rights Act 1998 (HRA), s 1.

24 HRA, s 6.

25 Before the Act came into effect there was a lively difference of view between Lord Justice Buxton, who took the view that the Act could not have any horizontal effect since the Convention was addressed solely to states: see Sir Richard Buxton 'The Human Rights Act and private law' (2000) 116 *LQR* 48, and Sir William Wade, who argued that it would have full direct horizontal effect: see Sir William Wade, 'Horizons of horizontality' (2000) 116 *LQR* 217.

26 Cf A. Clapham's writings before the Human Rights Act was passed, in which he discussed the privatisation of human rights: *Human Rights in the Private Sphere* (1993); and 'The privatization of human rights' (1996) 1 *EHRLR* 20.

covered in this collection but (drawing a parallel with European Community law and the effect of unimplemented directives) to be in terms of horizontality in varying degrees[27] or the 'private equivalent of Convention rights'.[28]

I. The role of the courts under the HRA

It will be convenient at this point to summarise briefly how the Act gives effect to Convention rights, focusing on the private sphere where appropriate. Section 2 of the HRA requires courts and tribunals to have regard to the jurisprudence of the European Court of Human Rights, though it does not require them to hold themselves bound by those decisions. To do so would be objectionable as a ceding of legislative power – the power to determine the law of the land – to the European Court of Human Rights. The decisions with which courts and tribunals may be concerned will be those involving the positive obligations of the parties to the Convention to secure that their legal systems provide protections in private as well as public law.[29] Section 3 of the HRA requires all bodies, including the courts, so far as possible to interpret legislation so as to be compatible with Convention rights: this applies to statutes that apply in the private sphere[30] (for instance,

---

[27] See, e.g., M. Hunt, 'The horizontal effect of the Human Rights Act' [1998] *Public Law* 423; G. Phillipson, 'The Human Rights Act, "horizontal effect" and the common law: a bang or a whimper?' (1999) 62 *MLR* 824; Sedley LJ in *Douglas v Hello! Ltd* [2001] QB 967, CA, at para 133. See also A. Barak, 'Constitutional Rights and Private Law' in D. Friedmann and D. Barak-Erez (eds), *Human Rights in Private Law* (2001), p 13.

[28] H. Beale and N. Pittam, 'The Impact of the Human Rights Act 1998 on English Tort and Contract Law' in D. Friedmann and D. Barak-Erez (eds), op. cit., p 137.

[29] See H. Quane, 'The Strasbourg jurisprudence and the meaning of a "public authority" under the Human Rights Act 1998' [2006] *Public* Law 106. E.g., *Belgian Linguistics case (No 2)* (1968) 1 EHRR 252; *Von Hannover v Germany* (2005) 40 EHRR 1. And in relation to the UK, *Young, James and Webster v UK* (1981) 4 EHRR 38. Note that the jurisprudence of the European Court of Human Rights on the right to privacy and the right not to be discriminated against was extensively discussed, and followed, in the case studies below.

[30] See N. Bamforth, 'The application of the HRA to public authorities and private bodies' (1999) 58 *CLJ* 159 and 'The true horizontal effect of the Human Rights Act 1998' (2001) 117 *LQR* 34.

consumer credit[31] and landlord and tenant legislation[32]) as much as those that apply between public authorities and individuals. This creates interpretive indirect horizontal effect in the private sphere. This aspect of the Act is considered further in the context of the anti-discrimination Article 14 of the ECHR in the first of the case studies below.

If, however, the courts do not find it possible to interpret legislation compatibly with a Convention right, they must give effect to it. They are not entitled to disapply it. If a court at the level of the High Court or above should find that a provision in an Act is incompatible with a Convention right it may, under section 4, make a declaration of incompatibility. This is the most interesting provision in the Act from a comparative law point of view. The Human Rights Act follows the New Zealand model more closely than the Canadian approach in this respect. The making of such a declaration triggers a power on the part of the responsible minister to introduce a remedial order (see below). This power is exercisable in order to remove the incompatibility.[33]

By summer 2006 only one declaration of incompatibility had been made and upheld on appeal[34] in relation to the private sphere: *Bellinger*[35] was a case about discrimination against those who

---

31 See, e.g., *Wilson v First County* [2002] QB 74, in which the Court of Appeal held that the Consumer Credit Act provisions disentitling lenders of money to repayment unless certain formal documents had been provided was incompatible with the protection of property provision in the first protocol to the ECHR. On appeal the House of Lords ([2004] 1 AC 816) found for the lenders in that case on another ground, but the Court of Appeal decision is nonetheless a useful illustration of how statutory provisions may affect rights in the private sphere and how the courts would deal with the provision in such a case. See also discussion of non-discrimination in landlord and tenant cases, below.

32 E.g., Rent Act 1977. See discussion of the *Fitzpatrick* and *Ghaidan* cases below.

33 Section 10 and Sch II, Human Rights Act 1998.

34 In *Wilson v First County* [2002] QB 74, the Court of Appeal made a declaration of incompatibility but this was reversed in the House of Lords.

35 *Bellinger v Bellinger* [2003] 2 AC 467, HL. See also *Wilkinson v Kitzinger and Attorney General* [2006] EWHC (Fam) 2022: a marriage that took place in Canada between same sex persons domiciled in England and Wales but valid by the law of Canada is not a valid marriage. That fact is not a failure in the right to respect for family life under Article 8 ECHR or a breach of the right to marry under Article 12, and hence there was no breach of the right not to be discriminated against under Article 14. It is not for the courts, by an exercise of purported interpretation, effectively to legislate in an area which only Parliament is equipped to evaluate. The case

had gone through gender reassignment surgery. The Matrimonial Causes Act 1973, s 11 provided that a marriage would be void unless the parties were 'respectively male and female'. The House of Lords held that the provision did not permit a person who had undergone gender reassignment surgery to be treated for the purposes of marriage as a member of her new sex. The Law Lords did not feel able to interpret the statute compatibly with the Convention, partly because of the potentially far-reaching ramifications of such a decision in many areas of the law. The matter required detailed legislation. The Law Lords made a declaration of incompatibility on the ground that the section interfered with the Article 8 right to privacy and the Article 12 right to marry and found a family. (The incompatibility has since been removed by the UK Gender Recognition Act 2004, which came into force in April 2006 and provides for transgendered people who have obtained a gender recognition certificate recognising their new gender to marry in their acquired gender.)

The duty of compatible interpretation under section 3 of the HRA displaces the general principle, that the courts should interpret legislation so as to give effect to the intention of Parliament at the time of legislating as expressed in the statutory text, where human rights are concerned. This represents a radical shift in the function of the courts in that, within the bounds of 'possible' interpretation, they are required to resist, rather than give effect to, apparent or even proven parliamentary intentions to interfere with Convention rights.

English courts have moved from an initial willingness to read in or read down legislation in a very strained way so as to give it a meaning that was compatible with Convention rights,[36] to the position that they should not go so far as to legislate rather than adjudicate, particularly where a strained interpretation would be inconsistent with a fundamental aspect of the scheme of the legislation in question.[37] It would be more appropriate, on this view, for a court to exercise its power under section 4 to declare a provision

---

law of the ECHR does not require recognition, partly because of a lack of consensus in Europe on the matter.

36 *R v Lambert* [2002] 2 AC 545, paras 79–81; *R v A (No. 2)* [2002] 1 AC 45, para 46.

37 See *Re S (Children in Care)* [2002] 2 AC 291; *R (Anderson) v Secretary of State for the Home Department* [2003] 1 AC 837; *Bellinger v Bellinger*, supra.

incompatible, thus giving rise to the ministerial power to introduce a remedial order, rather than, in effect, to legislate in a way that undermines a fundamental feature of the mechanisms put in place by Parliament. There have, in fact, been few cases on Convention rights in the private sphere where issues have been resolved by strained compatible interpretation, and, apart from the case of *Ghaidan v Godin-Mendoza*,[38] discussed below, these have tended to be on technical, procedural matters.[39]

Section 6 of the HRA provides that it shall be unlawful for a public authority to act incompatibly with a Convention right unless it is required to do so by an Act of Parliament. The Act thus gives direct vertical effect to Convention rights, subject to maintaining Parliament's power to legislate incompatibly by the use of plain words. 'Public authority' is defined to include 'persons certain of whose functions are functions of a public nature'.[40] It is beyond the scope of this volume to consider in any detail the difficulties caused by such concepts, but it is significant that where a body is held not to be exercising functions of a public nature, as in *R (on the application of Heather) v Leonard Cheshire Foundation*,[41] it has not even been argued that, nevertheless, the common law should be developed or statutory provisions should be interpreted so as to provide protection for Convention rights. This suggests that the scope for the development of human rights in the private sphere is not appreciated among practitioners.

Section 6 further provides that 'public authority' includes the courts,[42] and this has been taken to mean that the courts are under obligations to apply the law and develop the common law, including the law relating to the private sphere, compatibly with Convention rights. This approach gives effect to the fact that some of the case law of the European Court of Human Rights imposes positive obligations on governments to secure that Convention

38 [2004] 2 AC 557.

39 See Appendix to Lord Steyn's judgment in *Ghaidan*, supra, for an analysis of cases on compatible interpretation until July 2004.

40 HRA, s 6(3)(b).

41 [2002] 2 All ER 936, CA: a charity which provided residential care for disabled people was held not to be exercising functions of a public nature. Its decision to move the residents to another home could not therefore be challenged on the ground that it amounted to a breach of the residents' right to respect for their home.

42 HRA, s 6(3)(a).

rights enjoy legal protection in the private sphere.[43] But section 6 has not been interpreted in the English courts so as to give Convention rights 'direct' horizontal effect: it is not open to a claimant to plead their case directly on the basis of the articles in the ECHR. Instead, the claimant and her advocates must seek to persuade the court to develop English common law and equity, so as to be compatible with the Convention rights, in accordance with section 6 of the HRA.[44] They are to have effect via judicial development of the common law – developmental indirect horizontal effect. But given the ways in which, as we shall see, the courts have articulated the values that underlie Convention rights, for instance dignity and autonomy, and given the way in which they have been willing to do so in the private sphere, what is emerging in English law is the pervasive effect of Convention rights and their values in what Hunt has called 'all law' other than unavoidably incompatible legislation.[45] As we shall see in the second of the case studies below, the courts have been particularly active in relation to developmental indirect horizontal effect in the context of the law of privacy and achieving balances between the rights of an individual to privacy and of the press to freedom of expression.

By section 7 of the HRA, it is open to any 'victim' of a breach of a Convention right to raise the issue in litigation. Unlike the position in India, for instance, public interest groups may not rely on the Act. This does not, however, preclude such a group from finding a suitable applicant and assisting him to apply for a remedy. By section 8 the courts have the power to award such remedies, within their powers, as they consider to be just and appropriate.

2. *The legislative process*

The HRA sets up special procedural hurdles to reduce the likelihood of legislation being passed that is incompatible with Convention rights. By section 19, the Act requires the minister in charge of a bill in Parliament to make a statement that the bill is compatible with Convention rights or that it may not be but that

---

[43] See *Von Hannover*, supra and Chapter 14 in this book.

[44] See A. Young, 'Remedial and substantive horizontality: the common law and *Douglas v Hello! Ltd*' in [2002] *Public Law* 232 at 234–36.

[45] Hunt (1998) op. cit., pp 441–3.

the government wishes to proceed with the bill.[46] Thus, the government must apply its mind to the issue before introducing a Bill into Parliament. It is not, however, under any duty under the HRA to explain its reasoning in reaching that conclusion to Parliament.

The two Houses of Parliament have responded by creating a Joint Committee on Human Rights, which has the assistance of a specialist legal adviser, a human rights law expert, and which undertakes the scrutiny of all Bills for compliance not only with the ECHR but with other international human rights instruments. The Joint Committee reports to the two Houses on any provisions which appear to it to be incompatible with the Convention rights. Thus, Parliament itself may seek to rectify any defects in the legislation before the Bill receives the royal assent.

Lastly, in our summary of the provisions and working of the Human Rights Act, by section 10 a minister may make a remedial order by way of delegated legislation if either the European Court of Human Rights makes a finding that the United Kingdom is in breach of the Convention or a superior court in the United Kingdom makes a declaration of incompatibility. Before the minister lays such an order before Parliament, s/he must go through a 'notice and comment' procedure, and normally the order may not come into effect without parliamentary consent.[47] This 'fast track' procedure for securing the protection of Convention rights in the United Kingdom in statutory orders is the substitute for a power on the part of courts to disapply legislation which exists in some jurisdictions. The reason for the adoption of this approach is the commitment in the United Kingdom to the preservation of the doctrine of parliamentary sovereignty, which is rooted only partly in democratic theory and largely in the desire to preserve comity between the courts, on the one hand, and government and Parliament on the other, in our still predominantly political constitution.[48] It is, of course, also open to the government to introduce a Bill in

[46] Section 19. So far a statement that the Bill may not be compatible has only been made once, under the Communications Act 2003: restrictions on political advertising on television during elections were included in the Bill to secure a level playing field between parties, but it was not clear whether the ECHR would find such a provision to be incompatible with Article 10 free speech rights.

[47] HRA, Sch II.

[48] See J. A. G. Griffith, 'The Political Constitution' (1979) 42 *Modern Law Review* 1; D. Oliver, *Constitutional Reform in the UK* (2003).

Parliament that will bring UK law into compliance with the ECHR, and it has done this, for instance, in the Gender Recognition Act 2004, referred to earlier.

The working of the Act can be illustrated by two case studies, both on aspects of the Article 8 right to 'privacy' or, in the terms of the Article to 'respect for ... private and family life, ... home and ... correspondence'.

E. Case studies

1. Private life and a right to non-discrimination? An interpretive approach to indirect horizontal effect

An area in which the right to privacy or respect for private and family life, home and correspondence has generated English case law is the Article 14 right not to be discriminated against on grounds of sexual orientation. This latter right is 'parasitical' in the ECHR, in that it applies only to 'the rights and freedoms set forth in [the ECHR]'. The particular right to which non-discrimination attaches with which we shall be concerned is the right to 'respect for [one's] home'. The case law has developed quite radically since the Human Rights Act came into effect in 2000.

The background to the two contrasting cases we shall discuss is that, by the Rent Act 1977, certain people residing with a tenant of residential property at the time of his or her death are entitled, by statute, to remain in the property after death. If the survivor was a *spouse* of the deceased tenant, then he or she shall be the 'statutory' tenant by succession and enjoy certain benefits. A 'person who was *living with the original tenant as his or her wife or husband*' at the time of death shall be *treated as the spouse* of the original tenant. The survivor has security of tenure, the rent payable is a 'fair' rather than a 'contractual' or 'market' rent, and the landlord may obtain possession against him or her only if a court is satisfied that it is 'reasonable' to make such an order.

If, on the other hand, the survivor was a *member of the deceased tenant's family* residing with him or her at the time of death, that person is entitled to an 'assured' tenancy. This means that they may continue in occupation paying a market or contractual rent, but that they may be evicted for non-payment of rent at the option of the landlord as of right, subject to the landlord obtaining a court order for possession.

Fitzpatrick v Sterling Housing Association Ltd[49] was decided a year before the Human Rights Act came into force. Fitzpatrick had been the same-sex partner of the deceased tenant of a flat in which they lived together for some 18 years. On the death of the tenant, Fitzpatrick claimed to be treated as the surviving spouse, and therefore entitled to a statutory tenancy by succession. Alternatively, he claimed to be entitled to an assured tenancy under the Rent Act 1977 as 'a person who was a member of the original tenant's family ... residing with him ... at ... his death'.

The House of Lords held that the claimant could not be treated as the spouse of the deceased, as the reference to 'as his or her wife or husband' in the statute could not apply to a same-sex partner, though it could apply to a heterosexual partner. The words were gender-specific, connoting a relationship between a man and a woman. However, by a majority of three to two, the House held that a same-sex partner was capable of being a member of the original tenant's family for the purposes of the 1977 Act. 'Family', for these purposes, did not necessarily entail blood relationships or relationships through marriage or 'in-law' relationships. English case law in previous years had established that position. 'Family' involved a mutual degree of interdependence, the sharing of lives in a single family unit living in one home, caring and love, commitment and support. On the facts, the claimant met these criteria. In reaching the view that the claimant fell within the meaning of 'member of the family', Lord Slynn drew support from case law in other common law jurisdictions, notably the United States and Israel, both of which supported his view. He noted, however, that the European Court of Human Rights case law had not as yet accepted claims by same-sex partners to family rights.

We can see the difference that the Human Rights Act 1998 has made in the later, post-HRA case of *Ghaidan v Godin-Mendoza*.[50] The House of Lords was again faced with a case where the same-sex partner of a deceased tenant sought the right to remain in their home after the death of the tenant. The landlord sought possession of the flat. The defendant argued as follows: the HRA, which came into effect in October 2000, had changed matters since *Fitzpatrick*. It would amount to discrimination contrary to Article 14 of the

49 [2001] 1 AC 27.
50 [2004] 2 AC 557.

ECHR not to treat a same-sex partner as a spouse in this context, and thus the court was obliged under section 3 of the HRA to interpret 'spouse' so as to be compatible with the non-discrimination principle. The Convention right the claimant relied on was the right to respect for his home. While Article 8 did not itself give rise to an entitlement to security of tenure, the case law of the European Court of Human Rights established that if there were provisions for 'respect for the home' in the legal system they must not be discriminatory.[51]

The House of Lords was unanimous in holding that discrimination on grounds of sexual orientation was nowadays by common accord not acceptable as a basis for different legal treatment. Any difference in treatment of cohabiting homosexual partners did not pursue a legitimate aim. If a heterosexual partner has a right under legislation to respect for his home, then so should a same-sex partner. The court should therefore try to interpret the statute compatibly with Article 14 under section 3 of the HRA, and it did so. The majority held that the word 'spouse' in the 1977 Act was to be read so as to include the survivor of a same-sex partnership, since it was 'possible' so to construe the Act, as was required by the section 3 even if the Act were not ambiguous. One of the Law Lords did not, however, feel that it was possible so to interpret the Act.

Referring to the tests for 'possibly' compatible interpretation set out in the earlier case of *Re S (Children in Care)*,[52] it was noted that to interpret 'spouse' (which includes heterosexual partners) to include a same-sex partner was not inconsistent with any fundamental feature of the Rent Act. One of the judges in the case, Lord Nicholls, related this decision to the rule of law: any other finding would be the antithesis of fairness and bring the law into disrepute.[53]

One remarkable aspect of this case is that it was not even argued that the tenant's right to respect for his home should be balanced against the landlord's property rights under Article 1 of the First Protocol to the ECHR. This is a reflection, again, of the limited extent to which the potential for horizontal effect of Convention

---

[51] [2004] UKHL 411, paras 6, 12.

[52] [2002] 2 AC 291.

[53] Para 9. Lord Nicholls referred to ECHR case law, e.g. *Frette v France* (2003) 2 FCR 39 at 54, para 32.

rights has worked its way into the consciousness of legal practitioners in England. If the point had been argued, the court would have had to go through a balancing exercise, applying the proportionality principle as developed, for instance, in the House of Lords in *Douglas v Hello!*, discussed below.

It is also worth noting at this point some of the limitations to the situations in which the courts feel that it is possible, under section 3 of the HRA, to interpret statutory provisions so as to treat persons equally regardless of their sexual orientation, sex or gender – or marital status.[54] For instance, as we have seen, in *Bellinger v Bellinger*[55] the court would not treat a person who had undergone gender reassignment surgery as a 'female' when she had been born a 'male', for the purposes of capacity to marry, as to do so would have so many ramifications that Parliament was better suited to change the law. And in *Wilkinson v Kitzinger*[56] the President of the Family Division held that it was not for the court to recognise as a valid marriage in English law a marriage contracted by two domiciled English women in Canada, where it was recognised as a valid marriage, as to do so would be to legislate in an area in which Parliament was best equipped to decide on the matter, and the case law of the ECHR established that this was an issue in which states were entitled to a wide margin of appreciation, there being no consensus about it. (However, Parliament has recently legislated to equalise the position of some same-sex non-married persons in important ways,[57] but not so as to lead to a different result in the *Wilkinson* case.)

---

[54] See the decision of the Special Commissioners of Income Tax, *Holland v IRC* [2003] Simons Tax Cases (SCD) 43: a woman who had cohabited with the deceased man could not be treated as the spouse of the deceased for the purposes of inheritance tax. It was not possible to interpret 'spouse' so as to include a cohabitant. Taxing statutes taken together formed an interconnected code in which married persons were treated differently from persons living together as husband and wife. In other areas of the law married persons had mutual rights and obligations that did not apply in non-married relationships. The two kinds of relationship were not analogous. Therefore, the different tax treatment of married persons was not discriminatory; it was reasonable and proportionate and logically explicable in terms of policy towards marriage, and the difference in treatment was objectively justified.

[55] [2003] 2 AC 467.

[56] [2006] EWHC (Fam) 2022.

[57] Civil Partnership Act 2004.

2. *A right to privacy – or to confidentiality? Balancing privacy and the freedom of the press. A developmental approach to indirect horizontal effect*

Prior to the coming into effect of the Human Rights Act 1998, there was no common law or statutory right to privacy as such in English law. The courts had maintained, and continue to maintain,[58] that it is not appropriate for them to develop a tort of invasion of privacy. Parliament has not legislated on the matter. A number of official reports have considered the question of legislation to protect privacy.[59] A difficulty is that it is not easy to define privacy precisely.

There would be strong resistance from the British press to any attempt by Parliament to legislate to limit their right to freedom to publish. The issue is in this sense highly political. On the other hand, intrusions by the press into the private lives of individuals have generated pressure for some control and this has led to a system of self-regulation by the press, currently in the form of the Press Complaints Commission.[60] This body operates a code formulated by the industry and adjudicates – via a panel composed of a mixture of journalists and independent members – on complaints that the code has been breached. Its decisions do not, however, have legally binding force. The press almost always complies with its findings, largely because it is under threat of regulation by legislation if its self-regulatory controls prove to be ineffective. The clash between human rights in the private sphere and the difficulties in balancing them are then well illustrated in the field of privacy and the freedom of the press.

The ECHR does not in terms give any indication of the relative weights of Article 8 and Article 10 rights or how clashes between the two in the private sphere may be resolved. Article 8(2) only deals with interference with the rights by a public authority, and says nothing about interferences by private bodies. Article 10(1) provides: 'Everyone has the right to freedom of expression ....' Article 10(2) provides for restrictions on the exercise of the right to

---

58 See *Wainwright v Home Office* [2004] 2 AC 406, HL.

59 *Report of the Committee on Privacy* (the Younger Committee Report), Cmnd 5012, 1972.

60 *Report of the Committee on Privacy and Related Matters* (the Calcutt Committee) Cmnd 1102, 1990.

freedom of expression for the protection of the reputation or rights of others, and for preventing the disclosure of information received in confidence. But the text gives no guidance on achieving a balance. However, some of the case law of the European Court of Human Rights (discussed in another chapter in this volume) does give guidance on these matters. Significantly, in a series of cases – most recently *Von Hannover v Germany* – the Court held that 'there may be positive obligations ... [which] may involve the adoption of measures designed to secure respect for private life even in the sphere of the relations of individuals between themselves ...'.[61] And, when balancing the interests of the individual and the press, the court should consider: (i) whether the intrusion makes any contribution to a debate of 'general interest' (here it will be relevant whether the claimant exercised official functions and whether the publications relate exclusively to details of the claimant's private life); and (ii) whether the public has a 'legitimate interest' in knowing about the claimant's private life.[62] These important statements of principle have had a major effect on the extent to which English courts have developed the law of confidentiality. These tests were among those applied in the English cases of *McKennitt v Ash*[63] and *Douglas v Hello! (No. 3)*,[64] discussed below.

Even before the Human Rights Act came into effect the courts had been developing the tort of breach of confidence so as to give some protection to what in other jurisdictions would be regarded as privacy. The evolution of this tort is considered below. But the pre-Human Rights Act position of the English courts, that there was no right to privacy as such, meant that the courts were able to avoid making difficult balancing decisions by not recognising that the person complaining of breach of privacy had a cause of action. Since the Human Rights Act came into effect, however, the courts have accelerated the development of the law of confidentiality and other torts so as to provide much more extensive protection for

---

61 (2005) 40 EHHR 1, para 57. See also *Spencer v UK* (1998) 25 EHRR CD 105 at 112; *Plattform 'Arzte fur das Leben' v Austria* (1988) 13 EHRR 204; *X v Netherlands* (1985) 8 EHRR 235.

62 *Von Hannover*, supra, para 57.

63 [2005] EWHC 3003 (QB); upheld by the Court of Appeal sub nom *Ash v McKennitt* [2006] EWCA Civ 1714.

64 [2006] QB 125, CA.

privacy[65] than hitherto. In doing so, they have had to confront and deal with the need to delineate the extent of tortious rights, to balance the two Convention rights in Articles 8 and 10 and make decisions about such matters as defences to breaches of privacy and what remedies should be awarded for its breach. This, as we shall see, they have done pragmatically, by parallel analysis in which the starting point is a presumption of parity in that neither article had precedence over or 'trumped' the other,[66] articulating the values underlying the rights to privacy and free speech, developing a proportionality test, stressing the need to consider each case on its facts, and drawing on the case law of the European Court of Human Rights.

Despite the absence of an explicit statutory right to privacy in English law, by 2000, when the HRA came into effect, the courts had developed various torts which give increasingly broad, if not complete, protection to privacy. The torts of trespass and nuisance protect owners or occupiers of land from intrusions that would be regarded as breaches of privacy in jurisdictions in which a right was recognised. The tort of defamation protects individuals against defamatory publication. But truth is a justification (and so is fair comment on a matter of public interest), so the tort does not protect privacy as such, since generally the complainant in a privacy case is challenging the disclosure of accurate, but personal, information.

Turning to the ways in which the courts have developed the law so as to meet the requirements of Article 8, since the Human Rights Act came into effect in October 2000 the courts have, in exercise of their *equitable* jurisdiction, further developed a tort of breach of confidentiality which originated in the nineteenth century. Under this tort, confidential information may be protected by the granting of an injunction restraining publication (a discretionary remedy), and an award of damages, if such have occurred, for breach of the

---

65 See N. A. Moreham, 'Privacy in the common law: A doctrinal and theoretical analysis' (2005) 121 *Law Quarterly Review* 629; G. Phillipson, 'Transforming Breach of Confidence? Towards a Common Law Right of Privacy under the Human Rights Act' (2003) 66 *Modern Law Review* 726.

66 See *Campbell v MGN* [2004] 2 AC 457. See also the discussion of parallel analysis by Blackburne J in *HRH The Prince of Wales v Associated Newspapers (No. 2)* [2006] EWHC 522 (Ch) at paras 117–41.

duty of confidentiality. This development provides an interesting case study of how the courts have responded to concern about press intrusions and to the ECHR and the HRA by developing such rights in the private sphere.[67]

A brief history of the pre-HRA development of this equitable tort where publication of information is expected or has taken place serves to illustrate how the courts have moved towards protection of privacy. The first of the cases on the matter in England was *Prince Albert v Strange*:[68] the Vice-Chancellor in the Court of Chancery granted an injunction (an equitable, not a common law, remedy) preventing the publication by a third party of copies of etchings of his family by Prince Albert, Queen Victoria's consort, on the ground that publication without the consent of the Prince would be 'unconscionable' (a concept developed by the Courts of Equity). In this case there was a relationship involving a duty of confidentiality between Prince Albert and the printer to whom he had entrusted the plates for the printing of the etchings and from whom the defendant had obtained the plates 'surreptitiously'. That relationship and the fact that the information was confidential gave rise to a duty of confidentiality on the part of the third party.[69]

The circumstances which attract such protection have, as we shall see, been widened substantially, but incrementally, in the case law especially in the last decade or so. However, once information has lost the quality of confidentiality, for instance by publication, it will not normally be protected from further publication by the courts.[70]

The limitations of the extent to which the law of confidence could protect what in other jurisdictions would be regarded as privacy were illustrated in the pre-HRA case of *Kaye v Robertson*.[71] Photographs were taken of a famous actor who was lying unconscious in a coma in hospital. A newspaper proposed to publish the

---

67 See D. Feldman, *Civil Liberties and Human Rights in England and Wales* (2nd edn, 2002), ch 11.

68 (1849) 1 Mac&G 25. See also *Margaret Duchess of Argyll v Duke of Argyll* [1967] 1 Ch 302.

69 The court also based the jurisdiction to award an injunction in the law of property, trust and contract.

70 *A-G v Guardian Newspapers Ltd (No. 2)* [1990] AC 109. See also *McKennitt v Ash* [2005] EWHC 3003, QB (Eady J).

71 [1991] FSR 62.

photographs, together with what purported to be an interview with him. Through his representatives he claimed an injunction restraining publication on grounds of defamation, trespass to the person, passing off and malicious falsehood. The Court of Appeal found that the first three of these grounds were not established and so refused to grant an injunction. They found, moreover (which was not surprising at that time), that there was no right to privacy as such in English law. An injunction against publication was, however, granted for malicious falsehood, on the basis that publication would damage the commercial value to the actor of his story if in due course he wished to sell it to a newspaper. This was a rather strained and artificial ground for granting an injunction and was not related to any concept of a right to personal privacy. A significant point about this case was that it was not pleaded in confidentiality, since there was no pre-existing relationship between the person from whom the confidential material had been obtained and the plaintiff (as there had been in *Prince Albert v Strange*) and in the state of the case law at that time there could be no protection for such publications outside such relationships of confidentiality.

After *Kaye v Robertson*, however, the courts broadened the scope of the equitable tort of breach of confidentiality in various ways, even before the Human Rights Act came into force. They modified the need for a pre-existing relationship and extended the duty of confidentiality to those who come into possession of information the nature of which is obviously confidential, such as a private diary dropped in a public place.[72] Thus in a case between Princess Diana and the press, *HRH The Princess of Wales v MGN Newspapers Ltd*,[73] injunctions were granted restraining publication of photographs of Princess Diana taken in a private gymnasium which she frequented, despite the absence of a prior relationship between the Princess and the journalist.

Since the coming into force of the Human Rights Act 1998 in 2000, the courts have developed the tort of breach of confidentiality still further, to the point where there is, virtually, a right to privacy in relations between individuals and the press, in English

[72] *A-G v Guardian Newspapers Ltd (No. 2)* [1990] AC 109, per Lord Goff at 281.

[73] 1993, unreported but discussed by H. Fenwick and G. Phillipson, [1996] *CLJ* 447–55.

law, though limited in various ways by public interest considerations and the need to balance that right with the right to freedom of expression. In doing so the courts have focused on what they consider to be the values that underpin rights (sometimes referred to as 'legitimate interests'[74]) to privacy, namely the importance of human autonomy and dignity, which in the context of privacy and the press entails a right to control the dissemination of information about one's private life, a right to health and psychological welfare,[75] and the right to the esteem and respect of other people.[76] Where a balance has to be found between privacy and free speech, the courts have also focused on the values that they consider to underpin the right to freedom of speech, particularly freedom of the press: these include the importance of, and public interest[77] in, free political, intellectual, educational and artistic expression in a democracy.[78] This press interest is bolstered by section 12 of the HRA, which provides that in cases where the freedom of expression in relation to journalistic material is involved 'the courts must have particular regard to the importance of the Convention right to freedom of expression and to ... any relevant code'. We shall consider a number of recent cases which illustrate the development of the case law particularly well.

The requirement for a pre-existing relationship between the claimant and the defendant or the person via whom the material reached the defendant has gone. For instance, in *Douglas v Hello! Ltd*,[79] two film stars had sold the exclusive rights to publish their wedding photographs to OK! magazine. Unauthorised photographs of the wedding party were taken by photographers for another magazine, Hello!, with whom the couple had no relationship, and they sought, and won at first instance, injunctions restraining

---

74 See *McKennitt v Ash*, supra, para 56, citing case law of the European Court of Human Rights.

75 See per Lord Hope in *Campbell v MGN*, supra, at para 98, Baroness Hale at paras 144, 145, 157.

76 See per Sedley LJ in *Douglas v Hello! Ltd* [2001] QB 967 at para 126; Lord Hoffmann in *Campbell v MGN*, supra, at para 51.

77 See per Eady J in *McKennitt v Ash*, supra, at paras 54, 94.

78 See per Baroness Hale in *Campbell v MGN*, supra, at para 148.

79 [2001] QB 967, CA (re interlocutory injunction); *Douglas v Hello! (No. 3)* [2006] QB 125 (re substantive issues). See also *Venables v News Group Newspapers* [2001] 1 All ER 908, discussed below.

their publication. In deciding whether to grant injunctions, the courts seek a balance of convenience.[80] The Court of Appeal lifted the interlocutory injunctions against publication by Hello! on varying grounds, including that the couple's claim was not strong (per Brooke LJ), that they treated privacy as a commodity (per Sedley LJ), and that they had in fact arranged considerable publicity for the occasion (per Keene LJ). The Court of Appeal judges considered that, if a cause of action were found to lie for breach of confidentiality, damages would be a sufficient remedy.[81] This decision was made before the House of Lords' decision in *Campbell v MGN*,[82] discussed below, or the European Court of Human Rights decision in *von Hannover v Germany*[83] and, as we shall see, the Court of Appeal criticised this approach in a later *Douglas v Hello!* hearing.

One of the judges in *Douglas v Hello!*, Sedley LJ, stated that: '[W]e have reached a point at which it can be said with confidence that the law recognizes and will appropriately protect a personal right of privacy',[84] though at the same time he recognised that the right was still 'grounded in the equitable doctrine of breach of confidence'[85] and was not a separate free-standing right. The right remained in essence an *English* law right and was not a directly horizontally effective Convention right.

Brooke LJ, in the Court of Appeal, suggested that there might be a directly, horizontally effective *English* law right to privacy as such in certain matters, on the basis of the section 12 HRA provision, noted earlier, referring to 'any relevant code'. This brought the Press Complaints Commission Code of Practice on privacy into the picture, and Brooke LJ commented: 'A newspaper which flouts clause 3 of the code is likely in those circumstances to have its claim to an entitlement to freedom of expression trumped by art. 10(2) considerations of privacy.'[86] Equally, section 12 of the HRA gives

80 *American Cyanamid Ltd v Ethicon Ltd* [1975] AC 396.

81 Respectively at paras 60 and 95, 137 and 144 and 171.

82 [2004] 2 AC 457.

83 40 EHRR 1.

84 Para 110.

85 Para 125.

86 Para 94. Article 10(2) provides that 'The exercise of [freedom of expression] ... may be subject to such ... restrictions ... as are prescribed by law and are necessary in a democratic society, ... for the protection of the ... *rights* of others ...' The right in question would be the Article 8 right to privacy.

some express horizontal effect to the Article 10 right to free speech, since it requires special weight to be given to journalistic free speech, which would commonly arise as an issue where the press was the defendant in a case, i.e. not in vertical situations.[87] Indeed, it has been universally assumed (and the contrary has not even been argued) that the press are entitled to rely on Article 10 even in disputes with private parties to limit reputation and privacy rights.

Since then the case law on this point has moved on further: Lord Woolf CJ found in *A v B and others*[88] that 'a duty of confidence will arise whenever the party subject to the duty is in a situation where he either knows or ought to know that the other person can reasonably expect his privacy to be protected'. (In other contexts the phrases 'legitimate expectation' or 'legitimate interest' have been used and appear to carry the same meaning as 'reasonable expectation'.[89])

Jumping ahead in the story of the *Douglas v Hello!* litigation, having lost their claims for an injunction, the couple and the publishers of OK! Magazine pursued their claims in damages. At first instance[90] the couple had been awarded a modest sum including £3,750 each for the distress caused by the breach of confidence; OK! obtained an award in excess of £1 million against Hello! for breach of its commercial confidence and consequent loss of sales. On appeal to the Court of Appeal,[91] the awards to the couple and to OK! were upheld, but the court indicated that the interlocutory injunction should not have been lifted.

Liability, held the Court of Appeal, rested substantially on English domestic law rather than on the Convention rights, though developed so as to give effect to Articles 8 and 10 of the Convention. For a duty of confidence to arise in principle, the information had to be confidential in nature and imparted in circumstances where a duty of confidentiality arose or where it was

---

87 See per Sedley LJ in *Douglas*, supra, at para 133.

88 [2002] EWCA Civ 337.

89 The word 'expectation' in this context may be an English rendering of 'intérêt' (French) or 'interesse' (Italian). In fact, 'interest', which does not suggest (as 'legitimate expectation' does) that the defendant has done something to generate the expectation, might be a more appropriate term.

90 See *Douglas v Hello! (No. 2)* [2003] EWHC 786 (Ch), [2003] EWHC 2629 (Ch).

91 *Douglas v Hello! (No. 3)* [2005] EWCA Civ 595, CA.

plainly confidential or private; the test in English law was whether the would-be publisher knew or ought to have known that the claimants had a reasonable expectation that the information would remain private. But a balance has to be achieved between conflicting rights: the freedom to publish had to be weighed against the duty of confidentiality. This brought the court to the question of remedies.

The Court of Appeal held that, in retrospect, the injunctions should have remained in place in view of the subsequent decisions in *Campbell* and *von Hannover*, which indicated that the claimants' case was 'virtually unanswerable', there had been no real public interest in publication of the wrongly taken photographs, and a damages award, being necessarily small for mental distress, was not an adequate remedy nor an adequate deterrent against unlawful publication.[92] Ultimately, then, in *Douglas v Hello!* the ECHR was given indirect horizontal effect via the development of the common law. The level of damages award will be relatively low and consequently injunctions will be appropriate remedies in such cases.[93]

In the case of *Venables v News Group Newspapers*[94] too the court rested its protection for 'privacy' on English law, this time involving both confidentiality and, of particular weight, the common law and Convention rights to life and security. Two young men had been sentenced for the notorious murder of a toddler when they were aged about 12 years old. Both were coming to the end of their prison sentences and sought anonymity on their release to protect them from revenge attacks and to enable them to lead normal lives. They sought injunctions against the world restraining publication of information that could lead to their being identified. The President of the Family Division, Dame Elizabeth Butler-Sloss, granted the injunctions on the basis that they were necessary in order to protect the lives and physical security of the young men.[95]

---

[92] Paras 252–9.

[93] The decision is being appealed to the Appellate Committee of the House of Lords. As of December 2006 the appeal has not been heard.

[94] [2001] 1 All ER 908.

[95] See also *CC v AB* [2006] EWHC 3083, QB, in which Eady J granted an interim injunction restraining a cuckolded husband from publishing information about his wife's affair for revenge and for commercial gain. The judge's reasons included the need to protect the psychological health of the wife's lover's family.

She specifically held that claimants in private law proceedings could not rely on a free-standing application under the Convention – i.e. Article 8 had no direct horizontal effect.[96] She referred to Articles 8 and 10 of the ECHR and to the HRA, but maintained that they did not establish new law. They reinforced and gave greater weight to principles already established in the English case law.[97] As she put it, the HRA by section 6 required the courts to 'act compatibly with Convention rights in adjudicating upon existing common law causes of action'.

Although Butler-Sloss P referred to Articles 2 and 3, the rights to life and freedom from inhuman and degrading treatment articles, and the positive obligation on the state to secure their protection, it may very well be that she would have reached the same conclusion without reference to the HRA or the ECHR:

> In my judgment, the court does have the jurisdiction, in exceptional cases, to extend the protection of confidentiality of information, even to impose restrictions on the press, where not to do so would be likely to lead to serious physical injury, or to death, of the person seeking that confidentiality, and there is no other way to protect the applicants other than by seeking relief from the court.[98]

She stressed that it might not be appropriate to grant injunctions to restrict the press if Article 8 was the only article likely to be breached, and that she based her decision on the Articles 2 and 3 considerations.[99] It is significant that there was no relationship between the claimants and the press in this case.

The criteria for determining whether information was public or private and whether there is a public interest in receiving information about the private lives of celebrities were considered in *Campbell v Mirror Group Newspapers Ltd.*[100] A well-known model applied for an injunction restraining publication of information that she was receiving treatment for drug addiction. She had earlier denied to the press that she had an addiction. The parties agreed that she was not entitled to a remedy for the disclosure that she had this problem. By implication there is a public interest in revealing hypocrisy on the part of figures with a public profile,

---

96 Paras 27, 30.
97 Para 36.
98 Para 81.
99 Para 86.
100 [2004] 2 AC 457.

including, according to *A v B*,[101] those who may be regarded as role models by young people, and this public interest negates or overrides a right to confidentiality. Applying the approach of Lord Woolf CJ in *A v B*, it was accepted in *Campbell* that a person cannot have a reasonable expectation that information that discloses hypocrisy and lies will not be published. Campbell was, however, awarded damages totaling £3,500, including £1,000 in aggravated damages, for the breach of confidentiality in the publication of information about the treatment she was receiving.

The test applied by Lord Hope in *Campbell* was whether the information in question was public or private. Information about treatment was private in the sense that there was some interest of a private nature that the claimant wished to protect.[102] One way of resolving the issue in cases where it was not self-evident that the information was private was by asking what would be the reaction of a reasonable person of ordinary sensibilities in the position of the claimant if information of that kind were published about them.[103] Lord Hope was particularly influenced by the fact that the success of the treatment a person was receiving for a medical condition might be reduced by publication of the information. A risk to health was impliedly at stake in addition to the normal challenges to autonomy and dignity, including loss of esteem and respect, that invasions of privacy entail.

Even where a right to confidentiality or protection against misuse of information (or protection of private information[104]) is in principle established, however, the next question is how it is to be balanced against the right to freedom of expression, especially in cases between the individual and the press. Neither Article 8 nor Article 10 has pre-eminence the one over the other. Both articles recognise the need to respect the rights of others. Article 10(2), however, unlike Article 8, recognises that its exercise carries with it 'duties and responsibilities'. In *Campbell* Lord Hope looked to the

---

[101] *A v B and others* [2002] EWCA 337. (A famous footballer sought an injunction to prevent publication of a story that he had extra-marital affairs. The interim injunction that had been granted was lifted. Since the European Court of Human Rights decision in *von Hannover*, supra, the balance might go the other way in such a case in future.)

[102] Para 92.

[103] Paras 92–9.

[104] See N. A. Moreham (2005), op. cit.

jurisprudence of the European Court of Human Rights on the matter, as judges are required to do by section 2 of the HRA. He also took into account section 12(4) of the HRA, requiring the court to have particular regard to the importance of freedom of the press where journalistic material is involved: 'Essentially neither article 8 nor article 10 has any pre-eminence over the other in the conduct of this [balancing] exercise.' Lord Hope formulated the tests that the court should apply when balancing the right to privacy against freedom of expression as being: (i) does the publication have a legitimate aim? and (ii) are the benefits of publication proportionate to the harm that may be done?[105] He thus introduced a version of the proportionality test into the horizontal sphere. Baroness Hale was also explicit that the balance involved a proportionality test.[106] Having applied the test, Lord Hope, with the majority in the House of Lords, held that Campbell was entitled to damages for the publication of private, confidential information about her treatment.[107]

In the last of the cases we shall refer to as illustrations of the balancing of the rights to privacy and free speech in this case study, *McKennitt v Ash*,[108] the trial judge reviewed the case law of the European Court of Human Rights in considerable detail and synthesised the common law and a number of ECHR principles. This approach was approved by the Court of Appeal.[109] The plaintiff sought to restrain the publication of passages in a book written by a former friend which revealed details of her private life and of intimate conversations she had had with the author. The reasoning process adopted by the trial judge illustrates the adaptability of common law methodology.

First, Eady J sought to systematise the approach to be adopted. He set out the text of Article 8 and reviewed recent English case law and stated that, under the 'new methodology' (a phrase also used in *Campbell*) adopted under the Human Rights Act:

- neither article had precedence over the other;
- where there was conflict between the two rights there should be 'intense focus' on the comparative importance of the rights in the individual case;

---

105 Para 113.
106 At para 140.
107 Para 125.
108 [2005] EWHC 3003, QB, Eady J.
109 *Ash v McKennitt* [2006] EWCA Civ 1714.

- the court must take into account the justifications for interfering with or restricting the rights;
- and the proportionality test must be applied to each.[110]

Then, drawing on the Strasbourg case law and synthesising it with English case law, he noted that:

- 'private life' included a person's physical and psychological integrity and personality;
- individuals have a legally recognised 'legitimate expectation' of protection and respect for private life even where what takes place can be witnessed in a public place;[111]
- public interest or general interest in publication of information about a person's privacy is unlikely to arise where the person performs no public function;
- the public has no 'legitimate interest' in knowing about the plaintiff's private life;[112]
- the mere fact that information is 'anodyne or trivial' does not necessarily exclude it from the protection of Article 8, though it may do so; if such information is covered by confidentiality its triviality may be relevant to proportionality so that it may not be protected;[113]
- whether a person has a reasonable expectation[114] of protection of privacy may depend on the nature of the information or on factors such as the circumstances in which it was voluntarily imparted to another;[115]
- a right to respect, e.g. for one's home, means that 'correspondingly, there would be an obligation of confidence'.[116]

---

110 Para 48.

111 This ingredient was based on Strasbourg cases: paras 50–3.

112 These two elements draw on Strasbourg and English case law: paras 54–7.

113 This element draws on both Strasbourg and English case law: para 58; see also paras 134–5, 139, 141, 150.

114 On the meanings of 'reasonable expectation', see N. A. Moreham, op. cit.

115 Here the reference is to English case law only: paras 59–60.

116 Para 135. This neatly brings the English law of confidentiality and the Article 8 rights together.

Limiting principles include:

- whether the information is confidential (i.e. whether it has entered the public domain);
- useless or trivial information is not protected;
- whether the public interest in the protection of confidences is outweighed by a countervailing public interest in disclosure.[117]

Thus, Eady J held, in deciding whether Article 8 was engaged the first task was to identify whether there was a reasonable expectation of privacy, which was another way of asking whether the information had the 'quality of confidence',[118] and the second was to ask whether there was a countervailing public interest. On the countervailing public interest point he held that, while there might, according to the English case law, be a public interest in disclosing iniquity, 'a very high degree of misbehaviour must be demonstrated',[119] such as perjury or perverting the course of justice.[120] Not every peccadillo or foible cropping up in day-to-day life would be exposed.[121]

The reasoning process in this judgment in *McKennitt* is typically inductive rather than deductive: the Convention and the common law are woven together in a way that brings the common law into compliance with Convention rights so far as they are relevant to the particular case. But the end result of the case is that the freedoms of the press and, importantly, of private individuals (one of the defendants in the case was the author of the book) to publish information about the private life of an individual is quite strongly limited, as indeed the Strasbourg case law, notably *von Hannover*, requires. Although the defendant author was writing about her own private life, the right to do so and publish under Article 10 was limited by the right of the claimant under Article 8.[122] The presumption appears to be that once a right to privacy or confidentiality has been established it does trump the right of others, whether private individuals or the press, to publish information,

117 Here the references are to English case law: para 61.

118 Para 63.

119 Para 97.

120 Para 98.

121 Para 97.

122 Para 137.

unless the defendant can discharge the burden of convincing the court that there is a countervailing public interest in publication which outweighs the right to privacy. This position may not, however, differ from the pre-HRA position on the law of confidence, where the defendant was clearly required to show a public interest in disclosure.

The Court of Appeal upheld the judgment of Eady J. Lord Justice Buxton, giving the leading judgment, noted that the positive obligation imposed on states by the ECHR finds expression in section 6 of the HRA; that in fact the claimant could succeed in English law without reference to *von Hannover*;[123] but that that case could also be applied in support of the claimant's case;[124] and that the content of the English law of confidence is not to be found in Articles 8 and 10 ECHR.[125]

3. Summary

The influence of the HRA and its requirement of both developmental and interpretive approaches to indirect horizontal effect is very clearly illustrated in case law on same-sex couples in landlord and tenant cases and in relation to clashes between the right to privacy and freedom of the press.

Using techniques of compatible interpretation and common law development the English courts have gone a considerable distance to establish a right to privacy to meet the requirements of Article 8 ECHR. The change of direction in the *Ghaidan* case is obvious. The case law on privacy in relation to the press has developed greatly since the decision in *Kaye v Robertson*. If the facts in *Kaye v Robertson* were to arise nowadays, there is little doubt that the claimant would win. The court would probably decide that, the information having the quality of confidentiality, i.e. not being in the public domain, the claimant had a reasonable expectation that such photographs would not be published, their subject matter being private. In balancing the claims of the press to be entitled to publish against the interests of the claimant the court would hold that the rights of the claimant outweighed those of the press, damages

---

123 [2006] EWCA Civ, para 37.

124 Ibid at paras 40–2, 63.

125 Ibid at paras 10, 59.

would not be a sufficient remedy, and an injunction against publication would be a proportionate and legitimate restriction on the press's freedom, there being no sufficiently strong and proportionate countervailing *public* interest (such as the disclosure of serious hypocrisy) in the press publishing them as against the undermining of the claimant's dignity and autonomy that publication would entail.

However, as no doubt in most legal systems that seek to protect privacy, the English courts have not been willing to grant complete protection. They have to balance the right to privacy against freedom of speech, particularly of the press, and public interests, and in so doing they have elaborated some of the specific policy considerations at issue. In *Campbell* in the House of Lords the balance was held not to point one way or another *in principle*. The courts need to weigh the public interest in maintaining confidence and the countervailing public interest favouring disclosure in each case. The way in which the balance is made affects both the remedies that may be granted, and the extent of the right to privacy itself. On the one hand, is the public interest in, for instance, the exposure of hypocrisy and the commission of criminal offences, which the parties in the *Campbell* case agreed outweighed any right to privacy and therefore meant there could be no award of damages for publication of information only on that matter. Eady J in *McKennitt*, however, draws the line at peccadillos or foibles. On the other hand, in *Campbell* privacy did require non-disclosure of information that might damage a person's health, and damages were awarded for that damage.

What is striking about the development of the case law on discrimination and confidentiality since the coming into effect of the HRA is not only its rapidity and incremental nature, but also the ease with which the courts have adopted the proportionality tests required by the Convention in applying the new principle of compatible interpretation and developing the indirect horizontal effect of Articles 8 and 10 in *English* law. They have in fact made full use of the flexibility and subtlety of the common law method. In effect they have been checking English law against the requirements of the Convention without creating new causes of action. They differ in this from the courts in New Zealand, where a new tort of unreasonable invasion of privacy has been developed. The English courts have been fortunate in not having to grapple with the requirements of 'state action' doctrine, as courts in the United States have done, and in not having to engage with issues that frame the debate in Germany, for instance, around the appropriateness or otherwise of constitutionalising human rights in the private sphere. Their level of theorising has been less complex and sophisticated than that in some jurisdictions. On the other hand it has been deeply principled, focusing on universal underlying values that the courts consider to apply in both the public and the private sphere. Here the absence of a tradition of a public private divide in the common law means that there are fewer inhibitions than in, for instance, France, in importing values from one part of the law to another. English courts have been quite surprisingly explicit about the underlying values and rationales for the rights set out in the Convention and the development of the common law and statutory interpretation. In the cases we have considered and in many others they have referred to the importance of human dignity and autonomy as the values underlying human rights protection, and explained why discriminatory attitudes that earlier informed the law, such as preference for heterosexual over homosexual relationships, are no longer appropriate.

It is also notable that the balancing by the courts of the individual's right to privacy and press freedom has 'depoliticised' the issue. As we noted at the outset, successive governments have been reluctant to secure legislation on the matter for fear of the political backlash this would cause from the press. Yet the courts, exercising the functions allocated to them under the Human Rights Act, have felt able, outside the field of politics, to develop the law in a pragmatic and incremental way to secure results that would have been politically impossible if the parliamentary route had been taken and a Privacy and the Press Bill had been introduced.

F. Conclusions

It is suggested that the incremental approach adopted by courts in England has been an appropriate way of developing the law in these areas. Inductive reasoning which forms part of the culture of the common law allows for sensitive development of the law: the development of the common law and equity, and statutory interpretation, need to be sensitive to the underlying values of human rights. There would be acute problems in developing full direct horizontal effect, or even extensive indirect horizontal effect, of human rights because of the conflicts between rights and parties that they open up and the complexities where decisions disrupt fundamental features of an existing statutory scheme. The courts have displayed considerable common sense here.

The ability of the courts to secure that English law complies with the positive obligation of the United Kingdom under the ECHR to extend protection of human rights to relations between private individuals is, however, limited. There will no doubt be further successful challenges to the legal position between private parties in the European Court of Human Rights unless detailed legislation is passed to deal with the many and conflicting interests of diverse parties that might be affected by increasing the protection of rights. An alternative would be the development in domestic law of state liability for breaches of 'Convention rights' attributable to governmental failure to secure that English law provides the required protection in the private sphere. But this is not currently on any agenda in the United Kingdom.

Chapter 3: France Horizontal Application and the Triumph of the European Convention on Human Rights

Myriam Hunter-Henin

A. Introduction

The horizontal application of human rights, also known by the German word *Drittwirkung*, describes the application of human rights provisions in the private sphere. In other words, human rights are applied horizontally between private individuals and not only vertically (as originally conceived) to relations between the state and the individual citizen. By contrast, in litigation against the state, its bodies or agents, private individuals appear inherently weaker; their rights will thus be applied vertically, in order to protect them against encroachment from a much more powerful party.

The doctrine of horizontal effect originated in Germany, especially after the Second World War, where the Basic Law defines fundamental rights broadly. These are seen not only as protecting individuals against interference from public action but also as the manifestation of objective values permeating the entire legal system.[1] From this last thought follows the belief that individuals should be allowed to call upon judges to interpret legislation – whether it be in public or private law – in compliance with these values. After some hesitation, it has come to be accepted that in such instances the Constitution has an indirect and not direct effect in private law. In France, in contrast to German law, the horizontal application of human right provisions has mostly a direct effect. Moreover, this flows not so much from the Constitution as from the European Convention of Human Rights. These two features, i.e. the direct effect and the 'conventional' basis of human rights horizontal application, give French law its distinctive features.

---

[1] Cf. B. Markesinis, *The German Law of Obligation*, vol. II, *The Law of Torts: a Comparative Introduction* (3rd edn, 1997), p 355.

B. Key constitutional texts

It is interesting to explore why the horizontal application of human rights in France did not occur through the Constitution.

This situation is not linked to the absence of key constitutional texts on human rights: The French Constitution, albeit with scarce human rights provisions in the body of the text,[2] contains all the basic individual freedoms derived from the liberal tradition and several social rights, via a reference in its Preamble to, respectively, the 1789 Declaration on the Rights of Man and the Citizen and the Preamble of the previous 1946 Constitution.

Nonetheless, none of these French principles was given constitutional status until a 1971 decision of the Conseil constitutionnel;[3] and their provisions are vaguer than the list of rights provided for in the German Basic Law.[4] But is clarity a requirement for the constitutional interpretation of a text? In France, could not the vagueness of the French text be seized upon as an opportunity to develop a creative and imaginative constitutional case law highly protective of human rights? If the opportunity has never been seized by the Conseil constitutionnel, it is probably because the role of that body is restricted.

C. The limited role of the Conseil Constitutionnel

The intervention of the Conseil constitutionnel is limited to a non compulsory (pre-promulgation) and abstract (before litigation) examination of legislation recently passed by Parliament.[5] In these circumstances, it is unlikely that the Conseil constitutionnel will envisage – especially in the short time frame of one month available for its review[6] – the potential implications of the text for private

---

[2] See especially with potential implications in private litigation: Art 1: respect for individual beliefs; Art 66: individual freedom.

[3] Decision 71-44 DC 16 July 1971 *Liberté d'association, Rec.* 29.

[4] Cf. J. Rivero, 'La Protection des droits de l'homme dans les rapports entre personnes privées' in *René Cassin Amicorum Discipulorumque Liber,* III, *Protection des droits de l'homme dans les rapports entre les personnes privées* (1971), pp 311–22, esp p 320.

[5] Article 61 §1 of the Constitution.

[6] Article 61 §3 of the Constitution.

law. Potential future litigation is to some extent born in mind by the French Conseil constitutionnel when they declare that a piece of legislation complies with the Constitution provided it is interpreted in a certain way; these interpretation guidelines or *réserves d'interprétation* could have constituted a tool for the indirect horizontal application of human rights, ordinary judges being indeed instructed in future litigation to construe *lois* in compliance with the requirements – as defined by the Conseil constitutionnel – of constitutional human rights. But this has not happened.

The impact of the Conseil constitutionnel guidelines on private law has remained limited. In addition to those already stated, several factors account for the lack of obvious influence of the Conseil constitutionnel on the Cour de cassation (the Supreme Court for French private law).

First, few of the interpretation guidelines delivered by the Conseil constitutionnel are relevant to private law: most of the Acts submitted to it for scrutiny relate to public law or criminal law (whether substantive or procedural) where individual rights will again be opposed to the state.[7]

Secondly, in relation to the approach of the Cour de cassation, a lack of enthusiasm for a possible integration of constitutional case law in private law has been underlined by several authors.[8] Indeed, the Cour de cassation never openly refers to a constitutional guideline unless the piece of legislation invoked in the case is a provision that has been previously examined by the Conseil constitutionnel.[9] This is not to say, however, that constitutional case law has no

---

[7] Cf. M. Delmas-Marty, 'La Jurisprudence du Conseil constitutionnel et les principes fondamentaux du droit pénal proclamés par la Déclaration de 1789' in *La Déclaration des droits de l'homme et du citoyen et la jurisprudence*, 'recherches juridiques' (1998), p 151, describing the 1789 Declaration as mainly a list of criminal law provisions. Besides, most of the references to the Conseil constitutionnel in private law case law relate to criminal law, on the basis of Articles 8, 9 and 7 of the 1789 Declaration relating to habeas corpus, protection against discretionary criminal sanctions and the presumption of innocence. See figures given by N. Molfessis, *Le Conseil constitutionnel et le droit privé* (1997), p 531.

[8] Cf. G. Rouhette, 'La Jurisprudence du Conseil constitutionnel dans le droit privé' in G. Drago, B. François and N. Molfessis (eds), *La Légitimité de la jurisprudence du Conseil constitutionnel* (1999), pp 141–51.

[9] Respect for the Conseil constitutionnel's decisions in that case is indeed made compulsory by virtue of Article 62 §2 of the Constitution, which states that the Conseil constitutionnel's decisions bind public bodies and all administrative or judicial authorities.

bearing on that of the Cour de cassation. It is surely no coincidence that no conflicting interpretation of a particular human right between the Cour de cassation and the Conseil constitutionnel has ever been identified. Can the implicit nature of the (possible) recognition of constitutional case law by the Cour de cassation be seen as a sign of reluctance to be explicit on the matter, in view of the elliptical character of all of the Cour de cassation's decisions and its constant refusal to quote case law or a particular decision in support of any of its rulings?[10] The silence of the Cour de cassation about constitutional case law cannot therefore exclude the possibility of real influence of Constitutional freedoms – possibly implicitly used as a reference in construing applicable texts – in private litigation[11] – unless it is the Conseil constitutionnel which follows private case law[12] which, after all, has come first. However, this seems unlikely.

Reciprocal waves of influence between private and constitutional law can thus be detected, and this goes against the French tradition which advocates a clear divide between private and public law and which survives artificially because of the way several generations of lawyers were tightly trained on one or the other side of the border.[13] However, besides these educational (and changing) problems, the strict rules of jurisdiction constitute an insurmountable obstacle to the effective and rapid horizontal application of constitutional human rights by private law judges. In France, no individual is allowed to invoke the jurisdiction of the Conseil constitutionnel[14] nor is he/she authorised to invoke a constitutional

---

[10] Despite signs of evolution (see, e.g., *Les Revirements de jurisprudence*, Rapport sous la direction de M. le Professeur Nicolas Molfessis remis à M. le Premier Président Guy Canivet, La Documentation française, 2005) case law is indeed still not officially recognised as a source of French private law. The Cour de cassation still strictly complies for that matter with Art 17 of the 27 November 1790 Act, Art 1020 of the French Code of Civil Procedure and Art 5 of the French Civil Code.

[11] See, describing a hidden form of constitutional review by the Cour de cassation, M. Michel Jéol, premier avocat général à la Cour, *La Cour de cassation et la Constitution* (1995), p 69, quoted by J. Gicquel, 'La Cour de cassation et le contrôle de constitutionnalité de la loi au XXème siècle' in D. Chagnollaud (ed) *Aux origines du contrôle de constitutionnalité XVII ^{ème}-XX ^{ème}* siècles (2003), p 195.

[12] See N. Molfessis, *Le Conseil constitutionnel et le droit privé*, op. cit., pp 440–82.

[13] On the lack of a 'constitutional frame of mind' amongst French private lawyers and parties, see M. Frangi, *Constitution et droit privé* (1992), p 267.

[14] Since the 29 October 1974 reform, the Conseil constitutionnel has in effect been opened to political opposition. In 1974, 60 members of the lower house of the

principle in litigation, as this would be asking ordinary judges to check a piece of legislation against the Constitution, a task which exclusively belongs to the Conseil constitutionnel.[15] Depriving French law of any possible direct horizontal application of constitutional rights, this restrictive access to the Conseil constitutionnel moreover considerably limits any indirect application of such rights.

Although the possibility of implicit application of constitutional rights by the Cour de cassation has been considered above, one has to confess that the abstract formulation of principles by the Conseil constitutionnel makes their application in private litigation difficult. Even though the Conseil constitutionnel's decisions are much more detailed than those rendered by the Cour de cassation in private law cases (and indeed by the Conseil d'Etat in public law cases), the pre-promulgation nature of French constitutional review gives it an abstract style of reasoning which is quite foreign to the concrete disputes that lead to the Cour de cassation's rulings. It is true that at first sight, decisions by the Cour de cassation will also look very abstract. Indeed, Cour de cassation judges will not examine the facts of the case put before them but rather rely on the findings made by the lower courts. Moreover, their ruling will be based on a particular interpretation of the law and not on factual considerations. There is no doubt, however, that facts do play an important role in the Cour de cassation's decisions. Commentators always refer to the facts of a case in order to ascertain the ambit of a particular ruling by the Cour de cassation and to determine the underlying justification of a particular decision. Facts are more remote from the Conseil constitutionnel's decisions, as reviews of constitutionality do not stem from a dispute, from litigation but from a complaint made about a piece of legislation which has not been implemented and has never yet been applied. Facts will enter into the reasoning to some extent as French constitutional judges will speculate on the various potential factual implications of the text, but

---

French Parliament or 60 members of the upper house of the French Parliament were given entitlement, together with the four most eminent political figures – the President of the French Republic, the Prime Minister and the President of each of the French Houses of Parliament – to refer legislation to the Conseil constitutionnel (Art 61 §2 of the French Constitution).

[15] French ordinary judges have constantly refused to review the compatibility of French legislation with the French Constitution; cf. for administrative courts: CE 6 November 1936, *S.*1937.3.33, Conclusions X. Latournerie and for private law courts: Cass. Crim. 11 May 1833, *S.*1833.1.357.

the perspective will in any case remain vertical. The question put to the Conseil constitutionnel is indeed whether the state (or more specifically Parliament) has violated Constitutional rights in passing the piece of legislation in question. Hence, whenever the Conseil constitutionnel has touched on the issue of conflicting private rights, the matter has been dealt with swiftly. The Conseil constitutionnel has not given priority to certain rights over others, it has merely reminded the legislator of its duty to seek to reconcile constitutional principles and other values of equal standing.[16] The Cour de cassation is thus not given enough clues by the Conseil constitutionnel on how to balance conflicting constitutional human rights. It is, moreover, unable to submit preliminary questions to the Conseil constitutionnel for clarification, and nor is it willing to take the initiative of giving a more practical content to constitutional principles and later face possible contradiction from the Conseil constitutionnel.[17] Abstract principles are hard to handle in private litigation where judges are no longer only asked to confront two norms but are required to solve a dispute between two parties. Inevitably, a much more nuanced approach will be necessary and the blunt and solemn decisions of the Conseil constitutionnel – even tempered by interpretation guidelines – will be of little help.

D. The 'conventionalisation' of private law

Horizontal application of human rights has, however, taken place in France through the European Convention on Human Rights, which has become the key text on human rights in private law,[18] together with Article 55 of the Constitution, which allows the direct application of properly ratified international treaties by French courts.[19]

---

16 See Decision 181 DC 10 and 11 October 1984 *Entreprises de presse, Rec.* 73, §37.

17 See N. Molfessis, *Le Conseil constitutionnel et le droit privé*, op. cit., pp 537–8.

18 And indeed public law, thus undermining the public–private law divide. Cf. about the European Court's insensitivity towards the private/public law divide, P. Tavernier, 'La Convention européenne des droits de l'homme et la distinction droit public/droit privé' in *Liber amicorum M.-A. Eissen* (1995), p 399, esp p 400.

19 According to Art 55 of the Constitution, direct effect of international treaties is subjected to a condition of reciprocity. But this condition does not apply to a treaty on human rights. See F. Sudre, 'La Dimension internationale et européenne des libertés et droits fondamentaux' in R. Cabrillac, M.-A. Frison-Roche and T. Revet (eds), *Libertés et droits fondamentaux*, pp 35–56.

There is no more possibility for French ordinary judges to refer preliminary interpretation questions to the European Court of Human Rights than there is to consult the Conseil constitutionnel. However, in the European Convention context, at least since October 1981 when individual access to the Court was finally granted by France,[20] French judges can rely on a rich and detailed case law. Thus, through the influence of the European Convention, there has been both an indirect[21] and direct[22] effect of human rights in French private law.

If the direct horizontal application of the European Convention on Human Rights is grounded in Article 55 of the French Constitution, indirect application of the Convention stems from various provisions of the Convention[23] as well as, most of all, from the positive obligations imposed by the European Court on Member States.[24] Through its indirect dimension, horizontal application of the Conventional Human Rights relies on Member States whose duty it is, according to the European Court, to make sure that private parties under their jurisdiction do not violate the rights protected under the Convention. Member States are thus not only under the passive (negative) obligation to refrain from infringing the Convention human rights, they also have to take positive steps – hence the doctrine of positive obligations – to deter violations by private parties.

---

[20] Décret n°81-917 9 October 1981, *J.O.* 14 October 1981, p 2783.

[21] See, e.g., European Court of Human Rights, 29 April 1997 *HLR v France, RTDciv.* 1999, p 500, holding that the expulsion to his country of origin of a Columbian, convicted in France for drug offences, who claimed that his return would put him at risk of retaliation measures from local drug dealers, fell within the ambit of Art 3 of the Convention (protecting everyone against torture and inhuman and degrading treatment). Although in that case the threat was deemed not to be serious enough to justify a ruling against France, the application of the Convention was clearly upheld, notwithstanding the fact that the threats of inhuman treatment came from private parties (local drug dealers) and not state authorities.

[22] See numerous examples below.

[23] For a list of the relevant articles, see E. Albert Alkema, 'The Third Party Applicability or *Drittwirkung* of the European Convention on Human Rights in protecting Human Rights: the European Dimension' in F. Matscher and H. Petzold (eds), *Studies in Honour of Gerard J. Wiarda* (1988), pp 33–45, esp p 36; D. Spielman, 'Obligations positives et effet horizontal des dispositions de la Convention' in *L'Interprétation de la Convention européenne des droits de l'homme*, Actes du Colloque de l'IEDH à Montpellier des 13 et 14 mars 1998 (1998), p 161.

[24] See European Court, 26 March 1995 *X and Y v The Netherlands*, Série A, n°91.

Opposition to the horizontal application of human rights was (is?), however, strong in France, due to the fear of judge-made law. Such a fear is precisely the reason why the intervention of the Conseil constitutionnel is so strictly restrained in France.[25] If the 1958 Constitution for the first time conceived a form of censorship of the legislator, this is seen as the Conseil constitutionnel's prerogative and – as already pointed out – can only be exercised in limited circumstances. Ordinary judges were expected to be much more respectful of legislation and for a while the Cour de cassation was indeed reluctant to set aside an Act of Parliament which violated a fundamental right subsequently entrenched in an international convention. This reluctance still allowed an indirect application of human rights whereby Acts of Parliament were so far as possible interpreted in compliance with the European Convention. In the Jacques Vabre decision of 1975,[26] the Cour de cassation went one step further and, for the first time, set aside legislation which was in clear opposition to the provisions of a previous international Treaty.[27]

The way was thus opened for a flow of references to the European Convention on Human Rights by the Cour de cassation, leading to a true 'conventionalisation' of French private law and the direct horizontal application of ECHR human rights. The more the European Convention has been applied, the more incentive there has been to apply it in the future as French lawyers progressively realise the extraordinary mechanism that was available to them, and parties have become more and more aware of the endless source of rights on which they can rely.

Thus, horizontal application of human rights in France is specific in that it is carried out mostly directly and 'conventionally', i.e. via

---

[25] Initially, in 1958, the Conseil constitutionnel was only created in order to make sure that the legislator and the government each stayed within the sphere in which the Constitution allowed them to pass texts (See M. Dejean's comments in *Documents pour servir à l'élaboration de l'histoire de la Constitution du 4 octobre 1958*, La Documentation française, vol. 11 (1988), p 286). It is only in the early 1970s, with the bold decision 70-39 DC of 19 June 1970 (*Rec.*, p 15), that the Conseil constitutionnel conferred constitutional standing on the human rights barely mentioned in the Preamble and consequently unyield the power to review legislation violating individual freedoms (Decision 71-44 DC of 16 July 1971 *Liberté d'association (Rec.* 29)).

[26] Civ. 24 May 1975, *Jacques Vabre, D.*1975, p 496, Conclusions Touffait.

[27] The Jacques Vabre case deals with a provision of the EC Rome Treaty but its reasoning can be extented to the European Convention on Human Rights.

the European Convention on Human Rights. This situation has, however, attracted criticism: the new private law created is often accused of being an antidemocratic judge-made law which distorts both the concept of human rights[28] and the logic of private law categories.[29] Our own appraisal will be based on the study of the following important topics and cases.

E. Case studies

1. Privacy and family life – the home

(a) Employers and employees

In the *Spileers* case of 1999, an employee (a sales representative called Mr Spileers) was bound by his work contract to move his family home to his new working area within six months of his transfer to his new employment. First settled with his family in the Paris area from which he could cover the Paris region, the North and East of France, Mr Spileers was then transferred to the region of Montpellier in the South of France. The employee organised accommodation for himself near Montpellier during the week but refused to move his family home there and was consequently dismissed without any compensation. The lower courts (Employment Tribunal and Court of Appeal) pointed to the terms of the contract and held in favour of the employer. The Cour de cassation,[30] however, quashed the Court of Appeal's decision, stating that: 'Under article 8 of the European Convention on Human Rights, everybody has a right to freely choose his personal and family home.' In unequal relationships, whether of a public or private nature, the stronger party must therefore pay due consideration to the weaker party's family interests.

Decisions by the stronger party are thus subjected to a proportionality test: 'Restrictions by the employer to this freedom of choice can only be allowed if they are necessary to protect the firm's legitimate interests and there is proportionality between the

---

[28] P. Fraissex, 'Les Droits fondamentaux, prolongement ou dénaturation des droits de l'homme?' *RDP* 2001, pp 531–53, esp p 533.

[29] Cf. P. Malaurie, 'La Convention européenne des droits de l'homme et le droit civil français' *J.C.P.*2002.I.143.

[30] Cass. Soc. 12 January 1999, *Spileers v SARL Omni Pac, D.*1999, p 635.

position occupied, the functions carried out on the one hand and the goal pursued by the employer on the other,' added the Cour de cassation in *Spileers*.

A few commentators[31] have criticised the extension of the proportionality test to the private sphere. According to Jean-Pierre Marguénaud and Jean Mouly,[32] the horizontal application of conventional human rights relies on the doctrine of positive obligations.[33] This should be taken into account, wrote the two authors, in the interpretation of the proportionality test. Indeed, where the state is in principle required not to interfere (in vertical situations), the proportionately test is designed to allow those exceptional interferences which are proportionate to the legitimate goal pursued by the state. On the other hand, where the state is expected to take positive steps to ensure the respect of human rights by third parties, the proportionality test is a prerequisite to the existence of the positive duty itself; the purpose of the balancing exercise will then be to ascertain whether the existence of a positive duty will be too heavy a constraint on state action.

This analysis is in my view very convincing. However, one may criticise the claim that domestic judges applying Convention rights horizontally should, as a consequence, follow the approach adopted by the European Court in the context of state positive obligations. According to Jean-Pierre Marguénaud and Jean Mouly,[34] domestic judges applying Convention rights horizontally should either come to the conclusion that there is no state positive obligation or hold that the right in question has been violated. The approach, therefore, would be 'all or nothing' reasoning and would leave no room for any balancing exercise. But in *Spileers*, the question put to the Cour de cassation was not whether the French state had any positive duty to act to avoid employers encroaching on their employees' right to a family home. The question was whether the employer *Omni Pac* had failed to refrain from encroaching on his employee's fundamental right to choose his family home. The issue raised, therefore, dealt with negative obligations, the employer's duty NOT to interfere. In its indirect dimension, horizontal application of human rights relies on positive duties but in its direct dimension, horizontal

31 J.-P. Marguénaud and J. Mouly, *D.*1999, p. 635, esp p 647.

32 Ibid.

33 Cf. note 22, supra.

34 Ibid, p 647.

application of human rights may involve either positive or negative duties depending on the behaviour which is at the source of litigation. Therefore, the Cour de cassation in *Spileers* seems to have legitimately subjected its ruling to a balancing exercise between the firm's legitimate interests and the employee's rights.

The suggested 'all or nothing' approach would, moreover, lead to unacceptable results in practice. Either provision for a change of accommodation would have to be struck out of all employment contracts, or forced transfer of family homes would have to be systematically upheld. The first option would be very damaging to the economy and the stability of employment contracts; the second would, on the other hand, put employees under the discretionary powers of their employers. Surely the more balanced solution chosen in *Spileers* by the Cour de cassation, thanks to a proportionality test between all interests at stake, is to be preferred![35]

The proportionality test carried out in *Spileers* was also criticised for blurring the traditional divide between the making and performance of contracts. The proportionality test introduced by the Cour de cassation in this 1999 decision would subject the validity of a contractual term to circumstances posterior to the conclusion of the contract.[36] But a contractual term may be validly inserted in a contract (issue relating to the contracting stage) and still have its application later restrained by various conditions (issue relating to performance), typically the requirement that it should be carried out in good faith (Art 1134 §3 of the French Civil Code). The addition of a proportionality test, for the sake of family rights, does not in my view drastically alter the reasoning nor does it violate the traditional – and

[35] J.-P. Marguénaud and J. Mouly are not against any form of proportionality test as they would willingly accept that contractual terms covered by Art 8 of the ECHR in its horizontal dimension, i.e. according to these authors, exclusively terms which affect employees' personal life (as opposed to their professional life), should be subjected to a proportionality test by virtue of Article L. 120-2 of the French Labour Code (ibid., p 648). But the distinction between terms affecting personal life and those whose impact is limited to the professional sphere seems to me difficult to draw in practice. Moreover, in my opinion, the argument whereby a proportionality test could not be carried out under Art 8 of the ECHR when applied horizontally, does not – as above expressed – stand. J.-P. Marguénaud and J. Mouly's return to a balancing exercise at the end of their paper shows anyhow that judicial solutions on human rights cannot do away with a careful and delicate weighing of conflicting interests.

[36] Ibid, p 647.

anyway probably less and less useful[37] – division between the stages of contracting and performance. In any case, in my view, the Cour de cassation in *Spileers* does not purport to ascertain the validity of the contractual term but only to evaluate whether its application was reasonable and legitimate. The confusion stems from the ambiguity of the Cour de cassation's justification:

> In order to decide that the dismissal for non compliance with the contested contractual term relied on a serious and real ground, the Court of appeal considered the term to be valid ...; in so holding, without verifying that the transfer of a family home was a necessity for the firm ... especially as the employee was willing to transfer his personal residence to Montpellier; without verifying either that this restriction on the employee's freedom to choose his family home was proportionate to the goal sought by the employer ... especially as it was not apparent from M. Spileers' functions why his permanent presence in the Montpellier region was needed, the Court of appeal failed to give any legal basis to its decision.

The Cour de cassation does not in my view hereby assert that the contractual condition is not valid due to a disproportion in the degree of restriction imposed on the employee on the one hand and the legitimate interests of his firm on the other; it criticises the Court of appeal for failing to go beyond the question of the validity of the term. It is not only the wording of contractual terms but the way they are enforced by parties which must be compatible with human rights. The Court of appeal could not therefore uphold the dismissal without first examining how the employer had used the contractual provision allowing for the transfer of M Spileers' family residence. In my view, the Cour de cassation therefore not only respects the division between contracting and performance of contracts; it comes to a reasonable solution, highly protective of human rights. If protection was restricted to the stage of the making of the contract, abuse of legitimate contractual powers could not be punished and human right protection would have little practical impact. Theoretical divisions and categories must not hide or hinder the purpose of human rights, which, whether in a vertical or horizontal sense, is *le respect de l'Autre*.[38]

---

[37] Cf. recent contract case law undermining the distinction between conclusion and performance: A.P. 1 December 1995, *Bull. civ.*, n°7 (2 cases); Com. 22 October 1996 *Chronopost 1*, *Bull. civ.* IV, n°261.

[38] P. de Fontbressin, 'L'Effet horizontal de la Convention européenne des droits de l'homme et l'avenir du droit des obligations', *Liber amicorum Marc-André Eissen* (2005), pp 157–64, esp p 163.

Finally, the proportionality test may easily be linked to the 'spirit'[39] if not to the case law of the European Court.[40]

Despite the growing importance of the right to family life under Article 8 of the European Convention, both in European and Conseil d'Etat case law, it is difficult to state with absolute certainty that the *Spileers* case signals the beginning of a regular direct and horizontal application of that right by the Cour de cassation. Indeed, one cannot rule out the possible influence of a purely domestic provision – Article L. 120-2 of the French Labour Code – stating that 'any limitations by the employer to individual rights and freedoms must be justified by the nature of the tasks to be accomplished and proportionate to the goal pursued'. Although not applicable to the *Spileers* case because it was not yet in force at the time the contract was concluded, this provision emphasises the importance of proportionality and the protection of human rights in the working environment, thus sharing exactly the Cour de cassation's concerns. Could the Cour de cassation have therefore only relied on Article 8 of the European Convention because of the lack of applicability of Article L. 120-2? Would the domestic provision in future similar cases be preferred to a horizontal direct application of the Convention right? If the Cour de cassation wished implicitly to refer to Article L. 120-2 of the Labour Code, why depart from the terms of this provision in its *ratio decidendi*?[41] In my opinion, the *Spileers* case illustrates a clear instance of a horizontal application of Article 8 of the ECHR protecting the right to respect for a family home.

It is true that this increased protection comes along with increased control by the Cour de cassation. Whereas traditionally the existence of a legitimate and serious cause for dismissal was left to the discretion of lower courts,[42] the threat to a human right here justifies the Cour de cassation's intervention. One cannot, however,

---

[39] Cf. C. Uzan-Sarano, *L'Application de la Convention européenne des droits de l'homme par la Cour de cassation dans les relations interindividuelles de nature contractuelle*, Dissertation for l'IFRAC (2005), p 25.

[40] Cf. European Court 12 June 2003 *Van Kück v Germany*, req. n°35968/97, 2003-VII.

[41] As noted by A. Debet, *L'Influence de la Convention européenne des droits de l'homme sur le droit civil* (2002), n°455, p 431, whereas the Cour de cassation refers to a restriction 'indispensable to the post held and the work required', Article L. 120-2 provides that 'restrictions must be justified by the nature of the tasks to be done and proportionate to the goal pursued'.

[42] Cf. Soc. 10 December 1985, *D.*1986, p 120, note Boré.

wave against this decision the fear of judge-made law; it only leads to a transfer of powers from lower courts to the Supreme Court. In my opinion, uniformity and consistency of the law as well as individual freedoms have only to gain from such an evolution. This favourable conclusion needs, however, to be tempered in view of the risk of contradictory solutions. The direct horizontal application by the Cour de cassation of human rights *as interpreted by the European Court* is one thing; the direct horizontal application of conventional rights *as interpreted by the Cour de cassation* is another. In the latter situation, the solution reached by the Cour de cassation faces the risk of future contradiction by the European Court. Thus commentators on the *Spileers* case have underlined that the European Court never adopted such a wide definition of the right to respect for a home.[43] It seems to me unlikely, though, that the European Court would disapprove an interpretation which improves the protection afforded to the weaker party while insisting on the need to strike a balance between the interests of the two parties concerned. In *Buckley v United Kingdom*, the European Court held that Article 8 did not necessarily allow for individual preferences as to the place of abode to prevail over public interests and consequently saw no violation of Article 8 in the United Kingdom's refusal to allow a gipsy mother to settle in her caravan on her plot of land.[44] The comparison between *Spileers* and *Buckley*, sometimes drawn in order to prove the Cour de cassation's audacity,[45] on the contrary, seems to reveal a real harmony between the Cour de cassation and the European Court. In both cases the two courts considered that the right to choose one's home was covered by Article 8 but that violation of Article 8 depended on the results of a balancing test. Factual considerations may explain the ruling of violation in *Spileers*. The Court of appeal it seems had not found any legitimate reasons justifying, above the transfer of his weekly professional residence, transfer of the employee's family home.

The *Spileers* decision should therefore be wholly welcomed. By contrast, more caution is probably needed towards the horizontal direct application of Article 8 protecting the home in landlord–tenant relationships.

---

[43] Cf. J.-P. Marguénaud and J. Mouly, note on Soc. 12 January 1999, *Spileers*, *D.*1999, pp 645–8, esp p 646.

[44] §81, *RTDH* 1997, p 64, note O. de Schutter.

[45] J.-P. Marguénaud and J. Mouly, op. cit.

(b) Landlords and tenants

The first instance where protection of the home under Article 8 of the European Convention on Human Rights received a direct and horizontal application by the Cour de cassation was in a landlord–tenant relationship. In the 1996 *Mel Yedei* case,[46] the landlord sought to obtain termination of the tenancy agreement, claiming that the tenant had not respected her contractual undertakings. The latter had, indeed, housed the father (and his sister) of her two youngest children, in violation of a contractual term which stated that the flat was for the tenant and her children's exclusive benefit and that the tenant was to avoid action which was aimed at or could result in the presence of any kind of lodger in the flat. Both the lower courts and the Cour de cassation held in favour of the tenant. The Cour de cassation grounded its decision in Article 8 of the European Convention on Human Rights, stating that 'the terms of a tenancy agreement may not, by virtue of article 8-1 of the European Convention, deprive the tenant of the possibility to house people close to him/her'. The tenant's right to a home is thus a family home and must include the right to welcome *ses proches*. One may wonder whether these close connections should be welcome as temporary guests or could claim the right to stay in the rented premises throughout the duration of the tenancy.

If the duration of this right is uncertain, the *protected person* is by contrast clearly identified. The right protected in *Mel Yedei* is that of the tenant, Mrs Mel Yedei; her relatives would therefore not be able to rely on this decision to claim (against her will) a right to stay in her rented home; they can only hope for her invitation. But who exactly could benefit from the tenant's invitation? The Cour de cassation's wording is vague: the French word *proches* is sometimes used as a synonym for relatives, sometimes includes in a wider sense all people close to the person concerned: most of all, his/her partner but also his/her partner's own relatives and, more rarely, close friends. The tenant was here housing the father of two of her children and his sister. The word was therefore applied in its wider meaning. A commentator[47] saw in the *Mel Yedei* decision a

---

[46] Civ. 3ème 6 March 1996 *OPAC de la ville de Paris v. Mme Mel Yedei, D.*1997, p 167, note B. de Lamy.

[47] N. Van Tuong, note under Civ. 3ème 6 March 1996 *Mel Yedei, J.C.P.*II.22764, pp 31–2, esp p 32.

regrettable neglect for the institution of marriage, contrary to Article 12 of the Convention. But the application of Article 8 of the Convention beyond marriage and blood links is perfectly in line both with European[48] and administrative case law.[49] In identifying members of a family under Article 8 of the Convention, the effectiveness of the bonds matters more than their legal nature; and there is no reason why this approach should vary according to whether disputes concern immigration or whether tenancy disputes are involved. So far as possible, individual and family status should be seen in the same light in all areas of the law. One would therefore approve of the extension of Article 8(1) in the *Mel Yedei* case.

By contrast, the total lack of reference to the landlord's right is very unfortunate. *No proportionality test* was explicitly applied by the Cour de cassation. Yet the landlord could have had numerous legitimate reasons to limit his tenant's right to house her partner and his sister. The risk of over-occupation of dwellings is a real concern for landlords who might as a consequence face liability towards neighbours for the nuisance (extra noise) caused[50] and an increased probability of damage to the premises.[51] The landlord would then be entitled to sue his tenant for recovery of the sums paid to either renovate the premises or indemnify discontented neighbours, but why should the landlord be systematically the one bearing the hassle and cost of initiating an action against his tenant, not to mention the risk of insolvency on the tenant's part? In view of the risks of liability that rest on the landlord's shoulders, are not the unwanted and potentially numerous guests that could occupy his let premises too heavy a burden? The question could at least have been raised. Possibly, the Cour de cassation did not feel the need to point to the landlord's rights because it had implicitly weighed the landlord's and tenant's interests and reached the conclusion that the tenant's interests suffered a disproportionate restriction.

The specific nature of the landlord may also have encouraged the Cour de cassation's sympathetic ruling towards the tenant. In

---

48 Cf. European Court 28 May 1985 *Abdulaziz, Cabales & Balkandali*, supra, ignoring the legal issue raised of the validity of a wedding in order to consider rather the effectiveness of the bond.

49 Cf. R. Abraham, Conclusions under *Mme Babas*, CE 19 April 1991, *Rec.* p 182.

50 See, CA Paris 27 January 1955, *D.*1955, p 527; Civ. 2ème 8 July 1987, *Bull.* II, n°150.

51 Cf. B. de Lamy, note under Civ. 3ème 6 March 1996 *Mel Yedei*, *D.*1997, pp 167–9, esp p 169.

the *Mel Yedei* case, the landlord was indeed a semi-public body, l'OPAC, in charge of the management and letting of council premises. The tenancy agreements concluded were of a private nature and any litigation arising was therefore under the jurisdiction of the private law courts. However, the activities of l'OPAC respond to a public concern: the accommodation of people on low income. This goal added a strong public law flavour to the *Mel Yedei* case. If disregarded when carrying out public interest functions, one might argue[52] that the landlord's property rights are even more likely to yield when they are devoid of any public connotation. But one may also conversely defend the view that the more public interests the landlord represents, the more uneven will the landlord–tenant relationship be. Depending on the state of the market, tenants may well have real powers of negotiation against their private party landlords, but their hands will always be tied by tenancy agreements for council homes. The ongoing shortage of council premises means that all negotiating powers are vested in the landlord who, as the stronger party, is probably more of a threat to tenants' human rights. One is in any event left to speculate as the specific nature of the landlord was not raised by the plaintiff and the Cour de cassation consequently did not have to discuss the point.[53]

The extension of Article 8 protecting the right to a home in a landlord/tenant relationship, as in the *Spileers* case, thus provides judges with a tool to redress unequal contracts which potentially harm individual human rights. Unlike in *Spileers*, however, the Cour de cassation did not in *Mel Yedei* explicitly carry out a proportionality test to ensure that the weaker party's right to a home had not disproportionately been violated. One may say that explicit tests are only needed when the Court of appeal's decision is quashed for failure to balance the competing rights (or failure to do so correctly). This was indeed the criticism made of the Court of appeal in *Spileers*, whereas in *Mel Yedei*, the Cour de cassation just upheld the Court of appeal's decision in favour of the tenant. But why then did the Cour de cassation, when merely approving on that point the Court of appeal's decision, hold, on 27 February 1991, that the 'provisions of the 30 September 1953 decree relating to the renewal of commercial leases struck the right balance between the requirements of public interests and the necessity to protect individual

[52] See, A. Debet, op. cit., p 415, n°439.

[53] Ibid, quoting B. Wertenschlag, *La Location HLM* (1997), p 89.

fundamental rights and consequently complied with article 1 of the additional protocol to the European Convention on Human Rights'?[54] It is, in my opinion, unfortunate that the Cour de cassation in *Mel Yedei* did not make its reasoning more transparent and failed to have recourse to a proportionality test under Article 8(2)[55] of the European Convention.

As illustrated by the facts of the *Mel Yedei* case, the right to a home when applied to a horizontal situation may thus conflict with property rights. In asserting the tenant's rights under Article 8(1) of the European Convention, is not the Cour de cassation running the risk of ignoring property rights, also protected under the Convention umbrella?[56]

2. *Property rights*

In the only instance where the Cour de cassation has relied on property rights as fundamental human rights, it did so – unusually – by relying on the Constitution.[57] Referring to the constitutional nature of property rights, the Cour de cassation[58] quashed the decision of a divorce judge who had ordered the plaintiff to let out her agricultural premises to her ex-husband. The divorce judge had based his decision on Article 285-1 of the French Civil Code relating to the family home. However, the case at hand did not involve the family home but commercial, agricultural buildings. Applying Article 285-1 outside its ambit was, therefore, inappropriate. The

[54] *Bull*, III, n°67.

[55] Article 8(2) of the European Convention on Human Rights normally only applies to justify interferences from public bodies but, given the semi-public nature of the landlord in that case, Art 8(2) could probably have been extended to the facts of the *Mel Yedei* case.

[56] A. Debet, op. cit., p 416, n°440.

[57] See, however, Civ. 3ème 27 February 1991 (op. cit., note 55), relying on Article 1 of the additional Protocol. The Protocol also had an important indirect effect in inheritance law. Following condemnation of France by the European Court for violation of Article 1 of the Protocol protecting property rights (European Court 1 February 2000 *Mazurek, Droit de la famille* Feb. 2000, p 20, note B. de Lamy), Articles 759 and 760 of the French Civil Code were abolished by the new 3 December 2001 Act (cf. J. Casey, 'Droit des successions. Commentaire de la loi du 3 décembre 2001', *R.J.P.F.*2002-1/11). By virtue of these discriminatory articles, children who were born of adultery used, in presence of legitimate children or the spouse, to have their share to their married parent's estate cut by half.

[58] Civ. 1ère 4 January 1995, *Bull. civ.* I, n°4.

right to a home may legitimately outweigh the owner's right to enjoy his property, as both of these rights have a similar standing. The same, however, cannot be said for the right to stay in commercial premises. But did the Cour de cassation need to rely on the constitutional principle of property rights in order to quash the decision? Many private law authors[59] read the Cour de cassation's ruling as implying that Article 285-1 itself was contrary to the Constitution. Obviously it is not Article 285-1 of the French Civil Code which is to be blamed, but the way in which it was so widely construed by the lower judge.

The feeling that the Cour de cassation was actually reviewing the conformity of the text itself to the Constitution may only be linked to the fact that such is usually the purpose of constitutional principles. As constitutional principles are usually invoked by the Conseil constitutionnel in the process of review of legislation, the use of the same principles by the Cour de cassation may at first sight appear to be a checking of the compatibility of private law texts with the Constitution. If the Cour de cassation was effectively carrying out such a review, it would be acting beyond its powers.[60] However, the Cour de cassation is only criticised for giving the impression of carrying out such a check. To avoid any confusion, the Cour de cassation could have more appropriately relied on Article 285-1 itself and stated that its purpose is only to protect the family home. Unquestionably, the owner's constitutional property rights were involved but they were not directly threatened by the other party – her ex-husband. The threat came from the judge and his interpretation of the applicable legislation. This case is not, therefore, an instance of direct horizontal application of human rights; human rights are applied indirectly in support of a particular interpretation of legislative texts. This indirect application of a constitutional human right brings the Cour de cassation very close to review of compatibility of legislation with the Constitution, hence the feeling of uneasiness.

---

[59] Cf. P. Jestaz, 'Les Sources d'interprétation de la jurisprudence du Conseil constitutionnel' in G. Drago, B. François and N. Molfessis (eds), *La Légitimité de la jurisprudence du Conseil constitutionnel* (1999), pp 3–13, esp p 8.

[60] Nicolas Molfessis would be in favour, *de lege ferenda*, of a review of constitutionality carried out by ordinary judges as he claims that it is illogical that constitutional rights should only prevail over Acts which happen to have been submitted to the Conseil constitutionnel. Cf. 'La Dimension constitutionnelle des libertés et droits fondamentaux' in R. Cabrillac, M.-A. Frison-Roche and T. Revet (eds), *Libertés et droits fondamentaux* (2006) pp 81–99, esp p 98.

This isolated example of an indirect horizontal application of constitutional principles by the Cour de cassation thus proves *a contrario* that the French system is better suited to true direct horizontal application of conventional principles. Indeed, direct horizontal application of Article 8 of the European Convention of Human Rights has reshaped many areas of French Law. We have seen the impact of a right to a home in tenancy agreements and work contracts. In its personal component, granting a personal right to privacy, the same Article 8 has had an even greater influence.

3. Right to privacy and freedom of speech/freedom of the press

(a) Privacy in the work place

The right to privacy under Article 8 of the Convention is, like the right to a home under the same article, a tool enabling judges to protect employees from unwanted intrusion in their family or personal life. The right to privacy was used in the *Nikon* case[61] to challenge an employer's decision to dismiss an employee for misconduct. In that case, an employee who used his business computer for non-professional purposes was caught after his employer searched through his computer files and opened a file labelled 'private'. Thrown out for misconduct, the employee claimed compensation but lost his case in the Court of appeal, before finally winning before the court of last resort. The Cour de cassation, disregarding the employee's behaviour, held that the employer's conduct infringed Article 8 of the European Convention, together with Article 9 of the French Civil Code (also protecting the right to privacy), Article 9 of the French Code of civil procedure (requiring that evidence should be obtained by lawful means) and Article L. 120-2 of the French Labour Code (relating to individual's freedoms at work). The employer should not have opened his employee's personal (electronic) mail. This statement is made in general terms without any qualifications. However legitimate the employer's intentions may be, or serious the suspected misconduct on the employee's part may be, privacy, it seems, raises an impenetrable shield over all personal mail. This case, therefore, constitutes another example of a direct horizontal

---

[61] Soc. 2 October 2001, *Société Nikon France SA v M Onof, D.*2001, p 3148, note P.-Y. Gautier.

application of Article 8 of the European Convention in the context of unequal employer/employee relationships. However, unlike *Spileers*, the *Nikon* case contains no mention of any proportionality test. One should not, however, conclude that *Spileers* was overruled on that point; the lack of proportionality test in *Nikon* is rather due to the dishonesty that the employer showed in collecting evidence against his employee. *Nikon* is therefore more a case on the impropriety in the way used to discover private information than on privacy.[62] The absence of a proportionality test should not therefore be granted too much weight. Indeed, in privacy cases outside contractual work relationships, a proportionality test has become unavoidable.

(b) Privacy and freedom of speech

The press in France has since the end of the nineteenth century enjoyed large freedoms and a rather effective protection against the state.[63] The Act of 19 July 1881 on Freedom of the Press embodies the liberal philosophy that individual freedoms rely on a neutral sphere immune from state intervention. The press still has to respect individual rights to privacy, as enshrined into Article 9 of the French Civil Code by the 17 July 1970 Act and interpreted by a rich case law. At first, the right to privacy was seen as a personal prerogative and trials focused on the interpretation of the victim's consent. Was the intrusion by the press authorised by the victim? If so, did the press go beyond the extent of the authorisation?[64] If consent had been given and the extent of the authorisation had been respected, the 'victim' was not allowed to change his/her mind and withdraw his/her approval.[65] Otherwise, the press needed to prove very special circumstances to justify the intrusion.[66] The emphasis was

---

62 Cf. P.-Y. Gautier, note under Cass. Soc. 2 October 2001 *Nikon, D.*2001, pp 3148–53, esp p 3151.

63 See Ccel n°84-181 DC 10-11 October 1984, *Entreprises de presse, Rec.*, p 73.

64 Cf. Civ. 1ère 30 May 2000, *Bull. civ.* I, n°167: authorisation given for publication of a photograph on a brand of products may not afterwards be used to illustrate an article about the photographee.

65 Cf., e.g., Civ. 1ère 5 May 1987, *D.*1988, p 77, note Massip.

66 For instance, where the plaintiff is not the main subject of the photograph but only one of the component elements of a whole public subject, he cannot object to the publication of the photograph on the grounds of privacy and image rights: Civ. 1ère 25 January 2000, *J.C.P.*2000.II.10257, Conclusions Jerry Sainte-Rose.

therefore on privacy rights. Through the influence of the European Convention on Human Rights, there has been a complete shift in the French approach to privacy rights. These are now systematically balanced with the legitimate rights of the press to free speech. The Cour de cassation now relies simultaneously on Articles 8 and 10 of the European Convention, respectively relating to privacy and free speech. The aim is no longer to delineate the extent of a subjective (individual) right but to reach a fair balance between competing legitimate rights[67] and this requirement of proportionality, as the European Court reminded France in the *Plon* case,[68] extends to the remedies stage.[69]

When privacy rights are no longer involved, as when the victim of the intrusion died before the trial,[70] freedom of speech must then be balanced with the requirements, *in concreto*, of human dignity.[71]

4. Dignity

Strange though it may seem, the right to dignity, paramount in German Law, was, in French law, only recently recognised explicitly as a fundamental human right. Thus, it was not until 1994 that the Conseil constitutionnel[72] explicitly conferred constitutional status on this value. The right to dignity was, however, relied on by ordinary judges before the 1994 Conseil constitutionnel's decision.[73]

---

[67] See Civ. 1ère 23 April 2003, *D.*2003, p 1854, note C. Bigot, explicitly approving the Court of Appeal for having reached equilibrium between privacy rights and freedom of expression.

[68] European Court 18 May 2004 *Société Plon v France, D.*2004, p 1838, note A. Guedj.

[69] Cf. CA Paris 7 October 2003 *Cantat v Trintignant* (interim proceedings), *Légipresse*, Nov. 2003, p 67, note E. Derieux, where the Court of Appeal held that 'judges seized in emergency proceedings need to reconcile personality rights with freedom of expression and consequently order those remedies which are strictly necessary to alleviate the harm'.

[70] Cf. Civ. 1ère 14 December 1999, *Bull. civ.* I, n°345, p 222 where the Cour de cassation, overruling previous case law (e.g. TGI Paris 11 January 1977, *D.*1977, *IR*, p 83), held that protection of privacy did not extend beyond death.

[71] Cf. Civ. 2ème 4 November 2004, *D.*2005, p 696, note I. Corpart, insisting on the need for a balancing exercise between human dignity and the legitimate right of the public to be informed.

[72] C.Cel. n°94-343-344 DC 27 July 1994, *Rec.*, p 100.

[73] Dignity was, for example, the basis for the Conseil d'Etat's decision of 2 July 1993 decision in the *Milhaud* case where a doctor received a warning for having

In private horizontal litigation, the Cour de cassation has relied on human dignity to limit freedom of the press to photograph and report on victims of accidents.[74] In these cases, dignity serves to counteract the powers of the stronger party – the press – and directly protects the rights and desire of the weaker party – the victim – to be left alone. In a contractual relationship, dignity, through *ordre public* (public order or interest), can, however, intervene against the will of both parties and defend the weaker party, even against his/her wishes. Shows of dwarf-throwing were thus, for example, held to be illegal, despite the agreement reached by all parties involved.[75] Individuals may not agree to forfeit their dignity and no consideration may justify such an undertaking. Dignity is thus not only a subjective (individual) right, whose content is left to vary according to individual wishes; it is also an objective notion which protects a certain image of man. If the Conseil constitutionnel ensures that legislation complies with human dignity, the state, for the sake of public order and morality, will, at a lower level, ensure that private agreements also respect human dignity. This extension to private litigation is necessary for human rights to be fully enforced. Indeed, would it not be inconsistent to allow private parties to infringe rights that bind state powers? As a result, freedom of contract is inevitably restrained but this consequence is not surprising; freedom of contract has always been limited by public interests. Do dignity cases even illustrate a horizontal application of human rights?

Dignity was unquestionably the rationale for the Conseil d'Etat's decision in the dwarf case[76] but the principle of dignity itself was not explicitly asserted – let alone its constitutional status. The whole of the legal system is so immersed in the principle of human dignity that the latter hardly needs to be explicitly asserted at all, hence the late recognition of human dignity as a separate value of constitutional status. Moreover, when applied to a contract, its constitutional ranking is of little importance; the legal standing of public order (Art 6 of the French Civil Code) is enough to justify the limitations imposed on freedom of contract.

---

carried out a post mortem on a young man clinically dead: CE Ass 2 July 1993, *J.C.P.*1993.II.22133, note P. Gonod.

[74] Cf. Civ. 1ère 20 December 2000 *Erignac, J.C.P.*2001.II.100488, Conclusions J. Sainte-Rose.

[75] C.E. Ass. 27 October 1995, *Lebon*, p 372.

[76] C.E. Ass. 27 October 1995, *Lebon*, p 372.

5. *Freedom of conscience, religion*

So far the extension of human rights in the contractual sphere has resulted in new negative duties on the parties: the employer's duty *not* to open personal correspondence, *not* to ask unduly for the transfer of his employee's family home, the obligation, on both parties, *not* to enter in a contract whose object violates human dignity. The question is raised, however, whether one party could be forced to assume new positive contractual undertakings, for the sake of the other party's fundamental right to freedom of conscience and religion.

In the *Amar* case, the owner of a block of flats had installed an electrical digicode to secure entry on the premises. Several tenants of Jewish faith complained that this infringed their freedom of movement and their freedom of religion. As their faith forbade them to use electrical devices and equipment on days of *Shabbat*, they were forced either to ignore this religious prohibition (in violation to their freedom of religion) or to stay at home (in violation to their freedom of movement). Consequently, the tenants claimed that the landlord was under the positive obligation to have an ordinary mechanical lock installed. The Court of appeal recalled the landlord's general obligation to perform the contract in good faith (Art 1134 §3 of the French Civil Code) and considered that this implied taking steps necessary to ensure freedom of religion, as guaranteed by the Constitution and international texts. Under the reasoning of the Court of appeal, a stronger party can therefore be made to take action which is not at all mentioned in the terms of the contract and may have been completely unforeseeable. In the *Amar* case, the Court of appeal grants judges wide discretion to add, beyond contractual terms, obligations which are deemed necessary in order to protect individual freedoms. One may also cynically wonder whether freedom of religion could not conveniently be invoked to obtain extra services free of consideration.

This additional duty was, however, only imposed because, said the Court of Appeal, it did not alter the equilibrium of the contract. Presumably, therefore, heavy burdens could not be placed on the landlord even in order to satisfy human rights. Only minor duties could be added and, in this manner, freedom of contract would thus not be jeopardised. But what are 'minor' and 'heavy' or 'major' duties? Should parties not decide what obligations to undertake and decide for themselves what is light and what is too onerous? The Court of appeal in the *Amar* case probably took into account the fact that the landlord had taken the initiative in the first place to install a digicode. In the course of his action, the landlord should have had more consideration for his tenants' religious needs. A positive duty imposed in the course of conduct spontaneously undertaken is certainly less stringent than the duty to take action altogether.

Despite these limits (light duties and, on the facts, only in the course of conduct), the addition of positive duties on one of the parties undoubtedly runs counter to the golden rule of contract law: foreseeability. Was the landlord to know that a few tenants were of Jewish faith and would object to the installation of electrical devices? How far does the landlord have to investigate his tenants' background and beliefs before choosing a certain course of action? To avoid all liability, landlords could, before acting, make sure that their decisions are approved by all the tenants; but would this not introduce too much bureaucracy in private relationships? In view of the need for foreseeability and flexibility, the Cour de cassation[77] quashed the Court of appeal's decision in the *Amar* case, holding that: 'religious rites and behaviours do not, unless otherwise specified, enter in the contractual tenancy agreement and cannot impose on the landlord any specific positive duty.' This decision seems sensible. If a party enters into a contract for personal reasons, for instance under the mistaken belief that he would be entitled to a tax rebate, his mistake does not render the contract void. Unless otherwise expressly mentioned in the contract, the hope to benefit from a tax relief can be disregarded by the other party and will not affect the validity of the contract.[78] Similarly, it seems therefore logical for personal beliefs not to affect, unless otherwise expressly provided for in the contract, the way the contract is performed.

F. Conclusion

In Germany, horizontal application of human rights is linked to the Constitution and to some extent, to the paramount right of human dignity. By contrast, in France, human dignity, only officially grounded in the Constitution since 1994, has had very little impact on the reasoning of French judges and on freedom of contract.

---

[77] Civ. 3ème 18 December 2002, *Bull. civ.* III, n°262.

[78] See Civ. 1ère February 2001, *Bull. civ.* I, n°31.

Moreover, the constitutional text itself has hardly become a familiar tool for private lawyers and judges. This is not to say, however, that no process of horizontal application of human rights has ever taken place in France. On the contrary, human rights have provoked a revolution in methods and solutions in many areas of French private law, but the key text in this drastic change is not the Constitution but the European Convention on Human Rights and the most decisive right is not human dignity but the right to respect for privacy and to family life protected under Article 8 of the Convention. The introduction – horizontally and directly – of the Convention in French private litigation has compelled French judges to carry out balancing tests between conflicting human rights of equal standing. This is best exemplified in press cases, where the right to privacy, in the old days a subjective prerogative that could hardly be challenged, is now systematically balanced against freedom of speech. In contractual relationships, the horizontal application of conventional rights has led to negative duties imposed on stronger parties. The employer, the landlord, and others will thus have to make sure that contractual terms (or the way they are enforced) do not place an excessive restriction on their employee's or tenant's rights. Whether conventional human rights could and should also impose positive duties and force the stronger party to undertake a specific action is more doubtful; freedom of contract also deserves protection!

To use an analogy with another area of law, we may consider family relationships. The extensive use of human rights in this area was criticised for breaking up legal categories and undermining the logical links between legal institutions, in favour of an individualistic approach that has led to endless conflicts and litigation between members of a same family.[79] Whether this is the price to pay for more equality and fairness in family relationships is still the subject of much controversy.[80] Similarly, the tension between fairness and stability is to be found in contract law. There is a fear that the extensive reliance on human rights in contractual relationships may threaten

---

[79] For an example of the new approach derived from human rights in family law, see Civ. 1ère 22 February 2000, *D.*2001, p 398, note C. Courtin, balancing the interests of the child against his parents' right to privacy and right to freedom of religion and free speech.

[80] On the disorganisation caused by the introduction of human rights in French law, see M. Delmas-Marty, 'Réinventer le droit commun', *D.*1995, p 1, esp p 3.

stability and encourage parties who want to get out of a binding agreement to invoke a violation of their human rights in order to terminate the contract unilaterally without suffering any costs. It has even been suggested that the horizontal application of human rights in the contractual sphere might for example be an opportunity to introduce the doctrine of frustration in French contract law.[81] Indeed, one might argue that tying a party to the terms of an agreement that outside circumstances have made extremely onerous to fulfill is unfair (and probably economically unsound).[82] Whether any specific violation of human rights is, however, at stake seems more doubtful.[83] Human rights should not be an excuse for introducing reforms in contract law, however welcomed they may be. They should not either be a convenient way for so-called weaker parties to escape from binding agreements which they knowingly entered into. Is the distinction between positive (which could not be imposed on the stronger party) and negative duties (which could be) workable and useful in that respect?

The distinction between positive and negative duties is a fine one and, ultimately, it will be up to judges to strike the right balance between human rights and freedom of contract, as they do when they confront conflicting human rights. The horizontal application of human rights in France has therefore released huge powers for the judiciary and French private law is now largely a creation of judges, even in very codified areas, such as labour law.

---

[81] Cf. E. Garaud, 'Le relais législatif' in J.-P. Marguénaud (ed), *CEDH et droit privé, L'influence de la Cour européenne des droits de l'homme sur le droit privé français* (2001), p 171, esp p 185.

[82] See, however, rejecting the doctrine of frustration in French private law: Civ. 6 March 1876 *De Gallifet v Commune de Pelissane*, known as the *Canal de Craponne* case, *D.P.* 1876.1, p 193.

[83] The suggestion was to argue that the doctrine of frustration violated property rights by imposing on a party a ruinous contractual obligation for a small consideration, E. Garaud, op. cit.

Chapter 4: Germany
Drittwirkung in Germany

Jörg Fedtke

A. Early emergence and continued relevance of *Drittwirkung* in Germany

The relationship between private law and human rights provisions, codified in an entrenched constitution, is one of the *grands thèmes* of German post-1945 legal doctrine and jurisprudence. Summarised under the heading *Drittwirkung*, a typically Germanic compound word indicating – in abstract terms – the effect (*Wirkung*) of something which is regarded as essentially bipolar in nature (in this case fundamental rights) on an outsider to the relationship in question (a third party or *Dritter*), the issue has over the past decades attracted much attention on both sides of the country's fairly distinct public–private law divide. A series of important court decisions (mainly in the areas of family law, banking, employment relationships and personality rights) and a highly controversial government initiative designed to meet the requirements of European anti-discrimination law,[1] have in recent years yet again provoked keen academic, judicial and public interest in the issue.[2]

Neither the early emergence of the concept nor the ongoing debate which *Drittwirkung* has been able to generate in Germany is thereby coincidental. There are a number of 'local' reasons why the

---

[1] Entwurf eines Gesetzes zur Umsetzung europäischer Antidiskriminierungsrichtlinien, Drucksachen des Deutschen Bundestages (BT-Dr) 15/4538. This legislation aims to meet, inter alia, the requirements of EU Directives 2000/43/EC of 29 June 2000 (Official Journal L 180, 22 ff), 2000/78/EC of 27 November 2002 (Official Journal L 303, 16 ff) and 2002/73/EC of 23 September 2002 (Official Journal L 269, 15 ff).

[2] See, inter alia, J. Hager, 'Grundrechte im Privatrecht' (1994) *Juristen-Zeitung* (JZ) 373 ff.

Bundesverfassungsgericht, Germany's Federal Constitutional Court, was confronted with the problem as early as 1953, and it seems worthwhile, bearing in mind the comparative thrust of this study, to outline briefly a few particularly relevant aspects of the German development at the very outset of this chapter. A more detailed account of the country's legal system and the approach it has taken to *Drittwirkung* will be offered as the narrative develops.

I. Legal tradition and constitutional interpretation as starting points

At first blush, the German response to the question whether human rights provisions can affect the relationship between private individuals and/or legal entities is surprisingly straightforward, and in fact rather unlikely to cause much controversy.

There is, for one thing, the widely held view that human rights are, first and foremost, designed to protect individuals from the overly burdensome exercise of public authority (*status negativus*), and thus become operational predominantly (if not exclusively) between the state and its citizens, i.e. in vertical (as opposed to horizontal) relationships. This assumption is by no means compelling but finds ample support in the text of the Basic Law, the country's initially provisional but by now seasoned Constitution of 1949.[3] This document contains in its first section a Bill of Rights, of which only a single provision, Article 9(3) BL, expressly states that private activities are directly subject to a fundamental right – the right to form associations aimed at safeguarding and improving working conditions and, more generally, the economic environment of the country. Agreements that restrict or seek to impair this right are deemed null and void, measures directed to this end declared unlawful. Outside the Bill of Rights, Article 20(4) BL gives all Germans the right to resist 'any person' seeking to abolish the German constitutional order if and insofar as no alternative remedy is available.[4] Both constitutional provisions clearly impact on interpersonal relationships. They are seen as exceptional cases of a direct (*unmittelbare*) *Drittwirkung*[5] and,

---

[3] *Grundgesetz* (BL).

[4] The so-called *Widerstandsrecht* introduced in 1968 together with constitutional amendments relating to states of emergency. Article 20(4) has thus far hardly played a role in constitutional practice.

[5] V. Epping, *Grundrechte* (2nd edn, 2005), p 337.

argumentum e contrario, powerful indicators that all other provisions of the Basic Law address either issues of governance (the functions and powers of the state and the interaction between its various institutions) or (strictly vertical) the relationship between the state and its citizens (fundamental rights). In this respect, the Basic Law mirrors its predecessor, the Constitution of Weimar,[6] which envisaged the direct effect of human rights in only two cases, namely freedom of expression and (again) freedom of association, both of which were equally regarded as exceptional in terms of their protective scope.[7]

Today, this approach to the effect of human rights in the private sphere is further supported by Article 1(3) BL, which states that 'the following basic rights shall bind the legislature, the executive, and the judiciary as directly applicable law'. No mention is made, as in other constitutional documents such as those of Namibia (1990) and South Africa (1996), of 'natural and legal persons'.[8]

Set apart from and placed above the rest of the Bill of Rights, Article 1(1) BL seems to point in a similar direction. The provision establishes human dignity as the supreme value of the Basic Law and commits all public authorities to respect and – more importantly – protect actively the dignity of individuals against any form of violation by others. Private actors are, again, not mentioned in this context. According to German constitutional theory, however, human dignity is not subject to any restriction or, indeed, constitutional amendment,[9] and there is evidence that the authors of the Basic Law, though failing to articulate their approach *expressis verbis*, wanted to protect this value against both public *and* private interference. Article 1(1) BL is phrased 'in absolute terms', as Adolf Süsterhenn, Member of the Constitutional Council[10] and one of the leading architects of the Federal Republic, put it, and 'designed to protect against everyone, *whether public authority or private person*'.[11] As far as *Drittwirkung* is concerned, human dignity is thus considered,

---

6 Weimarer Reichsverfassung of 11 August 1919.

7 G. Anschütz, *Die Verfassung des Deutschen Reiches* (14th edn, 1933), Art 118 no. 5 and Art 159 no. 1; F. Poetzsch-Heffter, *Handkommentar zur Weimarer Reichsverfassung* (3rd edn, 1928), p 397.

8 Constitution of Namibia, Article 8; Republic of South Africa Act 1996, s 8(2).

9 See Article 79(3) BL.

10 Parlamentarischer Rat.

11 *Jahrbuch des Öffentlichen Rechts 1* (1951), p 51 (emphasis added).

by many, as a third exception to the rule that constitutional rights are not directly effective in the private sphere.[12]

This brief teleological, structural and historical interpretation of the Basic Law would thus seem to suggest, first, that the German approach to *Drittwirkung* is restrictive in the sense that human rights will affect private relationships only in exceptional cases, and, second, that the text of the Constitution itself identifies these exceptions more or less clearly. On this reading of the Basic Law, human dignity and freedom of association (in the specific context of employment relationships) are the only human rights that may be invoked in private disputes, complemented – in highly exceptional circumstances – by the right of all Germans to take any measures necessary to defend their constitutional order against both public authorities and fellow citizens in case of a severe constitutional crisis. All other rights, it seems, will offer no protection against horizontal interference.

Historical experience has, however, blurred this distinction and led to what has become known as an 'indirect' application of human rights in the private sphere or *mittelbare Drittwirkung*.

2. *Conflicting historical experience*

As is so often the case with unusual constitutional solutions found in Germany today, the experience of totalitarian rule between 1933 and 1945 is key to the understanding of this 'indirect' or 'radiating' effect of human rights.

The Basic Law is, in many respects, a reaction to the severe human rights violations committed in Germany following Hitler's rise to power in January 1933, violations committed not only by the state and its agents but also by single individuals or organisations outside any official context. The Third Reich created a climate of fear, terror and oppression, which went far beyond the many single instances of human rights infringements by the regime. Nazi ideology permeated society as a whole – the working environment, the arts, journalism, the scientific community, architecture, the church, schools and universities, social relationships, local communities where people

---

[12] See, e.g., BVerwGE 115, 189 at p 199 and P. Kunig in I. von Münch and P. Kunig, *Grundgesetz-Kommentar* (5th edn, 2000).

went about their daily lives, and even the allegedly safe nucleus of the family home. The Basic Law was designed as an antidote to this all-encompassing evil, and there is general consensus that its system of values must inform all spheres of society rather than be restricted to the most immediate interaction between the state and its citizens. Just as South Africa set out to combat 'privatised apartheid' in the 1990s following the demise of white minority rule and the enactment of individual constitutional rights vis-à-vis the state, so are human rights considerations – beyond their obvious importance as subjective (individual) safeguards against the unlimited exercise of public authority – regarded as a new paradigm for German society, or, in the words of the famous *Lüth* decision of 1958,[13] 'a fundamental and objective system of values' (*objektive Wertordnung*), which provides a blueprint for society as a whole. Instead of taking a 'neutral' stance, the German Constitution, in the words of the Federal Constitutional Court:

> erects an objective system of values in its section on basic rights ... This system of values, centering on the freedom of the human being to develop in society, must apply as a constitutional axiom throughout the whole legal system: it must direct and inform legislation, administration, and judicial decision. *It naturally influences private law as well; no rule of private law may conflict with it, and all such rules must be construed in accordance with its spirit.*[14]

Seen in this light, the more likely reaction to the former regime would thus have been a system of *directly* applicable human rights regardless of any public–private law distinction.

Conflicting historical experience, however, prevented the German system from embarking on that course. The shadows of Nazi rule certainly provided a powerful motive to push the influence of human rights considerations far into civil society, but much of this thrust was counterbalanced by a second concern, namely that the principle of private autonomy (*Privatautonomie*) – a highly cherished and constitutionally protected notion dating back to the nineteenth century struggle of an emerging middle class for economic freedom

---

13 BVerfGE 7, 198 ff of 15 January 1958.

14 Ibid. Translation by Tony Weir (emphasis added). For an English version of this case see the website of translated German legal materials of the Institute of Global Law (University College London) at http://www.ucl.ac.uk/laws/global_law/german-cases/cases_bverg.shtml?15jan1958.

and prosperity – could suffer too much damage on the way. Other arguments raised against direct *Drittwirkung* are linked to this concern.

There is, first, the fear that broadly phrased constitutional principles are simply unable to provide adequate solutions for the more intricate problems of private law. Others argue that the differences between weighing up interests of the state against those of its citizens in vertical relationships is fundamentally different from finding the right balance between the conflicting positions of individuals in horizontal relationships; the traditional concepts applied to the limitation of constitutional rights, including the principle of proportionality, would therefore at the very least require substantial modification. Both of these arguments against direct *Drittwirkung* will be discussed in more detail below; suffice it here to note that they are at least in part rooted in the preference for an autonomous civil society with which the state should interfere as little as necessary.

The protection of the weaker party in private disputes – mirror image of the relationship between state and citizen, and a theme which has influenced the debate concerning *Drittwirkung* in many systems – is also part and parcel of this equation. While the state (undoubtedly the stronger party in vertical disputes with its citizens) can under no circumstances invoke human rights protection, the opposite is true in the case of its counterpart in horizontal disputes between stronger and weaker private entities. *Both* sides to a private legal conflict (be they employers and employees, companies and customers, landlords and tenants, or the reporting media and the objects of its interest) are protected by human rights, and even the most odious exercise of private power by the stronger party remains an expression of the broad concept of freedom (in the guise of *Privatautonomie*) constitutionally protected by Article 2(1) BL.[15]

A number of interrelated questions arise at this point. Should such power really be restrained by human rights considerations? And if so, how and to what extent? Or is it not preferable to steer clear of such intervention, and rely on the ability of civil society to find its own equilibrium in terms of conflicting views, the distribution of material wealth, and, more generally, the balance of influence or power in private interaction?

---

[15] On this interpretation of Article 2(1) BL, see the leading case of the Federal Constitutional Court in BVerfGE 6, 32 ff of 16 January 1957 (Elfes).

The Germans have avoided the choice between absolute private autonomy and an equally absolute rule of constitutional values. A number of rights, such as human dignity, personality rights, the right to individual self-determination, freedom of expression, and equality have, over the years, gradually become operational in private law relationships, restraining, in many cases, the most blatant abuses of private power while at the same time stopping short of a direct application of human rights in the private sphere. This compromise, however, has come at a price. Indirect *Drittwirkung* created a grey area between two clear-cut positions, and has led to considerable uncertainty both as far as the conceptual foundations of the approach and the extent to which human rights may influence private relationships are concerned. This uncertainty has, in turn, sustained the debate over the issue ever since the problem first became virulent in the mid-1950s.

3. New values superimposed on an existing system of private law

A second feature of the German system (and this it again shares with, inter alia, the South African) is that the main corpus of private law – codified in the Civil Code (*Bürgerliches Gesetzbuch* or BGB) of 1900 – predates the Basic Law and the 'new' values it introduced in 1949. The younger constitutional text is thereby stronger than the revered Civil Code. Stopping short of declaring the Constitution 'supreme' (as is again the case, e.g., in South Africa and, more recently, in Iraq), there is no doubt that the framers of the text wanted all legislation to comply with the principles enshrined in the Basic Law and, more specifically, its human rights provisions. Article 1(3) BL expressly states this with respect to legislation by declaring, as pointed out above, that the legislator is bound by 'the following basic rights'. This, in itself, creates indirect effect for private relationships since legislation enacted in the area of private or labour law will have to comply with these constitutional principles (though, as will be discussed in the course of this chapter, the standard of review – or, put differently, the margin of appreciation granted to the political legislator in shaping parts of the legal order – could, arguably, be a different one here than it is in the area of public or criminal law). More importantly, *any* law (public or private) is potentially subject to judicial review by the Federal Constitutional Court, and can be declared void if in violation of human rights. This can happen at any stage; unlike the French *Conseil constitutionnel*, the *Bundesverfassungsgericht* may set aside unconstitutional legislation – including provisions which predate the Basic Law – at any point in time.

The introduction of a new and supreme constitutional order profoundly affected the whole legal system, which had to be brought in line with these new values. Though not superior in terms of hierarchy, private law was, until 1949, regarded as an essentially autonomous part of the legal order and independent of constitutional considerations. Human rights, moreover, were seen as general guiding principles rather than directly enforceable law. This relationship between the private sphere and constitutional values changed dramatically with the introduction of the Basic Law. While private law was previously often seen as a sphere of relative freedom from an otherwise interventionist and powerful state,[16] parts of the BGB suddenly fell foul of the standards established by the new constitutional order.

The most obvious candidate for an overhaul was the area of family law. Article 117(1) BL expressly called for conflicts between any legal provision and Article 3(2) BL (establishing equality between man and woman) to be resolved by 31 March 1953, and went on to declare that provisions contravening this basic constitutional principle would lose their legal force after that date.[17] Chancellor Adenauer's conservative government failed to adapt several provisions of the BGB which accorded the husband or father a privileged position in family relationships within the respite provided by this sunset clause. When the constitutional deadline passed without the task envisaged by Article 117(1) BL having been accomplished, the *Bundesgerichtshof* (BGH), Germany's highest court in private and criminal law matters, began to unpick one provision of the Civil Code after the other and re-fashion large parts of family law on a case-by-case basis. This approach, which triggered heated controversies about the competence of judges to 'create' law (at that time

---

[16] See, e.g., K. Hesse, *Verfassungsrecht und Privatrecht* (1988), p 10.

[17] Article 117(1) BL declares that: '(L)aw which is inconsistent with paragraph (2) of article 3 of this Basic Law shall remain in force until adapted to that provision, but not beyond March 31, 1953.'

certainly far more unusual in a civil law system than it is today), was endorsed by the *Bundesverfassungsgericht* in December 1953.[18]

This is certainly a particularly striking example of the influence human rights considerations have exerted on German private law, but, as a series of cases culminating in the *Lüth* decision (a freedom of expression case discussed in more detail below) were soon to show, this effect was not limited to family relationships, nor was it dependent on an express authorisation or, rather, prescription in the constitutional text. The fact that a complex set of new values had been superimposed on a pre-existent legal order thus created early tensions between the two, fuelling the discussions surrounding *Drittwirkung* in Germany.

4. *Specialised constitutional review*

A third local factor which has become increasingly important over the past years is the existence of a system of specialised courts, part and parcel of the distinction between public and private law, and the role played by the *Bundesverfassungsgericht*. All German courts are bound by the Basic Law and must take into account human rights considerations when interpreting legislation relevant to their respective areas of jurisdiction. With few exceptions following from the federal nature of the country, the *Bundesverfassungsgericht*, positioned alongside the other highest federal institutions of the land, thereby exercises final control over the constitutionality of legislative, administrative and judicial acts. Leaving aside for the moment the division of powers issue and the tensions that must inevitably arise between a legislator who opts for a particular legal solution and a court of law with the ability to invalidate this approach on the basis of a supreme constitution (this aspect will be discussed below in the context of the first abortion case of 1975[19]), it is the *specialised nature* of the review conducted by the Federal Constitutional Court which has caused debate. The Court is limited to the consideration of any *constitutional* questions arising from a particular dispute, and it is for the specialised private, labour,

---

18 BVerfGE 3, 225 ff of 18 December 1953. The court also refused to accept any extension of the deadline even in highly complex areas such as the financial settlement between spouses in cases of divorce.

19 BVerfGE 39, 1 ff of 25 February 1975.

criminal, administrative, social or fiscal courts to deal with all other legal issues. The borderline between constitutional matters and all other questions of law is difficult to draw in practice. This uncertainty has troubled the relationship between the *Bundesverfassungsgericht* and *all* supreme courts in Germany,[20] but it is indirect *Drittwirkung*, perched on the fence line between public and private law, which seems to have caused particular difficulties in this regard. Criminal, administrative, social and fiscal cases will usually involve some exercise of public authority – bringing these disputes in proximity to constitutional questions – while both labour disputes and private conflicts (including commercial, company, banking and family law cases) do not. In dealing with the latter, the *Bundesverfassungsgericht* has often been accused of going beyond its remit and encroaching on the competence of the private and labour law courts to interpret conclusively the law pertaining to their respective areas of expertise; more than anywhere else, the Court has been suspected of taking on the role of a supreme court in the American sense of the term, exercising final jurisdiction across the board. This raises the question who is ultimately authorised to shape private and labour law by determining the effect of constitutional provisions in the private sphere. This is an issue which legal systems operating an essentially unitary court structure will have far less difficulty coping with.

A fourth and last tributary to the discussion of *Drittwirkung* in Germany, which again distinguishes this system from many others, is procedural in nature and closely connected to the conflict surrounding the competence of the *Bundesverfassungsgericht* described in the previous paragraph. The Court can be drawn into private law disputes in two ways. First, any court confronted with a legal provision which it deems unconstitutional but nevertheless crucial for the outcome of a dispute may stay the proceedings and apply to the Federal Constitutional Court for a preliminary ruling concerning the validity of the law before proceeding to decide the case in the light of such guidance.[21] Only a few private or labour law disputes have reached the *Bundesverfassungsgericht* via this route.

---

[20] See, inter alia, R. Scholz, 'Fünfzig Jahre Bundesverfassungsgericht', Aus Politik und Zeitgeschichte, B 37-38/2001, pp 13 ff.

[21] See Article 100(1) BL. The same mechanism is found on the EU level when national courts or tribunals refer questions concerning the validity or interpretation of Community law to the European Court of Justice (see Article 234 of the EC Treaty).

A second path is the so-called individual constitutional complaint (*Verfassungsbeschwerde*), which may be filed with the Federal Constitutional Court by any person claiming that one of his or her basic rights or the rights specifically enumerated in Article 93(1) no. 4a BL[22] has been infringed by legislative, administrative or judicial activities of a public authority on any level of the system.[23] Access to the *Bundesverfassungsgericht* will require the applicant to exhaust all other available legal remedies first,[24] a requirement specifically designed to protect, inter alia, the exclusive right of all other courts to establish the facts of a case and deal with all non-constitutional questions of law. The final decision of a private or labour law court is thus, for the purposes of the constitutional complaint, regarded as an exercise of public (judicial) authority which can, potentially, constitute an infringement of human rights if based on unconstitutional legislation or an interpretation of the law which fails properly to take into account human rights considerations.

The relevance of this procedural twist is twofold. The constitutional complaint, first, gives parties in private law disputes direct access to the *Bundesverfassungsgericht* and allows them to overcome a court of final instance which has failed, in their view, to acknowledge or deal appropriately with a constitutional aspect decisive to their case. The mechanism thus places a final – constitutional – check on all other courts of law and brings private disputes into the constitutional arena. Second, it seems to overcome (albeit on a purely technical level) the objection that the effect of human rights should be limited to vertical relationships between the state and its citizens. A court of final instance undoubtedly exercises *public* (i.e. *judicial*) *authority* vis-à-vis the losing party/applicant in the guise of its own judgment, even if this happens to be a private or labour dispute. This does not, however, answer the more important question why judges adjudicating such cases should be obliged to

22 The latter are referred to as 'quasi-fundamental rights' (*grundrechtsgleiche Rechte*).

23 The court, though devoting a substantial amount of its resources to the resolution of human rights disputes (one of its two senates, the so-called *Grundrechtssenat*, is engaged exclusively in human rights jurisprudence) and despite repeated legislative initiatives aimed at reducing its workload, is confronted with approximately 5,000 to 6,000 *Verfassungsbeschwerden* every year. Less than 5%, however, are successful.

24 § 90(2) *Bundesverfassungsgerichtsgesetz* (BVerfGG), which regulates the procedure of the FCC.

take human rights considerations into account *in the first place* and, if they are, to what extent.

B. The constitutional background of the German approach

The preceeding sections, dealing with some of the reasons why Germany provided a particularly fertile ground for the development of *Drittwirkung*, will have already conveyed a flavour of the relevant constitutional background of this system. The main characteristics can thus be summarised as follows: (1) the existence of a supreme constitution which contains enforceable human rights provisions but expressly declares these applicable to private relationships only in exceptional cases; (2) a system of specialised courts; and (3) direct access of citizens to the Federal Constitutional Court. A few more details should be added in order to complete the picture.[25]

The *Bundesverfassungsgericht* has featured as the guardian of a fairly comprehensive system of human rights protection,[26] not only within the country but also on the European stage. Its two so-called *Solange* decisions[27] and the *Treaty of Maastricht* judgment[28] are only the most prominent examples of a series of much-discussed cases which have had implications for both German citizens and the development of human rights protection on the Community level.[29] Less well known is the fact that the 16 states forming the German Federation each have their own constitution, and that the majority of these documents offer an alternative (and sometimes even more extensive) source of human rights protection within the

---

[25] For a fuller description of the Basic Law see, e.g., D. Currie, *The Constitution of the Federal Republic of Germany* (1994).

[26] Articles 1-19 BL.

[27] See BVerfGE 37, 271 ff of 1974 and BVerfGE 73, 339 ff of 1986 (for English versions of these cases see the website of translated German legal materials at the Institute of Global Law (University College London) at http://www.ucl.ac.uk/ laws/ global_law/cases/german/bverfg/bverfg_29may1974.html (*Solange I*) and http://www.ucl.ac.uk/laws/global_law/cases/german/bverfg/bverfg_22oct1986.html (*Solange II*).

[28] BVerfGE 89, 155 of 1994.

[29] For a detailed account of this case law see J. Alter, *Establishing the Supremacy of European Law* (2001), pp 64 ff.

country. Together with the European Convention for the Protection of Human Rights and Fundamental Freedoms of 1950[30] and the emerging human rights jurisprudence of the European Court of Justice in Luxembourg, most German citizens thus have recourse to four different and overlapping human rights regimes established on the regional, national, Community and European levels.

The practical relevance of each of these systems is, of course, very different. It is safe to say that the vast majority of all contemporary disputes surrounding human rights in Germany are currently dealt with on the basis of the provisions found in the Basic Law and the case law of the *Bundesverfassungsgericht*. Due to substantial differences in their constitutional structures and the rich body of human rights jurisprudence which has developed in Germany over the past five decades (and despite a number of prominent decisions of the European Court of Human Rights and the ECJ in cases arising from the country[31]), German lawyers will in practice attach far less importance to the European Convention or the human rights protection provided within the context of the EU than their counterparts in many other European legal systems. Indeed, the German hierarchy of norms ranks the Convention below the Basic Law,[32] and the *Bundesverfassungsgericht* still claims ultimate – albeit currently dormant – jurisdiction over human rights issues arising in the context of the European Union.

The catalogue of human rights introduced on the federal level in 1949 is classical-liberal in character. It contains an extensive range of individual freedoms, and is based on the notion of human dignity as the core constitutional value.[33] The provisions that follow this first and pivotal statement of the Basic Law contain a number of specific rights, which include, inter alia, the right to life and physical integrity,[34] religious freedom,[35] free speech and freedom of the

---

30 Ratified by the Federal Republic of Germany on 5 December 1952.

31 See, e.g., the judgments of the European Court of Human Rights in *Streletz, Kessler and Krenz v Germany* (Application nos. 34044/96, 35532/97 and 44801/98) of 21 March 2001 and *von Hannover v Germany* (Application no. 59320/00) of 24 June 2004.

32 BVerfGE 74, 358 at 370 and BVerfGE 111, 307 at 317; H. D. Jarass in H. D. Jarass and B. Pieroth, *Grundgesetz für die Bundesrepublik Deutschland* (8th edn, 2006), Art 25 no. 10.

33 Article 1(1) BL.

34 Article 2(2) BL.

35 Article 4 BL.

press and the media,[36] protection of marriage and the family,[37] freedom of assembly[38] and association,[39] privacy of correspondence and telecommunications,[40] freedom of movement within the federal territory,[41] the protection of economic activity,[42] inviolability of the home,[43] and the protection of property.[44] Equality is protected in general terms,[45] in the form of a separate clause establishing equality between man and woman,[46] and, finally, in a more specific provision which identifies a number of grounds on which individuals may not be unfairly discriminated against.[47] Additional rights, accorded the same status for the purposes of a constitutional complaint as those enshrined in the Bill of Rights itself, are found in other parts of the Basic Law.[48] These include the right to resist attempts to abolish the constitutional order if no other remedy is available,[49] a range of political rights,[50] the right to participate in general, direct, free, equal, and secret elections,[51] and a number of important procedural safeguards in the event of criminal investigations.[52]

Finally, the German system tries to draw a clear distinction between the public and private spheres. This approach, though blurred in many areas, is reflected in the basic assumption that the exercise of any public authority (including that of the courts) is bound by human rights while private actors are, in principle, not; it permeates the whole legal system in the form of a specialised court structure with all its procedural and jurisdictional difficulties; and it may, on

---

36 Articles 5(1) and (2) BL.

37 Article 6 BL.

38 Article 8 BL.

39 Article 9 BL.

40 Article 10 BL.

41 Article 11 BL.

42 Article 12 BL.

43 Article 13 BL.

44 Article 14 BL.

45 Article 3(1) BL.

46 Article 3(2) BL.

47 Article 3(3) BL.

48 So-called *grundrechtsgleiche Rechte*; see Article 93(1) no. 4a BL.

49 Article 20(4) BL.

50 Article 33 BL.

51 Article 38 BL.

52 Article 101 BL (ban on extraordinary courts), Article 103 BL (the right to be heard in court in accordance with the law, protection from retroactive criminal laws and multiple punishment), and Article 104 BL (legal guarantees in the event of detention).

a less visible level, also affect academic debate in that many private lawyers instinctively seek to restrict the influence of the Basic Law on the private sphere while their counterparts in the field of public law tend to give constitutional values more leeway.

C. The choice between direct and indirect *Drittwirkung*

Over the last five decades, mainstream constitutional doctrine and jurisprudence have adopted an indirect approach to give effect to human rights in the private sphere. This solution, first applied in practice in the *Lüth* decision mentioned earlier, was preceded by an attempt of the Federal Labour Court (*Bundesarbeitsgericht*, BAG) to establish a more immediate effect of many human rights enshrined in the Basic Law.

I. Limited direct effect: Hans Carl Nipperdey and the Federal Labour Court

A limited direct effect of certain human rights in the private sphere was strongly advocated by Hans Carl Nipperdey, President of the Federal Labour Court from 1954 to 1963.[53] In an early decision of 3 December 1954 involving a worker and labour representative who had been dismissed by his employer for promoting the cause of the Communist Party by distributing pamphlets during working hours and subsequently challenged the dismissal, the Court discussed whether Article 3(3) BL (prohibiting discrimination against individuals on the basis of their political views) and/or Article 5(1) BL (freedom of expression) could place constitutional limits on the right of the employer to dismiss the plaintiff under labour law.[54]

In this much quoted case, the BAG challenged traditional wisdom that human rights are restricted to vertical relationships between the state and its citizens, and held that at least some rights could, in principle, directly affect private and labour law relationships.

---

[53] See L. Enneccerus and H. C. Nipperdey, *Allgemeiner Teil des Bürgerlichen Rechts* (15th edn, 1959), § 15 II 4 c; H. C. Nipperdey, *Grundrechte und Privatrecht* (1961), p 15.

[54] BAGE 1, 185 at pp 191 ff.

The Court stressed that, in its view, human rights had undergone a crucial functional change after 1949; in addition to providing protection for the fundamental freedoms of individuals against the undue exercise of public authority, they should now also be understood as basic guidelines (*ordre public*) for the organisation of social life in general. Fundamental values which bind the state – in particular human dignity, equality and the freedom to express religious, political or social views – thereby reflect basic constitutional choices which must find similar respect when it comes to employment issues within a company or contractual relationships between private parties in general.

The Court further supported this reasoning by drawing on what it described as a 'normative commitment' of the Basic Law to the idea of social justice (*Sozialstaatsprinzip*) enshrined in Articles 20 and 28 BL.[55] The underlying aim of this approach was to allow human rights considerations to intervene if individual freedom was at risk due to the unreasonable exercise of private power, an acknowledgment that substantial differences in the economic capacity of the parties involved in many private contractual relationships – in this case employer and employee – could in fact equal the disparity of power in classical 'vertical' disputes between state and citizen.

An interesting and surprisingly little-known feature of the judgment, however, is that the Federal Labour Court actually *upheld* the dismissal of the plaintiff *despite* this approach by tempering its reasoning with a heavy dose of proportionality. Only the most blatant abuse of power beyond the 'rule of reason' (the judgment actually uses this English phrase) ought to justify an intervention on the basis of human rights considerations. This, the Court held, could not be said of the defendant/employer in the case, who had exercised a high degree of tolerance towards similarly disruptive activities of the plaintiff on previous occasions, and had not dismissed him – as alleged – for expressing any *particular* political view (i.e. that of the Communist Party).

The essence of this decision, then, is threefold. First, human rights considerations penetrate the borderline between the strictly vertical state-citizen relationship and the private sphere, and should influence society as a whole. Second, certain rights (the Court only deals with equality and freedom of expression, and indicates that a selective

---

[55] BAGE 1, 185 at p 193.

approach may be necessary when considering the impact of other rights) can *directly* affect the interpretation and, possibly, validity of private agreements or decisions. Third, this effect is, however, limited to the most unreasonable exercise of private power – an important caveat which to a large extent reduces the danger of a too far-reaching limitation of private autonomy.

The *Bundesarbeitsgericht* followed this approach in subsequent decisions, often intervening in clearly phrased contractual agreements, until the early 1980s. A good example of this jurisprudence is a case involving the contract between a facility for mentally disabled persons and a trainee minder.[56] Here the Court held that a provision which automatically terminated the relationship between the parties in case the trainee should choose to marry was in contravention of Article 6(1) BL (protecting marriage) as well as Articles 1 and 2 BL (protecting human dignity and the general right to freedom), and therefore void. Under the rules of the training contract, trainees were obliged to live on the premises of the facility.

2. *The theory of indirect effect: Lüth, Blinkfüer and the 1975 Abortion Case*

The approach endorsed by Nipperdey and the Federal Labour Court did not prevail; mainstream German constitutional doctrine and jurisprudence today adhers to the theory of an 'indirect' or 'radiating' effect of human rights in the private sphere.

The first decision to develop fully the notion of human rights as an 'objective system of values' which must be taken into account both by the legislator when creating rules of private law and the courts when deciding private law disputes is the *Lüth* decision of 15 January 1958.[57] It is important to stress yet again that both legislator and courts are *themselves* in principle directly bound by human rights provisions when exercising public authority through the enactment of private or labour law, or through the adjudication of private or labour law disputes (hence the admissibility of constitutional complaints in case of the latter) – even if the level of judicial scrutiny may be lower here than that applied to all other types of

56 Case 1 AZR 249/57 of 10 May 1957 (*Zölibatsklausel*).
57 BVerfGE 7, 198 ff.

legislation (in particular administrative and criminal law) and despite the fact that a more limited range of human rights will usually be directly affected by court decisions than in the case of legislative or executive activity.[58] The indirect effect of human rights is thus restricted to the relationship between the parties to a private dispute, and has a knock-on effect on the deciding court only in the sense that it defines the standard of human rights protection which the judge must, in private or labour law cases, apply in order to appropriately discharge his duties. Indirect *Drittwirkung* involves, first, the interpretation of law (usually general clauses but also more specific rules) in the light of human rights considerations and, second, the constitutional duty of courts to apply this 'modified' law to the case at hand.

The facts of *Lüth*, which in many ways remains to the present day the leading German case concerning the application of human rights in the private sphere, centre around free speech. Veit Harlan, a prominent film director during the Nazi regime, had produced the anti-Semitic propaganda film *Jud Süß* in 1940. After the war, Harlan was held responsible for inciting hatred against Jews, but criminal charges were eventually dropped because it was thought that he could not have declined to participate in the project, nor could he have toned down the film contrary to Josef Goebbels' specific instructions without risking his own life. When Harlan produced his first film after these events, Erich Lüth, an author and high-ranking public official in the city-state of Hamburg, severely criticised him for his involvement in the Nazi regime and, in an open letter conveying harsh criticism of the controversial director, called for a boycott of Harlan's new film, *Unsterbliche Geliebte*. Both the producer and the distributing company applied successfully for an injunction prohibiting Lüth from repeating his statements, invoking the acquittal of Harlan in the previous criminal proceedings. The injunction was issued, the Court of Appeal (*Landgericht*) Hamburg accepting that Lüth's call for a boycott could, if successful, cause substantial harm to the financial interests of the applicants.[59] Lüth, in turn, raised a constitutional complaint against the court order based on Article 5(1) BL (free speech).

---

[58] Procedural safeguards and the principle of proportionality are by far the most frequently invoked rights in constitutional complaints against court decisions.

[59] See § 826 BGB.

The Federal Constitutional Court, confronted with this case, first dealt with the question whether the decision of a court in a private law matter could at all infringe human rights other than the specific procedural safeguards enshrined in the Basic Law. It held that the injunction was, objectively, indeed a limitation of Lüth's right to free speech, but that the judgment (representing the exercise of public authority) was not to be measured directly by the standards established in Article 5(1) BL, as human rights could only form a guideline for judicial activity if and insofar provisions of private law relevant to the case are at all influenced by constitutional values in the first place. It is here that the Court applied the theory of an 'indirect' effect of human rights, as developed by the constitutional lawyer Günther Dürig, who regarded them first and foremost as a protection of the individual against the exercise of state power, but also as an 'objective system of values' capable of reinforcing their effect outside the limited ambit of strictly vertical relationships. Free development of human personality and the protection of human dignity lie at the heart of the Basic Law, values which represent a fundamental constitutional choice of the framers of the German Constitution for all areas of the law and with which all law must comply.[60]

Interestingly, the Court drew a distinction between rules of private law which parties are free to adopt, change or ignore when establishing contractual relationships, and rules which are enforced regardless of the parties' intentions. The effect of human rights considerations will be the most intensive in the case of (but not restricted to) those rules of private law which are deemed so important for the protection of the general interest that they are not left to the disposition of private parties, and which can thus be compared to the equally binding rules of administrative or criminal law. General provisions of the Civil Code such as the principle of good faith (see § 242 BGB) or – as in *Lüth* – the prohibition against causing harm contra *bonos mores* (see § 826 BGB) are thereby inherently in need of interpretation by the courts and thus particularly open to the influence of constitutional values.[61]

Failure of the judge to take into account this 'radiating effect' of human rights on private law will thus not only infringe the 'objective system of values' but also the constitutional rights of the party

---

60 Ibid, at pp 204 f.

61 Ibid.

in question. The level of protection, however, is lower here than in cases where the constitutionality of legislation or the activities of public authorities are in question. Many situations which would trigger an intervention by the courts in a purely 'public law' setting will thus pass constitutional scrutiny in their 'private' guise simply because the decision to enter into a potentially restrictive private law relationship in the first place (such as the employment and training contracts in the two BAG cases of 1954 and 1957) will, in many cases, be an expression of private autonomy and, as such, a consequence of the free will of the parties. In subsequent decisions, the Federal Constitutional Court also stressed that private and labour courts enjoy considerable leeway when applying the law; only if judges fail completely to recognise the influence of constitutional values on the interpretation of particular rules or if their interpretation is completely at odds with the position of the *Bundesverfassungsgericht* will private parties be able to invoke human rights successfully against court decisions.[62]

Two further points should be mentioned in this context. The level of protection provided by the existence of a constitutional right in the private sphere depends, first, on the degree to which the Basic Law will, in principle, allow a limitation of the right. This posed a problem in the case of Article 5(1) BL, which may be limited by any 'general law' (defined by the *Bundesverfassungsgericht* as laws which are not designed specifically to restrict free speech[63]). An unqualified application of this wide limitation clause would, in general, have left free speech at the disposal of the legislator and, in the *Lüth* case, placed both the producer and distributor of Harlan's film at a huge advantage since the injunction had indeed been granted on the basis of such a 'general' law (§ 826 BGB). The high importance of free speech for a democratic society, however, prompted the *Bundesverfassungsgericht* to qualify this specific limitation clause. Article 5(1) BL thus, in turn, affects the interpretation of such (limiting) general laws. This process is termed *Wechselwirkung* or 'interplay of forces', and is a consideration courts need to take into account on a case-by-case basis when dealing with free speech disputes. This, second, leads to a proportionality analysis. Article 5(1)

---

[62] See, e.g., BVerfGE 73, 261 (*Sozialplan*) at pp 268 f. For further references see M. Ruffert, *Vorrang der Verfassung und Eigenständigkeit des Privatrechts* (2001), p 123.

[63] Ibid at p 209 f.

BL will thus prevail as long as it does not infringe the legally protected interests of another party which take precedence over free speech in the particular circumstances of a case.

Applying these criteria to the injunction against Lüth, the Court declared the decision of the *Landgericht* Hamburg unconstitutional. The *Bundesverfassungsgericht* thereby stressed the fact that Lüth had not directly pressurised anyone to follow his call for a boycott, but had only used the persuasive power of intellectual arguments in order to appeal to the moral conscience of his fellow citizens.

Another dimension of this indirect effect of human rights first became apparent in the *Blinkfüer* decision of the Federal Constitutional Court of 1969. While *Lüth* had made operational in the private sphere the classical 'defensive' function of a human right (free speech) against undue limitation (the court injunction) by identifying, as explained above, the limits of a particular right and balancing, where necessary, the interests of the private parties in the light of constitutional values, Blinkfüer went one step further by actually requiring courts to intervene in favour of one of the parties to a private dispute.

Blinkfüer was a small regional weekly magazine which published East German television and radio programme guides. On occasion of the 1961 Berlin crisis following the erection of the Berlin Wall, Axel Springer, a politically conservative publishing house which dominated the West German newspaper market at the time, called for a boycott of all publications which contained such guides, and threatened to terminate its commercial relationships with any newspaper agents who continued to sell such products. Blinkfüer, attempting to recover damages in tort for the infringement of its financial interests by Axel Springer (see §§ 823 and 826 BGB), lost its case in the *Bundesgerichthof* but succeeded with a constitutional complaint against that judgment.

The Federal Constitutional Court held that the BGH had erroneously given more weight to Axel Springer's right to free speech (the call for a boycott) than the legitimate commercial interests of Blinkfüer, failing to take into account the fact that the target of the boycott (the newspaper agents) were not more or less free to follow or ignore the call (as was the audience in the case of *Lüth*) but instead put under considerable pressure to dissociate themselves from certain products in order to retain their commercially vital links with the larger publisher.

While this was all still very much in line with its previous decision in *Lüth*, the Court then took matters one step further and in turn invoked the free speech rights of Blinkfüer (to publish the East German material) in order to require the private law courts to provide a remedy in tort, establishing, in effect, a duty of the state to actively protect one private party against the activities of another on the basis of overriding constitutional considerations (so-called *Schutzpflicht* or 'protective duty' of the state).

This approach was confirmed six years later in the (politically) highly controversial first abortion decision of the Federal Constitutional Court,[64] which – in balancing the rights of mother[65] and *nasciturus*[66] – held that the state was under a constitutional duty to protect the unborn child against infringements of its right to life (by the mother and the doctor performing the abortion) except in a very limited set of circumstances where continuing the pregnancy would place an intolerable medical or psychological burden on the mother. It is in this last case that the *Bundesverfassungsgericht* openly counteracted a law passed by a comfortable majority in Parliament, and provoked heavy criticism for apparently overstepping the boundaries of its review powers. These calls for judicial restraint were, however, not directed against the fact that the Court invoked the notion of an 'objective system of values' and regarded the duty of the state to intervene on behalf of unborn life as a case of indirect *Drittwirkung* by virtue of intervening legislation; more troubling was the fact that the *Bundesverfassungsgericht* was not merely content with striking down the abortion law in question and leaving it for the legislator to devise a new solution (a 'normal' procedure, after all, in a system which allows courts to test the constitutional validity of legislation) but rather spelt out in great detail its *own* version of a constitutionally acceptable approach with which the legislature would have to (and did in fact later) comply.

Other more traditional cases involving the use of constitutional rights in their classical 'defensive' function by private parties often involve freedom of the press and the media. An employer who published in an internal company journal critical remarks of unnamed employees concerning the work of union representatives sitting on

---

64 BVerfG 39, 1 ff.

65 To the protection of her life and physical integrity, Article 2(2) BL, to protection of the the most intimate sphere of life, Articles 2(1) and 1(1) BL, and to the protection of freedom in general, Article 2(1) BL.

66 The right to life, Article 2(2) BL.

the company's board thus successfully invoked Article 5(1) BL against decisions of the labour courts which had prohibited anonymous contributions in the journal in order to protect the parity of power between employers and the representatives of employees in labour relationships.[67] Free speech and personality rights were invoked by an applicant who had suffered sexual abuse by her father as a child, and who in later years went public with these facts. The civil courts had established that the allegations were indeed true, but prohibited the daughter from disclosing her own (maiden) name or the name of her father when interviewed by the press or presenting her story on television.[68] In interpreting the scope of the relevant provisions of the Civil Code,[69] the *Bundesverfassungsgericht* thereby balanced the general personality right of the father (which includes the right to determine, within limits, how one's own image is projected in public) with the right to free speech and (again) the personality rights of the daughter (here the right to discuss the – true – events of one's own life in public), and came out on the side of the daughter. Other examples involve the protection of the private sphere against intrusions by the press,[70] the permissibilty of shocking advertisement,[71] and disputes arising between landlord and tenant.[72]

D. Critique and further development

The theory of an indirect or radiating effect of human rights in the private sphere has, as indicated in the first part of this chapter, been subject to continued discussion in Germany. Critics have questioned, first, whether the rather hazy notion of an 'objective system of values' can actually provide sufficient justification for human rights to have an impact on private relationships – however 'indirect' this

---

[67] BVerfGE 95, 28 ff (*Werkszeitungen*).

[68] BVerfGE 97, 391 (*Missbrauchsbezichtigung*).

[69] §§ 823 and 1004 BGB.

[70] BVerfGE 101, 361 ff (*Caroline von Monaco II*).

[71] BVerfGE 102, 347 ff (*Schockwerbung*).

[72] See, e.g., BVerfGE 7, 230 ff (a decision handed down on the same day as *Lüth* which went in favour of a landlord who had prohibited a tenant from using the leased building to display political advertisements) and BVerfGE 90, 27 ff (establishing, in principle, the right of foreign tenants to attach parabol antennae to the building in order to receive foreign television programmes).

effect might be in practice; second, if and to what extent human rights should perform their classical 'protective' function in the private sphere; and, third, how intense the degree of judicial scrutiny should be when constitutional rights are invoked in private disputes. The last issue is closely linked to the debate concerning the limits of constitutional review as exercised by the *Bundesverfassungsgericht* in cases of this kind.

I. An alternative to the 'radiating' effect: protective duties of the state

It is certainly true that the Federal Constitutional Court has not wasted much ink on the justification of indirect *Drittwirkung*; in the past five decades, decisions of the Court have nearly always invoked the standard phrase developed in the initial *Lüth* case quoted above. Academic thinking has, by contrast, tried to come up with alternative justifications to explain the effect of human rights in the private sphere since the early 1980s.[73]

The most important of these attempts is the identification of positive constitutional duties of the state to intervene in certain private relationships for the benefit of a particular party (*Schutzpflichten*).[74] The *Bundesverfassungsgericht* has itself resorted to this explanation on single occasions when holding that the state was generally under an obligation to actively promote and safeguard the protection of human rights. An early example of this approach is the first abortion case mentioned above.[75] The focus here is on legislation designed and necessary to give effect to constitutional values. Protective laws are obviously the most efficient tool in this respect; the legislator is thus obliged to create a system of private law which balances competing private interests and ensures that individual freedom is adequately protected in private relationships.[76]

---

[73] See. e.g., C.-W. Canaris, 'Grundrechte und Privatrecht', AcP 184 (1984), pp 201–46.

[74] So-called *Schutzpflichten*.

[75] BVerfGE 39, 1 ff at p 42; see also the earlier decision BVerfGE 35, 79 ff at p 113.

[76] See, e.g., S. Oeter, '"Drittwirkung" der Grundrechte und die Autonomie des Privatrechts' (1994) *AöR* 119, pp 529 ff (at pp 537 f).

The courts, equally, are under an obligation to ensure the protection of constitutional rights if necessary.

This approach, however, encounters one fundamental difficulty. The Basic Law does not establish substantive limitations for legislative activity per se. Whereas state *intervention* in human rights protection must undoubtedly adhere to the strict limitation requirements spelt out in the constitutional text as well as the (uncodified) principle of proportionality, this is not the case where the legislator is not restricting rights for the sake of the public weal but rather identifying conflicting private interests and balancing these in the light of constitutional values when enacting rules of private law. This lower standard of protection was, in principle, accepted by the Federal Constitutional Court in its second abortion decision, where it held that the legislator is essentially free in the way it chooses to balance competing private interests unless it fails to provide the absolutely essential (minimum) level of protection required by the constitutional rights of one party. While state *intervention* in human rights must thus not be *excessive*, legislative or (if it becomes necessary in individual cases) judicial activity or inactivity in the area of private or labour law will fall foul of constitutional values only if it leaves this essential core of constitutionally protected interests at the risk of infringement by other private parties. This, however, still leaves the problem of identifying these 'essential' private interests in particular cases.

In a series of decisions not directly related to the effect of human rights in the private sphere, the *Bundesverfassungsgericht* has set up a number of additional requirements which will have to be met before the existence of protective duties can be assumed. The infringement (or danger) must thus be substantial and affect a right of sufficient importance,[77] and there must be a high probability that the individual will actually suffer damage.[78] Finally, courts will take into account the scope of existing state regulation in the given area,[79] as well as any competing rights of other private parties.[80] The Federal Constitutional Court has thus been reluctant to second-guess

---

77 See BVerfGE 46, 160 ff (*Schleyer*) at p 164.

78 See BVerfGE 49, 89 ff (*Kalkar I*) at p 142 and BVerfGE 53, 30 ff (*Mühlheim-Kärlich*) at p 57. For a more detailed analysis of this point see V. Epping, op. cit., note 5, p 45.

79 See BVerfGE 49, 89 ff (*Kalkar I*) at p 142.

80 See BVerfGE 88, 203 ff (*Schwangerschaftsabbruch II*) at p 254.

prognostical assumptions of the legislator unless these were obviously unfounded or based on blatantly insufficient data.

The *Bundesverfassungsgericht* has adopted this line of reasoning in a limited number of more recent cases such as the decision concerning the invalidation of suffocating personal financial security contracts between inexperienced and often very young individuals and the creditors, usually banks, of the family members they vouch for (*Bürgschaftsverträge*).[81] The most important feature of this jurisprudence is the fact that the political legislator is given a fair amount of leeway when choosing the method and tools with which constitutional rights are to be protected if, in principle, a duty to intervene in favour of individual interests indeed exists. This can, for one, be explained by the fact that legislation will usually have to take into account competing private rights, which may both enjoy constitutional protection. It is then up to the democratically legitimised legislator rather than the courts to strike an appropriate balance. In most cases, there will also be more than just one way of protecting the rights of the affected individual; the division of powers principle will then again demand that the courts accept the political decision in favour of a particular solution unless it infringes the minimum level of protection required by the Basic Law.[82] Judicial intervention is thus *ultima ratio*. The Federal Constitutional Court has, however, intervened where the state failed to provide any protection at all or if the measures taken were clearly insuffient.[83]

Finally, it should be noted that the existence of an *objective* duty of the state to protect individual private interests need not necessarily translate into a *subjective* right of individuals to invoke this protection in court. The Basic Law contains a number of provisions which identify particularly important societal goods (such as the environment[84]),[85] institutions (such as a free press), or abstract legal concepts (such as private property or freedom of contract).[86] These constitutional provisions affect the protection of private individual interests, albeit only indirectly in that the state is under an overall

---

[81] BVerfGE 89, 214 ff (*Bürgschaftsverträge*).

[82] See BVerfGE 56, 54 (*Fluglärm*) at p 81.

[83] See BVerfGE 77, 170 (*Lagerung chemischer Waffen*) at p 215 and BVerfGE 92, 26 (*Zweitregister*) at p 46.

[84] Article 20a BL.

[85] So-called *Staatszielbestimmungen*.

[86] So-called *Einrichtungsgarantien*.

obligation to safeguard the general good, guarantee the existence of particular institutions, or ensure that there are legal rules in place which allow contractual relationships to develop adequately or private property to exist. Most human rights provisions will, however, provide a platform for (potential) subjective or individual claims. This is, indeed, the main difference between the previous Constitution of Weimar, where human rights were little more than aspirational statements, and the Basic Law, which guarantees recourse to the courts if there is an infringement of rights.[87]

2. The 'defensive' function of human rights in the private sphere

Explaining the effect of human rights with a duty of the state to intervene for the benefit of particular individual interests begs the question whether this approach will also allow constitutional rights to be invoked in their classical 'defensive' thrust. Can human rights, in other words, be directly invoked against other private parties, private or labour court decisions, or legislation affecting private relationships if the key to making constitutional rights operational in the private sphere is indeed a duty of the state *to act* (as explained above) rather than a duty *to abstain from action* (as in their clerical vertical function)? The answer in mainstream German constitutional doctrine is different in each case.

With the exception of the particular rights highlighted in the introduction, private parties are not directly bound by human rights considerations; private and labour law will therefore in the overwhelming number of cases provide the exclusive basis for contractual, delictual or labour relationships. Courts, on the other hand, are directly bound by the procedural rights found in the Basic Law as well as the principle of equality. Apart from these special cases, however, court decisions will themselves only affect human rights if they fail to protect individuals against the infringement of core constitutional positions by other private parties; judicial intervention is only required (as in the *Blinkfüer* case) if the law does not offer the protection which the state is under a duty to provide. This approach potentially reduces the effect of human rights in the private sphere when compared to the more open-ended notion of

87 So-called *Rechtsschutzgarantie*; see Article 19(4) BL.

an 'objective value order' under the *Lüth* doctrine. Most commentators, however, argue that the legislator is *always* bound by human rights considerations, whether it is dealing with public, criminal, or private law issues. This is where the German system currently indeed comes close to direct effect of human rights in the private sphere. Any law must conform to the strict constitutional standards of Articles 1–19 BL, and can be challenged with a constitutional complaint if the applicant can show that it violates his or her constitutional rights. The theory of state duties to protect individual private interests is thus relevant only if the legislator has failed to act at all. Cases such as *Lüth*, the 1999 *Caroline von Monaco* decision,[88] and the dispute concerning shocking advertisement[89] all involved the scrutiny of legislation by the Federal Constitutional Court, and resulted either in the interpretation of statutes in the light of constitutional values or the invalidation of laws where they cannot be saved by restrictive interpretation. This limits the practical implications of the debate about *Drittwirkung* ('radiating effect' or 'duty concept') to single and rather exceptional cases *unless* one is prepared to go all the way and limit judicial scrutiny of legislation in the areas of private and labour law to a two-pronged inquiry into, first, the legislative duty to safeguard certain constitutional rights in the private sphere, and, second, whether the existing rules fail to offer a minimum level of protection.[90] This would not only recalibrate the balance between constitutional values and private autonomy; it would also have the effect of reducing the influence of the Federal Constitutional Court on the development of the private law.

3. *The scope of constitutional review and the division of powers agument*

One of the major differences between Germany and many other systems reviewed in this book is the existence of a specialised constitutional court, and much of the discussion concerning *Drittwirkung* is in fact a debate about the competence of the *Bundesverfassungsgericht* in a different guise.

---

88 Supra, note 70.

89 Supra, note 71.

90 As proposed, e.g., by V. Epping, supra, note 5, p 134.

It is important to distinguish the thrust of this debate from the more general division of powers issue. The Court has in the past indeed been criticised for encroaching on the competence of the legislator; on some occasions its judges have even been termed 'alternate makers of rules' (*Ersatzgesetzgeber*) – an indication of the considerable influence which this Court has exerted on the development of the German legal system in all areas of the law. The critique in the context of *Drittwirkung* is, however, different. As explained above, the Court has also been criticised for eroding the competence of the specialised courts and acting – beyond its undisputed final jurisdiction in most constitutional matters – as a general court of final instance. The *Lüth* approach does indeed open the door to an expanding constitutionalisation of the system, while the more restrictive theory of protective duties seems to strengthen both the competence of the legislator and the jurisdiction of the specialised courts in the area of private and labour law. This aspect of the German debate is, however, of only limited comparative interest, since it is the result of an unusual combination of factors: a specialised court system, a constitutional court with the overarching powers of the *Bundesverfassungsgericht*, and individual access to that court.

Closely linked to the role of the Federal Constitutional Court is, however, a question of wider importance – are constitutional rights really sufficiently precise so as to be made operational in the private sphere? And – related to this point – are judges really equipped to apply broad constitutional norms to the intricate problems of private disputes, or should not the legislator, within the boundaries of broadly defined constitutional limits, determine the correct balance between the competing interests of private parties? The German solution – indirect effect of constitutional rights – seems to address both points in that it acknowledges the importance of fundamental values while at the same time seeking to solve conflicts primarily through the prism of private law.

4. The protective potential of indirect effect?

The rich German case law on *Drittwirkung* seems to indicate that the indirect or radiating effect of constitutional rights has, in general, suceeded in its aim to protect the core values of the Basic Law in private relationships. The latest and perhaps most controversial discussion of the issue – the enactment of a federal statute prohibiting discrimination against individuals in the private sphere on the basis of a number of criteria – shows, however, that this may indeed not always be the case.

By the end of 2004, the then ruling Social Democratic/Green majority in Parliament finalised draft legislation aimed at combating discrimination in the private sphere. The so-called *Antidiskriminierungsgesetz* (ADG) was designed to meet European requirements contained in EU Directives 2000/43/EC, 2000/78/EC and 2002/73/EC.[91] The draft, however, reached far beyond the ambit of Community law, which is aimed mainly at the creation of equal opportunities in employment relationships. The ADG, by contrast, is designed to enforce the equal treatment of individuals with regard to gender, disabilities, religious and ideological views, sexual orientation, and age (§ 1 ADG) in wide areas of private law.[92]

The first draft of the ADG, eventually enacted in 2006, was heavily criticised by the (former) conservative and (current) liberal opposition in Parliament, which decried the initiative as an undue interference with the freedom of contract (*Vertragsfreiheit*).[93] The impact of the statute could indeed be substantial. The ADG aims to protect individuals against unequal treatment not only in the sphere of work but also in the formation, execution and termination of legal relationships which usually involve standard contract terms used by one party in relation to large numbers of other contracting parties, without special regard to the personal characteristics of the other. This includes many transactions of everyday life such as access to goods and services, including accommodation and private insurance contracts. If one party provides circumstantial evidence indicating that it may have been treated unequally on the basis of one of the personal characteristics specified by the statute, the other party bears the burden of proof of the absence of unlawful discrimination.[94] Any such discrimination must be stopped, and the affected party may ask for an injunction in case there is a danger of continued discrimination as well as compensation for any loss suffered, including equitable monetary compensation for pain and suffering.[95]

---

91 Supra, note 1.

92 See § 2(1) nos. 5-8 ADG.

93 See *Frankfurter Allgemeine Zeitung* (FAZ) of 22 January 2005, pp 1/2: *Streit im Bundestag über die Behandlung von Minderheiten.*

94 § 23 ADG.

95 § 22(3) ADG.

The history of the ADG is interesting in our context in that the Federal Government justified its legislative initiative with the need to enforce particular constitutional values in private relationships. Legislative intervention was thus considered necessary, inter alia, because of the limited effect of human rights in the private sphere;[96] experience had shown that the general clauses of private law (§§ 138, 242 and 826 BGB) do not provide adequate protection for individuals despite the existence of a comprehensive anti-discrimination clause in the Basic Law.[97]

While the cases discussed in this chapter thus indicate that the indirect effect of constitutional rights can provide protection in many situations, German experience also shows that the approach will need to be bolstered by the enactment of specific statutes designed to safeguard constitutional values in the private sphere. The 'indirect' constitutional route is, in many cases, simply not effective enough in legal practice.

E. Concluding remarks

The promise of an unrestricted – and thus, in principle, truly free – sphere of private human existence is attractive. Why not grant society maximum leeway to organise itself beyond the limitations of broad rights enshrined in a constitutional text and initially designed to protect against the undue exercise of public authority? German experience with totalitarian rule, however, called for a different approach. The indirect effect developed in *Lüth* is thus a compromise between the danger of suffocating state intervention via broadly phrased constitutional principles and an equally unattractive acceptance of unrestricted – often commercial – power in the private sphere. The notion of an 'objective value system' is, however, imprecise, and has attracted much criticism on that count.

It is also interesting to note that the German variant of 'direct' effect as developed by the Federal Labour Court in its early years basically leads to the same results as the 'indirect' effect endorsed by the *Bundesverfassungsgericht*, which eventually won the day. While approaching cases from completely different angles, both

---

96 Ibid, 17–18.
97 Ibid, 37.

theories tend to seek solutions in the grey area in between 'direct' and 'no' effect. The main explanation for this phenomenon lies in the unqualified subordination of all legislation to the human rights protection offered by the Basic Law. The Federal Labour Court thus instinctively invoked the (constitutional) principle of proportionality to temper its approach (and decline protection to the applicant in the initial case) while the *Bundesverfassungsgericht* opted for (only) a radiating effect of supreme constitutional values on the private sphere. Both solutions lead to the enforcement of constitutional values in the private sphere, but remain difficult to conceptualise with any degree of precision.

The identification of state duties to protect particular individual private interests can, by contrast, provide a more coherent explanation of the influence which constitutional values can and should exert on private relationships. It is, potentially, also more restrictive. The constitutional limits placed on *all* legislation (public and private) will, however, continue to characterise the German answer to *Drittwirkung*. It is, in essence, an indirect effect on the private sphere via the constitutional control of state legislation.

Chapter 5: Greece
Taking Private Law Seriously in the Application of Constitutional Rights

Christina Akrivopoulou

Introduction

The latest revision of the Greek Constitution of 1975 – enacted in 2001[1] – acknowledged the *Drittwirkung* of constitutional rights, as a constitutional principle,[2] by stating that '[T]hese rights also apply to the relationship between individuals wherever appropriate'.[3] This principle has been at the heart of renewed attention in Greek legal thinking concerning the relationship between the Constitution and private law. It is submitted that this principle provides the foundation for a 'judicial model' of application of constitutional rights in private law while also confirming the dialectic rather than conflicting relationship between the two areas. The following analysis approaches the adoption of such a model in the Greek legal order through three different lenses: (a) the controversy between direct and indirect *Drittwirkung* in the way it has initially been developed and understood by Greek legal theory; (b) the channels that the new constitutional principle creates for an exchange between the Constitution and private law, and between judge and legislator; and (c) the effect of the theoretical controversy on judicial practice and its own unique understanding of the issue.

---

[1] N. Alivizatos and P. Eleftheriadis, 'The Greek Constitutional Amendments of 2001' (2002) *South European Society & Politics* 63.

[2] Another example is Art 18(1) of the Portuguese Constitution; see B. Rodriguez Ruiz, 'Discourse Theory and the addresses of Basic Rights' (2001) *Rechtstheorie* 87 at note 62.

[3] Article 25(1), sub-s 3 of the Greek Constitution. For an English translation see D. Th. Tsatsos and X. I. Kontiadis (eds), *The Constitution of Greece 1975/1986/2001* (2001), p 34. A translation is also available on the website of the Greek Parliament at http://www.parliament.gr.

A. The introduction of *Drittwirkung* into Greek legal theory

The origins of theoretical discussion concerning the *Drittwirkung* of constitutional rights can be traced back to the mid-1970s, shortly after the establishment of a new democratic order and the adoption of a new Constitutional Charter in Greece. To say that the entire discussion was literally a loan from the classic *Drittwirkung* debate developed in German legal theory would probably be an understatement. Nevertheless, in a short period of time Greek thinking absorbed the problem (the effect of constitutional rights on private law and private relations), added its own unique and specific features, and articulated its own critical views and questions. In Greece, to begin with, the term *Drittwirkung* or 'third party effect' (*τριτενέργεια*), apart from its significance in identifying the issue – it is, after all, an internationally established term – was never accepted. Taking the view that individuals in their private relationships are not 'third parties' or 'outcasts' standing outside the classical state–citizen relationship, Greek jurists adopted differentiated and more descriptive terms such as 'horizontal effect' or 'interpersonal effect' of constitutional rights. Moreover, they focused strongly on tracing constitutional norms that could provide a stable and secure foundation for the acceptance of such a relationship between constitutional rights and the system of private law. A number of constitutional norms were suggested in this context, among them the principle of human dignity (Article 2(1)[4]), the right to free development of the personality (Article 5(1)[5]) and Article 25(1)[6] subsection 1, in which the protection of constitutional rights is guaranteed as a duty of the state and as an expression of the rule of law.

The subject that mainly occupied Greek constitutional theory was, after all, not the acceptance of the interpersonal effect of constitutional rights as such but rather the way that this effect was

---

4 'Respect and protection of the value of the human being constitute the primary obligations of the State.' See the translation by Tsatsos and Kontiadis, op. cit., at p 17.

5 'All persons shall have the right to develop freely their personality and to participate in the social, economic and political life of the country, insofar as they do not infringe the rights of others or violate the Constitution and the good usages.' See the translation by Tsatsos and Kontiadis, op. cit., at p 19.

6 'The rights of man as an individual and as a member of the society and the principle of the constitutional welfare state are guaranteed by the State.' See the translation by Tsatsos and Kontiadis, op. cit., at p 33.

actually to be implemented in judicial practice. It was thus never in doubt that constitutional rights, as principles, should bind persons in their private relationships; the question was rather how, to what extent, and in what form constitutional rights could play that role. In a nutshell, this debate reproduced the German controversy between direct and indirect *Drittwirkung*.[7]

The theoretical constructions of direct and indirect *Drittwirkung* share two common assumptions. First is the fact that certain principles follow from the substantive content of constitutional rights.[8] These principles normatively bind the legal system in its entirety, consequently affecting private law and individuals in their private relationships. Constitutional rights as principles influencing interpersonal relationships can, secondly, be distinguished from their former addressee, the state, and are held equally against private individuals. The main consequence of this second assumption is that both sides of a specific interpersonal dispute are acknowledged as the bearers of constitutional rights. This obliges both theoretical approaches (direct and indirect *Drittwirkung*) to accept the fact that the effect of constitutional rights in interpersonal relationships is, ultimately, not independent of the balancing of conflicting interests between individuals. These assumptions constitute the common ground on which the Greek notion of *Drittwirkung* developed.[9]

Apart from their 'family resemblances', the Greek proponents of direct and indirect *Drittwirkung* adopted their own lines of argument. Those supporting the direct effect of the Constitution in private law thus focused on the necessity of such an application in order to set clear boundaries and limits in any private activities that could undermine the principles deriving from constitutional rights. This necessity was based on a sense of realism, mainly on the observation that the development of technology in a modern society, the relocation of power from the state to private players, and the growing power of the media had created an unfriendly and potentially suppressive environment for the enjoyment of constitutional rights. Consequently, constitutional rights as the basic set of principles,

---

[7] A. Barak, 'Constitutional Human Rights and Private Law' in D. Friedman and D. Barak-Erez (eds), *Human Rights in Private Law* (2001), pp 13 ff at pp 15 and 22.

[8] M. Kumm, 'Constitutional Rights as Principles: On the Structure and Domain of Constitutional Justice' (2004) *I.CON* 574 at 576–8.

[9] R. Alexy, *Theorie of Constitutional Rights* (trans J. Rivers) (2002), pp 357–8.

commonly accepted by society in its entirety, should develop their protective effect beyond the classic state–citizen relationship and also cover interpersonal relationships. According to this approach, constitutional rights should be directly applied within the framework of a specific legal dispute between private individuals in order to guarantee effectively their protection. By 'directly' we mean that constitutional rights should be applied beyond the existing framework of private law, ignoring, discarding or altering any relevant private law norms. The effective achievement of the direct application of constitutional rights in interpersonal relationships was therefore considered to require implementing legislation.

This 'realistic' justification of direct application of constitutional rights in private law challenged an important normative constraint: the notion of separation of powers. The giving of direct effect to constitutional rights lay in the hands of the judge, broadening his discretion, while at the same time undermining the competence of the legislator to regulate interpersonal relationships via private law norms. In order to avoid a deadlock, the Greek proponents of direct *Drittwirkung* suggested ways of limiting its most dramatic effects. Among them were the proposed balancing between conflicting constitutional rights, the application of constitutional rights only in cases of 'power' relationships between private parties (e.g., labour relationships),[10] and the direct application of civil, but not political or social, rights.

These 'limited' versions appeared to be as problematic as the original 'direct' approach, though for different reasons. First, from a merely constructive point of view, it was difficult for the Greek legal system to adopt a model of direct application. This difficulty was a result of the Greek variant of judicial review, which does not involve a distinct legal action for the direct control of the 'constitutionality' of private law norms.[11] Moreover, the set of proposed

---

[10] B. Markesinis and S. Enchelmaier, 'The applicability of Human Rights as between Individuals under German Constitutional Law' in B. Markesinis (ed), *Protecting Privacy* (1999), pp 191 ff at p 200.

[11] In Greece, 'judicial review' has three unique characteristics: (a) it is exercised by courts of any kind and jurisdiction; (b) it is never the main object of legal reasoning and always exercised to the framework of a legal action of a private or public nature; and (c) it is 'specific' in the sense that it refers only to those legal norms which are of decisive importance for a judgment. See E. Spiliotopoulos, 'Judicial Review of Legislation Acts in Greece' (1983) *Temple Law Quarterly* 463 at 466.

limitations did not seem convincing. The identification of private power relationships seemed difficult and blurry, and its invocation did not lead to clear conclusions (though in real life in these kinds of relationship the infringement of constitutional rights seems to be more substantial) because in many cases even the relationship between equal parties can lead to similar results (e.g., the relationship between spouses). The distinction between directly applicable and non-applicable rights – based, in turn, on the difference between civil and political or social rights – was equally unclear, mainly for the reason that rights are complex in nature (e.g., the freedom of expression is both civil and political in character). In the end, the 'limitations' outlined above merely reproduced the stereotype of the classic state-citizen relationship, either by imitating it (e.g., relationships of private power) or by qualifying it (non-applicability of social and political rights between individuals). Apart from that, the notion of balancing was really a natural consequence of the fact that in private relationships both parties are equally bearers of constitutional rights. Moreover, its 'limiting' significance was reduced by the fact that the balancing of interests between opposing constitutional rights can provide sustainable arguments for both parties, and, thus, could often lead to serious deadlocks, such as controversial decisions and ambiguous justifications.[12]

The indirect *Drittwirkung* approach, on the other hand, seemed a lot more realistic and adaptable by the Greek legal system. Its invocation implies the joint application of constitutional rights and private law norms. According to its proponents, it implies a mild, friendly, purely hermeneutical relationship between the Constitution and private law. This approach was aimed at the legislator and based on a rather simple premise – that the private law system should combine its integrity and unity with a set of founding principles derived

[12] In the decision known as the 'Babiniotis Case' (13/1999), the Greek Supreme Civil Court dealt with a dispute between a Greek football team and the writer of a dictionary. The supporters of the team are often called 'Voulgarians' by their adversaries on the field, and this is considered to be offensive. The writer, Mr Babiniotis, included this term as an offensive interpretation of the word 'Voulgarian' in his dictionary. The Court was divided. The majority supported the writers' freedom of expression but the minority concluded – with the exact opposite reasoning – that the protection of the right of personality of the fans should prevail. Court cases referred to in this text and the footnotes are available by their number and year of publication at http://www.lawdb.intrasoftnet.com.

from constitutional rights. Constitutional rights appeared to provide fertile ground for a careful review of the private law system, enabling it to face new challenges and threats that interpersonal relationships and private activities could pose for the rights of the individuals. At the same time the private law system could preserve its unity, and the equilibrium between legislator and judge would remain intact. Under this approach, the 'interpersonal' effect of constitutional rights could be presented as an ongoing dialogue between discrete but mutually open legal systems – the constitutional order and private law. This scheme could involve both general clauses of private law or even specific norms which require further interpretation and concrete implementation, or should be understood in the light of principles derived from constitutional rights. It thereby acknowledged the effect of the Constitution on private law as being primarily hermeneutical in character. This notion could increase the normative importance of the Constitution for the entire legal order by improving the protection of the constitutional rights of individuals.[13]

B. The 'interpersonal' effect of constitutional rights as a constitutional norm, Article 25(1) subsection 3 of the Greek Constitution

As we have noted earlier, the constitutional revision of 2001 added to Article 25(1) of the Greek Constitution a third section stating that '[T]hese rights also apply to the relationship between individuals wherever appropriate'.[14] The explicit constitutional acknowledgement of the *erga omnes* effect of constitutional rights in interpersonal relationships put an end to the Greek theoretical discussion about its constitutional basis.[15] Furthermore, this acknowledgment strengthens an axiom, a fundamental premise of the legal order that cannot any longer be disputed. It is inconceivable that the horizontal effect of constitutional rights in interpersonal relationships could be contested following the introduction of Article 25(1), section 3 of the Constitution.

---

[13] G. Taylor, 'Why the common law should be only indirectly affected by constitutional guarantees: A comment on Stone' (2000) *MULR* 623 at 639–43.

[14] Ibid, note 2.

[15] E. Venizelos, 'La Constitution hellénique de 2001 et l' actualité du phènomène constitutionnel' (2002) *RDF CONST* 515 at 522.

The 'horizontal effect' does not only concern constitutionally acknowledged rights. The expression used – '[T]hese rights …' – refers to the first subsection of the article stating that: 'The rights of man as an individual and as a member of society and the principle of the constitutional welfare state are guaranteed by the State.'[16] The constitutional provision thus also includes any 'rights of man' deriving from European or international law (such as the European Convention of Human Rights). *Drittwirkung* as a constitutional principle thereby develops a rather interesting procedural relationship with rights (either human or constitutional). It functions as a mediating device which facilitates the application of constitutional or human rights in interpersonal disputes.

In the course of the Greek discussion surrounding *Drittwirkung* that was reopened by the constitutional acknowledgement of the theory, a set of arguments has been put forward concerning its modification in the light of Article 25(1), subsection 3. It has, in particular, been proposed that the constitutional norm serves as a legal justification for the interpersonal effect of constitutional rights.[17] The theoretical and legal justification of such an effect is, however, founded on the objective character of constitutional rights as principles. This is regarded as the common premise underlying both direct and indirect *Drittwirkung*. Any theoretical and legal justification of the interpersonal effect of constitutional rights thus lies in their very nature, and it is not a quality that can be granted to them by virtue of the Constitution. A constitutional norm can affirm but not confer on constitutional rights their objective character as principles radiating throughout the entire legal order.

Another argument specifically supports the identification of Article 25(1) of the Constitution with the theoretical construction of direct *Drittwirkung*.[18] This approach is based on a very simple argument: nowadays, threats to the rights of the individual are multiplied and stem from both public and private activities. The direct application of constitutional rights can address such threats and thus strengthen the protection of the individual. On the surface, the

---

16 Supra, note 2 at 33.

17 Ch. Anthopoulos, 'The "third party effect" (Drittwirkung) as constitutional Principle. An analysis of Art. 25 § 1 c of the Greek Constitution' (2005) *Revue Hellénique Des Droits De l' Homme* 707 at 708.

18 P. Eleftheriadis, 'Constitutional Reform and the Rule of Law in Greece' (2005) *West European Politics* 317 at 321.

principle seems to be neutral, considering the direct or indirect effect of constitutional rights in private law as equally acceptable solutions. There is a role for both the Constitution and private law to play as far as *Drittwirkung* is concerned. This role should thereby not consist either of a mere reduction of private law or a domination of the issue by the Constitution but to their mutual exchange and peaceful coexistence. To understand Article 25(1) of the Constitution as a case of direct *Drittwirkung* places far too strong limitations on the competences of the legislator, over-emphasises the discretion of the judge, and disrupts the equilibrium between the powers of the state. Seen in this light, it seems preferable to accept that the provision seeks to intensify the application of constitutional rights in private law and constitutes a guideline for the judge by asking him to focus on the protection of constitutional rights when resolving interpersonal disputes.

From this follows a third argument. Identifying Article 25(1) of the Constitution with direct *Drittwirkung* imposes an obligation on the judge and gives individuals a (corresponding) right or claim. This means that if the judge does not apply constitutional rights in an interpersonal dispute, he will himself breach an obligation deriving from a constitutional provision which establishes the right of the individual to enjoy constitutional rights. The question is, in other words, whether by not invoking the constitutional rights of individuals in an interpersonal dispute the judge might actually be infringing them.

There is no doubt that the judge has a key role to play in the application of constitutional rights in private law. His role is to ensure that constitutional rights take effect in private relationships. His main obligations and competences are, however, not determined by *Drittwirkung* as a constitutional principle but rather by his commitment to the notion of separation of powers, his respect both towards the legislator and the Constitution, and his obligation to grant judicial protection to the individual. Constitutional acknowledgment of *Drittwirkung* cannot trump these other commitments. Bearing these in mind, it is suggested that *Drittwirkung* as a constitutional principle obliges the judge to give effect to constitutional rights provided that their application has been requested by the parties involved. This means that he is obliged to take into consideration a claim that the constitutional rights of one of the parties were violated, meaning that he has to examine the credibility of the argument and balance it against the constitutional rights of the other party (even if that party has not raised a corresponding claim). Beyond that, it is part of his own discretion whether he will base his decision on the application of constitutional principles in order to resolve an interpersonal dispute or not. That will depend on the way he interprets the specific facts of the case: as an infringement of rights or as a violation of private law. Article 25(1) of the Constitution thus imposes on the judge a duty to justify any reluctance on his part to apply constitutional rights in private relationships if he has been specifically requested to do so by one or both the parties. He is, furthermore, not obliged to choose between direct or indirect effect of a constitutional right, between the application of constitutional principles or private law norms, or even to guarantee that the outcome of the balancing between the opposing interests of the parties involved is intrinsically fair. He is merely obliged to take into account the arguments of the parties concerning their constitutional rights, and to justify his decision to grant judicial protection or to deny it.

C. The judicial approach: four models of exchange between the constitution and private law

Article 25(1), subsection 3 is addressed to the judge. The judge, in addition to his key role in the process of applying constitutional rights in private law, is also in the important position of interpreting this constitutional provision. The question here is whether he identifies the constitutional principle of 'horizontal effect' of constitutional rights with one of the opposing theoretical approaches of *Drittwirkung* (the direct or indirect one).

While theory often acquires a one-sided view of such complex matters, legal practice forced to confront the ever-changing reality, is expected to provide concrete and justified solutions to specific interpersonal disputes and find a way to overcome theoretical debates such as the one concerning direct and indirect *Drittwirkung*. In Greek court practice we can identify arguments that show that both direct and indirect *Drittwirkung* – both the Constitution and private law – have a role to play in resolving interpersonal disputes. The Greek courts have not resolved the problem of giving interpersonal effect to constitutional rights via one route only – either direct or indirect effect. On the contrary, they seem to adopt a more substantive and less constructive way of bringing to bear on private law the effect of constitutional principles, treating *Drittwirkung* as a much more complex and wider issue than a choice between direct and indirect effect. Moreover, the judicial approach redirects our attention from the 'entrance' to the 'exit' of constitutional rights in private law, meaning that we can draw very interesting conclusions by analysing not only the way constitutional rights enter into interpersonal disputes but also, and mainly, by looking at legal outcomes. By focusing on the outcomes which the interpersonal effect of constitutional rights can achieve, we can overcome the distinction between the hermeneutical (indirect) and the potentially legislative (direct) interpersonal effect of constitutional rights – an effect in which the Constitution and the law both have their own clear and indispensable function.

Greek courts have gradually developed four models by which constitutional rights are invoked in interpersonal relationships. All of these models guarantee a balanced relationship between the Constitution and private law, though each of them has a different scope and adopts a distinct methodological approach or different construction: (a) via general clauses of private law (e.g., the clause preventing abusive enforcement of rights);[19] (b) by a joint application of constitutional rights and private law rights (e.g., the private right to personality);[20] (c) by interpreting and enforcing not general but specific norms of private law according to principles derived from constitutional rights (e.g., the legal action aiming at renunciation of paternity); and (d) by applying constitutional rights directly (without the mediation of private law norms) in order to determine the legitimacy of individual private activities (e.g., the unlawful use of tapes and videotapes in civil or criminal trials).

1. Constitutional rights and general clauses of private law

General clauses of private law, such as that preventing abuse of rights, play a very important and practical role in the realisation

---

[19] Article 281 of the Greek Civil Code declares: 'The exercise of a right is prohibited if it obviously exceeds the limits imposed by good faith or the good usages or the social or economic scope of the right.'

[20] Article 57 of the Greek Civil Code declares: 'Anyone who unlawfully experiences an infringement of his personality has the right to demand its termination and that such infringement is not repeated in the future.'

of the interpersonal effect of constitutional rights. Initially, such clauses were used as flexible, catch-all rules designed to provide 'just' or 'fair' results in private disputes. In addition to their classic function, nowadays these clauses facilitate the transfer of constitutional principles and values into the private law system, and are considered to be their *reflections*. In a legal order based on a normative liberal constitution, they thereby also function as expressions of equal autonomy between individuals or, in a more literal sense, as means for the protection of the weaker party in a private relationship (labour relationships, contracts). In other words, the general clauses of private law 'activate' the interpersonal effect of constitutional rights in private relationships in cases where the enjoyment of one individual's private autonomy suppresses or endangers the enjoyment of constitutional rights by another. The function of general clauses thus lies in their ability to create a minimum of equal autonomy enjoyed by both parties. Obviously, their importance is not limited to their role as 'entrances' or 'gateways'[21] for constitutional rights into private law. Their function is, from a purely constructive point of view, very important since they advance the metamorphosis of highly abstract and general constitutional norms into specific provisions (of private law) which can be applied in concrete legal situations and provide specific claims and remedies for the individuals concerned.[22] In addition, they facilitate a balancing between the conflicting rights and interests of individuals in interpersonal disputes.

A very interesting example can be drawn from Greek case law concerning labour relations and, more specifically, the right of the employer to 'manage' his enterprise. This right derives from private autonomy and is acknowledged in the Greek Civil Code. It enables the employer to make all choices necessary to maintain the viability of his enterprise, including his ability to dismiss his employees.

---

[21] G. Dürig, 'Grundrechte und Zivilrechtsprechung' in T. Maunz (ed), *Vom Bonner Grundgesetz zur gesamtdeutschen Verfassung, Festschrift für H. Nawiasky* (1956), p 157; T. Dieterich, 'Grundgesetz und Privatautonomie im Arbeitsrecht' (1995) *RdA* 129 at 132.

[22] O. Gerstenberg, 'Private law and the new European Constitutional settlement' (2004) *European Law Journal* 766 at 769: '... private law is ... the *geometric location* for formulating remedies for an infringement by one private individual on the constitutional right of another individual ...'

The Greek civil courts have gradually developed a set of general rules which limit this right of the employer by invoking the employee's constitutional right to personality via the general clause which prohibits abusive enforcement of rights (see Article 281 of the Greek Civil Code).[23] As the courts have stated on many occasions, the rights of the employer cannot be considered as absolute but are restrained – as any other private right – by the fundamental principles that follow from constitutional rights.[24] The constitutional protections of the personality and dignity of the employees thus stand as obstacles in the way of a one-sided decision of their employer to dismiss them when this decision cannot be justified by financial considerations, is not considered as an appropriate means to secure the viability of his enterprise, or in cases where it affects the constitutional rights of the employee in a disproportionate manner (e.g. the dismissal of an employee only two years before his retirement and after many years of loyal service).[25] Moreover, based on these rules, the employee has acquired the right to retain his position as a right deriving from the constitutional protection of his personality against unjustified or

[23] This was considered to be the basic line of argument in the decisions of the Greek Supreme Civil Court in such cases. In its judgments nos. 115/1992 and 34/1993, the S.C.C. has stated that as a result of the employer's right to regulate his enterprise, he has the right to deny the employees services, unless his denial is abusive (according to Article 281 of the Greek Civil Code).

[24] In Case No. 145/1998 of the Rodopi Court of First Instance, the protection of human dignity and the freedom that the individual enjoys to participate in social and financial activities are considered to be the boundaries of the employers 'management' rights. In judgment No. 1881/1996, the Athens Court of First Instance stated that the employee enjoys the right to his position as a substantial base of his social and economic existence. In Case No. 1910/1997, the Athens Court of First Instance considered the 'management rights' of the employer to be limited by the employees' dignity, free development of personality, and freedom to participate in social and financial life. Moreover, under these circumstances the employee enjoys the right to offer his services which the employer cannot reject without a legal justification.

[25] In Case No. 1881/1996, the Athens Court of First Instance applied a proportionality test on the employer's decision to dismiss an employee who had worked loyally in his business for many years, was very close to his retirement, and was financially supporting his wife and family. The proportionality principle guided the judge to weigh between the reasons of the dismissal and its effect on the employee's rights to livelihood, personality and dignity. The court held that the principle of proportionality obliged the employer to use milder means in order to pursue his financial interests and 'management' rights.

abusive decisions by his employer.[26] In this way the courts have been able to limit dismissals based on personal or political considerations[27] or motives of a clearly disproportionate nature.[28] It is obvious that the 'indirect' effect of constitutional rights is not crucial in these cases but rather the fact that constitutional rights can be developed in cases of conflict between private rights in interpersonal disputes, that they function as the foundation for the limitation of these private rights, and that they simultaneously create general rules which can serve as a foundation for claims, remedies or restrictions of the individuals involved.[29]

2. *Constitutional rights and rights established by private law*

Specific private rights cannot be equated with general clauses because the latter are the mediators of rights and their joint application with specific rights (either constitutional or established in private law, e.g., property rights) is the necessary precondition in order to provide claims and protection to the interests of the individual. The existence and significance of the (private) right of personality (article 57 of the Greek Civil Code) constitutes one of the special features of Greek *Drittwirkung*. This right has developed a very interesting relationship with a number of constitutional rights. Primarily, it

---

[26] In Case No. 3646/1992, the Athens Court of First Instance underlined the importance of using the proportionality principle in resolving labour disputes because of their character as relationships of power. Moreover, the court indicated that the employee's interest in retaining his position is constitutionally protected and socially desirable.

[27] In Case No. 259/1995, the Thessaloniki Court of Appeal dealt with the dismissal of an employee who was also a union member. The court performed a proportionality test on the reasons that had motivated his employer to dismiss him (his activities as a syndicalist). According to the judgment, the employee has the right to enjoy his freedom to express any idea, political or syndicalist, while the employer has the obligation to respect this freedom.

[28] Such as decisions of the employer which are degrading for the status of the employee (e.g., transfer of the employee, demotion, or verbal or sexual abuse). In Case No. 1227/1993, the Greek Supreme Civil Court concluded that these cases should be regarded as cases of unjustified dismissal, giving the employee the right to resign and claim damages.

[29] T. Ramm, 'Diritti fondamentali e diritto del lavoro' (1991) *GDLRI* 359.

retains a sufficiently distinct 'core' that can protect the individual effectively against a number of infringements. It protects the physical integrity, health, name and honour of the individual. Its qualities are nevertheless restricted to the 'civil' characteristics of the individual (concerning mainly his financial or contractual activities). Because of its strictly 'civil' nature, it seems inadequate to protect the individual in other equally vital dimensions of his personal and ethical integrity. In order to create new claims deriving from the private right of personality, the courts apply it together with specific constitutional rights. Their joint application has hermeneutical and normative consequences. It broadens the content of the private right of personality, which acquires new elements, new dimensions or even new rights (e.g., privacy, the protection of personal data, the protection of the image, or dignity).[30] Their joint application also has normative consequences in founding the claims necessary for individuals in order to protect their interests. What is very interesting is that after this process these rights and claims are added to the core of the (private) right of personality (in ways that resemble legal precedents) meaning that their joint application with specific constitutional rights is no longer needed in order to provide the necessary protection on future occasions.

The most interesting example is illustrated in a set of cases dealing with the protection of the environment as a specific aspect of the private right of personality. Greek courts have dealt with a

[30] In Case No. 1189/2001, the Athens Multimember Court of First Instance decided a dispute between a politician and an AIDS patient. The politician has been photographed with the patient during his visit to a hospital. He then printed the photograph in a brochure which he used for his electoral campaign, along with a comment about his humanitarian effort concerning AIDS patients. The AIDS patient invoked the protection of the private right to personality along with Article 9(1) sub-s 2 of the Greek Constitution, which acknowledges the right to privacy, and Article 2(1) (human dignity). The court accepted privacy and human dignity as interests protected by the private right to personality, ordered the politician to cease any present or future use of the photograph, and granted damages to the patient. Moreover, in Case No. 2364/2002, the same court dealt with a dispute between an actress and a magazine editor. The magazine had published a series of personal pictures of the actress without her consent. The court applied the private right of personality and Article 9(1) sub-s 2 of the Greek Constitution, which acknowledges the right to privacy, as well as Article 5(1), which protects the right of the individual to his own image. According to the judgment, privacy and the protection of the image (as dimensions of the private right of personality) could support the actress' claim for damages.

number of activities which either violate or degrade the cultural or physical environment as infringements of the private right to personality.[31] In a recent case,[32] Greek courts were confronted with a controversy between a famous Greek singer and the monastic community of Meteora.[33] The singer staged a video clip for her songs in the monastic city of Meteora. More specifically, she sang, danced, and was photographed and filmed inside the monastic area and in the presence of the monks. Afterwards, she used this audio-visual material to promote her music. The monks claimed that these activities breached their private right to personality. The court accepted their argument, basing its reasoning on the invocation of Article 24(1)[34] of the Greek Constitution. This provision protects the enjoyment of the cultural environment both as a civil and social right. Based on this constitutional principle, the courts concluded that the normative content of the private right of personality should also include the interest of individuals in the full respect of their natural and cultural environment. Following this approach, the courts identified certain claims and remedies which could be invoked by the monastic city, and developed specific prohibitions for the singer (to cease the present and abstain from any future use of the photographic or videotaped material). The characteristic feature of this case is the fact that a collective and constitutionally protected interest,

---

31 In Case No. 1531/2002, the Volos Court of First Instance considered the destruction of a small forest as an infringement of the private right of personality of the local residents. According to the court, the constitutional protection of the environment is a fundamental dimension of the civil personality of the individual. In Case No. 438/2001, the Syros Court of First Instance reviewed a dispute concerning the installation of an air wire station for transferring electric energy to the island of Tinos. The residents of the island considered the installation as detrimental to the environment. The court accepted the argument, considering the constitutional protection of the environment as an element of the private right of personality. In Case No. 304/2005, the Thessaloniki Court of Appeal was confronted with a dispute concerning an antenna serving cellphones on the roof of a building. The residents challenged this as a violation of their private right of personality. Invoking previous decisions, the court accepted their argument concerning the constitutional protection of the environment as an element of the private right to personality.

32 Case No. 349/2002 of the Trikala Court of First Instance.

33 Meteora is a holy Greek mountain where a monastic community has been located since the Byzantine era.

34 'The protection of the natural and cultural environment constitutes a duty of the State and a right of every person.' See the translation by Tsatsos and Kontiadis, op. cit., note 3, at 33.

such as the interest in the environment, can acquire an intense individualistic dimension when it is combined with a private law right.[35]

The synthesis between private law rights and constitutional rights, geared towards the creation of new rights that can protect the individual against modern risks and threats emanating from private society (e.g., technology or mass media), is a characteristic feature of the effect of constitutional rights on interpersonal relationships.[36] In addition, it provides a very interesting argument against those who claim that *Drittwirkung* (and especially its 'direct' variant) literally destroys the protection of private autonomy by the way it is constructed and made operational within the private law system. Nevertheless, the Constitution represents the main source of private autonomy and that is why constitutional rights, when applied jointly with rights protected by private law, are able to strengthen, expand and enrich their normative content. Consequently, limits to the private autonomy of individuals are not an issue of either the 'direct' or 'indirect' application of constitutional rights but rather the outcome of a balancing between the rights of the parties involved in a private relationship.

3. Constitutional rights and specific norms of private law

The theoretical construction of indirect *Drittwirkung* introduces an unjustified distinction between general clauses of private law and more specific legal norms. Despite the fact that general clauses of law offer the more appropriate framework for facilitating the exchange

35 A characteristic case concerning this argument is a Cypriot judgment known as the *Red Arrows* case (*Kostakis v Republic of Cyprus*), which was published on 4 August 2006 by the Provincial Court of Lemessos. The court dealt with a dispute concerning a contract between the British military base on the island of Cyprus and the Republic of Cyprus, which allowed British military aircraft (the 'Red Arrows') to fly near the city of Lemessos. Kostakis was an autistic child, suffering from an unusual form of acute hearing (meaning that the sound of the aircraft was intense for him). Kostakis claimed that due to flights that the Red Arrows had conducted not only near but actually over the city his physical and psychological condition was completely undermined. The sound of the aircraft, intensified in his ears, made his presence intolerable. The court considered the contract between the British base and Cyprus as infringing the environment and, in particular, infringing Kostakis' personality and inner privacy – thus transforming a general interest into an individual one.

36 G. Alpa, 'Il diritto costituzionale sotto la lente del giusprivatista' (1999) *RDC* 15 at 22.

between constitutional rights and private law, it would seem that the complete exclusion of legal norms with a more specific content from this function is not justified.[37] In Greek court practice, the effect of constitutional rights on specific norms of private law is based on the German notion of *verfassungskonforme Gesetzesauslegung*,[38] meaning a constitutionally minded interpretation of private law norms. This notion imposes on the judge the duty to choose from different but nevertheless acceptable interpretations of a specific norm of private law the one interpretation that is compatible with the principles deriving from constitutional rights. The most important feature of this method is that the effect of constitutional rights on private law is a consequence of an inherent balancing process which takes place between a specific norm of private law and constitutional principles. This feature distinguishes the approach from the previous two, where the effect of constitutional rights on private law was the outcome of a balancing exercise between the opposing rights and interests of the individuals involved in a dispute. The underlying justification of the notion lies in the fact that it enables the judge to avoid judicial review of private law and thus protects the intentions of the legislator. At the same time, the judge is in the position to 'amend' the content of a private law provision by means of a constitutionally minded interpretation of the legislative text.

Distinctive examples of such a constitutionally minded interpretation of private law can be found in a number of cases concerning the legal ability of the child to renounce his father.[39] In the early 1980s, children who were born in wedlock were automatically recognised as natural descendants of the mother's husband and were unable to renounce their father under the Greek Civil Code in case they were in fact not blood-related. This was a right the Greek Civil Code gave only to the legally acknowledged father (see Articles 1471 and 1475 of the Code). The Greek courts invoked Articles 2(1), 5(1) and 21(1)[40] of the Greek Constitution to find

---

[37] This argument was supported by the German Federal Constitutional Court. See C.-W. Canaris, 'Grundrechte und Privatrecht' (1984) *AcP* 201 at 223.

[38] K. Hesse, *Grundzüge des Verfassungsrecht der Bundesrepublik Deutschland* (20th edn, 1999), p 30.

[39] See Cases Nos. 10168/1982 and 9702/1984 of the Athens Court of Appeal.

[40] 'The family, being the cornerstone of the preservation and the advancement of the Nation, as well as marriage, motherhood and childhood, shall be under the

that human dignity, the free development of personality, and the constitutional protection of the family and child, in combination, include the right of a child to uncover its true origins and recover its true identity. On this constitutional basis, the courts re-interpreted the private law norms in question and gave the child a ground to support the legal action aimed at renouncing the legally recognised father. What the Greek courts did on this occasion was to avoid discarding as unconstitutional the specific norms of private law by reshaping their scope and meaning so as to be compatible with the invoked constitutional rights.

The Greek discussion on the topic considers constitutionally minded interpretation of specific norms of private law to be a form of direct *Drittwirkung*. This position is supported by the fact that the effect of constitutional rights under this approach is really not interpretative (indirect) but rather a way of creating legislation (direct). More specifically, the principles deriving from constitutional rights fill the 'gaps' in the law and thus function as a creative source of private law norms in those cases where the legislator has not predicted the need to regulate a particular legal relationship or has ignored the need to protect a certain legal interest. If this argument is indeed valid and we envisage these gaps as blank parts of the private law system (*tabulae rasae*), then allowing judges to fill these gaps directly, even with regard to constitutional principles, must be an infringement of the notion of separation of powers.[41] Even more difficult to understand is how a private relationship or an interpersonal controversy can be created in the absence of private law norms. In the cases commented on earlier, there was no existing legal 'gap' but merely an anachronistic private law norm which was modernised through the influence of principles derived from a set of constitutional rights. The judge did not create a new legal action, private right, claim or remedy but merely extended the existing private law protection in order to include both the child and the legally recognised father. What the judge did was to invoke constitutional rights in order to provide a foundation for adapting the existing norms of private law to evolving societal realities.

---

protection of the State.' See D. Th. Tsatsos and X. I. Kontiadis, op. cit., note 3, at 31.

[41] R. Alexy, op. cit., note 9, at 364.

4. Constitutional rights beyond private law norms

The constitutional amendment of 2001 in Greece added in Article 19(3) a norm stating that: '[U]se of evidence acquired in violation of this article and of Articles 9 and 9A is prohibited.' This norm is addressed to the judge and puts him under a binding obligation to exclude from consideration any unlawfully obtained evidence, especially evidence concerning the private sphere of the individual protected by Articles 9(1),[42] 9A,[43] and 19(1)[44] of the Greek Constitution. This norm has been strongly criticised in Greek theoretical discussion because of its absolute character and the deadlocks it causes in criminal proceedings where the search for truth is considered fundamental.[45] This is the reason why the courts in criminal trials allow the submission of evidence even when the private sphere is infringed in order to protect: (a) the value of human life; (b) the defendants' innocence until proven guilty; and (c) the search for truth.[46] In civil trials, by contrast, the protection of the private sphere is considered to be absolute, thereby restricting any submission of evidence that infringes privacy, the protection of personal data, or the secrecy of communication between individuals. Such a limitation seems less problematic in civil proceedings where the protection of private autonomy (and thereby of the private and personal life of the individual) is considered the core foundation of a fair trial. What is very characteristic about this approach is that the effect of constitutional rights is not an outcome of the balancing between the opposing rights of the concerned individuals but rather of a balancing between constitutional principles which takes place beyond the realm of private law and on a highly abstract level: human

---

[42] 'Every person's home is a sanctuary. The private and family life of the individual is inviolable.' See D. Th. Tsatsos and X. I. Kontiadis, op. cit., note 3, at 21.

[43] 'All persons have the right to be protected from the collection, processing, and use, especially by electronic means, of their personal data, as specified by the law.' See D. Th. Tsatsos and X. I. Kontiadis, op. cit., note 3, p 22.

[44] 'Secrecy of letters and all other forms of free correspondence or communication shall be inviolable.' See D. Th. Tsatsos and X. I. Kontiadis, op. cit., note 3, p 30.

[45] M. T. King, 'Security, scale, form, and function: The search for truth and the exclusion of evidence in adversarial and inquisitorial justice systems' (2002) *International Legal Perspectives* 185 at 189–90.

[46] These limitations were proposed in Case No. 42/2004 of the Greek Civil Court concerning the use of evidence in a criminal trial by the defendant, even though they were considered to infringe the private sphere.

dignity, privacy and freedom of communication versus the search for truth and the right of the individual to present evidence in order to support in court his or her arguments.[47] In this case we see a form of direct *Drittwirkung* due to the fact that Article 19(3) of the Greek Constitution is self executing, meaning that it is directly enforced in private disputes, without mediation by provisions of private law.

This high level of abstraction is evident in cases that preceded the constitutional amendment.[48] One of the leading decisions was Case No. 1/2001 of the Greek Supreme Civil Court.[49] Here the Court justified the absolute priority of the protection of the private sphere in civil cases concerning the admission of evidence with a set of constitutional principles. According to the Court's reasoning, the protection of human dignity and the private sphere of the individual provides the foundation for the enjoyment of the freedom of communication between individuals. As the Court emphasised, this freedom provides individuals with, inter alia, the right to express themselves freely at any time or place, and without fear that their thoughts or words are monitored or recorded. This freedom is so important to a democratic society that it justifies any absolute restriction on the submission of evidence which could possibly violate it. In a more recent decision, Case No. 3922/2005, the Supreme Administrative Court gave protection to the private sphere via the invocation of the constitutional right to privacy along with Article 8 of the European Convention of Human Rights. The case concerned a town mayor who had invited a young woman to his home, promising that he would hire her as a civil servant in exchange for sexual intercourse. The woman had videotaped their meeting and submitted the material to the Court, demanding his resignation.

---

[47] N. C. Alivizatos, 'Privacy and transparency: A difficult conciliation' in L. A. Sicilianos and M. Gavouneli (eds), *Scientific and Technological Developments and Human Rights* (2001), p 117; M. Cheh, 'Technology and privacy: Creating the conditions for preserving personal privacy' in ibid, p 99.

[48] Case No. 130/1996 of the Greek Supreme Civil Court concerned the dispute of a divorced couple in relation to the custody of their child. The ex-husband submitted evidence concerning his ex-wife's sexual affairs in order to support her inability to raise their child. The court commented in general on the conflict between the private sphere and the submission of evidence in a civil trial. Similarly, Case No. 748/2000 of the Greek Supreme Civil Court underlined the inherent conflict between privacy and the right to present evidence.

[49] The dispute was related to the existence of a testimony, which was, according to a tape-recorded discussion between the opposing parties, destroyed.

The Court referred to the *Caroline of Monaco* decision,[50] emphasising that even public figures enjoy a reasonable expectation of privacy, especially when their sexual life is concerned, and declined to consider the evidence.

These cases have developed another type of effect between constitutional rights and private law, which is characterised by an abstract invocation of the constitutional principles involved while reference to the 'real' events that led to the interpersonal dispute is rather limited. The balancing between constitutional rights provides the judge with the necessary principles to use as a standard in evaluating the circumstances in which the individuals obtained their evidence in order to support their respective positions in court. In this way, a purely procedural issue acquires a more substantive character. The effect of constitutional rights in such private disputes could be considered as 'direct', since any mediation of norms of private law is precluded by Article 19(3) of the Constitution, which is self-executing and directly effective in private law.

Under a normative (self-executing) Constitution, courts are obliged to enforce constitutional rights in interpersonal disputes even in the absence of private law norms. The legislator does not monopolise the protection of constitutional rights but provides the guidelines necessary for their application in interpersonal relationships. In the absence of such guidelines, the activity of the courts in applying constitutional rights is not prohibited, but it becomes much more difficult, the reason being that the 'direct' application of constitutional rights is intimately related to their balancing (which can often result in ambiguous outcomes). This danger is mainly a consequence of the general and abstract nature of constitutional norms and of the equality that individuals enjoy in their private relationships, which can render possible more than one constitutionally acceptable outcome in a particular case. The private law norms used as guidelines in such cases offer a helpful safety net for the judge, providing him with objective arguments in order to justify preferring one legal solution over another.

The most common argument against direct *Drittwirkung* is that it threatens the principle of the division of powers because it is considered to be a form of legislation. This argument often over-estimates

50 *Von Hannover v Germany*, European Court of Human Rights decision of 24 September 2004.

the judges' competence. The legislator is always able to change the law by introducing new norms and thus overcoming judicial solutions in matters concerning the application of constitutional rights, or even to change the normative foundations on which they were previously based. The problem with direct *Drittwirkung* does not lie in the judge substituting for the legislator but in the judge being identified with the constitutional text (considering himself as the 'constitutions mouthpiece'[51]). In cases concerning Article 19(3) of the Constitution and the absolute protection of the private sphere against unlawfully obtained evidence commented on above, it is not the direct application of the constitutional rights involved (privacy, the protection of personal data, and the secrecy of communication) that provokes criticism but rather the judgment being seen as an indisputable authority. The judge seems indifferent to the real facts of the case, does not seek a balance between privacy rights and the right to present evidence and supporting arguments in court (as part of a fair trial), and does not take into consideration that unlawfully extracted evidence in many cases uncovers criminal acts (e.g., extortion in case 3922/2005 of the Supreme Administrative Court and violation of the right to express the last will in case no. 1/2001 of the Greek Supreme Civil Court).

D. Conclusions: taking private law seriously in the application of constitutional rights

Contemporary Greek discussion of *Drittwirkung* is influenced by the acknowledgement of the principle in the Constitution and tends to overestimate the ability of constitutional rights to protect the individual in private relationships. As pointed out, the abstract character of constitutional principles renders them incapable of providing specific claims and remedies to the individual. Their co-existence with private law norms thus seems not only necessary but also indispensable. The system of private law should, moreover, not be underestimated (if for other reasons) as far as the interpersonal effect of constitutional rights is concerned. In many cases it incorporates constitutional values in the form of general clauses or (even) specific norms. It also has a 'constitutive' function in the application

---

[51] Rodriguez-Ruiz, op. cit., note 2 at 121.

of constitutional rights by providing the normative background for coherent and justified court decisions. The interpersonal effect of constitutional rights as a constitutional principle should, in consequence, lead to an ongoing exchange and mutual influence between the Constitution and private law. *Drittwirkung* is thus not merely a methodological concept but a reflection of the evolving dialogue between the Constitution and private law.

In this conceptualisation the role of the judge alters significantly while that of the legislator remains intact. The application of constitutional rights in private law enables the judge to strengthen the judicial protection granted to the individual against both society and the state. This intensified application of constitutional rights also facilitates the evolution of the private law system in order to embrace constitutional values which are considered to be of fundamental significance. At the same time, respect for private law norms seems to be critical in order to maintain the equilibrium between judge and legislator. In this relationship, the judge is obliged to apply both private law norms and constitutional rights in order to guarantee the judicial protection of individuals. Even after the constitutional acknowledgement of *Drittwirkung*, Greek courts seem to understand their role as one of mediators between the law and the Constitution, taking seriously their obligations towards the legislator as well as the protection of the individual. In the absence of a constitutional court in Greece, and in a constantly changing world which creates new threats for rights and moral issues such as abortion, euthanasia or bioethics in the very centre of the social and political dialogue, their role could nevertheless become even more substantial and dynamic.

Chapter 6: India
Protection of Human Rights against State and Non-State Action

*Mahendra P. Singh**

A. General

1. An overview of the Indian legal system

Generalisations about India or any society may reflect only a part of the totality. India's legal system does not fall within any of the major categories of legal systems of the world. It is in fact *sui generis*. However, for a comparative account like the one with which this chapter is concerned, the Indian legal system may be categorised as one of the variants of the common law, primarily because of the wide-ranging introduction of common law by the British until the end of their rule in 1947. Much of that law and many of its legal institutions have been retained and operate even in independent India. But this historical background should not lead us to conclude that the Indian legal system operates exactly as it does in United Kingdom or the United States or any other common law country.[1]

The Constitution of India adopted on 26 November 1949 and brought into force on 26 January 1950 forms the foundation of the current legal system of India. It is the highest law of the land and all laws, national or local, customary or statutory, past and future draw their validity and legitimacy from it. In its form and structure

---

* Vice-Chancellor, The W.B. National University of Juridicial Sciences, Kolkata, India; Formerly Professor of Law, University of Delhi, India. I thank Rajesh Kapoor for the research help rendered in the preparation of this chapter.

[1] R. David and J. E. C. Brierley, *Major Legal Systems in the World Today* (3rd edn, 1985) discuss the 'Law of India' among 'Other conceptions of Law and the Social Order' and not under 'The Common Law'.

the Constitution follows the Western liberal model of constitutionalism, but it has several features which are founded on Indian traditions and the special needs and circumstances of the society. It establishes a three-tier structure of central, state and local governments of the parliamentary form, elected every five years through universal adult franchise with an indirectly elected head of Indian state. All governments and their organs draw their power from the Constitution and are subject to it. The Constitution, besides the political checks and balances, provides for an independent and competent judiciary with powers to prevent and invalidate unconstitutional acts of any organ of the government and to provide appropriate remedies against them.[2] The judiciary is unitary, with the Supreme Court of India at the top, the High Courts in the middle and the subordinate courts at the bottom, established to interpret and implement all laws against all governments – central, state and local.

In the special human rights situation in India, provisions for the protection and realisation of rights are sprinkled all over the Constitution.[3] But they are primarily concentrated in Part III, read with Parts IV and IV-A. Part III, entitled 'Fundamental Rights' (FRs), primarily, but not exclusively, contains what are called the civil and political rights and may roughly be compared with the International Covenant on Civil and Political Rights (ICCPR), while Part IV, 'Directive Principles of State Policy' (DPs), contains what may primarily, but not exclusively, be called social and economic rights, roughly comparable to the International Covenant on Economic, Social and Cultural Rights (ICESCR). Part IV-A, 'Fundamental Duties' (FDs), may be puzzling in relation to a discussion of human rights and may not find any comparable instrument on the international plane except the draft Universal Declaration of Human Responsibilities.[4] Perhaps in the liberal perspective duties have little place in human rights discourse, but in the Indian context they perform an important role in the realisation

---

[2] On the position of judiciary in India see, among others, M. P. Singh, 'Securing the Independence of the Judiciary – The Indian Experience', (2000) 10 *Indiana International & Comparative Law Review* 245.

[3] See, e.g., Preamble, Citizenship, Art. 300-A, Part XIII, Part XVI, Part XVII, Schedules V & VI, etc.

[4] See, H. J. Steiner and P. Alston, *International Human Rights in Context* (2nd edn, 2000), p 351.

of the human rights of the masses, by obliging individual citizens to honour the rights of others or by creating rights in those to whom such duties are owed.[5] From the legal point of view, an important – in fact the only – difference between the FRs and DPs is that, while the former are enforceable in a law court – one of them specifically authorises the direct enforcement of all FRs in the Supreme Court – the DPs have been expressly excluded from judicial enforcement.[6] The FDs have not been so excluded from enforcement, but in their nature and spirit they can be enforced either through law or in association with one or more FRs. Although the interaction between these three parts of the Constitution is always relevant for understanding the rights under the Constitution of India, the purpose of the current chapter may be well served by confining our discussion to Part III (Fundamental Rights) of the Constitution.

Part III of the Constitution consists of Articles 12 to 35, which are divided into eight groups. Articles 12 and 13 are 'General'. The former defines 'the state', while the latter invalidates existing laws that are inconsistent with the FRs and prohibits the making of inconsistent law in the future. Articles 14 to 18 are grouped as 'Right to Equality'; Articles 19 to 22 as 'Right to Freedom', Articles 23 and 24 as 'Right against Exploitation', Articles 25 to 28 as 'Right to Freedom of Religion', Articles 29 and 30 as 'Cultural and Educational Rights'. Article 31, which constituted the 'Right to Property', was omitted in 1979. Articles 31-A to 31-C are grouped as 'Saving of Certain Laws' and Articles 32 to 35 are grouped as 'Right to Constitutional Remedies'. While most of these rights are guaranteed to the individual, e.g., Articles 14, 15(1), (2), 16(1)–(3), 18, 19–21, 22, 23–24, 25, 27, 28 and 32, a few of them are also guaranteed to groups of individuals, such as Articles 15(3), (4), 16(4)–(4-B), 17, 21-A, 26, 29 and 30. Again, while a few of the FRs are specifically guaranteed against the state, such as Articles 14, 15(1), 16, 18, 21-A, 29(2) and 30(2), the others are silent in

---

5 For relevance of duties in Indian tradition and for a criticism of their absence in the original Constitution see, P. V. Kane, *History of Dharmasastra* (1962), vol 5, Pt II, pp 1664–7.

6 For the position of the FRs and DPs in the Constitution, see M. P. Singh, 'The Statics and the Dynamics of the Fundamental Rights and the Directive Principles – A Human Rights Perspective' (2003) 5 *Supreme Court Cases (Journal)* 1.

this regard. From the latter, in some cases it may be inferred that they involve state action and therefore are protections against the state, such as Articles 19–21 and 22, while some others are inscrutable and from their nature it appears that they are primarily available against private parties or as much against such parties as against the state, e.g., Articles 15(2), 17, 23, 24, 25, 26, 29(1) and 30(1). Quite a few FRs, which were once considered to be available only against the state, or make provision to that effect, have been held to be available against private parties too. While we will pursue this aspect in detail a little later let me add that in addition to the fundamental right in Article 32 to approach or apply to the Supreme Court for the enforcement of any of the FRs, a person can also approach or apply to the High Courts under Article 226.[7] In this context it may also be mentioned that while the Constitution of India, like any other constitution, can be amended by the process of amendment provided in the Constitution, unlike many other constitutions its basic structure cannot be changed even by an amendment of the Constitution.[8] The power of the courts to review the actions of the other two branches of the government, especially their power under Articles 32 and 226, is part of this basic structure which cannot be taken away or curtailed even by an amendment of the Constitution.[9]

2. *India and international human rights*

India has been an active participant in the international human rights movement and in the establishment of international institutions ever since they started shaping up in the early half of the

---

[7] Under Art 32(3) Parliament has the power to authorise any court to exercise the powers of the Supreme Court to enforce the FRs. Under the Civil Procedure Code, Order XXVII-A, lower courts may also enforce fundamental rights so long as a new interpretation of the Constitution is not involved. But no one approaches these courts because of procedural hurdles, delays and ineffective remedies available with them.

[8] For this see Art 368 and any commentary on that article, e.g., M. P. Singh, *Shukla's Constitution of India* (10th edn, 2001), pp 880 ff. Among the major cases on the point, see *Kesavananda Bharati v State of Kerala*, AIR 1973 SC 1461 and *Minerva Mills v Union of India*, AIR 1980 SC 1789. For an instructive recent writing on the subject, see G. J. Jacobson, 'An Unconstitutional Constitution? A Comparative Perspective' (2006) 4 *Int'l Journal of Constitutional Law* 460.

[9] For this, see *L Chandra Kumar v Union of India*, AIR 1997 SC 1125.

twentieth century. Even before its independence, India became a member of the League of Nations and the International Labour Organization and actively participated in the drafting of the Universal Declaration of Human Rights. India has actively and unequivocally supported most of the international human rights instruments and has ratified all the major ones amongst them, such as the International Convention on the Prevention and Punishment of the Crime of Genocide, the International Convention on the Elimination of all forms of Racial Discrimination, the International Covenant on Civil and Political Rights, the International Covenant on Economic, Social and Cultural Rights, the Convention on the Elimination of all forms of Discrimination against Women and the Convention on the Rights of the Child. The only major instrument which she has not yet ratified is the Convention against Torture and other Cruel, Inhuman or Degrading Treatment or Punishment. Through judicial interpretation of FRs, domestic law has been fully brought in line with that Convention.[10] Domestic legislation implementing the provisions of these instruments has also been made in several cases.

The Constitution of India also directs the Indian state to 'foster respect for international law and treaty obligations in the dealings of organised peoples with one another'.[11] But it does not say that international law as such shall be part of or superior to the domestic law of India. As in other common law countries following the theory of dualism between international and domestic law, international law does not automatically become part of the domestic law of India. However, in line with developments in the status of international law world wide, general principles of international law are recognised as part of the domestic law of India and are observed in dealings within the domestic sphere. Although it is not yet conclusively settled, strong opinion is fast building towards the recognition of human rights among such general principles of international law binding on all nations. As regards international treaties and other instruments in general, they do not, ipso facto, become part of domestic law in the absence of supportive domestic legislation. The position in this regard too has, however, changed in respect of human rights treaties. The principle of the rule of law will not

---

[10] See, e.g., *DK Basu v State of West Bengal*, AIR 1997 SC 610 and 3017.

[11] Article 51 (c).

allow the rights of the individual to be curtailed by a treaty, which is considered to be an executive act. But a treaty containing or supportive of human rights instead of conflicting with the principle of the rule of law promotes it. It can, therefore, be enforced without legislative support. The courts in India have been accordingly giving effect to such treaties and international instruments, irrespective of whether India is a party to them or not, if such treaties or instruments are not inconsistent with any domestic law. With the support of such international instruments they have expanded the scope of FRs in several areas beyond expectation or imagination in a number of cases.[12]

3. *The public and private law dichotomy*

In line with the common law tradition, the Indian legal system maintains the unity of law and does not draw the kind of distinction that is drawn in the civil law countries between public and private law with definite consequences, institutions and procedures. Although differences between public and private law are not totally unknown to common law, they do not carry any practical consequences except in matters of legal remedies. While in civil law countries private and public law remedies are claimed in different branches of courts or tribunals, in India, as in other common law countries, these remedies are sought in the same courts. Some of these remedies are, however, peculiar to public law matters and not available in private law matters. The remedy of judicial review through various writs, directions and other devices that are available to the Supreme Court and High Courts is peculiar to public law and not available in private law. With respect to remedies and sometimes even with respect to general standards of behaviour of public authorities, the courts have emphasised the difference of approach in public and private law matters. The difference between the two, however, does not lead to the creation of separate courts and procedures as is done in the civil law countries. A constitutional amendment which provided for the creation of separate tribunals for the purpose of settling what could be categorised as public law disputes in the civil law countries has been invalidated

[12] See, e.g., *Vishaka v State of Rajasthan*, AIR 1997 SC 3011.

by the Supreme Court to the extent that it excluded judicial review of the decisions of the tribunals by the High Courts. The Court found such exclusion to be against the basic structure of the Constitution, which establishes judicial review of all legal determinations by independent courts in the judicial hierarchy.[13] The difference between private and public law remedies has, however, been taken to its logical conclusion of affording relief to the petitioner in the latter which he could not have obtained in the former.[14] The Court has also emphasised that, in respect of public law remedies, they have wide discretion to fashion them in order to serve their purpose, particularly of giving due effect to FRs.[15]

4. The Indian theory of human rights

In view of the Western origin of the current notion of human rights and the generally held belief that Asian societies are organised around duties rather than rights, any assertion of the existence of an Indian theory of human rights might be amusing. But I think such an assertion is well founded. I have examined this issue in detail elsewhere.[16] For the present it is enough to state that, going by history, absolute power in the state and its misuse during the Roman Empire, followed by similar exercises of power by the Church in the early half of the last millennium after wresting it from the king, and finally similar misuses of power by the state on its separation from the Church and its monopoly over secular affairs, led the West to limit the powers of the state by carving out an area for the individual into which the state could not enter.[17] The theory of human rights in the West evolved against an overbearing and oppressive state that could and did subject the individual to all kinds of indignities.

---

[13] *L Chandra Kumar v Union of India*, AIR 1997 SC 1125.

[14] See, e.g., *Nilabati Behera v State of Orissa* (1993) 2 SCC 746.

[15] See, e.g., *Bandhua Mukti Morcha v Union of India*, AIR 1984 SC 802; *MC Mehta v Union of India*, AIR 1987 SC 1086 and *Paramjit Kaur v State of Punjab* (1999) 2 SCC 131.

[16] M. P. Singh, 'Human Rights in the Indian Tradition – Alternatives in the Understanding and Realization of the Human Rights Regime' (2003) 63 *Zeitschrift fuer auslaendisches oeffentliches Recht und Voelkerrecht Heidelberg Journal of International Law* 551.

[17] For an analytical history of these developments, see H. J. Berman, *Law and Revolutions* (1983).

India did not experience either an absolute empire like the Roman, or a religious organisation like the Church, or separation between religion and state, or an absolute state monopolising all power in the so-called secular sphere.[18] At no stage in the history of India did either a political or religious organisation wield or claim absolute power. Any claims to that effect did not have any theoretical support and any attempts at its practice were repulsed by adverse reaction based on principled support from religious or cultural traditions. As the home of immigrants from near and far off from very early times in its history, India let these immigrants freely mix with one another as well as preserve their identity by letting them observe their custom, religion, language, laws, etc., subject to the state's responsibility of maintaining harmony and peace among them. The state did not claim or exercise the power of imposing common laws, religion, language or any other dogmas or practices that did not match with their identity.

Thus, unlike the West, until the establishment of British rule in the nineteenth century, the state in India never claimed or practised a monopoly of power in society, either in secular or in any other matters. It may be taken as underdevelopment of society and state in India, but the fact is that subject to a brief interlude under the British, people in India did not experience the absolute power of the state or for that matter of any other organisation in the society. This does not mean that people in India did not suffer any indignities and consequent violation of human rights at any stage of their history. Besides the indignities suffered in the past, the existence of such indignities is extensive and intense throughout the length and breadth of the land. But they have not resulted as much from state action as from the inaction or inadequate action of the state.

Therefore, instead of the current theory of human rights produced by the West as being designed to protect individuals against the excesses of the state, the theory of human rights in India must require the state to come forward with plans and strategies to remove all existing inequities and conditions that lead to those inequities in the society. If the state fails to do so, it violates human

---

[18] For details, see R. Thapar, *Ancient Indian Social History* (1978) and *History and Beyond* (2000).

rights and must be answerable for such violation.[19] The state must rather empower the impoverished masses of the people. So long as they are not empowered, their human rights are violated. Confining attention to violations of human rights only from the acts of the state or its officials will not change the on-the-ground reality of human rights in India. Such violations are far fewer in magnitude and intensity than the violations arising from state inaction. Therefore, an appropriate theory of human rights for India is not one which confines itself to the acts of state against human dignity, but the one which extends further and covers its non-action or inaction resulting in human indignity.

India's political and legal system adequately supports and justifies such a theory of human rights. We have already noted that the Constitution, which is the cornerstone of India's current political and legal system, besides prohibiting the state from interfering in the individual's affairs by way of FRs, also commands it through FRs and DPs to take certain steps to remove existing social, economic and political inequities through affirmative action, even to the extent of providing for the specific reservation of seats in political institutions such as the national and state legislatures, local bodies as well as in public services. It also expects the state to ensure the observance of FDs by citizens. This vision of the Constitution commanding the state to take affirmative action for remedying existing inequities is sufficient proof of the difference of India's vision of society and human rights from the one produced in the West. Thus the Constitution safeguards the rights of the individual not only against the state but also against those non-state actors who could violate them because of the non-action or connivance of the state.

B. State action

1. Concept of 'the state'

The existence of a distinct theory of human rights in India is further supported by an express provision in the Constitution for state

---

[19] For an early writing on the subject on those lines, see R. Kothari, 'Human Rights – A Movement in Search of a Theory' (1987) 5 *Lokayan Bulletin* 17. Also see, A. Varshney, *Ethnic Conflict and Civil Life* (2002), pp 23 ff.

action. If, as in the West, FRs in India were available only against the state there would be no need for either expressly using the expression 'the State' in some of the FRs or for defining that expression. As we have already noted, only a few of the FRs are expressly available against 'the State'.[20] For the purpose of these FRs, the Constitution provides a broad inclusive definition of the state in Article 12, which says: 'unless the context otherwise requires, "the State" includes the Government and Parliament of India and the Government and the Legislature of each of the States and all local or other authorities within the territory of India or under the control of the Government of India.' Subject to the condition that 'unless the context otherwise requires', Article 36 extends the same definition to DPs. Articles 12 and 36 are the first articles in Part III and Part IV respectively. In the common law tradition such definitions are generally given at the beginning of a statute. The definition helps in understanding the meaning of the defined word wherever it occurs in subsequent provisions of the statute. But it is not and cannot be used to restrict the scope of those provisions which have no reference to the defined expression. Accordingly, the definition of the state in Article 12 cannot be employed to restrict the scope of those FRs which have no reference to 'the state'. As the Constitution of India expressly departs from the traditional notion that the FRs are available only against the state action, there is no scope or justification for any presumption based on any theory or traditional understanding that the FRs are confined to state action only. The Constitution must be read as an evolving organic law in the light of its own freedom from the shackles of any theories and understandings developed in different contexts.

Initially, the Supreme Court of India was, however, influenced by the then existing Western precedents in confining the application of FRs to the state. Rejecting a petition for the enforcement of the right to property against a banking company, the Court held that 'The language and structure of Article 19 and its setting in Part III of the Constitution clearly show that the article was intended to protect those freedoms against the State action. ... Violation of rights to property by individuals is not within the purview of the Article'.[21] Repeating the same opinion a little later,

20 See, e.g., Arts 14, 15(1), 16(1) and (2), 18(1), 21-A, 30(2).

21 *PD Shamdasani v Central Bank of India Ltd*, AIR 1952 SC 59.

it observed: 'The whole object of Part III of the Constitution is to provide protection for the freedoms and rights mentioned therein against arbitrary invasion by the State.'[22] The position taken in the first case in respect of property right was also applied to the right to life and liberty in one of those early cases.[23] Without expressly overruling or referring to these decisions, however, the court soon started re-analysing the scheme of FRs in the Indian Constitution. In one such analysis in the early 1960s, it observed:

> Prima facie, these declarations [FRs] involve an obligation imposed not merely upon the 'State', but upon all persons to respect the rights so declared, and the rights are enforceable unless the context indicates otherwise against every person or agency seeking to infringe them. The rights declared in the form of prohibition must have a concomitant positive content; without such positive content they could be worthless. Relief may be claimed from the High Court or from this Court, against infringement of the prohibition, by any agency, unless the protection is restricted to State action.[24]

Since the late 1970s lessons learnt from the 1975-77 emergency have moved the pendulum completely in the direction of liberal interpretation and wider application of the FRs.[25] Better understanding of the Indian Constitution and its contextual setting, change in the nature of the state and expansion of human rights the world over have also led to the expansion of the definition of 'the State' in Article 12.

Even if the FRs are deemed to be available only against the state, the state may violate them as much indirectly as directly. While in the latter case its officials or agencies violate them, in the former it may let them be violated by others through its inaction or active connivance. The former violation may be as injurious as the latter. In such cases the state cannot escape its responsibility or liability for the protection of FRs on the plea that they are the actions of private individuals and not of the state. Accordingly, as we will see below, in several cases courts have given relief to the petitioner without going into the question whether violator of the FRs was the state. Such a reading of the Constitution is entirely consistent

---

[22] *State of WB v Subodh Gopal Bose*, AIR 1954 SC 92, 97.

[23] *Vidya Verma v Shiv Narain Verma*, AIR 1956, SC 108, 109.

[24] *State of West Begal v Union of India*, AIR 1963 SC 1241, 1264.

[25] A trendsetter in this regard has been *Maneka Gandhi v Union of India*, AIR 1978 SC 597.

with the background of the society for which the Indian Constitution is made. Unlike the West, where the constitutional guarantees were entrenched against an overbearing state which had monopolised all public power in the hands of those who controlled it, the Constitution makers wrote the FRs and DPs against the background of a pre-colonial tradition sustained by the colonial rule in which certain sections of people irrespective of their position in the state apparatus violated the rights of others, either in the absence of a powerful state or for the lack of its intervention. Therefore, the Constitution makers had to safeguard the rights of the individual not only against the state but also against those non-state actors who could violate them because of the non-action or connivance of the state. In the latter case, the individual could seek an appropriate direction from the court reminding the state of its obligation under the Constitution.

Further, since the crystallisation of the idea of rights into constitutional guarantees against the state, the nature of the state has substantially changed. From the monopoly of public power and functions in limited hands, it has moved to their diffusion and devolution into the hands of wider bodies and institutions unconnected or loosely connected with what was once considered the state. The rights which needed protection against the then state now need to be protected against this newly transformed state. They have not lost their value or relevance. The state cannot absolve itself from the responsibility of not violating them merely by dissolving itself into new bodies or by retransferring its powers into the hands of bodies unaccountable to people. If that were to be the case, all progress in the direction of human rights and liberties would be reversed.[26] Therefore, bodies which wield or have the potentiality of wielding public power of the kind which the state once wielded or could wield over the lives and affairs of the people have to be subject to the discipline of FRs. One could suggest that, if that were the case, the whole purpose of privatisation and liberalisation is defeated.[27] The answer to that question must be in the negative. Privatisation and liberalisation aim at reducing the size of the state in order to create more space for individual enterprise and

---

[26] See Krishna Iyer J in *Som Prakash Rekhi v Union of India*, AIR 1981 SC 212.

[27] See, e.g., R. R. Iyer, 'Public enterprises as "state" and article 12', (1990) XXV *Economic & Political Weekly* M-129.

for getting more efficient and less expensive public services, and not at reducing the scope and reach of FRs which are the foundation of private enterprise. The expansion of human rights the world over is in proportion, if not more, to the expansion of liberalisation and the market economy. Privatisation can no more return to the exploitation of past centuries. We must remember that recognition and protection of rights has brought us to the present stage of freedom and liberty. We have to move forward towards larger freedom and not return to serfdom. Development is not just profits but freedom.[28]

This background must guide us in the interpretation and application of Article 12 (which defines the state).[29] As is understandable, interpretation of Article 12 has not led to any serious controversy except in respect of the meaning of the expression 'other authorities'. The Supreme Court of India proceeded with a liberal approach from the very beginning. It declined to apply the ejusdem generis rule to the interpretation of this expression and held that the definition of the state in that article is only inclusive, and 'other authorities' would include all authorities created by the Constitution or statute on whom powers are conferred by law. It was not necessary that the statutory authority should be engaged in performing government or sovereign functions. Citing Articles 19(1)(g) and 298, which contemplate the engagement of the state in trade or business, and Article 46, which requires the state to promote the educational and economic interests of the weaker sections of the society, it stated that in these cases 'other authorities' would cover bodies created for the purpose of performing commercial activities or for promoting the educational and economic interests of the people.[30] This position was not changed in the next important case, though the majority in the divided court relied upon the distinction between bodies created by and under the statute.[31] As all the bodies in that case were created by statutes, they were found included in the definition. Concurring with the majority,

---

[28] See A. Sen, *Development as Freedom* (1999).

[29] Perhaps the Supreme Court ignored that background in *P D Shamdasani v Central Bank of India Ltd.*, AIR 1952 SC 59, where it made a somewhat overbroad statement that the purpose of Part III was protection of the individual from the state only, though the remarks could perhaps be justified in light of the facts of the case.

[30] *Electricity Board, Rajasthan v Mohan Lal*, AIR 1967 SC 1857.

[31] *Sukhdev Singh v Bhagatram*, AIR 1975 SC 1331.

Justice Mathew, however, did not agree with this distinction and relied upon the criteria of agency and nature of functions, i.e. whether the body was an agency of the state, or whether it was performing any public functions. In subsequent cases, the Court abandoned the distinction between the bodies created by and under the statute and developed the idea of agency, merging the nature of functions into one of the indices for the determination whether a body was the agency of the state.[32] The indices are:

1. If the entire share capital of the corporation is held by the government, it would go a long way towards indicating that the corporation is an instrumentality or authority of the government.
2. Where the financial assistance of the state is so much as to meet almost the entire expenditure of the corporation it would afford some indication of the corporation being impregnated with government character.
3. Whether the corporation enjoys monopoly status which is state conferred or state protected.
4. Existence of deep and pervasive state control may afford an indication that the corporation is a state agency or instrumentality.
5. If the functions of the corporation are of public importance and closely related to government functions, it would be a relevant factor in classifying a corporation as an instrumentality or agency of government.
6. If a department of government is transferred to a corporation, it would be a strong factor supporting the inference of the corporation being an instrumentality or agency of government.[33]

If, on a consideration of these factors, it is found that the corporation is an instrumentality or agency of government, it would be an authority and, therefore, the state within the meaning of Article 12. The expression 'corporation' is not confined to statutory or non-statutory corporations but also covers societies and other bodies. In that particular case, the Court held that the education society registered under the J & K Registration of Societies Act was an instrumentality or agency of the State and Central governments

[32] See *R D Shetty v International Airport Authority*, AIR 1979 SC 1628 and *Ajay Hasia v Khalid Mujib*, AIR 1981 SC 487.

[33] *Ajay Hasia v Khalid Mujib* (1981) 1 SCC 722 at 737.

because these governments had full control of the working of the society.

Following the law so laid down, several educational and research institutes,[34] co-operative banks,[35] registered societies,[36] public limited and government companies producing consumer goods,[37] a state aided school,[38] a medical college run by a municipal corporation,[39] several electricity boards,[40] Central Inland Water Transport Corporation Ltd, a government company jointly owned by the central government and two state governments,[41] a government company constituted as development authority under a state town planning Act,[42] regional rural banks established under the Regional Rural Banks Act,[43] and port trusts created under the Major Port Trust Act,[44] have all been held to be 'other authorities' within the meaning of Article 12. In one of the cases a unanimous constitution bench of the Court argued for including even non-government companies within the meaning of 'the State' if, for reasons of state control and regulation and the nature of functions they perform, they satisfy the test of being an agency or instrumentality of the state.[45] Without pursuing this argument any further, the court has subjected private educational institutions to the discipline of Article 14 (right to equality) on the ground that they were performing a

[34] E.g., Indian Statistical Institute: *BS Minhas v Indian Statistical Institute*, AIR 1984 SC 363; Indian Council of Agricultural Research: *PK Ramchandra Iyer v Union of India* (1984) 2 SCC 141; Sainik School Society: *All India Sainik School Employees' Assn v Sainik School Society*, AIR 1988 SC 88.

[35] *UP State Coop Land Development Bank Ltd v Chandra Bhan Dubey*, AIR 1999 SC 753.

[36] *Ajay Hasia v Khalid Mujib* (1981) 1 SCC 722.

[37] *Mahabir Auto Stores v Indian Oil Corpn*, AIR 1990 SC 1031.

[38] *Manmohan Singh Jaitla v Governor, Union Territory of Chandigarh*, 1984 Supp SCC 540.

[39] *Dinesh Kumar v Motilal Nehru Medical College, Allahbad* (1985) 3 SCC 156.

[40] E.g., *Rajasthan Electricity Board, supra, and Rohtas Industries Ltd v Bihar SEB*, 1984 Supp SCC 161.

[41] *Central Inland Water Transport Corpn Ltd v Brojo Nath Ganguly* (1986) 3 SCC 156.

[42] *Star Enterprises v City & Industrial Development Corpn of Maharashtra Ltd* (1990) 3 SCC 280.

[43] *Prathama Bank v Vijay Kumar Goel* (1989) 4 SCC 441.

[44] *Dwarkadas & Sons v Board of Trustees of the Port of Bombay*, AIR 1989 SC 1642.

[45] *MC Mehta v Union of India* (1987) 1 SCC 395.

function in furtherance of a state function, i.e. provision of education.[46] Later, a non-government company – the United India Insurance Co Ltd – was also subjected to the discipline of Article 14 because it had the trappings of the state.[47] Though sometimes the agency or instrumentality test with its above-mentioned indices has produced contradictory results, it has been upheld by a larger bench of the Court in *Pradeep Kumar Biswas v Indian Institute of Chemical Biology*[48] by 5:2. Later, in *Zee Telefilms Ltd v Union of India*,[49] a divided 3:2 Court expressed doubts about the long-standing agency test relied upon and confirmed in *Pradeep*. While relying upon *Pradeep*, the majority in *Zee* declined to entertain an Article 32 petition against the Board of Control for Cricket in India for the enforcement of a contract between the Board and the petitioner, on the ground that the Board was not an agency of the state. Expressing its disagreement with the agency test, the minority asked for its rejection in favour of functions test. Curiously, after recognising that some of the FRs are available against 'non-state actions including individuals', the majority took the stand that 'the pre-requisite for invoking the enforcement of a fundamental right under Article 32 is that the violator of that right should be a State first'.[50]

2. The judiciary

While the legislature and executive are expressly included in the definition of 'the State', the judiciary is missing. It means the Constitution does not intend to cover the judiciary within that definition. However, for this purpose a difference is drawn between the judicial and non-judicial functions of the judiciary. In respect of the former, it is not covered within the definition of 'the State', while in respect of the latter, it is. As regards judicial functions, they do not occasion the infringement of the fundamental rights; they involve determination of the scope of fundamental

---

46 *JP Unni Krishnan v State of AP* (1993) 1 SCC 645.

47 *Biman Krishna Bose v United India Insurance Co Ltd* (2001) 6 SCC 477.

48 (2002) 5 SCC 111.

49 (2005) 4 SCC 649.

50 Ibid at 681. For a critical comment on the case, see M.P. Singh, 'Fundamental Rights, State Action and Cricket in India' (2005) 13 *Asia Pacific Law Review* 203.

rights vis-à-vis a legislative or executive action. Unless the power to perform that function is excluded or restricted by the Constitution, the judiciary is competent to make a right or wrong determination.[51] A wrong determination in such a case does not constitute a breach of any fundamental right by the court. It is a genuine mistake which it is competent – though it is not expected – to make. The remedy against such a mistake is not to allege a breach of FRs by the court and approach the appropriate court under Article 32 or 226 for nullifying or voiding the determination, but to allege that the determination is not consistent with the FRs and approach the appropriate court with such allegation in appeal. Rejecting the request to issue a writ under Article 32 against a judicial order of a High Court, the Supreme Court held:

> It is singularly inappropriate to assume that a judicial decision pronounced by a Judge of competent jurisdiction in or in relation to a matter brought before him for adjudication can affect the fundamental rights of the citizens under Article 19(1). What the judicial decision purports to do is to decide the controversy between the parties brought before the court and nothing more.[52]

In case the determining court is the Supreme Court, the remedy lies in invoking its review or curative jurisdiction. A wrong determination of the Court cannot be corrected in writ proceedings.[53] While challenge to judicial determinations on the ground of violation of fundamental rights is appropriate in jurisdictions lacking provision for appeal, it is of no practical relevance for India where appeals are available as a matter of right within the unitary hierarchy of the Indian judiciary. It may be noted that the above immunity from challenge of a judicial determination extends only to determinations of the judiciary or courts as such and does not extend to tribunals of limited jurisdiction.[54]

---

[51] This statement must be read subject to *L Chandra Kumar v Union of India*, AIR 1997 SC 1125, where the court has held that judicial review is an essential feature of the Constitution which cannot be taken away even by an amendment of the Constitution.

[52] *Naresh S Mirajkar v State of Maharashtra*, AIR 1967 SC 1, 7–8.

[53] See, *AR Antulay v RS Nayak*, AIR 1988 SC 1531; *PSR Sadhanatham v Arunachalam*, AIR 1980 SC 856; *Khoday Distilleries Ltd v Registrar General, SC of India* (1999) 6 SCC 114; *Rupa Ashok Hurra v Ashok Hurra* (2002) 4 SCC 388.

[54] Even tribunals or quasi judicial bodies are not supposed to be violating FRs so long as they are acting within their jurisdiction and, therefore, if any of their

As regards the non-judicial determinations of the judiciary, they are as much subject to challenge on the ground of violation of FRs as of any other authority. For example, a rule made by a court in the exercise of its rule-making power can be challenged for the violation of FRs and an appropriate remedy may be granted under Article 32 or 226.[55] Similarly the administrative powers of the courts such as making of appointments or taking disciplinary actions is also subject to challenge on the ground of violation of FRs.[56]

C. Application of FRs to private action

Although the liberal and expansive application of the definition of 'the State' gives jurisdiction over much of the violation of FRs that could have escaped from scrutiny under the initial and traditional approach taken by the Court, several FRs which either expressly apply to private action or are ambiguous in their application or even the ones which are expressly available only against the state have found liberal application in the hands of the courts, thus ensuring the wide application and protection of human rights in India. Such an expansive use of FRs, as we have already noted, began primarily in the post-emergency period from 1978 onwards, in the light of the humiliation faced by the courts during the emergency primarily on the plea that they were using the FRs to protect the interests of the rich and powerful at the cost of, or ignoring the interest of, the poor and weak. The courts, therefore, under the leadership of some of the progressive judges such as P. N. Bhagwati, Krishna Iyer, Chinnappa Reddy, D. A. Desai and others, invented a new strategy for hearing cases for the poor and weak, who could not approach the Court for the enforcement and realisation of their FRs. The strategy came to be known as 'public interest litigation',

---

decisions is questioned on the ground of violation of FRs it must be done in the High Court under Article 226 and not in the Supreme Court under Article 32. See, *Ujjam Bai v State of UP*, AIR 1962 SC 1621 and *Coffee Board, Bangalore v Jt CTO*, AIR 1971 SC 870.

55 *Prem Chand Garg v Excise Commr*, AIR 1963 SC 996.

56 *State of Bihar v Balmukund Shah*, AIR 2000 SC 1296.

though some people prefer to call it 'social action litigation'.[57] After having made a beginning in some other cases,[58] the Court formulated that strategy in the following words:

> [W]here a person or class of persons to whom legal injury is caused by reason of a violation of a fundamental right is unable to approach the Court for judicial redress on account of poverty or disability or socially or economically disadvantaged position, any member of the public acting bona fide can move the Court for relief under Article 32 and a fortiori, also under Article 226, so that the fundamental rights may become meaningful not only for the rich and the well-to-do who have the means to approach the Court but also for the large masses of people who are living a life of want and destitution and who are by reason of lack of awareness, assertiveness and resources unable to seek judicial redress.[59]

This strategy opened the doors of the courts for those who suffered most from the violation of FRs. Although with the passing of time and retirement of the progressive judges who launched the strategy, the strategy has degenerated into bringing matters before the courts which do not really raise the concern of the weak and poor, it has given a new vigour and dimension to FRs, capable of taking them in the direction in which the Constitution makers wanted this nation to move.[60] We shall discuss some of these cases and relevant legislation under different heads given below. These heads are not exclusive, nor can every case be confined only to one head. Therefore, some overlapping and repetition is unavoidable.

1. The right to equality

The right to equality, as we have already noted, is found in Articles 14–18. Article 14 lays down the general principle of equality specifically directed to the state ('The State shall not deny to any person equality before the law or equal protection of the laws'),

---

[57] Professor Baxi coined the term social action litigation. See, U. Baxi, 'Taking Suffering Seriously: Social Action Litigation in the Supreme Court of India' (1979–80) 8–9 Delhi Law Review 91.

[58] The beginning was made primarily in *SP Gupta v Union of India*, AIR 1982 SC 149 at 216.

[59] *Bandhua Mukti Morcha v Union of India*, AIR 1984 SC 802, 813.

[60] For incisive survey of PIL see, P. Singh, *Annual Survey of Indian Law*, published by the Indian Law Institute, New Delhi for the current and past several years.

while the other provisions are partly directed to the state and partly to all persons. Within the prohibition on unequal treatment in Article 14 the Court has also developed a general principle of reasonableness which every state action must satisfy. 'It must ... now be taken to be well settled', it said in *Ajay Hasia v Khalid Mujib*,[61] 'that what Article 14 strikes at is arbitrariness, because an action that is arbitrary must necessarily involve negation of equality'. Applying this principle to contractual relationships, it has invalidated several contractual clauses or actions under them which it found unreasonable.[62] Several cases relating to the extension of the concept of 'the State' have also involved contractual relationships.[63] The right to contract falls within the scope of FRs and deserves protection as such. Such contractual obligations between a co-operative society and its members have been upheld by the Court against challenges on the ground of undue restriction on the alienation of property. The relationship between the society and its members has also been assigned the protection of the FR in Article 19(1)(c).[64] Thus the protection of Article 19 has also been invoked and upheld against private action.

But more notable in this regard is the sexual harassment in the workplace case *Vishaka v State of Rajasthan*.[65] In a Public Interest Litigation (PIL), the petitioners sought the enforcement of the FRs of working women under Articles 14, 19 and 21 against sexual harassment, which became imminent against the backdrop of gang rape of a social worker in the State of Rajasthan. Allowing the petition, the Court observed:

> Each such incident results in violation of the fundamental rights of 'Gender Equality' and the 'Right to Life and Liberty.' It is a clear violation of the rights under Arts. 14, 15 and 21 of the Constitution. One of the logical consequences of such an incident is also the violation of the

---

[61] (1981) 1 SCC 722 at 741.

[62] See, e.g., *Erusion Equipment & Chemicals Ltd v State of WB*, AIR 1975 SC 266; *Ram & Shyam Co v State of Haryana* (1985) 3 SCC 267 and *Harminder Singh v Union of India* (1986) 3 SCC 247.

[63] See, e.g., *Ramana Dayaram Shetty v International Airport Authority*, AIR 1979 SC 1628 and *Kasturi Lal v State of J&K*, AIR 1980 SC 1992.

[64] *Zoroastrian Coop Housing Society Ltd v District Registrar, Coop Societies* (2005) 5 SCC 632. For a critical comment on this case, see A. Chugh, 'Fundamental Rights – Vertical or Horizontal?' (2005) 7 *SCC (Jour)* 9.

[65] AIR 1997 SC 3011.

> victim's fundamental right under Art. 19(1)(g) 'to practise any profession or to carry out any occupation, trade or business.' Such violations, therefore, attract the remedy under Art. 32 for the enforcement of these fundamental rights of women.[66]

Relying further on Articles 42, 51A(a) and (e), 51(c), 253 and entry 14 of List I, the Court held that in the absence of domestic law international law could be employed. Taking support from the Convention on the Elimination of All Forms of Discrimination against Women, it legislated detailed guidelines for observance at the workplace both by state as well as private employers. It directed 'that the above guidelines and norms would be strictly observed in all work places for the preservation and enforcement of the right to gender equality of the working women. These directions would be binding and enforceable in law until suitable legislation is enacted to occupy the field.'[67]

Applying the definition of sexual harassment in *Vishaka*, the Court in *Apparel Export Promotion Council v AK Chopra*[68] reiterated that 'there is no gainsaying that each incident of sexual harassment, at the place of work, results in violation of the Fundamental Right to Gender Equality and the Right to Life and Liberty – the two most precious Fundamental Rights guaranteed by the Constitution of India'.[69] It allowed the appeal, emphasising the application of international human rights norms in situations where we do not have inconsistent domestic law.

A few FRs such as 15(3), (4), (5) and 16(4) provide for affirmative action from the state. I have elsewhere argued that these affirmative programmes may be demanded by an individual from the state.[70] The state in that case may be compelled to make special provisions for the specified groups, at least under Article 15, even against private persons and institutions. Equal protection of the laws in Article 14 has also been given a positive content,[71]

---

66 Ibid, 3012.

67 Ibid, 3017.

68 AIR 1999 SC 625.

69 Ibid, 634.

70 M. P. Singh, 'Are Articles 15(4) and 16(4) Fundamental Rights?' (1994) 3 *Supreme Court Cases (Journal)* 33.

71 *St. Stephen's College v University of Delhi*, AIR 1992 SC 1630, 1662; *Indra Sawhney v Union of India*, (2000) 1 SCC 168, 202. Also G. Austin, *Working a Democratic Constitution: The Indian Experience* (1999), p 669.

demanding favourable treatment for the disadvantaged which may also be enforced in the private sphere as decided in *Vishaka*.

2. Workers and allied rights

India has been a party to the ILO from its very inception and has ratified all major international instruments concerning labour matters. India's labour laws therefore meet international standards in general. It is also true that many of the labour rights, or any rights, are protected more by such laws than by FRs. However, the Constitution pays special attention to labour matters among FRs and DPs. Article 23 prohibits traffic in human beings and *begar* and other similar forms of forced labour and makes its contravention punishable by law. The Immoral Traffic (Prevention) Act 1956 provides punishment for traffic in human beings and the Bonded Labour System (Abolition) Act 1976 prohibits and punishes bonded labour system and *begar*. *Begar* is involuntary work without payment. It commonly connotes forced labour for which no wages are paid or, if some payment is made, it is grossly inadequate. It means making a person work against his will and without paying any remuneration.[72] In *Kahaosan Thangkhul v Simirei Shailei*[73] the Manipur High Court invalidated a customary practice requiring each of the householders in the village to offer one day's free labour to the village headman.

People's Union for Democratic Rights v Union of India[74] is a major example of the application of Articles 23 and 24. In a PIL the petitioner asked for the observance of various labour laws[75] in relation to workmen employed in the construction work of various projects connected with the Asian Games. Although the violators were private contractors, the contracts were awarded by the Union of India and the Delhi Development Authority (DDA) and therefore these authorities could not be absolved from their responsibility

---

[72] *S Vasudevan v SD Mittal*, AIR 1962 Bom. 53 at 67.

[73] AIR 1961 Mani. 1.

[74] AIR 1982 SC 1473. On minimum wages see also *Sanjit Roy v State of Rajasthan*, AIR 1983 SC 328.

[75] Particularly, the Contract Labour (Regulation and Abolition) Act 1970; the Minimum Wages Act 1948; the Equal Remuneration Act 1976; the Employment of Children Act 1938; the Inter-State Migrant Workmen Act 1979.

to enforce these laws. As regards FRs, the Court observed that: 'So far as Article 24 of the Constitution is concerned, it embodies a fundamental right which is plainly and indubitably enforceable against every one and by reason of its compulsive mandate, no one can employ a child below the age of 14 years in a hazardous employment.'[76] With respect to the non-observance of Equal Remuneration Act 1976, it said that it was a violation of Article 14 which the Union and DDA could not let its contractors do:

> If any particular contractor is committing a breach of the provisions of the Equal Remuneration Act 1976 and thus denying equality before the law to workmen, the Union of India, the Delhi Administration or the Delhi Development Authority as the case may be, would be under an obligation to ensure that the contractor observes the provisions of the Equal Remuneration Act 1976 and does not breach the equality clause enacted in Art. 14.[77]

Similarly, the Court found non-observance of contract labour laws and migrant workmen in violation of Article 21. It observed that these laws 'are clearly intended to ensure basic human dignity to the workmen and if the workmen are deprived of any of these rights and benefits to which they are entitled under the provisions of these two pieces of social welfare legislation, that would clearly be a violation of Article 21'.[78] Again, finding non-observance of the Minimum Wages Act to be a violation of Article 23, after observing that ' there are certain fundamental rights conferred by the Constitution which are enforceable against the whole world' and among them are Articles 17, 23 and 24, the Court said: 'Art. 23 ... is clearly designed to protect the individual not only against the State but *also against other private citizens*. Article 23 is *not limited in its application against the State* but it prohibits "traffic in human beings and beggar and other similar forms of forced labour" wherever they are found.'[79] The Court also refers to Article 4 of UDHR 'slave trade' as precursor of Article 23 but much wider in its scope.[80]

---

[76] AIR 1982 SC 1473 at 1483.

[77] Ibid, 1484.

[78] Ibid, 1485.

[79] Ibid, emphasis added.

[80] Ibid, 1486.

Following the same line of approach and citing the above case in *Bandhua Mukti Morcha v Union of India*,[81] which involved the plight of stone quarry workers near Delhi, the Court, referring to several legislative provisions including the Bonded Labour System Abolition Act and a few DPs, observed that their violation amounted to the violation of Article 21 and therefore:

> [T]he State is under a constitutional obligation to see that there is no violation of the fundamental right of any person, particularly when he belongs to the weaker sections of the community and is unable to wage a legal battle against a strong and powerful opponent who is exploiting him. The Central Government is therefore bound to ensure observance of various social welfare and labour laws enacted by Parliament for the purpose of securing the workmen a life of basic human dignity in compliance with the Directive Principles of State Policy.[82]

The court thus made the judicially non-enforceable DPs enforceable via the extension of FRs.

Again, the valiant PIL lawyer – M. C. Mehta – brought to the court the matter of children employed in the matches-making industry in Sivakasi in violation of various laws and international conventions as well as a violation of Articles 24, 39(e) and (f), 41 and 45. Relying upon these laws and constitutional provisions, the Court under the provisions of the Child Labour (Prohibition and Regulation) Act 1986 required the employers to pay an amount of Rs 20,000 for the employment of each child and also gave other detailed directions for their rehabilitation.[83] In another case, *Bandhua Mukti Morcha v Union of India*,[84] involving the carpet industry in Uttar Pradesh employing children below the age of 14, violation of Article 24 and derogation of Articles 39(e) and (f) and 45 read with the Preamble was alleged. Relying upon these articles as well as Articles 14 and 21 and the Convention on the Rights of the Child and decided cases including *MC Mehta's case*,[85] the court gave directions to the Union of India to take appropriate steps for the protection of the rights of the child. In *Ram Pal v Maishi Lal Raj Kumar*,[86] in a petition for the enforcement of Article 23 and

---

81 AIR 1984 SC 802.

82 Ibid, 812.

83 *MC Mehta v State of TN* (1996) 6 SCC 756.

84 AIR 1997 SC 2218.

85 *MC Mehta v State of TN* (1997) AIR SCW 407.

86 (1982) 2 SCC 349.

the Bonded Labour System (Abolition) Act 1976, the Court held that even if the bonded labourer owes some money to his employer under the terms of a contract which amounts to bonded labour, the labourer is entitled to walk away from the employer's premises or employment because bonded labour is prohibited by Article 23 and the Act.

Although the right to strike is not a Fundamental Right of the workers, it is open to a workman to go on strike or withhold his labour.[87] Such right is implied in the Industrial Disputes Act, 1947, subject to certain conditions.[88]

3. *Facets of the right to life*

In *MC Mehta v Union of India*,[89] the Court, without conclusively deciding whether the violator of the right – a public limited company – was 'the State' or not, held it responsible for death and injury to health caused by the leakage of olium gas. In *Vincent v Union of India*[90] the Court recognised the right to health under Article 21 in relation to the regulation of the sale and distribution of injurious drugs. Again, in *Ashok v Union of India*,[91] in a petition for the imposition of a ban on the production, distribution and sale of insecticides and chemicals hazardous to health, the court recognised the right to healthy life under Article 21 and directed the Union to take appropriate steps. *Parmanand Katara v Union of India*,[92] though a case against a government hospital for not giving immediate attention to an injured person resulting in his death, the Court, after holding that preservation of life is protected by Article 21, made a general observation relevant in our context. It said:

> Every doctor whether at a Government hospital or otherwise has the professional obligation to extend his services with due expertise for protecting life. No law or State action can intervene to avoid/delay the

---

[87] On the constitutional right to strike, especially of government employees, see *Kameshwar Prasad v State of Bihar*, AIR 1962 SC 1166 and *TK Rangarajan v Govt of TN*, AIR 2003 SC 3032.

[88] Sections 22 and 23.

[89] AIR 1987 SC 1086.

[90] AIR 1987 SC 990.

[91] AIR 1997 SC 2298.

[92] AIR 1989 SC 2039.

> discharge of the paramount obligation cast upon the members of the medical profession.[93]

Accordingly, no doctor contravenes any law if he attends to an injured victim without delay. The Court gave directions to that effect. It also said that 'every doctor wherever he be within the territory of India should forthwith be aware of this position' and, accordingly, the decision should be given due publicity. It is another clear instance of the application of Article 21 to private action. Again, in *Common Cause v Union of India*,[94] in a PIL petition under Article 32 bringing to the attention of the Court serious deficiencies and shortcomings in the matter of collection, storage and supply of blood in various blood centres, private as well as public, operating in the country, the Court gave wide-ranging directions to the Union for the administrative set-up as well as legislation for the purpose of ensuring that all chances of any risk to life or health guaranteed in Article 21 are eliminated in these processes.[95]

(a) Privacy, marriage and autonomy

In *X v Hospital Z*,[96] for reasons of confidentiality the facts do not disclose whether the hospital was government or private. The appellant charged the hospital with violating his privacy by disclosing the fact of his being HIV(+), as a result of which his marriage, to which he had a fundamental right under Article 21, was called off. The hospital defended the disclosure on the ground that the person to whom the appellant was going to be married also had the right to live a healthy life under Article 21 and in case of such a conflict of rights the right which promoted morality and public interest must have superiority. The Court referred to several marriage laws in which suffering from communicable diseases was a ground for annulment of marriage and rejected the claim of the appellant for the right to privacy.

---

93 Ibid, 2043.

94 (1996) 1 SCC 753.

95 Also, see *AS Mittal v State of UP*, AIR 1989 SC 1570 about observance of medical guidelines for organising eye operation camps.

96 (1998) 8 SCC 296.

In *T Sreetha v T Venkata Subbaiah*[97] the High Court of Andhra Pradesh applying the requirement of reasonableness of laws under Article 21 invalidated section 9 of the Hindu Marriage Act 1955 providing for the restitution of conjugal rights through judicial proceedings. The Court found 'the remedy of restitution of conjugal rights provided for by that section ... a savage and barbarous remedy, violating the right to privacy and human dignity guaranteed by Article 21'.[98] Although subsequently in two different cases, the Delhi High Court[99] and the Supreme Court,[100] disagreeing with *Sreetha*, have upheld the validity of section 9, no doubt was expressed, at least by the Supreme Court, on the requirement of reasonableness or of application of Articles 14 and 21 to matrimonial laws or non-penal laws. The Delhi High Court, 'applying the standard that the law has to be just, fair and reasonable as enunciated in Maneka Gandhi', found section 9 valid. So also the Supreme Court found that section 9 'serves a social purpose as an aid to the prevention of break-up of marriage' and therefore satisfied Articles 14 and 21. Although *Sarla Mudgal v Union of India*[101] dealt primarily with the DP in Article 44, it is also an instance of impermissibility of religious freedom to indulge in bigamy and evasion of punishment for bigamy. Entertaining a writ petition under Article 32 the Supreme Court has recently recommended the encouragement of inter-caste marriages and the provision of protection to those who enter into such an alliance.[102]

(b) Environmental protection

The environment is as much, if not more, spoiled by private action as by state action. The Supreme Court of India long back recognised that the right to a clean and healthy environment and preservation and protection of nature's gifts including the protection of wild life, forests, lakes, ancient monuments, fauna-flora, clean air, protection from noise, unpolluted water and ecological balance are

97 AIR 1983 AP 356.
98 Ibid, 373.
99 *Harvinder Kaur v Harmander Singh*, AIR 1984 Del. 66.
100 *Saroj Rani v Sudarshan Kumar* (1984) 4 SCC 90.
101 AIR 1995 SC 1531.
102 *Lata Singh v State of UP*, WP (Cri.) No. 208 of 2004 decided on 7 July 2006.

part of the right to life in Article 21.[103] *MC Mehta v Kamal Nath*[104] is an example of a petition under Article 32 against an individual on the ground of violation of the right to a clean environment under Article 21 and the FD under Article 51-A(g) as well as the DP under Article 48-A. The Court in that petition not only cancelled the deed of lease of land to the respondent but also asked him to pay compensation to the victims of environmental pollution as well as exemplary damages. MC Mehta has brought innumerable cases to the courts against the polluters of the environment in which most of the time culprits are private persons though they have been operating under the cover of state support. Among them, for example, are the two cases relating to the pollution of the Ganga river: *MC Mehta v Union of India*[105] and *MC Mehta v Union of India*,[106] in which detailed directions were issued to leather tanneries releasing pollutants in Kanpur and Calcutta respectively.

(c) The offence of rape

In *Bodhisattwa Gautam v Subhra Chakraborty*,[107] which was actually not a case for the enforcement of FRs but for the quashing of a complaint of rape against the appellant by the respondent, the Court, after observing that 'Fundamental Rights can be enforced even against private bodies and individuals'[108] also observed that rape 'is a crime against basic human rights and is also violative of the victim's most cherished of the Fundamental Rights, namely, the Right to Life contained in Article 21'.[109] We have noted above that

---

103 The number of cases on this issue is quite large. Some of them are: *Rural Litigation and Entitlement Kendra v State of UP*, AIR 1987 SC 2426; *Indian Council for Enviro Legal Action v Union of India* (1996) 3 SCC 212; *MC Mehta v Union of India* (1996) 4 SCC 750 and hundreds of other cases in his name; *Narmada Bachao Andolan v Union of India* (2000) 10 SCC 664. For more, see M. P. Singh, *Shukla's Constitution of India* (10th ed, 2001), p 167, note 62.

104 AIR 2000 SC 1997.

105 (1987) 4 SCC 463.

106 (1997) 2 SCC 411.

107 (1996) 1 SCC 490.

108 Ibid, 499.

109 Ibid, 500.

in *Vishaka* the Court found sexual harassment also as a violation of Article 21. In *Chairman Railway Board v Chandrima Das*,[110] though the rape was committed by railway employees, who were public servants, the Court recognised the right of the victim to get compensation for the violation of her right to life under Article 21.

(d) Right to safety

In *NHRC v State of Arunachal Pradesh*[111] the National Human Rights Commission approached the Supreme Court in a PIL under Article 32 on the ground that the Chakmas, who moved to India from the former East Pakistan, now Bangladesh, were being persecuted by sections of the citizens in the State of Arunachal Pradesh where they had been settled by the government. Such persecution, it was alleged, violated the right to life and liberty of Chakmas protected under Article 21. Allowing the plea of NHRC the Court gave several directions to the State and the Union of India for ensuring protection of 'life and personal liberty of each and every Chakma residing within the State' and for ensuring non-interference by anyone in settlement except according to law.[112]

In *Tarun Bora v State of Assam*,[113] though not a FR case, the Court made a remark which makes kidnapping by a private person a violation of Article 21: 'We may say that offence of kidnapping in any form impinge upon human rights and right to life enshrined in Article 21 of the Constitution.'[114]

4. 'Untouchability' and freedom of religion

Subject to public order, morality and health and other FRs, Article 25 guarantees to every person 'freedom of conscience and the right freely to profess, practice and propagate religion'. Similarly, Article 26 guarantees several rights to religious denominations. These rights have sometimes been exercised in India in breach of human dignity.

---

110 (2000) 2 SCC 465.
111 (1996) 1 SCC 742.
112 Ibid, 752.
113 AIR 2002 SC 2927.
114 Ibid, 2931.

One of the most blatant derogations has been the practice of 'untouchability', under which a large class of people is treated as untouchable on grounds of their 'birth-based pollution'. This practice has been a subject of condemnation for a long time, and finally the Constitution abolished it and forbade its practice in Article 17, which is one of the FRs. Article 17 also provides for punishment for any disability arising out of 'untouchability'. Parliament has enacted the Protection of Civil Rights Act 1955 for that purpose. Not many cases have come to the courts for the violation of this law but the one in which the matter reached the Supreme Court the Court upheld the punishment awarded to the culprit by the two lower courts but set aside by the High Court.[115] Denial of entry into temples to the untouchables or dalits has been one of the demonstrations of disabilities arising from that practice. To change the situation, temple entry laws have been enacted entitling everyone equally to visit the temples. Such laws have been upheld against the claims of religious freedom by religious denominations.[116] Laws abolishing the hereditary succession to the position of temple priests and other workers and opening such positions to qualified persons of any caste have also been upheld.[117] In *N Adithyan v Travancore Devaswom Board*[118] appointment of a non-Brahmin against the customary practice of appointing only Brahmins to the position of Poojaris/Santhikarans was upheld against the claims of Articles 25 and 26 and were found supportive of Article 17. The Court held that: 'Any custom or usage irrespective of even any proof of their having existed in pre-Constitution days cannot be countenanced as a source of law to claim any rights when it is found to violate human rights, dignity, social equality and the specific mandate of the Constitution and law made by Parliament.'[119] In *Surya Narayan Choudhary v State*[120] the Nathdwara temple administration which permitted entry to dalits subject to the condition of wearing a garland, sprinkling of Ganga water (holy water for purification) and carrying a few tulsi (a holy plant) leaves was found to be in violation of Articles 14, 15 and 17.

---

115 *State of Karnataka v Appa Balu Ingale*, AIR1993 SC 1126.
116 *Venkataramana Devaru v State of Mysore*, AIR 1958 SC 255.
117 See, e.g., *ERJ Swami v State of TN*, AIR 1972 SC 1586.
118 (2002) 8 SCC 106.
119 Ibid, 125.
120 AIR 1989 Raj. 99.

The right to propagate one's religion is vigorously pursued by Christian missionaries for the purpose of conversion from other religions to their own. People have complained of the use of unfair means for such conversions. The Court has held that such unfair practices violate one's right to freedom of conscience and the state may provide appropriate protection by law against such conversions.[121]

5. Freedom of expression and right to information

Article 19(1)(a) gives the right to 'freedom of speech and expression' to every citizen of India. Article 19 does not say that the rights in it are available only against the state. We have also noted above that in *Vishaka* the Court has read one of the rights in Article 19 to apply against private employers. There has not yet been a case in which the right to freedom of expression has been claimed against a private person. But in my view the right can be claimed against private employers by their employees and also by the general public on premises visited by the public. In *S Rangrajan v P Jagjivan Ram*[122] the SC has at least recognised a positive obligation of the state to protect freedom of expression from a hostile audience.[123]

The right to information has been recognised as part of the freedom of speech and expression under Article 19[124] as well as under Article 21.[125] For the effective implementation of this right, Parliament has enacted the Right to Information Act 2005. Primarily, the Act gives the right to seek information from public authorities but also entitles the seeking of information against private persons in the custody of or available to public authorities subject to certain procedural requirements. Except in case of trade and commercial secrets, such right to information against private

121 *Rev Stainislaus v State of MP*, AIR 1977 SC 908.

122 (1989) 2 SCC 574.

123 For indications to that effect, see *Kameshwar Prasad v State of Bihar*, AIR 1962 SC 1116.

124 See, *SP Gupta v President of India*, AIR 1982 SC 149, 234 and Secretary, Ministry of I & B, Govt of India v Cricket Assn of Bengal (1995) 2 SCC 161.

125 *RP Ltd v Proprietors, Indian Express Newspapers*, AIR 1989 SC 190, 202–203.

persons should be made available if the public interest in its disclosure outweighs in importance any possible harm or injury to a private person.[126]

D. Conclusion

This overview of the reach and application of human rights confined to civil and political rights in the form of FRs in the Constitution of India discloses the vision of the Constitution and its makers of the kind of society they aspired to establish in the country. The Constitution-makers were quite clear in assigning an equal role to each and every individual in the political process and decision-making. Not only did they provide for universal adult suffrage but they also provided for affirmative steps in the form of seat allocation or reservation in elected bodies for those who were incapable of competing in the political process at equal footing. For the effective participation in that process as well as for leading a dignified life, which they did not want to leave to the political process alone or postpone for the future, they also provided for Fundamental Rights which initially included what later became Directive Principles. The FRs and DPs, which have been designated as the conscience of the Constitution,[127] and harmony and balance between them, have been found to be among the basic features of the Constitution.[128] They are not confined to a vision of the individual free from state control in self-realisation and self-fulfilment, but aim at social transformation: the transformation of a society, which has ancient traditions and history and which has accommodated all sorts of people and cultures, but because of social and political reasons has lapsed into a system that does not fit well with the times and has become injurious to a life of dignity and fulfilment. The transformation of such a society does not depend merely on making it free from the shackles of the state, which were very few until some of them were experienced during British rule. It depends upon the active participation of the state as well as the individual in its realisation. The scheme of FRs in the

---

126 Section 11(1).

127 G. Austin, *The Indian Constitution: Cornerstone of a Nation* (1966), p 50.

128 *Minerva Mills v Union of India*, AIR 1980 SC 1789.

Indian Constitution is based on that vision which has been supplemented by the addition of Fundamental Duties (FDs).

In this scheme, therefore, FRs cannot be seen merely as guarantees against the state or reservation of a space for the individual free from state control and interference. Indian society stood at the time of commencement of the Constitution, and stands even today, at a stage where freedom from state control alone is no guarantee of human dignity. Such freedom will not only perpetuate the existence of already widespread indignities but will also strengthen and support them. It is a matter of some consolation that, after an initial distortion or lack of understanding of this vision on the part of legal fraternity trained in the Western vision of human rights, we have been for some time moving in the direction of realising that vision by reading positive guarantees in the FRs as well as by integrating them with the DPs and the FDs. Fortunately, the political process has never lost sight of that vision and has persistently, albeit slowly, been working towards its realisation by enacting necessary laws and taking administrative measures. But much more needs to be done in that direction and much faster. The judiciary, the legal profession and the intelligentsia in general must join in that move and contribute with full vigour and might.

Chapter 7: Ireland
Irish Constitutional Law and Direct Horizontal Effect – A Successful Experiment?

*Colm O'Cinneide**

A. Introduction

Private and public law are often conceptualised as occupying distinct and separate spheres.[1] The public/private distinction is particularly marked in both civil and common law systems when it comes to the applicability of constitutional norms. These are often seen as solely or predominantly binding upon public authorities, who, as organs of the state, are both established and have their powers and functions defined by the constitutional system. However, constitutional norms are often supposed to reflect and embody certain fundamental values, such as respect for human rights. Ensuring adequate and meaningful respect in practice for fundamental rights may require that non-state institutions are subject to some of the same legal controls as are imposed upon state bodies. In addition, private law is ultimately determined and enforced by state institutions, especially the courts: legal relationships in the private sphere are structured by regulation that ultimately is the product of state action.[2]

---

* Senior Lecturer in Law, University College London. An initial version of some of the arguments made in this paper was presented in C. O'Cinneide, 'Taking Horizontal Effect Seriously: Private Law, Constitutional Rights and The European Convention on Human Rights' [2003] 4 *Hibernian Law Journal* 77–108.

[1] This can take both substantive and procedural form. Certain legislation, such as the UK Human Rights Act and the Irish European Convention on Human Rights Act 2003, only applies to public authorities (and in the case of the HRA, to 'bodies exercising functions of a public nature' as provided by HRA, s 6), or 'organs of the state' in the Irish terminology. Certain other public law remedies can only be sought against bodies exercising public functions: see, e.g., Pt 54 of the Civil Procedure Rules 2000 (CPR).

[2] See O. Gerstenberg, 'Private Law and the New European Constitutional Settlement' (2004) 10(6) *European Law Journal* 766–86, 771–4.

Hence the problem of *Drittwirkung*: given the difficulty of drawing hard and fast distinctions between public and private law, to what extent should constitutional norms usually applied to public bodies be capable of also being applied to private bodies?

The answer to this question varies from jurisdiction to jurisdiction, often depending upon legal culture, constitutional tradition and conceptions of fundamental rights. A key factor is the status of the norms contained in the constitutional system. If these norms are envisaged as primarily concerned with controlling the functions of public bodies, then there may be some reluctance to apply them in the private sphere. However, if constitutional norms are seen as fundamental legal principles that should permeate all law, whether public or private, and which all legal actors should respect, then there may be much greater willingness to apply these norms in private law.

Ireland is an example of a jurisdiction that has adopted the latter approach: the fundamental rights and principles recognised by the Irish Constitution have been held by the Irish courts to be capable of being applied directly to private individuals and corporations. In particular, violations of constitutional norms by non-state actors can give rise to a cause of action known as a 'constitutional tort'. This doctrine has been identified by overseas commentators as one of the most interesting and salient features of Irish constitutional law from a comparative perspective.[3] Its application by the Irish courts has been often cited to demonstrate that the 'direct horizontal effect' of constitutional rights is possible, practicable and even desirable. For example, Stephen Gardbaum has argued that the Irish approach can and should be replicated in US constitutional law, as a replacement for the prevailing orthodoxy of the US 'state action' doctrine.[4]

The existence of this doctrine of direct horizontal effect is firmly established in Irish constitutional law, as is the ensuing availability of the 'constitutional tort' as a remedy for violations of fundamental

---

[3] See, e.g., A. S. Butler, 'Constitutional Rights in Private Litigation: A Critique and Comparative Analysis' (1993) 22 *Anglo-American Law Review* 1; M. Hunt, 'The "Horizontal Effect" of the Human Rights Act' [1998] *Public Law* 423; M. Forde, 'Who Can Remedy Human Rights Abuses? The "State Action" Question' in K. D. Ewing, C. A. Gearty and B. A. Hepple, *Human Rights and Labour Law: Essays for Paul O'Higgins* (1994) pp 221–39 at p 221.

[4] S. Gardbaum, 'The Horizontal Effect of Constitutional Rights' (2003) 102 *Michigan Law Review* 388–459.

rights by private actors. However, the actual impact of this doctrine has been mixed. Its existence means that Irish constitutional law is largely untroubled by complex and unsatisfactory attempts to differentiate between public and private bodies. The existence of the constitutional tort is widely seen as an essential safety net to protect fundamental rights from violations instigated by non-state bodies, if legislation and other forms of legal regulation do not do the job. However, the impact of the direct horizontal effect doctrine has often been muted and even nullified by the adoption of a cautious approach by the judiciary towards developing private law remedies to reflect rights norms, in particular where existing private law rules clearly apply to the matter at issue. In other circumstances, where existing private law rules do not clearly regulate a matter, and in particular where the Irish constitutional ban on abortion is at issue, the opposite has occurred: constitutional rights have been promiscuously treated as binding private individuals, without any real consideration of the appropriateness of blurring the public/private distinction in this context.

In general, the circumstances where the constitutional tort should be applied remain unclear and unsettled. There is a serious lack of conceptual clarity as to when and how horizontal effect should be given to fundamental rights. This uncertainty has been carried over into the legislation incorporating the European Convention on Human Rights into Irish domestic law: intended to reinforce rights protection in Ireland, this legislation manages to add new confusion as to when rights norms will be applied to private parties. The Irish experience therefore demonstrates both the potential benefits of direct horizontal effect, and the problems that can accompany it.

B. The *Meskell* doctrine: constitutional torts and direct horizontal effect in Irish constitutional law

Since independence from the United Kingdom in 1922, there have been two Irish Constitutions, the original Constitution of 1922 being superseded by the Constitution of 1937, known by its official name in Irish, *Bunreacht na hÉireann*. The provisions of the 1937 Constitution formally establish Ireland as a democratic state based upon respect for certain fundamental rights and a clearly delineated separation of powers structure. The rights explicitly listed in the text of the Constitution include the rights to equality, fair trial and *habeus corpus*, liberty, respect for the home and family life, freedom of religion and thought, education (including the right to free education for those under the age of eighteen), freedom of association, assembly and expression, and respect for property rights.[5] A highly controversial constitutional amendment in 1983 also inserted a reference to the 'right to life of the unborn child', a provision that, as discussed below, has had particular importance in the context of horizontal effect.[6]

Also of especial importance is Article 40.3.1° of the Constitution, which provides that 'the State guarantees in its laws to respect, and, as far as practicable, by its laws to defend and vindicate the personal rights of the citizen'. In a very important series of decisions, beginning with *Ryan v Attorney General*[7] in 1965, the Irish courts have recognised this provision as a source of unenumerated but fully enforceable constitutional rights, whose content is to be derived by judicial reasoning from the nature of the Irish state and the relationship between the citizen and the state as envisaged by the text of the Constitution taken as a whole.[8] Rights recognised as derived from Article 40.3.1° include the right to personal privacy,[9] the right to earn a livelihood[10] and the right to communicate.[11]

In Irish constitutional law, the provisions of the 1937 Constitution are the supreme source of legal validity and all other legal norms must conform to the requirements of the Constitution. Therefore, all legislation must be compatible with these constitutional rights and values, whether enacted prior to the coming into force of the Constitution in 1937 or afterwards. Similarly, all common law rules must comply with constitutional norms, even if they only have application between private bodies. Nothing can be a 'law' that clashes with the Constitution. This constitutional norm can even extend to

---

[5] See Articles 40–44 of the Constitution.

[6] See Art 40.3.3°.

[7] [1965] IR 294.

[8] For discussion of the controversy that still surrounds Ryan and the doctrine of unenumerated rights, see G. Hogan, 'Unenumerated Personal Rights: Ryan's Case Evaluated' (1990–92) 25 *Irish Jurist* 95; J. W. Parker, 'Must Constitutional Rights Be Specified? Reflections on the Proposal to Amend Article 40.3.1' (1997) *Irish Jurist* 102.

[9] *McGee v AG* [1974] IR 284.

[10] *Murtagh Properties Ltd v Cleary* [1972] IR 330.

[11] *AG v Paperlink* [1984] ILRM 373.

nullify common law rules that are incompatible with, or run fundamentally against the grain of, the underlying values of the constitutional order, even if they are not specifically contrary to a fundamental right or another express textual provision of the Constitution. The classic example of this is the famous decision of *Byrne v Ireland*,[12] where the Supreme Court decided that the common law concept of the royal prerogative, and 'linked' doctrines such as state immunity, were incompatible with the underlying framework of values underpinning the Irish constitutional order.[13]

The Irish Constitution therefore confers both subjective rights upon individuals against the state and also generates objective norms that determine the validity of all other forms of law within the Irish legal system. This means that, in private law actions, litigants are able to challenge the constitutionality of the legislation or common law rule at issue as part of the proceedings, even where no state action is directly involved. This is because a private litigant in the private law case can assert that the law being challenged is not a binding legal norm, on the basis that it is incompatible with the Constitution, and therefore should not be applied in the case, or alternatively should be applied in a manner compatible with the Constitution.

For example, the Supreme Court granted injunctive relief in the case of *Educational Co of Ireland v Fitzpatrick (No. 2)*,[14] where a strike called by a trade union against a private company to enforce a closed shop arrangement was deemed to be contrary to the constitutional right of freedom of association. In seeking an injunction to restrain picketing by the union, the company argued that the protection given to industrial disputes by the Trade Disputes Act 1906 should not be applied to union action directed towards compelling association with a union. By a slender majority of 3 to 2, the Supreme Court agreed, finding that the 1906 Act could not make lawful action that was designed to nullify the freedom to associate protected in Article 40.6.1°iii of the Constitution.[15]

---

12 [1972] IR 241.

13 See B. Lenihan, 'Royal Prerogatives and the Constitution' (1989) 24 *Irish Jurist* 1; K. Costello, 'The Expulsion of the Prerogative Doctrine from Irish Law: Quantifying and Remedying the Loss of the Royal Prerogative' (1997) 32 *Irish Jurist* 32 at 145; G. Hogan and G. Whyte, *Kelly: The Irish Constitution* (3rd edn, 1994), pp 24–36.

14 [1961] IR 345.

15 For similar decisions also involving alleged trade union interference with freedom of association where the legislation was interpreted to secure conformity with

Similarly, in *Murtagh Properties Ltd v Cleary*,[16] a trade union placed a picket on the plaintiff's bar as a result of the plaintiff employing female staff, which the union alleged was a breach of an industrial agreement. Kenny J granted an interlocutory injunction restraining the picketing, even though it was in furtherance of a trade dispute, on the basis that the industrial action was unlawful as it was intended to force the plaintiff to dismiss the female employees and deprive them of their unenumerated constitutional right to earn a livelihood, which was deemed to constitute a 'personal right' of the citizen recognised by Article 40.3.1°. The trade union legislation was interpreted and applied to prohibit this specific type of industrial action, and therefore to ensure conformity with fundamental rights.

Thus, in a dispute between two private parties, the Supreme Court is prepared to disapply or interpret legislation to ensure that individual constitutional rights are not infringed. In comparative terms, this is not so unusual. A similar approach is adopted in other common law constitutional systems, even those without a doctrine of direct horizontal effect.[17] However, the Irish constitutional jurisprudence goes further. The Irish courts are under a constitutional duty to vindicate the individual rights guaranteed under the Constitution, by ensuring their effective protection. This guarantee of effective protection constitutes an objective norm of the Irish constitutional order: the organs of the state, including the courts, are to take the

---

constitutional norms, see *NUR v Sullivan* [1947] IR 77 and *Murphy v Stewart* [1973] IR 97. For similar decisions in other contexts (i.e. outside the sphere of trade union regulation), see *O'Brien v Keogh* [1972] IR 144; *Tuohy v Courtney* [1994] 3 IR 1; *Re Tilson* [1951] IR 1; *Mayo-Perrott v Mayo-Perrott* [1958] IR 336.

[16] [1972] IR 330.

[17] In the UK, the House of Lords has been prepared to allow litigants in private actions to challenge the compatibility of legislation with the Human Rights Act: see e.g. *Mendoza v Ghaidan* [2004] UKHL 30 and *Bellinger v Bellinger* [2003] UKHL 21. The Canadian Supreme Court has done likewise: see *M v H* (1999) 171 DLR (4th) 577. In practice, the availability of this remedy to private litigants can considerably blur the issue of whether rights guarantees can be applied in private relationships. The distinction between striking out a law that offends against constitutional rights and applying a constitutional right directly to the conduct of private individuals may often not be conceptually very distinct. For an illustration, see the discussion in D. Mead, 'Rights, Relationships and Retrospectivity: the Impact of Convention Rights on Pre-existing Private Relationships following *Wilson* and *Ghaidan*' [2005] *Public Law* 459.

necessary steps to prevent a breach of fundamental rights, or to provide a remedy for breaches of fundamental rights.[18]

This positive obligation appears to apply, irrespective of the source of any infringement. In the case law of the Supreme Court, it does not seem to matter whether an infringement stems from a public, private or mixed public/private legal entity: the Constitution is interpreted as requiring the Irish legal system to prevent or compensate for a violation of a right, and this can involve, if necessary, the imposition of legal restraints upon non-state actors. In other words, Irish constitutional law recognises the possibility that a legal remedy can be obtained against any legal actor, including private individuals and bodies corporate, where interference with fundamental rights has occurred or is threatened.[19] The Irish courts have therefore treated the Constitution as establishing the existence of a 'constitutional tort' action, which can be brought against a private individual or organisation. Through this tort action, the rights protected under the Constitution can be applied directly to regulate the conduct of private actors.[20]

The existence of this 'constitutional tort' as a mechanism for giving 'direct horizontal effect' to provisions of the Constitution was confirmed by the Supreme Court in a sequence of decisions in the early 1970s, including *Meskell v CIE*,[21] and *Glover v BLN Ltd*.[22] These decisions held that interference with the constitutional rights of individuals by private individuals, companies or trade unions constituted a 'constitutional tort', to which the Irish courts will provide a remedy via injunctive relief and/or damages.[23] Public authorities

---

18 See *East Donegal Co-Op Livestock Mart v Attorney General* [1970] IR 317, esp at 368–9, per Walsh J.

19 Similar approaches have been adopted to varying extents in the Netherlands, Spain, Malta, Czech Republic and Switzerland: see A. Barak, 'Constitutional Human Rights and Private Law' in D. Friedmann and D. Barak-Erez, *Human Rights in Private Law* (2001) pp 13–42 at pp 25–28.

20 See Butler, op. cit., note 3, pp 20–21; J. Temple Lang, 'Private Law Aspects of the Irish Constitution' (1971) 6 *Irish Jurist* 237 at 244–49; F. von Prondzynski, 'The Protection of Constitutional Rights: Comparisons Between Ireland and Germany' (1980) 2 *DULJ* 14.

21 [1973] IR 121.

22 [1973] IR 388.

23 See T. Kerr and T. Cooney, 'Constitutional Aspects of Irish Tort Law' (1981) 3 *Dublin University LJ* 1.

could also be liable for 'constitutional torts', but no particular significance is attached to whether a body is designed as 'public' or 'private': liability under the 'constitutional tort' may vary according to the nature of the right at issue and the nature and responsibilities of the body being sued, but its public/private status is rarely treated as a determining factor.

Meskell is the decision which is regularly cited as the major precedent establishing the existence of the constitutional tort and its potential applicability to anyone who infringes a constitutional right. In this case, CIE, then a fully nationalised Irish public transport company, agreed with the four major unions represented in its workforce to terminate all existing employee contracts and offer all employees new contracts, which however would oblige all employees to join one of the four unions. The plaintiff refused to sign the new contract and was dismissed. The Supreme Court held that CIE had attempted to violate the plaintiff's constitutional right of free association (which had been recognised in the *Educational Co* decision discussed above to also incorporate a right to disassociate) and therefore had acted unlawfully.

Walsh J in *Meskell* stated the rationale behind this decision in straightforward terms:

> ... if a person has suffered damages by virtue of a breach of a constitutional right or the infringement of a constitutional right, that person is entitled to seek redress against the person or persons who have infringed that right.[24]

No distinction was made between public and private entities, and no real discussion took place as to whether CIE as a nationalised corporation constituted an organ of the state. The Supreme Court was content to find that a violation of a constitutional right entitled the victim to redress from the body responsible.

The *Meskell* decision involved a semi-state nationalised corporation providing essential public services: therefore, the ratio of the decision cannot necessarily be interpreted as clearly establishing a precedent that purely private bodies are subject to an obligation to respect constitutional rights. However, in the subsequent decision of *Glover v BLN Ltd*,[25] the board of directors of a private company were required as a matter of constitutional justice to conduct an

---

24 [1973] IR 121 at 133.
25 [1973] IR 388.

inquiry to ascertain whether the plaintiff was in breach of his contract with them. In other words, constitutional rights were applied directly to regulate the internal affairs of a private body. Walsh J stated that 'the dictates of constitutional justice require that statutes, regulations or agreements setting up machinery for taking decisions which may effect rights or impose liabilities should be construed as providing for fair procedures'.[26] In *Rodgers v ITGWU*,[27] this rule was subsequently applied to trade unions in their conduct of their internal affairs. Private bodies, including limited companies and trade unions, are therefore bound by the requirement to respect certain constitutionally mandated norms of procedural fairness, which have been established by judicial interpretation of the provisions of the Constitution governing fair trial and the administration of justice. Therefore, the *Meskell* and *Glover* decisions taken together establish that constitutional norms can be applied directly to private bodies.

C. Residual uncertainties

The approach taken in *Meskell* reflects the strongly 'activist' approach adopted by the Irish Supreme Court in the 1960s and early 1970s, guided by the then Chief Justice O'Dalaigh CJ (later to be President of Ireland) and in particular by Walsh J, the author of the leading opinions in *Byrne*, *Meskell*, *Glover* and a host of other important decisions. This era of Supreme Court jurisprudence also produced the *Ryan* decision, with its recognition of the existence of unenumerated constitutional rights, as well as a considerable expansion of the scope of the rights expressly recognised in the text of the Constitution, and a decisive break with the earlier, more cautious jurisprudence of the Court in interpreting constitutional guarantees. This judicial activism was the result of a number of factors. Of particular importance was the influence of Catholic natural law theory, with its emphasis on the overriding value of human dignity and the existence of inherent rights vested in the individual. Other significant contributing factors included the comparative example of the activist US Supreme Court jurisprudence of the same time

---

26 Ibid at 424.

27 [1978] ILRM 51 (the right to participate in trade union decision-making procedures was derived from the right to freedom of association in Art 40.6).

period, the gradual emergence of European human rights standards and the strong rhetorical commitment in Irish constitutional and political discourse to a democratic rights-based culture.

This combination of influences resulted in a 'style' of Supreme Court jurisprudence that was very protective of fundamental rights and the overriding authority of constitutional norms, and which resulted in the recognition of sweeping new forms of rights-based remedies such as the constitutional tort action. It was also characterised by a certain impatience with the incremental common law style of judicial reasoning. *Meskell* as a decision exemplifies this 'style' perfectly, with its reliance upon overarching statements of constitutional principle and the absence of much reasoning from analogous cases, or of any attempt to delineate with precision how this new constitutional tort should be applied in other contexts.[28] It also reflects natural law influence in its lack of concern with the maintenance of a strongly distinct public/private distinction, which tends not to be accorded a particularly significant status in natural law theories.[29]

However, in recent years, the Supreme Court has tended to adopt a more cautious approach, incrementally developing existing constitutional doctrine in a more recognisable common law mode of adjudication while being slow to expand or to contract the scope of rights protection established by the activist O'Dalaigh court.[30] The Court has also tended to jettison reliance upon natural law theory in favour of more emphasis upon liberal state theory. Irish society has also changed dramatically, becoming closer in economic development and moral views to the European/North American mainstream. These trends raise some questions about the current scope and status of the *Meskell* doctrine. How is the sweeping principle

[28] Note that *Murtagh Properties* was also decided during this period, and *Educational Co* dates from the initial stages of this shift towards a more active style of constitutional interpretation.

[29] See B. McMahon and W. Binchy, *Law of Torts* (3rd edn, 2000), para 1.78, p 24.

[30] See, e.g., the decision in *Sinnott v Minister for Education* [2001] 2 IR 545, which saw the Supreme Court refuse to extend the protection conferred by constitutional rights in the socio-economic rights field beyond that which was well-established in the existing case law. For a sample of the debate that followed this decision, see G. Hogan, 'Directive Principles, Socioeconomic Rights and the Constitution' (2001) *Irish Jurist* 174.

enunciated in *Meskell* and *Glover* to be applied to the wide range of circumstances where it might potentially 'bite'? Can it fit into the more incremental common law approach now favoured by the Supreme Court, or will its scope have to be clipped or contained? Is the Irish 'direct horizontal effect' doctrine capable of being applied in a society with greater levels of social and economic complexity, but perhaps less consensus on core values?

Considerable uncertainty still shrouds the scope and extent of the *Meskell* doctrine.[31] As happened with the abolition of the royal prerogative in *Byrne*, the Supreme Court in *Meskell* and *Glover*, in sweepingly asserting the supremacy of constitutional values within the Irish legal order, left the definition of the scope of the new doctrine to future court decisions.[32] In neither case was there any real discussion of the legitimacy of the direct horizontal effect approach, as contrasted with vertical 'state action' approaches, or indeed alternative horizontal effect doctrines. There was also no real discussion of the types of alleged violations, justifications and methods of balancing competing rights claims that could be pleaded in support or defence of a constitutional tort claim. In other words, there was no real blueprint laid down as to how the constitutional tort action would be applied to non-state bodies.

Some of the uncertainties left in the wake of *Meskell* even cast some doubt over whether it is firmly established in the case law that Irish constitutional law actually gives direct horizontal applicability to constitutional rights. Previous court decisions that pre-dated *Meskell* and the 'activist' approach of the O'Dalaigh court had rejected the applicability of specific constitutional rights provisions in private disputes. For example, in *Schlegel v Corcoran*,[33] Gavan Duffy J considered that the constitutional right to freedom of religion and the prohibition of state discrimination on the basis of religion in Article 44.2.3° were not relevant in a private dispute about a landlord's refusal to consent to a sub-let on the basis of anti-Semitic

---

31 See McMahon and Binchy, *Law of Torts*, op. cit., para 1.66, p 22.

32 For an analysis of the *Byrne* decision and the subsequent attempt in *Webb v Ireland* [1988] IR 353 (SC) to fill some of the gaps in common law doctrine left by the abolition of the royal prerogative, see J. Kelly, 'Hidden Treasure and the Constitution' (1988) 10 *DULJ* 5; D. G. Morgan, 'Constitutional Interpretation' (1988) 10 *DULJ* 24.

33 [1942] IR 19.

prejudice against the proposed new tenant, a Jewish dentist.[34] As mentioned above, the *Meskell* decision itself concerned a nationalised transport company, even if *Glover* did concern a private company. In addition, the lack of any extended analysis in either decision, and in particular the lack of any sustained examination of alternative constitutional approaches to the issue of horizontal effect, leaves a certain degree of doubt as to whether the Supreme Court in either *Meskell* or *Glover* was establishing a firm and fixed doctrine of direct horizontal effect.

Given this ambiguity in the key precedents, one of the leading Irish constitutional commentators, Michael Forde, has questioned whether direct horizontal approach has actually been established as a fixed constitutional doctrine in Irish constitutional law.[35] He has argued that the *Meskell* decision concerned a semi-state nationalised body, while *Educational Co* and the other trade union cases cited in *Meskell* in support of the decision just involved the constitutional interpretation of legislative provisions.[36] Therefore, in his view, the *Meskell* decision has not given a definitive answer as to the degree of horizontal effect constitutional rights have in the Irish legal system: in fact, it could be open to the Irish courts to adopt a vertical 'state action' approach, similar to the approach taken in US constitutional law, and the doctrinal position that Forde himself would prefer.[37]

Forde's analysis is correct in pointing out the somewhat uncertain foundations of the assumption that the Irish Constitution has a firm and fixed doctrine of direct horizontal effect. However, these cases, and *Meskell* and *Glover* in particular, were clearly decided on the assumption that no significant difference exists between public and private bodies in giving direct application to constitutional

---

[34] James Casey argues that this decision would clearly not be followed if a similar case arose now, due to the horizontal effect of the Constitution: see J. Casey, *Constitutional Law in Ireland* (3rd edn, 2000), p 701. Interestingly, he cites the US decision of *Shelley v Kramer* (1948) 334 US 1 as indicating the appropriate approach to resolving such a problem, but not *Meskell*. This is an example of how the constitutional tort action has a relatively low profile in Irish constitutional commentary.

[35] See Forde, 'Who Can Remedy Human Rights Abuses? The "State Action" Question', op. cit., note 3 supra.

[36] It could be argued that the reference to *Educational Co* in *Meskell* could have indicated a certain lack of clarity on the part of the Supreme Court as to this distinction between interpreting legislation to comply with constitutional values and giving constitutional rights direct horizontal effect.

[37] Forde, op. cit., note 3, p 234.

norms. There is no indication in any of these cases that the Supreme Court recognised the existence of any meaningful public/private divide when issues of the enforceability of constitutional rights are at stake: in fact, the wording of the *Meskell* judgment indicates the contrary.

In any case, a succession of subsequent High and Supreme Court decisions have repeatedly applied constitutional rights in private law disputes,[38] with no real concern about whether the scope of these rights is confined to the 'vertical' citizen-state relationship. Many of these cases relate again to trade unions. In *Crowley v Ireland*, McMahon J held that industrial action brought by a teachers' trade union which had shut down several national schools constituted an unlawful interference with the children's right to education, as explicitly protected in Article 42.4 of the Constitution.[39] Subsequently, in *Hayes v Ireland*,[40] damages were awarded, inter alia, against the union for a violation of the right to education. Carroll J ruled that as the action was a *Meskell*-style claim for vindication of constitutional rights, the immunity from tort liability conferred on trade unions by s 4 of the Trade Disputes Act 1904 did not apply. Similarly, in *Conway v INTO*,[41] the Supreme Court approved the award of exemplary damages against a trade union for directing that other schools should not accept pupils from the school at the centre of an industrial dispute.[42] These cases differ from *Educational Co* and the other trade union cases cited above, in that the cause of action in all three cases was the alleged violation of constitutional rights in question, not a private law claim for interference with contractual relations: the constitutional rights in question were being used as a sword, not merely as a shield to strike out the application of statutory defences that would otherwise have applied.

---

38 As Forde recognises, see op. cit., note 3, pp 231–3.

39 [1980] IR 102.

40 [1987] ILRM 651.

41 [1991] 2 IR 305 (SC).

42 See also *Cotter v Ahern and others*, unreported, High Court, Finlay P, 25 February 1977, where damages were awarded against a trade union for pressurising a school manager to terminate a contract of employment with the plaintiff, a newly appointed school principal, on the basis that the union's action was done to punish the plaintiff for exercising his constitutional right of choosing not to be a union member.

Nor are these more recent cases confined to the trade union sphere. In *Lovett v Grogan*,[43] the Supreme Court held that a transport company whose business had been substantially damaged by the defendant's actions (which had continued notwithstanding the imposition of a reasonably minimal fine for the breach of statutory regulations, which was the only statutory remedy available) were entitled to an injunction to uphold the constitutional entitlement to earn one's livelihood.[44] In *Doyle v Croke*,[45] the High Court followed the earlier decision of *Rodgers v ITGWU* in finding that internal trade union procedures had to respect constitutional requirements of natural justice. *Glover* was also explicitly followed by the Labour Court as recently as 2005 in the religious discrimination case of *Icon Clinical Research Ltd v Tsourova*.[46]

In addition to these decisions, numerous judicial dicta have recognised that private bodies are subject to a constitutional obligation to respect fundamental rights, and that a failure to do so will leave them open to the application of the constitutional tort remedy.[47] Academic commentary has tended to accept that the constitutional tort action is firmly established in Irish law. The Supreme Court regarded this as a settled aspect of Irish constitutional law in the highly controversial abortion cases of *Attorney General (Society of the Protection of Unborn Children) v Open Door Counselling and Dublin Well Woman Centre*[48] and *X v Attorney General*,[49] where the courts were prepared to place severe restraints upon the conduct and movement of private individuals so as to give effective protection to the constitutional right to life of the unborn child, inserted into the Irish Constitution by a referendum in 1983. Interestingly, in many of these cases, and in particular in the abortion decisions, no real argument took place before the courts on the issue of the applicability of constitutional rights directly to private individuals

---

[43] [1995] 1 ILRM 12.

[44] See also *Parsons v Kavanagh* [1990] ILRM 560 (HC); *O'Connor v Williams* [1996] 2 ILRM 382 (HC).

[45] Unreported, High Court, Costello J, 6 May 1988.

[46] (2005) ED/04/2, Determination No. 054. Note again that in *Glover*, there was little or no discussion about whether private companies should be treated differently from see e.g. public bodies.

[47] See also the cases discussed below in the context of the recent 'taming' of the *Meskell* doctrine. *PH and others (infants) v John Murphy & Sons Ltd* (1987) IR 621.

[48] [1988] IR 593.

[49] [1992] 1 IR 1.

and bodies. This could be taken as confirming the settled nature of the constitutional tort and of the direct horizontal effect in general of the Irish Constitution: it could also reflect a lack of engagement with the issue of the public/private distinction, a point which will be discussed further below.

Forde suggests that the decision of the Supreme Court in *McGrath and O'Rourke v Trustees of Maynooth College*[50] is an example of the Irish courts adopting an alternative 'vertical state action' approach. The two plaintiffs in this case were dismissed from their teaching posts at Maynooth College, which was originally a privately funded Catholic seminary but was now funded as a state third-level institution, while still retaining its Catholic ethos. Both plaintiffs were dismissed because as clerical members of staff, their teaching and conduct conflicted with Catholic orthodoxy, and they were both in the process of laicisation (leaving the clergy). The plaintiffs contended that Maynooth as a state-funded institution should not discriminate on the basis of religious belief and conduct. The Supreme Court held that, notwithstanding Maynooth's receipt of state funding, it remained a religious institution and was entitled as such to require conformity with its statutes and ethos.

This case certainly stands out from the mainstream of constitutional case law, as the Supreme Court actively engaged with the issue of whether Maynooth College should be classified as a public or private body. However, it cannot be seen as an example of the horizontal effect of constitutional rights being rejected. *McGrath* was decided on the basis of the textual wording and appropriate interpretation of the specific constitutional right of non-discrimination on the grounds of religious belief, not on the basis that constitutional rights could not be applied to private bodies in general.[51] At no point did the Supreme Court rule out the application of all fundamental rights to private institutions, even private institutions with a strong religious character. Indeed, the Court was willing to examine closely

---

50 [1979] ILRM 166.

51 The Supreme Court placed great emphasis on the fact that this constitutional right was expressly limited in scope and could only apply to the activities of the state, which it held were not at issue in this case, as Maynooth College was best classed as a religious institution. Casey suggests that the Supreme Court was too quick to accept the formal characterisation of the institution as a seminary and too slow to take into account the reality of the institution's funding and status as it had developed over time. See Casey, *Constitutional Law in Ireland*, op. cit., pp 705–6.

the specific Catholic doctrinal law on laicisation that applied to one of the plaintiffs, to assess whether the College was abiding by its own rules and regulations, and thereby complying with general constitutional norms of fairness and non-discrimination.

Therefore, the doctrine that constitutional rights can bind private bodies, via the constitutional tort action, appears to be firmly rooted at this stage in Irish constitutional law. In the mainstream of Irish constitutional commentary, this doctrine is regarded as consistent with the Constitution's status as *lex superior* and the obligation to give effective protection against violations of constitutional rights. It would require a substantial deviation from existing precedent for this doctrine to be uprooted, notwithstanding its slightly obscure birth.

D. The uncertain scope of the constitutional tort

However, Forde is entirely correct to argue that the merits and constitutional justification of the direct horizontal approach have never been clearly set out or debated in the jurisprudence of the Irish courts.[52] It is also true that considerable uncertainty remains as to how this approach should be applied in practice via the constitutional tort action. The *Meskell* doctrine has remained a rule of unclear scope, lacking any systematic judicial or academic exegesis.

The leading authorities on Irish tort law, McMahon and Binchy, suggest that the circumstances in which a constitutional right will give rise to a cause of action against private bodies remain extremely uncertain.[53] They suggest that there is a lack of clarity as to what conduct on the part of a private body will generate a cause of action for violation of constitutional rights, and in particular when proof of fault will be required.[54] They also highlight persistent uncertainty as to whether a constitutional right should only be actionable on proof of actual damage, as is the norm for most torts, or whether it should be actionable per se, as with the torts of interference with

52 See Forde, op. cit., note 3, p 234.

53 McMahon and Binchy, *Irish Law of Torts*, op. cit., note 29, para 1.66.

54 See McMahon and Binchy, *Irish Law of Torts*, op. cit., para 1.68, p 22. See also Temple Lang, op. cit., note 20, p 247.

the person.[55] In addition, McMahon and Binchy argue that 'completely undeveloped in Irish judicial analysis of the action for infringement of constitutional rights is the investigation of whether *all* constitutionally protected rights are enforceable against the state and against individuals without discrimination.'[56] The case-by-case basis on which the Supreme Court has adjudicated constitutional tort claims has meant that no overarching test has been established to determine whether a constitutional right will be given horizontal effect, and if so, to what degree and extent.

Even when particular rights are well established in the case law as clearly suitable for the application of the constitutional tort remedy, problems remain. It will often be unclear how a specific right should be applied across the diverse range of circumstances in the private sphere where it could have an impact. The bulk of Irish constitutional rights jurisprudence relates to public authorities and other organs of the state: therefore, it will often not provide much guidance to courts in applying constitutional rights in the private sphere. The case law that does exist on horizontal effect is very context-specific: the emphasis in decisions like *Meskell*, *Lovett* and *Open Door* is on delineating the scope of the constitutional right at issue, and then applying it to the specific facts, rather than on establishing rules of general application to the private sphere.

This lack of guidance on horizontal effect is a real problem. How a public institution should respect a fundamental right may differ considerably from how a private body or individual might be expected to respect the same right. Big differences might also exist between the obligations imposed on different private bodies to respect the same right. Different rights may have to be balanced against each other when they come into conflict in the private sphere, and again little guidance exists on how this should be done in the Irish constitutional case law.

This chronic lack of precision as to how and when constitutional rights will be given direct horizontal effect inevitably generates considerable uncertainty, and raises concern about the possibility

---

55 While preferring the later option as more compatible with respect for fundamental rights, McMahon and Binchy note that '*Meskell* offers no guidance on the general question whether some, or all, infringements of constitutional rights are actionable *per se*'. Ibid, paras 1.61–1.65, pp 20–21.

56 Ibid.

of ad hoc unstructured judicial law-making. It also could impact upon personal autonomy, not least through the lack of legal certainty that this uncertainty generates: private individuals and bodies may be unsure or unaware of the constitutional obligations that may be imposed upon them.[57] This lack of clarity can also deter lawyers, judges and litigants from making use of the constitutional tort action. For a doctrine of such potential sweep, the direct horizontal effect of the Irish Constitution has been notably under-utilised by judges and practitioners. Its prominent status in comparative constitutional commentary on the horizontal effect of human rights instruments is not matched by a similar profile internally within the Irish legal system.[58]

E. The constitutional equality clause and direct horizontal effect

An example of the deeply rooted uncertainty about the scope of the constitutional tort action is the doubt that exists in the academic literature as to whether Article 40.1, the constitutional equality clause, applies as between private individuals.[59] The wording of the text of Article 40.1 refers to the right to be recognised as 'equal before the "law" by the 'State ... in its enactments'. This could suggest that the equality clause is envisaged as just applying to the organs of the state. John Kelly, the leading exponent of Irish constitutional law, considered that the Irish courts should follow the German approach in not generally applying the equality guarantee to the private sphere.[60]

Similarly, the Constitution Review Group (a group of experts established in 1995 to report on reforms to the Constitution) felt that it was inappropriate for Article 40.1 to be given direct horizontal

---

[57] See Forde, op. cit., note 3, pp 234–7.

[58] A wholly unscientific survey by the author of acquaintances practising in the Irish Law Library indicated a high degree of lack of knowledge about the existence and scope of the doctrine.

[59] See also J. Casey, *Constitutional Law in Ireland* (3rd edn, 2000), p 475. The Supreme Court in *In re Article 26 and the Employment Equality Bill 1996* [1997] 2 IR 321 mentioned this issue but felt it unnecessary to determine the applicability of Art 40.1 to the area of private law (Hamilton CJ for the court, at 346).

[60] J. Kelly, 'Equality Before the Law in Three European Jurisdictions' (1983) XVIII *Irish Jurist* 259 at 266–7; see also J. Kelly, *The Irish Constitution* (2nd edn, 1984), p 447.

effect. The Group's Report argued that it would 'constitute an unjustified intrusion upon individual autonomy'. It also considered that giving horizontal effect to the equality clause in the private sphere would generate real difficulties as to how to identify when, where and to whom it would apply. The Review Group also expressed concern about its potential impact on the separation of powers: giving horizontal effect to this constitutional right would open up a vast and uncertain terrain where judicial decisions would determine the application of this right to private relationships, which might conflict with or cut across legislation passed by the *Oireachtas*, the legislative branch of government.[61]

However, despite the Group's singling-out of Article 40.1 for special attention (it did not examine the suitability of any other right for direct horizontal application), all of its arguments in favour of not giving the equality clause horizontal application could in a similar manner be applied across the full spectrum of constitutional rights. For example, Article 40.3 requires the 'State' to vindicate the 'personal rights of the citizen'. This has as discussed above been interpreted as requiring the organs of the state to respect a range of unenumerated personal rights, which can be rationally derived from an underlying constitutional concept of human dignity.[62] If these unenumerated personal rights are applied horizontally, they may have a considerable impact on private autonomy. They would also give rise to complex questions about how to balance the rights of different private parties.

Therefore, all the arguments that the Review Group considered in rejecting giving direct horizontal effect to Article 40.1 apply in the context of Article 40.3 as well.[63] However, the Supreme Court in *Lovett v Grogan* has already given direct horizontal effect to the unenumerated right to earn a livelihood derived from Article 40.3. It is likely that a similar approach will be adopted in respect of the unenumerated right to personal privacy that is now firmly established in the case law. Costello J in *X v Flynn and others*[64] granted a series of interlocutory injunctions restraining the publication of press material, on the basis that the plaintiff had made out a serious issue to be tried

---

61 See Report of the Constitution Review Group (1996), pp 224–6. See also J. Casey, *Constitutional Law in Ireland* (3rd edn, 2000), p 475.

62 [1965] IR 294.

63 In addition, the text of Article 40.3 refers only to the 'State', as does Article 40.1.

64 Unreported, High Court, 19 May 1994.

as to whether the invasion of her privacy violated her unenumerated constitutional right to privacy recognised in *McGee v Ireland*[65] and *Kennedy v Ireland*,[66] rather than on common law principles.[67]

Therefore, the Review Group's discomfort with giving horizontal effect to Article 40.1 is inconsistent with how horizontal effect has already been given to Article 40.3 by the Supreme Court.[68] It also appears to be out of step with the constitutional logic that underlies the direct horizontal effect doctrine in the first place. The Irish courts have recognised that the Article 40.1 right to equality confers a positive right upon individuals to be free from unjustified discrimination:[69] why should this particular right not be applied in the private sphere when others are given direct horizontal effect, especially when the right to equality is particularly vulnerable to infringement by private actors? However, the qualms about giving Article 40.1 direct horizontal effect via the constitutional tort action reflect not alone a lack of clarity in this area; they also indicate that concerns exist about the impact of the horizontal effect doctrine upon legal certainty and separation of powers principles.

F. Problems with direct horizontal effect: the abortion cases

These concerns are not wholly unfounded. The 'abortion case' of *Attorney General v Open Door Counselling* serves as a valuable

65 [1974] IR 284.

66 [1987] IR 587.

67 See P. Walley, 'Privacy Law in Ireland: A Jurisprudential Cinderella' (1999) 3(1) *Irish Intellectual Property Review* 6 at 12. In *Aherne v RTE* [2005] IEHC 180, the High Court considered that the unenumerated constitutional right to privacy could be applied to the Irish public sector broadcaster RTE, the Irish equivalent of the BBC. There was no analysis of whether RTE should be considered to be a public or private body, but following the logic of *Meskell*, this privacy right would appear to be equally applicable to private sector media companies.

68 It should also be noted that the right of association in Article 40.6.1°iii, which has a similar wording to Article 40.1 and a similarly wide potential impact upon private bodies if given horizontal effect, was regarded without any real debate in *Meskell* as being capable of applying to private bodies.

69 See *In the matter of Article 26 of the Constitution of Ireland and in the Matter of the Employment Equality Bill* [1997] 2 IR 321, in particular Hamilton CJ's comments at 347.

cautionary tale about the inherent uncertainty of the Irish direct horizontal effect doctrine and its potential severe, unpredictable and far-ranging impact upon private conduct. The *Open Door* case involved relator proceedings brought by a very prominent anti-abortion pressure group, the Society for the Protection of the Unborn Child (SPUC), through the name of the Attorney General to prevent women's health clinics and advice centres from distributing information on how to obtain an abortion in the United Kingdom.[70] The Supreme Court held that the right to life of the unborn child, as recognised by Article 4.3.3° of the Irish Constitution,[71] required the courts to take effective steps to vindicate this right. It therefore granted an injunction restraining the defendants from disseminating the information in question. This was followed by a subsequent decision in *SPUC (Ireland) Ltd v Grogan (No. 1)*, which saw SPUC obtain injunctions restraining student unions in two of Dublin's leading universities from distributing similar information.[72]

These decisions have been extensively analysed in terms of their controversial preference for giving priority to the constitutionally recognised right to life of the unborn child over free speech rights, which was subsequently found to be incompatible with Article 10 of the ECHR.[73] Much less attention has been focused upon the fact that these decisions are based upon the application of the constitutional direct horizontal effect doctrine. The Supreme Court imposed constitutional norms directly to restrain the actions of the private health clinics, advice centres and student unions, despite the fact that the defendants had at no stage acted contrary to any specific common

---

70 See J. Casey, *The Irish Law Officers* (1996) pp 157–67. See also *SPUC (Ireland) Ltd v Coogan* [1989] IR 734, where the Society for the Protection of the Unborn Child were held to have the locus standi to bring legal proceedings seeking an injunction against the University College Dublin Students' Union, as they were a body with a bona fide interest in the subject matter at issue.

71 This was inserted into the Irish Constitution by a popular referendum in 1983, partially due to fears that an activist Supreme Court could at some future date follow the US Supreme Court decision in *Roe v Wade* 410 US 113 (1973) and recognise that a constitutional right to have an abortion could be inferred from the unenumerated right to personal privacy, which was recognised as a 'personal right' in *McGee v Attorney General* [1974] IR 284.

72 [1989] IR 753.

73 *Open Door Counselling Ltd v Ireland* (1993) 15 EHRR 244.

law or legislative rules. This was justified as necessary to ensure effective respect and protection for the right in question. However, it severely infringed the freedom of action and communication of the defendants, who prior to the granting of the injunction could not have known that they were necessarily acting contrary to Irish law.

There is a notable lack of analysis in both the *Open Door* and *Grogan* decisions as to the appropriateness of applying the right to life of the unborn child directly to the defendants, even though the constitutional provision in question, Article 40.3.3°, suffers from a lack of clarity in its wording and is explicitly directed towards the state. There is also little real consideration of how the competing rights in question should be balanced, given the non-public nature of the defendants. The fact that the plaintiff in these actions was another private body, and that the entire situation was characterised by a lack of legal clarity, also did not feature prominently in the Court's decisions. There was also no guidance given as to the limits of the obligations that could be imposed upon private persons in the name of securing respect for the right to life of the unborn child.

The extent to which personal autonomy could be restricted by the direct horizontal effect of this provision became apparent in the case of *Attorney General v X*.[74] This decision involved a 12-year-old girl who had been raped, become pregnant and decided to go to England to have an abortion. When her father contacted the Irish police to see whether a DNA sample from the foetus would be useful as evidence, the matter was brought to the notice of the Attorney General, who felt obliged to seek an injunction preventing the girl travelling to obtain an abortion. Costello J in the High Court granted an injunction, on the basis that this was necessary to vindicate the right to life of the unborn child in line with the Supreme Court decisions in *Open Door* and *Grogan*.

This decision caused huge controversy, as might be expected. The Supreme Court subsequently held by a four to one majority that, as the girl in question was threatening to commit suicide if she was forced to continue with the pregnancy, her right to life had to take priority and she had a right to obtain an abortion in the specific circumstances of the case. This resolved the immediate issue. However, once again, there was no analysis of the legitimacy of

---

74 [1992] 1 IR 17.

requiring an individual to conform to a constitutional norm, irrespective of the cost to that person's autonomy, or of the distinction between a public body and a private individual.

The *X* case can be seen as an example of direct horizontal effect gone out of control, with the constitutional norm being treated as all-encompassing and no differentiation made between the respective responsibilities, obligations and freedom of action of the private individual and the organs of the state. Subsequent constitutional amendments in the wake of *X* have guaranteed the right to receive information on abortion services in other countries and the right to travel, thus nullifying the immediate impact of the *Open Door*, *Grogan* and *X* decisions. However, these cases remain as precedents establishing that the right to life of the unborn child can have extensive and far-reaching direct horizontal effect.

Interesting issues remain unresolved as a consequence. For example, can a mother be prevented from acting in a particular way, such as smoking or drinking excessively, if it could impinge upon the right to life of her unborn child?[75] Could advocating the legalisation of abortion in the Republic of Ireland (as distinct from the (now) constitutionally permitted provision of information 'relating to services available in another state') be subject to legal sanction, on the basis that it would constitute an attempt to undermine respect for a constitutional right? In the aftermath of *Open Door* and *X*, the Supreme Court would in all likelihood be much more willing to distinguish between private and public bodies in delineating what Article 40.3.3° requires. However, real uncertainty persists.

Forde has argued perceptively that if the Supreme Court had adopted a vertical 'state action' approach to Article 40.3.3°, they would have 'saved a lot of trouble'.[76] Nevertheless, the right to life of the unborn child remains a constitutionally protected fundamental right at present, notwithstanding its intensely controversial status, and the Irish courts have been at least consistent in giving it a degree of horizontal effect. The problems that have arisen in the abortion context may be unique in certain respects. However, they also reflect

---

[75] The Canadian Supreme Court refused to extend existing tort law to provide for such an action in *Winnipeg Child and Family Services (Northwest Area) v G (DF)* (1998) DLR (4th) 193, on the basis that such an extension would exceed the permissible limits of the judicial role.

[76] Forde, op. cit., p 233.

wider difficulties with the lack of clarity and certainty in the current Irish approach to horizontal effect. In particular, they stem from the absence of any real analysis in the case law of how the distinctions that can exist between private and public bodies should be reflected in giving constitutional rights direct horizontal effect. A similar problem could be said to exist in some of the horizontal effect cases involving trade unions, such as *Doyle* and *Crowley*. While these decisions may be much less controversial than the abortion cases, they suffer from a lack of analysis as to whether a trade union should be treated differently from other bodies, in particular when it comes to issues of freedom of association.

G. The 'taming' of *Meskell*

A further problem exists with the current Irish approach to horizontal effect. Since the early 1990s, the Irish courts have showed greater caution in applying constitutional rights in the private sphere, where existing private law clearly regulates a matter within the scope of application of a constitutional right. Well-established private law rules, whether common law or legislative in origin, are presumed to be consistent with constitutional norms: only in exceptional circumstances will they be subject to constitutional scrutiny, and horizontal effect will only come into play where the existing private law is clearly and manifestly out of line with the Constitution.

This cautious approach reflects the gradual and cautious re-entrenchment of the Irish constitutional jurisprudence since the activism of the O'Dalaigh court and a concern to avoid judicial overstretch and excessive annexation of state power. It also could perhaps stem from the uncertainty of the *Meskell* doctrine, driven in particular by attempts to apply it in commercial contexts. In *Carna Foods Ltd v Eagle Star Insurance Co Ltd (Ireland) Ltd*,[77] McCracken J expressed concern as to the effect of imposing constitutional rights directly in the context of purely commercial relationships between private parties, describing it as a 'serious interference in the contractual position of parties in a commercial contract'.

The key decision is that of the Supreme Court in *Hanrahan v Merck Shape and Dohme*,[78] where the Court held that it would not

[77] [1995] 1 IR 526.
[78] [1988] ILRM 629 (SC).

in usual circumstances intervene to supplement the extent of protection given in common law to constitutional rights. In this case, the plaintiffs in the course of their nuisance action argued, inter alia, that the defendant had violated their constitutional rights to property and bodily integrity by polluting their land, and that the state's duty to vindicate these rights required the court to shift the onus of proof in relation to this matter to the defendants, as otherwise effective vindication of this right would be very difficult to secure in practice. The Supreme Court disagreed. It treated the existence of the tort of nuisance in Irish common law as implementing the state's duties under the Constitution to protect individuals against damage to the enjoyment of their property, but refused to supplement the existing scope and parameters of the tort. In other words, they refused to reshape the existing rules to give more effective protection to the plaintiff's constitutional rights in private law.

Henchy J expressed the rationale for this as follows:

> So far as I am aware, the constitutional provisions relied on have never been used in the courts to shape the form of any existing tort or to change the normal onus of proof. The implementation of those constitutional rights is primarily a matter for the State and the courts are entitled to intervene only when there has been a failure to implement or, where the implementation relied on is plainly inadequate, to effectuate the constitutional guarantee in question. In many torts – for example, negligence, defamation, trespass to person or property – a plaintiff may give evidence of what he claims to be a breach of a constitutional right, but he may fail in the action because of what is usually a matter of onus of proof or because of some other legal or technical defence. A person may of course in the absence of a common law or statutory cause of action, sue directly for breach of a constitutional right (see *Meskell v CIE*); but when he founds his action on an existing tort he is normally confined to the limitations of that tort. It might be different if it could be shown that the tort in question is basically ineffective to protect his constitutional right. But that is not alleged here.[79]

The position adopted by the Supreme Court in *Hanrahan* is therefore that the Irish courts will not develop the parameters of an existing tort or provide a supplemental remedy under their jurisdiction to uphold constitutional rights, unless the existing scope of the tort in question is 'basically ineffective' or 'plainly inadequate' to secure the protection of the constitutional rights at issue.[80] In other words,

79 Ibid, at 636.

80 See McMahon and Binchy, op. cit., para 1.19, pp 8–9.

the direct horizontal effect of constitutional rights would remain suspended and would not be used to alter or modify existing private law rules, except where it was obviously and unequivocally necessary to do so to vindicate these rights.

This approach was confirmed by Costello J in *W v Ireland (No. 2)*.[81] This case concerned an attempt to claim damages from the state by a victim of a confirmed paedophile, who claimed to have suffered psychiatric shock from the delayed extradition of the paedophile from the Republic of Ireland to Northern Ireland. This delay was alleged to have been caused by the negligence of the Attorney General. Costello J held initially that the Attorney General owed no duty of care in tort to the plaintiff in this context. He went on to dismiss the plaintiff's related claims for damages for violation of his constitutional right to bodily integrity. Costello J distinguished between two classes of constitutionally guaranteed rights: those that were regulated and protected by existing common law or legislation independently of constitutional jurisprudence, and those that were not. Where the alleged breach of a right fell into the second category, the Irish courts should give the Constitution direct effect by applying the constitutional tort remedy where appropriate. Where, on the other hand, the alleged breach fell into the first category, then the approach of the Supreme Court in *Hanrahan* was to be followed: in the absence of the manifest inadequacy of existing causes of action, no expansion or supplementing of the existing remedies was required.[82] In this case, Costello J held that existing tort law regulated where and how a plaintiff could claim for damages for negligence by public authorities. The plaintiff could not recover damages under this existing law, but no manifest deficiency existed in this law from a constitutional perspective, so no separate constitutional tort action could be sustained.[83]

---

[81] [1997] 2 IR 141 (HC).

[82] Costello J considered it unnecessary for a court to look beyond existing causes of action in such hypothetical cases as when a person was injured by an army lorry or in the case in point, in the absence of any such plain inadequacy. Ibid, at 142. See also N. Gaughran, 'Tort, Public Policy and the Protection of Constitutional Rights' (1998) 6 *Irish Law Times* 88.

[83] While *W* differed from *Hanrahan* in involving the state as a party, the applicability of constitutional rights to both public and private sector parties via the 'constitutional tort' action recognised in *Meskell* meant that the involvement of the state as a party in the litigation did not alter the impact of this judgment, which would apply as precedent in purely private actions as well.

The Supreme Court in *McDonnell v Ireland*[84] again reaffirmed the *Hanrahan* position. The Court found in this decision that the Statute of Limitations applied to a constitutional tort action in the same manner as to any other tort action: in the absence of any manifest deficiency in the existing law, the standard procedural rules and time-limits would apply even in respect of claims linked to the assertion of constitutional rights. Barrington J observed that:

> The general problem of resolving how constitutional rights are to be balanced against each other and reconciled with the exigencies of the common good is, in the first instance, a matter for the legislature. It is only when the legislature has failed in its constitutional duty to defend or vindicate a particular right ... that this Court ... will feel obliged to fashion its own remedy. If however a practical method of defending or vindicating the right already exists, at common law or by statute, there will be no need for this court to intervene ... constitutional rights should not be regarded as wild cards which can be played at any time to defeat all existing rules.[85]

This comment could be said to narrow even further the circumstances where the constitutional tort action can be applied, and thereby where direct horizontal effect will have an impact. Barrington J appears to suggest that the constitutional duty upon the state is not to guarantee respect for constitutional rights in the private sphere as well as in the public sphere, but just to enact a legal framework to enable these rights to be vindicated in general.[86] If the private law framework that is established is sufficient *in general* to uphold these rights, then there will be no space for a *Meskell*-style constitutional tort action. Costello J in *Hosford v John Murphy & Sons Ltd* appeared to take a similar approach.[87]

The approach adopted in *Hanrahan* and the subsequent cases of limiting the scope of application of the *Meskell* doctrine to cases where existing private law is 'plainly inadequate' in terms of upholding constitutional values could be seen as a solution to the lack of clarity and certainty that has bedevilled the development of direct horizontal effect in Irish constitutional law. Butler has praised the *Hanrahan* decision as a model example of a 'co-ordinate' approach,

---

84 [1998] 1 IR 134 (SC).

85 Ibid at 147–8.

86 McMahon and Binchy, *Law of Torts*, op. cit., paras 1.23–1.28, pp 10–11.

87 [1988] ILRM 300 (HC).

whereby the courts will give due respect to existing legislative or common law attempts to regulate the issues at hand, and thus avoid excessive judicial intervention.[88] It certainly helps to ensure a degree of clarity and order, where private law clearly regulates an issue. The existing private law norms will remain untouched, subject to a last resort 'override' if constitutional rights are not sufficiently respected: this arrangement therefore preserves the possibility of direct horizontal effect, where it is absolutely necessary to apply this doctrine.

However, the approach taken in *Hanrahan*, *W* and *McDonald* will not apply where private law does not sufficiently and fully 'control' a particular area. Many of the main horizontal effect decisions of the Irish courts cited above, in particular the key cases of *Meskell*, *Glover*, *Doyle* and *Open Door*, could be classified as situations where there was no clear legislative or common law set of norms governing the situation in question. Therefore, the *Hanrahan* approach does by no means provide clarity and certainty across all of private law, and, as argued by McMahon and Binchy, uncertainty persists as to when an existing private law remedy will be deemed to be 'plainly inadequate'.[89]

However, McMahon and Binchy also suggest that the impact of the approach adopted in *Hanrahan* could in practice effectively insulate large areas of Irish private law from the influence of constitutional norms. They suggest that if the general reasoning and approach of the Irish courts in *Hanrahan* and the subsequent decisions continue to be applied in cases where a private party alleges an infringement of his or her constitutional rights by another third party, then constitutional rights will only come into play in the private sphere where the existing private law framework clearly does not provide effective protection *in general* for a particular right (as opposed to providing effective protection and a suitable outcome in a particular case). Therefore, the *Meskell* constitutional tort action will not be usable except in circumstances where there is little or no existing private law regulation, or where the legislative or common law framework governing a particular area of private law is manifestly out of line with constitutional norms. Indeed, if

---

[88] See Butler, 'Constitutional Rights in Private Litigation: A Critique and Comparative Analysis', op. cit., note 3, pp 32–3.

[89] Ibid, para 1.20, p 9, paras 1.73–1.74, p 23.

Barrington J's approach in *McDonnell* is followed, the courts will only give effect to constitutional norms in private law action when the *legislature*, as distinct from the private parties involved, have failed in their 'constitutional duty' to uphold fundamental rights, a test which might be extremely difficult to satisfy. Outside of these unusual circumstances, the judgments in *McDonnell* seemed to suggest that constitutional norms had no role to play in private law adjudication: existing private law, in the absence of 'plain inadequacy' or legislative dereliction of duty, is to be considered to be entirely in conformity with the Constitution and immune from alteration.

McMahon and Binchy suggest that the impact of these decisions has been to 'tame' the *Meskell* doctrine of direct horizontal effect, and reduce it to a narrow and limited sphere of operation. They argue that:

> the judiciary ... has largely tamed the beast *Meskell* released by shackling it to the pre-existing tort law ... they have sought to mitigate its practical effects by looking to the pre-existing law as the medium through which the constitutional remedy should be challenged ... the conceptual difficulties relating to the principle are left unanswered ... whilst new difficulties arise ...[90]

For them, the 'idea that [the] corpus of common law is surrounded by a shroud through which the light of the Constitution can penetrate only in narrow shafts is difficult to understand'.[91] The approach adopted in *Hanrahan* and *McDonnell* sits uncomfortably with the existence of the *Meskell* constitutional tort, and may insulate private law from constitutional influences in a manner that seems out of step with the general thrust of Irish constitutional law, with its emphasis upon the overriding supremacy of constitutional norms and values.

McMahon and Binchy argue that a more appropriate approach would be to recognise a role for constitutional rights in shaping the interpretation and evolution of private law norms even in the absence of 'plain inadequacy'. In other words, in addition to the constitutional tort serving as a safety net, there is a need for the Irish courts to give constitutional rights some degree of effect via the gradual evolution and development of private law, in a manner analogous to how 'indirect horizontal effect' is applied in other jurisdictions.

However, whether due to the *Hanrahan* line of authority, or the caution exhibited by Irish courts since the high water mark of judicial

90 McMahon and Binchy, op. cit., para 1.60, p 20.
91 Paras 1.20, p 9.

activism in the 1960s and 1970s, or a perhaps excessive reverence for how the existing Irish private law framework has developed, the Irish courts have been reluctant to shape existing private law in line with constitutional principles where the constitutional tort has not been triggered. As a consequence, the Irish courts have in certain respects lagged behind the UK, Canadian, German and South African courts in ensuring that private law remedies evolve to reflect constitutional rights concerns.[92]

For example, existing Irish tort law has been set in amber, rather than being developed to reflect the fundamental rights guarantees that are supposed to underpin the Irish constitutional order.[93] In the specific context of defamation, the Advisory Group on Defamation noted that Irish defamation law was out of step with developments in other jurisdictions with a similar legal tradition, with the case law of the European Court of Human Rights and with constitutional values.[94] This to a considerable extent has been due to the reluctance of the Irish courts to give indirect effect to the constitutional guarantee of free speech in developing defamation law.[95] There has been little or no use of constitutional principles until recently

---

[92] See E. O'Dell, 'Does Defamation Value Free Expression? The Possible Influence of *New York Times v Sullivan* on Irish Law' (1990) 12 *Dublin University LJ* 50.

[93] This is not to suggest that the Supreme Court was necessarily wrong in the individual cases of *Hanrahan* and *McDonald* in refusing to modify the common law in the particular manner sought by the litigants in each case. A more appropriate response might, however, have been to leave open the possibility of constitutional rights playing a role in shaping the evolution of private law, even in the absence of 'plain inadequacy', while rejecting the necessity for altering existing law in these individual cases. The same applies to Costello J's decisions in *W* and *Hosford*.

[94] *Report of the Legal Advisory Group on Defamation* (Dublin: Department of Justice, Equality and Law Reform, 2003), para 11, p 7. See also the conclusions of the Law Reform Commission in 1991 that the existing law of defamation did not strike the appropriate balance between the constitutionally recognised rights of free speech and reputation: Law Reform Commission, *Report on the Civil Law of Defamation* (1991) Appendix A, 'The Constitution and the Law of Defamation' (1991).

[95] See W. Binchy, 'Some Unanswered Questions in Irish Defamation Law', in J. Sarkin and W. Binchy (eds), *Human Rights, the Citizen and the State* (2001), pp 243–63. See also M. Boyle and M. McGonagle, *A Report on Press Freedom and Libel* (1988), note 113; M. McDonald, *Irish Law of Defamation* (2nd edn, 1989); E. O'Dell, 'Does Defamation Value Free Expression? The Possible Influence of *New York Times v Sullivan* on Irish Law' (1990) 12 *DULJ* 50; S. Frazier, 'Liberty of Expression in Ireland and the Need for a Constitutional Law of Defamation' (1999) 32 *Vanderbilt Transnat JL* 391.

to re-shape the outmoded nineteenth-century structure of common law defamation. McMahon and Binchy have described the impact of the constitutional guarantee of free speech in this area as equivalent to a '*tabula rasa*'.[96]

The recent decision of the High Court in *Hunter v Blom-Cooper* may signal a new approach. In this case, the scope of the common law qualified privilege defence to defamation actions was expanded by O'Caoimh J, who referred both to the constitutional right to free speech and to English case law, itself the product of the UK courts being willing to give indirect horizontal effect to the ECHR.[97] However, in general, the Irish courts tend to adopt an approach based upon deference towards existing private law positions, which *Hanrahan* reinforces by apparently sealing off well-developed areas of private law from the influence and impact of constitutional norms. Giving direct horizontal effect to constitutional rights via the constitutional tort is increasingly treated as a 'nuclear option' in case of private law remedies being manifestly inadequate, or where private law does not regulate a particular factual circumstance. Outside of these situations, the horizontal effect of the Irish Constitution has tended to be muted, with the use of the constitutional tort being increasingly corralled within this narrow scope of application, and little sign of indirect horizontal effect being evidenced in the evolution of private law remedies.

H. Time to change? Lessons from the Irish experience of direct horizontal effect

What then are the lessons that can be extracted from the Irish experience of giving constitutional norms direct horizontal effect? Writing in 1992, Andrew Butler suggested that the experience of direct horizontal effect in Ireland had largely been an unqualified success. He suggested that the Irish jurisprudence had ensured the 'maximum protection of fundamental rights compatible with the minimum amount of interference with autonomy and institutional interests'.[98]

---

96 McMahon and Binchy, op. cit., para 34.08, p 882.

97 See *Hunter v Duckworth & Co Ltd and Blom-Cooper*, HC (unreported, 31 July 2003); see also M. Kealey, 'New Privilege for the Press to Report Without Fear', *The Irish Times*, August 2003.

98 Butler, 'Constitutional Rights in Private Litigation: A Critique and Comparative Analysis', op. cit., note 3, p 40.

In particular, he argued that by developing the constitutional tort action, the Irish case law had recognised the potential for third-party violation of fundamental rights and the power that private bodies such as companies and trade unions could exercise over individuals, while using the *Hanrahan* doctrine and locus standi rules to restrain this application of direct horizontal effect from going out of control.[99]

However, this paints too rosy a picture. There is a lack of clarity and certainty that afflicts the *Meskell* doctrine of direct horizontal effect and makes it difficult to define its parameters with any sort of precision. The abortion cases demonstrate that the application of the horizontal effect doctrine to private individuals has not been unproblematic. The *Hanrahan* doctrine does restrain uncontrolled application of constitutional rights in the private sphere to a degree, albeit at the price of generating uncertainties of its own and insulating much of private law from the influence of constitutional norms. In recent years, the application of direct horizontal effect in Irish constitutional law has tended to be slightly schizophrenic: strong judicial passivity in respect of existing private law rules has been combined with the occasional spasmodic use of the blunt instrument that is the constitutional tort. The profile and salience of the *Meskell* doctrine is also low: judges and lawyers are slow to apply the constitutional tort. It also has not been paralleled by the evolution of any complementary indirect approaches to developing private law remedies in line with constitutional norms. This can be contrasted unfavourably at times with the more fluid, norm-driven development of private law via indirect horizontal effect in other jurisdictions such as Germany and South Africa.[100]

McMahon and Binchy suggest that the *Meskell* doctrine 'has been less than successful ... No judge has gone so far as to declare the *Meskell* experiment over. Yet the product of over twenty years of judicial development of *Meskell* has been surprisingly modest'.[101] As

---

[99] As an example of the courts using locus standi rules in this area to control the application of direct horizontal effect doctrine, Butler cites the decision of O'Hanlon J in *Lennon v Ganly* [1981] ILRM 84 (HC) to the effect that the plaintiff did not have the standing to seek an injunction against the Irish Rugby Football Union sending a touring team to apartheid South Africa.

[100] See C. O'Cinneide, 'Taking Horizontal Effect Seriously: Private Law, Constitutional Rights and the European Convention on Human Rights [2003] 4 *Hibernian Law Journal* 77–108.

[101] Paras 1.81–1.82, p 25.

Catherine Donnelly has recently argued, the doctrine of direct horizontal effect also tends to encourage complacency about the lack of legal controls in public–private partnerships: as the constitutional tort is always lurking as a nominal safety-net, then the shrinking of the state is not seen as a matter of immense concern, notwithstanding the real problem with the constitutional tort as it currently stands.[102] With increased 'contracting-out',[103] this casual reliance upon the *Meskell* doctrine as a constitutional 'long-stop' may become more and more problematic. The lack of clarity that persists at the moment makes its application difficult to predict. In addition, the *Hanrahan* approach may discourage the courts from intervening where well-established private law regulatory regimes govern public–private agreements, notwithstanding the fact that these agreements may not be designed with fundamental rights in mind and, while not being so 'plainly inadequate' as to trigger direct effect, may be insufficiently adequate remedies to vindicate core constitutional entitlements.

In light of these difficulties afflicting the Irish doctrine of direct horizontal effect, is it then time to abandon this doctrine? As discussed previously, Forde argues for this step and advocates the adoption in its place of a US-style 'state action' doctrine, citing in support the 'near-universal adoption of a state action principle' in the constitutional law of various states.[104] However, much of comparative constitutional law is actually characterised by the adoption of indirect horizontal approaches: very few jurisdictions now adopt a purely vertical approach, and rarely achieve coherence when they do.[105] The adoption of a UK-style indirect horizontal effect is another potential option, as is German-style *Drittwirkung*. However, the *Meskell*

---

[102] C. Donnelly, 'Public Authorities, Private Bodies and the European Convention on Human Rights Act 2003', paper presented at the Society of legal Scholars (Ireland) conference, 17 February 2006, Trinity College Dublin.

[103] See, e.g., the partnerships contemplated by the following legislative instruments: the Prison Bill 2005 ss 2–7 (private prisoner escort services); State Authorities (Public Private Partnership Arrangements) Act 2002; Local Government Act 2001, s 128(2)(d). (All of these examples are listed in Donnelly, op. cit.).

[104] Forde, op. cit., p 234.

[105] See S. Gardbaum, 'The Horizontal Effect of Constitutional Rights' (2003) 102 *Michigan Law Review* 388–459; C. O'Cinneide, 'Taking Horizontal Effect Seriously: Private Law, Constitutional Rights and the European Convention on Human Rights [2003] 4 *Hibernian Law Journal* 77–108; M. Hunt, 'The "Horizontal Effect" of the Human Rights Act' [1998] *Public Law* 423; A. Clapham, 'The Privatisation of Human Rights' [1995] *EHRLR* 20–32.

doctrine is firmly embedded in Irish constitutional law. More importantly, the periodic difficulties in applying direct horizontal effect should not conceal the essential validity of the *Meskell* approach in the Irish constitutional context, or its potential to combat injustice and abuses of private power, which was the original underlying rationale for its introduction.

Private law is the product of an aggregation of different principles and rules shaped over a long period of historical and legal development, much of which predated the coming into force of the Irish Constitution and modern human rights values. As a result, private law was not intended or designed to achieve the task of vindicating fundamental rights: in addition, it tends to focus upon the conduct of the defendant, rather than on the entitlements of the plaintiff.[106] All of this means that existing private law norms may often be an inadequate tool to deliver sufficient protection for an individual's constitutional rights. Permitting constitutional norms to shape private law directly if necessary conforms to the concept of the Constitution as *lex superior*. It also reflects the prioritisation of constitutional rights norms, which from the inception of the new state has been central to the Irish constitutional imagination.

The potential for rights to be given direct horizontal effect also goes some way to ensuring that all of the legal rules of the Irish system fulfil the goal of being 'consistent in principle', which has been identified by Dworkin as a key ingredient of legal coherence, i.e. that they 'express a single and comprehensive vision of justice'.[107] It also avoids the trap of artificially creating separate private and public spheres. As Gerstenberg and Van der Walt have argued, all private law ultimately derives its legal force status from its recognition by the state:[108] private and public law are intertwined and inseparable, and coherence throughout an entire legal system is more likely to be achieved through some method of ensuring a common set

---

[106] See McMahon and Binchy, paras 1.70–1.71, p 23.

[107] See R. Dworkin, *Law's Empire* (1986), pp 134, 167, 184.

[108] See O. Gerstenberg, 'Private Law and the New European Constitutional Settlement' (2004) 10(6) *European Law Journal* 766–86, 771–4; see also J. Van der Walt, 'Progressive Indirect Horizontal Application of the Bill of Rights: Towards a Co-Operative Relation Between Common-Law and Constitutional Jurisprudence' (2001) 17 (3) *SAJHR* 341 at 347–8, where he comments 'one can never take the vertical relation or involvement of the state out of horizontal or private legal relations, be these relations founded upon statutory private law or common law private law'.

of values apply in both areas than by creating unsustainable barriers. Neither Forde's preferred vertical 'state action' nor even a German-style indirect *Drittwirkung* approach chimes fully with the structure, aspirations and current development of the Irish Constitution.[109] The rationale of the direct horizontal approach – its recognition that rights abuses can be caused by private actors, that the law should reflect a consistent vision of justice and that direct horizontal effect may be necessary to ensure this – is essentially sound and, in Dworkinian terminology, constitutes the 'best fit' with the values of the Irish constitutional order.[110]

However, the *methods* used by the Irish courts in giving rights direct horizontal effect are very questionable. The *Meskell* doctrine has suffered from a lack of coherent systemisation or sustained judicial exegesis. More importantly perhaps, it could be argued that a reassessment of how the doctrine is applied and its normative underpinnings is necessary. McMahon and Binchy have argued that the Irish adoption of a direct horizontal effect is partially rooted in the strong influence of natural law philosophy upon Irish constitutional

---

[109] It may be the case that the German approach does not in practice vary greatly in terms of end results from the Irish approach, especially if the *Meskell* doctrine is developed as suggested below in this paper. The differences between direct and indirect horizontal effect can be greatly exaggerated, especially if an obligation to achieve a result in total conformity with constitutional norms exists under both approaches: this tends to make the distinction purely a matter of tactics. However, as Gerstenberg argues (above, at note 108), the German doctrine makes a differentiation between the public and private spheres that may be logically difficult to sustain, and which is out of step with Irish constitutional approaches that tend to place much less emphasis upon the private/public distinction.

[110] The Constitutional Review Group recognised this in its review of the Constitution in 1996. While initially affirming that it was mainly an issue for the Oireachtas to determine the extent to which third parties should be obliged to respect an individual's rights, the Review Group did recognise that there were circumstances where it would be desirable to require third parties to respect constitutional rights even in the absence of legislative obligations to do so. It also noted in particular that attempts to constrain the scope of constitutional guarantees to the 'state' ran up against the difficulty of defining what exactly constituted the state. The Review Group did acknowledge the difficulties in defining what obligations should be imposed upon different private entities, and the potential for conflicts of rights. It also however accepted the difficulty in trying to make an a priori distinction between different situations: it therefore recommended that while no express obligation to respect fundamental rights should be imposed upon third parties, the courts should decide on a case-by-case basis when rights should be directly enforceable against third parties. See *Report of the Constitution Review Group* (1996), pp 266–7.

law, which was particularly pronounced in the jurisprudence of the 'activist' Supreme Court of the 1960s and 1970s.[111] Natural law theories regard rights as inhering in individuals by virtue of their basic humanity: the existence and authority of these rights claims are not dependent upon the activity of the State for their generation or establishment. The maintenance of a strongly distinct public/private distinction is not given a particularly significant status in natural law approaches, especially when compared to the overriding normative obligation to uphold the fundamental right in question.[112]

However, Irish constitutional jurisprudence is now abandoning its reliance upon natural law theory in favour of a new engagement with liberal democratic theory, along with a new emphasis upon maintaining the separation of powers and other traditional pillars of liberal constitutional architecture.[113] These liberal norms are founded upon the recognition and acceptance of the existence of social and political difference, and place greater priority upon liberal autonomy. In simple terms, they place priority upon achieving the 'right' rather than the 'good' and make more room for differentiation between institutions and actors than do natural law approaches, with their overriding emphasis upon giving effect to the 'good'.

This shift should be reflected in how the *Meskell* doctrine is applied by the Irish courts. There needs to be more analysis of the appropriateness of subjecting different public and private bodies to particular rights norms, and what these rights norms should require from these different and varying bodies. There also needs to be more emphasis on achieving clarity and precision in the application of constitutional norms: a complex society that recognises disagreement and differentiation needs to have more transparent and accessible norms than the *Meskell* doctrine provides at present. However,

111 B. McMahon and W. Binchy, *Law of Torts*, op. cit., para 1.77, p 24.

112 McMahon and Binchy also argue that Irish constitutional law has placed a heavy emphasis on the maintenance of an extensive sphere of judicial authority, especially when constitutional principles are at issue: the executive power has been made largely answerable to the courts across a wide range of its functions, and this subordination of executive power means that the Irish courts are less concerned with maintaining strict boundaries between state and non-state action. See McMahon and Binchy, op. cit., para 1.78, p 24.

113 See the very significant decision of *In re Article 26 and the Regulation of Information Bill* [1995] I IR 1.

none of this should require the jettisoning of *Meskell*, merely a revision of how constitutional norms are applied in the private sphere.

To implement this new approach, the Irish courts should be prepared to take a leaf out of the constitutional practice of the German and South African courts: the application of constitutional norms in the private sphere should in normal circumstances start from the existence of the relevant common law and statutory private law frameworks, and then develop that law to ensure that its application meets the requirements of the Constitution. Such an approach would 'piggyback' upon the greater certainty and precision of existing private law, utilising it as a stable and relatively clear framework, while modifying it as necessary to achieve the constitutionally appropriate result: this indirect approach would be similar to that utilised in South Africa and Germany, and increasingly in the United Kingdom.[114] A key ingredient of this approach would be an analysis of the scope and nature of the right at issue and the extent to which it is capable and appropriate to utilise it to alter the legal rights and obligations of individuals. Rights that are not suitable for being applied to private individuals or bodies within the relevant context should be deployed very cautiously, if used to modify existing private law. At the least, it is imperative that a court engages in an analysis of the content and scope of the right in question, and not gloss over the issue as occurred in *Open Door*.

In other words, an 'indirect' effect similar to that deployed by the German and South African courts should be the first port of call for the Irish courts in giving horizontal effect to constitutional rights. This may require a modification of the *Hanrahan* approach: existing private law should no longer be immune from modification except where it is 'manifestly inadequate'. Only if this approach cannot generate a satisfactory outcome should the constitutional tort action be deployed as the fallback weapon of last resort. However, this remedy should remain available as an ultimate remedy: the *Meskell* doctrine of direct horizontal effect remains sound constitutional law, but needs some development and more nuance in its application, and the development of complementary indirect horizontal effect approaches.

[114] See C. O'Cinneide, 'Taking Horizontal Effect Seriously: Private Law, Constitutional Rights and the European Convention on Human Rights', pp 77–108.

I. Incorporation of the ECHR

The necessity for the Irish courts to adopt this new and preferable approach to the horizontal effect of the Irish Constitution has not been rendered redundant by the incorporation of the ECHR into Irish law, which was achieved by the European Court of Human Rights Act 2003. Section 2 of the 2003 Act provides that when interpreting a 'rule of law', the courts must as far as possible do so in a manner compatible with the ECHR, with 'rule of law' defined in s 1 as including the common law. This interpretative obligation may require the Irish courts to adopt a broadly similar approach to that taken by the UK courts in interpreting the HRA, and this is reinforced by the incorporation of Article 13 (unlike the UK) with its obligation to provide effective remedies for the violation of Convention rights.

However, s 1 of the Act exempts courts from the 'organs of state' that are subject to a duty under s 3 to perform their functions in a manner compatible with the ECHR. This may ensure that unlike the provisions of s 6 of the Human Rights Act, the Irish courts will not be subject to an explicit duty to apply ECHR norms in their decision-making. As yet the Act has generated little case law and none on this particular issue.[115] The consequences of the absence of a duty on the courts to give effect to the Convention in how they perform their functions are therefore not yet clear. However, the presence of a duty upon the courts in the United Kingdom, South Africa and elsewhere to give horizontal effect to fundamental rights has been an important factor in ensuring that indirect effect is given to fundamental rights provisions. Such a duty can be particularly useful in encouraging courts that might otherwise be suspicious or uncertain about the introduction of 'new' rights norms into a national legal system to apply these new norms in private litigation. The absence of such a duty in the 2003 Act means that the superior legal norms of the Constitution will in all probability remain the

---

[115] Ibid. This paucity of case law reflects a widespread view that the Act is both flawed and adds little to existing constitutional rights protection. For the general limits of the Act, see D. Connell, 'The ECHR Act 2003: A Critical Perspective', in U. Kilkelly (ed), *ECHR and Irish Law* (2004) pp 1–11; R. Murphy, 'The Incorporation of the ECHR into Irish Domestic Law' (2001) 6 *European Human Rights Law Review* 640.

principal vehicle for injecting fundamental rights considerations into the development of private law: hence the need for a reinvigoration of the *Meskell* doctrine.

J. Conclusion

The development of the direct horizontal effect doctrine in Irish constitutional law was a groundbreaking and, by international standards, precocious recognition of the importance of protecting constitutional rights against violations of those rights by private bodies. Commentators such as Gardbaum and Butler who have advocated the Irish approach as the most appropriate method of ensuring protection for constitutional rights in the private sphere are not wrong in highlighting its attractions as legal doctrine. However, at present, its charms appear more enticing in the abstract and when viewed from afar then when they are examined up close.

The doctrine of direct horizontal effect has been inadequately developed, and insufficient attention has been paid to defining its scope and the extent to which particular rights are or should be applicable to private actors. It has also been 'tamed' and rendered partially toothless in relation to its potential impact upon private law, via the *Hanrahan* approach of limiting its scope to where existing private law is manifestly inadequate. Van der Walt has commented that there is an 'age-old tension between clear-cut rules and open-ended principles ... which is central to common law institutions', and that 'the drive towards closure ... always seems to gain the upper hand in the course of time'.[116] The taming of *Meskell* is a perfect example of this. New thinking is now needed to rejuvenate and reinvigorate the doctrine of direct horizontal effect in Irish constitutional law, to give it more nuance, clarity and subtlety, and to develop complementary 'indirect' approaches to developing existing private law norms.

---

116 Van der Walt, see note 108, supra, 360–2.

Chapter 8: Israel
Human Rights in Private Law – The Israeli Case

Daphne Barak-Erez and Israel Gilead***

A. Human rights in Israel: From an unwritten constitution to a written constitution

The protection of human rights in Israeli private law has to be understood in the context of the broader framework of Israeli constitutional law and it's unique history. When the State of Israel was established, the first elected Parliament (the Knesset) was expected to adopt a written Constitution for the new state. It soon became apparent that the required consensus could not be reached. The ideological rifts and gaps were unbridgeable. It was therefore decided that Israel's Constitution should be written in piecemeal manner, chapter by chapter. The enactment of these chapters, entitled 'Basic Laws', was deferred to future times. By the dawn of the 1990s, ten basic laws had been enacted. Yet, these dealt with the structure and powers of governmental institutions such as the Knesset, the government and the courts. None of these actually dealt with human rights and freedoms.

During this long period, the Israeli Supreme Court had recognised and enforced human rights on the basis of unwritten constitutional principles. This judicial recognition of human rights was not merely empty rhetoric, but rather an operative recognition in the sense that the Court enforced human rights when they were infringed by actions taken by government authorities. The main limitation of this form of judicial protection of human rights was its

---

* Stewart and Judy Colton, Professor, Faculty of Law, Tel-Aviv University.

** Bora Laskin Professor of Law, Faculty of Law, Hebrew University.
We thank Magi Otsri for her assistance.

loyalty to traditional views regarding legislative sovereignty, which means that it fell short of invalidating infringing legislation.[1]

A major step toward the creation of a formal constitutional bill of rights took place in 1992 with the enactment of two additional basic laws – Basic Law: Freedom of Occupation and Basic Law: Human Dignity and Liberty. These basic laws declare that their purpose is to safeguard the rights enumerated in them, 'in order to anchor in a Basic Law the values of the State of Israel as Jewish and Democratic state'. Basic Law: Freedom of Occupation deals with the relatively specific 'right to engage in any occupation, profession or trade',[2] whereas Basic Law: Human Dignity and Liberty protects several basic rights, including the right to life, bodily integrity and human dignity,[3] the right to property,[4] the right to personal liberty,[5] the right freely to enter and leave the country[6] and the right to privacy.[7] Notably, these two basic laws were soon interpreted by the Supreme Court as empowering the courts to carry out judicial review of primary legislation.[8] Unfortunately, however, the controversy as to whether these two basic laws do empower the courts to conduct judicial review of legislation, and the interpretation of these laws by the Supreme Court, stalled the enactment of the additional basic laws required to complete the bill of rights. It is now doubtful whether they will be enacted in the foreseeable future.

B. The traditional approach: the focus on human rights vis-à-vis the government

As in many other countries, the protection of human rights in Israel was traditionally perceived as aimed at limiting governmental power. The implicit assumption was that, as a rule, the protection of human rights is only relevant in the context of relationships between citizens and the government. This assumption was inspired by the liberal

---

1 See D. Barak-Erez, 'From an Unwritten to a Written Constitution: The Israeli Challenge in American Perspective' (1995) 26 *Colum Hum Rts L Rev* 309.

2 Section 3 of Basic Law: Freedom of Occupation.

3 Sections 2 and 4 of Basic Law: Human Dignity and Liberty.

4 Section 3 of Basic Law: Human Dignity and Liberty.

5 Section 5 of Basic Law: Human Dignity and Liberty.

6 Section 6 of Basic Law: Human Dignity and Liberty.

7 Section 7 of Basic Law: Human Dignity and Liberty.

8 C.A. 6821/93 *United Hamizrahi Bank Ltd v Migdal Kfar Shitufi*, 49(4) PD 221.

tradition, which feared government tyranny. For many years, this assumption was not even discussed but rather regarded as an uncontroversial baseline. This general assumption obscured the fact that at least some human rights have always been protected by private law.

Tort law has traditionally protected basic human rights. The Civil Wrong Ordinance [New Version],[9] Israel's core and major tort legislation, defines 'damage' as 'loss of life, or loss of, or detriment to, any property, comfort, bodily welfare, reputation or other similar loss or detriment'.[10] This definition is broad enough to include harms caused by violations of human rights, and these rights were indeed protected, to differing degrees, by traditional tort law. Such protection was provided both by the general torts of negligence[11] and breach of statutory duty,[12] which protect a wide variety of interests ranging from bodily integrity to 'pure' mental anguish, and by a variety of specific torts and liability arrangements within and outside the Ordinance. Bodily integrity, for example, has been protected by the general torts (negligence and breach of statutory duty), by specific torts such as assault and public nuisance,[13] and by special tort arrangements that impose absolute and strict liability with regard to road accidents and defective products.[14] Dignity has been protected, inter alia, by the Defamation (Prohibition) Law 1965, and privacy has been protected by the Protection of Privacy Law 1981. Property has been protected by the general torts and by a variety of specific torts such as trespass (land), conversion (goods) and passing off (commercial reputation).[15] In the context of contract law, the principle of 'public policy' has been used to invalidate contracts that infringe upon human rights in their private sphere aspects. Accordingly, the courts have, for example, invalidated broad limitations on future post-employment of workers, thus protecting their right to freedom of occupation.[16]

In general, however, although early case law recognised the relevance of human rights to some private law issues, they remained at the margins of private law. In the context of tort law, the theme

---

[9] Hereinafter 'Civil Wrongs Ordinance' or the 'Ordinance'.

[10] Section 2 of the Civil Wrongs Ordinance.

[11] Sections 35 and 36 of the Civil Wrongs Ordinance.

[12] Section 63 of the Civil Wrongs Ordinance.

[13] Sections 23 and 43 of the Civil Wrongs Ordinance.

[14] Road Accidents Victims Compensation Law 1975; Defective Products Liability Law 1980.

[15] Sections 29, 52 and 59 of the Civil Wrongs Ordinance.

[16] See C.A. 283/73 *Shar'abi v Chamzani*, 28(1) PD 85; C.A. 4/74 *Berman v 'Amal' Ltd*, 29(2) PD 718; C.A. 369/74 *'Tromasbast' Ltd v Zakai*, 30(1) PD 793;

of human rights was mainly discussed under defamation law with regard to the balancing process between free speech and the protection of reputation.[17] In the context of contract law, the case law showed utmost hesitation with regard to invalidating contract provisions for the sake of protecting freedom of occupation, and was therefore inclined to do so only in relatively extreme cases.

C. The gradual change toward the application of human rights in the private sphere

Although it is not possible to point at any concrete development that has triggered this change, the Israeli Supreme Court has gradually demonstrated a greater openness to the understanding that constitutional rights should be applied in the context of private law as well. This development may have been influenced by the fact that, since the 1980s, Israel has been undergoing a significant privatisation process which has shifted power from administrative authorities, governed by public law, to private entities, governed by private law. This increase in the power of some private actors emphasises the need for private law to counterbalance unequal power between the parties with the protection of human rights. This justification has not, however, been put forward as such by the courts.[18]

Obviously, and as we shall see, the enactment of the two basic laws on human rights in 1992 was a major factor in the 'constitutionalisation' of private law and had an important impact on the growing trend to apply human rights in the private sphere. It should be noted, however, that the tendency to apply human rights also in the sphere of private law was not based only on these basic laws. It is customary to regard the dictum of Justice Barak in the

---

C.A. 566/77 *Dicker v Moch*, 32(2) PD 141; C.A. 618/85 *'Ma'ayanot HaGalil HaMaravi' Ltd v 'Tavori' Ltd*, 40(4) PD 343.

[17] C.A. 723/74 *Ha'aretz v Israel Electricity Company Ltd*, 31(2) PD 281. The court also adopted a rule which severely restricts preliminary injunctions in defamation cases in order to avoid prior restraint, especially in public matters or regarding public figures. See: C.A. 214/89 *Avneri v Shapira*, 43(3) PD 840.

[18] The imbalance of power as the core justification for applying human rights in the private domain was stressed by Frances Raday. See: F. Raday 'Privatising Human Rights and the Abuse of Power' (2000) 13 *Canadian Journal of Law and Jurisprudence* 103. In fact, Raday criticises the application of human rights in the private sphere in a neutral manner which does not address the question of power.

Kastenbaum case[19] as an important turning point in the application of human rights to the private sphere. In this matter, which related to the relevance of human rights principles for invalidating contracts under the public policy principle, Barak stated in a general manner that human rights also apply to relationships between private parties, without basing his view specifically on the basic laws.[20] Moreover, this decision addressed litigation which had started before the new basic laws were enacted.

D. Direct and indirect applications of human rights

A preliminary question to be addressed is whether the application of human rights in the private sphere derives from a *direct* application of the 1992 basic laws to all relevant parties, or only from the *indirect* influence of the basic laws and the culture of human rights on the interpretation of open-textured legal notions and on the balancing process within private law doctrines.

This question arises because the basic laws do not address the question of their application to private actors. They only declare their application to government authorities.[21] On the one hand, this express application to government authorities could have been interpreted as excluding the possibility of application in the private sphere. On the other hand, it is possible to argue that the basic laws do not address this matter at all, but rather only emphasise the duty of government authorities to abide by the human rights protected by the basic laws.

The common view is that the jurisprudential approach which serves as the basis for the application of human rights in Israeli private law is the model of indirect application. According to this model, the 1992 basic laws do not apply to private parties, but rather serve as a source of inspiration for the interpretation of open-textured terms in private law legislation, such as 'public policy', 'unlawfulness' and 'good faith', and affect the balancing between rights and

---

[19] H.C.J 294/91 *Hevra Kadisha 'Jerusalem Community' v Kastenbaum*, 46(2) PD 464.

[20] According to Barak: 'Human rights are not directed only against the authorities. They spread also in the relationships between individuals.' op. cit., p 530.

[21] In their so-called application clauses – s 5 of Basic Law: Freedom of Occupation and s 11 of Basic Law: Human Dignity and Liberty.

interests conducted within them.[22] Yet, as we shall see, there are some judicial statements that do leave the door open for a direct application of the basic laws in some cases.

There are several reasons to prefer the indirect application model of the basic laws in the private sphere. First, formally speaking, the basic laws state that government authorities should respect the specified rights but they make no reference to their application in the private sphere. Second, on the substantive level, the balancing of human rights against collective interests in the public sphere is significantly different from the balancing conducted in the private sphere, where one human right is often balanced against another human right. Thirdly, as mentioned, the project of basic laws is not yet completed and therefore important human rights are still not protected by basic laws, at least explicitly. Obviously, affording enhanced direct protection only to some human rights but not to others is most problematic. At present, the basic laws do not mention several rights, including the rights to freedom of speech (and freedom of association), to freedom of religion and conscience and to equality. Indeed, the Israeli Supreme Court has tried to cope with this partiality by interpreting the basic laws in a broad manner, stating, for example, that freedom of speech and equality are derivatives of human dignity,[23] but this mode of interpretation has its limits as well.

Against this background, the following sections will review and analyse the main developments regarding the application of human rights in Israeli private law, concentrating on two major branches of it – contract law and tort law.

E. Human rights in contract law

Israeli law recognises the relevance of human rights for contract law in both the contractual and the pre-contractual phases. Nevertheless, it seems that the Israeli Supreme Court is still more

---

[22] A. Barak, 'Constitutional Human Rights and Private Law' in D. Friedmann and D. Barak-Erez (eds) *Human Rights in Private Law* (2001) pp 13, 29.

[23] This broad interpretation was suggested by Aharon Barak CJ and has gradually gained support. The argument that the right to equality should be inferred from the right to human dignity was recently accepted as the view of the Supreme Court in H.C.J. 6427/02 *The Movement for Quality Government in Israel v The Knesset* (11.5.06) and H.C.J. 7052/03 *Adalah – The Legal Center for Arab Minority Rights v Minister of Interior* (to be published, 14.5.06).

inclined to invalidate provisions which consist of significant infringements of human rights in the contractual stage than to enforce contracts on those who refused to enter into them for discriminatory reasons. With regard to the legal mechanism for introducing human rights to the contractual arena, the case law uses the indirect application model. This approach is sometimes complemented by specific legislation, which directly applies some human rights norms to the parties to the relationships regulated by that legislation.

I. Contractual limitations on freedom of occupation

As already noted, even early case law recognised the possibility of invalidating contract provisions which imposed significant limitations on freedom of occupation. Since the 1990s, however, the courts have demonstrated a determined application of this principle. This change was originally initiated by the Israeli National Labor Court, and later also adopted by the Israeli Supreme Court.

In the *Frumer* case,[24] the National Labor Court ruled in favor of the appellant, a software engineer who signed a contract with his previous employer which limited his right to work for a competing company for a period of 22 months. Whereas in the past the courts were willing to accept limiting clauses which did not exceed several years, the National Labor Court invalidated this provision. According to the Court, the restrictions on the appellant's freedom of occupation were unreasonable, especially since there was no risk of disclosure of trade secrets.[25] The Supreme Court has continued and strengthened this new direction of legal reasoning in the *AES* case,[26] which also dealt with a provision limiting future employment of computer personnel. The Court explained that the basic

---

[24] L.A. 164/99 *Frumer & Check-Point v Redguard Ltd*, 34 LPD 294.

[25] The National Labour Court based its reasoning on several factors: the values of the new basic laws, the inherent inequality between employers and employees, the importance of freedom of occupation not only for subsistence but also for self-fulfilment, the contribution of competition on workers for the market and the value of the flow of information in the market. Therefore, it would be possible to restrict freedom of occupation for the sake of protecting trade secrets or due to special training afforded to the employee but not otherwise. In addition, the court emphasised the importance afforded to the issue of compensation for provisions restricting freedom of occupation and the issue of good faith of both the employer and employee.

[26] C.A. 6601/96 *AES System Ltd v Sa'ar*, 54(3) PD 850.

laws set a system of values that also serve as a framework for the development of private law, and that the aspiration to block effective commercial competition is not a legitimate interest which the law should be willing to protect.[27]

2. Contractual limitations that offend human dignity

The *Kastenbaum* case, already mentioned,[28] serves as an example for invalidating a contractual provision perceived as infringing on human dignity. The case dealt with a standard contract used by a burial association which allowed only the use of Hebrew letters and Hebrew dates for inscriptions on gravestones. Family members of a deceased who signed this contract wanted to resist this mandate and argued against its enforcement on them. The majority opinion written by Justice Barak invalidated this provision, which was understood as infringing the human dignity of the family members of the deceased and limiting their autonomy and their freedom of expression.

3. Contractual limitations on the freedom to organise

Another development led by the National Labor Court was the willingness to enforce employment contracts on employers who had fired workers because of their trade union activities. A decision to lay off in such circumstances infringes on the workers' right to organise, and the effective answer to such an infringement is to invalidate the lay off decision and accordingly to enforce the employment contract (as an exception to the general principle against enforcement of contracts for personal services). The enforcement of employment contracts in such circumstances was first introduced by the National Labor Court in the *Yaniv* case,[29] which dealt with a decision to dismiss workers due to their activities as workers' representatives. In a similar manner, in the *Horn* case,[30] the National Labor Court ruled in favour of workers who were dismissed after a strike. The court based its ruling on the constitutional right to organise and on the principle of equality. According to the court,

---

27 Ibid, at p 873.

28 See the text accompanying notes 19–20, supra.

29 L.C. 3-209/96 *Tahanot Factories Ltd v Yaniv*, 33 LPD 289.

30 L.C. 1008/00 *Horn and Leibovitz Ltd v New Labour Union*, 35 LPD 145.

the right to strike is one of the only means of pressure that workers can exert on their employers in a labor dispute. The court expressed its concern that a ruling against the workers may have severe consequences on the rights of current and future workers. Later on, the same norm of enforcing an employment contract following a decision to lay off which offends the right to organise was also adopted by specific legislation.[31]

4. Contractual limitations on access to justice

Contracts which include provisions limiting the possibility to bring a law suit infringe upon the right to free access to the courts, and the court may therefore invalidate them, or at least refrain from enforcing them.

The *Levin* case[32] dealt with an alimony contract signed between spouses during the course of their separation. According to the wording of this contract, it was not to be used for any purpose, including for the purpose of presenting it before a court of law. Justice Zamir ruled that free access to the court is a fundamental right. Therefore, a contract should be interpreted in accordance with the presumption that the parties did not intend to limit this right. When such an interpretation is not possible, a provision of this kind may be invalidated as infringing public policy. In the circumstances of the case, Zamir eventually preferred the non-enforcement option over the invalidation option. As a result, for practical purposes, the provision which professed to limit the use of the contract for purposes of litigation was not given any effect. In a number of other cases, the Supreme Court adhered to interpretive choices which left room for access to court over other interpretive choices which denied it.[33]

5. Contractual discrimination in collective bargaining

The Supreme Court used the principle of equality to invalidate collective agreements tainted with group discrimination on several occasions. The Court considers this form of intervention to

---

[31] Collective Agreements (Amendment 5) Law 2001.

[32] C.A. 3833/93 *Levin v Levin*, 48(2) PD 862.

[33] C.A. 3369/98 *The Israel Land Administration v Rosenthal*, 55(4) PD 52; C.A. 7608/99 *Locki-Project Execution (Construction) 1989 Inc v Mitspe Kineret 1995 Inc*, 56(5) PD 156.

be relatively lighter because the weight attached to the personal autonomy of the parties to the contractual relations is diminished in the context of collective bargaining.

Several cases in this context have dealt with discrimination against female employees.[34] In addition, the same principle was applied to discrimination on the basis of sexual orientation[35] and age.[36] In the vast majority of the circumstances discussed in these cases, the same result can be reached now also under express legislation on employment.[37] Still, it is important to note the willingness of the Israeli Supreme Court to apply equality in these contexts even outside the contours of specific legislation.

6. *Discrimination in the pre-contractual stage*

A greater challenge to the traditional concepts of contract law was the use of equality in the pre-contractual stage for the purpose of enforcing a contract against a party who refused to enter it for discriminatory reasons.

This dilemma was first raised in the *Beit Yules* case[38] in the context of a private tender. More specifically, the question was whether a private actor who conducts a tender has to treat all bidders in an equal manner. Since equality as such is not a principle of contract law, the question was whether the duty to act in good faith also mandates the equal treatment of the bidders. The majority opinion answered this question in the negative, resting on traditional concepts of contractual autonomy. In contrast, the minority justices thought that although the principle of equality does not apply in the context of a private tender (or in other private law contexts) the duty to treat bidders equally was implied in the circumstances of the case by the private law principle of good faith which applies to the pre-contractual stage. Formally speaking, the majority opinion has set the precedent in this matter. Nevertheless, the minority opinion is no less important. First, it was handed down by two of the

34 See H.C.J 104/87 *Nevo v The National Labor Court*, 44(4) PD 749; H.C.J 6845/00 *Niv v The National Labor Court*, 56(6) PD 663. These two cases dealt with discrimination against women regarding retirement age.

35 H.C.J 721/94 *El-Al Israel Airlines Ltd v Danielowitz*, 48(3) PD 749.

36 F.H. 4773, 4191/97 *Rekanat v The National Labor Court*, 54(5) PD 337.

37 Mainly Equal Opportunities in Employment Law 1988, as amended.

38 F.H. 22/82 *Beit Yules v Raviv*, 43(1) PD 441.

most influential justices of the Israeli Supreme Court – Chief Justice Shamgar and Justice Barak, his predecessor as the Chief Justice of the Court. Second, the decision was given in the early 1980s, when the application of human rights in Israeli private law was still in its early stages, before the enactment of the new basic laws. Third, it is important to note that the case addressed simple economic discrimination which did not involve forbidden forms of group discrimination. It is possible that a different result may be reached with regard to constitutionally forbidden group discrimination.

Later decisions given by lower courts have indeed proved that Israeli law is inclined toward intervening in pre-contractual discrimination when group discrimination is involved. The legal principles behind these rulings are not always clear, but the firm conviction that such discrimination should not be permitted is clear enough. One influential decision given by a Jerusalem Magistrate Court is the *Na'amne* case.[39] This decision dealt with an incidence of discrimination against Israeli Arabs who were not admitted to a private water resort. The court ruled that the advertising of the park constituted an offer to the public, and that a rescission of such an offer is impossible vis-à-vis those who already relied on it and came to the park, or at least should be considered as conducted in bad faith. Alternatively, the decision also offered a tort-based argumentation – an infringement of statutory duty with reference to the duties implied by Basic Law: Human Dignity and Liberty (which was assumed to apply also to private actors).[40]

A similar decision was given in the *Shamsian* case,[41] which dealt with a refusal to allow the entrance of a woman with a walking disability to a bar where a singles party was being held. The Tel-Aviv Magistrate Court was willing to accept the lawsuit based on a similar legal argumentation, referring to the impossibility to rescind an offer made to the general public once it has already been relied upon.

The *Na'amne* and the *Shamsian* cases reflect the openness of the courts to apply human rights principles in the context of private law. At the same time, these cases reveal the shortcomings of the traditional doctrines in the pursuit of effective protection of human

---

39 C.F. (Jerusalem) 11258/93 *Na'amne v The Kibutz Kalia Water Park* (unpublished, 24.9.96).

40 This alternative argumentation is dealt with below.

41 C.F. (Tel-Aviv) 15/97 *Shamsian v Ganey Rosemari Restaurant* (unpublished, 12.1.99).

rights in the pre-contractual stage. In both cases, the legal reasoning relied heavily on the fact that the defendants had advertised an offer to the public. This reasoning falls short of providing a solution for cases of pre-contractual discrimination when the relevant business was open and clear about its discriminatory policy. For dealing with such cases, specific legislation would be necessary, as will be explained below.

7. *Specific human rights legislation on discrimination*

In addition to the general judicial willingness to apply human rights through open-textured terminology in private law statutes, in the form of indirect application, another route for action has been legislation to promote human rights in specified areas. This method of specific legislation was used at a relatively early stage in the area of employment law.[42] Another major development was achieved through the Prohibition of Discrimination in Products, Services and Entry to Places of Entertainment and Public Places Law 2000.[43] Section 3(a) of this law prohibits people whose trade is in the supply of products or services, or in managing a place to which the public has right of access from discriminating on the basis of race, religion, nationality, land of origin, sex, sexual orientation, views, political views, personal status, parenthood or disability.[44] The significant advantage of this law is that it addresses the relatively neglected pre-contractual stage. In addition, such legislation deals with the direct application of certain rights (mostly, the right to equality) to the relationships regulated by it. The shortcoming of the Prohibition of Discrimination in Public Places Law from the perspective of contract law is that it defines prohibited discrimination as a tort, and does not provide for the enforcement of the refused contract.

F. Human rights in tort law

The relevance of human rights to tort law is even more obvious, considering the pre-existing protection of human rights by traditional

42 See supra note 37.

43 Hereinafter 'Prohibition of Discrimination in Public Places Law'.

44 Unfortunately, this law does not mention discrimination on the basis of 'age'.

tort law.[45] Not only has tort law protected human rights, it has been well equipped to extend this protection in various ways: through the open-ended concepts of 'carelessness' and 'duty of care' in negligence; by admitting more enacted duties into the general framework of breach of statutory duty; and through a human-rights-inclined interpretation of specific torts and liability arrangements. In addition, extended protection could be provided by the enactment of new torts that directly protect human rights.

Against this background, the questions are: first, in what ways have the new basic laws contributed to the protection of individuals against damage caused by violation of human rights and what has been their effect on tort law in this regard; and, second, what are the main developments in the scope of the protection that tort law, now inspired by the basic laws, provides to human rights.

As in the context of contract law, the approach adopted by the Israeli Supreme Court regarding the impact of the new basic laws on tort law has generally followed the indirect application model. A direct application model means that claims for damage caused by an infringement of any right recognised by the basic laws could be based directly on the basic laws, and be brought either in conjunction with a 'traditional' tort claim,[46] or as a sole and independent claim. For example, a person whose property has been damaged, may, according to this approach, sue on both counts: a traditional tort claim for trespass[47] or negligence, and a constitutional claim for infringement of the protected right to property.[48] Similarly, a person whose reputation has been damaged may sue for defamation under traditional tort law and, in addition, for violation of the constitutional right to dignity.

The Israeli Supreme Court has been reluctant to adopt this 'direct application' approach, and for good reasons. Such an approach, if taken, would have necessarily led to the creation of a judge-made law of torts, 'constitutional law of torts' alongside the existing, legislated tort law. Undoubtedly, the creation of a distinct constitutional

---

[45] See the text accompanying notes 9–15, supra.

[46] In principle, Israeli law allows for different causes of action to concur. See: F.H. 20/82 *Address Building Materials v Harlow & Jones*, 42(1) PD 221; C.A. 5768/94 *Ashir Import Production and Distribution v Forum Avizarim and Consumption Products*, 52(4) PD 289.

[47] Sections 29 and 31 of the Civil Wrongs Ordinance.

[48] Section 3 of Basic Law: Human Dignity and Liberty.

law of torts, originating directly in the basic laws, is problematic. The basic laws refer to the protected rights only in a very general manner, stating, for example, that 'the dignity of any person shall not be violated'. They do not specify the extent of the protection and the concrete factual and mental elements required to establish liability. It would therefore be a most demanding task for courts to attribute concrete meanings to such general formulas, especially if this involves the development of a new set of underlying doctrines, such as causation, vicarious liability, multiplicity of liabilities rules of remedies and defences. Moreover, the development of such a new law of compensation may well create numerous problems of overlap and conflict between the new and the old law of torts, and therefore erode and undermine the latter, for example, by circumventing existing limits on the scope of liability.

Another reason to prefer the indirect application of the basic laws is the balance ingrained in tort law between individuals' rights on the one hand and social values and interests on the other hand. The indirect application of human rights through tort law would therefore be a better guarantee that the weights attached to collective values and interests are not too small. A prominent example in this regard is the liability of public authorities. This liability may have negative side-effects such as over-deterrence ('defensive frame of mind' of public officials), flood of suits (the 'floodgate' argument) and 'second-guessing' by the judiciary of administrative decisions which disturbs the separation of powers.[49]

The reluctance of the Israeli Supreme Court to embark upon developing an independent constitutional law of torts is exemplified by the *Da'aka* case.[50] This decision dealt with the question of liability for the failure to provide a patient with adequate information concerning a treatment, where it was established that the patient would have agreed to the treatment even if the information had been provided. It was held that the claimant is entitled to compensation because she was deprived of the right to decide for herself,

---

[49] See, e.g., C.A. 915/91 *State of Israel v Levi*, 48(3) PD 45, where liability of governmental authority for the exercise of a 'broad discretion' that harmed the claimant was severely restricted due to these 'pragmatic' considerations. It should be noted, however, that recent decisions tend to expand the liability of public authorities. See, e.g., C.A. 2906/01 *Municipality of Haifa v 'Menorah' Insurance Company Ltd* (to be published, 25.5.06).

[50] See C.A. 2781/93 *Da'aka v 'Carmel' Hospital*, 53(4) PD 526.

on the basis of the relevant information, whether to undergo medical treatment. Although the damage originated in violation of the claimant's right to dignity and autonomy, the justices were reluctant to base their decision only on Basic Law: Human Dignity and Liberty. One justice commented that developing a constitutional law of compensation is a complex task that raises as yet unanswered questions concerning the protected rights, their scope and the available remedies. At this stage, it was argued, it would be better for the courts to adhere to tort law, the law of negligence in this case, as inspired also by the value of autonomy. Another justice commented that it was unclear whether under constitutional tort law the criteria applied to the assessment of damage would differ from the criteria of ordinary tort law in this matter. Eventually, the majority opinion of the court did impose liability in this case, but it did so by developing the tort of negligence, as inspired by the value of autonomy protected by Basic Law: Human Dignity and Liberty, thus following the indirect application model.

It should be noted, however, that although the direct application of the basic laws on private actors is generally excluded, it may nevertheless be recognised, in exceptional circumstances, as a *residual* basis for liability. In the 2004 *Tenenbaum* case,[51] the question was whether the relatives of a person abducted by a terror organisation are entitled to an injunction prohibiting publication of information that may endanger his life. It was stated that in principle (but not in this case) they do, namely, that Basic Law: Human Dignity and Liberty does directly provide for such a right to an injunction between private persons, when the injunction is required to protect life and bodily integrity, and provided that this remedy is unattainable under another field of law. This form of direct application has been based on the well-recognised principle of *ubi ius ibi remedium* (where there is a right there is a remedy).

I. The indirect application of the basic laws and its effect on the balancing process of tort law

Given the judicial tendency not to apply the new basic laws directly in the private sphere, what does the alternative of 'indirect application'

---

[51] C.A. 9185/03 *Tenenbaum v Ha'aretez Newspaper*, 58(1) PD 359, 365–6.

mean in the context of tort law? The answer focuses on the effect the constitutionalisation of human rights has had on the balancing process that lies at the core of tort law. In deciding whether liability should be imposed on an activity that causes damage, the courts have to balance the rights and interests of the actors against those of the persons who suffer the damage, as well as the rights and the interests of affected third parties and the interests and the values of society at large. This balancing process requires that weights be attached to each interest, right or value. When given rights are constitutionalised, they gain greater weight in the course of this process. As a result, they may receive greater protection in the framework of tort law in comparison to their protection in the past and even gain protection that was not afforded at all before. This is, in a nutshell, the main effect of the indirect application of human rights on tort law. The constitutionalisation of the right to dignity, for example, has increased the relative weight attached to this right in the balancing process and, as a result, different aspects of this right, such as autonomy, have gained stronger and even novel forms of protection. The impact on this balancing process is most significant in the area of negligence law where such balancing determines whether a given activity is negligent and whether a duty of care should be recognised.

Two comments are important in this regard. First, the greater weight attached to the constitutionalised rights reinforces their protection by tort law in both the private sphere (vis-à-vis private actors) and the public sphere (vis-à-vis public authorities). The constitutionalisation of dignity, for example, had influenced also the decision to impose liability on the police for failure to protect the claimant's dignity from being infringed by criminal offenders.[52] Second, the outcomes of the balancing process may remain unchanged despite the constitutionalisation of the rights relevant to this balancing. Generally speaking, this would be the case where the rights of the two parties to the dispute are constitutionalised. For example, the prevailing view is that both freedom of speech and the right to good reputation are derivatives of the right to dignity. Therefore, the balancing of the two against each other in the framework of defamation law was not affected by the enactment of Basic Law: Human Dignity and Liberty.[53]

---

52 C.A. 1678/01 *State of Israel v Weiss*, 55(5) PD 167.

53 See F(6) infra.

2. *The protection of dignity by specific tort legislation (sexual harassment and unlawful discrimination)*

Basic Law: Human Dignity and Liberty has highlighted the importance that society attaches to the value of human dignity. This has undoubtedly contributed to the enactment, a few years later, of two laws that protect important aspects of human dignity in the private sphere.

The Prevention of Sexual Harassment Law 1998[54] establishes a new tort action for sexual harassment. The law states that no person shall sexually harass another and imposes tort liability (as well as criminal liability) for such behaviour.[55] Sexual harassment, as defined, includes, in addition to the already existing criminal offences of sexual blackmail and indecent acts, repeated propositions of a sexual nature directed towards a person who has indicated to the harasser that he or she is uninterested in the stated propositions; repeated references directed towards a person, focused on his or her sexuality, where that person has indicated that he or she is uninterested in the said references; and intimidating or humiliating references directed towards a person with respect to his or her sex or sexuality, including his or her sexual orientation. The law empowers courts to award compensation for sexual harassment up to a given ceiling even without proof of damage.

The Prohibition of Discrimination in Public Places Law has already been mentioned with regard to discrimination in contract making.[56] It provides that where people whose trade is in the supply of products or services, or in managing a public place, discriminate on the basis of race, religion, nationality, land of origin, sex, sexual orientation, views, political views, personal status, parenthood or disability, this discrimination is an actionable tort. Here too compensation may be awarded up to the statutory ceiling without proof of damage.[57]

Interestingly, and in accordance with the preceding analysis, the two laws stress that their aim is not just to protect the rights of the individual (dignity, liberty, privacy, non discrimination) but also to promote equality in society and between the genders, that is, to promote social values as well.

---

54 Hereinafter 'Prevention of Sexual Harassment Law'.

55 Sections 3, 4 and 6 of the Prevention of Sexual Harassment Law.

56 See the text accompanying notes 43–44, supra.

57 Section 5 of Prohibition of Discrimination in Public Places Law.

3. *Protection of human rights by rights – promoting legislation through the tort of breach of statutory duty*

A question which has not yet been fully answered is the extent to which liability for infringements of enacted duties that protect human rights can be imposed through the general tort of breach of statutory duty.

The tort of breach of statutory duty consists of a failure to perform a duty imposed by any enactment other than the Civil Wrongs Ordinance itself, provided that it was intended for the benefit or protection of the person who suffered damage, and that the damage was of the kind or nature contemplated by the enactment. If such a failure harms the claimant then he is entitled to the remedies provided by the Civil Wrongs Ordinance, unless the intention of the enactment was to exclude such a remedy.[58]

May the basic laws themselves serve a basis for liability through this general tort? In the *Na'amne* case it was argued that they may.[59] In this case, let us recall, the magistrate court imposed contractual liability on owners of a water resort who did not allow the admission of Israeli Arabs, but stated further that tort liability is also generated in the circumstances of the case through the tort of breach of statutory duty. The statutory duty referred to was the duty not to discriminate, inferred from the right to dignity. Although the outcome of the *Na'amne* case is desirable, this statement should be further studied.[60] To start with, on the jurisprudential level, it is far from clear whether the basic laws, being superior to ordinary statutes, may be considered regular 'statutory' duties for the purposes of the tort of breach of statutory duty. Second, since the basic laws define the protected rights in a very general manner, without specifying the extent of their protection and the concrete factual and mental elements required to establish liability, courts will have to fill these gaps by creating an independent body of judicial constitutional tort law, that may either overlap or conflict with traditional tort law, thus raising similar questions to those posed by the possibility of a direct application of the basic laws to private parties. In fact, the very general nature of the constitutional duties

[58] Section 63 of the Civil Wrongs Ordinance.

[59] See supra notes 39–40.

[60] Since the *Na'amne* decision was given by a magistrate court, it is not a precedent.

inferred from the basic laws may prevent the application of this tort to them in the first place. There are judicial statements that enacted duties can serve a basis for the tort of breach of statutory duty only if they are sufficiently concrete and detailed.[61]

In contrast, concrete statutory duties to respect human rights may well generate tort liability through the tort of breach of statutory duty and enhance their protection. A prominent example is the enacted duty of a husband not to divorce his wife without her consent. It was held that a unilateral act of divorce constitutes the tort of breach of statutory duty and that the offended wife is entitled to compensation.[62] Another example, discussed below, is the duty under the Patient's Rights Law 1996[63] to provide information before medical treatment.

4. *Removing the barriers regarding compensation for 'pure' losses in negligence law*

The ability of traditional tort law to effectively protect the wide spectrum of human rights otherwise than by special legislation was limited also by 'exclusionary' rules that denied or severely restricted liability under the tort of negligence for 'pure' losses – pecuniary and non-pecuniary. 'Pure' losses are losses that are neither physical losses nor losses consequential on physical damage to the claimant's body or property. As violation of human rights often involves such 'pure' losses, especially 'pure' non-pecuniary harms to one's dignity or autonomy, tort liability for such violations was basically restricted to those 'pure' losses that were protected by specific torts and liability arrangements such as false imprisonment, malicious prosecution, defamation, private nuisance and deceit. The major source of tort liability – the law of negligence – could not be used. Over the years, however, these barriers have been gradually removed. Recovery for a pure economic loss under negligence has become available in the 1950s in a case of negligent misrepresentation and its scope has grown ever since. Recovery for a pure non-pecuniary loss became available in the early 1980s, in a case of negligent prosecution and imprisonment,[64] and has been extended

---

61 *Levi* case, supra note 49, at 90; C.A. 5379/95 *Sahar Insurance Co v Israel Discount Bank*, 54 (4) PD 464.

62 C.A. 245/81 *Sultan v Sultan* (1984) 38(3) PD 169.

63 Hereinafter 'Patient's Rights Law'.

64 C.A. 243/83 *City of Jerusalem v Gordon*, 39(1) PD 113.

since by the Supreme Court to include offended autonomy in cases of uninformed consent to medical treatment,[65] sorrow and frustration caused by loss of ability to become a parent,[66] disgust caused when it became known that one had drunk milk containing harmless silicon,[67] insult suffered when being treated in an dishonest way by public authorities[68] and frustration caused to a client by his lawyer's negligent tax assessment.[69] It is the removal of this barrier that paved the road for negligence law to assume its major role in the protection of human rights. The removal of the barrier can, to a large extent, be attributed to the growing sensitivity to human rights and the indirect effect of the 1992 basic laws.

5. *Protecting patients' autonomy and the right to receive information*

When a patient agrees to medical treatment on the basis of insufficient information regarding the benefits and risks of this treatment or its scope, the unjustified failure of the medical personnel to provide adequate information and the ensuing medical treatment violate the patient's autonomy and offend his dignity. The development of the protection afforded by tort law to this aspect of dignity is interesting and illustrative. At first, liability in such cases of 'uninformed consent' was imposed through the tort of assault. The 'uninformed' consent was considered defective and void and that rendered the medical treatment an assault. Liability, however, was imposed not for the offended dignity but rather for the bodily injury caused by the medical treatment. Later on, such claims were allowed under the tort of negligence on the grounds that the failure to provide adequate information amounts to negligent conduct as well. But there is a difference between these two causes of action. Assault focuses on the subjective mindset of the patient. Information should be provided in order to meet the patient's subjective need to know. Negligence, in contrast, focuses on the objective standard of provision of information, a standard that takes into account, inter alia, time and budgetary constraints, paternalistic attitudes and custom. It centres on the question of

---

65 See F(5) below.

66 C.A. 398/99 *Kupat Cholim Klalit v Dayan*, 55(1) PD 765.

67 C.A. 1338/97 *Tnuva Agriculture Marketing v Rabi*, 57(4) PD 673.

68 C.A. 1081/00 *Avna'al Shoes Distribution Co v State of Israel* 59(5) PD 193.

69 C.A.153/04 *Robinovitch v Rozenbeum* (6.2.06).

sufficient information from the perspective of a reasonable member of the medical profession. Given these differences, courts wisely merged these two approaches into the 'reasonable patient' test, which combines the subjective (patient) with the objective (reasonable). The next development came with the enactment of the Patient's Rights Law, which embraced the 'reasonable patient' test and specified in detail the information that should be provided to patients.[70] Accordingly, it was held that a breach of the enacted duties under this law constitutes liability under the tort of breach of statutory duty.[71] Another important aspect of the autonomy and dignity of the individual that gained enhanced protection under the Patient's Rights Law is the right not to be subjected to forced, paternalistic, medical treatment.[72]

In 1999, the *Da'aka* case, already mentioned,[73] moved even further with regard to a failure to provide adequate information. In these circumstances, a causal link between the failure to provide information and the damage caused by the treatment was not established and therefore the only damage was that the claimant was deprived of the right to decide for herself, on the basis of the relevant information, whether to undergo medical treatment. The court held that this deprivation constitutes a damage to autonomy and dignity and that such damage is recoverable under negligence and possibility under assault.[74]

6. The tension between the protection of reputation and free speech

The constitutionalisation of the right to dignity has implied the possibility that the right to good reputation should receive enhanced

---

70 Section 13 of the Patient's Rights Law 1996.

71 See: C.A. 6153/97 *Shtandel v Prof Sadeh*, 56(4) PD 746.

72 Under s 15 of the Patient's Rights Law only a special ethical committee (a lawyer, two medical experts, a psychologist or social worker, and a priest or public figure) has the authority to approve forced treatment. Moreover, even this committee cannot approve a treatment when there are no reasonable grounds to assume that the patient would, *after the fact*, agree to the treatment. In other words, when the cause of the patients' refusal is ideological, medical treatment cannot be enforced.

73 See supra note 50.

74 As mentioned, the justices were reluctant to reach the same outcome by a direct application of the Basic Law: Human Dignity and Liberty.

protection. However, enhanced protection of good reputation may well lead to a corresponding curtailment of freedom of speech. As noted, freedom of speech was not explicitly included in the rights that were constitutionalised under the Basic Law: Human Dignity and Liberty. Does it follow that the very delicate and sophisticated balance between reputation and free speech, established by the Defamation (Prohibition) Law 1965, should be shifted towards reputation and away from free speech?[75] The Israeli Supreme Court answered this question in the negative. It held that freedom of speech was also a derivative of human dignity and therefore retains its relative weight in the balancing process, vis-à-vis reputation.[76] The Court's reluctance to change the balance in favor of reputation reflects the weight attached to freedom of speech as the cornerstone of democracy. Indeed, recent decisions of the Supreme Court in defamation cases indicate an even greater tendency to 'sacrifice' the individual's right to protected reputation for the sake of free speech as a collective value, especially when that individual is a 'public figure'.[77]

7. The protection of human rights in marital relations

The enhanced protection of dignity, autonomy and equality in Israeli law is evidenced by the role that tort law now plays in marital relations. As already indicated, tort liability was imposed long ago under the tort of breach of statutory duty for the breach of an enacted duty not to divorce one's wife without her consent.[78] Recent decisions of magistrate courts have imposed tort liability in negligence on husbands who refused to divorce their wives for the mental anguish ensuing from such a refusal.[79] In another marital

---

[75] In C.F. (Tel-Aviv) 942/93 *Thermokir v Hamagen Co* [1994] (3) PM 177 (a district court decision) it was indeed argued that a greater weight should now be attached to reputation. Ibid at 185.

[76] C.A. 6781/94 *Rinat v Rom*, 56(4) PD 72. In the same direction, the court preserved its principled aversion to preliminary injunctions in defamation cases. See R.C.A. 10771/04 *Reshet Communication and Productions (1992) Ltd v Etinger*, 59(3) PD 308.

[77] See C.A. 4534/02 *Shoken Newspapers v Hertsikovitz*, 58(3) PD 558, where it was held that even the 'objective,' factual, question whether a given statement is defamatory should be answered with reference to public policy considerations.

[78] The *Sultan* case, supra note 63.

[79] See, e.g., F.F. (Jerusalem) 19270/03 *Anonymous v Anonymous* (not published, 21.12.04).

relations matter, the Supreme Court ruled that not just husband and wife but also unmarried partners who live together are entitled as dependents to compensation for loss of support from the tortfeasor who killed their partner.[80]

8. Increasing awards of compensation

Another manifestation of the enhanced protection of dignity and autonomy in tort law is the increase in sums awarded for an infringement of these rights. A prominent example regarding autonomy is a recent 2005 'informed consent' case, in which the sum awarded for breach of the patient's right to autonomy was ten times the sum awarded in an earlier 1999 case establishing liability for such damage.[81] Another example is a substantial sum awarded for the mental anguish suffered as a result of a prolonged criminal harassment.[82]

Interestingly, in a recent Supreme Court decision, the court claimed to promote autonomy and equality through the criteria used in awarding compensation for 'lost earnings'. It was held that, in assessing the future lost earnings of a minor who suffers bodily injury, the court should disregard the fact that the minor belongs to a minority group in which the average income is lower than the average income within the general population. The values of autonomy and equality, said the court, justify the adoption of a judicial presumption that minorities which are disadvantaged at present will enjoy equal opportunities in the future and therefore their earnings will eventually equal the earnings of the general population.[83]

G. Conclusion

Israeli law shows a growing willingness to protect human rights also in the private law sphere. The tendency to do so changes from one context to another. In general, contract law has proved to

---

80 C.A. 2000/97 *Lindorn v Karnit*, 55(1) PD 12.

81 From about €3,000 in the *Da'aka* case, supra note 50 to about €30,000 in C.A. 9817/02 *Weinstein v Dr Bergman* (to be published 16.6.05).

82 About €120,000 awarded in the *Weiss* case, supra note 52.

83 C.A. 10064/02 *'Migdal' Insurance Company Ltd v Abu-Hana* (to be published 27.9.05). See also C.A. 6111/03 *Sharogo v Knesset-Yehuda Synagogue* (to be published 21.11.05).

be more suspicious towards the application of human rights, due to the clear tension with the basic assumption of freedom of contract. At this stage, however, the question is no longer whether human rights should be protected within contract law but only to what extent they would be so protected. Tort law has proved to be more willing and assertive in this regard, gradually but systematically pushing outward the boundaries of liability to provide greater protection of dignity, autonomy, equality and other human rights.

The enactment of the 1992 basic laws has been a major driving force behind the process of providing enhanced protection of human rights in the private sphere. The approach chosen for this protection has usually been the indirect effect of these basic laws on existing doctrines of private law and not their direct application to private actors.

In sum, Israeli private law, inspired by the 1992 basic laws, has developed to play an important role in the protection of human rights. As the relative weights attached to human rights are steadily growing, it appears that the depth and width of this protection will undoubtedly increase in future years. The potential of private law in this regard is still far from being tapped.

Chapter 9: Italy
The Protection of Constitutional Rights in the Private Sphere

*Chiara Favilli and Carlo Fusaro**

A. Introduction and general constitutional background

The present Italian legal system is based upon a written and rigid Constitution which entered into force on 1 January 1948 and is protected by a relatively centralised judicial review of legislation; it is mostly up to the courts (and here to any kind of court) to refer to the Constitutional Court a law required to decide a specific case so that the Court may decide whether legislation infringes the Constitution or not. Decisions concerning the constitutional legitimacy of laws are therefore centralised, but the right to initiate such proceedings is decentralised. This allows for a permanent and broad constitutional control of legislation.

It must be emphasised, however, that judicial review conducted by the Italian Constitutional Court concerns only the law itself (only legal provisions adopted either by Parliament or a regional legislative body); it does not include findings on the actual case between the two parties, although it is such actual cases which prompt the referring court to approach the Constitutional Court.[1] More precisely, ever since its very first decisions back in June 1956, the Constitutional Court has held that the object of its ruling would not merely be the textual provisions of a particular piece of legislation but the rules

---

* This article has been conceived by the two authors together, so they both share full responsibility for it. However, Chiara Favilli has laid down parr. C. 1-5 and D.3; Carlo Fusaro has laid down the rest.

[1] It should be noted that when a court refers a law to the Constitutional Court it must suspend the proceedings, which will start again only when the Court has provided its decision. The suspension is mandatory in relation to that specific case only; however the decision is made public through the 'Gazzetta Ufficiale' of the Italian Republic, so that all other courts will be informed and might also autonomously decide to suspend similar cases (Law 11 March 1953, no. 87).

derived from them by the referring courts through their interpretation. In other words, what the Constitutional Court evaluates is how legislation is interpreted; in many (if not most) instances, the Court thereby tends to uphold legislation if it may be interpreted in a way that is consistent with the Constitution (possibly specifying which alternative readings of the law might be unconstitutional and ought to be avoided). This is relevant to our main topic because it is an approach which reduces those instances in which legislator might have fulfilled inadequately his function to mediate between constitutional provisions and the regulation of conflicting interests which the courts have to cope with.

For this reason, it is primarily up to each individual court to identify the correct legal rule (that is to say the appropriate law) on the basis of which to solve a specific case. The judge is subject to the law (Article 101.2 Italian Constitution[2]) and to the law only; and there is no doubt that when the Constitution refers to the 'law' in most cases it does refer to law enacted either by Parliament or a regional legislative body. There is a presumption that the courts will always look for rules based on enacted law, and this is regarded within the Italian constitutional order as the most important guarantee for the protection of constitutional rights. However, there is no monopoly of the Constitutional Court in the interpretation of the Constitution;[3] wherever necessary, it is up to the individual judge to seek an interpretation of legislation which is best suited to respect the Constitution.

Part I of the Italian Constitution (Articles 1 to 50) includes as wide and complete a bill of rights as could be laid down in the years immediately following the Second World War; it is no accident that its founding fathers meant to ensure the protection of the most relevant constitutional rights, specifying that any limitation of protection ought to be reserved to parliamentary legislation (so-called *riserva di legge*). They also prescribed that limitations permitted by parliamentary law would be subject to a strict interpretation and ought to be applied or authorised only by the judiciary (so-called *riserva*

[2] Unless stated otherwise, articles quoted always refer to the updated text of the Italian Constitution.

[3] V. Onida, 'L'attuazione della Costituzione fra magistratura e corte costituzionale' in *Aspetti e tendenze del diritto costituzionale. Scritti in onore di C. Mortati*, vol. IV (1977), pp 592–4.

di giurisdizione). According to the prevailing positivist approach, the *riserva di legge* is still regarded by many as a precious guarantee against judicial subjectivism.[4]

That said, in order to resolve a conflict of interests between private parties, each court will first of all search for legislative provisions capable of supporting its decision either directly or on the basis of a suitable interpretation. A court will, for instance, try to draw the boundaries of a legal rule in compliance with the protection of a right recognised by the Constitution; only if no suitable interpretation is found, will the court refer the law to the Constitutional Court. In their interpretative activity, wherever this might be necessary, Italian courts may recur to what we could define as forms of *mittelbare Drittwirkung*, a concept developed by some German scholars.[5] In a much more limited set of cases, characterised by the total absence of applicable legislation, a court will try to base its decision directly upon some constitutional provision in the form of *unmittelbare Drittwirkung*.[6]

In both instances (*mittelbare* and *unmittelbare Drittwirkung*), conventional provisions deriving from international treaties on human rights (and the related jurisprudence of international courts) can also be employed by Italian courts to either interpret national legislation or, in admittedly rare cases, in order to decide the case directly. This leaves in question the status of such international law within the Italian legal systems (see part C., below 3).

Some other features of the Italian constitutional system should be emphasised by way of introduction in order to understand the approach followed in Italy concerning the horizontal effects of constitutional provisions. These features are linked to both principles expressed in the Italian Constitution and issues which have *not* been dealt with in that text. As far as the latter is concerned, we would remind the reader of the following features of the Italian system:

(a) There is no *recurso de amparo* (individual constitutional complaint or *Verfassungsbeschwerde*); individuals or legal persons are not given direct access to the Constitutional Court.

---

[4] A. Pace, 'Costituzionalismo e metodi interpretativi dei diritti fondamentali' in G. Rolla (ed), *Tecniche di garanzia dei diritti fondamentali* (2001).

[5] E.g., by Günther Dürig in 1984.

[6] See W. Leisner (1960) and H. C. Nipperdey (1962); in Italy: G. Lombardi, *Potere privato e diritti fondamentali* (1970).

(b) There is no national *ombudsman* (grievance officer) or other independent authority.[7] The protection of constitutional rights (not their implementation, which is, of course, a duty of administrative bodies) is therefore reserved for courts of law, more specifically to *ordinary* courts (with the exception of a limited set of issues where administrative courts or the *Corte dei conti*, the Court of Auditors, is competent).
(c) The Italian Constitution lacks provisions expressly establishing *Drittwirkung* (as is the case with the German, the Portuguese, the South African and the Greek Constitutions[8]).
(d) Until 2001, the Italian Constitution also lacked provisions establishing the supremacy and the direct application of international treaties and conventions (as is the case with the French and Spanish Constitutions).[9]

The Italian Constitution includes several provisions dealing with matters traditionally reserved for private law. This has prompted some scholars to claim that one of its features is the abolition of a clear distinction between public and private law. In fact, this distinction is still widely used for the sake of teaching and in order to distinguish between subjects in the curricula of law schools; the basic content and the notion of constitutionalism underlying the 1948 Italian Constitution, however, definitely militate against a clear-cut separation between public and private law. The supremacy of the Constitution and its widespread and deeply influential recognition of human rights (including social rights) also means that, in spite of the constitutional recognition of a substantial degree of autonomy of both a variety of institutions (Regions, municipalities) and private individuals and associations (see Articles 2, 5, 18, 29,

---

7 In fact the last *Report of the Commissioner for Human Rights* (A. Gil-Robles) concerning the actual protection of human rights in Italy recommends the establishment of a national mediator or *ombudsman* and the creation of a national agency for the implementation of human rights in compliance with the UN Resolution 48/134 of 20 December 1993. The chamber of deputies is presently discussing a bill which would establish such as agency, see XV Leg., AC 626-1090-1441-2018. It should be added that in Italy there are independent authorities in charge of the protection of specific rights (e.g., the *Garante per la protezione dei dati personali*, who is in charge with the protection of privacy).

8 In the same order, see Art 1(3) BL, Art 18(1) of the Portuguese Constitution, s 8(2) of the Constitution of the Republic of South Africa, and Art 25(1) Ell. Const.

9 In the same order, see Art 55 of the French Constitution and Arts 10(2) and 96 of the Spanish Constitution.

33, 39 and 49 Italian Constitution), these may all be restricted in order to guarantee a fuller protection of fundamental rights. The civil code – once regarded as the *true* constitution of the land – is now limited by constitutional provisions and must be interpreted in a way which complies rigorously with them. The old theory of 'subjective public rights' is widely regarded as outdated; neither are rights only protected *against* the state nor only *by* the state.[10] This theory of subjective public rights implied a supremacy of the state, which has ceased to exist and is not consistent with the supreme principles of the Italian Constitution. Fundamental rights are firmly entrenched in a superior law and cannot depend upon policy choices of simple parliamentary majorities.

The acceptance of and emphasis on *Drittwirkung* comes as a consequence of this constitutional reasoning; as rights do not depend upon the will of a majority in society or upon the will in form of 'ordinary' state legislation (which are, in principle, the same), they must have effects not only vis-à-vis public authorities but also within the context of private relationships. Although (as indeed anticipated) little room is left for *Drittwirkung* in a highly regulated (and, according to many, even over-regulated) system as the Italian, it is difficult to find constitutional scholars willing to deny that constitutional provisions may, at least in principle, be directly applied within the private sphere and therefore have horizontal or third party effects. Interestingly, many private law experts appear to be much more cautious.

It is particularly interesting to note that historical circumstances triggered a fairly early interest in an application of *Drittwirkung* in Italy after the Constitution entered into force. The new Constitution demanded an extensive legislative initiative in order to clear existing law of the many provisions which did not comply with the new supreme law and to implement the protection of the rights it recognised by new ordinary legislation. The Cold War heavily influenced and slowed down this process; as late as June 1956 the Constitutional Court was not yet operational. As a consequence, the enforcement of the Constitution was ultimately devolved to the Supreme Court of Cassation (the *Cassazione*, the higher body of the judiciary) formed by judges trained and educated during the

[10] A. Barbera, 'La libertà tra diritti e istituzioni' in *Aspetti e tendenze del diritto costituzionale. Scritti in onore di C. Mortati*, vol. I (1977).

previous regime. The application and implementation of the Constitution became a major constitutional and political issue. Opinions conflicted upon the direct application of *all* constitutional provisions (not to mention those meant to protect fundamental rights) and even upon their validity towards pre-constitutional law. The latter approach was thereby based on the theory that only *newly adopted* laws should have to comply with the Constitution.

In absence of new laws (due to the reluctance by the parliamentary majority at the time) and without a functioning Constitutional Court the burden of applying the Constitution rested entirely upon the ordinary courts; and it was thanks to lower courts in particular that first attempts to directly apply constitutional provisions in order to acknowledge specific claims were conducted. Within the private sphere this occurred first in the area of labour relations. This was the consequence of converging circumstances: the high practical relevance of social conflicts in the field of employer–employee relationships; the pivotal role expressly given to labour and to workers' rights by the new Constitution (starting with Article 1: 'Italy is a democratic Republic founded on labour'); and the more general idea that property rights and rights connected to private economic activity are not absolute and do not share the same status as fundamental rights (more about this later). In summary, when – as early as 1952 – the courts had to face claims concerning the salary earned by workers not organised in trade unions who asked for the same pay as that determined by the contracts of union workers, the courts directly applied Article 36 of the Constitution, stating that the salary of union workers specified the amount of renumeration 'proportionate to the quantity and quality of work ... and in any case sufficient to ensure ... a free and honourable existence', as granted by that provision.[11] The same soon occurred with respect to the direct application of Article 37.1 (which grants men and women equal pay); Article 37.4 (protection of the work of minors); and Articles 36.2 and 36.3 (recognition of the right to leave and to one free day per week to all employees).

The idea of *Drittwirkung* emerged soon although it was absorbed by the more general debate concerning the direct application of the provisions of the new Constitution *in general* (not only within

[11] Article 2099.2 Civil code establishes that the amount of salary is determined by the court when no contract is available.

the private sphere but even between public authorities and individuals). The first scholarly research devoted to the subject must be attributed to Giorgio Lombardi and was published in 1970, a few years after the first German works to which it was indebted.[12] This Italian author emphasised the trend to limit the rights concerning free and private enterprise and private property in order to protect traditional and new rights as recognised to every human being both as an individual and as a member of a social group (see Article 2 Italian Constitution).[13] Third party effects of these rights were envisaged as restrictions on both the autonomy of private parties among themselves and the internal powers within associations which individuals might become members of. The result would be reached by a combined reading of the relevant constitutional provisions and Article 24.1, which declares that 'all may bring a case before a court ... in order to protect their rights ...' . The rationale advanced by Lombardi recognised that, in many instances, the equality of private parties (as the conceptual base of their right to determine the rules of their relationships freely) is a fiction; in reality, there is disparity, and the direct application of the Constitution can help to overcome its consequences when these differences in power infringe the constitutional rights of the weaker party.[14]

In fact, ever since 1965, the Italian Magistrates Association (ANM) has openly advocated the duty of each judge to directly apply all suitable constitutional provisions in order: (i) to interpret all legislation in force; (ii) to interpret general clauses such as bona fide and fairness (*correttezza*) within the law of contract; and (iii) to grant third party effects to constitutional rights such as the right to good health (Article 32 Italian Constitution).

That said, it must be added that there is relatively little proportionality reasoning on the part of the ordinary courts both because

---

[12] Lombardi accurately explains the basic reasoning of Nipperdey, Leisner and Dürig, as well as of more traditional authors such as Forsthoff and Mangoldt; op. cit., note 3, pp 63 ff.

[13] According to Article 2 Italian Constitution: 'the Republic recognizes and guarantees the inviolable rights of man, both as an individual and as a member of the social groups in which one's personality finds expression, and it requires the performance of imperative political, economic and social duties.'

[14] Among private law scholars, a leading role in affirming the direct application of the Constitution in the area of contracts was played by Stefano Rodotà thanks to his formative publications of 1964 and 1967.

of the civil law system and because of how the process of constitutional review is structured: proportionality and reasonableness are mostly matters of the Constitutional Court to look into, and the balancing is generally left to the legislator or to the Constitutional Court (which may sanction the former for having improperly balanced or for having failed to balance conflicting but relevant constitutional rights and interests – for instance, for failing to protect the right to privacy in order to protect the right to inform).

B. How the protection of human rights is granted in Italy

The most relevant difference between the previous constitutional order and the Italian Constitution of 1948 is the radical shift from a state-centred system to a system centred on the human being or natural person (*persona umana*), which is deemed as instrumental to the implementation and protection of his/her rights. Such legal personalism permeates the Constitution (starting with Articles 2 and 3[15]), and it has proven a strong conceptual tool in the effort to update and expand the interpretation of the Italian Bill of Rights as entrenched in Part I of the constitutional text. The courts, and in particular the Constitutional Court, along with the – at times slow – legislator have made their contribution to this development.

There is no word about *human rights* as such within the Constitution of Italy nor about *fundamental rights*; the text speaks of rights and freedoms. However, it does mention 'the inviolable rights of man' in general terms, and does label some of the rights listed in Articles 13 to 50 as such (personal freedom in Article 13; personal domicile in Article 14; freedom of correspondence and of every other form of communication in Article 15). In spite of a great amount of scholarly debate, there is, as a recent paper by the Constitutional Court puts it, a widespread tendency to use terms such as *human rights*, *inviolable rights*, *constitutional rights* or *fundamental rights* in a promiscuous and indiscriminate way. What these terms have in

---

[15] Article 3 affirms that all mean are equal in social status and before the law 'without distinction as to sex, race, language, religion, political opinions, and personal and social conditions'. Furthermore, it states that 'it is a duty of the Republic to remove all economic and social obstacles which ... prevent the full development of the individual'.

common, however, is that they all tend to indicate rights which must be recognised by every person as such.[16] For the sake of brevity, we will thus summarise some basic assumptions emerging from the constitutional jurisprudence on *constitutional rights*:

(a) Apart from political rights, all rights are granted to every person, regardless of citizenship (see decisions 104/1969, 219/1995 and 432/2005[17]).
(b) Inviolable rights in particular are binding for all,[18] cannot be alienated, can never extinguish (even if not claimed for a long time), and cannot be renounced or disposed of.[19]
(c) There are rights whose recognition is so strictly connected with the *supreme principles* underlying the Constitution that they may not be restricted, not even through the procedures of a legal constitutional amendment.
(d) The Constitutional Court has emphasised its duty and right to evaluate the constitutional legitimacy of laws revising the Constitution itself (see decision 1146/1988); this applies to international law as well as Community law (see decisions 48/1979 and 170/1984).
(e) Based upon Article 2 of the Constitution, which is regarded as an *open textured provision* and/or based upon one of the other specific guarantees, the Court has constantly expanded the list of rights protecting all human beings.

---

[16] See Corte costituzionale. Servizio studi, *I diritti fondamentali nella giurisprudenza della Corte costituzionale* (2006). *Human rights* are often referred to as the rights recognised by international treaties, while the phrase *fundamental rights* is used to indicate a more inclusive set of *all* (civil, political, social, third generation and so on) constitutional rights. But these are just stipulations. We will mostly use the term 'constitutional rights,' which seems more appropriate.

[17] We will refer to the jurisprudence of the Constitutional Court by quoting each decision with its number and year. Starting from 2003, an abstract in English of the most relevant decisions is available (see http://www.cortecostituzionale.it/eng/attivitacorte/pronunceemassime/abstract/abstract_2006.asp). E.g., decision 432/2005 declared constitutionally illegitimate a law of the Regione Lombardia because it did not extend its provisions concerning the right to freely use public transportation to disabled *non*-citizens (grounds: breach of Article 3 in connection with Article 2 Italian Constitution).

[18] See decision 122/1970; but also decisions 455/1990 and 292/1991.

[19] Inviolable rights might be regarded as the *preferred freedoms* in the wording of Justice Cardozo in *Palko v State of Connecticut* 302 US 319, 1937.

(f) Some of the previously mentioned wider interpretations have allowed forms of direct or indirect *Drittwirkung* (see, for instance, the recognition of a *right to personal physical integrity* or the *right to life*).
(g) The Court has expressly stated that *inviolable rights* are to be automatically recognised – at least in their core elements – within all sub-national (autonomous) jurisdictions (for example, the regions) as well as within the private sphere.

For many years now one of the most debated issues has been how to interpret Article 2 of the Constitution, one of the most important provisions, already referred to above. Back in 1972, a pioneering work by Augusto Barbera put forward the idea that Article 2 was a suitable gateway for the recognition of rights not already expressly entrenched in the Constitution or capable of being derived from the specific guarantees provided for by Articles 13 to 50 of Part I. This interpretation is not nowadays still shared by such authoritative scholars as Paolo Caretti, Franco Modugno, Damiano Nocilla and Alessandro Pace, who believe that it is more appropriate to interpret the specific clauses of Articles 13 ff broadly (they fear that the 'creation' of *new* rights based upon Article 2 might lead to the restriction of rights *expressly recognised* by the Constitution). Others have followed Barbera's approach (Antonio Baldassarre, Alessandro Pizzorusso and Piero Perlingieri). The Court has always been very cautious on this point and recently reaffirmed that a difference between a right directly protected by the Constitution and a right derived from an interpretation of Article 2 does exist; in the latter case the legislator has more room for own discretion (see decision 121/2004). However, since with decision 561/1987, the Court has in fact started to base the recognition of new rights on Article 2 (see decision 561/1987, involving the right to sexual freedom; decision 404/1988, involving the right to have a home; decision 139/1990, involving the right to privacy; decision 278/1992, involving the right to emigrate; decision 13/1994, involving the right to one's own identity, which was already developed by the earlier decision Cassaz. 22 June 1985, no. 3769; decisions 372/1994 and 223/1996, involving the right to life; and other cases involving the right to one's name, the right to marry, and the right to one's reputation).

The relevance of Article 2 of the Constitution cannot be overemphasised. In many instances, courts have supported the direct application of other constitutional provisions in order to rule on specific claims, supporting their reasoning with further reference to Article 2; in other cases, they have based their decision mostly if not entirely on Article 2 (for instance, where a specific right is not directly guaranteed by other constitutional provisions); finally, they have based the direct or indirect application of provisions deriving from international law (starting with the European Convention on Human Rights) on Article 2 (see part C., below).

The Constitutional Court, however, has not been the single driving force behind the improvement of the protection of fundamental rights – Parliament has not always been lazy or reluctant to act. In general, there are numerous laws passed by the Italian Parliament and by regional legislators which are designed to implement the protection of constitutional rights and the protection of human rights stemming from international instruments signed up to by Italy. Because of a variety of historic circumstances, the single piece of legislation which has exercised the greatest impact has probably been the so-called Charter of the Employees' Rights (*Statuto dei lavoratori*), Law of 20 May 1970, no. 300.[20] In 1982, Parliament also passed a law granting the right of a person to change his/her name following a change of his/her sex by medical operation, a right which had been denied by the Constitutional Court. Previously, Parliament had included a provision granting the right of doctors and nurses not to perform abortions based on their freedom of conscience. In both instances, the constitutional ground was Article 2 of the Constitution. Legislation indeed remains the most relevant ordinary instrument to implement the protection of constitutional rights as well as rights recognised by provisions belonging to other systems of law but which are closely intertwined with the Italian (in particular Community law and the European Convention on Human Rights).

C. The impact of the international instruments to which Italy is a party

1. The multi-levelled protection of rights in Europe

As a consequence of the close relationship between international, Community and national jurisdictions (each with its own sphere of

---

[20] Amended by law of 9 December 1977, no. 903, which forbade all discriminations on the labour market on the grounds of gender.

competence, inter alia, in the area of fundamental rights), there is a lot of discussion among constitutional lawyers in Europe about the so-called *multi-levelled* protection of human rights and about *multi-levelled constitutionalism* in general. This trend is especially apparent since the adoption of the Charter of Fundamental Rights of the European Union in Nice in 2000 but it had already emerged before that based on Article 6 of the Treaty on European Union of 1992, which expressly refers to the European Convention on Human Rights.[21] Ingo Pernice in Germany may have been the first author to draw attention to this issue.[22] The unfortunate difficulties that the Treaty Establishing a Constitution for Europe has run into has dampened this enthusiasm but not changed the overall picture.

One could identify up to four levels of protection in Europe: (a) rights guaranteed by internal constitutional provisions or by rules at least based upon national constitutional provisions; (b) rights directly or indirectly guaranteed by the European Union or Community law; (c) rights guaranteed directly or indirectly by the European Convention on Human Rights; and (d) rights indirectly guaranteed by other international instruments. The role of Italian courts differs, of course, in each case, although a trend has started to emerge which assimilates the European Convention and Community law (see below).

2. *Human rights treaties and Italy*

In addition to its own constitutional provisions, Italy is party to many international treaties, adopted either at the international or

21 This has prompted ECJ jurisprudence to grant protection to ECHR rights recognised as *general principles of community law* based upon Articles 6(2) and 46(d) of the Treaty on European Union.

22 See I. Pernice, 'Multilevel Constitutionalism and the Treaty of Amsterdam: European Constitution-making revisited?' in (1999) 36 *Common Market Law Review* 703–50. In Italy, see R. Bifulco, M. Cartabia and A. Celotto, *L'Europa dei diritti: commento alla Carta dei diritti fondamentali dell'Unione Europea* (2001); P. Falzea, A. Spadaro and L. Ventura, *La Corte costituzionale e le Corti d'Europa* (2003); P. Bilancia and E. De Marco, *La tutela multilivello dei diritti* (2004); C. Casonato, *The Protection of Fundamental Rights in Europe: Lessons from Canada* (2004); D. Tega in L. Califano, *Corte costituzionale e diritti fondamentali* (2004); S. Panunzio, *I diritti fondamentali e le corti in Europa* (2005); and G. Silvestri, *Verso uno* +ius commune *europeo dei diritti fondaemntali*, in (2006) 26 *Quaderni costituzionali* 7–24. Since vol. XXIII (2003), the most prominent Italian constitutional review (*Quaderni costituzionali*) has hosted an exhaustive section of 'Notes from Europe' edited by M. Cartabia.

regional level, either general or devoted to a specific issue, and either multilateral or bilateral.

At regional level, the most important role is played by the European Convention on Human Rights and Fundamental Freedoms ratified in 1955 (ECHR), including Protocols 1, 4, 6 and 7,[23] and many other conventions among which it is worthwhile mentioning the European Social Charter (revised in 1996).

At the international level, Italy is part of almost all United Nations conventions such as the Convention on Refugee Status (1951) and the related Protocol of 1967; the Convention on the elimination of all forms of Racial Discrimination (1965); the 1966 Covenants, also accepting the jurisdiction of the Human Rights Committee in relation to individual complaints and the Second Optional Protocol to the Civil and Political Rights aiming at the Abolition of the Death Penalty (1989); the Convention on the Elimination of All Forms of Discrimination against Women (1979); the Convention against Torture and Other Cruel, Inhuman or Degrading Treatment or Punishment (1984); the Convention on the Rights of Childhood (1989); and the Rome Statute on the International Criminal Court (1998). As far as specialised organisations are concerned, Italy is party to several ILO[24] and UNESCO[25] Conventions.

3. *The system of incorporation and the status of conventional provisions within the Italian hierarchy of law*

The way in which human rights treaties are incorporated into the Italian system does not differ from the one applied to any other treaty. The Constitution regulates only the adherence to international *customary* law. Article 10.1 of the Constitution thus states that 'the

[23] Before the entry into force of Protocol no. 11, Italy had also accepted the optional clauses of Articles 25 and 46, recognising the competence of the Convention's bodies to receive individual complaints and to interpret the ECHR.

[24] ILO Convention (no. 29) on Forced Labour (1930); ILO Convention (no. 100) concerning Equal Remuneration for Men and Women Workers for Work of Equal Value (1951); ILO Convention (no. 111) concerning discrimination in respect of Employment and Occupation (1958); ILO Convention (no. 143) on Rights of Migrant Workers (1975).

[25] UNESCO Convention against Discrimination in Education (1960); UNESCO Convention on Cultural Diversity (2005).

Italian legal system shall conform with the generally recognised rules of international law', a provision which displays openness to international law; international customary law is automatically part of Italian law since it is immediately effective at the international level and judges can apply it without any further act. Moreover, international customary law takes effect on the constitutional level, which means that in case of a conflict between the international provision and the Constitution, the first shall prevail over the latter with the exception of those fundamental rights which cannot be changed even by constitutional amendment (see decision 48/1979 of the Constitutional Court[26]).

As far as treaties are concerned, the Constitution regulates the ratification procedure, binding the government to ask for an authorisation by Parliament before concluding the most relevant treaties (see Articles 80 and 87.8). Standard practice has been to adopt an ad hoc law (so-called *ordine di esecuzione*), which is usually part of the legislative act authorising the ratification of the treaty. The *ordine di esecuzione* is a very short provision, stating that 'full and entire execution is given to the treaty ...'.[27] This is considered a 'special' system of incorporation because the international treaty is not rewritten in the form of an internal act but can be applied directly by judges or administrative authorities if it is self-executing (i.e. if its provisions can be applied without the need to modify existing national law; see Cassaz. 25 January 1989, no. 1418 and 16 April 1996, no. 2549).

Experience in fact shows that the non self-executing character of international law is often proclaimed by claiming that the treaty in question is incomplete or of a political nature in order to avoid its immediate application (see the Constitutional Court decisions 188/1980 and 62/1981 as well as Cassaz. 6 February 1999, no. 1062; *contra* Cassaz. 8 July 1998, no. 6672). This has typically occurred to conventional provisions in the area of human rights; claiming

26 In this decision the Constitutional Court established that customary laws in existence before the entry into force of the Constitution could prevail over *every* constitutional provision while the others must respect the fundamental values of the Italian Republic. See more recently and in the same sense, Cassaz. 3 August 2000, no. 530.

27 Generally, the first Article is devoted to the authorisation to ratify and the second one to the execution order. This means that, again generally, the execution is ordered *before* the entry into force of the treaty (for Italy). As soon as the treaty does enter into force, it can be immediately applied thanks to the execution order.

their uncertain formulation (for instance in the area of so-called social rights, often expressly subordinated to a 'step by step' or gradual application), states tend to argue that international human rights provisions oblige them to adopt the necessary internal laws, in default of which the international provisions may not be applied directly (see Cassaz. 23 February 1999, no. 98). To avoid similar abuse, some authors maintain that the non self-executing nature of provisions in international conventions must be subject to strict interpretation.[28] In particular, a treaty could be interpreted as non self-executing only when it allows more options, when there is a need to create or modify a procedure, or to establish a (new) body or authority.[29] In Italy, the *Cassazione* has recognised the direct application of human rights treaties and, despite some divergent decisions, there is wide acceptance of this approach (see Cassaz. 12 May 1993).

A large number of international human rights treaties that Italy has ratified are therefore part of Italian law, despite the absence of an internal act of incorporation. This system ensures strict coherence between national law and international treaties in terms of interpretation and the continued existence of the treaty (which can be affected by reservations or termination); on the negative side, it tends to make the knowledge of the international provisions of this kind less widespread for those jurists who are not international law experts. As a consequence, many lawyers do not refer to international law in their petitions and many judges (especially in the lower courts) do not apply it in their decisions.[30] This may be particularly true for conventions protecting human rights due to the belief, shared both by many scholars and courts, that internationally guaranteed human rights are already substantially embedded in the Italian Constitution itself; many human rights treaties are thus seen as the natural reflection of what is already entrenched in Italy (for a similar reasoning see Constitutional Court decisions 388/1999, 10/1993 and 161/1985). At times, the Constitution is, furthermore, regarded as providing a more extensive protection than that granted by international conventions (see Constitutional Court decisions

[28] B. Conforti and F. Francioni, *Enforcing International Human Rights in Domestic Courts* (1997).

[29] B. Conforti, *Diritto internazionale* (2006).

[30] Italy then formally respects the treaty while its effective protection may not be guaranteed.

98/1965, 148/1999 and 29/2003). In summary, court decisions enforcing fundamental human rights rarely refer to international law, and when they do, this is mostly in order to merely confirm an interpretation apparently already derived from the Italian Constitution.

4. The lack of constitutional entrenchment (no constitutionalisation of international conventions): the novelty of Article 117.1 of the Italian Constitution after the revision of title V in 2001

Beside the lack of constitutional provisions regulating the incorporation of treaties, there was, until 2001, also a lack of constitutional entrenchment for international conventions.[31] Problems always arose in case of conflicts between subsequent internal legislation and the provision ordering the execution of an international treaty, since the latter was entitled the same legal force as the act of execution, mostly an ordinary law (see Constitutional Court decision 73/2001; Cassaz. 14 April 2003, no. 5902). Being of the same rank among the sources of law, the latter should, in principle, prevail over the former (see Constitutional Court decision 188/1980). In this case, however, there is no clear and generally accepted method to resolve the conflict, a problem which is generally left to the judges. Judges are thus confronted with two conflicting laws regulating the same object; if they focus on the succession of the laws in time as a criterion, they might have to apply the most recent internal law, thereby possibly infringing the international treaty. In order to avoid the conflict, they should interpret national laws in compliance with the international treaty. Interpretation is the best way to resolve the issue, though it may not always be available, e.g., when the wording of the law does not leave sufficient space for an interpretation in compliance with the international provision. For this reason, a general trend has emerged which accords international law a 'special' force (or higher status) so as not to incur international responsibility.

When the provision of an international treaty can be linked to a constitutional right, the issue is resolved with respect to the higher

[31] Article 10.2 binds the legislator to respect international law but only insofar as it regulates foreigners' status; Article 11 allows limitations to national sovereignty intended to favour a legal system that will ensure peace and justice.

status of the Constitution, which is then interpreted in the light of the covenant. In these cases, a conflicting (later) ordinary law would violate not only the international treaty but also the Constitution which enshrines the same right even if the treaty allows a more extensive interpretation of the same right (see Constitutional Court decision 168/1994).

In order to grant a higher status to provisions in international conventions, some scholars have tried to argue that Article 10.1 of the Constitution also applies to treaties,[32] but this theory has not been followed because of the wording of the text of Article 10 and because the proceedings of the Constitutional Assembly show that the constitutional legislator expressly wanted to exclude international treaties (see Constitutional Court decisions 15/1982, 323/1989 and 496/1991). More convincing is a theory according to which the execution order is 'special' law and that it prevails on subsequent legislation. The law that executes an international treaty can thus be regarded as special or 'atypical' – not because of its content but because of its international origin and the duty not to violate an international obligation. In case of a 'special' law, only when the legislator has expressly adopted an act with the express intention to regulate the matter differently would it be legitimate to allow the subsequent law to prevail over the execution order, with all the consequences resulting from Italy's international responsibilities.

The Constitutional Court appeared ready to follow this new course when it adopted decision 10/1993 and stated that the International Covenant on Civil and Political Rights (Article 14.3) and the European Convention on Human Rights (Article 6.3) should still be applied even after the new Italian Criminal Code introduced conflicting provisions because 'they are laws deriving from an atypical competence which may not be cancelled or amended by ordinary law'. The same position was adopted by the *Cassazione* in Cassaz. 10 July 1993, when it stated that the provisions of the European Convention on Human Rights have a particular status vis-à-vis ordinary law, adding that the same applies to the case law of the European Court of Human Rights.

These decisions, however, have gained only limited acceptance by the jurisprudence (but see Cassaz. 14 June 2002, no. 8503), and until the adoption of Constitutional Law 3/2001 the framework

---

[32] R. Quadri, *Corso di diritto internazionale pubblico* (1968).

remained unchanged. Constitutional Law 2001 no. 3 then radically revised Title V of the second part of the Italian Constitution. In particular, the new Article 117, which modified the allocation of powers between State and Regions, also changed the relationship between ordinary laws (both national and regional) and international law. In particular, Article 117.1 of the Constitution now states that 'legislative powers shall be exercised by the State and by the Regions in accordance with the Constitution and within the limits set by EU law and international obligations'. Scholars share different opinions about how these new provisions should be interpreted. Some tend to diminish their effects (see also Cassaz. 17 December 2002, no. 17564) while others stress their importance because they grant a stronger status to international (and European) law in relation to internal ordinary law. Even the latter, though, believe that Article 117.1 must be interpreted with some restraint; the general reference to 'international obligations' should not be understood as to include *executive agreements*, since the government could otherwise limit parliamentary powers on the basis of international agreements signed without the participation or even knowledge of the latter.[33]

The Constitutional Court has not shed any light on this issue as yet. In our opinion it should not be ignored that Article 117 of the Constitution grants a constitutional framework designed to respect international obligations (to say the least). The new provision does not, of course, change the procedure by which treaties are ratified (see above). What Article 117.1 of the Constitution should, however, allow is a review of legislation by the Constitutional Court based on the provisions of international conventions (used as parameters). Few cases have been submitted to the Constitutional Court on these grounds, but the Court has been reluctant to take advantage of the new constitutional provision. The constitutional duty to respect international obligations based on Article 117.1 can

---

[33] An intermediate opinion considers Article 117.1 as a synthesis of the fundamental values given by the interaction of the 'multileveled protection of human rights'. Article 117.1 would refer to the three different law systems (based upon the Constitution, Community law, and international law) that the legislator (national or regional) must take into account; P. De Stefani, *L'incorporazione dei diritti umani. L'adattamento al diritto internazionale e il nuovo art. 117 della Costituzione*, Research Papers 1/2003, at http://www.centrodirittiumani.unipd.it/a_attivita/research.asp?menu=attivita.

also reinforce the obligation of ordinary courts to interpret national law in compliance with the system of protection established by the European Convention on Human Rights. As already pointed out, interpretation in compliance with international provisions is instrumental (not only in Italy) to guarantee the respect for international obligations. This should also be the case within the new constitutional framework, leaving it to the Constitutional Court to review tensions in a residual role.

In theory, there could be a conflict between some international human rights provisions and Italian constitutional law. This is unlikely, however, to happen in practice; constitutional provisions do generally reflect (and contain a – possibly implied – link to) international law. On the other side, rights do not exist separately and the level of protection of a specific right depends on how other rights are protected, on how the monitoring body interprets each of them, and on how the balance between potentially conflicting rights is reached. It cannot therefore be entirely ruled out that a conflict may arise. In this case, and from a legal and technical point of view, internal constitutional law shall prevail.

5. The difference between the European Union system and the ECHR system (the absence of preliminary references in the latter)

The EU legal system differs from every other international treaty, including the system established by the European Convention on Human Rights, which does not expressly hold a special status in Italian law.

Following a discourse between the European Court of Justice and the Italian Constitutional Court,[34] the latter has abandoned the more 'traditional' theory formulated in its decision 14/1964 and has, based on Article 11 of the Constitution, recognised the supremacy of European Union law and (consequently) the inapplicability of national laws which are contrary to directly applicable Community law or Community law with direct effect (see decision 170/1984).

In view of the clear reference to the European Convention on Human Rights in Article 6.2 of the EU Treaty, some court decisions

---

[34] G. Gaja, *Introduzione al diritto comunitario* (2005), pp 121–41.

have argued that the Convention might have the same status as Community law. The first of such decisions can be found in Cassaz. 19 July 2002, no. 10542, and, previously, in two decisions of ordinary tribunals (see Trib. Genova, 4 June 2001 and Corte d'app. Roma and Torino 11 April 2002).[35] The latter decisions in particular refused to apply an Italian law, justifying this approach with the same principles which determine the relationship between Community law and national law (see ECJ Case 6/64 of 15 July 1964 – *Costa* – and ECJ Case 106/77 of 9 March 1978 – *Simmenthal*).

This interpretation goes too far. The European Convention on Human Rights can assume this 'special' status only in a matter regulated by the European Union and acting as a parameter for the legitimacy of Community law. This means that in case of conflict between a national law enacted in a sector ruled by Community law and a general principle established by the Convention, national judges could ask the European Court of Justice for a decision about the true effects of that principle. The tension will then be resolved by applying a 'principled' interpretation or, where this is not possible, by dismissing national law. A direct dismissal by the national judges can take place only when a particular principle has been already clarified by the ECJ (see ECJ Case 283/81 of 6 October 1982 – *Cilfit*). The lack of a direct link between national judges and the Strasbourg Court (such as the one established by the preliminary reference procedure enshrined in Article 234 of the EC Treaty), is considered as one of the major hindrances in the recognition of the Convention through the direct dismissal of national law by common judges; for lack of this opportunity to refer questions to a (European) court, only the supreme (national) court is able to support the decision of the single judge. According to the Italian Constitutional Court, the preliminary reference procedure also performs another function: while declining to directly qualify itself as bound to refer questions directly to the ECJ (Ordin. 536/1995), the Court has asked the lower courts to refer cases to the ECJ in order to ascertain whether potential conflicts between Community law and particular Italian constitutional values truly exist or not. If this is the case, then the Italian court will be obliged to refer the issue to the Constitutional Court as the supreme guardian of (national) fundamental rights.

---

35 A. Guazzarotti, 'I giudici comuni e la CEDU alla luce del nuovo art. 117 Cost.' in (2003) 1 *Quaderni costituzionali* 25–51.

Even after the new Article 117.1 of the Constitution entered into force, there is no room for ordinary judges to dismiss a national law which seems to directly contradict the European Convention as interpreted by Strasbourg. Direct application of the Convention does not allow conflicting national law to be dismissed. Indeed, this is not foreseen either in the Convention itself (which 'only' asks for the respect by Member States of the Council of Europe) nor, indeed, by the case law of the European Court of Human Rights. Checks on the lack of respect for the Convention and the Court's case law tend to be more political than judicial.[36]

It is worthwhile mentioning that special relevance is attached to the case law of the European Court of Human Rights (see Article 46 of the Convention), at least with respect to violations of the right to a fair trial guaranteed by Article 6 of the Convention. With four decisions issued in 2004, the *Cassazione* has established the binding force of decisions of the European Court of Human Rights, stating that these must be respected by Italian courts (see the decisions of 26 January 2004, nos 1338, 1339, 1340 and 1341). A new law has recently been passed concerning the execution of Strasbourg case law, conferring on the Prime Minister the duty to take all the necessary measures to conform with these decisions, to promptly inform parliamentary committees about them, and to submit an annual report on compliance with Italian human rights obligations to Parliament.[37]

D. *Drittwirkung* in a highly regulated legal system

It follows from the points outlined above that direct application of higher law which dictates provisions for the protection of human rights may therefore be based on: (a) provisions expressly formulated in the Constitution; (b) principles and rules which are implied by constitutional provisions or are the product of their interpretation; and (c) provisions deriving from international instruments.

---

[36] For this reason Guazzarotti, op. cit., argues that the decision to allow courts to directly strike down national laws does not depend on a decision of the Constitutional Court but it could be a necessary 'political' decision, a conferral of that power to the courts and the recognition of the special status to the ECHR system.

[37] Law 9 January 2006, no. 12. On 30 November and 1 December 2005, the Presidents of the two Chambers sent a letter to the Presidents of each Standing Committee asking them to take into adequate account the obligations deriving from ECHR, particularly in view of the legislative proceedings in these bodies.

We have already indicated that the first examples of *Drittwirkung* within the private sphere in the Italian system date back to the 1950s and became consolidated in the 1960s in the area of labour relations (see below). We present here a review of some leading cases in this and other areas concerning the protection of constitutional rights both in contract law and the law of torts (contractual and non-contractual obligations). We will quote decisions of both ordinary courts and the Constitutional Court. In evaluating this jurisprudence, the foreign reader should be reminded that while the Constitutional Court is the final judge of the constitutional legitimacy of primary law, the highest ordinary tribunal is the *Corte di cassazione*; the latter is in charge of the correct interpretation of law (under the assumption that its compliance with the Constitution is not in question).[38]

1. Labour relations (Articles 2, 3, 19, 36, 37, 41 and 42 of the Italian Constitution)

Back in the early 1950s, the *Cassazione* established the legitimacy of a direct application of Article 36 of the Italian Constitution by lower courts in order to use the salaries agreed upon by collective labour agreements as the parameter to determine the salary of non-union workers (see Cassaz. 10 August 1953, no. 2696). In fact, the Constitution (Article 39) devolves to registered trade unions the task to strike agreements on behalf of all workers (with *erga omnes* effect). However, this provision has never been implemented because trade unions never allowed themselves to be submitted to registration requirements or to the membership census meant to determine their respective importance. In order to achieve a similar outcome, civil tribunals started referring directly to Article 36 of the Constitution, which recognises the right of workers to 'remuneration proportionate to the quantity and quality of their work, and in any case sufficient to ensure to them and their families a free and honourable existence'. This opinion was confirmed by the Constitutional Court in decision 129/1963 (see also decisions 156/1971 and 177/1984). In 1966, the Court extended the same right to days not paid for by social security in case of accident or illness (see decision 74/1966).

---

[38] Otherwise the *Cassazione* as well as any other court would have to refer the issue of constitutional legitimacy of the law to the Constitutional Court.

Article 36 of the Constitution also states that 'workers shall be entitled to a weekly day of rest and to annual paid holidays' (an *absolute* right which 'cannot be relinquished'). In 1962, the Constitutional Court confirmed a trend to directly apply this constitutional provision (see decisions 76/1962 and 150/1967).

Article 37, on the other hand, establishes that 'working women shall be entitled to equal rights and, for comparable jobs, the same pay as men'. Before the general law prohibiting discrimination in labour relationships was adopted (Law of 20 May 1970, no. 300, as modified by Law 903/1977), courts directly referred to this provision to deal with claims raised by women in order to obtain the same pay as men for the same work; the same can be said about the direct application of Article 37.3 of the Constitution in the context of minors (also entitled to equal pay for comparable work). In these cases we can see instances of an *unmittelbare Drittwirkung*. In another leading case (decision 17/1987), the Court clearly affirmed that the principle of equality between men and women as workers 'has general effects towards all parties'; and it denied the right of an employer to fire a woman because one of his clients had refused to be served by her. The court held that 'any contractual clause which implies a discrimination against women is null and void; *neither can it legitimate the decision by an employer not to hire or to fire a woman* ...'.

More recently, the courts have developed a contractual liability of employers vis-à-vis their employees in cases of mobbing perpetrated by other employees (for having neglected to adopt all measures required to prevent violations not only of the right to good health but, primarily, of the right to human dignity which every person and every worker is entitled to on the basis of Article 2 of the Constitution). Article 2087 of the Civil Code, in fact, states that employers must protect the physical integrity and the dignity of their employees. Not preventing mobbing from taking place within the workplace is sufficient to trigger employer's liability (not to mention the general clauses of *bona fide* and *fairness* in implementing obligations as established by the Civil Code for all contracts; see Articles 1175 and 1375 Civil Code).[39] The *Cassazione* has stated that the decisive factor, aside from specific acts, is the *global unlawful behaviour* of the employer who does little or nothing (and in

39 These two general clauses have been recurred to more than once in relation to the breach of constitutionally entrenched rights (a case of *mittelbare Drittwirkung*).

any case not enough) in order to prevent mobbing practices to take place within his/her enterprise (see Cassaz. 23 March 2005, no. 6326 and, previously, Cassaz. 4 May 2004, no. 8438). By doing so, the Court has *de facto* created a new model situation capable of attracting compensation on the basis of a combined reading of an article of the Civil Code (which was never so interpreted before) and Articles 2, 32 and 36 (the latter two in part) of the Constitution.

In the area of labour relations, it has also been recognised that Article 41.2 of the Constitution (which prohibits to use one's own economic rights in any such way that may 'harm the security, the freedom, or the dignity of any natural person') implies that – regardless of contractual freedom – the constitutional rights of employees (for instance the freedom of religion protected by Article 19 of the Constitution) may be limited (on acceptance by the worker) but only insofar as required by the production process. Furthermore, the employer has the duty to adopt production processes which do not infringe the protection of religious rights wherever possible (see Cassaz. 18 Feb. 2000, no. 1892).[40] This is another case of a direct application of constitutional provisions.

As has become clear, in no other area of the law has there been such a long-lasting effort to implement the idea that individuals are an end in themselves and that the law cannot treat them as mere instruments.[41]

2. Constitutional rights protection through extended compensation

By far the most extensive application of a variety of forms of *mittelbare Drittwirkung* within the Italian jurisdiction must be credited to a long-lasting trend by the courts to widen the indirect protection of constitutional rights through new heads of damage in the area of non-economic loss or compensation for non-pecuniary damages both in contract and in tort law.

By the time it becomes a matter of financial compensation, the violation of a fundamental right has, in most cases, of course already

---

40 V. Pacillo, *Contributo allo studio del diritto di libertà religiosa nel rapporto di lavoro subordinato* (2003).

41 R. Del Punta, *Diritti della persona e contratto di lavoro* (paper given in 2005).

taken place; and yet, along with compensation, the claimant might be able to obtain full protection of his/her rights from the time being while the courts' decisions – if sufficiently consistent and supported by the *Cassazione* (and, possibly, by the *Corte costituzionale*) – can grant some advanced protection of the involved rights by encouraging parties to comply in the first place and ensuring that those rights are not violated so as to avoid liability and related judicial costs. In time, the trend might eventually even prompt Parliament to intervene.

The basic conceptual scheme is similar to that followed (for other reasons) within the framework of the European Convention, which seeks to protect the rights included in Section I of the Convention by imposing on the Member States an obligation to secure to everyone those rights, or at least to grant the effective remedy established by Article 13, and granting as an alternative the (pecuniary) 'just' satisfaction established by Article 41.

This outcome is reached by the courts' innovative and integrative interpretation of liability clauses as they are presently regulated by the Italian Civil Code. The basic approach is to trump the restrictions and pre-conditions dictated by the Civil Code on the basis of a proper reading of the relevant constitutional provisions.

According to both the *Cassazione* (see decisions Cassaz. 31 May 2003, nos 8823 and 8828, but also Cassaz. 15 July 2005, no. 15022) and the Constitutional Court (see decision 233/2003), non-pecuniary damage attracts compensation even if no criminal offence is committed when they are the consequence of a violation of a fundamental right recognised by the Constitution (such as health, reputation, freedom of thought); basing its decision upon this concept, the Council of State thus recently denied compensation to a young woman who had not been selected in a competitive entrance examination intended to fill the position of a college researcher (see Cons. Stato 15 December 2005, no. 6960). The quoted *Cassazione* decision textually referred to a 'constitutionally oriented interpretation' of Article 2059 of the Civil Code, based on the principle of so-called *Drittwirkung* according to which constitutional provisions reflecting inviolable values or right of individuals do not only bind public authorities but also have an immediate and direct effect within the private sphere. Not only therefore must those cases directly identified by existing legislation be regarded as non-pecuniary damage but also any other instance in which there is an unlawful violation of constitutionally guaranteed human rights – under the condition that from such a violation may arise harm which is not capable of being quantified in economical terms and beyond any restrictions following from the *riserva di legge* (the need of a specific legal authorisation). The point is that Article 2059 of the Civil Code states that non-pecuniary loss may be compensated 'only in the cases established by law' – and legislation only provides for compensation if harm is caused by a crime. But not all violations of constitutional rights will, of course, constitute a criminal offence (neither in Italy nor anywhere else). In Cassaz. 31 May 2005, no. 8828, the judges explained that 'within the present system of law, based upon the Constitution's supremacy, which recognizes and guarantees the inviolable rights of man, non-pecuniary loss must be regarded as a broader head of damage, including all instances in which a value connected with the human person is violated'. In this case the Court recognised compensation for non-pecuniary loss as a consequence of the loss of parental relationships (a son had died in a car accident, with no crime having been committed). In Cassaz. 10 May 2005, no. 9801, compensation was awarded to a spouse for both pecuniary and non-pecuniary loss as a consequence of the violation of the right to enjoy a full sexual life; the other spouse had neglected to inform him/her of his/her sexual malfunctions which made intercourse impossible (see also the earlier Constitutional Court decision 561/1987, based on Article 2 of the Constitution, which recognised the 'right to sexual freedom'). And as early as the mid- to late-1970s, the *Cassazione* awarded compensation for non-pecuniary loss in all cases in which the defendant inflicted on the claimant some injury to his/her psychical or physical health (in these cases Article 32 of the Constitution was referred to; see Cassaz. 7 June 2000, no. 7713 and Constitutional Court decisions 88/1979, 455/1990 and 202/1991, where the Court held that 'the recognition of the right to good health as a fundamental right and a constitutionally guaranteed primary interest operates fully within the private sphere ...').

In this sense, a vast jurisprudence exists, supported by a leading decision of the Constitutional Court which stated that, according to the Constitution (which is primarily meant to guarantee the values related to the human person), the articles of the Civil Code on the basis of which compensation for both pecuniary (see Article 2043 Civil Code) and non-pecuniary loss (see Article 2059 Civil Code) is awarded 'shall be read in connection to the various provisions of the Fundamental Charter ... and are therefore in a way capable of compensating the harm inflicted on those values as a consequence of any wrongdoing …'. The most recent leading case is Constitutional Court decision 233/2003, where the Court overruled the interpretation of those tribunals which continued to interpret the law as meaning that non-economic loss should not be awarded in cases where the defendant's fault is not proven in trial, but only established on the basis of a legal presumption. The Court declared that this interpretation was no longer in line with the present legal and jurisprudential order; 'jurisprudence', the Court confirmed, 'has for some time now established further cases of substantially non-economic loss arising from injuries to constitutionally protected interests for which damages may be awarded, notwithstanding the absence of criminal intent …'.

The great potential of the reported trend in favour of an evergrowing extension of compensation for non-pecuniary loss in tort has been emphasised by several recent works.[42] Riccardo Del Punta, for example, conducts an inquiry into a wide range of constitutionally guaranteed interests which have been or might be recognised as a legitimate basis for compensation if violated: reputation, identity, privacy, dignity, life, wrongful life, the environment, the disturbance of peace, constitutional rights within labour relationships, and even 'spoiled holidays'.

3. *Prohibition of discrimination (Article 3 of the Italian Constitution)*

The principle of equality has played a crucial role in the Italian system. The inclusion in the Constitution of a general statement emphasising the principle of equality (Article 3),[43] has allowed the Constitutional Court to address all the disparate treatments not

---

[42] See G. Comandé (ed), *Diritto privato europeo e diritti fondamentali: saggi e ricerche* (2004); M. L. Chiarella in Comandé, op. cit.; E. Navarretta (ed), *I danni non patrimoniali* (2004); R. Del Punta, *Diritti della persona e contratto di lavoro* (paper given in 2005).

[43] Article 3.1 states that: 'all citizens possess an equal social status and are equal before the law, without distinction as to sex, race, language, religion, political opinions, personal and social conditions.' Article 3.2 declares that: 'it is the duty of the Republic to remove all economic and social obstacles which, by limiting the freedom and equality of citizens, prevent the full development of the individual and the

based upon a reasonable case-by-case differentiation in respect to the principles embedded in the Constitution and nurtured by the general values of Italian society.

The large number of Constitutional Court decisions based on Article 3 of the Constitution is a striking contrast to the absence of a direct application of that principle within the private sphere. Actually, the principle of equality as expressed in Article 3 has been interpreted by the majority as binding only the legislator and also often in conjunction with other fundamental rights protected by the Constitution.[44]

This can also explain why the legislator has never adopted a specific law forbidding discrimination in order to implement the constitutional principle of equality per se (for labour relations, see above).[45] Indeed, the first acts adopted in this field which also applied within the private sphere were issued to implement international conventions (such as Law 13 October 1975, no. 654, on racial discrimination[46]) or Community law (such as Law 9 December 1977, no. 903, on sex discrimination). The first genuine 'national' initiative in this field took place only in 1998 thanks to Law 40/1998 (now Legislative Decree 286/1998), which for the first time granted a specific civil action against discrimination based on

---

participation of all workers in the political, economic and social organization of the country.' The list of grounds for forbidden distinctions included in Article 3.1 is not a closed list but affirms a presumption of discrimination of any different treatment based upon those grounds. Moreover, the 'social origin' ground listed in Article 3.1 is a formula capable of including other implicitly forbidden discriminations which everyone is entitled the right to be protected against.

44 We could say that Article 3 has been interpreted much more like Article 14 ECHR than the EU general principle of non-discrimination.

45 Even before the coming into force of the Constitution, there were laws directly or indirectly prohibiting discrimination. The old Royal decree of 6 May 1940, no. 635, Art 187, e.g., already stated that shopkeepers shall not deny their services to any customer who asks and pays for them; and some protection of privacy was granted by the law 633/1941, which was meant to grant copyrights (Arts 93–95). An entire set of criminal law provisions, both included within the criminal code (*codice penale*) and in specific laws, are meant to protect fundamental rights. Other statutes protect privacy (law 31 December 1996, no. 675) and expressly extend the protection of fundamental human rights as recognised by internal law and by international covenants to all foreigners (legislative decree 25 July 1998, no. 286, Art 2).

46 Later amended by Law 20 May 1993 and Article 13 Law 85/2006. It is worth mentioning that the criminal law approach of this Act has had little success; it has not prevented violations and only too rarely has someone been found guilty.

race, colour, descent, national or ethnic origin, and religious beliefs in all situations in which both a private subject or the public administration has caused discrimination ('the judge can order the interruption of the detrimental behaviour and adopt any other adequate measure').[47] There is no direct link between these provisions and the constitutional principle of equality; (indeed the wording of Article 43 legislative decree 286/1 does reflect its international inspiration, since discrimination is defined in terms which recall the definition used by the International Convention and also limits its scope of application to the enjoyment of fundamental rights). In 2003, Parliament adopted two legislative decrees nos 215 and 216 of 9 July in order to implement Directives 2000/43/EC and 2000/78/EC (aimed at granting equal treatment of all regardless of race, ethnic origin, religion or belief, disability, age and sexual orientation) and finally avoided reference to fundamental rights. Both Decrees also apply to the private spheres, although the latter concerns only the employment and occupation sectors (reflecting the same limited scope of application as Directive 2000/78/EC).

Even after the adoption of these laws, it is very difficult to find much jurisprudence in this field, in particular cases invoking discrimination within the private sphere. Only three decisions based on Article 44 of Legislative Decree 286/1998 dealt with this issue, and they all ended with the conviction of the alleged perpetrator of the discrimination.[48] The first two involved estate agents that discriminated between European and non-European citizens in the text of house offers (see Trib. Milano, 30 March 2000 and Trib. Bologna, 22 February 2001); the third involved a coffee shop which had asked different prices from citizens and foreigners, mainly non-European citizens (see Trib. Padova, 19 May 2005). The estate agents and the coffee shop were not allowed legally to discriminate between citizens and foreigners in providing their services because this is forbidden by law and there is no room for the exercise of

---

47 The wording of Article 43 reflects its international inspiration as discrimination is defined in terms which recall the definition used by the International Convention against Discrimination.

48 The other cases concern decisions on housing and jobs within the public administration.

private choices justified by economic freedom; this distinction is forbidden and has no economic rationale. Indeed, it is the Constitution itself (Article 41.2 as explained above) which allows the legislator to set limits on private property and economic activity when these limits are socially oriented and justified by the need to protect other fundamental interests guaranteed by the Constitution.

Gradually, a debate among scholars is developing concerning the application of these limits to private property and to individuals in their private lives (apart from their job or professional activities). A case of this kind could, for example, involve the refusal to rent an apartment to an Arab, Asian, or any other person belonging to a specific ethnic group. It has also been argued that in this case it might be difficult to prove discrimination and that, in any event, there may be room to regard as legitimate such a behaviour on the basis of the right to privacy (which is protected through Article 2 of the Constitution), though only as long as there is no publicity.[49]

It is worth mentioning that in all the (few) cases based on Articles 43–44 of Legislative Decree 286/1998, neither constitutional principles nor provisions of international law have even been quoted.[50] It seems that lawyers do not recognise in these laws the implementation of a fundamental right. While equality is deemed one of the main values and purposes for the legislator, non-discrimination has been considered only as one of the effects of the former but not as an autonomous principle. Discovering the link between national laws and Community or international provisions forbidding discrimination can promote the affirmation of the principle of non-discrimination and its application within the private sphere. Speaking of 'non-discrimination' instead of 'equality' also has the advantage of stressing the recognition of the difference in question and the protection against disparate treatments based on that difference. The non-discrimination principle allows to make legally relevant all those

49 P. Morozzo della Rocca, *Immigrazione: profili normativi e orientamenti giurisprudenziali* (2004, 2005); B. Nascimbene (ed), *Il diritto degli stranieri* (2004).

50 Only in one case is there a reference to Article 2 Italian Constitution in order to protect not only the right to equality but also the right to privacy, and to protect one's own person, Trib. Bologna 6/17 October 2000. Another exception is Trib. Verona 24 February 2005: here the court applied law 654/1975 and referred to all relevant national and international law, and especially to the ECHR, developing a coherent set of provisions meant to fight racial discrimination.

differences of treatment which would otherwise run the risk of being melded together with other forms of different treatment which are legally neutral and regarded as the natural outcome of the freedom of choice.

In summary, the application of the non-discrimination principle within the private sphere is only devoted to legislative acts backed by Article 41.2 of the Constitution, but it is very difficult, in practice, to find much jurisprudence in this particular area. The international or Community origin of these laws might be a reason why there is little awareness of the potential of the non-discrimination principle in particular within the private sphere.

4. Political rights: freedom of political propaganda versus property rights (Articles 18, 21, 41, 42, 48 and 49 of the Italian Constitution)

A rather isolated but very interesting case concerns the balancing between the freedom of political propaganda (fully recognised by the Constitution) and property rights. A group of political activists involved in canvassing during an electoral campaign in 1999 had started to distribute flyers in a new shopping centre near the city of Verona, but were disturbed by the private guards of the company. They appealed to the tribunal in order to obtain an urgent order against the defendant[51] forcing him to stop interfering with the claimants when these are distributing their leaflets (at least in the parking lots and in the open areas within the mall). The defendant argued that the shopping centre was private property and that, according to Article 832 of the Civil Code, the owner was entitled the full right to stop any unauthorised activity.

In its decision, the Court (Trib. Verona 7 June 1999) underlined the conflict between freedom of expression (Article 21 of the Constitution), the free exercise of political rights (Articles 48 and 49 of the Constitution), and private property (Article 42 of the Constitution) – emphasising, however, that the Constitution allows to restrict the protection of property 'in order to ensure its social function'. The court openly referred to the concept of *Drittwirkung*

---

[51] As regulated by Article 700 of the Code of Civil Procedure (urgent *interim* measures).

and proved to be aware of the content of Article 1.3 of the German Basic Law (which it quoted); and although it also quoted some decisions of the Constitutional Court which urge ordinary judges to look for interpretations of existing law in compliance with the Constitution (rather, the judges wrote, than flooding the Court with issues of constitutional legitimacy), it bluntly 'created' a rule based entirely upon its own direct balancing of the conflicting constitutional interests involved in the case. The Court thus ordered the defendant to allow the distribution of flyers as long as it would take place not within the shops but only in the larger common areas, internal squares, and aisles (including the parking lots), and as long as the activists did not use any furniture or equipment belonging to the centre.

There is no doubt that it actually was a case of *unmittelbare Drittwirkung* because (and in spite of some of the reasoning conducted by the Verona tribunal in its judgment) it was only thanks to the higher relevance accorded to the freedom to engage in political propaganda that it was possible to pass over and limit the property rights which the defendant had invoked; freedom of expression was recognised as a 'trump card' able to overcome private property.[52] There was no specific legal provision to interpret in a new and different way – there was only the need to integrate existing law.

In a system which does not provide for *stare decisis*, a ruling such as the one given by the Verona tribunal would, of course, not ensure that an identical case would be resolved in the same way in future disputes.[53] This is, however, not just a matter of differences between a common law and a civil law jurisdiction. More importantly, it is actually the true difference nowadays between ordinary courts and the Constitutional Court; contrary to what some believed in the past, they *both* interpret and apply the Constitution, but *only* the Constitutional Court can decide issues with *erga omnes* effect (in case it decides to declare a law unconstitutional and deprives the related provisions of their effect). Ordinary courts may only rule on specific claims.

---

52 See O. Chessa, '*Drittwirkung* e interpretazione: brevi osservazioni su un caso emblematico' in E. Malfatti et al. (eds), *Il giudizio sulle leggi e la sua 'diffusione'* (2002).

53 This concept applies to all non-constitutional jurisprudence in the Italian legal order.

5. *Freedom of expression versus freedom of association within religiously oriented social institutions (Articles 2, 3, 7–8, 18, 19, 21, 24 and 111, 33, 41 of the Italian Constitution)*

There is a small set of cases in which the courts have had to deal with the conflict arising between some fundamental rights (and here in particular freedom of expression, Article 21 of the Constitution, religious freedom, Article 19 of the Constitution, and the right to be heard in court and to have a fair trial, Articles 24 and 111 of the Constitution) and other fundamental rights, such as the freedom of association (which includes the right to freely profess one's own religious beliefs in association with other individuals, Articles 18 and 19 of the Constitution), the right freely to establish schools and educational institutions (Article 33.2), freedom of economic enterprise (Article 41.1) and the right of religious denominations to organise themselves freely (Article 8).

Particularly in Constitutional Court decisions 195/1973 and 18/1982 as well as in the recent Consiglio di stato 18 April 2005, no. 1762, it was stated that no claim can be brought to court against the (free) decision of Catholic Church authorities to approve or not approve the appointment (and firing) of professors in charge of teaching at a Catholic private college; the freedom of such ideologically oriented institutions would be infringed if they could not choose their teachers taking into account their personality and their conformity to the ideological orientation of the institution which hires them. Previously, the Constitutional Court had accepted that teachers of ideologically oriented private schools might have to abide by a set of cultural, religious and ideological orientations (see decision 195/1972, which attempted to determine the balance between the conflicting constitutional values of individual freedom of expression and the right to establish private schools).

On the other hand, it is clear since Constitutional Court decision 18/1982 that Italian courts must verify whether rulings by courts belonging to other jurisdictions (for instance, the ecclesiastical tribunals of the Catholic Church) were based on procedures capable of guaranteeing the parties' constitutional rights. Consistent with this trend, the Court in Trib. Bari 12 December 2004 stated that the basic rules of fair trial ought to apply to the disciplinary process which ended with the expulsion of a believer from the Jehovah's Witnesses Congregation. The allegation by the Congregation, according to which the decision to expel its (former) member was not subject to review by a state tribunal, was not accepted. However, in Cassaz. 27 May 1994, no. 5213, the Court refused to accept a claim of a former member of a religious denomination against expulsion. According to the reasoning of the *Cassazione*, this result derived from the fact that that specific denomination had signed a particular agreement with the Italian State based upon Article 8.3 of the Constitution. The same could not be said of Jehovah's Witnesses. The *Cassazione*'s opinion remains unconvincing; the rights of autonomous organisations are recognised by the Constitution in Article 8.2 and should be granted to all denominations regardless of agreements with the Italian State.

In another case, the *Cassazione* upheld the principle that the right of a member to withdraw from an association may not be made subject to preconditions in the case of ideologically oriented associations; contrary to what happens in all other associations, freedom of expression (which means the freedom to withdraw immediately) trumps the right of all associations to organise freely recognised by both the Constitution and the Civil Code.

E. *Drittwirkung* in the Italian jurisdiction – conclusions

In conclusion, we can say that the application of constitutional rights in the private sphere is basically taken for granted within the Italian legal system, but at the same time it is nowadays a fairly marginal issue. In fact, in a civil law jurisdiction (such as the Italian one) it is rare that the protection of any kind of constitutional right may not be directly or indirectly derived from some statutory provision.

Cases of *Drittwirkung* may arise where the judge registers a total absence of legislation or where he is unable to find a valid law which is open to interpretation in compliance with the constitutional provisions designed to grant the right requiring protection. Where a law does exist but can be interpreted only in a way which renders it ineffective with regard to the aim of granting the required protection, there is, in the Italian system, no other outcome than a referral to the Constitutional Court. The ordinary judge cannot ignore the existence of an ineffective but binding law unless he accepts the risk of being overruled by another court or the *Cassazione*.

It is not a paradox that this was not so during the long phase during which the Italian Constitution (including the Bill of Rights) was waiting for its exceedingly slow implementation. The set of ordinary laws then suited to grant the protection of the rights established within the Constitution displayed more than one gap, and especially in the area of social and labour rights progressive courts were prompted to allow the direct application of a Constitution which was not really regarded as immediately effective and binding. The widely accepted interpretation of Articles 41 and 42 of the Constitution, confirmed by several decisions of the Constitutional Court, helped; the inviolable rights which belong to the inalienable protection of all human beings do not include economic freedoms (see Constitutional Court decisions 11/1956 and 16/1968). In the absence of statutory provisions striking a different balance, a balancing in favour of social rights was therefore possible.

Within this framework, direct (*unmittelbare*) *Drittwirkung* appears as an option which a court might decide to try in order to close real or apparent legislative gaps. At times it can be referred to in order to foster the recognition of new rights not specifically enumerated by the Constitution (in this case Article 2 provides the legal 'leverage' needed to enlarge the list of constitutionally recognised rights).

More often, the courts will resort to *mittelbare Drittwirkung*. In this case the text and the 'living' Constitution (the Constitution as interpreted by the courts themselves, in particular the Constitutional Court) will be used in order to interpret existing law in even very innovative ways so as to expand the protection of rights – possibly along the lines of existing international law, which may be very helpful in this exercise thanks to their broader legitimacy (whether or not they can be given a superior position within the Italian hierarchy of norms). International case law can also be referred to for the same purpose. Contract and tort law have often been interpreted in order to pave the way towards a more effective protection of constitutional rights. *Unmittelbare Drittwirkung* is also suited to be used in order to bypass the constitutional jurisprudence when it has proven exceedingly cautious or 'slow' (instead of referring legislation to the Constitutional Court so that it may evaluate its constitutionality, the courts interpret it in a constitutionally oriented way or directly apply a constitutional provision, at times also relying on international provisions).[54]

[54] A. Guazzarotti, 'I giudici comuni e la CEDU alla luce del nuovo art. 117 Cost.' in (2001) 1 *Quaderni costituzionali* 25–51.

Drittwirkung has, of course, a lot to do with the idea of a constitution which is shared within a legal system. To this end it can be said that in Italy the belief that the Constitution is law, and, more importantly, a binding law of a superior kind and likely to trump conflicting legislation, is widely shared. The interpretation of the Constitution is not the exclusive business of the Constitutional Court; there is ample room for judges to reinforce and extend the protection of rights within the private sphere as well.

As a consequence, the idea of a sharp separation between private and public law is regarded as outdated by most authoritative scholars. It is clear that, within a system based on a written constitution as the supreme law, there is no room for private law performing the function of a 'sacred constitution of the private sphere' when this supreme constitution openly recognises social rights while at the same time protecting property and economic rights in a somewhat limited way.[55] There is only one constitution and this constitution is public law by definition. No one could interpret it in a way so as to render null and void the core of private enterprise or private property (all constitutional rights when subject to a balancing process with other constitutional rights deserve at least *some* measure of protection regarding their core) but there is, equally, no doubt that fundamental rights or inviolable rights (starting with human rights) will invariably come first. The private sphere is bound to be subordinated to the protection of the core rights accorded to every human being, and the courts will find the necessary mechanisms to make this protection effective.

55 Another example which appropriately shows how difficult it is to maintain barriers between private and public law is the autonomous jurisdictions in the area of sports: the effort to consider sport federations' internal disciplinary procedures exempted from the strict application of the basic principles of a fair trial as recognised by the Constitution (Article 24) and ECHR law (Article 6) is losing ground. The law now provides some protection by tribunals (see law 17 October 2003, no. 280), and as recently as 22 August 2006 the Lazio Administrative Tribunal stated that to deny any 'public' jurisdiction over the decisions of internal sports courts would infringe basic constitutional principles. In this and in similar cases the conflict is between the freedom of association and property rights, especially within those sports associations where the role of professionals is crucial and teams are even owned by public limited companies (in the case of football, for instance). Labour law is another field where public and private law tend to merge via osmosis.

Chapter 10: New Zealand Taking Human Rights into the Private Sphere

Paul Rishworth

[This case] falls into a special area where, in the New Zealand context, a sharp boundary between public and private law cannot realistically be drawn.

Cooke J, for the New Zealand Court of Appeal
in *Finnigan v New Zealand Rugby Union Inc*[1]

---

[1] [1985] 2 NZLR 159, 179 (per Cooke J, for the Court). The New Zealand Court of Appeal 'stopped the All Blacks tour' to South Africa in 1985. It was the era of South African apartheid. Two rugby-playing New Zealand lawyers had commenced proceedings in the High Court to challenge the Rugby Union's decision to send the New Zealand national rugby team, the All Blacks, to South Africa and so to maintain sporting contacts at a time when the Commonwealth, along with many liberal New Zealanders, called for sporting boycotts. By sending the team, they claimed, the Rugby Union would act outside its constitutive rules, which required it to 'promote, foster or benefit the game of rugby in New Zealand'. The claim was struck out in the High Court on the grounds that, not being members of the Rugby Union, the plaintiffs had no standing to sue to enforce its rules. The Court of Appeal disagreed: the plaintiffs' challenge was important, bearing on the future of the game in New Zealand. If the plaintiffs were not accorded standing there was no other way of testing the lawfulness of the Rugby Union's actions. The appeal was allowed; the action reinstated. The rest is (New Zealand) history. A trial on the merits commenced but, late on a Saturday afternoon with the case only part heard and the team due to leave the following Monday, the trial judge issued an interim injunction to stop the tour. The Rugby Union elected not to appeal and no tour took place. For discussion see M. Taggart, 'Rugby, the Anti-Apartheid Movement and Administrative Law' in R. Bigwood (ed), *Public Interest Litigation* (2006), p 69.

A. Introduction

New Zealand law distinguishes public from private law obligations, recognising the 'special area' where the boundary is difficult to define. In the last two decades New Zealand courts have been increasingly drawn into that area, the contraction of government in an era of corporatisation and privatisation making challenges to the decisions of non-governmental bodies more likely than in earlier times.[2] The courts have asked whether such a body bears some extra legal burden on account of its being 'public',[3] performing functions that are 'public',[4] being affected by a 'public interest',[5] or doing things that have 'public consequences'.[6] The result of bearing that burden may vary according to the nature of the case, but, in the main, it is that the party's impugned action is amenable to some degree of judicial review. The party will need to have acted 'reasonably and in good faith and upon lawful and relevant grounds of public interest'.[7] The enactment of the New Zealand Bill of Rights Act 1990, which applies to government and to bodies that perform 'public functions', provided a further reason for exploration of that

---

2 Most recently, *Ransfield v Radio Network Ltd* [2005] 1 NZLR 233 (HC); *Hosking v Runting* [2005] 1 NZLR 1 (CA); *Dunne v CanWest TV Works Ltd* [2005] NZAR 577.

3 The general availability of judicial review in respect of bodies that are part of the executive branch of government is not contested, or, if it is, the contest arises out of some feature of the case other than the nature of the decision-maker.

4 See *Federated Farmers of New Zealand (Inc) v New Zealand Post Ltd* [1990–92] 3 NZBORR 339.

5 See *Sky City (Auckland) Ltd v Wu* [2002] 3 NZLR 621 (CA), two of three judges being attracted to the view that a casino favoured with a statutory licence to operate is as a result affected by a public interest, such that it could exclude patrons only for good reason. The applicable legislation, however, unequivocally ousted that argument. But the court noted that the general proposition was 'soundly based in New Zealand law and in economic good sense' (para 22). See also *Vector Ltd v Transpower New Zealand Ltd* [1999] 3 NZLR 646 and authorities cited in that case.

6 This formulation was used in *Phipps v Royal Australian College of Surgeons* [1999] 3 NZLR 1 (CA), [2000] 2 NZLR 513 (PC) and in *Dunne v CanWest TVWorks Ltd* [2005] NZAR 577.

7 H. W. R. Wade and C. F. Forsyth, *Administrative Law* (9th edn, 2004), p 355, earlier editions of which were cited with approval in *Webster v Auckland Harbour Board* [1983] NZLR 646 at 650 and *Webster v Auckland Harbour Board* [1987] 2 NZLR 129 at 131, per Cooke P (CA).

special area: Bill of Rights constraints provide further, and substantive, grounds for administrative challenges.[8]

But it is possible, of course, to go further and suggest there is no true boundary at all between the public and the private: that every human interaction involving law is, and always has been, susceptible to infusion with values that are 'public'. Indeed, the label 'private' may do no more than describe the result in those cases where the reasons for individual autonomy (and non-intervention by a court) override the reasons for imposing 'public' obligations on a defendant at the suit of an aggrieved plaintiff. Every case, in other words, is open for review and to the possibility that human rights and concomitant obligations will operate 'horizontally'. Private law, no less than public law, embodies conclusions about rights. This argument is not a new one, but it has taken on a new form since enactment of the New Zealand Bill of Rights, which, by s 3(a), binds the judicial branch of government as well as the two branches that initiate governmental action. It is now said that the judiciary is positively bound to resolve *all* cases in a Bill of Rights-consistent manner, even those between private litigants fought over the scope and impact of the common law. And this, it is said, means the Bill of Rights operates in the manner that is generally described as 'indirect horizontality'.

This chapter explores the way in which these issues are developing in New Zealand's law. It has to be said that no clear position has emerged. But the pattern of existing law along with developing case law in the Bill of Rights fields suggests the following tentative conclusions:

1. Virtually all law, common law and statutory, is explicable at some level as being about human rights – as that term is now understood – whether as rights against the state, against other citizens, or both. That is to say, rights horizontality (rights operating between citizens in private litigation) is, once one looks for it, intrinsic to the system of law we have. The ubiquity of horizontality can be masked because in a great number of cases the prevailing right or interest is that which results in the relationship being characterised as private. The relative paucity of litigated cases making this point is explicable by reason of its

8 See s 3(b) of the New Zealand Bill of Rights Act 1990, discussed further below.

obviousness. There has been no litigation, for example, arguing for remedies for discrimination in the selection of a person's friends or dinner guests, or for arbitrary detention of children in their bedrooms, and very little litigation seeking judicial review of commercial decisions (save in the marginal cases where it is argued for special reasons that the actor is public or performs a public function).[9]

2. In the last half-century the rise to prominence of a body of human rights law, comprising the imperatives of the various international treaties as well as domestic statutes, has prompted a reassessment of many of the judgments embedded in common law and legislation that bear upon the meaning of rights in practice, including their operation between private citizens. That is to say, given modern sensibilities, some points no longer seem as obvious as they once did. The location of the public–private boundary is, in that sense, contestable; the scope for uncontrolled private action depends upon the resolution of those contests by the courts in different eras (recognising, of course, the possibility of parliamentary action to countermand judicial decisions).
3. In New Zealand it is the legislative branch that has, as might be expected, taken the lead in 'rights-promoting' legal reforms designed to operate between citizens, as well as between citizen and government. The private sphere is always susceptible to organisation and control, and it is first and foremost a political decision as to how far this will go. Occasions for judicial re-evaluation of rights-reflecting balances in the common law are fewer and, given the nature of adjudication, somewhat accidental. That said, both legislative and judicial reassessments of human rights issues are increasingly taking place using the language and concepts suggested by human rights instruments (the international treaties and, in New Zealand's case, the New Zealand Bill of Rights Act 1990).
4. The impetus of the call for advancing human rights – passing over for the moment the many areas of contention about what rights actually mean in particular cases and what counts as advancing them – is, ultimately, much more important than the language of the instruments in which those rights happen to

---

[9] *Mercury Energy Ltd v Electricity Corporation of New Zealand Ltd* [1994] 1 WLR 521 (PC).

be currently expressed. To put it another way, there is considerable commonality between New Zealand, Canada, South Africa, the United Kingdom and the United States of America in the field of human rights (and, in particular, in relation to their possible horizontal application). This is so even though one can point to differences in the wording of the relevant charters or bills of rights – as to whether, say, they bind the 'judicial branch' of government (which New Zealand's does but Canada's does not); whether they apply to private bodies performing 'public functions' in addition to the executive branch (as New Zealand's and the United Kingdom's do but Canada's does not); and whether they apply to the common law (as South Africa's explicitly does in contrast to all others, where it is left to various degrees of inference). These differences count for less than one might think, first because they are irrelevant to political calls for legislative reforms based on the affirmed rights; and second, because judicial developments in the cause of protecting rights will depend, ultimately, on judges being persuaded that such developments are necessary and possible – at which point the real question is whether anything in the bill or charter *stops* such a development. In short, the affirmation of rights and freedoms in bills and charters supplies the language for argument about possible refinement or development of common law doctrine for rights-protecting reasons. But any reform that might ensue is still a product of common law reasoning, which judges are bound to undertake because they are judges.

5. In some quarters the conclusion just outlined is regarded as claiming too little for the New Zealand Bill of Rights. Some say the Bill of Rights positively *compels* a rights-consistent common law, making the Bill of Rights an instrument of empowerment to redress rights violations in the private sphere. It is said that judges should apply not just the 'values' of a bill of rights but the bill of rights itself, with the implication that the latter approach is somehow more demanding – that it requires the evaluation of any limits placed on rights in the crucible of the applicable 'reasonable limits' clause. I will suggest, however, that in New Zealand there is no evidence of any practical difference between the 'Bill of Rights as values' approach and the 'Bill of Rights as positive compulsion' approach. And there are reasons for thinking that the New Zealand jurisprudence to date is best explained on the 'values' approach.

6. The overall conclusion is consistent with rights in the New Zealand Bill of Rights operating horizontally. There will be cases where, upon consideration, the balance between rights in settled law is adjusted, and other cases where it is undisturbed. The point is that all law must ultimately meet Bill of Rights values, but – importantly – those values include the liberty and autonomy of private actors, as well as the rights and interests of those acted upon.

The above is offered as an explanation of New Zealand developments, with no claim that it is necessarily germane elsewhere.

How, then, to make these claims in more detail? Some description of New Zealand's constitutional arrangements is a necessary starting point. I then turn to consider the impact of the Bill of Rights on the common law of New Zealand, and it is through this inquiry that the points made above will be expanded.

B. New Zealand's constitutional arrangements

As things stand, no single document claims to be New Zealand's 'Constitution'. Instead, the Constitution of New Zealand is an amalgam of a small number of parliamentary statutes, important for their 'constitutional' subject matter, along with constitutional conventions and fundamental common law principles. Also firmly in the mix, yet so far in a benignly unarticulated way, is the Treaty of Waitangi – the treaty made in 1840 between the English Crown and numerous Maori chiefs, following which the Crown proclaimed sovereignty over the islands of Aotearoa/New Zealand. More could be said about the Treaty of Waitangi, and the continuing Maori institutional autonomy that it implies, for this generates some indigenous issues about the public–private divide in Maoridom. But that must be left for another occasion.[10]

---

[10] Having evolved our political constitution to the point where Maori, operating through tribes, are said to be the Crown's 'Treaty partner', there are some important consequential questions about representation and mandate in Maoridom, and the nature of Maori institutions. One aspect concerns arguably illiberal practices affecting women in Maori protocol. Some of these are addressed in C. Charters, 'Maori, beware the Bill of Rights Act!' [2003] NZLJ 401 and 'BORA and Maori: the Fundamental Issues' [2003] NZLJ 459.

The 'constitutional canon' of important statutes comprises, most agree, the Constitution Act 1986, the Electoral Act 1993 and the New Zealand Bill of Rights Act 1990.[11] No more need be said about the Electoral Act 1993, and the Bill of Rights features shortly, but the Constitution Act needs a little more explanation – its name might suggest more than it delivers. It is essentially a *description* of the legislative branch of government: it does not create or empower it.[12] The Constitution Act is itself an Act of the New Zealand Parliament, so the source of legislative power obviously lies elsewhere. Empowerment came, historically, from a series of UK statutes commencing with the New Zealand Constitution Act 1852.[13] Progressively greater power was conferred by successive imperial statutes, including a power to amend the Constitution Act locally, to the point where by 1947 a 'sovereign' legislative power was enjoyed by New Zealand's General Assembly (as it was then called). With no formal legal restrictions, and a power (so it seemed) to define its own power, the General Assembly was analogous to the UK Parliament. When in 1968 a judge in a criminal case questioned Parliament's powers to legislate extraterritorially,[14] that question was shortly answered by the New Zealand Constitution Amendment Act 1973 (amending, that is, the original 1852 constitution enacted by the UK Parliament). The 1973 Parliament asserted a power to legislate even with extra-territorial effect, relying upon its amending power to extend its law-making power.

---

[11] See, generally, P. Joseph, *Constitutional and Administrative Law in New Zealand* (2nd edn, 2001), p 21. Joseph makes the point that a great number of statutes include provisions that bear on constitutional matters, including for example the State Sector Act 1988 (the public service); the Legislature Act 1908 (Parliamentary privilege); the Judicature Act 1908 and District Courts Act 1947 (creation of High Court, Court of Appeal and District Courts); the Ombudsmen Act 1975 (forum for complaint about administration of government); Citizens Initiated Referenda Act 1993 (possibility of non-binding referenda if sufficient numbers seek it); and so on. But the Constitution Act 1986, Electoral Act 1993 and the Bill of Rights are at the core. For further discussion see P. Rishworth, G. Huscroft, S. Optican and R. Mahoney, *The New Zealand Bill of Rights* (2003), pp 2–4.

[12] As to the judicial branch, the Constitution Act protects High Court judges from removal from office, save by the Sovereign or Governor-General on an address by Parliament (s 23), and protects their salaries (s 24). It does not purport to establish and empower courts and judges.

[13] New Zealand Constitution Amendment Act 1857 (UK); Statute of Westminster 1931 (UK); New Zealand Constitution (Amendment) Act 1947 (UK).

[14] *R v Fineberg* [1968] NZLR 119.

The Constitution Act 1986 then completed the series. Prompted by an unrelated controversy (about the transition between governments at election time), the 1986 Act asserted in s 15 that Parliament has 'full power to make laws'. Simultaneously, s 26 provided that the various imperial statutes that had brought Parliament into being were thereafter to be of no force or effect in New Zealand. This was likened – by legal academics at least – to sawing off the branch of the tree on which one sits, or travelling back in time to shoot one's grandfather. That is, the 1986 Act was arguably a technical revolution, producing an autochthonous constitution whereunder Parliament's power rests on the assent of the New Zealand people and not on any historic empowerment by the United Kingdom. An alternative view is that no-one was shot; it is simply a case of freedom, once conferred, being irrevocable.[15]

In any event, all agree that New Zealand's Parliament has no higher law to constrain it. And most agree its legitimacy rests on the continuing assent of the New Zealand people, and not the historic 'top-down' grant of a once-Royal power. This is significant, because the idea of 'rights' now pervades political debate, helpfully or not, and Parliament is increasingly scrutinised for how it deals with rights. The New Zealand Bill of Rights Act 1990, to which I come shortly, is the natural focus of this discourse and scrutiny, but rights-talk occurs across the spectrum of political activity, in every field from health, welfare and education through to the environment and Maori concerns. In some fields the rights discourse produces policy and legislation explicitly taking rights into the private sphere where they may operate between citizens – notably in the field of employment and information privacy, of which a little more later.

Back to Parliament's legally unlimited powers. Some, notably the late Lord Cooke of Thorndon, believed that a set of judicially enforceable common law limits circumscribes the New Zealand Parliament's law-making power.[16] That debate happily remains theoretical. All agree there are no express limits. One serious attempt

---

[15] See the discussion in Joseph, op. cit., note 11, at pp 453–60.

[16] See Lord Cooke of Thorndon, 'Fundamentals' [1988] NZLJ 158, and the commentary by M. D. Kirby, 'Lord Cooke and Fundamental Rights' in P. Rishworth (ed), *The Struggle for Simplicity in Law: Essays for Lord Cooke of Thorndon* (1997), p 331.

was made to change that. In 1985 the newly elected Labour government proposed a supreme law Bill of Rights, releasing a White Paper with a suggested text and promotional commentary. But the process of public consultation that followed revealed no public sentiment in favour of a greater power for judges and, in some quarters, downright antagonism. The government's response was remarkably deft – strategic withdrawal coupled with a somewhat anaemic Trojan Horse. That is, the people were taken to have rejected only a *supreme law* Bill of Rights, not the idea of a Bill of Rights itself. And so a *statutory* Bill of Rights was proposed. This was duly enacted as the New Zealand Bill of Rights Act 1990, on the votes of government members over those of the opposition.[17] This made for an inauspicious legislative history, the new Bill of Rights being initially remarked upon only for what it was not, the supreme law that its principal protagonist, Attorney General and Prime Minister Sir Geoffrey Palmer, had wanted. Greeted by an apathetic legal profession and (with some exceptions)[18] a sceptical bench, the Bill of Rights was initially fodder only for the criminal defence lawyers.[19]

But things changed very quickly. The New Zealand Bill of Rights Act soon blossomed into a significant pillar of the unwritten Constitution. It could hardly have been otherwise, for the rights and freedoms it affirmed were essentially the contemporary expressions of English law's ancient concerns, reinforced by the late twentieth

[17] See P. Rishworth, 'The Birth and Rebirth of the Bill of Rights' in G. Huscroft and P. Rishworth, *Rights and Freedoms* (1995), p 1.

[18] Notably Lord Cooke of Thorndon, then Sir Robin Cooke, President of the New Zealand Court of Appeal. His first Bill of Rights decision, *Flickinger v Crown Colony of Hong Kong* [1991] 1 NZLR 439, saw him cite the famous dictum about the need, when interpreting constitutional instruments, to eschew the 'austerity of tabulated legalism'. This located the Bill of Rights in the international constitutional discourse. The 'tabulated legalism' reference goes back to S. De Smith in *The New Commonwealth and its Constitutions* (1964), p 194.

[19] Notably *Ministry of Transport v Noort; Police v Curran* [1992] 3 NZLR 260 (CA), which determined that a road-side breath alcohol stop by police constituted a detention under the Bill of Rights and this triggered the, albeit reasonably limited, right to consult counsel contained in s 23(10(b); *R v Laugalis* (1993) 10 CRNZ 350 (CA) is also significant from this era, with the search powers contained in the Misuse of Drugs Act 1975 read down in light of the right to be free from unreasonable searches and seizures contained in s 21 of the Bill of Rights.

century's international call for human rights. From around 1994,[20] then, the Bill of Rights came to be re-imagined, shedding the limitations of its humble beginnings. A few things helped in the process: the renaissance of the international human rights movement; the end of apartheid and a new rights-based constitutionalism in South Africa; the clarion call of human rights as a way to end ethnic conflict in battle zones around the world. These all put the phrase 'human rights' into public consciousness, and now it seemed that New Zealand had been only just a little ahead of its time in affirming a domestic set of human rights in the 1990 Act. In the United Kingdom, at about this time, there was a groundswell of support for 'bringing rights home' from Europe.[21] With the mother country regarding our Bill of Rights as a model for hers, the New Zealand legal profession and bench seemed to look more fondly upon what we had. And model it was, for by this time it was clear that even a parliamentary affirmation of rights, instructing judges to prefer rights-consistent interpretations of enactments where possible, augured a form of judicial review of legislation that elevated judges in the scheme of rights-protection. After all, only after a suggested meaning of an enactment is reviewed for its consistency with a bill of rights can courts obey the mandate to prefer consistent over inconsistent meanings. And if they conclude that a consistent interpretation is impossible, that is effectively a 'declaration' of the provision's 'incompatibility'.[22] This underscored the essential commonality of the enterprise in which the constitutional courts of the common law world were now engaging: measuring the actions of government, legislative and otherwise, against human rights standards set out in

---

[20] A critical case in the re-imagining of the Bill of Rights was *Simpson v Attorney-General (Baigent's Case)* [1994] 3 NZLR 667 (CA), in which it was held that the Bill of Rights implicitly created a public law cause of action for compensation for breach of its provisions. The case traversed constitutional jurisprudence from around the world, so locating New Zealand's Bill of Rights in that realm.

[21] This culminated in the enactment of the Human Rights Act 1998 (UK).

[22] Section 4 of the New Zealand Bill of Rights requires that a court apply an inconsistent enactment notwithstanding the inconsistency. The point, however, is that a court needs first to have found inconsistency before the section has any 'bite'. In effect, reliance upon s 4 to apply an enactment is tantamount to a declaration of inconsistency. The Court of Appeal said in *Moonen v Film and Literature Board of Review* [2000] 2 NZLR 9 that it would make declarations of inconsistency when that was required. That case was decided when the Human Rights Act 1998 (UK) had been enacted but before it had come into effect.

bills or charters of rights. Strong form constitutionalism involves judicial invalidation; weak form involves finding interpretative solutions and declarations of incompatibility.[23] But both involve judicial review of legislation.[24]

From the idea of judicially cognisable standards in bills of rights it was only a small step to the question of indirect horizontality. Do those new human rights standards bind private persons? Do they do so indirectly by requiring government to protect private persons from infringements of rights by others? How far do they extend into the private sphere by the device of their being applicable to 'public functions' carried out by non-governmental bodies? And – the question about horizontality – if the Bill of Rights binds the judges does that mean that the common law must be made rights-consistent?

Even at the White Paper stage in 1985, the question of horizontality had been seen as an issue with which judges would wrestle once a New Zealand Bill of Rights was enacted. The key White Paper advisers had, it transpired, been schooled in US constitutional law, couching their commentary on what we now term horizontality in the American language of 'state action'.[25] Their draft Article 2 guaranteed the rights and freedoms against 'acts done by the legislative, executive and judicial branches of government', as well as 'acts done by persons or bodies in the performance of a public function'. By way of commentary, they said:[26]

> In a broad sense Bills of Rights are thought of as documents which restrain the great powers of the State. They are not seen as extending to private actions. Such actions are rather to be controlled by the general law of the land; that law will be adequate to deal with private action or can be made so.

---

[23] The idea of strong and weak form constitutionalism is explored in Tushnet, 'Weak-Form Judicial Review; Its Implications for Legislatures', in G. Huscroft and I. Brodie (eds), *Constitutionalism in the Charter Era* (2004), p 213.

[24] The point is developed in P. Rishworth, 'The Inevitability of Judicial Review under Interpretive Bills of Rights: Canada's Legacy to New Zealand and Commonwealth Constitutionalism?' in G. Huscroft and I. Brodie, op. cit., p 233.

[25] The drafting of the White Paper was entrusted to a committee of lawyers from the public and private sector under the direction of Professor Kenneth Keith (now Sir Kenneth Keith, a member of the International Court of Justice). Sir Kenneth and a leading private lawyer on the committee, David A. R. Williams, had done postgraduate degrees at Harvard Law School.

[26] *A Bill of Rights for New Zealand* (1985), para 10.20.

They referred to *Shelley v Kraemer*,[27] where the Supreme Court of the United States said that the Fourteenth Amendment 'erects no shield against merely private conduct, however discriminatory or wrongful'. But, as they observed, that led inexorably to the question: how is the line between public and other actions to be drawn? A series of illustrative scenarios was put, drawn from New Zealand and American examples including the facts of *Shelley v Kraemer* itself (a racially discriminatory restrictive covenant that the Supreme Court refused to enforce). The discussion concluded, presciently it turns out, with the observation that the provisions of draft Article 2 could 'only be a first step in the drawing of the line between public action, which would be caught by the Bill, and private action, which would not be'.[28] That was a frank admission of the difficulty of capturing in words the complexity of the necessary inquiries into whether something, or some body, is public or private. I return to the problem of language a little later.

In the end, as has been said, the White Paper version of the Bill of Rights was not enacted. Draft Article 2 became, with minor changes, s 3 of the statutory Bill of Rights in 1990:[29]

> 3. **Application**—This Bill of Rights applies only to acts done—
>
> (a) By the legislative, executive, or judicial branches of the Government of New Zealand; or
>
> (b) By any person or body in the performance of any public function, power, or duty conferred or imposed on that person or body by or pursuant to law.

The statutory Bill of Rights was not capable of invalidating inconsistent legislation, but its potential impact in taking human rights into the private sphere was the same as the White Paper version. After all, cases at the cutting edge of horizontality or state action were never likely to involve the constitutionality of legislation. They were much more likely to be about the common law, or about particular acts done by private bodies but in the performance of functions claimed to be public. In short, all the scenarios in the

---

27 334 US 1 (1948), p 13.

28 Note 26, para 10.23.

29 The word 'only' in the first line (not in the White Paper draft) seems to have reflected an unwarranted fear that, without it, s 3 might have been seen as simply a statement that the Act bound the Crown, leaving the inference that the Bill of Rights was in other respects intended to bind everyone.

White Paper commentary were still capable of occurring under a statutory Bill of Rights; indeed, a number already have.

In the early days of the New Zealand Bill of Rights Act 1990, then, the attention of academic commentators turned to whether and how it would apply to private litigation involving the common law. Some pointed to the express inclusion of 'acts done' by the judicial branch in s 3, an obvious point of difference from s 32 of the Canadian Charter of Rights and Freedoms, which by 1990 had been held by the Supreme Court of Canada not to apply directly to the common law in private litigation (although the Charter could influence the common law through its 'values').[30] It was suggested, on that textual basis, that the New Zealand judges were directly bound by the Bill of Rights and required to declare a rights-compliant common law, essentially making the Bill of Rights operative in the realm of purely private litigation. Others, of whom I was one, suggested that the Canadian approach was still apt; that Bill of Rights values should inform common law but that this did not flow from the proposition that the judicial act of deciding cases fell within the concept of 'acts done' by the judiciary.[31] My reason was essentially the pointlessness of any argument that judges, by reason of being mentioned in s 3(a), became 'bound' by the Bill of Rights. Where, really, did such an argument lead? That a judge might 'breach' the Bill of Rights by making – as a disappointed litigant would see it – the *wrong* decision on a rights claim involving the common law? If so, could that judge then be sued by the litigant, along with every other unobliging judge in succession, with potentially infinite regression or at least until the litigant attained a pleasing result? And then, given that suing a judge is impossible anyway, is anything really gained by arguing that judges are somehow 'bound' by the Bill of Rights to develop a rights-compliant common law?[32] Much better, it seemed to me, to say that the Bill of

---

30 *RWSDU Local 580 v Dolphin Delivery Ltd* [1986] 2 SCR 573, 603. An early New Zealand commentator who pointed to the textual differences between New Zealand and Canada was A. Butler, 'The New Zealand Bill of Rights and Private Common Law Litigation' [1991] *NZLJ* 265.

31 See P. Rishworth, G. Huscroft, S. Optican and R. Mahoney, *The New Zealand Bill of Rights* (2003), pp 98–109.

32 A similar point is made by L'Heureux-Dubé in *Dagenais v Attorney-General (Canada)* [1994] 3 SCR 835 at para 145.

Rights should *inform* the development of common law, to the extent that the considered demands of the newly affirmed rights and freedoms might well supply reasons for the common law's extension or refinement. (As to what *was* meant by the concept of 'acts done' by the judicial branch in s 3(a) of the Bill of Rights, the more appealing view was that it covered non-adjudicative acts such as delaying judgment so as to unreasonably delay a trial, refusing an interpreter, and so on. And even then the effect was not to make the judge himself or herself liable; rather the aim of s 3(a) was to make it clear that such things counted as breaches by the government to which the Bill of Rights spoke.)

As it has turned out, New Zealand courts have quite properly operated on the basis that, one way or the other, the Bill of Rights is indeed germane to their adjudication of private litigation. No considered ruling on exactly how or why has yet been felt necessary. But there are dicta of various types, some supporting each of the two possible views as to how and why the Bill of Rights applies to private litigation. I discuss the cases shortly. But enough has been said to sketch the basic features of the New Zealand constitution: a Parliament that is acknowledged to be supreme and have only political, not legal, constraints, allied with a statutory Bill of Rights that affirms a set of civil and political rights to which legislators ought to have regard when enacting laws, and to which judges ought to have regard when interpreting them.

Three other salient features of the constitution, from a rights perspective, should quickly be mentioned. First, s 7 of the Bill of Rights requires that the Attorney General must advise Parliament if he or she considers that any provision in a Bill is inconsistent with the affirmed rights and freedoms. This has in fact occurred on 39 occasions between 1990 and August 2006, 21 times in relation to private members' Bills, and 18 times in relation to government Bills. Nothing prevents enactment of a Bill that has attracted one of these 's 7 reports' and this has happened a number of times. Generally, one of two explanations then applies: that the House disagreed with the Attorney General's advice and considered the Bill to be consistent with the Bill of Rights, or that it accepted that advice but wished to enact the Bill regardless.[33]

---

[33] Happily, very few cases are in that last category, and some of these concern the special case of social welfare legislation that did not recognise same-sex

A second rights-protecting feature deserving mention is the judicial obligation in s 6 of the Bill of Rights to prefer, where possible, rights-consistent meanings of enactments.[34] An unstated but inevitable consequence is the concomitant power to declare that a consistent interpretation of an enactment can *not* be given – and this is the 'declaration of inconsistency' that was recognised by the Court of Appeal as part of its remedial weaponry in *Moonen v Film and Literature Board of Review*,[35] and which is a very close cousin of the explicit power given English courts to make a declaration of 'incompatibility' under s 6 of the Human Rights Act 1998 (UK).

Third, a word is necessary about the impact of the United Nations human rights treaties (there are no regional human rights treaties in the Pacific). The International Covenant on Civil and Political Rights, along with the other principal human rights treaties, has been ratified in New Zealand. It is not 'incorporated' into New Zealand law, if by incorporation one means the simple replication of its provisions in a domestic statute. Rather – to adopt the usual New Zealand terminology about treaty obligations – it is 'given effect' in domestic law by the enactment of particular statutes designed to ensure that the affirmed rights are protected under law (at least to the extent it is felt they are not already protected by existing statutes or common law principles). As described below, the enactment of the first Human Rights Act in 1977 was prompted by the then looming ratification of the ICCPR: the Act conferred rights in relation to public and private sector discrimination and so gave domestic legal expression to the equivalent rights in the treaty. But most other rights – to life, to fair trials, and to freedom of expression and religion, for example – were judged to be adequately

---

relationships. These Bills were enacted at a time when it was known that a more comprehensive reform of the area was shortly to come, so their passage may not have seemed too problematic for legislators who believed they contained discriminatory features. For a more general discussion of s 7 see Rishworth et al., op. cit., note 32.

[34] Section 6 requires a consistent meaning where it 'can be given', a formulation that is not unlike the 'where it is possible to do so' in the Human Rights Act 1998 (UK). Some claim to see a difference in the two formulations, and describe the New Zealand provision as 'weaker' (see Lord Steyn in *R v A (No. 2)* [2001] 2 WLR 1546). For my part, I see no distinction between that which can be done and that which it is possible to do. See also G. Marshall, 'The Lynchpin of Parliamentary Intention: Lost, Stolen or Strayed' [2003] *PL* 236 at 240.

[35] [2000] 2 NZLR 9 (CA).

protected by existing legislation. Back in 1977, no one claimed that a Bill of Rights was necessary to give effect to rights in the ICCPR. That said, when the proposal for a supreme law Bill of Rights surfaced in 1985, the ICCPR text was, along with the Canadian Charter of Rights and Freedoms, the principal source upon which the drafters relied for the wording of the various rights.[36] And subsequently, when the statutory Bill of Rights was enacted in 1990, the preamble affirmed that it was a measure to 'affirm New Zealand's commitment to the ICCPR'.[37] The year before – 1989 – New Zealand had acceded to the ICCPR's Optional Protocol allowing individual communications to the Human Rights Committee. So far there have been 11 such communications.

With that brief account of the rights-protecting component of the New Zealand constitution, I turn to look at the way in which human rights have operated horizontally, between citizens. I begin with the position that has long applied, quite independently of the Bill of Rights.

C. Horizontality's heritage

The short point here is the ubiquity of rights operating horizontally. The ability of citizens to claim basic human rights against each other derives first and foremost from the law of tort and crime, protecting liberty, autonomy, bodily integrity, reputation, along with the possession and enjoyment of property. As a matter

[36] The Charter's main influence was one of design – New Zealand adopted a general 'reasonable limits' clause (now s 5 of the Bill of Rights) that was very similar to s 1 of the Charter. The text of most of the rights was more closely aligned with the ICCPR, but by no means identical. Some ICCPR rights were wholly omitted, such as the right to marry and found a family (Article 23), the right to privacy (Article 17), the right to compensation for wrongful conviction (Article 14(6), to which New Zealand had entered a reservation) and the general right to be equal before the law (Article 26). Some rights had no direct ICCPR analogue, notably the right to observance of the principles of natural justice in s 27 of the Bill of Rights.

[37] More recently, there have even been claims that proper compliance with the ICCPR actually requires a state to have the affirmed rights protected by constitutional arrangements whereunder they are enshrined in a supreme law. This appears to be the Human Rights Committee's view, but it has not been found persuasive in New Zealand. See discussion in P. Rishworth, 'Bill of Rights, Human Rights' [1998] *NZ Law Rev* 585 at 590–2 on whether the ICCPR requires a state to have a higher law constitution protecting rights.

of history, the body of law classed as 'tort' might be quite recent, and its early entwinement with criminal law somewhat complex,[38] but there seems no reason to doubt that its driving force as a category of legal wrongs has always been the idea that persons have 'rights' that others ought not to violate. In large part, contemporary debates about the operation of bills of rights in the private sphere arise now only because of lacunae (as they are perceived) in the standard common law protections – that tort protects reputation but not privacy, or that defamation law is too solicitous of reputation at the expense of robust political commentary. This should not obscure the essential horizontality of human rights that produced the extensive reach of the criminal and tort law we have. It is no surprise that legal arguments for the extension and adjustment of the law between citizens are now made in terms of the rights affirmed in bills and charters of rights. In a sense, that has always been so: the rights were affirmed because they were already regarded as fundamental. The contemporary question seems, in New Zealand at least, to have transmuted into an almost trivial one as noted earlier: whether the Bill of Rights represents a change in the common law method of 'doing' law? That is, whether judges are now *compelled* by bills of rights to reach rights-consistent results in private litigation, with the attendant requirement that the common law *must* be changed to allow such results? As foreshadowed, my answer is that this is not a helpful or realistic approach. It seems to assume that there will be cases where a judge is persuaded that the common law can and ought to be changed to better accommodate human rights, yet would not make that change unless compelled by a bill of rights to do so. I doubt that such a phenomenon could or should occur. Certainly it has not in New Zealand.

But that is to get ahead. The present point is that some fundamental rights have long operated horizontally, and that this has come about through common law development and statutes over a long period. The recent enunciation of international human rights standards in treaties provides, in large part, an ex post facto obligation to maintain rights-protecting statutes in place – criminal law protects life and bodily integrity, education statutes confer rights to education, and so on. With a little effort most statutes can

---

[38] See T. F. T. Plucknett, *A Concise History of the Common Law* (5th edn, 2001), p 455 ff.

be sheeted home to some conception of a civil, political, social or economic right. Civil and political rights have sometimes been called negative rights, but it is a truism that most dictate various forms of positive action, if only to avoid a breach of the negative right.[39] In any event, a set of negative prohibitions has always seemed a sterile sort of charter for conduct, and it is no surprise that even the most famous of them – the Ten Commandments – was described as summarised by the (positive) commandment to love one's neighbour.[40] Likewise, to take but one example, the Human Rights Committee interpreting the right to life in Article 6(1) of the International Covenant on Civil and Political Rights explains that it requires 'all possible measures to reduce infant mortality and to increase life expectancy'.[41]

D. Horizontality and rights-protecting legislation: the first wave of the human rights renaissance

Rights-threatening lacunae in common law are generally capable of redress through parliamentary legislation, and this has been the general pattern in New Zealand. It is convenient to go back to the origins of the modern human rights movement, the United Nations Declaration of Human Rights in 1948. The covenants and conventions that then followed were catalysts for successive legislated protections of domestic human rights. These filled some major gaps left by the common law, principally in the realm of rights against discrimination. In the field of contract-making, be it for employment, accommodation or for goods and services, the prevailing value in the common law had been the autonomy, privacy and dignity of the contract makers. They could subscribe to their own values without having to answer to values prescribed by the state, or by anybody else. To this there were notable exceptions, as in the cases of innkeepers[42] and certain others who were under a legal

[39] See, e.g., H. Quane, 'The Strasbourg Jurisprudence and the Meaning of a "Public Authority" under the Human Rights Act' [2006] *PL* 106 at 108.

[40] See Romans, chapter 13, verse 10; Galatians, chapter 5, verse 14.

[41] General Comment 6, UN Doc HRI/GEN/1/Rev.1 at 6, para 5.

[42] *Constantine v Imperial Hotels* [1944] 1 KB 693.

duty to deal with all who could pay a reasonable fee. Some amelioration of the harshness of the common law's approach was possible in other ways – racial covenants in real estate transactions might be held contrary to public policy, for example[43] – but the sort of development required to introduce meaningful prohibitions on discrimination required legislation. International human rights law was the catalyst in New Zealand. In 1972 New Zealand ratified the Convention for the Elimination of Racial Discrimination,[44] and in keeping with its practice of first making any required legislative changes the New Zealand Government procured the passage of the Race Relations Act 1971 through Parliament the previous year. That Act prohibited, as CERD required, discrimination on the grounds of national, racial or ethnic origin in the spheres of employment, accommodation, goods and services, education, and access to public places. The Act applied in public and private sectors. A few years later, anticipated ratification of the International Covenant on Civil and Political Rights[45] resulted in enactment of the Human Rights Commission Act 1977, prohibiting discrimination on a range of further grounds: sex, marital status, and religious or ethical belief. The common law had not supplied any tort of discrimination, and once these statutes entered the field it was unlikely then to do so.[46] The Human Rights Commission Act 1977 established a forum for low-level resolution of complaints about discrimination. The Human Rights Commission was created to receive and mediate complaints, referring unresolved matters to a 'Proceedings Commissioner', who was empowered to commence litigation before the Equal Opportunities Tribunal on the complainant's behalf. Sixteen years later, the Human Rights Act 1993 made a major revision, adding age, disability, employment status, political opinion, family status and sexual orientation as prohibited grounds.

---

43 *Re Drummond Wren* [1945] 4 DLR 674 (Ont HC).

44 660 UNTS 291, entered into force 4 January 1969. New Zealand's ratification, 22 November 1972, 848 UNTS 256.

45 999 UNTS 272, entered into force 12 November 1968. New Zealand's ratification 28 December 1978, 1120 UNTS 489-90.

46 The Supreme Court of Canada in *Seneca College of Applied Arts and Technology v Bhadauria* (1981) 124 DLR 3d 193 held there to be no tort of discrimination at common law and no cause of action for breach of the human rights code, which was instead a complete code of administrative remedies for discrimination.

Other legislation similarly took rights into the private sphere. The Official Information Act 1982 wrought improvements in the public's 'right to know', with a forum for complaint (the Ombudsman) if official agencies failed to respond. The Privacy Act 1993 set out principles for the use by public and private sector agencies of citizens' personal information, again with rights of complaint to a dedicated Privacy Commissioner and the availability of a tribunal to redress unresolved complaints. This idea of legislated statements of individual rights as a legal device for accountability and quality control spread to other fields. In the health context, for example, a Code of Patients Rights was promulgated, giving New Zealand's health and disability service consumers the ability to complain to a Health and Disability Commissioner about their treatment by health institutions and practitioners.[47]

The enactment of the Bill of Rights in 1990 can be seen as part of the march of human rights law. While its origins, as we saw, lay in the proposal for a supreme law, its subsequent popular validation owes much to the idea – an idea as intrinsically appealing as it is complex and contestable – that respect for human rights is part of the natural order of things and that the New Zealand state ought to be subject in a meaningful way to the international human rights obligations it has solemnly assumed, as well as subject to the same human rights restraints that it imposes upon private people. On a range of specific issues a rising human rights consciousness both inside and outside government has wrought continuing reforms throughout the 1980s and 1990s. The field of family law, for example, underwent child-centred reforms,[48] as well as being opened up to include de facto and same-sex couples.[49] The Civil Union Act 2004 brought marriage-in-all-but-name for same-sex couples (and civil unions are equally available to male-female couples). These reforms were driven essentially by rights-based arguments centred on international treaties such as the Convention on the Rights of the Child and (for unmarried and same-sex couples) on the anti-discrimination principle in s 19 of the Bill of Rights. At the same

[47] See Health and Disability Commissioner Act 1994, s 22.

[48] See the Children's Commissioner Act 1993 and the Children, Young Persons and Their Families Act 1989.

[49] Property (Relationship) Act 1976, this being the new title conferred in 2001 on the Matrimonial Property Act 1976 consequent upon amendments to extend its provisions to de facto and same sex couples.

time, it is fair to say that the impetus for such reforms owes as much to a change in attitudes that is not attributable to particular treaties or laws. Indeed, the sorts of legal arguments about civil unions that many found compelling in 2004 were actually available, as a matter of law, a decade or more earlier: that the concept of marriage discriminated on the grounds of sex and indirectly on the ground of sexual orientation. But the arguments were either not made then or were readily dismissed. There are times and tides in the affairs of men and women.

In a similar vein, the current 'smacking debate' in New Zealand travels a similar path to that in the United Kingdom and Canada, and so exemplifies the ubiquity of 'horizontality'. A statutory defence of 'reasonable force by way of correction' is available to assault charges under s 59 of New Zealand's Crimes Act 1961, yet there is unease in some quarters when it is invoked by parents and leads to acquittals in what seem, from media reports, to have been serious cases. This has prompted a private member's Bill to abolish the defence, and at the time of writing the Bill is before Parliament. As in the United Kingdom, the arguments for the Bill owe much to the idea of a state obligation to protect citizens from each other.[50] But it is not as if this is a new idea. The vast bulk of criminal law already does just that. As with the 'gaps' in common law that permit irremediable rights abuses (as judged by modern sensibilities) so, too, the horizontality argument is, in this respect, a new form of political argument for rights-protecting legislation.

For its part, the field of public and private sector employment law has, for some considerable time, been infused with the public law values of good faith, fairness and natural justice. Indeed, a 2004 amendment to New Zealand's Employment Relations Act 2000 waxed lyrical about what is entailed in good faith between employer and employee (emphasis added):[51]

---

[50] See *A v United Kingdom* (1998) 20 EHRR 611 (United Kingdom held in breach of European Convention on Human Rights for maintaining a law that failed to protect the right of the child under Article 3). See also *Canadian Foundation for Children Youth and the Law v Canada (Attorney-General)* [2004] 1 SCR 76 (defence of reasonable force restrictively interpreted for better protection of children's rights).

[51] Section 4(1A) of the Employment Relations Act 2000.

The duty of good faith ...

(a) is wider in scope than the implied mutual obligations of trust and confidence; and

(b) requires the parties to an employment relationship to be *active and constructive* in establishing and maintaining a productive employment relationship in which the parties are, among other things, *responsive and communicative.*

Largely as a result of employment law reforms over the past two decades – legislative and judicial – it is fair to say that the term 'natural justice' has lodged firmly in the lexicon of New Zealanders, and it would assuredly not be seen as something limited to their dealings with government. It is part of the sense of 'fair play' to which most New Zealanders aspire.

In the realm of freedom of expression, legislation in the 1990s wrought restrictions explicitly calculated to promote equality and non-discrimination amongst the citizenry. In the realm of broadcasting these have been relatively non-controversial; codes of practice require broadcasters not to transmit material that denigrates people on account of those characteristics that are prohibited grounds of discrimination.[52] These standards have been applied in the realm of religious programming that is critical of homosexuality, where a line has had to be drawn between the permitted expression of religious ideas and the prohibited propagation of denigrating material.[53]

Much more controversially, a similar approach was adopted in the realm of censorship law under the Films, Videos and Publications Classification Act 1993. For some time the Chief Censor and the tribunal to which first level appeals are taken each operated on the basis that they could ban, as 'objectionable', any material that depicted a person or group as 'inherently inferior' by reason of such a prohibited ground. On that basis the tribunal banned two American-made videos, one presenting a fundamentalist Christian critique of homosexual behaviour and its link to AIDS

---

52 See Free-to-air Television Code of Broadcasting Practice, reg 6g.

53 Broadcasting Standards Authority, Decision No. 2004-001, 26 February 2004 (Voice of Islam programme on community television station said that the Islamic position on homosexuality was 'death'; the complaint was upheld). In Broadcasting Standards Authority, Decision No. 2004-001, 26 February 2004 a Christian programme that expressed the view that homosexual acts were immoral was held not to reach the threshold of denigration.

and the other making an essentially political case that, in the United States, sexual orientation ought not to be a ground of prohibited discrimination. On appeal to the New Zealand Court of Appeal in *Living Word Distributors Ltd v Human Rights Action Group*,[54] the tribunal defended its censorship decision on the grounds that censorship legislation was designed to promote equality amongst citizens,[55] and that it was entitled to ban *any* publication or video that advanced the idea that persons might be inferior by reason of sexual orientation. The Court of Appeal, however, restored the previous understanding of censorship law: that it arose only in relation to publications depicting 'sex, horror, crime, cruelty or violence'. Mere expression of opinion could not be liable to censorship. The Court of Appeal rejected also the tribunal's view that the rights of groups to be free from discrimination (in s 19 of the Bill of Rights) trumped the freedom of expression of the video-makers and their audiences (under s 14).

It is significant that this decision prompted calls in some quarters, including from the Human Rights Commission, that it be legislatively overturned so that publications tending to reinforce discriminatory views in the citizenry might be susceptible to prior restraint through banning. Ultimately, those calls transmuted into calls for further restrictions on 'hate speech' – that New Zealand's existing hate speech provisions be extended beyond racial vilification so as to protect religious and sexual minorities as well. No such extension has yet taken place, but the episode illustrates the salience that a liberty-restricting but (as they would see it) horizontal equality-enhancing regime of expression holds for some New Zealanders.

Enough has been said to make the point that legislation has done much to take human rights into the private sphere. Much of the action has been in the realm of promoting equality and anti-discrimination law, with natural justice protections also being prominent in employment. But there are gaps. The Human Rights Act regulates affairs between private citizens but does not deal with the full panoply of human rights. The engine room of the Human

---

54 [2000] 3 NZLR 570 (CA). I disclose that I was counsel for the video importers.

55 The tribunal drew on the work of US academic Mari Matsuda, 'Public Response to Racist Speech: Considering the Victim's Story' (1989) 87 *Mich LR* 2320.

Rights Act is its set of prohibitions on discrimination. Nothing in the Human Rights Act affirms freedom of expression or religion, nor rights against unreasonable search and seizure, nor any of the other substantive rights that are found in the New Zealand Bill of Rights.[56] For its part, the Bill of Rights confers these rights, as we saw, 'only' against the executive, legislative and judicial branches of government, and against other persons or bodies who perform 'public functions'.

That takes us to the next question. To what extent, then, has the Bill of Rights taken human rights into the private sphere, especially those rights not taken there already through specific legislation?

E. The indirect horizontal effect of the New Zealand Bill of Rights

I noted above the views of commentators on the question whether the New Zealand Bill of Rights applies directly to the common law and so, indirectly, to private persons whose affairs are then regulated by that law. In 16 years of Bill of Rights litigation, two relevant propositions have emerged: first, that the Bill of Rights does not apply directly to 'wholly private conduct';[57] second that the Bill of Rights requires a rights-consistent common law.[58] The first proposition seems unexceptional in the face of s 3, which applies the Bill of Rights 'only' to the three branches of government and to bodies performing a public function. The second proposition is intuitively appealing, but the extent to which it negates the first has not yet been explored in any case. That is, does a truly rights-compliant common law require that private citizens be placed

---

[56] It is true, however, that freedom of expression and freedom of religion can indirectly be protected by anti-discrimination law in many contexts. The right to be free from religious discrimination can be a proxy for freedom of religion, and the political opinion ground of prohibited discrimination protects expression.

[57] The phrase is that of Richardson P in *R v N* [1999] 1 NZLR 713 at 718 (CA). Similar sentiments are expressed in *R v H* [1994] 2 NZLR 143 at 147; *R v Grayson & Taylor* [1997] 1 NZLR 399 at 407; and *Living Word Distributors Ltd v Human Rights Action Group* [2000] 3 NZLR 570, para 41.

[58] At trial in *Lange v Atkinson* [1997] 2 NZLR 22 at 32 Elias J (as she then was) said: 'It is idle to suggest that the common law need not conform to the judgments in [the New Zealand Bill of Rights Act 1990]. They are authoritative as to where the convenience and welfare of society lies.'

under legal duties to observe the rights of others? Would that bind private persons to observe the Bill of Rights, despite the apparent intention behind s 3 that it apply 'only' to the state and public actors?

A large part of the answer lies, I believe, in understanding what a Bill of Rights-compliant common law might be like. It cannot be one that requires private persons to respect the same rights that a state owes to citizens. This is not just because many of the rights in a Bill of Rights are simply inapt for that sort of transposing – consider the criminal procedure rights, for example, and the right to vote. More fundamentally, a common law that demanded that A refrain, say, from discrimination against B carries the risk that A's liberty and autonomy is itself unduly restricted. It must reckon not just with B's 'horizontal' right to be free from discrimination, but with A's vertical right to be free from forced association (or to be free from penal or civil consequences for deciding not to associate). In fact, just this sort of judgment has long been made in New Zealand's Human Rights Act. The prohibitions on discrimination are restricted to fields where the social interest in equal access and opportunity is strong. The Act applies to employment, accommodation, education, goods and services, and access to public places. But it also draws lines that presuppose a zone of continuing liberty, in which people are not required to conform to the state's general vision of equality. Clubs, for example, are wholly exempted from the prohibitions on discrimination when it comes to choosing their members.[59] Persons seeking room-mates to share their homes are not bound to refrain from otherwise prohibited discrimination (although landlords who will not be allow sharing the accommodation are so bound).[60] And religious organisations choosing and ordaining pastors and priests are exempted to the extent their doctrines and rules require.[61] Each of these exceptions, and there are others, represents a judgment about how the anti-discrimination value is to be reconciled with competing values.

The clash and reconciliation of value and principle has long been the province of the common law (although much of the field is now occupied by legislation that, as we have just noted, embodies

59 Human Rights Act 1993, s 44(4).

60 Ibid, s 54.

61 Ibid, s 39 (as to qualifications and licensing); s 28(2)(b)(i) (as to employment).

values and principles of its own). The point is well illustrated by the most recent case in the field, the New Zealand Court of Appeal's decision in *Hosking v Runting*,[62] which concerned the plaintiffs' claim to restrain an alleged violation of privacy. Mr Hosking, a minor celebrity, sought to prevent a magazine publishing pictures of his two infant children taken in a city street. New Zealand law recognised no general tort of violating privacy, and the Hoskings had lost at first instance.

The outcome of the case was a 3:2 decision affirming the existence of a tort of unreasonable invasion of privacy, albeit that the tort was not established on the facts of the case (the pictures having been taken in a public place). On the plaintiffs' side of the argument was the right to privacy, affirmed in the ICCPR but not explicitly in the Bill of Rights. On the defendant's side lay freedom of expression in s 14 of the Bill of Rights. Both plaintiff and defendant were private persons, neither directly bound by the Bill of Rights. In reaching their conclusion that a tort of invading privacy existed, two judges in the three-judge majority (Gault and Blanchard JJ) said:[63]

> Without addressing the complex question of the extent to which the courts are to give effect to the rights and freedoms affirmed in the Bill of Rights Act in disputes between private litigants, it cannot be contended that limits imposed to give effect to rights declared in international conventions to which New Zealand is a party cannot be demonstrably justified in a free and democratic society.

Note the structure of this reasoning. First, for reasons independent of the Bill of Rights – not mentioned in the quotation but essentially the value of privacy, a right affirmed in the ICCPR – these judges were minded to recognise a new tort of invasion of privacy applicable between private persons. Second, the restriction that such a judicially created tort would impose on private citizens had to meet the standard set by the Bill of Rights – that it be no more than a reasonable limit demonstrably justified in a free and democratic society. In so deciding, these judges, despite their disavowal, *did* address (at least in part) the complex question of when the

62 [2003] 3 NZLR 385 (CA). See also A. Geddis, 'The Horizontal Effects of the New Zealand Bill of Rights Act, as Applied in *Hosking v Runting*' [2004] *NZ Law Rev* 681.

63 Para 44.

courts are to give effect to the Bill of Rights in disputes between private litigants. They ran the law they were minded to declare over the Bill of Rights template, concluding that it met the standard demanded. That was entirely appropriate, for s 5 of the Bill of Rights says that the rights affirmed shall be subject only to 'reasonable limits prescribed by law' that are 'demonstrably justified in a free and democratic society'. The judges were prescribing a law that would limit a right; they sought to ensure it was no more than a reasonable limit.

For Tipping J, the third judge in this 3-2 decision to declare the existence of a new tort, the entire locus of the case could be put in Bill of Rights terms. For Tipping J the impetus for the tort of invasion of privacy could be found in the text of the Bill of Rights itself, and the values that that text revealed. The right against unreasonable search and seizure in s 21 was, he said, 'not very far from an entitlement to be free from unreasonable intrusions into personal privacy'.[64] The judge recognised that the Bill of Rights is designed to operate between citizen and state, but went on to say that it was appropriate for the values recognised in that context to inform the development of the common law. The judicial branch, he said, should give 'appropriate weight' to rights in the Bill of Rights when undertaking that exercise. Note the expression give 'appropriate weight'. Not 'apply'. I come back to that important distinction shortly. So privacy was discerned as a Bill of Rights value, and the law of tort developed to reflect that value. And, as with the other two judges, Tipping J assessed the legitimacy of that development against the standard set by the Bill of Rights.

Two judges dissented. Keith J and Anderson J held that the development of the new tort of privacy would unreasonably infringe the right to freedom of expression in the Bill of Rights. But that, of course, was a disagreement over the merits of the case for a new tort. All judges, then, saw the Bill of Rights as relevant in shaping the law of tort between citizens. There was common ground in holding that the common law ought not to be developed to the point that it works an *infringement* on protected rights (with the judges dividing on the merits of whether the majority's formulation did just that). One judge saw the positive impetus for a privacy tort as lying in values that the Bill of Rights reflected, while two judges

64 Para 224.

located those same values in the ICCPR. These conclusions may be drawn:

(a) Positive doctrines of common law that limit protected rights must meet the Bills of Rights standards.
(b) Bill of Rights values help judges assess whether a lacuna exists in the common law, and in the development of doctrine to remedy that lacuna.

Is this, then, the 'Bill of Rights colonisation' of private law? Is all private law then 'constitutionalised' in the sense that it must meet Bill of Rights standards? The answer is no; it is simply the common law method now expressed in the language of rights. It is reasoning within the common law paradigm, in which the values of New Zealand society declared in a fundamental enactment passed by Parliament are given appropriate weight in formulating that law.

The earlier important case of *Lange v Atkinson*[65] in 1998 is illustrative. The issue in *Lange* was whether the common law of defamation in New Zealand ought to be ameliorated (as media defendants would see it) by a defence along the lines of *New York Times v Sullivan*.[66] The claim was that a media defendant's freedom of expression in s 14 of the Bill of Rights would be unreasonably limited by the continued operation of defamation law if there were no defence for reasonable error. The Court of Appeal was persuaded that some such amendment to the common law was called for, influenced by the importance of free expression on political affairs. Significantly, the Court went on to pay attention to whether such a law change could legitimately be made within the paradigm of common law incrementalism, or whether a law change was a matter for the legislature. In the end it concluded that judicial change was possible and appropriate. Although there is no discussion of exactly this point, it seems to me that the Court's concern for legitimacy in taking the desired step reveals that the Court was

65 [1998] 3 NZLR 424 (CA). The case went on appeal to the Privy Council ([2000] 1 NZLR 257) who did not address Bill of Rights applicability but referred the case back to the Court of Appeal for reconsideration in light of the then recently decided *Reynolds v Times Newspapers Ltd* [1999] 3 WLR 1010 (HL). The Court of Appeal issued a further judgment ([2000] 3 NZLR 385), without addressing Bill of Rights applicability afresh.

66 376 US 254 (1964).

engaging in common law reasoning, rather than making a 'Bill of Rights decision'. That is, it did not see itself as positively bound by the Bill of Rights to make the desired change. After all, if it were truly bound, the Court's inquiry into the legitimacy of its proposed actions, in common law terms, would have been misplaced. It would have had a statutory mandate to make the desired change under the Bill of Rights.

This reflects similar sentiments in the South African case of *Carmichele v Minister of Safety and Security*, that common law must be developed in a way that meets the requirements of the Constitution 'but must be done in a way most appropriate for the development of the common law within its own paradigm'.[67] Indeed, the New Zealand Court of Appeal's approach in this regard resonates with that required by the text of the South African Bill of Rights. Under the interim constitution, it will be recalled, the Constitutional Court had ruled that the South African Bill of Rights operated only with 'indirect horizontality', in that its values might influence the common law but that the rights did not operate directly in a horizontal manner.[68] In the Final Constitution, however, the relevant provision of the Bill of Rights reads:

> **Application**
>
> 8. (1) The Bill of Rights applies to all law and binds the legislature, the executive, the judiciary, and all organs of state.
> (2) A provision of the Bill of Rights binds natural and juristic persons if, and to the extent that it is applicable, taking into account the nature of the right and of any duty imposed by the right.

But this purportedly direct horizontality remains close to indirect. Much work is done by the words 'to the extent applicable', and 'taking into account the nature of the right and any duty imposed'. These require judgment and evaluation and suggest the continued application of the common law method. In addition, Currie and de Waal report that the invitation to direct horizontality in s 8(2) of the South African Bill of Rights is almost routinely eschewed by the South African courts in favour of the indirect horizontality referred

---

[67] 2001 (4) SA 938 (CCSA) at para 56.

[68] *De Klerk v Du Plessis* 1996 (3) SA 850 (CCSA).

to in s 39(2) – that is, through development of the common law.[69] The former point is exemplified in the extra-judicial writings of Justice Ackermann, who observed that while *Shelley v Kraemer* would be decided the same way in South Africa as in the United States, a complaint about a racially motivated eviction from, say, a bridge club held in a private home would most likely be resolved in favour of the autonomy of the home owner.[70] I would agree, and I think it a moot point whether this result is achieved by 'taking into account the nature of any right or duty imposed' in terms of s 8(2) or whether it arises by virtue of discerning and applying appropriate common law values under s 39(2). I am inclined to think these are the same thing. Either way, there is a judgment that the horizontality of the right in that context would come at too great a cost to liberty.

Now, some in New Zealand might see this approach to Bill of Rights applicability in common law cases as a 'watering down' of the imperatives of the Bill of Rights. A harder-edged, more insistent infiltration of common law by the Bill of Rights might be thought desirable – perhaps a methodology that reduces judicial choices. I am not sure this is realistic. In the end it is all about the adjustments, if any, to settled balances in common law doctrine that are suggested by rights in the Bill of Rights. This is common law methodology. The Bill of Rights does not supply the answers, only the terminology. And it does not assist to say that judges are positively bound to make rights-consistent decisions about the common law. Could one usefully argue that the minority judges in *Hosking*, who refused to develop a tort of privacy, somehow *breached* the Bill of Rights? If the majority judges had reached a less 'expression-protecting' conclusion about the nature of the privacy tort, might they be at risk of being sued by media for unreasonably limiting freedom of expression? Just to pose these questions is to realise how fruitless is the proposition that judges are 'bound' by the Bill of Rights.

---

69 *The Bill of Rights Handbook* (2005), para 3.3(b)(iii)(aa). Section 39(2) reads: 'When interpreting any legislation, and when developing the common law or customary law, every court tribunal or forum must promote the spirit, purport and objects of the Bill of Rights.'

70 L. W. H. Ackermann, 'The Legal Nature of the South African Revolution' [2004] *NZ Law Rev* 633 at 667.

The true position, exemplified in the cases above, is that the Bill of Rights generates reasons that may persuade judges to develop rights-protecting doctrine, but also requires that such doctrine impose no more than reasonable limits on protected rights. The reason why this is so is persuasively argued by Amnon Reichman, speaking of the Canadian Charter rather than the New Zealand Bill of Rights:[71]

> As an instrument of reason, the Charter may indeed present a reason-based argument with which the common law must take issue. But such a role is not one of hierarchical review, since there is no higher reason, there are only better or weaker arguments, and stronger or weaker coherence with other reason-based norms. Thus, the Charter can and ought to be invoked in common law adjudication as an interpretive aid, as part of a claim that the courts have failed in the past to fully grasp the principles that flow most convincingly from the concept of out ability (and desire) to engage in moral reasoning. The essence of the process is not one of judicial review of common law norms for their compatibility with superior Charter norms, but rather one of elucidation of common law principles, integral to common law methodology.
>
> The duty to develop the common law in light of constitutional values, therefore, is not derived from the supremacy of the Charter, but form the common law itself.

What, then, of remaining New Zealand case law? There are numerous instances of the Bill of Rights being considered and applied in litigation between private parties. In some the basis for application of the Bill of Rights is taken for granted and not explicitly considered. The cases may be put into several categories.

First, there are those that, while between private litigants, engage the criminal law of contempt of court. In *Duff v Communicado Ltd*,[72] where the defendant sought sanctions against the plaintiff for prejudicial radio comments, the trial judge readily accepted the relevance of the plaintiff's right to freedom of expression in the Bill of Rights, albeit finding that a contempt had been committed. That is plainly right; the underlying law, though invoked by the defendant as a private litigant, is analogous to criminal law and the case is really one of vertical application of the Bill of Rights.

---

71 'A Charter-Free Domain: In Defence of Dolphin Delivery' (2002) 35 *UBC LR* 329 at 343.

72 [1996] 2 NZLR 89. See also *Progressive Enterprises Ltd v North Shore City Council* (2006) 2 NZLR 262.

Second, there is a series of cases in which injunctions are sought in private litigation to restrain the use of information, whether through contract, intellectual property claims, or the equitable law of confidence. Not all these cases are pure exemplars of the horizontality question: in some there were statutes operating, and hence the operation of the Bill of Rights is explicable on the routine basis that legislative incursions into rights must be no more than reasonable.[73] But others were purely contractual or equitable claims, and the right to freedom of expression was explicitly considered when determining whether speech-restricting injunctions ought to be granted. Such cases, therefore, do indicate a horizontal application, but the point is not discussed in great depth in any of them.[74] The right to freedom of expression is brought to bear as a factor affecting remedy and not – to the extent the two can be separated, of course – as influencing the underlying legal rule. But such cases can be seen as exemplifying the points already made: in the calculus of reasons why remedies ought to be granted or withheld in these common law cases, the right to freedom of expression in the Bill of Rights is plainly a pertinent consideration. This is especially so in relation to expression whose restriction might bear upon the openness of the court system. While it may suit some private litigants to keep public values out of their litigation, the courts must give proper regard to the wider interests.

This is exemplified in the most recent case, *Television New Zealand Ltd v Rogers*,[75] in where the plaintiff (Rogers) was seeking an injunction to prevent TVNZ's broadcasting of a videotape recording his confession to murder. That confession had in earlier criminal litigation been ruled inadmissible, and Roger had subsequently been acquitted at a trial. At some stage the videotape had passed into the hands of TVNZ, in circumstances not detailed in the judgment and not regarded as relevant to the issue. After the

---

[73] See, e.g., *PC Direct v Best Buy Ltd* (1997) 7 TCLR 452; *Cosco (NZ) Ltd v Port of Napier* (HC Napier, CP 7/999, 31 March 1999, Wild J).

[74] See, e.g., *Attorney-General for England and Wales v Television NZ Ltd* (1998) 44 IPR 123 (CA), holding that s 14 of the Bill of Rights was a critical consideration in deciding whether to grant an injunction to prevent a television broadcast, allegedly in breach of contractual obligations owed by a former member of the SAS, who had served with the Bravo Two Zero patrol in Iraq, to the United Kingdom Government, his former employer.

[75] [2006] 2 NZLR 156 (CA).

acquittal, TVNZ indicated that it wished to air the video confession in a documentary about the case. The High Court granted a permanent injunction to prevent this on the grounds that it would violate the plaintiff's right to privacy. The Court of Appeal allowed an appeal, the majority holding that although the elements of the tort of invasion of privacy had been established, the defence of 'legitimate public concern' applied. The third judge, agreeing in the result, was not satisfied that the privacy tort was made out at all (in particular, he doubted there was a reasonable expectation of privacy in an on-the-record confession that it is known will be used at public trial). For that judge, TVNZ's freedom of expression in s 14 was said to be relevant to determining the matter, which he felt was otherwise equally poised. That same judge also said:[76]

> I recognise that there is scope for debate as to the extent to which rights guaranteed by the New Zealand Bill of Rights Act 1990 can or should be enforced horizontally (cf the comment in *Hosking* at [114] per Gault P and Blanchard J). For myself, however, I think that the case engages the right to freedom of expression recognised in s 14 of the New Zealand Bill of Rights Act; this is because Mr Rogers is seeking to invoke the coercive powers of the Courts and the Courts are subject to the Act (cf *Attorney-General for England and Wales v Television New Zealand Ltd* (1998) 44 IPR 123 (CA)). I do not understand the judgments in *Hosking* to suggest otherwise. In Canada, the Charter provision corresponding to s 14 has been utilised to dismiss claims seeking relief by way of prior restraint: *Little Sisters Book and Art Emporium v Canada* [2000] 2 SCR 1120.

In light of developments to date, the following conclusions are possible in New Zealand:

(a) All accept that the Bill of Rights ought to inform the development of the common law. Whether this is a matter of obligation under s 3(a), or simply the phenomenon of judicial reasoning in light of fundamental values, is not resolved but this is not a controversy that can be expected to affect the outcome in any particular case.
(b) Rights-limiting doctrines that already exist, or that are under consideration for enshrinement as a new cause of action (or extension of an existing one) must pass muster under the reasonable limits section (s 5).

[76] Para 114.

(c) Rights in the Bill of Rights can also be the impetus for the development of limits (the right of privacy in *Hosking*).
(d) In the field of remedies (principally affecting freedom of expression) the courts will seek to preserve freedom of expression so far as possible even in cases fought between private litigants. This may be explicable on the basis that expression, above all rights, has a public value that transcends its significance between the litigants: that is, others have an interest as well. In cases about the operation of the justice system this is especially so. This explains the contempt cases and *Rogers*, for example.

To these points some might respond that the Bill of Rights operates as something of a 'make-weight' – that because the values it affirms are already operative in the realm of legal principle and argumentation, nothing has been truly altered by invocation of them as rights in the Bill of Rights. But the point may be admitted, and is not a troubling one. The Bill of Rights itself says that the rights are 'affirmed', not created. Indeed, in the *Lange v Atkinson* case the Court of Appeal rested its amelioration of defamation law on a number of bases, of which the right to freedom of expression in the Bill of Rights was simply one (the others being developments in comparative law and what the Court referred to as 'freedom of expression in its wider context', namely the writings of Milton, Mill and Sir James Fitzjames Stephen).[77] The contribution of the Bill of Rights is to supply a framework or methodology, especially in relation to the assessment of the reasonableness of limits under s 5. The Bill of Rights did not invent the rights it affirms. Rather, it prescribes a standard that the state must meet when dealing with them.

That standard is ultimately set by the word 'reasonable' in s 5, which is an analogue of s 1 of the Canadian Charter of Rights and Freedoms and of the various limitations clauses attached to particular rights in the European Convention on Human Rights and ICCPR. Section 5 of the New Zealand Bill of Rights reads in full:

> 5. **Justified limitations**—Subject to section 4 of this Bill of Rights, the rights and freedoms contained in this Bill of Rights may be subject only to such reasonable limits prescribed by law as can be demonstrably justified in a free and democratic society.

---

[77] [1998] 3 NZLR 425 at 460.

The opening reference to s 4 can happily be ignored in the present context; it simply makes the point that a statute imposing unreasonable limits on rights is not invalid or unenforceable.[78] The clause has no 'bite' in cases about common law. As it happens, there is precious little indigenous jurisprudence that expounds upon or even applies the test of reasonable limits in s 5. In two cases the Court of Appeal has briefly essayed what it believes to be involved in determining the reasonableness of legislated limits on rights. Both of these cases have been in the context of legislation rather than common law. The more recent of the two cases is *Moonen v Film and Literature Board of Review*, where the Court of Appeal said this:[79]

> [In applying s 5] it is desirable first to identify the objective which the legislature was endeavouring to achieve by the provision in question. The importance and significance of that objective must then be assessed. The way in which the objective is statutorily achieved must be in reasonable proportion to the importance of the objective. A sledgehammer should not be used to crack a nut. The means used must also have a rational relationship with the objective, and in achieving the objective there must be as little interference as possible with the right or freedom affected.

That passage covers the bases familiar to students of Canadian Charter and European Convention jurisprudence: identifying a statutory provision's objective, inquiring into the rationality of the means used to attain the objective and assessing the proportionality between the objective and the rights-infringing impact of those means. This balances rights against public interests, but amongst those interests, of course, may well be the perceived need to protect rights operating horizontally. There remain some technical issues about the Court's suggested approach – for example, if the statutory means are truly in '*reasonable* proportion' to the objective will the statute pass muster even if it does not achieve as '*little interference as possible*'? But, to date, none of these wrinkles has actually mattered in any decided case. Indeed, no case at appellate level has really turned on application of the s 5 test. This is only partly because the Bill of Rights is not supreme law – a fact that obviously

---

[78] Section 4 says that no enactment shall be invalid or ineffective or held impliedly repealed by reason only of its inconsistency with the Bill of Rights.

[79] [2000] 2 NZLR 9 at 16–17. The earlier case was *Ministry of Transport v Noort*, supra, note 20.

discourages litigation of the 'constitutional' type familiar in North American jurisdictions. It is also because, even in those contexts where the Bill of Rights can generate meaningful results for litigants (such as when administrative decisions or provisions of delegated legislation are challenged for inconsistency), the cases to date have simply tended not to generate s 5 questions. In contrast to the courts, the government's legal advisers reckon with the reasonable limits test routinely, when assessing proposed legislation for consistency with the Bill of Rights.

In any event, the present concern is with whether and how s 5 operates in cases fought over the content of the common law, or over judicial orders in cases between private litigants. Here a number of points may be made. First, as noted, the Court is enjoined by s 5 of the New Zealand Bill of Rights to ensure that limits prescribed by law – and this includes *common* law – are reasonable. As we saw, all judges in *Hosking v Runting* purported to make this inquiry. But it is significant that the Court saw no reason to ascribe burdens of proof or persuasion in dealing with s 5 in common law cases. Certainly the Canadian position is that the party seeking to impose the limit – normally government – bears these burdens, and in part the reluctance to apply the Charter directly to Canadian common law is attributable to a desire not to impose these burdens on private litigants who may not be placed to meet them. It seems inevitable that the same allocation of burden will generally prevail in New Zealand when it is *legislation* being defended, for evidence may well be needed to support the imposition of limits on rights. But it seems correct for questions of burden not to enter into the resolution of common law disputes. Indeed, there was no suggestion that it was unfair to place Mr Hosking in the position of arguing for a privacy tort that needed to track the contours set by Mr Runting's guaranteed freedom of expression. There is no suggestion that this involved Hosking's lawyers in marshalling their case in a manner qualitatively different from that in which sophisticated common law argumentation has always been presented. Litigants arguing about the proper scope of the common law must always address the broader justifications for and against the positions they espouse.

Second, because common law is necessarily expressed at a high level of generality, it may preserve on its face the requisite respect for rights, effectively delegating the task of accommodating rights to the judges who apply the doctrine in particular cases. The point is well illustrated by the *Hosking* court's strategic insertion of a 'legitimate public concern' defence into the tort of invasion of privacy:[80]

> [T]he scope of privacy protection should not exceed such limits on the freedom of expression as is justified in a free and democratic society. A defence of legitimate public concern will ensure this. The significant value to be accorded freedom of expression requires that the tort of privacy must necessarily be tightly confined.

This is very close to holding that the newly minted tort should never be applied when doing so would constitute an unreasonable limit on freedom of expression. In other words the very definition of the tort expresses the rights-protecting qualification that is needed to track Bill of Rights concerns. Unless there is some problem with the definition of the tort itself (I recognise that those who say there should be no privacy tort at all would claim there is), its application in actual cases ought therefore to result in outcomes consistent with the promises of the Bill of Rights. No case ought to end in a person being unable to publish something which, in a free and democratic society, he or she must be able to publish. This turns out to be broadly similar to the situation that applies where statutes confer general discretions or decision-making power: the effect of the Bill of Rights is to require that each exercise of the discretion or power be rights-consistent.

The above point is illustrated by the outcome in *Rogers*, where the Court of Appeal held that the 'legitimate public concern' defence to a privacy claim was operative and that TVNZ was entitled to broadcast the video. Some might dispute that conclusion in the particular case, but that is simply an argument about how the balance was drawn in that case. The underlying common law tracks the Bill of Rights protections, for it preserves the ability to publish if there is a legitimate public interest.

F. Conclusion

New Zealand's experience with human rights operating horizontally is, on the whole, a successful and relatively uncomplicated one. I have suggested that this is the result of two factors. First, it

---

80 Para 130.

has been the legislature that has taken the lead in bringing rights into the private sphere, and it has done this through legislation prompted either by international human rights treaties or by more generalised concern for human rights expressed in and through the political process. The eradication of discriminatory provisions against gay persons and same-sex couples is a good example. Here the Bill of Rights operates in a conventional way, requiring that legislative intrusion into the private sphere tracks the guarantees of individual liberty. And political argument has been sophisticated enough to recognise that the Bill of Rights can be the reason *for* the taking of human rights into the private sphere, and not merely a constraint to be observed when doing so.

The second development I have outlined is judicial use of the Bill of Rights when developing the common law in private litigation. This judicial use in the realm of the privacy tort tracks the same two dimensions: the Bill of Rights (or the ICCPR) as an impetus *for* change, and as guide to the *nature* of the change. I have suggested that this is a continuation of orthodox and legitimate judicial method, in which litigants press reasons for the development of common law. They are now using the language and concerns of the Bill of Rights.

I have argued that none of this turns on the fact that, by s 3(a), the New Zealand Bill of Rights expressly binds the judicial branch of government. The developments I have outlined would, I think, have occurred whether or not that was so, just as similar developments have occurred in countries with different constitutional arrangements and wordings. It is fair also to say that the debate about indirect horizontality of human rights in New Zealand has been transacted at a fairly technical level. This is in contrast, say, to Canada where the discourse over the legitimacy of the public–private divide has tended to include political claims: notably that the private sphere can be a site of oppression and inequality to which the Charter *ought* to speak, empowering remedies and dealing with unequal distribution of wealth and opportunity, and that it ought not to be relegated to being merely a limit on the power of governments. New Zealand, as already noted, has not produced that sort of debate. This is probably because the statutory nature of the Bill of Rights meant that it was never fastened with any great hopes for social transformation. It is a modest instrument in its design and history. That said, in its substance it is a contemporary statement of utmost importance, affirming many of the recognised human rights as well as setting a standard to be met when those rights are limited by law. That courts have recourse to those rights and that standard when setting the parameters of common law is not surprising. Nor is it surprising that, when such recourse is made, the dictates of human rights may often point in different directions – equality for some may come at the cost of liberty to others, privacy at the cost of freedom of expression, and so on. In the end, balances of competing rights are called for. And, when this is done in cases about common law, it is really the continuation of established common law method. What the New Zealand Bill of Rights has done, then, is prompt new arguments for the revision of settled doctrine, and it supplies some of the language in which the revision takes place. This looks like the taking of human rights into the private sphere. But it is not a wholly new enterprise, for human rights in some form or other were there already. New balances of rights are being made, not because the judges are somehow 'bound' by the Bill of Rights to do so, but because they are persuaded that the reasons for doing so are good ones.

Chapter 11: South Africa
From Indirect to Direct Effect in South Africa: a System in Transition

Jörg Fedtke

A. A changing constitutional landscape

The most prominent feature of South Africa's constitutional landscape over the past 15 years has been the speed with which the system has changed. Since the former President Fredrik Willem de Klerk officially announced the beginning of negotiations with the African National Congress (ANC) and its allies in November 1990, the country has lived under no fewer than three constitutions – the last apartheid Constitution of 1983,[1] the so-called 'Interim' Constitution of 1993 (IC),[2] and the current 'Final' Constitution of 1996 (FC).[3] Constitutional change on this scale is difficult for any society, and a challenge for academics – both local and abroad – wishing to keep abreast of developments. At the same time, the transition from apartheid to present-day South Africa has been particularly exciting and rewarding for the comparativist; the last decade and a half has seen the country borrow, discard, and modify transplanted constitutional ideas and concepts from a wide range of systems,[4] with the legislator paving the way and open-minded judges seizing the opportunity to blend local traditions and experience with foreign approaches.[5]

---

1 Republic of South Africa Constitution Act 110 of 1983.

2 Constitution of the Republic of South Africa Act 200 of 1993.

3 Constitution of the Republic of South Africa Act 108 of 1996.

4 See J. Fedtke, *Die Rezeption von Verfassungsrecht. Südafrika 1993-1996* (2000).

5 The South African judiciary exerted much influence on the legal transplants contained in the two Constitutions and today still continues to play an exceptional role in the use of foreign ideas. The Constitutional Court in particular (itself a legal transplant) has repeatedly referred to foreign material in order to shape the country's new and developing body of constitutional doctrine. On the use of comparative methodology by judges in seven legal systems, including South Africa,

Drittwirkung is no exception. The inclusion of enforceable human rights provisions in the post-apartheid constitutional settlement – though not disputed in principle – was fraught with difficulties,[6] and the question if and to what extent constitutional rights should become operational in the private sphere was one of the most contentious during the Multi-Party Negotiation Process (MPNP)[7] leading up to the Interim Constitution.[8] The conflict between so-called 'anti-horizontalists'[9] and those in favour of direct horizontal effect eventually ended in a stalemate, and it was left to the Constitutional Court, as in the case of the death penalty, to come up with a solution to the problem. This happened in the *Du Plessis* decision of May 1996,[10] a defamation case and one of the most comparative judgments handed down by any major national court over the past years. The majority of judges thereby came out in favour of an indirect effect of human rights on private relationships, a solution closely modelled, as shall be seen, on the German approach.

By that time, transition had, however, already moved on. The two-stage process leading from the 1983 Constitution to the final settlement of 1996 gave the newly elected Parliament (convened as a Constitutional Assembly between 1994 and 1996) an opportunity to revisit the matter in the light of both judicial developments and changed political majorities. The result – section 8 FC – not only declares the Bill of Rights applicable to all law and binding on the legislature, the executive, the judiciary, and all other organs of the state;[11] it also says that human rights shall bind natural or juristic persons if, and to the extent that, they are applicable, taking into account, first, the nature of the right and, second, the nature of any duty imposed by the right.[12] This approach has moved the system from indirect towards a more direct effect of many constitutional

---

see Sir B. Markesinis and J. Fedtke, *Judicial Recourse to Foreign Law. A New Source of Inspiration?* (2006).

6 See the comments by I. Currie and J. de Waal, *The Bill of Rights Handbook* (5th edn, 2005), p 32.

7 Held at Kempton Park (outside Johannesburg) in 1993.

8 See the *10th Report of the Technical Committee on Fundamental Rights* (5 October 2003) at 1.2.

9 Which included, inter alia, the National Party and the South African Communist Party.

10 *Du Plessis and another v De Klerk and another*, 1996 (3) SA 850.

11 Section 8(1) FC.

12 Section 8(2) FC.

rights, though the implications of this change have been rather limited in practice.

B. The current constitutional blueprint

The political parties competing for South Africa's constitutional future agreed, as indicated above, on a two-stage reform process while restructuring the country's new legal order in the 1990s. This led to the negotiation of an interim settlement, which entered into force in 1994, and – following the first free elections held in April that year – the 'final' 1996 Constitution. Both documents were strongly influenced by foreign constitutional ideas, the German Basic Law (BL) of 1949 proving one important source.[13] Among the other systems and legal instruments which inspired the framers we also find the United States, Canada, India, Namibia, the European Union, and the European Convention on the Protection of Human Rights and Fundamental Freedoms. Both Constitutions are thus, not surprisingly, a blend of many different legal traditions, including that of the most important former colonial power in the region, the United Kingdom. This foreign influence has, as we shall see in the course of this chapter, also affected the discussion surrounding the application of human rights in the private sphere. Looking at the wide spectrum of systems that were consulted on the topic, ranging from the United States (with a predominantly vertical effect) to Germany (indirect effect) and Namibia (direct effect), this is, again, no surprise.

German constitutional thinking is particularly evident in four areas: human rights,[14] the influence of the *Rechtsstaat* idea,[15] the establishment of a specialised constitutional court similar to Germany's *Bundesverfassungsgericht*, and the introduction of quasi-federal structures.[16] Of particular importance for our topic here are the

---

[13] The degree of German influence is quite remarkable given that Germany was the only country outside the common law world and the English-speaking legal community which received such attention from the framers of the new South African constitutional order.

[14] The essential content clause in s 33(1)(b) IC, the protection of juristic persons in ss 7(3) IC and 8(4) FC, and the inclusion of occupational freedom (*Berufsfreiheit*) in s 22 FC are remarkable examples of legal transplants in this area.

[15] Counterpart of the English rule of law.

[16] Pertaining to, inter alia, the distribution of legislative competence between the central and provincial levels as well as the concept of 'co-operative government' (*kooperativer Föderalismus*).

clauses dealing with the application of the Bill of Rights, sections 7 IC and 8 FC, which resemble Article 1(3) BL and reveal both the basic foundations of South Africa's human rights regime *and* interesting differences from their German model. The allocation of constitutional review to a specialised court is the second important legal transplant in this context.

In a shift of seismic proportions, South Africa has moved away from the principle of parliamentary sovereignty, inherited from the English legal tradition and used for decades to legitimise white minority rule, and made the exercise of all state authority – including legislative power – subject not only to formal (procedural) safeguards but also substantive constitutional requirements. The Constitution is now the supreme law of the land, and all law or conduct inconsistent with it is regarded as invalid.[17] More specifically, section 8 FC declares that the Bill of Rights applies to all law, and binds the legislature, the executive, the judiciary, and all organs of state.[18] Human rights are defined as a 'cornerstone of democracy in South Africa'[19] which the state must 'respect, protect, promote and fulfil'.[20] An interesting difference between the Constitutions of 1993 and 1996 is the role of the courts in this respect. While section 7(1) IC stopped short of declaring the Bill of Rights binding on the judiciary, section 8(1) FC fully adopts the German text of Article 1(3) BL, making all court decisions subject to human rights considerations. We will return to this difference in more detail later. Ultimate control is exercised by the Constitutional Court, which was created in 1994 and allocated a specialised and final jurisdiction in all constitutional matters.[21]

The Bill of Rights is extensive, covering a wide range of classical liberal rights such as human dignity,[22] life,[23] freedom and security of the person,[24] privacy,[25] freedom of religion, belief and opinion,[26]

---

[17] Section 2 FC.
[18] Section 8(1) FC.
[19] Section 7(1) FC.
[20] Section 7(2) FC.
[21] Section 167(3) FC.
[22] Section 10 FC.
[23] Section 11 FC.
[24] Section 12 FC.
[25] Section 14 FC.
[26] Section 15 FC.

freedom of expression,[27] freedom of assembly and association,[28] political rights,[29] and the protection of property.[30] The Constitution also features extensive socio-economic rights such as the right to fair labour practices,[31] a healthy environment,[32] rights to housing,[33] health care, food, water and social security,[34] special children's rights,[35] and the right to basic education.[36] Access to information held not only by the state[37] but also – where required for the exercise or protection of any rights – private individuals,[38] a right to just administrative action[39] and access to courts,[40] and a number of rights for arrested, detained and accused persons[41] are also guaranteed. Equality is protected both as a general principle and in the form of two anti-discrimination clauses addressed to the state and private parties.[42] The introduction of the (interim) Bill of Rights in 1994 had an immediate impact on litigation. Courts on all levels of the system, usually exercising general jurisdiction (the Constitutional Court being the most important exception), have been confronted with human rights issues from day one of the post-apartheid era.

Finally, it is interesting to note that South Africa is not only a blend of different constitutional traditions but also a 'mixed' or 'hybrid' system in terms of its private law roots, which combine the English common law with strong Roman-Dutch elements.[43]

---

27 Section 16 FC.
28 Sections 17 and 18 FC.
29 Section 19 FC.
30 Section 25 FC.
31 Section 23 FC.
32 Section 24 FC.
33 Section 26 FC.
34 Section 27 FC.
35 Section 28 FC.
36 Section 29 FC.
37 Section 32(1)(a) FC.
38 Section 32(1)(b) FC.
39 Section 33 FC.
40 Section 34 FC.
41 Section 35 FC.
42 Sections 9(1), (3) and (4) FC.
43 On this see, e.g., F. Stone, 'The End to be Served by Comparative Law' (1950/1951) *Tulane Law Review* 325 ff; K. Zweigert and H. Kötz, *An Introduction to Comparative Law* (3rd edn, 1998), pp 227 ff; G. Erasmus, 'Thoughts on private law in a future South Africa' (1994) *Stellenbosch Law Review* 105 ff.

Customary law is a third important source.[44] While distinctions between legal families in the area of private law are of little importance when it comes to questions of constitutional or administrative law, and despite the strong trend towards a convergence of legal cultures in general, common law systems more than their continental European counterparts still tend to have a different perception of the role that judges should play in developing the law. While Continental systems instinctively place more emphasis on the legislator as the most legitimate source of law (while accepting that many, including constitutional, developments are in fact strongly affected and sometimes even driven by judges), common law systems will, in principle, have no difficulty in accepting the role of the courts in shaping a legal system. When it comes to the effect of human rights in the private sphere, courts will thus, more than this is the case in civil law systems, be accepted as an intervening force. In Germany, by contrast, much energy is still spent on explaining that courts are in fact not applying human rights to the case at hand unless the overall importance of constitutional considerations require core values to be taken into account in exceptional situations. The more the judge is perceived as a legitimate source of law, the less, it seems, may such justification be necessary. South Africa with its common law heritage is a good example.

C. The Interim Constitution of 1993 and the *Du Plessis* decision of 1996

I. Drittwirkung *in the negotiations leading to the Interim Constitution*

As already indicated above, the issue of a possible *Drittwirkung* of constitutional rights led to one of the most heated debates in the negotiations leading up to the Interim Constitution. This political conflict ended in a highly ambiguous constitutional text, which avoided the clear language proposed, for example, by the Technical Committee on Fundamental Rights, an independent body of legal

---

[44] On the development and influence of South African customary law, see, e.g., N. Olivier, 'The judicial application of African customary law' in A. J. G. M. Sanders (ed), *The Internal Conflict of Laws in South Africa* (1990), pp 41 ff and G. Devenish, 'The making of the Interim Constitution' (1997) *THRHR* 612 at 627.

experts responsible for the scientific support of the party delegates discussing the issue. Noting, first, the extreme differences of power which can equally exist in relationships outside the traditional domain of state authority and, second, the international trend towards a stronger *inter partes* effect of constitutional rights, the Committee in its 5th Report of June 1993 had proposed to make human rights binding, 'where appropriate, on all social institutions and persons'.[45] This approach was inspired by the Constitution of Namibia[46] and reflected the proposals of the ANC[47] and the Democratic Party (DP).[48] The de Klerk Government, on the other hand, tried to limit the operation of human rights to vertical relationships, conceding only an indirect effect through inherent limitations (rights should thus not be exercised to the detriment of others), the interpretation of existing private law in the light of constitutional values, and the binding effect of a supreme constitutional settlement for future legislation.[49] The Technical Committee tried to bridge this gap between the parties by proposing, first, to make the provisions of the Interim Bill of Rights applicable 'to other bodies and persons to the

---

[45] See the *5th Report of the Technical Committee on Fundamental Rights* (11 June 1993) at 3.1.

[46] Which declares in Article 5 that the fundamental rights and freedoms enshrined in that document 'shall be respected and upheld by the Executive, Legislature and Judiciary and all organs of the Government, its agencies and, where applicable to them, by all natural and legal persons in Namibia, and shall be enforceable by the Courts in the manner hereinafter prescribed'.

[47] Article 17(1) of the ANC Proposal of 1992 declared: 'The terms of the Bill of Rights shall be binding upon the State and organs of government at all levels, and where appropriate, on all social institutions and persons.'

[48] Article 1 of the DP proposal of 1993 declared: 'This Bill of Rights guarantees the rights enshrined in it. They shall be respected and upheld by all organs of the State and government, whether legislative, executive or judicial, and, where applicable, by all persons in South Africa, and shall be enforceable by the Supreme Court of South Africa.'

[49] See 'Republic of South Africa Government's Proposal on a Charter of Fundamental Rights' (1993) *African Journal of International and Comparative Law* 436 f: 'The Draft Charter is based on four principles. Firstly, the principle of verticality. This means that the Charter primarily regulates legal relations between the State and the subject. It does not directly regulate relations among citizens themselves, although the Charter will have an "over-flow" effect on such horizontal relations. For instance 'rights are required by the Charter to be exercised responsibly with due regard to the rights of others. Also, the principles of the Charter will serve as guidelines in the interpretation of statutes dealing with legal relations among subjects. These principles will also materially influence the substance of future laws.'

extent expressly provided for' in the Interim Constitution[50] and, second, by insering a further qualification into the application clause (binding effect only 'where just and equitable').[51] The first solution envisaged the identification of particular rights which could have been given a direct effect in the text of the 1993 Constitution while the second approach relied heavily on the courts to achieve an appropriate level of human rights protection in the private sphere. The 7th Report thus put on record that:

> (T)he Committee thought it best ... not to be prescriptive as regards the horizontal application of fundamental rights during the transition. Instead the suggested formulation ... leaves room for the evolutionary and natural development of the concept of the horizontal enforcement of rights in the jurisprudence of the designated judicial authority.[52]

This solution was rejected not only by the South African Communist Party (SACP)[53] but also, and more importantly, by the judiciary, which came out strongly against a direct effect of constitutional rights on the common law for fear of 'great legal uncertainty and social insecurity'. Judges also felt that the courts should not become embroiled in the task of distinguishing constitutional rights which have direct effect in the private sphere from those that do not. The question was regarded as a 'policy issue' rather than one which should be allocated to the judiciary.[54]

---

50 6th Report (15 July 1993).

51 7th Report (29 July 1993).

52 Ibid at 1(1)(b).

53 See L. du Plessis and H. Corder, *Understanding South Africa's Transitional Bill of Rights* (1994), p 111.

54 See M. Corbett, *Memorandum submitted on behalf of the Judiciary of South Africa on the Draft Interim Bill of Rights* (3 September 1993) at 3: 'This clause will create great uncertainty and confusion. The reference to the application of the Bill to "other bodies and persons" implies the horizontal application of the Bill. This entails the application of the Bill to, inter alia, the actions of companies and corporations (whether public or private), partnerships, societies and clubs, and all individuals. In consequence, all private relationships will be governed by the Bill of Rights. The phrase quoted above can, and notionally will, be interpreted to mean that the provisions of the Bill override the common law. For example, clause 9 entrenches freedom of speech. If clause 1(1)(b) remains, it may be construed as meaning that A can defame B freely; B's common law protections and remedies are nullified by A's constitutional rights. Is this the intention? If so, it must be realised that the effect of the Bill may be to supersede large parts of our established common law, and that it may well lead to great legal uncertainty and social insecurity. We suggest that what the drafters of the interim Bill probably had in mind was to eliminate privatised discrimination,

The solution eventually codified in the Interim Constitution was a political compromise which involved a careful balancing of several provisions and which, in effect, left the question undecided. Section 7(1) IC was, on the one hand, rephrased so as to exclude the judiciary from the binding effect of the Bill of Rights. The interpretation clause was, on the other hand, expanded by a provision which opened the door to an indirect effect of constitutional rights along the lines developed by the German Federal Constitutional Court in the *Lüth* decision of 1958.[55] Section 35(3) IC thus declared that '[I]n the interpretation of any law and the application and development of the common law and customary law, a court shall have due regard to the spirit, purport and objects' of the Bill of Rights. Similar provisions had previously been suggested by the South African Law Commission (with specific reference to the German model)[56] and by the de Klerk Government.[57] The Interim Constitution also acknowledged the indirect influence of human rights via legislation in section 7(2) IC, declaring that the Bill of Rights shall apply to all law in force, and section 33(4) IC, a provision which specifically addressed the possibility of legislation designed to prohibit unfair discrimination by private parties. Section 33(2) IC, finally, specifically prohibited any law – 'whether a rule of the common law, customary law or legislation' – from limiting constitutional rights unless the limitation was, in particular, proportionate.[58]

---

i.e. unfair discrimination by legal entities and individuals in private affairs. If so, it is necessary to demarcate, clearly and unambiguously, the precise field of impermissible discrimination (e.g., employment) from those areas of highly personal affairs where one should be free to choose one's own associates (e.g., religion, cultural organisations, private home life, etc.).'

55 BVerfGE 7, 198 of 15 January 1958 (see the chapter on Germany for a detailed discussion of this influential case).

56 South African Law Commission, *Project 58: Group and Human Rights – Interim Report* (1991), section 39.

57 In 1993, the Government proposed the following provision under the heading *Operation of the Charter Against Third Parties*: '(1) No provision of this Charter shall be construed so as to create or regulate legal relations other than those between the State and a person as contemplated in Section 1. (2) In the interpretation of any law regarding legal relations among persons *inter se*, the spirit, objects and purport of this Charter shall be taken into account. (3) Where a person exercises or enjoys a right recognised by this Charter, such a person shall do so in a manner which will not infringe the rights of any other person.'

58 Section 33(1) IC.

2. Academic interpretation of the Interim Constitution

If the political parties were unable to come up with a clear answer to the problem of *Drittwirkung* in 1993, how then did the new constitutional settlement work in practice? Academic opinion was equally divided on the matter, some authors suggesting an indirect effect similar to the German model[59] while others argued in favour of a direct application of human rights in the private sphere.[60] The first group felt that constitutional rights should influence private relationships by 'seepage' or, closer to the German model, a 'radiating effect' on private law. Policy considerations and open-ended standards or principles were identified as the most appropriate links between private law and constitutional values. Fairness, justice and good faith, or the notion of an equitable compensation for loss in ideally balanced contractual relationships are, according to this approach, examples of suitably flexible elements of private law through which constitutional rights can be made operational; wrongfulness, legal causation, remoteness and negligence were suggested in the area of tort law. The effect of these 'gateways' was, however, to be limited; only in exceptional circumstances should human rights call for judicial intervention. As Annél van Aswegen remarked:[61]

> Policy considerations are usually applied in instances where the traditional area of application of a settled rule has to be expanded to meet changed social, scientific or technological circumstances, or where settled rules apparently conflict or give rise to contradictory consequences,

---

59 See, e.g., L. du Plessis and H. Corder, op. cit., note 53, pp 113 ff and 116; L. du Plessis, 'A Background to Drafting the Chapter on Fundamental Rights' in B. de Villiers (ed), *Birth of a Constitution* (1994), pp 93 ff; D. Basson, 'South Africa's Interim Constitution: the Challenges to Diversity and Identity' (1995) *Verfassung und Recht in Übersee* 421; J. Kruger, 'Is interpretation a question of common sense? Some reflections on value judgments and section 35' (1995) *Comparative and International Law Journal of South Africa* 1 at 7; A. Henderson, 'Operation of the constitution between private actors,' (1995) *De Rebus* 439 at 440; G. Erasmus, 'Limitation and Suspension,' in D. van Wyk et al. (eds), *Rights and Constitutionalism* (1994), p 632.

60 See, e.g., J. D. van der Vyver, 'The private sphere in constitutional litigation' (1994) *Tydskrif vir Hedendaagse Romeins-Hollandse Reg* 47 ff; D. Davis, 'Equality and Equal Protection' in D. van Wyk et al. (eds), op. cit., note 59, pp 210 f; H. A. Strydom, 'The private domain and the bill of rights' (1995) *South African Public Law* 52 ff; A. Cachalia et al. (eds), *Fundamental Rights in the New Constitution* (1994), p 122.

61 A. van Aswegen, 'The Implications of a Bill of Rights for the Law of Contract and Delict' (1995) *South African Journal on Human Rights* 50 at 56, 60.

> and occasionally where settled rules have to be altered to accommodate novel factual circumstances. ... Obviously, legal rules formulated with reference to policy considerations furnish the most effective method of incorporating the values underlying the protection of fundamental rights into the fabric of private law. It can be assumed that the bill of rights reflects the fundamental values accepted in a society, and as such it represents a crystallised form of public policy. The policy considerations determining the contents and application of open-ended rules can therefore to a significant extent be extracted from the provisions of the Bill of Rights.

The main reason for this careful approach was the fear of the negative consequences which a more direct effect could have on the principle of private autonomy.[62] Legal certainty, a consideration voiced by the judiciary, also played a strong role.[63]

These fears were not shared by the 'horizontalists'. Apart from arguments based on the wording of the Interim Constitution, three important points were raised in favour of direct effect. There was, first, much criticism of the uneven distribution of (private) power and wealth in post-apartheid South Africa, and, coupled with this, the fear that past discrimination by the state could continue within the sanctuary of private law. Full application of human rights in the private sphere was regarded as the most appropriate safeguard against 'privatised apartheid'.[64] Direct effect was, second, regarded as preferable in terms of legal certainty because it renders unnecessary the difficult distinction between public and private action.[65] Finally, supporters of direct effect felt that a limited impact of human rights on judge-made common law would be a contradiction to the full subordination of the legislator to human rights considerations: '[T]he mere form of law should not dictate a difference in result.'[66] Some academics thereby accepted that particular areas of private

---

62 E. de Wet, 'Indirect Drittwirkung and the Application Clause' (1995) *South African Journal on Human Rights* 610 at 613.

63 J. de Waal, 'A Comparative Analysis of the provisions of German Origin in the Interim Bill of Rights' (1995) *South African Journal on Human Rights* 1 at 14.

64 A. Cachalia et al, op. cit., note 60, p 20; J. W. G. van der Walt, 'Justice Kriegler's disconcerting judgment in *Du Plessis v De Klerk*: Much ado about direct horizontal application (read nothing)' (1996) *Tydskrif vir die Suid-Afrikaanse Reg* 732 at 733.

65 S. Woolmann, 'Limitations,' in M. Chaskalson et al. (eds), *Constitutional Law of South Africa* (1996), pp 10–15.

66 S. Woolmann, ibid, pp 10–14 f and 11–2; F. Naude and V. Terblanche, 'The Interim Constitution – Effect of private litigation on our common law' (1994)

law might be insulated from the effect of constitutional rights; the internal rules of private organisations or purely private transactions such as the sale of a house or the contractual relationships between a hotel and its guests could thus be regarded as an 'a-constitutional private sphere' in which human rights considerations could become effective only through specific anti-discrimination laws.[67]

3. *Case law in the interim phase*

The courts, confronted with this highly ambiguous constitutional text, adopted very different solutions. Two divisions of the Supreme Court restricted, in principle, the effect of human rights to vertical relationships between the state and its citizens while at the same time accepting some measure of indirect influence.[68] Section 35(3) IC is thus:

> ... intended to permeate our judicial approach to interpretation of statutes and the development of the common law with the fragrance of values in which the Constitution is anchored. This means that whenever there is room for interpretation or development of our virile system of law that is to be the point of departure.[69]

This restrictive approach was justified mainly with the traditional argument that human rights operate first and foremost between the state and the citizen. The legislator of 1993, so the argument went, had been aware of this but had nevertheless opted against an expansion of human rights considerations into the private sphere. The court in *De Klerk and another v Du Plessis and others* also felt that this was in line with the historical experience of the country, where individuals had suffered primarily at the hands of public authorities.[70] The broad language of constitutional rights was, finally,

---

De Rebus 609 at 613; D. Spitz, 'Eschewing Silence coerced by Law: The Political Core and Protected Periphery of Freedom of Expression' (1994) *South African Journal on Human Rights* 301 at 317.

[67] J. D. van der Vyver, op. cit., note 60, at pp 389 f and 393 f; E. de Wet, op. cit., note 62, at p 614.

[68] See, *De Klerk and another v Du Plessis and others*, 1994 (6) BCLR 124 (T) – this decision was later reviewed by the Constitutional Court – and *Potgieter en 'n Ander v Kilian*, 1996 (2) SA 276.

[69] *De Klerk and another v Du Plessis and others*, 1994 (6) BCLR 124 (T) at p 133.

[70] Ibid, at p 130 f.

regarded as too imprecise; well-developed principles of private law could not readily be modified or even exchanged by the direct application of the Bill of Rights. The court in *De Klerk* thus held:

> The alternative, that it was intended that the Bill of Rights have horizontal effect, is extremely unattractive. It entails that all private rights, contracts and relationships are henceforth to be tested by the Constitutional Court against broad and vaguely defined principles. Legal uncertainty on an unprecedented scale would be the result.[71]

Most other courts, however, came out in favour of direct effect. The most influential of these decisions was *Gardener v Whitaker* of the Eastern Cape Division of the Supreme Court,[72] which identified three distinct areas of private activity with different levels of judicial scrutiny in terms of human rights considerations. 'Societal activities not directly prescribed by law' were thus not subject to human rights, and could only be affected by constitutional values through legislative intervention aimed specifically at the prohibition of certain forms of discrimination.[73] Direct effect, however, was assumed for most parts of the legal system. The courts, in the view of the Eastern Cape Division, were thus obliged to protect individuals against threats to their constitutional freedoms by direct application of human rights in private relationships.[74] 'Merely apparent and insubstantial conflicts' should, finally, be resolved by adapting the common law to constitutional values as envisaged by sections 35(1) and (3) IC.[75] Interestingly, the Court acknowledged the values of the new constitutional settlement while at the same time calling for a cautious approach to the review of long-standing common law rules. Not all human rights provisions would, moreover, lend themselves to direct effect. There is, in the words of the Court:

> ... no uniform and single answer to the question whether an alleged breach of a fundamental right contained in Chapter 3 of the Constitution can found an action between private individuals and entities, or whether it only applies between individuals and State organs.

---

71 Ibid, at p 131.

72 1994 (5) BCLR 19 (E).

73 At p 28, with specific reference to J. D. van der Vyver, op. cit., note 60.

74 The indirect effect of human rights on the private sphere through their binding effect on legislation was already emphasised in an earlier decision of the Orange Free State Provincial Division of the Supreme Court in *Walton's Stationary Co (Edms) Bpk v Fourie and another*, 1994 (1) BCLR 50 (O).

75 1994 (5) BCLR 19 (E) at p 30.

> It all depends on the nature and extent of the particular right, the values that underlie it, and the context in which the alleged breach of the right occurs.[76]

An intermediate position was, finally, adopted by the Witwatersrand Local Division of the Supreme Court, which rejected the notion of an unqualified horizontal effect of human rights in *Holomisa v Argus Newspapers Ltd.*[77] Much emphasis was, however, placed on section 35(3) IC, which could even justify a complete overhaul of pre-Constitutional law.[78]

4. The **Du Plessis** *decision of the Constitutional Court*

The interpretation of the Interim Constitution was eventually resolved by the Constitutional Court in *Du Plessis and others v De Klerk and another*,[79] an appeal against the *De Klerk* decision of the Transvaal Provincial Division of the Supreme Court mentioned above. A defamation case involving the Pretoria News, the judgment resolved the question in favour of indirect effect.

In February and March 1993, the Pretoria News had published a series of six articles dealing with the supply of weapons and other material to the Angolan rebel movement UNITA. In a nutshell, the paper wrote that South African citizens were involved in these covert operations, which were conducted in contravention of air traffic control regulations. The Pretoria News criticised the supply of arms to UNITA, and suggested that those responsible for organising the flights were fuelling the war in Angola for personal gain. The last two articles of the series mentioned Gerd de Klerk and his company,

---

[76] Ibid, at p 31.

[77] 1996 (6) BCLR 836 (W).

[78] Ibid, at p 850: 'Section 35(3), far from supplanting the common law or declaring it redundant, requires its "development" in the light of the new basic norm the Constitution posits. But the requirement that the fundamental rights gurantees be given "due regard" may entail that even the high authority of pre-Constitution judicial determinations may be superseded. To have "due regard" to something means to take it into proper account, to give appropriate consideration to it. The phrase "spirit, purport and objects" is broad and encompassing. It includes values which underlie the Constitution, the objectives the Constitution as a whole seeks to attain, and the enactment's sense, tenor and ostensible meaning. The directive in section 35(3) in my view therefore requires the fundamental reconsideration of any common law rule that trenches on a fundamental rights guarantee.'

[79] 1996 (3) SA 850.

Wonder Air (Pty) Ltd, as one of several private air operators which the South African Department of Foreign Affairs had called in for questioning in the context of these illegal flights. De Klerk issued a combined summons claiming damages of 750,000 Rand for injury to his reputation and his feelings; Wonder Air claimed a total of 5 million Rand for loss of business and damage to its commercial reputation. The Pretoria News admitted to publishing the articles but denied that the material had presented de Klerk and his company as being involved in illegal activities or that it was, indeed, defamatory. The newspaper also invoked the public interest defence of fair comment; as far as the articles were an expression of opinion, these constituted a fair comment made in good faith on matters of public interest, and were based on facts truly stated in the articles themselves. More importantly, the exercise of the constitutional right to free speech as enshrined in section 15(1) IC was later added to the defence after the coming into force of the Interim Constitution on 27 April 1994. This last aspect was at issue in the Constitutional Court. Not only had the Transvaal Provincial Division decided that the case was to proceed without reference to the Interim Constitution since it had been filed before the enactment of the new constitutional settlement;[80] the lower court had also accepted the argument of the plaintiffs that the new Bill of Rights could not, in principle, be applied to horizontal relationships.

The leading judgment of Kentridge AJ emphasised, first, that the Bill of Rights was binding only on the executive and legislative branches of government. The courts, in applying statutory law and developing the common law, are bound only indirectly by virtue of the interpretative rule contained in section 35(3) IC, which would be redundant if constitutional rights were to be understood as having direct effect. Human rights are thus directly relevant in private law disputes only insofar as they form a constitutional standard with which all law has to comply.[81] Interestingly, Kentridge AJ also invoked procedural considerations in this context. Section 98 IC thus restricted the jurisdiction of the newly created Constitutional Court to the invalidation of formal statutes, while it was left to the Supreme Court to develop and, if necessary, adapt the common law to the values of the new constitutional order. A final and overarching

---

80 Invoking an exemption of pre-Constitutional cases contained in section 241(8) IC.

81 1996 (3) SA 850, at p 879.

(constitutional) control by the Constitutional Court would, in the view of the majority, have run counter to the logic of the new court structure established by the Interim Constitution:

> The consequence would be that appeals in all such cases would lie to the Constitutional Court and the Appellate Division [of the Supreme Court] would be deprived of a substantial part of what has hitherto been seen as its regular civil jurisdiction. At the very least, appeals to the Appelate Division would routinely result in referrals of common law cases to the Constitutional Court. I do not believe that such a state of affairs could ever have been intended by the framers of the Constitution.[82]

Other judges, such as Ackermann J[83] and Sachs J, supported this argument, the latter pointing out that direct application of human rights by the Constitutional Court would deprive the system of its necessary flexibility and infringe the division of powers principle. An indirect effect of constitutional rights on the development of the common law by the Supreme Court would thus maintain the right of the legislator to shape private relationships through the enactment of statutes, while final and binding judgments of the Constitutional Court precluded further legislative intervention short of constitutional amendments.[84] This approach maintained the common law jurisdiction of the Appellate Division of the Supreme Court.[85]

The solution adopted by the majority of the Court was one of indirect horizontal effect. In line with the new specialised jurisdiction of the Constitutional Court, the German model was thereby regarded as particularly relevant. A flexible interpretation of all law in the light of constitutional values, as envisaged in section 35(3) IC, was preferable to a control of the common law by the Court, which could only invalidate but not constructively shape the private legal order. Indirect effect would, by contrast, allow:

> ... the development of the common law and customary law by the Supreme Court in accordance with the objects of [the Bill of Rights].

---

[82] Ibid, at p 883.

[83] Ibid, at p 906.

[84] Ibid, at p 931 f.

[85] In *National Media Ltd v Bogoshi*, 1999 (1) BCLR 1 (SCA), the Appellate Division thus heard an appeal based on the alleged unconstitutionality of a common law rule on defamation, and adjusted its own past jurisprudence on the matter without directly applying constitutional rights but rather examining the compatibility of the new rule with the spirit, purport and objects of the Bill of Rights.

> This is provided for in section 35(3): ... The presence of this subsection ensures that the values embodied in [the Bill of Rights] will permeate the common law in all its aspects, including private litigation.[86]

Referring with approval to the Canadian case of *Bank of British Columbia v Canadian Broadcasting Corporation*, Kentridge AJ then continued that:

> [T]he [Canadian] Court ruled out direct application of the Charter, but emphasized that the common law must be interpreted in a manner which is consistent with Charter principles. This obligation is simply the manifestation of the inherent jurisdiction of the courts to modify or extend the common law in order to comply with prevailing social conditions and values.[87]

Individuals are therefore not directly bound by the constitutional rights of others but the courts were under an obligation to interpret and develop the common law in the spirit of the Bill of Rights. Kentridge AJ was, however, also willing to concede that single constitutional rights could in certain circumstances exert a more direct effect; the Court was anxious only to exclude '*general* direct horizontal application' of the Bill of Rights.[88]

Two judges, however, argued forcefully in favour of direct effect. The opinion of Kriegler J, in particular, focused on the historical background of the Interim Constitution and emphasised the need for fundamental changes in the South African legal order. Any resolution of private disputes with the help of legal instruments activates, in Kriegler J's view, the supremacy of the Constitution: 'All organs of the State in all their decisions and actions are bound by the terms of the rights. So, too, are any resorts to law by anybody.'[89] Freedom to organise one's private life beyond the ambit of constitutional values existed only in areas not regulated by any law unless the legislator decided to intervene in order to prevent discrimination. This did not render section 35(3) IC superfluous. The provision,

---

86 Ibid, at p 885. Ackermann J saw in section 35(3) IC a legal transplant of the German theory of indirect effect and invoked the German counterpart of the rule of law, the *Rechtsstaatsprinzip*, to reject direct effect as a too unpredictable mechanism in the area of private law. Indirect effect, made operational through general clauses and concepts such as public policy considerations, the *boni mores*, unlawfulness, reasonableness, fairness and the like, would, by contrast, allow a gentle seepage of constitutional values into all areas of the law (ibid, at p 903).

87 Ibid, at p 886.

88 Ibid, at p 887 (emphasis added).

89 Ibid, at p 916.

in his view, established a duty of the courts to take constitutional values into account even where the parties had chosen not to invoke them in private law disputes.[90] Madala J, finally, suggested that the question of direct or indirect effect should be reviewed on a case-by-case basis and with a view to the particular constitutional right involved.

Finally, it is worthwhile reflecting on this judgment from a methodological point of view. As indicated, it made extensive use of comparative law for two reasons. There were, first, clear signs that the political parties negotiating the constitutional settlement of 1993 had contemplated various solutions found abroad. For political reasons, the agreement eventually found was highly ambiguous, and in interpreting this text it made good sense for the judges of the Constitutional Court to apply their minds to the arguments put forward in the drafting process. Comparative law suggested itself as a valuable method. Second, the issue had obviously been left undecided by the legislator. Here, we encounter a similarity with the well-known death penalty dispute,[91] which was equally left for the courts to resolve. In both cases, South African judges were thus given a mandate by the political process – a mandate, one could argue, not only to apply traditional *judicial* but also *legislative* techniques, which no doubt include the use of comparative law. Taking into account this legislative background, it is thus no surprise that *Du Plessis* is probably one of the most comparative judgments ever published. Foreign law also had exceptional impact on the reasoning of the judges because the issue at hand – the inter partes application of fundamental rights – has, at one time or the other, riddled most societies with a system of human rights protection.[92]

---

[90] Ibid, at p 917: 'Section 35(3) answers the question what courts do when there is no direct infringement or claim of an infringement of a right protected under [the Bill of Rights]. This includes cases dealing with statutory law, common law and customary law. It mandates that all courts ... in interpreting statutory law and when applying and developing common and customary law, always have regard to the spirit, purport and objects of [the Bill of Rights]. This includes courts with constitutional jurisdiction and courts without constitutional jurisdiction. The purpose is that this Constitution is to permeate all that judges do, just as it is to permeate all that the legislature and the executive do, conformably under section 7(1).'

[91] *The State v Makwanyane and Mchunu* (Case No. CCT/3/94 of 6 June 1995).

[92] Stephen Gardbaum describes the issue as 'currently one of the most important and hotly debated in comparative constitutional law'. See 'The "Horizontal Effect" of Constitutional Rights' [2003] 102 *Michigan Law Review* 387 at 388.

Before embarking on an extensive analysis of US, Irish, Canadian and German law, as well as the work of Chief Justice Barak in Israel, Kentridge AJ nevertheless emphasised the need to bear in mind the specific characteristics of the *South African* setting.[93] As in other decisions of the Court, there needs to be a balance between a line of reasoning which focuses on the provisions of the 1993 Constitution and the discussion of foreign ideas. The latter are not only used to *confirm* a 'South African' solution; references to Canadian and German law show that some foreign ideas were actually used to *shape* the result in *Du Plessis*. Kentridge J describes remarks on considerations of policy cited from the opinion of McIntyre J in *Dolphin Delivery* as 'fully applicable to Chapter 3 of our own Constitution',[94] and explains that the German approach to the interpretation of private law by a specialised constitutional court is of particular interest to South Africa. We thus find the following passage at [60] of the judgment:

> The model of indirect application or, if you will, indirect horizontality, seems peculiarly appropriate to a judicial system which, as in Germany, separates constitutional jurisdiction from ordinary jurisdiction. This does not mean that the principles evolved by the German Constitutional Court must be slavishly followed. They do however afford an example of how the process of influencing the common law may work in practice.

Another element which specifically enhanced the influence of German law on the thinking of some judges is the close genealogical relationship between South African law and the German legal system. The provisions of the 1993 Constitution relevant in *Du Plessis* may not have been *direct* legal transplants (as indicated by Ackermann J) but there *was* certainly substantial influence of German legal thinking on the work of the Multi-Party Negotiating

---

93 At no. [33]: 'There can be no doubt that the resolution of the issue must ultimately depend on an analysis of the specific provisions of the Constitution. It is nonetheless illuminating to examine the solutions arrived at by the courts of other countries. The Court was referred to judgments of the courts of the United States, Canada, Germany and Ireland. I would not presume to attempt a detailed description, or even a summary, of the relevant law of those countries, but in each case some broad features are apparent to the outside observer. A comparative examination shows at once that there is no universal answer to the problem of vertical or horizontal application of a Bill of Rights.'

94 At no. [58].

Process related to the question of *Drittwirkung*. This thinking continued to exert its influence in *Du Plessis*.[95]

Finally, it should be pointed out that the use of comparative law was not uncontroversial. In dissenting from the majority of the Court, Kriegler J emphasised the unique character of the South African constitutional arrangement, and cautioned against too much reliance on foreign experience.[96]

The approach developed in *Du Plessis* was confirmed by the Constitutional Court in *Gardener v Whitaker*,[97] and applied by the lower courts in a series of subsequent cases.[98] As shall be seen below,

---

[95] One can see this clearly from the following passage from the opinion of Ackermann J: 'That the drafters of our Constitution had recourse to or were influenced by certain features of the German BL in drafting our Constitution is evident from various of its provisions. The marked similarity between the provisions of section 35(3), enjoining courts "[i]n the interpretation of any law and the application and development of the common law and customary law" to "have due regard to the spirit, purport and objects of [Chapter 3]," and the indirect horizontal application of the basic rights in the German BL in German jurisprudence cannot, in my view, simply be a coincidence. It provides a final powerful indication that the framers of our Constitution did not intend that the Chapter 3 fundamental rights should, save where the formulation of a particular right expressly or by necessary implication otherwise indicates, apply directly to legal relations between private persons.'

[96] Writing at [127]: 'It is therefore no spirit of isolationism which leads me to say that our Constitution is unique in its origins, concepts and aspirations. Nor am I a chauvinist when I describe the negotiation process which gave birth to that Constitution as unique; so, too, the leap from minority rule to representative democracy founded on universal adult suffrage; the Damascene about-turn from executive directed parliamentary supremacy to justiciable constitutionalism and a specialist constitutional court, the ingathering of discarded fragments of the country and the creation of new provinces; and the entrenchment of a true separation and devolution of powers. Nowhere in the world that I am aware of have enemies agreed on a transitional coalition and a controlled two-stage process of constitution building. Therefore, although it is always instructive to see how other countries have arranged their constitutional affairs, I do not start there. And when I do conduct comparative study, I do so with great caution. The survey is conducted from the point of vantage afforded by the South African Constitution, constructed on unique foundations, built according to a unique design and intended for unique purposes.'

[97] 1996 (6) BCLR 775 (CC).

[98] See, e.g., *Ryland v Edros*, 1997 (1) BCLR 77 (C); *Rivett-Carnac v Wiggins*, 1997 (4) BCLR 562 (C); *McNally v M and G Media (Pty) Ltd and others*, 1997 (6) BCLR 818 (W); *Mistry v Interim National Medical and Dental Council of South Africa and others*, 1997 (7) BCLR 933 (D); *Buthelezi v South African Broadcasting Corporation*, 1997 (12) BCLR 1733 (D).

it also remains extremely influential under the provisions of the current constitutional settlement.

D. The final Constitution of 1996

Du Plessis was heavily criticised by a number of academic authors.[99] Beside invoking those sections of the Interim Constitution which could be read as establishing direct effect, the inability of indirect *Drittwirkung* to address discrimination effectively in the private sphere was a frequently voiced concern.[100] Many commentators also rejected the comparative approach of the Constitutional Court; Germany and Canada, the two most important models for *Du Plessis*, were regarded as too different in terms of their socio-economic environment to provide workable templates for South Africa.[101]

Negotiations concerning the Final Constitution had, in the meantime, reached a crucial stage as far as the application of human rights in the private sphere was concerned.[102] The first free elections held in April 1994 had shifted the balance of power in favour of those parties which supported direct effect; the National Party (NP) was now the only political group to promote a more restrictive approach, arguing that the application of constitutional rights to private relationships would limit the ability of the private legal order to function properly.[103] Most other parties represented in the Constitutional Assembly felt, however, that a restriction of human

---

99 See, e.g., S. Woolmann and D. Davis, 'The Last Laugh: *Du Plessis v De Klerk*, Classical Liberalism, Creole Liberalism and the Application of Fundamental Rights under the Interim and Final Constitution' (1996) *South African Journal on Human Rights* 361 at 363 ff; H. Cheadle and D. Davis, 'The Application of the 1996 Constitution in the Private Sphere,' (1997) *South African Journal on Human Rights* 44 at 51 ff; S. Woolmann, 'Application' in M. Chaskalson et al. (eds), *Constitutional Law of South Africa* (2nd edn, looseleaf), pp 31–23 ff.

100 See, e.g., S. Woolmann and D. Davis, op. cit., p 403: '(T)he application doctrine adopted by the majority of the Constitutional Court in *Du Plessis v De Klerk* has the potential to immunise from direct constitutional scrutiny a whole range of feudal and racist relationships created and sustained by previous apartheid regimes.'

101 S. Woolmann and D. Davis, op. cit., at p 404.

102 For a more detailed account of the relevant deliberations in the Constitutional Assembly, see H. Cheadle, 'Application' in H. Cheadle et al. (eds), *South African Constitutional Law: The Bill of Rights* (2002), pp 26 ff.

103 Theme Committee 4, *Explanatory Memorandum* (9 October 1995), p 266.

rights to vertical relationships would undermine seriously the trust of South Africa's citizens in the final constitutional settlement.[104]

Regardless of this shift of opinion, political opposition against direct effect nevertheless continued. Uncertainty concerning the consequences following from the various approaches eventually prompted the Technical Committee advising the Constitutional Assembly on human rights issues to present a further report as late as October 1996, in which it put on record that the differences between indirect and direct effect were, in fact, negligible in practice. The Committee supported its position with four arguments. Constitutional and common law values were, first, in most cases very similar (if not identical), so that courts would usually continue to apply private law without recourse to the Constitution. If, however, constitutional rights indeed required a different solution in single cases, even a horizontal approach would in all likelihood utilise the open-ended clauses of the common law to cover the situation. The notion of *boni mores* had, third, always been used to introduce considerations of the public good into South African contract, tort, and inheritance law. As long as the Final Constitution offered access to the courts in cases of human rights infringements, judges would probably continue to use this mechanism and come to results very similar to the German concept of indirect effect. Finally, conflicts between competing constitutional values could be resolved through a balancing of interests, a technique already well-known to common lawyers.[105]

Despite this analysis, the Committee nevertheless proposed to qualify the new application clause by insering the caveat 'where applicable' into the text. It also suggested binding the judiciary to the Bill of Rights (as is the case in Namibia and Germany); courts confronted with private disputes, so the argument ran, would in any case be bound by human rights considerations only to the extent to which these are, in principle, applicable to private relationships, while certain constitutional rights such as the right to a fair trial are clearly addressed to judicial activity.[106] These suggestions of the Committee were eventually incorporated in sections 8(1) FC, dealing

---

[104] See Theme Committee 4, *Report on Nature and Application of the Bill of Rights* (May 1995).

[105] Theme Committee 4, op. cit., note 103, pp 270 f.

[106] See Theme Committee 4, op. cit., note 103, p 272 f: 'Including the judiciary in the binding clause does not imply that it is bound to apply the Bill of Rights in a

with the effect of human rights on vertical relationships, and section 8(2) FC, which establishes direct horizontal application.

Section 8(3) FC was designed to reflect the more active role of the judge in common law jurisdictions by specifying that a court, when applying a provision of the Bill of Rights to a natural or juristic person, must apply, or if necessary develop, the common law to the extent that legislation does not give effect to that right,[107] and may develop rules of the common law to limit a right, provided that such limitation is in accordance with the general limitation clause and, in particular, the principle of proportionality.[108] These last-minute additions to the text of the Final Constitution were clearly meant to protect in particular the common law from the potentially disruptive effects of horizontally applicable constitutional rights.

The substance of section 35(3) IC was maintained as an 'interpretational directive'[109] in section 39(2) FC. The provision has subsequently been understood not as an expression of the German theory of indirect effect but rather as a general guideline for the courts to respect human rights in all cases and irrespective of whether the parties actually invoke them or not.[110] The provision also addresses the procedural concern voiced by a number of judges in *Du Plessis*, namely that the Constitutional Court had no jurisdiction to develop the common law in order to give effect to constitutional rights in the private sphere.[111]

Finally, the 1996 Constitution removed the procedural obstacle to direct application of human rights identified by the Constitutional Court in *Du Plessis*. The High Courts, the Supreme Court of Appeal and the Constitutional Court now exercise a shared jurisdiction over constitutional matters. This had a knock-on effect on the whole structure of the legal system in that constitutional law

---

totally unqualified way. The judiciary in deciding on matters concerning relationships between private parties (like the legislature in making laws, and the executive in their execution) can only be bound by the Bill of Rights to the extent that the Bill of Rights can be applied to such relationships.'

107 Section 8(3)(a) FC.

108 Section 8(3)(b) FC.

109 Constitutional Committee, *Supplementary Memorandum on the Bill of Rights and Party Submissions* (9 November 1995), section 38 at 1.2.

110 I. Rautenbach and E. F. J. Malherbe, *Constitutional Law* (1994), p 305; H. Cheadle and D. Davis, op. cit., note 99, p 55.

111 See, e.g., I. Rautenbach and E. F. J. Malherbe, *Constitutional Law* (4th edn, 2004), p 314.

and common law are no longer regarded as distinct areas, with constitutional values affecting private law indirectly, but rather as one unified system of law with the Constitution at its apex.[112]

As far as the substantive provisions of the Bill of Rights themselves are concerned, it is important to note that some rights are expressly designed to regulate private relationships while others, by virtue of their content, operate only vertically. Section 9(4) FC thus provides that no person may unfairly discriminate directly or indirectly against anyone on one or more of the grounds identified in section 9(3) FC, and thus has an immediate impact on the private sphere. The same is true for section 32(1)(b) FC, which establishes the right of access to information held by another person and required for the exercise and protection of any rights. A person's right to citizenship,[113] just administrative action,[114] or the rights of arrested, detained and accused persons[115] are, by contrast, obviously limited to the relationship between the state and its citizens. Direct effect will, moreover, depend on the protective scope of a right, which may be limited to particular individuals such as adult citizens,[116] children,[117] workers and employers,[118] or persons belonging to a cultural, religious or linguistic community.[119] Academic commentators have stressed the danger of compiling a formal list of rights and duties that can have an effect in the private sphere and those which cannot; the details of the particular case under consideration should always be taken into account.[120]

Direct effect of human rights has been invoked in a large variety of situations including defamation cases,[121] the freedom not to

---

[112] See *Pharmaceutical Manufacturers Association of South Africa: In re: ex p President of the Republic of South Africa*, 2000 (2) SA 674 (CC), where the Constitutional Court held that: '[T]here are not two systems of law, each dealing with the same subject matter, each having similar requirements, each operating in its own field with its own highest court. There is only one system of law. It is shaped by the Constitution which is the supreme law, and all law, including the common law, derives its force from the Constitution and is subject to constitutional control.'

[113] Section 20 FC.

[114] Section 33 FC.

[115] Section 35 FC.

[116] Section 19(3) FC.

[117] Section 28 FC.

[118] Section 23 FC.

[119] Section 31 FC.

[120] I. Rautenbach and E. F. J. Malherbe, op. cit., note 111, p 314.

[121] *National Media Ltd v Bogoshi*, 1999 (1) BCLR 1 (SCA).

attend religious observances in private schools,[122] or the contractual undertaking not to use loudspeakers to broadcast calls to prayer from a suburban mosque.[123] It is, however, important to note that the notion of directly enforceable human rights has in practice been rendered practically redundant. Since *Du Plessis*, courts have routinely tackled the problem of *Drittwirkung* through the indirect application of constitutional values to the common law. The reasons for this could lie in the very similar – if not equal – outcome of cases under both regimes, the flexibility of common law remedies, and the fact that indirect effect has since *Du Plessis* offered a familiar template for the resolution of human rights issues in private disputes.[124]

One exception in this context is the decision of the Constitutional Court in *Khumalo v Holomisa*,[125] a defamation case involving the leader of the United Democratic Movement (Bantu Holomisa) and the newspaper Sunday World over a report that alleged that Holomisa was involved in criminal activities and under police investigation. The Court held that the Bill of Rights must find direct application to the common law wherever appropriate and, in balancing the Final Constitution's commitment to human dignity with freedom of expression, came out in favour of Holomisa. The Constitutional Court did not, however, provide a workable approach to the application of section 8(2) FC,[126] in particular as far as the distinction between direct horizontal application and the binding effect of human rights on all law (including the common law) is concerned, and it remains to be seen whether the case will indeed have a long-term effect on the development of *Drittwirkung* in South Africa.

---

122 *Wittmann v Deutscher Schülerverein, Pretoria*, 1998 (4) SA 423 (T).

123 *Garden Cities Incorporated Association Not for Gain v Northpine Islamic Society*, 1999 (2) SA 268 (C).

124 On this see I. Currie and J. de Waal, op. cit., note 6, pp 50 f; C. Springman and M. Osborne, 'Du Plessis is not Dead: South Africa's 1996 Constitution and the Application of the Bill of Rights to Private Disputes' (1999) *South African Journal on Human Rights* 25 ff.

125 2002 (5) SA 401 (CC).

126 See the criticism by S. Woolmann, supra note 99, pp 31–42 ff and I. Curie and J. de Waal, supra note 6, p 51 f.

E. Concluding remarks

The Constitutional Court spoke of 'horizontal application' when dealing with section 8 FC in its second Certification Judgment.[127] Many commentators have, however, observed that the solutions of Kentridge AJ (indirect effect but full application of constitutional values on statutory provisions, common law and customary law) and Kriegler J (direct effect of human rights between private parties) in *Du Plessis* amount to very much the same thing, and that the Final Constitution had adopted a *via media* rather than introduced a revolutionary form of direct effect.[128] An interesting remark made by Mahomed J in *Du Plessis* points in a similar direction:

> Having examined the detailed reasons given by Kentridge AJ and those given by Kriegler J, I have come to the conclusion that on any approach the practical consequences are substantially the same ... The only residual area of potential disagreement arises in the case where what is sought to be attacked is some or other rule of the common law in litigation between private parties not involving any legislative or executive authority. But even in this limited area the true debate is effectively not whether the rights articulated in [the Bill of Rights] are capable of horizontal effect, but whether or not such horizontality is to arise in consequence of the direct application of the relevant ... right or through the mechanism of interpreting, applying and developing the common law by having regard to the spirit, purport and objects of the [Bill of Rights] pursuant to section 35(3) ... *The difference in the theoretical approaches favoured by Kriegler J and Kentridge AJ therefore seem to me to involve no substantial practical consequences.*[129]

The fact that human rights considerations have affected private relationships predominantly through the indirect application of constitutional values enshrined in the Final Constitution seems to confirm this view.

Two final points should be made in this respect. The 1996 Constitution, first, does not expressly provide a new constitutional remedy for the infringement of human rights in private relationships. Making constitutional rights operational in the private sphere remains an interpretative – and thus, structurally, 'indirect' – task in

---

[127] *In Re: Certification of the Constitution of the Republic of South Africa, 1996*, 1996 (10) BCLR 1253 (CC), at p 1280 f.

[128] K. Govender, 'Horizontality revisited in the light of *Du Plessis v De Klerk* and clause 8 of the Republic of South Africa Constitution Bill 1996' (1996) *Human Rights and Constitutional Law Journal of Southern Africa* 20 at 22.

[129] 1996 (3) SA 850, at p 891 (emphasis added).

the sense that the common law as a whole provides the link between constitutional values and the private sphere. Constitutional 'action' in private disputes is thus in most cases still mediated through the common law, which must be applied and, if necessary, developed in order to give effect to human rights.[130] The difference between the South African approach and its German model, then, is one of degree rather than substance. By limiting the radiating effect of human rights mainly (though not exclusively) to general clauses contained in the German Civil Code, German indirect *Drittwirkung* tends to be more restrictive. This is, however, largely a consequence of the structural differences between common law and civilian systems of private law. Second, the South African legislator, too, is (vertically) bound by the Bill of Rights. The mere existence of a supreme constitution will in itself have a strong impact on the private sphere through judicial review of an ever increasing amount of parliamentary legislation regulating private relationships.

---

[130] Section 8(3)(a) FC.

Chapter 12: Spain
A Jurisdiction Recognising the Direct Horizontal Application of Human Rights

Andrea Rodríguez Liboreiro[1]

A. Introduction

Since 1812, the year of enactment of its first Constitution, Spain has had eight constitutional texts. It is said that the failure, until recently, of the Spanish constitutionalist movement has been mainly due to three factors. One has been social or socio-economic: the slow modernisation of Spanish society in the XIX century (both social and economical). Another has been political: the lack of a culture of negotiation and compromise among the members of the elites who led each process of change, and who, with few exceptions, preferred the imposition of ideas and formulations of one or other ideology to agreement or compromise with their opponents.[2] The last factor has been ideological: the understanding of the Constitution as a mere political document and not as a legal one. The conception of the Constitution as a *norma normarum* and not as a *lex*, superior over the rest of the norms of the legal system.[3] These three factors had disappeared in the political transition, from the end of Franco's dictatorship in 1975 to the enactment of the present Constitution in 1978.[4]

---

[1] I would like to thank Miguel Angel Ramiro Avilés and Javier Mijangos y González of the University Carlos III Madrid and Colm O'Cinneide of University College London for their comments on earlier drafts of this chapter.

[2] F. Balaguer Callejón, *Manual de Derecho Constitucional* (2005), p 30.

[3] See the excellent work of R. Blanco Valdés, *El valor de la Constitución: separación de la ley y control de constitucionalidad en los origenes del Estado liberal* (1994).

[4] The 1978 Constitution was influenced by the Republican Spanish Constitution of 1931, which was the most important Constitution before 1978. The 1931 Constitution established a unicameral Parliament and a Republican Government; a democracy based on universal suffrage, a lay state and political des-centralisation.

The Spanish Constitution of 1978 marks the end of the Franco regime and reflects the optimism of a new democracy. Its aim was to establish a political system within the Western tradition which would guarantee citizens certain rights and freedoms. The 1978 Constitution itself combines a progressive approach, offering extensive individual rights, with a strong role for the state, the hope being that this Constitution would not suffer the same fate as those of the nineteenth century.[5]

The 1978 Constitution, written and codified, is not just a norm, but the first of the norms of the legal system, the fundamental norm, the *lex superior*.[6] It is the one which the other norms always have to conform with. The Constitution reveals its aims in the Preamble: to grant justice, freedom and security, to promote the wellbeing of those who belong to the Nation, and to establish and maintain a state that recognises and guarantees the rule of law, and protects all Spaniards in the exercise of their human rights. However, it is specifically the wording of Article 1.1, the primary and fundamental norm of the Spanish constitutional system, which articulates this conception. When proclaiming Spain 'a Welfare and Democratic State that recognizes the rule of law', Article 1.1 establishes freedom, justice, equality and political pluralism as the higher order values of the legal system.

The political objective of the Spanish democratic state is to guarantee and protect human rights and freedoms, which are the foundation both of the legal system (and give expression, in its specific provisions, to its higher order values) and of the political order and social peace.[7] The Spanish constitutional text has a broad section dedicated to the subject of fundamental rights and duties. Even though the main section on rights is proclaimed in Title I (Articles 10–55), there are other rights located in other sections of the Constitution, such as the right to petition (Article 77) or the right to use the Castilian language (Article 3).

It recognised economic and social rights and created the *Tribunal de Garantías Constitucionales* (Court of Constitutional Guarantees), precursor of the actual Spanish Constitutional Court.

5 C. Villiers, *The Spanish legal tradition* (1999), p 17.

6 E. García de Enterría, *La Constitución como norma y el Tribunal Constitucional* (2001) (1st edn, 1981), p 49.

7 Article 10.1. F. Balaguer, op. cit., note 2, p 44.

Although human rights are guaranteed by the Spanish Constitution, Spain is also a party to a number of treaties which grant and recognise human rights. Article 96 provides that international treaties become, following the monist system, automatically part of Spanish law once they are signed and ratified, without requiring any further implementation. Amongst others, Spain is party to the Universal Declaration of Human Rights, the International Covenant on Civil and Political Rights 1966, the International Covenant on Economic Social and Political Rights 1966 (both signed in 1976 and ratified in 1977), the European Convention for the Protection of Human Rights and Fundamental Freedoms 1950 (signed in 1977, ratified in 1979), and the European Social Charter 1961 (signed in 1978, ratified in 1980). Article 10.2 of the Constitution states expressly that rights and liberties contained in the Constitution are to be interpreted in accordance with the Universal Declaration of Human Rights and other treaties to which Spain is party. The Constitutional Court has held consistently that, in accordance with Article 10.2 of the Constitution, international treaties on human rights to which Spain is party are binding in relation to the interpretation of the human rights recognised by the Constitution.[8] That means that when any court, in any proceedings, has to apply a human right recognised by the Constitution, which has its counterpart in an international treaty on human rights, it must adopt the interpretation of the human right which is most in harmony with the international treaty. However, the Constitutional Court has held that international treaties cannot create new human rights in the Spanish legal system. The violation of a right which is only recognised by a Treaty but does not have a counterpart in the Constitution, is not remediable, unless the Constitutional Court derives the new right, recognised by the Treaty, from a right which already exists in the Constitution through an exercise in interpretation.[9]

Not all rights in the Spanish Constitution are similar in nature, nor do they enjoy equal protection. Article 53 of the Constitution distinguishes three categories of rights: firstly, those

---

[8] See, e.g., STC 38/1985, 36/1991, 254/1993.

[9] For an overview of the subject, see L. M. Díez Picazo, *Sistema de Derechos Fundamentales* (2005) (1st edn, 2003), pp 159–87; A. Sainz Arnaiz, *La aperture constitucional al derecho internacional y europeo de los derechos humanos: EL Artićulo 10.2 de la constitutien Española* (1999); R. De Asís Roig, *Jueces y Normas: La decisión judicial desde el Ordenamiento* (1995).

rights recognised in Section 1 of Chapter II of Title I (Articles 15–29), referred to as 'fundamental rights in the strict sense,' which are guaranteed as described in Article 53.1 and 53.2. Secondly, the rest of the rights proclaimed in Chapter II of Title I (Articles 30–38: 'rights and duties of citizenship') which only enjoy the guarantees laid down by Article 53.1. Technically, they are not 'fundamental' rights but mere 'constitutional rights' or 'citizenship rights'. However, this latter category contains very important rights such as the right to private property, the right to work or the right to collective bargaining and freedom of enterprise within the framework of the market economy. These two sets of rights (15–29) and (30–38) and Article 14, have a system of guarantees sufficiently precise to make it possible for them to be normatively, institutionally and jurisdictionally enforced in case of any violation. Finally, there are principles which guide social and economic policy (39–52), which, as set out by Article 53.3, effectively require further legislation to be passed in order to have any practical effect.

Leaving aside for a moment the principles which guide social and economic policy, the two groups of rights, 15–29 (fundamental rights in the strict sense) and 30–38 ('constitutional rights') have in common the guarantees of Article 53.1. First, they are directly and automatically binding on all public authorities. In this way these rights are not just rules which the legislator is required to put into effect, rather they have immediate effect and bind courts and judges. Secondly, the exercise of such rights can only be regulated by law, in English terms Act of Parliament, that respects the essential content of those rights. Respect for such essential content means that a law regulating one of those rights must contain the main features that makes a right recognisable and must respect the interests which the right aims to protect.[10]

The differences between the guarantees for the two groups of rights are set out in Article 53.2, which only applies to 'fundamental rights in the strict sense'. Judicial protection of those rights is achieved in two ways: by the use of a preferential and summary procedure[11]

---

10 STC, 11/981.

11 The 'preferential and summary' procedure is regulated by the Ley 62/78, of 26 December, as *Proteccion Jurisdiccional de los Derechos Fundamentales de la Persona* (hereafter 'LJPDP – Jurisdiccional Protection of Fundamental Rights of the Person'). The three sections into which the law was divided have been derogated from by Ley 29/1998, of 13 July, *Regulaciona De La Jurisdicción Contencioso Administrativa* (Law 29/1998 concerning Regulation of the Contentious-Administrative Jurisdiction);

before *ordinario* courts[12] and by means of *recurso de amparo* in the Constitutional Court. Both procedures will be explained later in the chapter. Although not within the formal section on fundamental rights, Article 14 (the right to equality before the law) can also be invoked by a preferential and summary procedure and can be protected through *recurso de amparo*. Article 30.2 (conscientious objection) also enjoys the protection of the *recurso de amparo* but cannot be invoked by a preferential and summary procedure.[13]

A further difference between the two sets of rights is that any constitutional modification of 'fundamental rights in the strict sense' will have to go through the special ('aggravated') procedure for constitutional reform, while constitutional rights may be amended by the ordinary procedure for constitutional reform. An ordinary procedure requires that the proposed amendment has to be approved by a majority of three-fifths, both in Congress and Senate, a higher majority than required for any normal legislative procedure; if such majority is not obtained in the Senate, and only if in such chamber an absolute majority favours the amendment, the proposed amendment of the Constitution will be approved if it achieves a majority of two-thirds in the Congress.[14] An 'aggravated' procedure of amendment is required when the proposal for amendment is one which affects the whole Constitution, the Preliminary Title, the Second Chapter of the First Section of I Title ('fundamental rights and public liberties') or Title II ('The Crown').

Ley 1/2000 of 7 January concerning the Enjuiciamiento Civil (Law 1/2000 concerning the Civil Proceedings), and Ley 38/2002 of 24 October, *de retur ma Parciac de la ley de enjuiciamiento criminal para ei enjuiciamiento rápido einmediato to de determinados delitos y faltas y de moorcacos dec abatiron* (Law 38/2002 concerning Quick Proceedings for Offences and Misdemeanours).

[12] 'Ordinario' courts are all Spanish courts except the Constitutional Court, which is independent of the Judiciary and the highest interpreter of the Spanish Constitution.

[13] See L. M. Díez Picazo, (2005), op. cit., note 9, p 79. For an opposite view see M. Carrasco, *Procesos para la tutela de los derechos fundamentales* (2002), p 62, who believes that Article 30.2 can be the object of a 'preferential and summary' procedure, since it was incorporated to the LJPDP through the Ley Orgánica 8/1984, of 26 December, *por la que se regula el Régimen de Recursos en caso de objeción de conciencia y su régimen penal* (Law 8/1984 regulating the Regimen of Appeals in case of Conscientious Objection and its Criminal Regimen).

[14] Moreover, the reform approved by both Chambers would be submitted to a referendum, if this is requested within 15 days of the approval of the reform, by a

Such amendment must be approved by a majority of two-thirds in both Congress and Senate, and the chambers must then be immediately dissolved. The newly elected Parliament must ratify the new Constitution by a majority of two-thirds (over the whole text) in each Chamber. Once the amendment has been approved it will have to be ratified in a referendum effectively requiring a second involvement of the electorate, which may be difficult to achieve in practice. Finally, the regulation of rights by law is also different as between the two types of rights: fundamental rights may be regulated only by organic law, while constitutional rights may be regulated by an ordinary law. Whilst an organic law can only be approved, modified or derogated from if it obtains an absolute majority (half of the members plus one) in the Congress, an ordinary law only requires a simple majority of the members of Congress present and voting for its approval, modification or derogation.

The third chapter in Title I contains the guiding principles of social and economic policy. Those principles are not directly legally binding. They require further legislation in order to have any practical effect. Their effectiviness depends on the enactment of appropriate legislation. This does not mean that they have a mere rhetorical character. Since the Constitution itself has normative force (i.e. it binds public authorities and private individuals: Article 9) they can work as criteria for the constitutionality of the laws.[15] Those laws, or in English terms Acts of Parliament, which do not conform to them can be held to be unconstitutional.[16]

The principle of the institutionalised and directly judicially enforceable guarantee of human rights comes from German law and it is based on the reality that the mere rhetorical recognition or recitation of human rights in a constitution is not sufficient for the realisation or enjoyment of those rights. Such rights require to be given effect as well as being stated in a written constitution. This principle is reinforced by the structural mechanism of institutionalised

---

tenth of the members of whichever chamber. Once approved, the reform would need to be sanctioned and promulgated by the King, in order for it formally to become law.

15 It goes without saying that in practice it is very difficult to declare the unconstitutionality of a law on the basis of the mere invocation of the violation of any of these principles of chapter three.

16 A different issue would be whether public authorities are obliged to develop the appropriate legislation to give effect to these guiding principles. Their effectiveness

guarantees of such rights, the view being that such rights would have little value if they were not effectively constitutionally guaranteed.

The guarantees of human rights extend to all the measures that the legal system provides for the protection, guardianship and safeguard of fundamental rights. These guarantees can be divided into four groups: (a) guarantees of rights before the legislator; (b) guarantees of rights before the administration and the judiciary; (c) preferential and summary procedure; and (d) *recurso de amparo*.[17]

First, substantive rights guarantees may not be removed by the legislator. The rigid character of the Spanish Constitution prevents its being amended or tacitly derogated from or impliedly repealed by law in English terms, Act of Parliament. Rights are seen as the insurmountable barrier imposing restrictions on majoritarianism (a doctrine of rights as limits to public authorities).[18] The procedure for scrutiny laws for constitutionality, the 'recourse of unconstitutionality', is another guarantee which aims to preserve the rigidity and supremacy of the Constitution, thus safeguarding fundamental rights. A 'recourse of unconstitutionality' can be filed by the President of the Government, the Ombusdman, 50 members of Congress, 50 members of Senate, the executive organs in the autonomous communities, the assemblies of the autonomous communities or the judiciary (in which case it is a 'question of unconstitutionality'). A 'recourse of unconstitutionality' can be filed, in the Constitutional Court, against laws or normative provisions with the force of law which allegedly violate the Constitution. There is no appeal from the decision of the Constitutional Court. The main difference between the 'recourse of unconstitutionality' and the *recurso de amparo*, is the effect of the decision. A decision which grants *amparo* will only invalidate the unconstitutional provision for the specific case. The decision of the 'recourse of unconstitutionality', on the other hand, results in the invalidation of the

---

requires a considerable amount of economic resources, thus legislation giving effect to those principles depends on the decision (and priorities) of public authorities elected by the majority of the citizens.

17 For an excellent account of the guarantees of human rights and liberties, see L. M. Díez Picazo, op. cit., note 9, pp 73–95. See also, G. Peces Barba, *Curso de Derechos Fundamentales. Teoría General* (1999) (1st edn, 1991).

18 See, e.g., R. de Asís, *Las paradojas de los derehcos fundamentales como límites al poder* (2000) (1st edn, 1992).

law, or that part of the law, which has been declared unconstitutional, with general effect.

Secondly, the guarantees of rights before the administration and the judiciary are set basically by the requirement that rights 15–38 are to be regulated only by law (Article 53.1.) and the principle of legality. Thus, the administration,[19] which can only enact regulations which are of inferior rank to the law (i.e. subordinate or delegated legislation), cannot lay down norms which affect fundamental rights.[20] As has been said, both the administration and judicial organs, as public authorities, are bound by the legal norms regarding fundamental rights. If the administration or the judiciary believes that a norm violates a fundamental right, the only possible solution will be for a judge or tribunal competent to hear the matter to refer a 'question of unconstitutionality'[21] to the Constitutional Court. The norm can only be set aside by the Constitutional Court. There is a final guarantee of fundamental rights specifically before the administration: the 'reservations of jurisdiction'. That is, the Constitution provides in places that certain decisions which affect fundamental rights may only be made by a judge or a tribunal, or else required prior judicial authorisation. This is the case in relation to the deprivation of liberty (Article 17) and the interception of communications (Article 18). However, this only applies to the adoption of individuated decisions in relation to specific individuals and not in relation to general norms. Courts and tribunals may

---

19 See L. M. Díez Picazo, op. cit., note 9, p 77.

20 The immediate consequence of Article 53.1 is that it impedes primary and fundamental aspects of the right from being regulated by a norm of inferior rank than the law in question, allowing only subordinate legislation enacted by the administration to regulate secondary aspects of the right normally related to how the law, in English terms Act of Parliament, should be executed. L. Prieto Sanchís, *Estudios sobre derechos fundamentales* (1990), pp 167–83 believes that the repeated holdings of the Constitutional Court (STC 111/1983 FJ 8, STC 60/1986, (FJ 4) and STC 3/1988 of 21 January) that, as a matter of fundamental rights, the only thing the 'Decreto-Ley' (provisional legal dispositions that the government can dictate in case of urgent and extreme necessity – Article 86) cannot do is 'regulate or define the general legal regime of fundamental rights' or 'integral elements of the rights', leaves a door open for the administration to regulate, or at least tangibly have a bearing on, fundamental rights. (However, it is necessary to bear in mind that the 'Decretos Ley' are norms with legal force and not subordinate legislation as such.)

21 If during proceedings a judge or a court doubts whether a law (i.e. Act of Parliament) or a norm with force of law is unconstitutional, they can file a 'question of

not engage in 'abstract review'. The ultimate objective of these reservations is to prevent the administration, which is managed by organs of a political nature (as opposed to the judiciary, which is seen as an impartial organ) from adopting certain decisions regarding fundamental rights.

Thirdly, proceedings under Articles 14–29 have priority (they are 'preferential') and they can only deal with alleged violations of fundamental rights and not with other questions which arise in the case (they are 'summary'). The aim of this procedure is to create a fast judicial track for the violations of fundamental rights.

Finally, the *recurso de amparo* is an exceptional measure of protection before the Constitutional Court which protects all citizens from the violation of fundamental rights and liberties.[22] The Constitutional Court is a national court, independent of the judiciary, and is the highest level interpreter of the Constitution. Its remit is to guarantee respect for the Constitution by other institutions, organs of the state *and private parties*, and thereby to act as a guarantor of respect for the fundamental rights and public liberties provided by the Constitution. The Ley Organica 2/1979 of 3 October, del Tribunal Constitucional (Law 2/1979 regarding the Constitutional Court, hereafter LOTC) establishes, in Article 41.2 that the *recurso de amparo* protects all citizens, under the terms established by the aforementioned law, from the violation of human rights and liberties contained in Articles 14–30. Those violations must originate, according to the same article, in 'dispositions,

---

unconstitutionality' with the Constitutional Court, for it to decide about the constitutionality of such law. A 'question of unconstitutionality' can be filed if the law or norm with force of law is applicable to the case which the court is judging and if the finding depends on whether or not that law is constitutional. The proceedings will be suspended until the Constitutional Court gives a verdict. Once the Constitutional Court has given judgment, the judge or court will have to decide its case in conformity with such decision.

22 There is a double justification or *raison d'être* of the *recurso de amparo* on the one hand, during the period prior to the enactment of the Constitution there was a degree of distrust regarding the willingness of the judiciary to make others comply with constitutional norms, and especially those regarding human rights – thus the creation of a process by which the Constitutional Court could review the decrees of other courts on fundamental rights. On the other hand, the *recurso de amparo* has a function of unification of the criteria of interpretation and application of the norms regarding human rights, especially needed in a judiciary, like the Spanish one, characterised by its division into different jurisdictional orders (civil, criminal, contentious-administrative, social and military). See L. M. Díez-Picazo, op. cit., note 9, p 93.

judicial actions or simply "vía de hecho"[23] by public authorities of the State, Autonomous Communities and any other public entity of a territorial, corporate or institutional character as well as its employees or agents', that is, acts (or omissions) of public authorities (the legislature, the administration and the judiciary, see Articles 42–44 of the LOTC). In the case of the legislature, laws cannot be the object of a *recurso de amparo*, the reason being that any law which violates a fundamental rights, and is therefore allegedly unconstitutional, can only be challenged, as has been seen above, through the procedure of *recurso de inconstitucionalidad*. Although not expressly stated in the Constitution or in the LOTC, there will also be *recurso de amparo* for the violation of fundamental rights in *private relationships*, as will be seen later in this chapter. A *recurso de amparo* can be filed by any natural or legal person who invokes a legitimate interest, the Spanish Ombudsman and the Ministerio Fiscal (in English terms the Crown Prosecution Service) (Article 161.2b of the Constitution and Article 46 of the LOTC). The function of the *recurso de amparo* is not only to offer another guarantee to the citizen whose rights have been violated but also to control how judges and *ordinario* courts give effect to fundamental rights. When the Constitutional Court grants a *recurso de amparo*, it is not only re-establishing a fundamental right that has been violated but is also giving guidelines for *ordinario* courts and judges to follow in future interpretations and applications of fundamental rights. Lastly, the *recurso de amparo* is only available if rights of appeal against the decision in the *ordinario* courts have been exhausted. There is no further appeal from the *recurso de amparo*.

Within this constitutional framework, the substantive question to answer is whether, in Spain, human rights apply to protect individuals from violation of those rights by public authorities only (vertical effect) or whether rights guarantees can apply in appropriate circumstances to protect individuals from violations of their human rights by other *private parties* (horizontal effect). The aim of this chapter is to explain and analyse the direct horizontal application of human rights in the private sphere in Spain. The impact of

---

23 *Voie de fait*: principle of administrative law whereby a public body, government or local authority is empowered to embark on a course of action without legal warrant and prior to the settlement of the issue subject to later judicial review and to the possibility of having to indemnify any person whose rights are infringed by the effects of the *fait accompli*.

human rights *inter privatos* under this jurisdiction does *not* occur merely via the courts exercising power to take into account constitutional values when interpreting, applying and developing the law in line with those values (weak indirect effect), nor through the duty upon the courts to ensure the compatibility of all existing law with constitutional rights and not just values (strong horizontal effect). In Spain, rights are directly enforceable against both public authorities and private parties either before the *ordinario courts* or the Constitutional Court.

B. The Spanish approach to human rights in the private sphere[24]

Spain, like Germany, contends that human rights have a dual function, subjective and objective.[25] Fundamental rights are not only used as governing principles of the legal system, i.e. they are objective rights, but they also have a direct impact on private relationships as 'constitutionally reinforced' subjective or individual rights. Fundamental rights as set out in the Constitution are directly horizontally applied in the Spanish legal system. Unlike the position in Germany, in the Spanish legal system fundamental rights do not undergo a 'transmutation'[26] of their legal nature when applied in *inter privatos* relationships, because they have a bearing on all relationships, whether public or private, as both subjective and objective rights.[27]

In order to understand the direct horizontal application of fundamental rights in relationships between private individuals in Spain, it will be necessary to try to explain in depth the particular characteristics of the Spanish jurisdiction, a legal system largely unknown to the English reader, which make it a system where the application of fundamental rights is direct. There are three characteristics to consider. First, the binding of both citizens and public

---

24 For an excellent explanation of direct horizontal effect in Spain, see J. Mijangos y Gonzalez, *La vigencia de los derechos fundamentales en las relaciones entre particulares* (2004).

25 See, e.g., M. C. Barranco Avilés, *La teoría jurídica de los derechos fundamentales* (2000).

26 J. M. Bilbao Ubillos, *La eficacia de los derechos fundamentales en las relaciones entre particulares: Analisis de la Jurisprudencia del Tribunal Constitucional* (1997), p 327.

27 J. Mijangos y Gonzalez, op. cit., note 25, p 29.

authorities to the norms of fundamental rights; second, the role of judicial organs vis-à-vis the application of the Constitution; and finally, how fundamental rights are protected.

1. The binding of both citizens and public authorities to the norms of fundamental rights

On the face of it there is no textual basis in the Spanish Constitution for the direct horizontal application of fundamental rights between private individuals. However, the Constitution does not explicitly exclude this mode of application

Article 1.1 of the Constitution establishes, as the superior values of the Spanish State and its legal system, freedom, justice, equality and political pluralism. The article does not limit these values to the public sphere. Private law must also abide by them.

Article 9.1 of the Constitution establishes that 'citizens and public authorities are subject to the Constitution and to the rest of the legal system' and by doing so it breaks from the paradigm of a Constitution directed from and to public authorities. Furthermore, public authorities have a duty under Article 9.2 to foster the necessary conditions for the freedom and equality of individuals and any groups that they form to be 'real and effective'. Public authorities are also duty bound to remove any obstacles which impede the fulfilment of freedom and equality in society and 'to facilitate the participation of all citizens in the political, economic, cultural and social life'. It draws no distinction between public and private, and it is arguable that freedom and equality cannot be 'real' or 'effective' if excluded from private relationships.[28]

The extension of these values, and necessarily of fundamental rights, to the private sphere can be seen as inevitable due to Article 10.1, which states that a person's dignity and the inviolable rights inherent in it are the foundation of the political and social order. The Constitutional Court held in case 25/1981, that Article 10.1 entails the double function of fundamental rights as both objective and subjective.[29]

---

[28] R. Naranjo de la Cruz, *Los limites de los derechos fundamentales en las relaciones entre particulares: la Buena Fe* (2000), p 209.

[29] See also STC 19/1985, STC 88/1985, STC 6/1988, Buena fe and STC 177/1988. Moreover, the Constitutional Court has said that it is a court with a

Article 53 could lead to the mistaken conclusion that it is only possible to have a direct application of fundamental rights in a state–individual relationship as it lays down that rights and liberties recognised in Chapter II (Articles 14–38) of Title I bind all public authorities.[30] However, what can be deduced from Article 53's position under Chapter IV, entitled 'of the Guaranteeing of Liberties and Fundamental Rights', is that the binding of public authorities to fundamental rights is the most important guarantee of those rights.[31] The objective of Article 53.1 is to guarantee that the human rights contained in Chapter II of Title I will not require legislative enactment in order to be applied by the public authorities, particularly courts and judges.[32] Thus, Article 53.1 does not refer to the addressee (public or private) of fundamental rights but to those norms that even without enactment by the legislator are directly applicable rights.[33] Reference to the addressee of the constitutional norms, and thus of fundamental rights, is made in Article 9.1 of the Constitution.

Nevertheless, it is important to point out that the binding of citizens to the Constitution does not have the same intensity or scope as the binding of public authorities. In the Constitutional Court's words, the binding of Article 9.1 'is translated as a different duty for citizens and public authorities, while citizens have a general negative duty to abstain from any act which will violate the

---

double function, on one hand the protection of subjective (individual) rights and on the other the objective guardianship of the Constitution. See STC 1/1981, 26 January, STC 11/1982, STC 62/1983, and STC 36/1983. See L. M. Diez-Picazo, 'Dificultades prácticas y significado constitucional del recurso de amparo' (1994) 40 *Revista Española de Derecho Constitucional* 9–37; P. Cruz Villalon, 'Sobre el amparo' (1994) 41 *Revista Española de Derecho Constitucional* 9–23.

30 For an opposite view, see S. Varela Diaz, 'La idea de deber constitucional' (1982) 4 *Revista Española de Derecho Constitucional* pp. 77–78: he believes that Article 53.1 cancels the possibility of direct horizontal application. J. Alfaro Aguila-Real 'Autonomía privada y derechos fundamentales' (1993) XLVI *Anuario de Derecho Civil* 60, believes that Article 53.1 refers to public authorities and there is no such reference within the Constitution to private individuals.

31 R. Naranjo de la Cruz, op. cit., note 28, p 210.

32 J. Mijangos y González, op. cit., note 24, p 33.

33 Regarding the direct applicability of human rights see STC 21/1981, (FJ 17), STC 77/1982, STC 15/1982.

Constitution ... public authorities also have a positive right to exercise their functions in accordance with the constitutional text'.[34]

Moreover, it is not to be understood that *all* fundamental rights are effective in private relations, because fundamental rights do not form a homogeneous category within the Constitution. On the one hand, there are multi-directional rights capable of binding both private individuals and public authorities. Such is the case of the rights to life and to physical integrity (Article 15). Similarly, freedom to belong to a trade union[35] under Article 28.1 can be directly applied in the relationships between private employer and employee. Furthermore, some of the constitutional rights by definition would 'have no meaning if they [could] not be asserted against other citizens'.[36] The right's existence in itself 'presupposed its application in the field of private relations'.[37] This is the case with the right to strike (Article 28.2 of the Constitution), which is practically left empty of meaning if not binding on private employees.

On the other hand, there are fundamental rights which are unidirectional and as such exclusively bind public authorities. Thus the right to obtain a fair hearing from judges and courts (Article 24), the right to be a conscientious objector (Article 30) and rights affiliated to the principle of legality (Article 25.1) are justiciable only against the State. With regards to other rights, the question remains open.

Ultimately, the final decision as to the horizontal effect of a given right is made on a case-by-case basis. It must be noted that, in a general sense, there is no obstacle to fundamental rights applying directly in private relationships. Whether or not a fundamental right actually exists in any given relationship will be conditional on the nature of that relationship, and this is a separate issue.[38] Moreover, in relationships between individuals there will often be a collision of constitutionally protected rights, which necessitates a balancing between them by the court. The invocation of a fundamental right is not unequivocal. Its existence does not preclude a balancing by

---

34 STC 101/1983, (FJ 3), STC 19/1983, (FJ 1) and STC 129/1989, (FJ 2). See also L. Prieto Sanchis, 'Artículo 53. Protección de los derechos fundamentales' (1994) IV *Comentarios a las Leyes Politicas: Constitucion Española de 1978*, pp 461.

35 See J. M. Bilbao Ubillos, op. cit., note 26, pp 356–7.

36 E. Alonso García, 'La Jurisprudencia Constitucional' (1998) 1 *RCEC*, pp 206–7.

37 Ibid.

38 T. de la Quadra-Salcedo Fernández Castillo, *El recurso de amparo y los derechos fundamentales en les Relagones entre Particulairs* (1981), p 72.

the court of one fundamental right as against another constitutionally protected entitlement.

Spanish case law has accepted from the beginning the horizontal application of human rights in private relationships. In case 2/1982, the Constitutional Court established that 'neither the freedom of thought, nor the freedom of association and protest allow the possibility to exert moral violence of an intimidating character over private parties, because this is contrary to constitutionally protected entitlements ... which ought to be respected not only by public authorities but also by citizens, in compliance with article 9 and 10 of the Constitution'. This is reinforced by Case 177/88, which held that 'relationships between private individuals ... are not excluded from the ambit of the application of the principle of equality and the principle of autonomy, and must respect the constitutional principle of non discrimination and the constitutional or 'ordinario' [i.e. non constitutional legal] rules from which will be derived the need for equality of treatment'.

(a) Employment law: a case study

Undoubtedly, the most important decisions of the Constitutional Court have been in the area of employment law. In case 88/1985 the Court had to decide on the constitutionality of the dismissal of a worker as a sanction for his public criticisms of the functioning of the company. It held that 'an employment contract does not mean the deprivation for one of the parties, the worker, of the rights that the Constitution gives him as a citizen ... [T]he freedom of establishment under Article 38 of the Constitution does not mean that those employed by the company have to endure deprivation of rights' for the period of the contract.[39] Although the jurisprudence of the Constitutional Court has admitted that a worker's right to freedom of expression vis-à-vis the employer has to be exercised in good faith (STC 120/1983, 88/1985 and 6/1988), the requirement of good faith must not be confused with the existence of a generic duty of loyalty of the worker to the company, a duty which entails the subjection of the worker to the company's interest (STC 120/1983, 88/1985, 128/1989, 126/1990, 134/1994, 6/1995, and 186/1996). 'A necessary equilibrium between the obligations of the worker arising from the contract and the

---

[39] See also STC 1/1998 and STC 153/2000.

ambit – restricted by the contract but nevertheless continuing – of his constitutional liberty' must be preserved (STC 6/1998 FJ 8). The restriction of the ambit should only take place 'to the extent that is strictly necessary for the correct and efficient development of the productive activity' (STC 99/1994 (FJ 4), STC 196/1996 (FJ 5).

Moreover, in its decision 99/1994, where the Constitutional Court declared unfair the dismissal of an employee for the violation of the right to one's image, the Court summarised its doctrine of direct effect in employment law as 'an employee's contract cannot be an entitlement which justifies or constitutes a curtailment of the fundamental rights that the employee, like any citizen, has and which he does not lose when he joins a private organization' (STC 88/1985). Notwithstanding the existence of this principle, it cannot be overlooked that, as a consequence of the existence of Article 35 (right to employment) and Article 38 (freedom of establishment), the employer can, when strictly necessary, restrict those rights to promote the adequate development of the activity for which he has been employed.'[40] In Case 6/1988, the Constitutional Court reaffirmed the principle laid down in its earlier decision of 11/1981: 'the use of a fundamental right ... cannot be punished.' Therefore, had the employee been dismissed because of a legal exercise of his fundamental rights, the dismissal would have been unfair. Finally, in Case 98/2000 the Constitutional Court explained that in 'an employment contract there can only be a limitation of a fundamental right either if the nature of the work entails the restriction of that right ... or there is a proved need or interest of the company. In order to limit the fundamental right of the employee a mere invocation of the need or necessity does not qualify.'[41]

2. *The role of the judicial organs vis-à-vis the application of the Constitution*

Article 7.1 of the Ley Orgánica 6/1985 del Poder Judicial[42] affirms Articles 9.1 and 53.1 of the Constitution as it establishes that rights

---

[40] FJ 4. This has been reaffirmed by the court, amongst other cases in STC 106/1996; STC 86/1996; STC 90/1997 and STC 98/2000.

[41] FJ 5.

[42] Ley Orgánica 6/1985, of 1 July, del Poder Judicial (Organic Law 6/1985, of 1 July, concerning the Judiciary).

and liberties under Chapter II of Title I of the Constitution bind, in their entirety, all judges and courts and are guaranteed by the right to fair proceedings. 'Courts' includes both the judiciary 'ordinario' and the Constitutional Court. The existence of the Constitutional Court is not an obstacle to the *ordinario* jurisdiction. The only monopoly that the Constitutional Tribunal has is the declaration of unconstitutionality under Article 163 of the Constitution. Thus the Constitution provides for all courts to apply constitutional norms, and especially fundamental rights, in all claims that they hear. The *ordinario* judge will apply and interpret the law in conformity with the Constitution and especially in compliance with the meaning most favourable for the exercise and enjoyment of fundamental rights.[43]

3. *How human rights are guaranteed*

As seen above, Article 53.2 of the Constitution states that any citizen shall have cases involving their fundamental rights as recognised in Article 14 and Section I of Chapter II heard by a court of the ordinario jurisdiction in a 'summary and preferential' procedure. When applicable the case will also be heard by the Constitutional Court. Article 53.2 confirms that the Constitution enables both the *ordinario* judiciary and the Constitutional Court to protect fundamental rights. It does not create specialised courts for fundamental rights cases because the application and interpretation of those constitutional guarantees is incumbent upon all courts.

A reading of Article 53.2 in isolation could lead to the conclusion that fundamental rights which are not included in Article 14 and section 1 of Chapter II (15–29) lack constitutional protection. However, Article 53.2 is not the only manner in which constitutional rights are protected.

(a) 'Ordinario' jurisdiction

Article 53.2 of the Constitution provides a specific system of protection of certain rights, Articles 14–29 and 30.2, notwithstanding

---

[43] See STC 76/1987, (FJ 2); STC 24/1990, (FJ 2), STC 146/1999, (FJ 6) and 148/1999, (FJ 3). For a criticism of this principle see M. Medina Guerrero, 'Comentario al articulo 1' in *Comentarios a la Ley Orgánica del Tribunal Constitucional* (2001), pp 85–86.

the ordinary protection offered by Article 24.1, which specifies that all courts must give effective protection to all rights of the Constitution.[44] If any of the rights mentioned in Article 53.2 are violated the person or body who suffers the grievance can file a claim either via Article 24.1 or via Article 53.2 ('summary and preferential' proceedings) or both, if it is understood that the 'summary and preferential' proceedings have the objective of examining the possible violation of fundamental rights in accordance with their constitutional definition and not the solution of other problems of legality, which have to follow the normal procedure.[45] If the right violated falls outside those mentioned in Article 53.2 (14–29 and 30.2), those who claim to have suffered the violation will be able to file a claim via Article 24.1. The effective protection of any constitutional guarantee is granted whether the violation is by a public authority or a private individual. The public/private character of the violator is irrelevant to the effective protection of rights.[46]

The German legal system differs from the Spanish one as private individuals in the German system do not have an action *ex constitutionae* to claim a violation of fundamental right by another private individual. The German *ex constitutionae* action is restricted to violations by public authorities. In German law the individual's right to invoke human rights in the private sphere is confined to *ordinario* courts applying the law in conformity with the Constitution. The 'radiation effect' is the only way that fundamental rights can 'infiltrate' private relations in German law.

The classic formulation of fundamental rights as subjective or individual rights, that is, rights as limits to the conduct of public authorities, only partly characterises the Spanish legal system. Private individuals have the right to obtain effective judicial protection against violations of their rights via Article 24.1 and/or Article 53.2, whether that violation has come from public authority or private individuals. This is the same as saying that neither public

---

[44] Article 117.3 provides that the effective protection of constitutional rights is incumbent upon courts and judges.

[45] J. M. Bilbao Ubillos, op. cit., note 26, p 44 and P. Garćia Manzano, 'El ámbito de protección del proceso de la Ley 62/78' (1993) *Estudios de Derecho Publico en Homenaje a Ignacio de Otto* pp 223–228. See also STC 34/1989, (FJ 3) and 98/1989, (FJ 2).

[46] See J. M. Bilbao Ubillos, op. cit., note 26, pp 42–43.

authorities nor private individuals may, legally speaking, violate someone's right. Private individuals, like public authorities, will be obliged to respect fundamental rights, and are exposed to legal liability if this obligation is not fulfilled.

(b) 'El recurso de amparo'

As has been explained, the *recurso de amparo* is an exceptional measure of protection before the Constitutional Court. The LOTC establishes that the *recurso de amparo* protects citizens from the violation of the rights contained in Articles 14–30 of the Constitution derived from acts (or omissions) of public authorities (any acts of the judiciary and the administration and non-normative acts of the legislative power). An initial analysis seems to suggest that there will be no *recurso de amparo* for the violation of fundamental rights in private relationships. However, the Constitutional Court held in Case 171/89 that an individual might violate the fundamental right of another individual (i.e. that the duty to respect fundamental rights extends to individuals, who thus act unlawfully if they breach them), and accepted since its earliest decisions the possibility that the violation of fundamental rights in *private relationships* could reach the Constitutional Court after having exhausted the *ordinario* jurisdiction. However, an individual who has his rights violated does not prima facie have a right to have the case heard in front of the Constitutional Court, as there is no direct access. Private individuals can appeal to the Constitutional Court on the ground that the *ordinario* jurisdiction has failed to comply with its duty to give effect to the fundamental right in the private relationship. The failure to protect the individual's right by the *ordinario* court constitutes itself a violation of the right to effective judiciary protection stated in Article 24 and this gives rise to the constitutional claim. Nevertheless, the need for a previous intervention by a judicial organ should not be understood as importing the German notion of indirect horizontal application of fundamental rights into the Spanish legal system.

The decision of the *ordinario* jurisdiction is not therefore the only way of enforcing the direct horizontal application of fundamental rights. It is only in cases where this jurisdiction has failed in its duty to protect the individual's rights, and the party appeal against the decision of the *ordinario* court through a violation of

Article 24 of effective judicial protection, that the *recurso de amparo* kicks in as a final protection.[47]

In Germany, the intervention of judicial organs is required to sidestep its traditional conception of fundamental rights as limits on public authorities. It is through the duty of the courts to take into account the objective dimension of fundamental rights that such a right is introduced into the private sphere. The German Constitutional Court, when resolving claims of unconstitutionality, does not decide as to possible violations of fundamental rights in private relations, but as to the failure of the lower courts to take into account the objective dimension of fundamental rights.[48] By contrast, in the Spanish legal system judicial intervention when a fundamental right is violated is not needed in order to incorporate the fundamental right into the private dispute: fundamental rights already apply directly and automatically to *inter privatos* relationships. Judicial intervention is simply a procedural mechanism to allow access to *recurso de amparo* in conformity with Article 44.1 of the LOTC. Whilst in Spain it is a legal instrument, the LOTC, which imposes the requirement of an act of the judiciary for the individual to have access to the *recurso de amparo*, in Germany it is the notion, per se, of fundamental rights which requires the mediation of a public authority for the right to be introduced in the private sphere.

In sum, the direct applicability of fundamental rights in *inter privatos* relationships in Spain is not based on the possibility of having access to the exceptional protection provided by the *recurso de amparo* but on the effective protection of the *ordinario* jurisdiction. Nonetheless, the *recurso de amparo* is a further corroboration that fundamental rights in the Spanish legal system directly bind private individuals.

C. Conclusion

In conclusion, it is plain that fundamental rights in Spain bind directly, as objective and subjective rights, both public authorities and private individuals. A direct application model like the Spanish one is the only approach which offers a full, coherent answer to the question of the application of human rights in legal relations

---

47 J. Mijangos y González, op. cit., note 24, p 39.

48 J. M. Bilbao Ubillos, op. cit., note 26, pp 322–23.

between private individuals. In Spain, human rights do not need the act of a public authority as a condition *sine qua non*, to be implanted in *inter privatos* relationships. They are configured as both objective and subjective rights for every relationship.

Whether through *ordinario* proceedings or through the *recurso de amparo* there is always a possibility of the direct recognition and enforcement of them as human *rights* and not as mere guiding principles. Direct application does afford the best level of protection for human rights in both public–private and private–private relationships, and it does so with a clear, methodical and rigorous approach. The question is not who has violated the right, but whether the right can be applied in the case in question. This analysis is directed to the characteristics of the right and not to the characteristics of the violator of the right. However, not all fundamental rights are effective in private relations, as fundamental rights do not form a homogeneous category. It is an analysis of the content of the right and not of the violator of the right which helps the court to decide whether or not the right applies. Focusing on the content of the right avoids the obscure and sometimes arbitrary exercise of interpretation of who is a private individual or party. Moreover, the approach is also logical, eliminating the superficial and nonsensical private/public distinction in this area. Finally, in relationships between individuals there will often be a collision of constitutionally protected rights which will need to be balanced by the court. What natural limits to rights exist in private relationships would constitute the subject of another essay.[49]

---

[49] This is referred as 'the collision problem' by R. Alexy, *Teoría de los Derechos Fundamentales* (2001) (1st edn 1993). See also J. M. Bilbao Ubillos, op. cit., note 26, pp 360–82 and R. Naranjo de la Cruz, op. cit., note 28, pp 161–246.

Chapter 13: The United States and Canada: State Action, Constitutional Rights and Private Actors

*Eric Barendt**

A. Introduction

Comparisons between constitutional law in the United States of America and Canada are often striking. Both countries have federal constitutions. But powers are divided differently in them. While in the US Constitution (1787) specific powers are granted to the federal Congress and President and residual powers reserved for the states, under the Canadian Constitution[1] the federal Parliament has a general legislative power and the Provinces have competence to legislate only on specified matters. Fundamental rights were introduced into the US Constitution by a series of Amendments, initially in 1791, and subsequently in 1865–70 following the Civil War. Similar rights were only introduced recently into Canadian law by the Charter of Rights and Freedoms (1982) which forms part of the Constitution. Canadian courts frequently refer to US decisions when interpreting Charter provisions concerning, for example, freedom of expression and the right to a fair trial, but they also emphasise that they are concerned to develop distinctive Canadian constitutional principles.

It is, therefore, interesting to compare how far US and Canadian courts have been prepared to hold private persons and institutions bound to respect the fundamental human rights guaranteed by their constitutions, or – a different proposition – to hold that these rights affect the application of private common law. In both jurisdictions courts have been unwilling to give full (or direct) horizontal effect to constitutional rights; in neither are private individuals and bodies

* I am grateful for the comments of Paul Bender and James Weinstein on the part of this chapter dealing with United States law.

[1] The Canadian Constitution Act 1982 replaced the United Kingdom British North America Act 1867, when the Charter of Rights and Freedoms was introduced.

directly bound in the same way as the state and other public authorities to honour such rights. In the United States constitutional rights are engaged only when there is governmental or state action. There must be some element of state involvement in a private action or decision for a constitutional right to be implicated; this is known as the 'state action' doctrine. Nevertheless, courts in both the United States and Canada may sometimes be required to take account of constitutional rights in litigation between private persons; both jurisdictions recognise to different degrees some indirect horizontal effect or impact of constitutional rights on private persons.

B. The United States

1. Origins and key texts

It is clear constitutional law in the United States, both from the text of the Amendments and the jurisprudence of the Supreme Court, that constitutional rights bind only government and public authorities. For example, the First Amendment to the federal Constitution provides that '*Congress* shall make no law … abridging the freedom of speech, or of the press …' (emphasis added), while the Fifth and Sixth Amendments providing for, among other rights, the right against self-incrimination and the right to a 'speedy and public trial', were obviously framed to provide individuals with protection against arbitrary conduct by the police and the courts – part of the state machinery.[2] So individuals are not directly bound to honour constitutional rights; editors and publishers do not, for instance, violate the freedom of speech guaranteed by the First Amendment if they decline to publish material submitted to them. Private universities, unlike state universities, need not respect constitutional rights. Nor is a private employer, unlike a state or public authority, required to observe due process procedural requirements under the 14th Amendment if it disciplines or dismisses its employees.[3] Privacy as

[2] The First Amendment binds the federal executive, as well as Congress, so the courts do not take an overly literal approach to constitutional interpretation. More generally, federal constitutional rights bind the states under the doctrine of incorporation: the rights are incorporated in the Due Process Clause, part of the 14th Amendment set out below in the text.

[3] See *Rendell-Baker v Kohn*, 457 US 830 (1982), where it was held that a private school was not a state actor, even though public funds accounted for 90% of its

a constitutional right could not be claimed against the media or private detective agencies. But under the state action doctrine developed by the Supreme Court in Washington constitutional rights may be successfully claimed if the state was involved in some way in the conduct of, or the decision taken by, a private individual or institution.

The origins of the state action doctrine are to be found in the *Civil Rights Cases*,[4] in which the Supreme Court held that the post Civil War Amendments to the Constitution did not empower Congress to enact the Civil Rights Act of 1875; the statute proscribed (private acts of) racial discrimination in public accommodations such as inns, transport and places of entertainment. The key constitutional provision is section 1 of the 14th Amendment (1868), which provides:[5]

> No State shall make or enforce any law which shall abridge the privileges or immunities of citizens of the United States; nor shall any State deprive any person of life, liberty, or property, without due process of law; nor deny to any person ... the equal protection of the laws.

For the Court, Bradley J ruled that the Amendment proscribed only 'state action' such as legislation infringing citizens' due process and equal protection rights. These constitutional rights were only guaranteed against infringement by the state; they were not protected against a private act unless that act was supported by state authority. The Amendment was not intended to interfere with private discriminatory conduct; that could be corrected by state law.

Another term of the Constitution should be set out. Article VI, known as the Supremacy Clause, provides that the Constitution '... shall be the supreme law of the Land; and Judges in every State shall be bound thereby... ', irrespective of what a state law or constitution provides. All state law, including common law rights and freedoms, is subject to the federal Constitution, which of course guarantees the constitutional rights set out in its Amendments. That means that

---

budget. It could therefore dismiss teachers for supporting student criticism of its policies; the teachers could not claim that their free speech and due process rights had been infringed.

4 109 US 3 (1883).

5 Section 5 gives Congress power to enforce the Amendment. The earlier 13th Amendment (1865) abolishing slavery, and enabling Congress to enforce that abolition, clearly binds private persons, viz. slave owners. It was, however, held inapplicable to the discrimination at issue in the *Civil Rights Cases*.

when a private individual relies on a state law, whether statutory or common law, state courts must apply that law subject to federal constitutional rights. The Supremacy Clause might have resolved some important cases where individuals relied on state common law rights, the enforcement of which infringed others' constitutional law rights.[6] Arguably, therefore, it was unnecessary to fashion a distinct 'state action' doctrine under which a court must find some element of state involvement before it considers whether a constitutional right has been infringed. The only issue which a court need resolve is the scope of the particular constitutional right: does the First or the 14th Amendment, for example, on its proper interpretation constrain private conduct or not?[7]

Be that as it may, the Supreme Court has never departed from its reasoning in the *Civil Rights Cases*, and has developed a distinctive state action doctrine. The requirement of state action has become one of the most complex areas of US constitutional law. Forty years ago it was described as a 'conceptual disaster area';[8] decisions in the last few decades have done little to clear up the mess. Before I examine some of these difficulties, it may be helpful briefly to examine the arguments usually put forward to justify the requirement of state action.

2. *Justifications of the state action doctrine*

The two principal justifications of the requirement of state action were neatly stated by the Supreme Court in *Lugar v Edmondson Oil Co*:[9] it 'preserves an area of individual freedom by limiting the reach of federal law and federal judicial power'. This statement emphasises the doctrine's role in immunising the decisions and conduct of individuals from constitutional challenge, while also underlining the constraints it imposes on federal law and courts.

---

[6] In particular, see *Shelley v Kraemer*, 334 US 1 (1948) and *New York Times v Sullivan*, 376 US 254 (1964).

[7] See S. Gardbaum, 'The "Horizontal Effect" of Constitutional Rights' (2003) 102 *Michigan Law Rev* 387 at 390–91, 418–22.

[8] C. Black, 'Foreword: "State Action," Equal Protection, and California's Proposition 14' (1967) 80 *Harvard Law Rev* 69 at 95.

[9] 457 US 922, 936 (1982).

(a) The doctrine protects individual freedom

In the absence of a state action doctrine, individuals would be as liable as public authorities to honour constitutional rights. Private employers, for example, would be required to ensure that their employees enjoy full First Amendment freedoms of speech and religion, and they themselves would have to observe the Due Process and Equal Protection (or non-discrimination) obligations imposed by the 14th Amendment. That would significantly limit the freedom of individuals, in particular the freedom to choose with whom they associate. Contractors and testators would not be free to make arrangements, without at least considering whether these arrangements would be open to challenge, as violating, say, freedom of religion or equal protection rights. The boundary between public and private would be eroded. The Constitution would 'become ... a vehicle of regulation and annoyance as the populace is forced continually to look over its collective shoulder in fear that its actions might be in contravention of the judiciary's demarcation of another's constitutional rights'.[10]

This argument has, however, been challenged. In a classic article, Erwin Chemerinksy pointed out the contradictory character of this defence of state action: the protection of constitutional rights, say, to freedom of speech and assembly is limited, in order to protect individual freedom.[11] Moreover, the freedom safeguarded by the state action requirement may be the freedom of a few very powerful people, for example, media corporations. Indeed, one criticism is that the doctrine does not articulate the character of the individual freedom it protects; another is that the doctrine ignores its impact on the constitutional right at issue in the case. Its effect is to preclude any claim to the protection of that constitutional right, merely because it is infringed by a *private* actor. As Chemerinsky puts it, albeit very tendentiously: '... state action enhances freedom only if it is believed that the liberty to violate the constitution always is more important than the individual rights that are infringed'.[12]

---

10 W. P. Marshall, 'Diluting Constitutional Rights: Rethinking "Rethinking State Action"' (1986) 80 *Northwestern Univ Law Rev* 558 at 569–70.

11 (1986) 80 *Northwestern Univ Law Rev* 503 at 536–42.

12 'Rethinking State Action' Ibid, 537.

(b) The doctrine protects states' rights and federalism

It is now more usual for academic commentators to defend state action as limiting the power of Congress and the federal courts with regard to the states; it protects federalism.[13] It is for the states to determine the extent to which federal, as well as state, constitutional rights should be protected against infringement by private actors. This argument was indeed crucial in the *Civil Rights Cases*; the Court pointed out that individuals could vindicate their rights by resort to state laws and courts.[14] In the absence of a state action requirement, arguably many state crimes and wrongs might also be constitutional infringements under the 14th Amendment; homicide might perhaps be regarded as a deprivation of life without due process, whether committed by a private person or by, for example, the police.

Powerful though this argument is, it is not altogether persuasive. It appears to assume that states will ensure the enforcement of those federal constitutional rights and implementing legislation which should be interpreted to bind private persons as well as public authorities – notably, the Equal Protection right against racial discrimination.[15] If some states were to enforce, say, First Amendment rights to speech and religion against private actors, but other states did not, it would arguably make nonsense of these rights as *federal* constitutional rights. In principle, such rights should be respected consistently throughout the federation. That is the point, of course, of the Supremacy Clause, designed to ensure that the federal Constitution trumps inconsistent state law.[16] Even if the state action requirement were abolished, it would still be open to the states to fashion appropriate remedies for the redress of federal rights against private persons; the values of federalism would not disappear altogether.

3. Modifications to the state action doctrine

This section briefly discusses in general terms modifications to a pure state action doctrine under which the mere fact that the fundamental

---

13 See L. Henkin, '*Shelley v Kraemer*: Notes for a Revised Opinion' (1962) 110 *Univ of Pennsylvania Law Rev* 473, and J. Choper, 'Thoughts on State Action: The "Government Function" and "Power Theory" Approaches' [1979] *Washington Univ Law Q* 757.

14 *Civil Rights Cases*, 109 US 3, 17 (1883).

15 See Chemerinsky, op. cit., note 11, p 511–16.

16 See p 401–2 above.

right was directly infringed by a *private* actor would mean that no constitutional claim to that right could be entertained. Many of these claims were made in contexts other than standard private common law disputes; but they bring out some of the difficulties in drawing a bright line between state or public action on the one hand, and private acts on the other. Some of the more important instances where constitutional rights have been claimed in the context of what appear to be private law disputes are given fuller consideration in section (4).

(a) Delegation of state responsibilities to private bodies

In some contexts state action has been found when a state responsibility or public function is delegated to, or discharged by, a private body. A classic example of this modification to the strict doctrine are the voting rights cases, where the Supreme Court held there was state action when African-Americans had been excluded from primary elections conducted by the Texas Democratic Party or from a pre-primary election conducted by the Jaybird Democratic Association whose candidate had generally run unopposed in the Democrats' primaries.[17] Texas had delegated to political parties the responsibility of regulating primary elections; political parties, like the state itself, must not violate the 15th Amendment (1870), which provides that citizens' voting rights are not to be denied by any state on the basic of colour or race. Similarly, the Court has held that a town owned by the Gulf Shipbuilding Corporation could not ban the distribution of religious literature on its pavements; the private managers of the town were no more free to infringe the First Amendment freedom of speech than a public local authority was.[18] The company town had assumed a public function. But more recently it has been held that a privately owned shopping mall may forbid meetings and leafleting on its premises.[19] The Court has also refused to hold that a private utility company performs a public function; so an electricity company can cut off defaulting

---

[17] *Smith v Allwright*, 321 US 649 (1944); *Terry v Adams*, 345 US 461 (1953).

[18] *Marsh v Alabama*, 326 US 501 (1946).

[19] *Hudgens v NLRB*, 424 US 507 (1976), overruling *Amalgamated Food Employees Union v Logan Valley Plaza*, 391 US 308 (1968), which had applied the principle in *Marsh* to protect picketing in a private shopping centre. For discussion of these cases, see E. Barendt, *Freedom of Speech* (2005), 286–7.

customers without giving them notice and observing due process requirements.[20]

(b) State involvement in private action

In *Burton v Wilmington Park Authority*[21] a 6-3 majority of the Supreme Court held that a private restaurant owner violated the 14th Amendment prohibition of racial discrimination, when he declined to serve black people; as the restaurant was situated in a building owned by a state-created parking authority and leased from that authority, there was sufficient public involvement in the private decision to satisfy the state action doctrine. By taking rent from the restaurant owner, the state had significantly involved itself with his discriminatory practices. But the case has frequently been distinguished, and the 'state involvement' modification eviscerated, in later decisions. For instance, the Court held there was no state action when a licensed private club refused service to blacks.[22] The club owned its own premises; the exercise by the state of its licensing and regulatory powers over the club did not amount to state involvement and action.

Members of the Court have also been reluctant to find state involvement in private decisions in free speech cases.[23] In *Columbia Broadcasting System (CBS) v Democratic National Committee*[24] three Justices held there was no state action when the Federal Communications Commission (FCC) ruled that the broadcaster was not required to accept political advertisements, though Brennan and Marshall JJ, in dissenting judgments, considered that the federal regulation of broadcasting combined with the specific FCC approval of CBS's decision did amount to state action. The majority of the Court declined to find state action when Congress granted the United States Olympic Committee (a private organisation) exclusive rights to use, and authorise the use of, the word 'Olympic', which the

---

20 *Jackson v Metropolitan Edison Co*, 419 US 345 (1974).

21 365 US 715 (1961).

22 *Moose Lodge v Irvis*, 407 US 163 (1972). Also see *Jackson v Metropolitan Edison* (note 20, supra), where the court held that approval by a public utility commission of the electricity company's practices did not amount to state action.

23 But see the cases considered in the next section at pp 410–12.

24 412 US 94 (1973).

Committee used to stop the petitioner describing its games as the 'Gay Olympic Games', arguably an exercise of its free speech rights.[25]

(c) State law enforces or permits private 'infringement' of constitutional rights

There is considerable overlap between this category of case and that discussed in the previous paragraph. One important example of state approval of private 'infringements' of constitutional rights may occur through *judicial* decisions, say, enforcing racially discriminatory covenants or testamentary dispositions. Leading decisions in that context are discussed in the next section. The decision in *Reitman v Mulkey* should be mentioned here, as it shows how the Court has on occasion modified the state action doctrine to protect constitutional rights.[26] An amendment to the Constitution of California, approved in a state-wide referendum, prevented the state or any public authority from limiting or interfering with an owner's right to decline to sell or lease his property to anybody he chose. By a 5-4 majority the Court ruled that this amendment to the state constitution infringed the 14th Amendment. It was clear to the majority that it authorised a right (in this context) to discriminate on racial grounds; persons practising discrimination could invoke state constitutional support for their decision. In dissent Harlan J argued that no distinction should be drawn between an explicit statutory provision or constitutional amendment and the implicit approval by the state legislature of the common law. In his view the implication of the Court's decision was that any refusal by a state to interfere with private discriminatory conduct must now be regarded as state action.

4. Specific contexts and leading cases

This section discusses a few leading cases in which constitutional rights have been claimed in what might be regarded as essentially

---

[25] *San Francisco Arts and Athletics Inc v United States Olympic Committee*, 483 US 522 (1987). The dissent pointed out that the legislation authorised public funding of the Committee, and the US President was its Honorary President.

[26] 387 US 369 (1967). For criticism of the decision, see Choper, op. cit., note 13, 771–3.

private law contexts. In some of them the Court has held there is state action when the courts are called on to enforce laws – either common law or statutory – which might lead to an infringement of constitutional rights; in others it has declined to take that step.

(a) Property rights and equal protection

In its best known state action decision the Supreme Court held in *Shelley v Kraemer* that enforcement by state courts of restrictive covenants providing that properties in a block should be sold only to whites amounted to state action.[27] The equal protection rights of the black people to whom the property had been freely sold were infringed by enforcement of the covenants. Vinson CJ for the unanimous Court, reversing the decision of the state courts, made it clear that the covenants themselves and any voluntary compliance with them did not involve state action, but state judicial action did, whether it was to enforce a common law right, as in this case, or a statute. But the distinction drawn by the court is unconvincing. Ultimately, all private law rights are dependent on court action for their recognition or enforcement. Suppose black people had applied for a declaratory judgment that the covenants infringed their constitutional right to equal protection? Or had sued the vendor for breach of contract when the latter, realising that the buyers were black, had refused to go through with the sale? The state court would almost certainly have dismissed those suits, for the simple reason that the covenants themselves and the vendor's reliance on them would not involve state action. But on a broad reading of *Shelley* any state court decision to that effect would have amounted to state action.[28] The Supremacy Clause, moreover, would require a state court to give effect to the rights conferred by the federal Constitution in preference to incompatible state common law.

The broad interpretation of *Shelley* was applied by three members of the Court in *Bell v Maryland*.[29] State criminal trespass laws could not be applied to enable a restaurant owner to evict blacks

---

[27] 334 US 1 (1948).

[28] For an exploration of the difficulties in *Shelley v Kraemer*, see L. Pollak, 'Racial Discrimination and Judicial Integrity' (1959) 108 *Univ of Pennsylvania Law Rev* 1; and L. Henkin, op. cit., note 13.

[29] 378 US 226 (1964).

from the premises. But a strong dissent from Black J took a narrower view of the earlier case: *Shelley* should be interpreted to preclude only judicial interference, as in that case, with a sale by a willing vendor to a willing purchaser. It did not invalidate private acts of discrimination by unwilling vendors or restaurant owners. The state trespass laws, unlike the restrictive covenants at issue in *Shelley*, were on their face neutral. Clearly, they did not in themselves infringe equal protection rights. But their use by state courts to enforce private acts of discrimination could plausibly be said to involve the state in an infringement of the constitutional right to equal protection.

What is the impact of equal protection on testamentary freedom? This question was considered in *Evans v Abney*.[30] In 1911 a US Senator left some land on trust to the Mayor and Council of Macon, Georgia, which (after the death of his wife and daughters) was to be used as a park for the enjoyment of whites only. In 1966, the Supreme Court held that the management of parks, like the police and fire services, was a public function; even after the resignation of City councillors as its trustees, the park was to be regarded as public, and therefore had to be open to everyone, irrespective of race or colour.[31] When the case went back to the state courts, they ruled that the trust had failed and the park should revert to the Senator's heirs. In a subtle, but far from persuasive, judgment, Black J for the Court, 7-2, affirmed their ruling. It was for the Georgia courts to interpret the will, and they had held that the Senator would have preferred termination of the trust rather than integration of the park. Application of the principles of interpretation of wills did not involve state action. There was no evidence that the state judges were motivated by any racial intent. *Shelley* was distinguished on the ground that in this case the park was closed, so the loss was shared by whites and blacks alike. Black J concluded that the loss of charitable trusts, as here, 'is part of the price we pay for permitting deceased persons to exercise a continuing control over assets owned by them at death ... [an] aspect of freedom of testation ...'[32] In dissent, Brennan J considered *Shelley* indistinguishable; the record, in his view, indicated that the City Council to whom the property had been left were willing to integrate the park;

---

30 396 US 435 (1966).
31 *Evans v Newtown* (1966) 382 US 296.
32 Note 30, supra, p 447.

as in that case, the state courts were enforcing a private decision to discriminate on the basis of race.

(b) Common law rights and freedom of speech

Reference has been made already to decisions holding that free speech rights could not be claimed in the absence of state action: neither private shopping centres, nor broadcasting corporations (even with FCC approval), infringe the constitutional right to freedom of speech when they refuse claimants access to their premises, or wavelengths, to communicate their messages. In some contexts, however, the Court has summarily dismissed the argument that there was no state action to engage freedom of speech and the press. The best-known instance of this is its historic ruling in *New York Times v Sullivan*,[33] where it held that state libel laws had to be assessed against the First Amendment rights to freedom of speech and of the press. The Alabama state courts had dismissed the newspaper's free speech claim, holding that Sullivan, the libel plaintiff, had brought a private action; there was no state action. The Supreme Court had no time for this. It ruled that the Alabama courts had applied state rules of libel law which, it was claimed by the *New York Times*, inhibited free speech. It was immaterial that libel law was applied in a civil action 'and that it is common law only, though supplemented by statute'.[34] As will be seen, this robust approach contrasts sharply with that of the Canadian Supreme Court, which has declined to subject common law rights, including reputation rights, to strict constitutional scrutiny.[35] The *New York Times* decision adopts the same approach as the Court had taken, on the broader reading of its decision, in *Shelley v Kraemer*:[36] there is state action, and not a purely private decision, whenever a state rule of law, whether statutory or common law, is at issue in private litigation.[37] The decision arguably could have been reached on the basis of the Supremacy Clause without invoking the state action principle; a state court is bound by federal constitutional law and

---

33 376 US 254 (1964).

34 Ibid, at 265.

35 See p 420 below.

36 Page 408 above.

37 See Gardbaum, op. cit., note 7, 429.

rights when it applies state law, including common law.[38] At any rate, *New York Times* evidences that in some contexts the Supreme Court is prepared to give strong indirect horizontal effect to constitutional rights.[39]

A less familiar example of the same approach is the decision in the *Claiborne Hardware* case.[40] The Court held unconstitutional as applied to the defendants' boycott of segregated shops, state common law rules imposing liability for conspiracy and malicious interference with business. An action had been brought by white traders whose business had been damaged by the boycott – private action. The Court did not appear to consider there was any state action difficulty and held the defendants could not be sued in respect of exercise of their First Amendment right of political protest.

At first glance it may be a little puzzling why the Supreme Court had no difficulty in sweeping away any threshold issue of whether there was state, or only private, action in those cases, when it had refused to hold that freedom of speech was even engaged in the shopping centre or broadcasting cases referred to earlier in this chapter. Recognition of the First Amendment claim in the *CBS* case[41] would entail holding that the broadcasters – a private network – were *directly* bound to respect the free speech rights of the group claiming the right to advertise its political cause on the network. Another related explanation is that, in both the broadcasting and the shopping centre cases, the free speech claims were themselves problematic; their acceptance would have meant, for instance, that an owner of a shopping centre would have to allow his property to be used for speech he might disagree with or feel was irritating to its users.[42] Courts are often unwilling to recognise positive access rights to freedom of speech.[43] Rather than balance the owner's property and economic rights against a problematic free speech right, it was easier to invoke a threshold principle of state action and hold that free speech was not even engaged. The libel and economic boycott cases

38 See p 401–2 above.

39 See Gardbaum, op. cit., note 7, 435–7.

40 *NAACP v Claiborne Hardware*, 458 US 886 (1982).

41 Note 24, supra.

42 In the broadcasting case the Democratic National Committee was claiming a positive free speech right to use the CBS channel; recognition of such a right would clash with the broadcasters' editorial freedom to use their channel as they wished.

43 Barendt, *Freedom of Speech*, op. cit., note 19, ch III, s 6.

do not involve the same difficulties. At all events, those cases show that in the US the constitutional right to freedom of speech does have some *indirect* horizontal impact on common law rights to reputation and the conduct of business.[44]

(c) The enforcement of statutory liens and due process rights

In *Flagg Brothers v Brooks*[45] the Supreme Court held that a warehouseman was entitled to enforce his statutory lien by selling goods he had been storing for the respondent, Shirley Brooks, after a dispute about unpaid storage charges, without affording her due process rights. The Supreme Court reversed the District Court's decision in favour of the respondent. Rehnquist J for the majority held that the warehouseman was entitled to sell by virtue of his property interest – the lien on the goods – rather than because the New York Commercial Code authorised the sale. (It was clear that the goods could have been sold at common law; the Commercial Code authorised, and to some extent limited, exercise of the common law right.) The mere existence of a body of state property law did not in itself amount to state action.[46] It would have been different if the Code had compelled the sale of the bailor's goods, which otherwise would have been unlawful. Moreover, there was no involvement of any public official or court in the sale. Rehnquist J understandably did not consider the state had delegated to the warehouseman a distinctive public function.

Stevens J, dissenting with two other members of the Court, considered the existence of the Commercial Code provision was itself enough to implicate the state in the warehouseman's decision; in his view, no sharp line could be drawn between statutes compelling and statutes authorising sales to enforce liens, or more generally between public and private action. It was clear from earlier authorities that if a creditor has to obtain a summons from a court clerk before obtaining a remedy to safeguard his position, there is some element of state action and due process is required to protect the debtor.[47]

---

[44] See Gardbaum, op. cit., note 7, 440–46.

[45] 436 US 149 (1978).

[46] Ibid, at 160.

[47] See, e.g., *Sniadach v Family Finance Corp*, 395 US 337 (1969) and *North Georgia Finishing v Di-Chem Inc*, 419 US 601 (1975).

But in Stevens J's view, it was ludicrous 'to base judicial review on the fortuity of such governmental intervention ...' which often would be little more than an administrative formality.[48] What was crucial was that there was a state statute which could have protected the respondent, but did not. For Stevens J that meant that the state had implicitly authorised or approved of the warehouseman's sale, so there was state action. But suppose there had been no state statute at all, and Shirley Brooks had gone to court to stop the sale? Would a judicial decision denying her relief amount to state action? Rehnquist J indicated that state acquiescence in private action does not amount to state action.[49] That must be right, if any distinction is to be drawn between state and private action in this context. But on a generous reading of *Shelley*, a judicial decision in favour of the warehouseman, in effect denying Shirley Brooks due process, might be treated as state action.[50]

(d) No state duty to protect life, liberty, or property

The final example shows perhaps more clearly than any other discussed in this section the distinction between state and private action. *DeShaney v Winnebago Department of County Services*[51] concerned a civil action for deprivation of constitutional rights brought by Joshua, a 4-year-old boy, and his mother. After the boy had been admitted to hospital with multiple bruises, the county social services team considered there was insufficient evidence of abuse to keep him in the custody of the court. But it decided to supervise his welfare at home. Despite monthly visits by a caseworker, after which she reported suspicious injuries, the social services department took no action. Eventually, Joshua was so severely abused by his father that he fell into a coma and was expected to spend the rest of his life in an institution. His argument was that the state, Wisconsin, had deprived him of his liberty by failing to protect him against his father's violence; it had therefore infringed the Due Process Clause of the 14th Amendment. The majority of the Court,

---

48 Note 45, supra, at 174.

49 Ibid, at 164.

50 For a discussion of the difficulties of this case, see P. Brest, 'State Action and Liberal Theory: A Casenote on *Flagg Brothers v Brooks*' (1982) 130 *Univ of Pennsylvania Law Rev* 1296.

51 489 US 189 (1989).

5-4, in a judgment given by Chief Justice Rehnquist, held that the purpose of the Clause 'was to protect the people from the State, not to ensure that the State protected them from each other'.[52] There might be a remedy in state law, but there was no state action to engage the due process right. For the dissenters, notably Brennan J, the state of Wisconsin had assumed responsibility for Joshua's welfare; its consequent inaction was consequently as clear an abuse of state power as any positive decision might have been.

The Court's reasoning is certainly open to criticism.[53] The distinction between state action and inaction is not as clear as Rehnquist J suggested; it is virtually impossible to draw this line where, as in this case, a public social services agency assumed some responsibility for the child's welfare and arguably acted with gross carelessness. Its failure to intervene could have been characterised as an abuse of state power. But it remains the case that the boy's federal constitutional rights not to be deprived of his life or liberty without due process cannot be claimed against a private person. The successful prosecution of the father in Wisconsin provided a state law remedy; the boy could have sued in tort, though it is doubtful whether he could have obtained much compensation.[54] The *DeShaney* case is unusual, because state law almost invariably provides satisfactory remedies to protect people from the violence of other individuals. If, however, the state remedy is inadequate, as it probably was here, and there has been significant intervention by the public services – whether the police, the prison authorities, or a state hospital – the argument for finding some state action in order to protect the constitutional right not to be deprived of liberty without due process is a strong one.

5. Conclusions on the US position

The state action doctrine is indeed a complex and confusing area of law. The difficulties should not, however, be exaggerated. Some cases are so plain that they are hardly ever litigated: the decisions and conduct of the media, of private employers, and of business corporations cannot be challenged, even when there would clearly

---

[52] Ibid, at 196.

[53] D. A. Strauss, 'Due Process, Government Inaction, and Private Wrongs' [1989] *Supreme Court Rev* 53.

[54] Ibid, p 56.

be an infringement of a fundamental constitutional right to freedom of speech, freedom of religion, privacy, or due process, as the case may be, if a comparable decision had been taken by the state or by a public authority. The freedom of individuals and private institutions to discriminate may however be limited by equal protection rights; the Supreme Court has sometimes been willing to find state action, either in the enforcement of the discriminatory conduct by state courts (*Shelley*, *Bell)* or in the mere enactment of state law or constitutional amendment (*Bell*, *Reitman*).[55] Many other instances of discrimination are governed by the federal Civil Rights Act of 1964 prohibiting racial and other forms of discrimination in restaurants and other facilities open to the public, and by private employers. That measure is valid under the Commerce Clause, giving Congress full power to regulate inter-state commerce.[56]

Outside the civil rights context, and more particularly in recent years, the Court has been unwilling to find state action implicated in disputes between private persons or institutions. This caution is shown its decisions or judgments, for instance, in the Gay Olympics case,[57] in *Flagg* and in *DeShaney*; in all of these cases a strong minority of the Court was prepared to find an element of state action and to uphold the right to freedom of speech or to due process. The Court has refused to uphold the argument that the mere provision of a legislative framework, with an opportunity to limit the exercise of private decision-taking, necessarily entails state action.[58] That approach seems right. Otherwise, the state action doctrine would be abandoned; apart from pure common law disputes, there is always some legislative framework governing individual conduct. It might be right, either for reasons of principle[59] or because of the Supremacy Clause,[60] to hold that the application of any state law,

---

[55] The absence of any state action obstacle to the enforcement of freedom of speech in *New York Times v Sullivan* and in *NAACP v Claiborne Hardware* could also be explained in terms of the civil rights context of these cases.

[56] Article I, s 8(3) of the US Constitution.

[57] See note 25, supra.

[58] See the decisions in *Jackson* (note 20, supra), *Flagg* (note 45, supra) and the Gay Olympics case (note 25, supra).

[59] See the arguments of Chemerinsky, op. cit., note 11, for abandoning the state action doctrine.

[60] Gardbaum, op. cit., note 7, 458–9, argues that the Supremacy Clause renders private choices 'indirectly subject to the Constitution, whenever an individual relies on the law to protect or enforce them …'

whether by state organs or private persons, must respect federal constitutional rights. But that conclusion is not uniformly reflected in the decisions of the Supreme Court and does not represent the position in the United States.

C. Canada

1. Origins and key texts

The approach in Canada to the relationship of constitutional rights and private action was determined by the seminal ruling of its Supreme Court in *Retail, Wholesale and Development Store Union v Dolphin Delivery*.[61] This was one of the first decisions of the Court on the scope of the right to the freedom of expression, guaranteed by section 2(b) of the Charter of Rights and Freedoms 1982. The question was whether secondary picketing by a trade union was covered by that right and, if so, whether the right applied to private litigation, in this case, an application brought by the respondents for an injunction to restrain the threatened picketing. The Supreme Court held that the picketing would have involved an exercise of the right to freedom of expression. Moreover, the Charter does apply to the common law. But it applies to the common law 'only in so far as the common law is the basis of some governmental action which … infringes a guaranteed right or freedom'.[62] The Charter does not apply to private litigation, so the respondents could apply for an injunction to stop the picketing on the basis of common law principles, unconstrained by the union's constitutional right to freedom of expression.

The Court's approach was determined by its interpretation of two key texts of the Constitution Act 1982, of which the Charter constitutes Part I. Section 52 provides that 'any law that is inconsistent with the provisions of the Constitution is, to the extent of the inconsistency, of no force or effect'. The Court understood that to mean that the Charter does apply to the common law. It would be contrary to the language of the provision to exclude it from Charter application.[63] Since much of the common law is concerned with

[61] [1986] 2 SCR 573.
[62] Ibid, at 599.
[63] Ibid, at 593.

the rights and freedom of the individuals, it would have been reasonable to infer that the Charter applies to private litigation. But in the Court's view that inference was precluded by another key provision of the Constitution, section 32(1). It provides:

> This Charter applies (a) to the Parliament and government of Canada in respect of all matters within the authority of Parliament ...; and (b) to the legislature and government of each province in respect of all matters within the authority of the legislature of each province.

According to the Court, that means that only the legislative, executive, and administrative branches of federal and provincial government are bound by Charter rights. The Court declined to equate court orders with governmental action; if it had made that equation, then the Charter would have applied to the enforcement of common law rights in private litigation.[64]

The Court's interpretation of the text was supported by arguments of principle. The balancing of constitutional rights against individual common law freedoms is more appropriately done in legislation than by judicial decision. The human rights codes of the provinces made ample provision for equality rights against discrimination by private employers or private institutions providing services.[65] If Charter rights were applicable to private litigation, their scope would be radically increased. They would constitute an 'alternative tort system' in some contexts, for example, when a private person wrongfully arrested or detained an individual.[66]

So the Court concluded that the Charter is not directly applicable to private litigation. But that does not mean it is entirely irrelevant; courts ought to develop the common law consistently with the fundamental values of the Constitution.[67] The significance of this weak form of indirect application of Charter rights to private litigation will be discussed in the next section. Arguably, this obligation is inconsistent, at least in spirit, with the Court's decision that judicial enforcement of individual common law rights does not engage the Charter.[68] Another difficulty is that the Court agreed

---

64 Ibid, at 600. (The court's decision on this point contrasts sharply with that of the US Supreme Court in *Shelley v Kraemer*, note 27, supra).

65 Ibid, at 595–6.

66 Ibid, at 597.

67 Ibid, at 603.

68 B. Slattery, 'The *Charter's* Relevance to Private Litigation: Does *Dolphin* Deliver?' (1986–87) 32 *McGill LJ* 905 at 921–2.

that individuals are bound to respect Charter rights, when they act on the basis of powers conferred by legislation or delegated legislation. In Quebec private rights are based on the Civil Code, so it would seem to follow that most private relations there are open to Charter scrutiny.[69] In a federal system it makes little sense to allow the Charter a wider scope in one province, merely because it provides a statutory basis for individual rights and freedoms, while other provinces base these freedoms on the common law.

The Court discussed the questions of principle again in *McKinney v University of Guelph*,[70] where the particular issue was whether university decisions should be regarded as government or private activity. La Forest J, in the majority judgment of four members of the Court, emphasised that the exclusion of private activity from the Charter was deliberate. Historically, bills of rights, like that in the United States, are aimed at government. If powerful private institutions trample on the rights of individuals, they can be regulated by the state. The application of Charter rights to private activity would diminish freedom, notably freedom of contract, and would burden the courts.[71] The arguments are strikingly similar to those made in defence of the US state action requirement.[72]

2. *The common law and Charter rights*

The significance of Charter rights for the common law has been fully explored in two major Supreme Court decisions. The first of these cases, *Dagenais v Canadian Broadcasting Corporation* (CBC),[73] concerned the compatibility with freedom of expression of a court ban on the broadcast by the CBC of a fictional series chronicling sexual abuse of children in a religious institution; the ban had been imposed on the ground that the series would prejudice the contemporaneous trial of four members of Catholic orders on charges of child abuse.

---

69 Ibid, at 916.

70 [1990] 3 SCR 229. (For further discussion of the particular issues in the case, see 3 below.)

71 Ibid, at 261–3. Also see A. McLellan and B. Ellman, 'To whom does the Charter apply? Some recent cases on section 32' (1986) XXIV *Alberta Law Rev* 361, cited by La Forest J.

72 See pp 202–4 above.

73 (1994) 3 SCR 835.

The judgment of five members of the Court was given by Lamer CJ. He held that it was inappropriate after adoption of the Charter for courts to continue to apply a common law rule favouring fair trial rights over the right to freedom of expression. The Court should develop the common law in a manner consistent with Charter values. In this context that meant that a publication ban should only be ordered when it was necessary to prevent a real and substantial risk to the fairness of a trial, because other alternative measures would not prevent the risk.[74] Lamer CJ's judgment followed the approach taken in the *Dolphin Delivery* case; the common law should be developed in accordance with Charter values.

McLachlin and LaForest JJ took a different approach. The judgment of the former was particularly clear. The principles in *Dolphin Delivery* only applied to court orders regulating a purely private dispute. They did not apply to court orders in the criminal sphere which affect Charter rights and which are subject to full Charter scrutiny. In this context court orders can be equated with government action.[75] That is surely correct; a number of Charter rights such as the rights of criminal defendants under section 11 and the section 12 right not to be subject to 'cruel and unusual treatment or punishment' are primarily guaranteed against court orders. *Dolphin Delivery* was, therefore, distinguished here, although *Dagenais* involved civil, not criminal, proceedings. (McLachlin J went on to hold in agreement with Lamer CJ that the restraint on freedom of expression was not justified, as the lower court had not considered alternative measures.) It should be pointed out that McLachlin J's approach is identical to that taken in this context in the United States: contempt of court orders are regarded as state action, which fully engage (and are in practice inconsistent with) the right to freedom of speech guaranteed by the US First Amendment.[76]

---

74 These alternatives include postponing or changing the venue of the trial, and the issue of strong directions to the jury to avoid consideration of matter not introduced in evidence.

75 McLachlin J followed two earlier Supreme Court decisions which had held court orders fully subject to Charter scrutiny for infringement of the parties' rights to a fair trial: *R v Rahey* [1987] 1 SCR 588; *BCGEU v British Columbia (Attorney General)* [1988] 2 SCR 214.

76 *Bridges v California*, 314 US 252 (1941), which was cited approvingly in *Shelley v Kraemer*, discussed at p 408 above.

In *Hill v Church of Scientology of Toronto and Manning*,[77] the Court considered the impact of the Charter right to freedom of expression on the protection of reputation. Hill, a government lawyer, took libel proceedings against the defendants who had accused him of misleading a court in earlier proceedings and of other improprieties in connection with that action. The Court first held that there was no government action involved in bringing the defamation action. The proceedings were private; Hill was bringing them on his own initiative and not under the direction of the Attorney General or the government. Cory J for the Court distinguished *Dagenais*; that case did not involve a purely private dispute, but a type of government action – a court order – in the context of civil proceedings. Secondly, following the principles it had formulated in the *Dolphin Delivery* case, the Court considered whether the common law of libel, including the defences of justification, fair comment and privilege, was compatible with Charter values. In the context of civil cases involving private litigants, the Charter applies to the extent only that the common law is inconsistent with Charter values. The courts should be cautious in amending the common law and leave fundamental changes to legislation.[78] Most importantly, it is for the party challenging the common law to bear the burden of showing that it is so inconsistent with the Charter that its provisions can no longer be justified. That is in contrast to the position where a Charter right is limited by government action; it is then for the government to show that right has been subjected to a reasonable limit which is 'demonstrably justified in a free and democratic society'.[79]

On the basis of this approach, the Canadian Supreme Court concluded that the common law of libel was consistent with Charter values, allowing defendants adequate freedom of expression through its defences of truth, fair comment and privilege. Further, the right to reputation was itself linked to the right to privacy which was guaranteed by the Charter. The Court specifically rejected import of the 'actual malice' rule formulated by the United Supreme Court

---

77 [1995] 2 SCR 1130. For a comparative discussion of this case, see L. Leigh, 'Of Free Speech and Individual Reputation: *New York Times v Sullivan* in Canada and Australia' in I. Loveland, *Importing the First Amendment* (1998), 51, 57–62.

78 Ibid, at 1170–1.

79 Section 1 of the Charter. For the application of this provision in freedom of expression cases, see Barendt, op. cit., note 19, 56–7.

in *New York Times v Sullivan*,[80] under which public official libel claimants have to prove that the defendant published the allegations knowing that they were false or reckless whether they were true or not. More importantly, for the purpose of this book, the Canadian Supreme Court did not adopt the approach taken by the US Supreme Court to the impact of freedom of speech (or expression) on the common law right of individuals to protect their reputation. The latter was prepared to find state action through the mere existence of judicially enforced libel laws, in effect giving strong indirect horizontal effect to the constitutional right to freedom of speech. In contrast, the Supreme Court in Canada gave the right only weak horizontal effect, merely examining whether the common law of libel was consistent with its underlying values. Of course, if Ontario libel law had been codified in a statute, the Court's approach would necessarily have been quite different; in that event, freedom of expression would have been restricted by legislation, rather than by the common law, and Hill would have had to show that the restrictions imposed by statutory libel law were clearly justified. The right to freedom of expression would then have had strong indirect horizontal effect.

3. The boundary between government and private action under statute

One important consequence of the approach taken to the horizontal impact of Charter rights in *Dolphin Delivery* is that it becomes crucial to determine the scope of governmental action, or, put differently, the boundary between such action and private action. Under section 32 of the Charter, only governmental action fully engages Charter rights. The previous section has discussed the extent to which court orders can be treated as governmental action; this is concerned with how the conduct of other institutions which may have an impact on Charter rights should be categorised. One fascinating decision is that of the Supreme Court in *McKinney v University of Guelph*.[81] It involved a challenge to university mandatory retirement policies on the ground that they infringed the equality rights

---

[80] Note 33, supra.

[81] [1990] 3 SCR 229.

guaranteed by section 15 of the Charter.[82] A majority of the Court ruled that universities were not part of government for the purpose of section 32. It was immaterial that they were set up by statute and liable to judicial review; nor was it important that they performed a 'public function', a criterion which in its view was too uncertain to be applied satisfactorily.[83] Although they were funded and to some extent regulated by government, the appellant universities enjoyed a substantial degree of autonomy, so it would be wrong to treat them as part of it. The Court invoked the principle of academic freedom and pointed out that the mandatory retirement policies were freely chosen by the universities themselves, not imposed by government.[84] In her long dissenting judgment, Wilson J concluded that as the universities were heavily funded and regulated by government, their decisions should be regarded as governmental. They discharged a traditional government function on its behalf.

A different result from that in *McKinney* was reached in a later case where the issue was whether a hospital should be regarded as part of government for the purpose of section 32 of the Charter.[85] The Court confirmed that the mere fact that an institution performs a public service is not enough to make it part of government.[86] What was important was whether it was implementing a specific governmental policy or programme. An entity could be regarded as governmental by its nature or by virtue of the degree of governmental control for the whole of its actions, or alternatively particular acts could be regarded as governmental. The Court held that, when they provide specific services required by legislation, hospitals implement governmental objectives and are therefore bound to respect Charter rights.

---

[82] Equality rights include the right to equal benefit of the law without discrimination based on (among other things) age.

[83] Note 81, supra, at 265–8.

[84] Ibid, at 269–74. The court referred to the US Supreme Court decision in *Jackson v Metropolitan Edison Co* (note 20, supra) and to *Greenya v George Washington University* 512 F 2d 556 (DC Cir 1975), where the DC Circuit of Appeals held a private university was not a state body, even though it was established by government charter and received federal funds.

[85] *Eldridge v British Columbia (Attorney General)* [1997] 3 SCR 624.

[86] In *Stoffman v Vancouver General Hospital* [1990] 3 SCR 483, decided contemporaneously with *McKinney*, the court had held that as the routine aspects of its medical work were not subject to government control, the hospital should not be regarded as part of government.

In the most important recent case, *Dunmore v Attorney General for Ontario*,[87] the question was whether there was governmental action when the Ontario legislature repealed agricultural labour relations legislation, which had extended trade union and collective bargaining rights to agricultural workers. As a result of the repeal, farm workers were subject to the Labour Relations Act 1995, under which they were excluded from the protection of the statutory labour relations regime. Employers were therefore free not to recognise their unions. The appellants challenged the repeal and their exclusion from the general statutory labour relations regime as infringing their right to freedom of association, guaranteed by section 2(d) of the Charter. With only one dissenter, the Court allowed their appeal, holding unconstitutional both the repealing legislation and the provision of the Labour Relations Act 1995 which excluded agricultural workers from protection. The judgment for seven members of the Court was given by Bastarache J. Although the decision not to recognise an agricultural workers' union would be taken by employers, and therefore would be private, he held there was state or government responsibility. The appropriate remedy for the state's failure to discharge its responsibility was the declaration of unconstitutionality of the legislation. In this case, 'the government is creating conditions which in effect substantially interfere with the exercise of a constitutional right ...'[88] The legislation in effect permitted employers not to recognise the union rights of farm workers, an aspect of their freedom of association; moreover, the general labour relations legislation was under-inclusive in excluding agricultural workers from its protection. In a more general comment, Bastarache J said that 'this Court's understanding of "state action" has matured since the *Dolphin Delivery* case and may mature further in light of evolving Charter values'.[89]

The separate concurring judgment of L'Heureux-Dubé had less difficulty with the requirement of government action. She pointed out that section 32(1)(b) of the Charter makes it clear that it applies to the legislature of a province in respect of all matters within its authority; the provision did not require a positive act on its part. It could infringe a Charter right by a failure to take adequate steps to

87 [2001] 3 SCR 1016.
88 Ibid, para 22.
89 Ibid, para 26.

protect a Charter right.[90] The object of the legislation was clearly to prevent agricultural workers from unionising; it compelled them in effect to abandon their efforts to form a union and so it infringed freedom of association. Only Major J dissented. In his view the fundamental freedoms guaranteed by section 2 of the Charter did not impose a positive obligation on Parliament or the government to protect them; the appellants had therefore failed to prove that the state was causally responsible for their inability to exercise freedom of association.[91]

What is not clear is whether the Court would have held there had been an infringement of freedom of association in this case, if the Ontario Parliament had never enacted legislation to protect the freedom of association rights of agricultural workers and subsequently repealed it. One observation of Bastarache J suggests the Court attached importance to the particular legislative history: '[o]nce the state has chosen to regulate a private relationship such as that between employer and employee, I believe it is unduly formalistic to consign that relationship to a "private sphere" that is impervious to Charter review.'[92] The concurring judgment of L'Heureux-Dubé clearly takes a broader view; there is government action whenever legislation is framed to restrict the effective exercise of a Charter right, even though the immediate infringement is occasioned by a private decision, in this case the decision of private farmers not to accord union rights to groups of agricultural workers. On this broader view, the decisive questions concern the scope of the Charter right: what in this case does freedom of association mean? Does it entail a right to form an effective association with which employers will negotiate? It will be relatively easy to find government action whenever legislation fails to protect a right, particularly if the omission is clear and deliberate.

---

[90] In *Vriend v Alberta* [1998] 1 SCR 493 the court held the omission of a particular group, in the case homosexuals, from the protection of provincial non-discrimination legislation, could amount to an infringement of the Charter guarantee of equality rights. The court rejected the argument that the effect of Charter application was to regulate the private activity of those discriminating against homosexuals: ibid, at 534–5.

[91] Note 87, supra paras 211–14.

[92] Ibid, at 29.

D. A comparison of the US and Canadian positions

Some comparisons can be made, even though there is relatively little Canadian case law to match the rich US jurisprudence and the complex doctrinal development of the state action requirement. In neither jurisdiction are private persons and institutions bound to respect constitutional rights in the same way as the government and public authorities. Both require state action to implicate these rights. (Indeed, the term 'state action' was used by the Canadian Supreme Court in *Hill* and *Dunmore*; the earlier ruling in *Dolphin Delivery* referred to a requirement of 'government' or 'governmental' action.) There is strong support for a state action requirement in the texts of the 14th Amendment to the US Constitution and in section 32 of the Canadian Charter; in both the United States and Canada inferences from the text have been backed up by similar arguments that it would be wrong to increase the coverage of constitutional rights, so that they replace state or provincial law and its remedies. Relationships between individuals are better regulated by the common law and specific human rights codes. Both the US and Canada, therefore, reject direct horizontal effect for constitutional rights.

But there is a clear contrast between the approach of the United States Supreme Court in *Shelley* and *New York Times* (and a few other cases) on the one hand and that of the Canadian Supreme Court in *Dolphin Delivery* and *Hill* on the other; the former has recognised that, at least in some contexts, the judicial enforcement of common law rights is state action, so that a private individual relying on a freedom to discriminate or on her reputation right is constrained by the constitutional right of equal protection or freedom of speech, as the case may be. As a result, these rights have a strong indirect horizontal effect on the common law. The Canadian Supreme Court has declined to take that step; the common law must be consistent with Charter values, but that is a much weaker requirement than scrutiny of laws limiting the exercise of Charter rights. As already pointed out, it seems hard to defend this position in principle; it means that a statutory law of libel would be subject to stricter scrutiny than the common law, although they are equally concerned to balance reputation and freedom of expression interests. But that position is the implication drawn by the Court from section 32 of the Charter, which makes it applicable only to the legislature and government of Canada and of the provinces. Courts are not regarded as part of government in Canada. Nor, as *McKinney* held, are universities. In the United States, in contrast, the decisions of public universities and (sometimes) the courts are regarded as state action and therefore engage constitutional rights. The difference can be explained perhaps in terms of the constitutional texts: section 32 of the Charter refers to 'government', while the 14th Amendment prohibits the 'State' – a broader concept – enacting or enforcing laws abridging constitutional rights.

It is often hard to categorise institutions which have both public and private characteristics; they may perform what may be regarded as traditional public functions, such as street management, education, or health care, yet equally may enjoy much the same autonomy and freedom from state control as commercial corporations. The strict line drawn in the United States between, for example, public schools and state universities which must observe the due process and free speech rights of their students and employees, and private schools and universities which need not, seems hard to defend in principle: why, for example, should an employee of a state university such as the University of California enjoy First Amendment rights which are not enjoyed by, say, the employees of Stanford or Princeton University? Perhaps in this context the approach of the Supreme Court of Canada is more sensible; it considered all the relevant factors in determining whether a college or university should be regarded as part of government for Charter purposes, and has taken a similar approach in cases concerning hospitals. But flexibility may be purchased at a high cost; complex judgments such as that in *McKinney* make it difficult for other 'mixed' institutions to predict whether or not they are bound to observe Charter rights. Finally, the recent decision of the Canadian Supreme Court in *Dunmore* indicates that it is now prepared, at least in some circumstances, to find state action where legislation permits private persons to infringe Charter rights, in that case freedom of association. Its approach may be contrasted with the more conservative position of the US Supreme Court in the *Flagg* warehouseman case; the Court there held that New York legislation merely permitting, but not requiring, a private person to take a decision which would breach due process if taken by a government official did not involve state action. In this context, in contrast with common law cases, it may be easier now in Canada than it is in the US to find an element of state action and so give protection to constitutional rights where the immediate cause of infringement is private action.

Chapter 14: The European Convention on Human Rights The European Court of Human Rights*

Dean Spielmann

A. Introduction

The question of the extent and limits of the applicability of the European Convention on Human Rights to the behaviour of private parties is controversial. Generally described by the notion of 'horizontal effect' or the German term *Drittwirkung*,[1] the Convention's application to the private sphere, of relations amongst individuals themselves, has been undoubtedly extended by the European Court of Human Rights. However, it has not as yet been fully conceptualised.[2]

---

* The author is very much indebted to Ms Leto Cariolou, Legal Officer of the European Court of Human Rights for her comments and very valuable suggestions on an earlier draft of this chapter. The author wishes also to express his gratitude to Ms Gergana Grigorova for the research accomplished during her study visit at the Court. The views expressed are in the author's personal capacity.

[1] On the evolution of German Constitutional Law, see, B. Markesinis, 'Privacy, Freedom of Expression, and the Horizontal Effect of the Human Rights Bill: Lessons from Germany' (1999) *Law Quarterly Review* 47. For a comparison with the European Convention on Human Rights system, see, D. Spielmann, *L'effet potentiel de la Convention européenne des droits de l'homme entre personnes privées* (1995).

[2] See H. Pauliat and V. Saint-James, 'L'effet horizontal de la CEDH' in J.-P. Marguénaud, *CEDH et droit privé. L'influence de la jurisprudence de la Cour européenne des droits de l'homme sur le droit privé français* (2001), p 75. For an early approach, see, e.g., M.-A. Eissen, 'La Convention et les devoirs de l'individu' in *La protection internationale des droits de l'homme dans le cadre européen* (1961), p 167 and by the same author, 'La Convention européenne des Droits de l'Homme et les obligations de l'individu: une mise à jour', *René Cassin Amicorum discipulorumque liber III* (1971), p 156. See also E. A. Alkema, 'The Third-Party Applicability or "Drittwirkung" of the ECHR', in F. Matscher and H. Petzold (eds), *Protecting Human Rights. The European Dimension. Studies in Honour of G.J. Wiarda* (1988), p 33.

It has often been stated that the authors of the Convention did not intend it to have a 'third-party' effect.[3] Such an intention has most notably been expressed in Article 34 of the Convention, which poses a procedural obstacle to claims introduced against private parties.[4] However, despite any such intentions, the text and spirit of many articles of the Convention indicate that its rights may concern and be applied in purely private relationships.[5] The Court has employed a variety of methods to apply the Convention to the relations between private parties.[6] On the basis of the Convention's textual indications, and in particular by virtue of Article 1 of the Convention, the Court has developed its 'positive obligations' doctrine, which has constituted a robust tool for the enforcement of the Convention rights, in conferring indirect horizontal effect on the substantive provisions of this treaty. This was indeed required by the primary principle of enforcing 'practical' and 'effective' rights. In ensuring respect for the same principle, the Court has further required the domestic courts of the Contracting States to interpret private law instruments in a manner compatible with the Convention. Moreover, the Convention's applicability amongst third parties has been expanded by the Court's resort to balancing of competing rights in the private sphere. In substance, the scope of many of the Convention's provisions has been extended to carry implications relevant for private parties.[7]

B. The procedural obstacle to claims against private parties

Article 34 of the Convention provides as follows:

> The Court may receive applications from any person, non-governmental organisation or group of individuals claiming to be the victim of a violation by one of the High Contracting Parties of the rights set forth in the Convention or the Protocols thereto. The High Contracting Parties undertake not to hinder in any way the effective exercise of this right.

---

[3] See, inter alia, A. Drzemczewski, 'The European Human Rights Convention and Relations between Private Parties' (1979) 2 *Netherlands International Law Review* 168.

[4] Further analysis in section B below.

[5] See section C below.

[6] See section D below. These methods are set out in a description sence and do not demote any theoritical distinctions.

[7] See section E.

Under this provision, the Court has systematically declined to examine complaints directed against private parties in finding that in such cases it lacks jurisdiction *ratione personae*. For instance, in the case of *Florin Mihăilescu v Romania*, it was stated that:

> ...according to Article 34 of the Convention, it (the Court) can only deal with applications alleging a violation of the rights guaranteed by the Convention claimed to have been committed by State bodies. The Court has no jurisdiction to consider applications directed against private individuals or businesses.[8]

Judge Lech Garlicki has recently observed in this respect that '[a]lthough there have been examples of the Court's generosity in determining the scope of its jurisdiction, the Convention imposes certain limits that must be respected by the Court'.[9]

However, the fact that a state chooses to delegate some of its powers to be exercised by a private entity cannot be decisive for the question of state responsibility *ratione personae*.[10] In the Court's view, the exercise of state powers which affects Convention rights raises an issue of state responsibility regardless of the form in which these powers are exercised; for instance, by a body whose activities are regulated by private law.[11] If the Court is satisfied that the public element existing in a case is predominant, it entertains jurisdiction notwithstanding the fact that the respondent is classified as a private body under the relevant domestic law concerned.[12] However, the nature of any involvement by public authorities in a given infringement of a right protected by the Convention may well be unclear. In order to determine the extent of such involvement and

---

[8] *Florin Mihăilescu v Romania* (dec.), no. 47748/99, 26 August 2003. See also *Sevo v Croatia*, no. 53921/00, decision of 14 June 2001; *Shestakov v Russia* (dec.), no. 48757/99, 18 June 2002 and *Scientology Kirche Deutschland eV v FRG*, no. 34614/96, Commission decision of 7 April 1997, *Decisions and Reports* 89A, 163, at p 171; *Proszak v Poland*, no. 25086/94, Commission decision of 17 January 1995, § 3.

[9] L. Garlicki, 'Relations between Private Actors and the European Convention on Human Rights' in A. Sajo and R. Utiz (eds), *The Constitution in Private Relations: Expanding Constitutionalism* (2005), p 130, note 3.

[10] See, mutatis mutandis, *Costello-Roberts v United Kingdom*, judgment of 25 March 1993, Series A no. 247-C, p 58, § 27.

[11] *Woś v Poland* (dec.), no. 22860/02, ECHR 2005-IV, at para 72.

[12] *Mykhaylenky and others v Ukraine*, nos. 35091/02, 35196/02, 35201/02, 35204/02, 35945/02, 35949/02, 35953/02, 36800/02, 38296/02 and 42814/02, §§ 45-46, ECHR 2004-XII.

establish whether a respondent state should be absolved from responsibility, the Court has developed the test of 'sufficient institutional and operational independence from the State'.[13] In this respect the Court is prepared to thoroughly examine whether a respondent body is owned by the state, whether it is exercising any public function and in general the extent to which the state is exercising effective control over it.[14]

C. The text and spirit of the Convention

While the text of the Convention does not *explicitly* require horizontal effect for its substantive provisions, such an effect is not excluded. The wording of many of these provisions suggests that the Convention's protection extends beyond state action. First, there is the general duty to protect human rights under Article 1, of the Convention. Pursuant to Article 1, '[t]he High Contracting Parties shall secure to everyone within their jurisdiction the rights and freedoms defined in Section I of [the] Convention'. This provision has proven to be of utmost importance where the Court has had to deal with the responsibility of the state in connection with acts of private parties. In this respect the Court has consistently held, since its judgment in *Young, James and Webster v United Kingdom,*[15] that the responsibility of a state is engaged if a violation of one of the Convention's rights is the result of non-observance by that state of its obligation under Article 1 to secure those rights and freedoms in its domestic law to everyone within its jurisdiction. A state's responsibility may also be engaged on account of acts which have sufficiently proximate repercussions on rights guaranteed by the Convention, normally of individuals within its jurisdiction. In certain cases such responsibility, however, may be extended to repercussions occurring outside its jurisdiction.[16] Article 1 makes no distinction as to the type of rule or measure concerned and does not exclude any part of the Member

[13] *Mykhaylenky and others v Ukraine*; cf. note 8, supra and, mutatis mutandis (with reference to Article 34 of the Convention), *Radio France and others v France* (dec.), no. 53984/00, ECHR 2003-X.

[14] See *Mihăilescu v Romania*, note 8, supra.

[15] Judgment of 13 August 1981, Series A no. 44, p 20, § 49.

[16] *Ilaşcu and others v Moldova and Russia* [GC], no. 48787/99, § 317, ECHR 2004-VII; *Soering v United Kingdom*, judgment of 7 July 1989, Series A no. 161, p 35.

States' 'jurisdiction' from scrutiny under the Convention.[17] Further, a state may be held responsible even when its agents are acting *ultra vires* or contrary to clear instructions. This is based on a concept of strict liability of state authorities for the conduct of their subordinates, which are under a duty to impose their will and cannot shelter behind their inability to ensure that it is respected.[18]

Accordingly, the state cannot absolve itself from responsibility *ratione personae* by delegating its obligations to private bodies or individuals.[19] The undertakings given by a Contracting State under Article 1 of the Convention include, in addition to the duty to refrain from interfering with the enjoyment of the rights and freedoms guaranteed, positive obligations to take appropriate steps to ensure respect for those rights and freedoms within its territory.[20] The Court has been clear in this respect that the acquiescence of a state in the acts of private individuals which violate the Convention rights of others within its jurisdiction may render that state responsible under the Convention. In the landmark case of *Cyprus v Turkey*, the Court held that:

> As to the applicant Government's further claim that this 'jurisdiction' must also be taken to extend to the acts of private parties in northern Cyprus who violate the rights of Greek Cypriots or Turkish Cypriots living there, the Court ... confines itself to noting ... that the acquiescence or connivance of the authorities of a Contracting State in the acts of private individuals which violate the Convention rights of other individuals within its jurisdiction may engage that State's responsibility under the Convention. Any different conclusion would be at variance with the obligation contained in Article 1 of the Convention.[21]

Article 1 of the Convention has thus constituted one of the basic provisions implementing state responsibility for private action, notably

---

[17] *United Communist Party of Turkey and others v Turkey*, judgment of 30 January 1998, *Reports of Judgments and Decisions* 1998-I, p 17–18, § 29.

[18] *Ilaşcu*, ibid, at para 319; *Ireland v United Kingdom*, judgment of 18 January 1978, Series A no. 25, p. 64, § 159; see also Article 7 of the International Law Commission's draft articles on the responsibility of states for internationally wrongful acts ('the work of the ILC') in J. Crawford, *The International Law Commission's Articles on State Responsibility. Introduction, Text and Commentaries* (2002), 106 et seq.

[19] See, mutatis mutandis, *Costello-Roberts v United Kingdom*, judgment of 25 March 1993, Series A no. 247-C, p 58, § 27.

[20] *Z v United Kingdom* [GC], no. 29392/95, § 73, ECHR 2001-V.

[21] *Cyprus v Turkey* [GC], no. 25781/94, § 81, ECHR 2001-IV. See also *Ilaşcu and others v Moldova and Russia* [GC], no. 48787/99, § 318, ECHR 2004-VII.

by forming the foundation of the doctrine of 'positive obligations'.[22] However, in addition to Article 1, the wording of some of the substantive provisions of the Convention suggests that its provisions may extend to the private sphere. For instance, Article 13 of the Convention, requiring an effective remedy 'before a national authority notwithstanding that the violation has been committed by persons acting in an official capacity', suggests that a violation may be committed by private actors. As Clapham observes, 'one can complain that there is no avenue to effectively review the governmental policy which has led to interference with the right by the non-state actor'[23] and 'the lack of an effective remedy before an national authority to ensure respect by a private person of a Convention right … could give rise to a violation of Article 13, and could be sanctioned at the international level'.[24]

Furthermore, Article 17 of the Convention clearly prohibits the abuse of the Convention's rights, inter alia, by private groups or persons in providing that:

> Nothing in (the) Convention may be interpreted as implying for any State, group or person any right to engage in any activity or perform any act aimed at the destruction of any of the rights and freedoms set forth herein or at their limitation to a greater extent than is provided for in the Convention.[25]

Finally, in a similar vein, the limitation clauses in Articles 8–11 refer explicitly to the rights and liberties of others. The developed case law on the issue of the 'rights of others' suggests that private law disputes may well fall within the scope of the Convention. But the responsibility of the state, under the Convention, can only be engaged if an action or omission may be attributed to a public authority.

---

22 See below section D, subsection 1.

23 A. Clapham, *Human Rights Obligations of Non-State Actors* (2006), p 420.

24 A. Clapham, op. cit., pp 358 and 420.

25 See A. Spielmann, 'La Convention européenne des droits de l'homme et l'abus de droit' in *Mélanges en homage à Louis Edmond Pettiti* (1998), p 673; S. van Drooghenbroeck, 'L'article 17 de la Convention européenne des droits de l'homme: incertain et inutile?' in *Pas de liberté pour les ennemis de la liberté? Groupements liberticides et droit* (2000), p 139. For rare cases where this provision has been applied, see, e.g., *Garaudy v France* (dec.), no. 65831/01, ECHR 2003-IX (extracts); *Norwood v United Kingdom* (dec.), no. 23131/03, ECHR 2004-XI.

D. Three means of applying the Convention in the relations between private parties

Although the court has stated its reluctance in elaborating some general theory at applicability of the convention on purely private relations,[26] it has nevertheless managed to play a significant role in improving the relations between private actors in light of basic human rights principles. Thus, on the basis of individual applications it has constructed a significant body of case law on this subject matter, from which three main methods of extending the scope of the Convention may be discerned.

There are three main methods employed by the court in applyiing certain requirements of the convention on private parties: the first one involves the analysis and expansion of the doctrine of 'positive obligations'; the second concerns the obligation imposed on the domestic courts to interpret private law instruments in a manner compatible with the protection of the Convention rights and the third is based on the Court's resort to the balancing technique to deal with competitions between fundamental rights and other public interests. The reference and analysis of these methods is persued in a discriptive sense. Indeed, the latter two could fairly be described as applications of the doctrine of positive obligations. Moreover, such means are not mutually exclusive; they have often been combined in dealing with issues concerning the relations between private parties.[27]

1. The doctrine of positive obligations

The primary objective of the 'positive obligations' doctrine is to indicate that in some situations the state is not only under the duty to

---

[26] See, inter alia, *Vgt Verein gegen Tierfabriken v Switzerland*, no. 24699/94, § 46, ECHR 2001-VI, where it was stated *obiter* that: '[t]he Court does not consider it desirable, let alone necessary, to elaborate a general theory concerning the extent to which the Convention guarantees should be extended to relations between private individuals *inter se*.'

[27] E.g., in *Craxi (no. 2)*, no. 25337/94, 17 July 2003, the Court balanced the different interests under Articles 8 and 10 of the Convention, whilst insisting on the importance of the procedural obligation under Article 8. In *Appelby*, no. 44306/98, ECHR 2003-VI, the Court was faced with the competition between the right to protest and the right to property, and while balancing between the different interests at stake, it also had to establish whether or not positive obligations existed under Article 10 of the Convention.

refrain from interference with human rights, but it is also obliged to take 'positive' action to ensure the effective implementation of the Convention's rights.[28] This has had significant implications in respect of the acts or omissions of the state and its agents, as well as in respect of the conduct of private actors operating within that state's jurisdiction. The Court inaugurated the 'positive obligations' doctrine as early as 1968 in the *Belgian Linguistics* case concerning the right to education guaranteed in Article 2 of the Protocol, by stating that:

> [t]he negative formulation indicates, as is confirmed by the 'preparatory work' (especially Docs. CM/WP VI (51) 7, page 4, and AS/JA (3) 13, page 4), that the Contracting Parties do not recognise such a right to education as would require them to establish at their own expense, or to subsidise, education of any particular type or at any particular level. However, it cannot be concluded from this that the State has no positive obligation to ensure respect for such a right as is protected by Article 2 of the Protocol. [A]s a 'right' does exist, it is secured, by virtue of Article 1 of the Convention, to everyone within the jurisdiction of a Contracting State.[29]

In *Marckx v Belgium*, the Court confirmed that:

> [b]y proclaiming in paragraph 1 the right to respect for family life, Article 8 (art. 8-1) signifies firstly that the State cannot interfere with the exercise of that right otherwise than in accordance with the strict conditions set out in paragraph 2 (art. 8-2). As the Court stated in the 'Belgian Linguistic' case, the object of the Article is 'essentially' that of protecting the individual against arbitrary interference by the public authorities (judgment of 23 July 1968, Series A no. 6, p. 33, para. 7). Nevertheless it does not merely compel the State to abstain from such interference: in addition to this primarily negative undertaking, there may be positive obligations inherent in an effective 'respect' for family life.[30]

As to the extent of a state's 'positive obligations' under the Convention, the Court has itself admitted on numerous occasions that:

> [t]he boundaries between the State's positive and negative obligations ... do not lend themselves to precise definition. The applicable principles are nonetheless similar. In both contexts regard must be had to the fair balance that has to be struck between the competing interests of the individual and of the community as a whole.[31]

---

[28] L. Garlicki, op. cit., p 132.

[29] *Belgian linguistics case* (merits), judgment of 23 July 1968, Series A no. 6, p 31, § 3.

[30] *Marckx v Belgium*, judgment of 13 June 1979, Series A no. 31, p 15, § 31.

[31] *Stjerna v Finland*, judgment of 25 November 1994, Series A no. 299-B, pp 60–61, § 38; see also the *Keegan v Ireland* judgment of 26 May 1994, Series A no. 290, p 19, § 49.

The requirements of the 'proportionality test' when applied in cases involving a state's positive obligations are not substantively different from those concerning negative obligations. In this respect, the Court has noted in its judgment in the case of *Powell and Rayner*, that:

> Whether the present case be analysed in terms of a positive duty on the State to take reasonable and appropriate measures to secure the applicants' rights ... or in terms of an 'interference by a public authority' ... the applicable principles are broadly similar. In both contexts regard must be had to the fair balance that has to be struck between the competing interests of the individual and of the community as a whole; and in both contexts the State enjoys a certain margin of appreciation in determining the steps to be taken to ensure compliance with the Convention ... Furthermore, even in relation to the positive obligations flowing from the first paragraph of Article 8 (art. 8-1), 'in striking [the required] balance the aims mentioned in the second paragraph (art. 8-2) may be of a certain relevance.[32]

Further, ever since its judgment in *Abdulaziz, Cabales and Balkandali*, the Court, in dealing with positive obligations, has referred to a wider 'margin of appreciation' enjoyed by the domestic authorities:

> ... especially as far as those positive obligations are concerned, the notion of 'respect' is not clear-cut: having regard to the diversity of the practices followed and the situations obtaining in the Contracting States, the notion's requirements will vary considerably from case to case. Accordingly, this is an area in which the Contracting Parties enjoy a wide margin of appreciation in determining the steps to be taken to ensure compliance with the Convention with due regard to the needs and resources of the community and of individuals ...[33]

In balancing the different competing interests at stake, the Court uses the 'proportionality test' in an inverted way. Indeed, as van Drooghenbroeck points out, in a classical vertical relationship, the proportionality requirement triggers a 'prohibition of excess' in action, whereas in a 'positive obligations' situation the same principle implies a similar prohibition, but of excessive inaction of the

---

32 *Powell and Rayner v United Kingdom*, judgment of 21 February 1990, Series A no. 172, § 41. See also the *Rees* judgment of 17 October 1986, Series A no. 106, p 15, § 37, as concerns para 1) (Art 8-1), and the *Leander* judgment of 26 March 1987, Series A no. 116, p. 25, § 59, as concerns para 2) (Art 8-2). For further analysis, see F. Sudre, 'Les "obligations positives" dans la jurisprudence européenne des droits de l'homme' in P. Mahoney, F. Matscher, H. Petzold and L. Wildhaber (eds), *Protecting Human Rights. The European Perspective, Studies in memory of Rolv Ryssdal*, (2000), p 1359 et seq, esp p 1372.

33 *Abdullaziz, Cabales and Balkandali v United Kingdom*, Judgement of 28 May 1985, Series A no. 94, § 67.

public authorities. This nuance is of great importance because positive obligations are only obligations of means as opposed to obligations of result characterising the traditional vertical approach of human rights protection.[34]

The doctrine has proved to be a successful tool in granting indirect horizontal effect to the Convention. The scope of 'positive obligations' is not limited to the mere abstention of a state to acts being tantamount of a violation of the Convention. The obligations concern also the state's failure to react properly to an interference with a right attributable to an individual. Keir Starmer has identified five broad categories of positive duties, namely, a duty to establish a legal framework providing for the effective protection for Convention rights, a duty to prevent unlawful interferences with the Convention rights, a duty to provide information and advice on matters concerning the Convention rights, a duty to respond to breaches of Convention rights and finally a duty to provide resources to individuals to ensure respect for their rights.[35] In the context of a private interference with human rights, the 'positive obligations' theory was developed from 1981 by the Court primarily in the context of freedom of association and the protection of private life of individuals. It was soon extended to the whole of the Convention and its additional protocols.

Recent case law of the Court shows the doctrine's impact on the right to property guaranteed in Article 1 of Protocol No. 1.[36] For instance, in the case of *Öneryıldız v Turkey*, the Court was faced with the consequences of a methane explosion in a rubbish tip, which caused a landslide of waste engulfing some ten slum dwellings situated below it, including the applicant's dwelling. The Grand Chamber

---

[34] See on this important distinction, S. van Drooghenbroeck, 'L'horizontalisation des droits de l'homme', in H. Dumont, F. Ost and S. van Drooghenbroeck, *La responsabilité, face caché des droits de l'homme* (2005), p 372 et seq.

[35] K. Starmer, 'Positive Obligations Under the Convention' in J. Jowell and J. Cooper (eds), *Understanding Human Rights Principles* (2001), p 146 et seq.

[36] Article 1 of Protocol No. 1 reads as follows:

> 'Every natural or legal person is entitled to the peaceful enjoyment of his possessions. No one shall be deprived of his possessions except in the public interest and subject to the conditions provided for by law and by the general principles of international law. The preceding provisions shall not, however, in any way impair the right of a State to enforce such laws as it deems necessary to control the use of property in accordance with the general interest or to secure the payment of taxes or other contributions or penalties.'

of the Court chose to examine the complaint concerning the loss of the applicant's house under the general rule contained in the first limb of the first paragraph of Article 1 of Protocol No. 1 laying down the right to the peaceful enjoyment of possessions. The Court stated that:

> Genuine, effective exercise of the right protected by that provision does not depend merely on the State's duty not to interfere, but may require positive measures of protection, particularly where there is a direct link between the measures which an applicant may legitimately expect from the authorities and his effective enjoyment of his possessions.[37]

More recently, this technique has also been extended as a tool of vigorous control concerning the Convention's unqualified rights as well as in relation to the right to protection from unlawful detention, as the examples presented in section E of this chapter demonstrate.

2. *The obligation to interpret private law instruments in a manner compatible with the Convention*

The dynamic nature of the obligation to secure respect for the right guaranteed by the Convention even in the sphere of the relations of individuals between themselves is illustrated well by the case of *Pla and Puncernau v Andorra*. This concerned the decisions of the domestic courts barring the first applicant, as an adopted child, from inheriting the estate of his grandmother. The latter prepared her will in 1939, which stipulated that her son was to pass on his inheritance to a child or grandchild 'from a legitimate and canonical marriage'. In 1995 the applicant's father bequeathed the property he had inherited to the applicant. In the context of subsequent court proceedings, the Andorran High Court of Justice held that the first applicant, as an adopted child, could not be considered as 'a child of a lawful and canonical marriage' and could not, therefore, inherit the relevant estate. This decision was upheld on appeal by the Constitutional Court.

The applicant complained that the domestic court decisions contravened Article 8 of the Convention guaranteeing the right to respect for private and family life and were discriminatory and, as such,

---

[37] *Öneryıldız v Turkey* [GC], no. 48939/99, ECHR 2004-XII, (2005) 41 EHRR 325, at para 134. See also *Broniowski v Poland* [GC], no. 31443/96, § 144, ECHR 2004-V.

contrary to Article 14.[38] In its judgment of 13 July 2004,[39] the Court observed that the national courts were better placed than an international court to evaluate, in the light of local legal traditions, the particular context of the legal dispute submitted to them – especially when interpreting an eminently private instrument such as a clause in a will – and the various competing rights and interests. Accordingly, an issue of interference with private and family life could only arise under the Convention if the national courts' assessment of the facts or domestic law were manifestly unreasonable or arbitrary or blatantly inconsistent with the fundamental principles of the Convention.[40]

The High Court of Justice's interpretation of the testamentary disposition deprived the applicant, as an adopted child, of his right to inherit his grandmother's estate despite the fact that the instrument in question made no distinction between biological and adopted children. Such an interpretation amounted to the judicial deprivation of an adopted child's inheritance rights.[41]

Further, it was reiterated that the Convention is a living instrument whose text must be interpreted dynamically and in the light of present-day conditions. Thus, the domestic courts' interpretation of the will could not be reached solely on the basis of the social conditions existing at the time when the will was drafted, especially since a period of approximately 60 years had elapsed between its drafting and the transfer of the estate to the relevant beneficiaries. In light of the length of such period, during which profound social, economic and legal changes had occurred, the courts could not ignore new realities. The same was true with regard to wills: in the event of their interpretation an effort should be made to ascertain the testator's intention and render the will effective, while bearing in mind that the testator could not be presumed to have meant what he or she did not say and without overlooking the importance of interpreting the clauses in the will in the manner that most closely corresponded to

---

38 Article 14 of the Convention reads as follows:

> 'The enjoyment of the rights and freedoms set forth in [the] Convention shall be secured without discrimination on any ground such as sex, race, colour, language, religion, political or other opinion, national or social origin, association with a national minority, property, birth or other status.'

39 *Pla and Puncernau v Andorra*, no. 69498/01, ECHR 2004-VIII.

40 §§ 46 and 59.

41 § 60.

domestic law and to the Convention as interpreted in the European Court's case law.[42] The Court therefore found that there had been a violation of Article 14 read in conjunction with Article 8.[43]

Judge Garlicki dissented from the Court's majority opinion. In his view, the real question arising from the circumstances of the case was the extent of the Convention's 'indirect third-party effect' and the responsibility of States to intervene in actions by private parties. Specifically, he stated that:

> Nevertheless, it seems equally obvious that the level of protection against a private action cannot be the same as the level of protection against State action. The very fact that, under the Convention, the State may be prohibited from taking certain action (such as introducing inheritance distinctions between children – see *Marckx v. Belgium*, judgment of 13 June 1979, Series A no. 31; *Vermeire v. Belgium*, judgment of 29 November 1991, Series A no. 214-C; and *Mazurek v. France*, no. 34406/97, ECHR 2000-II) does not mean that private persons are similarly precluded from taking such action. In other words, what is prohibited for the State need not necessarily also be prohibited for individuals. Of course, in many areas such prohibition may appear necessary and well-founded. However, it should not be forgotten that every prohibition of private action (or any refusal to judicially enforce such action), while protecting the rights of some persons, unavoidably restricts the rights of other persons. This is particularly visible in regard to 'purely' private-law relations, such as inheritance. The whole idea of a will is to depart from the general system of inheritance, that is, to discriminate between potential heirs. But at the same time, the testator must retain a degree of freedom to dispose of his/her property and this freedom is protected by both Article 8 of the Convention and Article 1 of Protocol No. 1. Thus, in my opinion, the rule should be that the State must give effect to private testamentary dispositions, save in exceptional circumstances where the disposition may be said to be repugnant to the fundamental ideals of the Convention or to aim at the destruction of the rights and freedoms set forth therein. As in respect of all exceptional circumstances, however, their presence must be clearly demonstrated and cannot be assumed.
>
> No exceptional circumstances of the above-mentioned kind existed in the present case. The testatrix had taken a decision, which was perhaps unjust, but cannot, even by present-day standards, be regarded

---

42 § 62.

43 §§ 63–64. On this case, see also, R. S. Kay, 'The European Convention on Human Rights and the Control of Private Law' [2005] *European Human Rights Law Review* 466 et seq; D. Spielmann, *The European Court of Human Rights. Recent developments*, lecture delivered at the Lauterpacht Research Centre for International Law, Cambridge, 14 January 2005, on file, Library of the European Court of Human Rights, Strasbourg.

> as repugnant to the fundamental ideals of the Convention or otherwise destructive of Convention rights. Thus, the State was under a duty to respect and give effect to her will and was neither allowed nor expected to substitute its own inheritance criteria for what had been decided in the will.[44]

There is merit in the submission that the whole idea of a will might well be to depart from the general system of inheritance and to discriminate. However, in this particular case, the Court made it clear that in ascertaining the validity of such instruments and in the absence of an express disownment of adopted children by the testator, the domestic courts must apply the principles of the Convention.

Another case where the importance of consistent interpretation of the domestic law with the principles of the Convention was emphasised was *Sovtransavto Holding v Ukraine*.[45] The application concerned certain domestic proceedings during which the applicant company's shareholding had been reduced and consequently its ability to manage and control another company had been limited. The Court observed that the Member States are under an obligation to afford judicial procedures that enable the domestic courts to adjudicate fairly in disputes between private persons. The Court's role in the exercise of its supervision was to verify whether the consequences of the domestic courts and tribunals' interpretation and application of the domestic law were compatible with the principles laid down in the Convention.

3. Balancing competing rights and public interests in the private sphere

The Court's approach in cases involving the need for adjudication between competing fundamental rights has been to resort to the employment of a balancing test.[46] A most interesting example is the *von Hannover v Germany* case. Princess Caroline von Hannover was campaigning since the beginning of the 1990s to prevent the publication of photographs revealing her private life. On this basis she unsuccessfully applied on several occasions to the German courts

---

[44] Dissenting opinion of Judge Garlicki, ECHR 2004-VIII, at p 248.

[45] No. 48553/99, ECHR 2002-VII.

[46] For an interesting comparison under German Law, see, B. Markesinis, 'Privacy, Freedom of Expression, and the Horizontal Effect of the Human Rights Bill: Lessons from Germany' (1999) *Law Quarterly Review* 47.

to obtain an injunction preventing any further publication of a series of photographs which had appeared in the 1990s in the German magazines *Bunte*, *Freizeit Revue* and *Neue Post*. She claimed that they infringed her right to protection of her private life and her right to control the use of her image.

In a landmark judgment of 15 December 1999, the Federal Constitutional Court granted the applicant's injunction regarding the photographs in which she appeared with her children on the ground that their need for protection of their intimacy was greater than that of adults. However, the Constitutional Court considered that the applicant, who was undeniably a contemporary 'public figure,' had to tolerate the publication of photographs of herself in a public place, even if they showed her in scenes from her daily life rather than engaged in her official duties. The Constitutional Court referred in that connection to the freedom of the press and to the public's legitimate interest in knowing how such a person generally behaved in public.[47]

The applicant maintained that the decisions of the German courts infringed her right to respect for her private life, as guaranteed by Article 8 of the Convention, since they failed to afford her adequate protection from the publication of photographs taken without her knowledge by paparazzi on the ground that, in view of her origins, she was undeniably a contemporary 'public figure'. She also complained of an infringement of her right to respect for her family life.

In its judgment of 24 June 2004,[48] the Court observed at the outset that there was no doubt that the publication by various German magazines of photographs of the applicant in her daily life either on her own or with other people fell within the scope of her private life. Article 8 of the Convention was accordingly applicable. It was therefore necessary to balance the protection of the applicant's private life against freedom of expression, as guaranteed by Article 10 of the Convention.[49]

---

[47] In the context of balancing competing rights, it is interesting to note that the President of the Chamber of the Court granted leave under Rule 61 § 3 of its Rules, to the Association of German Magazine Publishers (*Verband deutscher Zeitschriftenverleger*) and another company, Hubert Burda Media Holding GmbH & Co KG, to submit written observations as third parties.

[48] *von Hannover v Germany*, no. 59320/00, ECHR 2004-VI.

[49] § 53 and § 58.

Although freedom of expression applied to the publication of photographs, this was an area in which the protection of the rights and reputation of others took on a particular importance, as it did not concern the dissemination of 'ideas,' but of images containing very personal or even intimate 'information' about an individual. Furthermore, photographs appearing in the tabloid press were often taken in a climate of continual harassment which induced in the person concerned a very strong sense of intrusion into their private life or even of persecution.[50]

The Court considered that the decisive factor in balancing the protection of private life against freedom of expression should lie in the contribution that the published photographs and articles made to a debate of general interest. In the case before it, the photographs showed scenes from the applicant's daily life, engaging in activities of a purely private nature. The Court noted in that connection the circumstances in which the photographs had been taken: without the applicant's knowledge or consent and, in some instances, in secret. It was found that they made no contribution to a debate of public interest, since the applicant exercised no official function and the photographs and articles related exclusively to details of her private life.[51]

Furthermore, while the general public might have a right "to information", including, in special circumstances, the interest to be informed at the private affairs at public figures, no such right existed in the instant case. The general public did not have a legitimate interest in knowing Caroline von Hannover's whereabouts or how she behaved generally in her private life even if she appeared in places that could not always be described as secluded and was well known to the public. Even if such a public interest existed, just as there was a commercial interest for the magazines to publish the photographs and articles, such as interest would have to yield, in the Court's view, to the applicant's right to the effective protection of her private life.[52]

The Court reiterated the fundamental importance of protecting private life from the point of view of the development of every human being's personality and said that everyone, including people known to the public, had to have a 'legitimate expectation' that his or her private life would be protected. The criteria that had been established

---

[50] § 59.

[51] §§ 60 et seq.

[52] § 77.

by the domestic courts for distinguishing a figure of contemporary society *par excellence* from a relatively public figure were not sufficient to ensure the effective protection of the applicant's private life and she should, in the circumstances of the case, have had a 'legitimate expectation' that her private life would be protected.[53]

Having regard to all the foregoing factors, and despite the margin of appreciation afforded to the state in this area, the Court considered that the German courts had not struck a fair balance between the competing interests. Accordingly, it held that there had been a violation of Article 8 of the Convention and that it was not necessary to rule on the applicant's complaint relating to her right to respect for her family life.[54]

In the more recent case of *Craxi (No. 2)*,[55] concerning the publication of a private conversation, the Court in balancing the different interests at stake, namely that of freedom of the press and the right to privacy, applied the same test as it usually applies in examining the justification of an interference by public authorities:

> 65. However, public figures are entitled to the enjoyment of the guarantees set out in Article 8 of the Convention on the same basis as every other person. In particular, the public interest in receiving information only covers facts which are connected with the criminal charges brought against the accused. This must be borne in mind by journalists when reporting on pending criminal proceedings, and the press should abstain from publishing information which is likely to prejudice, whether intentionally or not, the right to respect for the private life and correspondence of the accused persons (see, *mutatis mutandis*, *Worm v. Austria*, judgment quoted above, *ibidem*).
>
> 66. The Court observes that in the present case some of the conversations published in the press were of a strictly private nature. They concerned the relationships of the applicant and his wife with a lawyer, a former colleague, a political supporter and the wife of Mr Berlusconi.

---

53 Especially § 78.

54 § 79. On this case, see also D. Spielmann, *The European Court of Human Rights. Recent developments*, lecture delivered at the Lauterpacht Research Centre for International Law, Cambridge, 14 January 2005, on file, Library of the European Court of Human Rights, Strasbourg and also 'Freedom of press, Protection of Privacy and presumption of innocence. Balancing competing rights', address delivered at the 7th Annual Meeting of the 'Alliance of Independent Press Councils of Europe', Luxembourg, 30 September 2005 (2005) 15 *Annales du droit luxembourgeois*, to be published (on file, Library of the Palais des droits de l'Homme, Strasbourg).

55 *Craxi v Italy (No. 2)*, no. 25337/94, 17 July 2003.

> Their content had little or no connection at all with the criminal charges brought against the applicant. This is not disputed by the Government.
>
> 67. In the opinion of the Court, their publication by the press did not correspond to a pressing social need. Therefore, the interference with the applicant's rights under Article 8 § 1 of the Convention was not proportionate to the legitimate aims which could have been pursued and was consequently not 'necessary in a democratic society' within the meaning of the second paragraph of this provision.

This important development is rightly pointed out by van Drooghenbroeck as a transposition at horizontal litigation of the same reasoning applied in 'vertical' cases.[56] Further, the Court extended the application of the procedural obligation usually existing in respect to Articles 2 and 3 of the Convention in respect to Article 8. It specifically observed that:

> [I]t does not appear that in the present case an effective inquiry was carried out in order to discover the circumstances in which the journalists had access to the transcripts of the applicant's conversations and, if necessary, to sanction the persons responsible for the shortcomings which had occurred. In fact, by reason of their failure to start effective investigations into the matter, the Italian authorities were not in a position to fulfil their alternative obligation of providing a plausible explanation as to how the applicant's private communications were released into the public domain.
>
> 76. The Court holds, therefore, that the respondent State did not fulfil its obligation to secure the applicant's right to respect for his private life and correspondence. There has consequently been a violation of Article 8 of the Convention.[57]

---

[56] S. van Drooghenbroeck, 'L'horizontalisation des droits de l'homme' in H. Dumont, F. Ost and S. van Drooghenbroeck, *La responsabilité, face caché des droits de l'homme*, (2005), at p 376. See *Fuentes Bobo v Spain*, no. 39293/98, 29 February 2000 quoted by van Drooglenbrock, op. cit. et. loc. cit.

[57] At para 75. See the very interesting partly dissenting opinion of Judge V. Zagrebelsky, where he observed that:

> 'Up till now, only in cases concerning Articles 2 and 3 has the Court imposed on the States a procedural obligation to carry out an effective investigation subsequent to acts leading to a person's death, torture or inhuman or degrading treatment. But such a requirement is clearly and understandably justified by the necessity to protect such a fundamental right as the right to life and to prevent torture or ill-treatment. I do not think that that aim of the Court can easily be expanded so as to cover any possible violation of the Convention, beyond rights of such an importance as to be subject to no derogation even in time of emergency (article15 § 2).'

The *Appleby* case[58] concerned the setting up of a stall and canvassing of views in 'The Galleries', a shopping mall that had effectively become the town centre. The applicants were refused permission to solicit signatures for a petition in a privately owned shop. The manager of the Galleries informed the applicants that permission had been refused because the owner took a strictly neutral stance on all political and religious issues. In this case the right to protest was pitched against the right to property enjoyed by the company which owned the Galleries and the town centre.[59]

The Court, applying the positive obligations technique, insisted on striking a balance:

> In determining whether or not a positive obligation exists, regard must be had to the fair balance that has to be struck between the general interest of the community and the interests of the individual, the search for which is inherent throughout the Convention. The scope of this obligation will inevitably vary, having regard to the diversity of situations obtaining in Contracting States and the choices which must be made in terms of priorities and resources. Nor must such an obligation be interpreted in such a way as to impose an impossible or disproportionate burden on the authorities (see, *inter alia*, *Rees v. the United Kingdom*,

---

It was further observed in relation to the newly introduced procedural requirement under Article 8, that:

> 'one has to be realistic about this. The Court should take into account the fact that normally the only effective method is to compel journalists to reveal their sources or to make use of very intrusive procedures against them, such as intercepting their communications or searching their homes or offices. However, this kind of investigation was found to be in violation of the Convention (Article 10) in *Roemen and Schmit v Luxembourg* (judgment of 25 February 2003, no. 51772/99) and the protection of journalistic sources is one of the basic conditions for press freedom. Without such protection, sources may be deterred from assisting the press in informing the public on matters of public interest (a public interest that could hardly be questioned in this case) ... The Court was unable to find any direct responsibility of the State for the leak. In my view, by putting the onus on Contracting States to conduct an effective inquiry, while at the same time reversing the burden of proof (see § 75 of the judgment), the Court has without sufficient reason adopted the scheme of positive State duties under Articles 2 and 3 of the Convention and imposed on the States an arduous, if not impossible, task to fulfil. In so doing, the judgment concludes by imposing on the State a kind of objective responsibility. And that, in my view, is hardly acceptable within the Convention system.'

58 *Appleby and others v United Kingdom*, no. 44306/98, ECHR 2003-VI.
59 See Clapham, op. cit., p 412.

> judgment of 17 October 1986, Series A no. 106, p. 15, § 37, and *Osman v. the United Kingdom*, judgment of 28 October 1998, *Reports of Judgments and Decisions* 1998-VIII, pp. 3159-60, § 116).[60]

It was found that while freedom of expression was an important right, it was not unlimited. The property rights of the owner of the shopping centre also had to be taken into consideration. The Court was not convinced that there should be automatic rights of entry to private property (or even all state-owned property), but if a bar on access to property were to result in the lack of any effective exercise of freedom of expression, the Court would not rule out the possibility that a positive obligation could arise for the State to protect the enjoyment of Convention rights by regulating property rights.[61]

In the present case, however, the applicants had alternative means of communicating their views to the public and were not actually prevented from doing so as a result of the limited restriction imposed on them by the owner of the shopping centre. Whether they would have obtained more signatures in support of their petition if they been able to set up their stands in the shopping mall was mere speculation. The Court did not find that the government had failed to comply with any positive obligation to protect the applicants' freedom of expression.[62] Largely identical considerations arose in respect of their right to freedom of assembly.[63]

The balancing test has also been eemployed by the Court when a right protected under the Convention entered into conflict with a mere public interest; the latter being inferior to a right protected under the Convention. The *Verliere* case illustrates well this exercise. Verliese alleged that her surveillance by private detectives employed in the context of an insurance dispute had infringed Article 8 of the Convention. She relied on the civil remedy that was available to her but her action was dismissed. In its decision of 28 June 2001, the Court rejected the application as being manifestly ill-founded on the following grounds:

> The Court notes that the domestic courts carried out a thorough analysis of the competing interests of the insurer and the applicant. They had regard in particular to the fact that the insurer was under an obligation to verify whether the victim's claim for compensation was justified, as

60 At para 40 of its judgment.

61 §§ 43 et seq.

62 § 48.

63 §§ 51 et seq.

> it was also acting in the interests of all the insured collectively. On that basis, they considered that the insurer was entitled to conduct private investigations and that the victim was under a duty to cooperate in establishing the facts and to accept that the insurer might conduct investigations, even without the insured's knowledge, when that was necessary to achieve the aim pursued. They found that in the instant case the insurer's investigations, which were conducted from a public place and were confined to ascertaining the appellant's mobility, had been aimed solely at protecting the insurer's pecuniary rights. The domestic courts had thus found that the insurer had an overriding interest that made the interference with the applicant's personality rights lawful.
>
> In the light of the foregoing, the Court considers that Switzerland has complied with its positive obligation inherent in the notion of effective respect for family life, at both the legislative and judicial levels.[64]

E. The extension of certain of the Convention rights to private parties

In section E of this chapter, examples of the extension of certain of the Convention's rights to private parties are presented. It is proposed to follow mainly a chronological approach outlining the Court's case law, bearing in mind, as Andrew Clapham rightly states, that '[n]early all of the Articles of the Convention and its Protocols could be implicated with regard to the application of human rights in the private sphere'.[65] It is, however, impossible within the limited space of this presentation to give a full picture of the whole case law of the Court.[66]

1. *Freedom of assembly and association*

One of the first areas in which the Court found the existence of positive obligations, as early as 1981, was the right to freedom of association. In *Young, James and Webster*, the Court confirmed that the

64 *Verliere v Switzerland* (dec.), no. 41953/98, ECHR 2001-VII.

65 Op. cit., at p 418. The Court considered 'positive obligations' even in the context of Article 1 of Protocol no. 1. See *Sovtransavto Holding v Ukraine*, no. 48553/99, ECHR 2002-VII.

66 For many examples of the Court's case law, see S. van Drooghenbroeck, 'L'horizontalisation des droits de l'homme' in H. Dumont, F. Ost and S. van Droogenbroeck, *La responsabilité, face caché des droits de l'homme* (2005), p 355.

state has to ensure the protection of freedom of association rights in the context of a private employment relationship:

> Under Article 1 (art. 1) of the Convention, each Contracting State 'shall secure to everyone within [its] jurisdiction the rights and freedoms defined in ... [the] Convention'; hence, if a violation of one of those rights and freedoms is the result of non-observance of that obligation in the enactment of domestic legislation, the responsibility of the State for that violation is engaged. Although the proximate cause of the events giving rise to this case was the 1975 agreement between British Rail and the railway unions, it was the domestic law in force at the relevant time that made lawful the treatment of which the applicants complained. The responsibility of the respondent State for any resultant breach of the Convention is thus engaged on this basis. Accordingly, there is no call to examine whether, as the applicants argued, the State might also be responsible on the ground that it should be regarded as employer or that British Rail was under its control.[67]

Further, the principle of positive obligations imposes a requirement on state authorities to ensure that the participants in a demonstration must be able to demonstrate without having to fear that they will be subjected to physical violence by counter-demonstrators. It was held that the genuine and effective freedom of peaceful assembly cannot be reduced to a mere duty on the part of the state not to interfere; a purely negative conception would not be compatible with the object and purpose of Article 11.[68] In the case of *Sibson v United Kingdom*, the Court confirmed that although the action complained of was not attributable to the state, the latter may be under an obligation to ensure that its laws sufficiently protected the applicant.[69] Most recently, in the case of *Sørensen and Rasmussen v. Denmark*,[70] the applicants complained about the application of pre-entry closed shop agreements in the context of their employment in the private sector. The Court observed that the impugned acts did not involve the direct intervention by the state. However, Denmark's responsibility was still

---

[67] *Young, James and Webster v United Kingdom*, judgment of 13 August 1981, Series A no. 44, p. 11, § 23.

[68] *Plattform 'Ärzte für das Leben' v Austria*, judgment of 21 June 1988, Series A no. 139.

[69] *Sibson v United Kingdom*, judgment of 20 April 1993, Series A no. 258-A. See also, concerning the obligation to join a private taxi drivers' association, *Sigurður A. Sigurjónsson v Iceland*, judgment of 30 June 1993, Series A no. 264.

[70] *Sørensen and Rasmussen v Denmark* [GC], nos. 52562/99 and 52620/99 ECHR 2006-I.

engaged in light of the failure on its part to secure to the applicants under the domestic law their negative right to freedom of association.

2. *Private and family life*

The main area in which the Court has had the opportunity to expand the Convention's applicability on the relations between private parties has been that of private life. Article 8 provides that:

> 1. Everyone has the right to respect for his private and family life, his home and his correspondence.
>
> 2. There shall be no interference by a public authority with the exercise of this right except such as is in accordance with the law and is necessary in a democratic society in the interests of national security, public safety or the economic well-being of the country, for the prevention of disorder or crime, for the protection of health or morals, or for the protection of the rights and freedoms of others.

The leading case in this area is that of *X and Y v The Netherlands*, which concerned the unavailability of criminal proceedings against the perpetrator of sexual assault on a minor girl who was suffering from a mental handicap.[71] The Court observed in this respect that:

> Although the object of Article 8 is essentially that of protecting the individual against arbitrary interference by the public authorities, it does not merely compel the State to abstain from such interference: in addition to this primarily negative undertaking, there may be positive obligations inherent in an effective respect for private or family life ... These obligations may involve the adoption of measures designed to secure respect for private life even in the sphere of the relations of individuals between themselves.[72]

Disputes within the family are particularly concerned with the principles laid down in Article 8 of the Convention. Concerning family relations, and in particular in the context of child abduction cases, the Court has established that there is a state duty to ensure that a divorced or separated parent is not prevented from maintaining contact with his/her children by the other party, and the state must

---

71 D. Spielmann, 'Obligations positives et effet horizontal des dispositions de la Convention', in F. Sudre (ed), *L'interprétation de la Convention européenne des droits de l'homme* (1998), p 140, quoted by L. Garlicki, op. cit., at p 134.

72 *X and Y v The Netherlands*, judgment of 26 March 1985, Series A no. 91.

prevent the abduction of children by one of the parents.[73] In *Karadžić v Croatia*,[74] the Court recalled that:

> the State's positive obligation under Article 8 includes a right for parents to measures that will enable them to be united with their children. However, the national authorities' obligation to take such measures is not absolute, since the reunion of a parent with a child who has lived for some time with the other parent may not be able to take place immediately and may require the taking of preparatory measures. The nature and extent of the measures will depend on the circumstances of each case, but the understanding and cooperation of all concerned are always an important ingredient. Any obligation to apply coercion in this area must be limited since the interests and the rights and freedoms of all concerned must be taken into account, and more particularly the best interests of the child and his or her rights under Article 8. Where contact with the parent might appear to threaten those interests or interfere with those rights, it is for the national authorities to strike a fair balance between them.[75]

Neighbourhood disputes have also given the Court the opportunity to develop its case-law.[76] The right to respect for one's home and interference by private individuals has been examined in recent cases. As an example, in a recent judgment, the Court emphasised the importance of positive obligations concerning private life endangered by noise pollution. In *Moreno Gómez v Spain*, the applicant complained of the existence of extreme noise and of being disturbed at night by nightclubs near her home. She alleged that the Spanish authorities were responsible and that the resulting noise pollution constituted a violation of her right to respect for her home, as guaranteed by Article 8 of the Convention. The Court,[77] noted that the applicant lived in an area that was indisputably subject to night-time disturbances that clearly unsettled her as she went about her daily life, particularly at weekends. These disturbances had been reported on a number of

---

[73] *Salgueiro da Silva Mouta v Portugal*, no. 33290/96, ECHR 1999-IX. See also, *Ignaccolo-Zenide v Romania*, no. 31679/96, ECHR 2000-I.

[74] Judgment of 15 December 2005.

[75] *Karadžić v Croatia*, no. 35030/04, § 52, 15 December 2005. See also *Hokkanen v Finland*, judgment of 23 September 1994, Series A no. 299, p 22, § 58 and *Sylvester v Austria*, nos. 36812/97 and 40104/98, § 58, 24 April 2003.

[76] See amongst others, *López Ostra v Spain*, judgment of 9 December 1994, Series A no. 303-C, concerning nuisance caused by a waste treatment plant close to housing.

[77] *Moreno Gómez v Spain*, no. 4143/02, ECHR 2004-X.

occasions. In the circumstances of the case, there appeared to be no need to require, as the Spanish authorities had done, a person from an acoustically saturated zone to adduce expert evidence of a fact of which the municipal authority was already officially aware.[78] In view of the volume of the noise, which went beyond permitted levels, and the fact that it took place during the evenings and had continued over a number of years, the Court found that there had been a breach of the rights protected by Article 8. Although the City Council had adopted measures intended to secure respect for the rights guaranteed by the Convention, it had tolerated, and thus contributed to, the repeated flouting of the rules which it had itself established.[79]

Thus, the Court found that the applicant had suffered a serious infringement of her right to respect for her home as a result of the authorities' failure of take action to deal with the night-time disturbances and held that the respondent state had failed to discharge its obligation to guarantee her right to respect for her home and her private life, in breach of Article 8 of the Convention.[80]

3. *The right to property*

Recent case law on the scope of Article 1 of Protocol No. 1 to the Convention has accepted that a state's responsibility may be involved in respect of interferences with the peaceful enjoyment of an applicant's possessions resulting from transactions between private individuals.[81]

A violation of this provision was found, for instance, in the case of *Allard v Sweden*, which concerned the demolition of a house built on jointly owned land without the consent of all joint owners and while proceedings concerning the division of ownership

---

78 §§ 57–59.

79 §§ 60–61.

80 §§ 61–62. See D. Spielmann, *The European Court of Human Rights. Recent developments*, lecture delivered at the Lauterpacht Research Centre for International Law, Cambridge, 14 January 2005, on file, Library of the European Court of Human Rights, Strasbourg. On the *Moreno Gómez v Spain* case and the protection of the environment in general under the Convention, see L. Loucaides, 'Environmental Protection through the Jurisprudence of the European Convention on Human Rights' (2004) 75 *British Yearbook of International Law* 249.

81 *Gustafsson v Sweden*, judgment of 25 April 1996, *Reports of Judgments and Decisions* 1996-II, p 658, § 60.

were pending.[82] More recently, in the case of *Fotopoulou v Greece*, the Court examined a complaint about the construction of an extension to a wall by the applicant's neighbours which effectively blocked her sea view. A violation of the right to effective protection of the applicant's property was found.[83]

4. Unqualified rights

(a) Right to life

The requirement of measures of positive action is of particular importance when the Convention's unqualified rights are at stake. There seems to be no difficulty to accept that Article 2 of the Convention, protecting the right to life and imposing the positive duty on public authorities to protect the life of others, concerns also private action inconsistent with this right. As Clapham correctly states:

> [t]he issue of the obligations of the non-state actor as regards the right to life hardly arises in practice. Taking a life is clearly illegal under national law and there would normally be no reason to raise this before a national court in terms of human rights law ... The issue does arise, however, in relation to whether non-state actors might themselves have positive obligations to protect life, and the parallel obligations of the state to ensure that the non-state actor fulfils these obligations with regard to everyone within the state's jurisdiction.[84]

The Court has developed criteria for the duty to protect the right to life from non-state actors. The leading case is *Osman v United Kingdom*, concerning the alleged failure of authorities to protect the right to life of the first applicant's husband and the second applicant from the threat posed by an individual. Another relevant issue was the lawfulness of restrictions on the applicants' right of access to a court to sue the authorities for damage caused by the said failure.[85] The Court held that:

> bearing in mind the difficulties involved in policing modern societies, the unpredictability of human conduct and the operational choices which must be made in terms of priorities and resources, such an obligation must

---

[82] *Allard v Sweden*, no. 35179/97, ECHR 2003-VII.

[83] *Fotopoulou v Greece*, no. 66725/01, 18 November 2004.

[84] Clapham, op. cit., pp 368–9. On the duty to rescue, see also below.

[85] *Osman v United Kingdom*, judgment of 28 October 1998, *Reports of Judgments and Decisions* 1998-VIII, p 3124.

be interpreted in a way which does not impose an impossible or disproportionate burden on the authorities. Accordingly, not every claimed risk to life can entail for the authorities a Convention requirement to take operational measures to prevent that risk from materialising. Another relevant consideration is the need to ensure that the police exercise their powers to control and prevent crime in a manner which fully respects the due process and other guarantees which legitimately place restraints on the scope of their action to investigate crime and bring offenders to justice, including the guarantees contained in Articles 5 and 8 of the Convention.

In the opinion of the Court where there is an allegation that the authorities have violated their positive obligation to protect the right to life in the context of their above-mentioned duty to prevent and suppress offences against the person (see paragraph 115 above), it must be established to its satisfaction that the authorities knew or ought to have known at the time of the existence of a real and immediate risk to the life of an identified individual or individuals from the criminal acts of a third party and that they failed to take measures within the scope of their powers which, judged reasonably, might have been expected to avoid that risk. The Court does not accept the Government's view that the failure to perceive the risk to life in the circumstances known at the time or to take preventive measures to avoid that risk must be tantamount to gross negligence or wilful disregard of the duty to protect life (see paragraph 107 above). Such a rigid standard must be considered to be incompatible with the requirements of Article 1 of the Convention and the obligations of Contracting States under that Article to secure the practical and effective protection of the rights and freedoms laid down therein, including Article 2 (see, *mutatis mutandis*, the above-mentioned *McCann and Others* judgment, p. 45, § 146). For the Court, and having regard to the nature of the right protected by Article 2, a right fundamental in the scheme of the Convention, it is sufficient for an applicant to show that the authorities did not do all that could be reasonably expected of them to avoid a real and immediate risk to life of which they have or ought to have knowledge. This is a question which can only be answered in the light of all the circumstances of any particular case.[86]

The case of *Mahmut Kaya v Turkey* concerned the insufficient investigation into the murder of a doctor by counter-guerrilla groups established outside the formal framework of the state, but nevertheless targeting individuals perceived to be acting against state interests, with the acquiescence, and possible assistance, of members of the state's security forces.[87] In its judgment of 28 March 2000,

---

86 Ibid at para 116.

87 *Mahmut Kaya v Turkey*, no. 22535/93, ECHR 2000-III.

the Court found that the authorities had failed to take the reasonable measures which were available to them in order to prevent the real and immediate risk to the life of the deceased.[88]

In addition to the obligation to implement preventive measures to ensure the protection of life within a state's jurisdiction, requirement imposed by Article 2 is the obligation to conduct an effective investigation into losses of life and punish private individuals and other non-state actors that are found responsible.[89]

The procedural dimension of many rights has been promoted especially in recent judgments and decisions of the European Court.[90] The *Menson* decision of 6 May 2003[91] is of special importance as it concerns a racial killing. The Court first held that the applicants did not impute responsibility to the authorities of the respondent state for the death of Michael Menson; nor was it suggested that the authorities knew or ought to have known that Michael Menson was at risk of physical violence at the hands of third parties and failed to take appropriate measures to safeguard him against that risk. The case is therefore to be distinguished from cases involving the alleged use of lethal force either by agents of the state or by private parties with their collusion[92] or where the factual circumstances imposed an obligation on the authorities to protect an individual's life,

---

88 § 101.

89 See *Ergi v Turkey*, judgment of 28 July 1998, *Reports of Judgments and Decisions* 1998-IV, p 1751; *Yasa v Turkey*, judgment of 2 September 1998, *Reports of Judgments and Decisions* 1998-VI, p 2411; *Tanrıkulu v Turkey* [GC], no. 23763/94, ECHR 1999-IV; and *Paul and Audrey Edwards v United Kingdom*, no. 46477/99, ECHR 2002-II. See also *Menson v United Kingdom* (dec.), no. 47916/99, ECHR 2003-V. See also Clapham, op. cit., p 136 et seq.

90 See numerous references by F. Tulkens and S. Van Drooghenbroeck, 'La Cour européenne des droits de l'Homme depuis 1980. Bilan et orientations' in W. Debeuckelaere et D. Voorhoof (eds), *En toch beweegt het recht*, Tegenspraak, cahier 23 (2003), pp 211–35; F. Tulkens, 'Le droit à la vie et le champ des obligations des Etats dans la jurisprudence récente de la Cour européenne des droits de l'homme' in *Libertés, justice, tolérance, Mélanges en hommage au Doyen Gérard Cohen-Jonathan,* (2004), p 1605 et seq, at 1623 et seq; J.-P. Costa, 'La Cour européenne des droits de l'homme: Un juge qui gouverne?' in *Etudes en l'honneur de Gérard Timsit* (2004), p 68 et seq, esp at p 73.

91 *Menson v United Kingdom* (dec.), no. 47916/99, ECHR 2003-V.

92 The Court referred to, e.g., *McCann and others v United Kingdom*, judgment of 27 September 1995, Series A no. 324; *Hugh Jordan v United Kingdom*, no. 24746/94, judgment of 4 May 2001, ECHR 2001-III (extracts); *Shanaghan v United Kingdom*, no. 37715/97, judgment of 4 May 2001, ECHR 2001-III (extracts).

for example where they have assumed responsibility for his welfare,[93] or where they knew or ought to have known that his life was at risk.[94] The Court held that:

> the absence of any direct State responsibility for the death of Michael Menson does not exclude the applicability of Article 2. It recalls that by requiring a State to take appropriate steps to safeguard the lives of those within its jurisdiction (see *L.C.B. v. the United Kingdom*, judgment of 9 June 1998, *Reports* 1998-III, p. 1403, § 36), Article 2 § 1 imposes a duty on that State to secure the right to life by putting in place effective criminal law provisions to deter the commission of offences against the person, backed up by law enforcement machinery for the prevention, suppression and punishment of breaches of such provisions (see *Osman*, cited above, § 115).

Concerning the case and with reference to the procedural obligations under Article 2, the Court observed that the obligation to secure the installation of a law enforcement system requires an effective investigation in cases where there is reason to believe that an individual has sustained life-threatening injuries in suspicious circumstances. The purpose of such an investigation would be to identify those responsible with a view of bringing them before justice. At the same time, in cases where death results, the relevant investigation becomes even more important since it would constitute the main means of ensuring respect for the right to life guaranteed by the Convention. The state is entitled to choose the means by which it implements the duty of investigation which is bound to vary in different circumstances. However, the Court was clear that:

> [W]hatever mode is employed, the authorities must act of their own motion, once the matter has come to their attention. They cannot leave it to the initiative of the next of kin either to lodge a formal complaint or to take responsibility for the conduct of any investigative procedures ... [A] prompt response by the authorities in investigating a use of lethal force may generally be regarded as essential in maintaining public confidence in their adherence to the rule of law and in preventing any appearance of collusion in or tolerance of unlawful acts.

The Court further established that the requirement of an effective investigation also applies to circumstances involving a life-threatening

---

[93] The Court referred to *Paul and Audrey Edwards v United Kingdom*, no. 46477/99, judgment of 14 March 2002, ECHR 2002-II.

[94] The Court referred to, for example, *Osman v United Kingdom*, judgment of 28 October 1998, *Reports of Judgments and Decisions* 1998-VIII, p 3124.

attack on an individual regardless of whether or not death results. Special significance is attributed to cases of racially motivated attacks, where the relevant investigation must be pursued with vigorous impartiality, having regard to the need to reassert continuously society's condemnation of racism and to maintain the confidence of minorities in the ability of the authorities to protect them from the threat of racist violence.[95] In addition to the requirement of an effective

---

[95] Concerning the facts, the Court noted that it:

> 'must have regard at the outset to the fact that the police investigation into the death of Michael Menson ultimately led to the identification and arrest of the culprits between March 1999 and May 1999. They were all convicted and received heavy prison sentences later that same year. It is also to be observed that a public inquest into the cause of Michael Menson's death was held shortly after he died and a Coroner's jury returned a verdict of unlawful killing in September 1998. The Court cannot but note that the first findings of the official inquiry into the police's handling of the case in the early stages appear to be critical of the way in which certain officers of the MPS reacted to the attack on Michael Menson. Indeed, the evidence advanced before the Coroner's jury and at the trial of the accused clearly indicates that there were very serious defects in the handling of the attack on Michael Menson and which were entirely at odds with the requirements of an effective investigation as outlined above.
>
> The applicants maintain that these defects have their basis in racism within the MPS [Metropolitan Police Service], in particular the refusal of certain police officers to deal with an attack on a black victim with an open and independent mind as regards the cause of his injuries. However, it is not for the Court, in the context of Article 2 and in the circumstances of this case, to pronounce on these claims, including the applicants' allegations of an institutional cover-up of police misconduct and harassment of them at various stages of the investigation.'

The Court in any event proceeded to declare the application as being manifestly ill-founded on the basis of the relevant circumstances. Its reasoning reads as follows:

> 'In the first place, the legal system of the respondent State ably demonstrated, in the final analysis and with reasonable expedition, its capacity to enforce the criminal law against those who unlawfully took the life of another, irrespective of the victim's racial origin. For the Court, this must be considered decisive when deciding whether the authorities complied with their positive and procedural obligations under Article 2. Secondly, the inquiry into the applicants' complaints has not yet terminated. It appears from the communication of the PCA [Police Complaints Authority] to the applicants' solicitor, dated 31 December 2002, that the report prepared by the Chief Constable of Cambridgeshire Constabulary into the applicants' complaints has been forwarded to the Crown Prosecution Service ("CPS") for consideration. Thirdly, although the applicants' stress the authorities' failure to secure the

investigation, the Convention may require in certain circumstances the availability of recourse to criminal law.[96]

The scope of positive obligations in connection with the right to life has been clarified by the jurisprudence of the Court. This jurisprudence is summed up eloquently by Andrew Clapham who has usefully summarized it in the following terms:

> These cases have extended the international law of human rights into new realms. First the right to life in the Convention covers situations where the killer was a private or non-state actor, as well as situations where it is not clear whether the killing was carried out by state agents or others. In short, it is not necessary to show who carried out the killing to come within the protective scope of Article 2. Second, the Court has extended the procedural guarantees in Article 2 to situations where the killing is not necessarily attributed to state actors. Third, the positive obligations of the state have been articulated and applied in ways that seek to ensure that states put in place procedures at the national level which will avoid the need for the European Court of Human Rights to investigate the facts of each loss of life. These developments have radically changed the way in which one thinks about the right to life in human rights law.[97]

He adds an interesting consideration on the extent of positive obligations on individuals expectations, i.e. the duty to rescue.[98] Many member states have used their criminal laws to sanction failure to rescue, or *non-assistance à personne en danger*. The question arises whether, under the positive obligation to protect life, states are bound to legislate in this area. The Court has not, as yet, had the opportunity to give a final answer to this question and, in particular, to whether a *criminal law* remedy, as opposed to a *civil law* one, is always required. However, the role of the private, sector in health

---

> accountability of the police for the alleged discriminatory approach to the investigation, this is a matter which falls to be examined, if at all, under Article 6 of the Convention and, since they are close family members of the deceased, under Article 13. Article 2 is primarily concerned with the assessment of a Contracting State's compliance with its substantive and procedural obligations to protect the right to life. That Article does not guarantee as such an applicant a right to a remedy in respect of any alleged defects occurring in the discharge of those obligations.'

See also, L. Garlicki, op. cit., p 136.

[96] See *Kılıç v Turkey*, no. 22492/93, § 62, ECHR 2000-III, and *Mahmut Kaya v Turkey*, no. 22535/93, § 85, ECHR 2000-III.

[97] Op. cit., p 368, footnote omitted.

[98] Ibid.

care has been examined in *Calvelli and Ciglio*.[99] In the context of medical negligence, the Court has held that:

> [I]f the infringement of the right to life or to personal integrity is not caused intentionally, the positive obligation imposed by Article 2 to set up an effective judicial system does not necessarily require the provision of a criminal-law remedy in every case. In the specific sphere of medical negligence the obligation may for instance also be satisfied if the legal system affords victims a remedy in the civil courts, either alone or in conjunction with a remedy in the criminal courts, enabling any liability of the doctors concerned to be established and any appropriate civil redress, such as an order for damages and for the publication of the decision, to be obtained. Disciplinary measures may also be envisaged.[100]

(b) Prohibition of torture

It is clear that the acts of private parties which interfere with the right of others under Article 3 of the Convention providing that '[n]o one shall be subjected to torture or to inhuman or degrading treatment or punishment' may contravene the Convention. The Court has had the opportunity to elaborate its jurisprudence in this respect, *inter alia*, in cases concerning corporal punishment in private schools,[101] physical abuse inflicted on minors by members of their families,[102] parental neglect,[103] and rape.[104] Two examples of the Court's approach may be referred to. The first concerned corporal punishment inflicted in a private school where the respondent state argued that, notwithstanding its obligation towards securing the rights guaranteed by Articles 3 and 8 of the Convention, its responsibility was not in fact engaged because the domestic legal system had adequately secured such rights by prohibiting the use of

---

99 *Calvelli and Ciglio v Italy* [GC], no. 32967/96, ECHR 2002-I.

100 At para 51 of its judgment. See also *Vo v France* [GC], no. 53924/00, ECHR 2004-VIII. D. Spielmann, 'La Convention européenne des Droits de l'Homme et le droit pénal' (2004) 14 *Annales du droit luxembourgeois* 55.

101 *Costello-Roberts v United Kingdom*, judgment of 25 March 1993, Series A no. 247-C.

102 *A v United Kingdom*, judgment of 23 September 1998, *Reports of Judgments and Decisions* 1998-VI, p 2692.

103 *Z and others v United Kingdom* [GC], no. 29392/95, ECHR 2001-V.

104 *MC v Bulgaria*, no. 39272/98, ECHR 2003-XII.

any corporal punishment which was not moderate or reasonable. The Court observed that:

> Accordingly, in the present case, which relates to the particular domain of school discipline, the treatment complained of although it was the act of a headmaster of an independent school, is none the less such as may engage the responsibility of the United Kingdom under the Convention if it proves to be incompatible with Article 3 or Article 8 or both (art. 3, art. 8).[105]

In *A v United Kingdom*[106] the Court, in examining a case concerning the abuse of a child by his stepfather, stated that:

> ... [T]he obligation on the High Contracting Parties under Article 1 of the Convention to secure to everyone within their jurisdiction the rights and freedoms defined in the Convention, taken together with Article 3, requires States to take measures designed to ensure that individuals within their jurisdiction are not subjected to torture or inhuman or degrading treatment or punishment, including such ill-treatment administered by private individuals (see, *mutatis mutandis*, the H.L.R. v. France judgment of 29 April 1997, *Reports* 1997-III, p. 758, § 40). Children and other vulnerable individuals, in particular, are entitled to State protection, in the form of effective deterrence, against such serious breaches of personal integrity (see, *mutatis mutandis*, the X and Y v. the Netherlands judgment of 26 March 1985, Series A no. 91, pp. 11–13, §§ 21–27; the Stubbings and Others v. the United Kingdom judgment of 22 October 1996, *Reports* 1996-IV, p. 1505, §§ 62–64; and also the United Nations Convention on the Rights of the Child, Articles 19 and 37).
>
> 23. The Court recalls that under English law it is a defence to a charge of assault on a child that the treatment in question amounted to 'reasonable chastisement' (see paragraph 14 above). The burden of proof is on the prosecution to establish beyond reasonable doubt that the assault went beyond the limits of lawful punishment. In the present case, despite the fact that the applicant had been subjected to treatment of sufficient severity to fall within the scope of Article 3, the jury acquitted his stepfather, who had administered the treatment (see paragraphs 10–11 above).
>
> 24. In the Court's view, the law did not provide adequate protection to the applicant against treatment or punishment contrary to Article 3. Indeed, the Government have accepted that this law currently fails to provide adequate protection to children and should be amended.

---

105 *Costello-Roberts v United Kingdom*, judgment of 25 March 1993, Series A no. 247-C, § 28.

106 *A v United Kingdom*, judgment of 23 September 1998, *Reports of Judgments and Decisions* 1998-VI, p 2692.

> In the circumstances of the present case, the failure to provide adequate protection constitutes a violation of Article 3 of the Convention.[107]

(c) Expulsion

Private conduct may also be relevant in expulsion cases. In *Ahmed v Austria*[108] the Court did not accept that the fact that a threat coming from a non-state actor was sufficient to take the case outside the scope of the Convention.[109] A similar approach has been adopted by the Court in *HLR v. France*,[110] concerning threats from a criminal organisation:

> It is therefore necessary to examine whether the foreseeable consequences of H.L.R.'s deportation to Colombia are such as to bring Article 3 into play. In the present case the source of the risk on which the applicant relies is not the public authorities.
>
> According to the applicant, it consists in the threat of reprisals by drug traffickers, who may seek revenge because of certain statements that he made to the French police, coupled with the fact that the Colombian State is, he claims, incapable of protecting him from attacks by such persons.
>
> Owing to the absolute character of the right guaranteed, the Court does not rule out the possibility that Article 3 of the Convention (art. 3) may also apply where the danger emanates from persons or groups of persons who are not public officials. However, it must be shown that the risk is real and that the authorities of the receiving State are not able to obviate the risk by providing appropriate protection.

(d) Prohibition of slavery and forced labour

The recent judgment of the Court in the case of *Siliadin v France*[111] highlights the relevance of the prohibition of slavery in the modern era. The case concerned the appalling working conditions imposed

---

107 §§ 22–24.

108 *Ahmed v Austria*, judgment of 17 December 1996, *Reports of Judgments and Decisions* 1996-VI, p 2195.

109 See Clapham, op. cit., at p 377.

110 *HLR v France*, judgment of 29 April 1997, *Reports of Judgments and Decisions* 1997-III, p 745, at paras 39–40.

111 *Siliadin v France*, No. 73316/01, ECHR 2005-VII.

on a Togolese national, who was essentially a 'maid without pay'[112] for a couple in Paris. The Court emphasised the need for effectiveness of the prohibition of 'modern slavery' and compulsory labour which would render the prohibition incorporated into Article 4 of the Convention applicable to the acts of private parties. Pursuant to Article 4 of the Convention:

> 1. No one shall be held in slavery or servitude.
>
> 2. No one shall be required to perform forced or compulsory labour.
>
> 3. For the purpose of this article the term 'forced or compulsory labour' shall not include:
>
> (a) any work required to be done in the ordinary course of detention imposed according to the provisions of Article 5 of [the] Convention or during conditional release from such detention;
>
> (b) any service of a military character or, in case of conscientious objectors in countries where they are recognised, service exacted instead of compulsory military service;
>
> (c) any service exacted in case of an emergency or calamity threatening the life or well-being of the community;
>
> (d) any work or service which forms part of normal civic obligations.

The applicant complained that the state did not fulfil its positive obligations entailed in this provision by installing an effective system of criminal law capable of preventing, prosecuting and punishing private actors' involvement in 'modern slavery'. The Court considered its case law on positive obligations, as well as relevant international treaties and documents[113] and proceeded to reach a finding of a violation of the Convention on the following grounds:

> In those circumstances, the Court considers that limiting compliance with Article 4 of the Convention only to direct action by the State authorities would be inconsistent with the international instruments specifically concerned with this issue and would amount to rendering it ineffective. Accordingly, it necessarily follows from this provision that Governments have positive obligations, in the same way as under Article 3 for example, to adopt criminal-law provisions which penalise the practices referred to in Article 4 and to apply them in practice (see *MC v Bulgaria*, cited above, § 153).[114]

---

112 Clapham, op. cit., p 383.

113 §§ 77–89 and § 111.

114 At para 89 of its judgment.

The Court concluded that the criminal law legislation in force did not afford the applicant, who was only a minor at the relevant time, practical and effective protection against the actions of which she was a victim.[115]

5. The right to be protected from unlawful detention

In the case of *Storck v Germany*,[116] the Court had to examine the case of an applicant who had been placed in a locked ward of a private psychiatric clinic at her father's request, following various family conflicts. In this respect Article 5 § 1 of the Convention, which reads as follows, was relevant:

> 1. Everyone has the right to liberty and security of person. No one shall be deprived of his liberty save in the following cases and in accordance with a procedure prescribed by law:
>
> (a) the lawful detention of a person after conviction by a competent court;
>
> (b) the lawful arrest or detention of a person for non-compliance with the lawful order of a court or in order to secure the fulfilment of any obligation prescribed by law;
>
> (c) the lawful arrest or detention of a person effected for the purpose of bringing him before the competent legal authority on reasonable suspicion of having committed an offence or when it is reasonably considered necessary to prevent his committing an offence or fleeing after having done so;
>
> (d) the detention of a minor by lawful order for the purpose of educational supervision or his lawful detention for the purpose of bringing him before the competent legal authority;
>
> (e) the lawful detention of persons for the prevention of the spreading of infectious diseases, of persons of unsound mind, alcoholics or drug addicts or vagrants;

---

[115] At para 148 of its judgment. See also D. Spielmann, 'La Convention européenne des Droits de l'Homme et le droit pénal' (2004) 14 *Annales du droit luxembourgeois* 55.

[116] *Storck v Germany*, No. 61603/00, ECHR 2005-V. See by contrast the case of *Nielsen v Denmark* (judgment of 28 November 1988, Series A no. 144), where the Court concluded that the hospitalisation of the applicant did not amount to a deprivation of liberty within the meaning of Article 5, but was a responsible exercise by his mother of her custodial rights in the interest of the child and that, accordingly, Article 5 was not applicable in the case.

(f) the lawful arrest or detention of a person to prevent his effecting an unauthorised entry into the country or of a person against whom action is being taken with a view to deportation or extradition.

The Court considered that:

> 100. [T]he special circumstances of the applicant's case also warrant an examination of the question whether her detention is imputable to the respondent State in that the State breached a positive obligation to protect the applicant against interferences with her liberty by private persons.
>
> 101. The Court has consistently held that the responsibility of a State is engaged if a violation of one of the rights and freedoms defined in the Convention is the result of non-observance by that State of its obligation under Article 1 to secure those rights and freedoms in its domestic law to everyone within its jurisdiction (see, *inter alia*, *Costello-Roberts v. the United Kingdom*, judgment of 25 March 1993, Series A no. 247-C, p. 57, § 26, and *Woś v. Poland* (dec.), no. 22860/02, § 60, ECHR 2005-). Consequently, the Court has expressly found that Article 2 (see, among other authorities, *L.C.B. v. the United Kingdom*, judgment of 9 June 1998, *Reports of Judgments and Decisions* 1998-III, p. 1403, § 36), Article 3 (see, *inter alia*, *Costello-Roberts*, cited above, pp. 57-58, §§ 26 and 28) and Article 8 of the Convention (see, *inter alia*, *X and Y v. the Netherlands*, judgment of 26 March 1985, Series A no. 91, p. 11, § 23, and *Costello-Roberts*, ibid.) require the State not only to refrain from an active infringement by its representatives of the rights in question, but also to take appropriate steps to provide protection against an interference with those rights either by State agents or by private parties.

It was found that the applicant, who had notably tried to flee from the clinic on several occasions, had not agreed to her continued stay there and had therefore been deprived of her liberty within the meaning of Article 5 § 1. The Court found Germany responsible for that deprivation of liberty in three respects: first, the authorities became actively involved in the applicant's placement in the clinic when the police, by use of force, had brought her back to the clinic from which she had fled; secondly, the national courts, in the compensation proceedings brought by the applicant, had failed to interpret the provisions of civil law relating to her claim in the spirit of Article 5; and thirdly, Germany had violated its existing positive obligation to protect the applicant against interferences with her liberty carried out by private individuals. As there had been no court order authorising the applicant's confinement to the private clinic, her detention had not been lawful within the meaning of Article 5 § 1. Consequently, the applicant's confinement to the private clinic amounted to a breach of her right to liberty as guaranteed by Article 5 § 1.[117]

F. Conclusion

Although the Court has not made a clear pronouncement on the extent of the direct effect of the Convention and its protocols between private parties, it has established through its consistent case law, that member states are bound to secure respect for human rights, even in the sphere of the relations of individuals amongst themselves. Relying on the text and spirit of the Convention, the Court has evolved the doctrine of 'positive obligations' which has served as it's primary tool to implement human rights between private actors. At the same time, the Court has insisted on the duty of the domestic authorities to interpret even private law instruments in a manner compatible with the Convention. This obligation will bear a great impact in the development of areas of law traditionally thought of as distant from human rights adjudication. Further, the Court's employment of the balancing technique has involved considering competing Convention rights and public interests concerning private actors in a manner resembling the normal function of civil law courts.

The need to safeguard the dignity of individuals within the Convention's reach has led the Court to establish that its endeavours are governed by the principle of effectiveness that the Convention rights are not 'theoretical' or 'illusory'. This will inevitably require at times the application of the Convention rights in the sphere of the relations of private actors amongst themselves.

---

[117] The Court found also that the applicant's medical treatment, which had been carried out against her will, interfered with her right to respect for private life. The Court, referring to its findings with respect to Article 5 § 1, found that Germany was responsible for that interference. As the applicant's confinement to the clinic for medical treatment had not been authorised by a court order, the interference with her right to respect for private life had not been lawful within the meaning of Article 8 § 2. Consequently, there had been a violation of Article 8. On this case, see I. Soumy, 'L'effet horizontal de l'article 5 § 1, première phrase comme limite à la tyrannie familiale: L'affaire *Storck c. Allemagne* du 16 juin 2005' (2006) 17 *Revue trimestrielle des droits de l'homme* 237 et seq.

PART III: Comparative Analysis

Comparative Analysis

Dawn Oliver and Jörg Fedtke

A. Introduction

We now turn to the comparative aspects of this project. In what follows section we shall try to draw comparisons and lessons from the material on the 14 national jurisdictions and the European Convention on Human Rights compiled in Part II above. We will also look briefly at the situation in the European Union, which today brings together most of the systems covered in this study. Inevitably, we shall be drawn to speculate about some of the comparative points that we make, but will aim to base our analysis as far as possible on the material presented in the previous chapters.

First, however, it is worth reminding ourselves that for many of the jurisdictions that we have considered, private sphere protection has been a departure from the traditional presumption that human rights apply only 'vertically' (as between the individual and the state). This assumption was made initially in relation to the European Convention on Human Rights as well, though it was realised soon after that instrument came into effect that the text and spirit of many of the articles did in fact envisage at least some 'horizontal' effect. The European Court on Human Rights has developed extensive private sphere protection through its case law over the years, from its initial 'state action' starting point to the current 'state responsibility' and 'positive obligation' approaches. But a presumption in favour of a vertical application of *constitutional* rights protection is also evident in many domestic jurisdictions, notably in this study Germany, France, Canada and the United States. In Canada and the United States, of all our jurisdictions, the verticality doctrine is based on express provisions in, respectively, the US Constitution and the Canadian Charter of Rights, and is strongly adhered to. Broad interpretations of the 'state' element of the 'state action' requirement in the US Constitution have, however, resulted in the judicial development of some human rights protection where allegations are made against broadly 'private' defendants. In other jurisdictions, too, the concepts of 'state' or 'public function' and the like have been developed to extend the scope of human rights protection beyond the classic state institutions. Our focus in this project has, however, been on the effect of human rights in the 'purely' private sphere. We have deliberately not extended our consideration of human rights protection to the other side of the public–private law divide (however this line may be defined in single jurisdictions) save in relation to the European Convention, the 'state action' doctrines in the United States and Canada, and (in passing) some other jurisdictions where this seemed necessary (as, in particular, India); to do so would have taken up more space than is available to us on this occasion, and thus limited our ability to focus on purely private sphere protection. Suffice it therefore to note at this point that the trend to privatise functions traditionally performed by public authorities – from public transport and roads to schools and universities, health systems, prisons, or the provision of utilities such as water, gas, electricity or telecommunication services – may have prompted courts in many systems to expand the ambit of human rights protection in an attempt to soften the impact a retreating welfare state must inevitably have on the protection of individual interests. The legal and political implications of what has been identified in Germany as attempts of the state to escape into the less restrictive realm of private law (so-called *Flucht ins Privatrecht*) are closely linked to the issues covered in this study and may provide a worthwhile topic for future comparative work.

How, then, do constitutional rights become operational in private relationships? The legal systems of all the countries we have included in this collection give considerable protection to the normal range of civil and political rights in the private sphere in their ordinary private law (contract, tort, property law and so on), whether this protection is based in the common law, in civil law codes, or in specific statutory provisions (for instance, in relation to anti-discrimination issues, employment, or landlord and tenant relationships). We have been particularly concerned, however, to explore and compare the ways in which *additional* protection is given to these interests as 'rights' in the private sphere. As indicated in the introduction, here we mean that the 'right' in question has a special legal status which extends to private relationships and enjoys a measure of increased protection from legislative or executive interference, for example by constitutional provisions, special entrenchment, principles of interpretation, or judicial duties to develop the law in a 'rights compatible' way. Such a special private sphere status derives, in the countries considered in this study, from one or more of the following mechanisms:

1. The country's (written) constitution, as in Denmark, Germany, Greece, India, Ireland, Italy, South Africa, and Spain.
2. A special bill or charter of rights separate from the written constitution, as in Canada (the Charter of Rights), Denmark (the ECHR as incorporated in 1991), England and Wales (the Human Rights Act 1998), Ireland (the European Convention on Human Rights Act 2003), and Israel (the two Basic Laws of 1992 dealing with human dignity, freedom, and economic activity).
3. Legally recognised fundamental or otherwise underlying *values* – found either in the texts of constitutional documents or established by the courts. In Israel these include dignity, equality, and non-discrimination; Germany, France, Ireland and Italy identify human dignity as the principal value; in Greece, special importance is given to human dignity and personality rights; in England and Wales core values are human dignity and autonomy; and in Spain emphasis is placed on freedom, justice and equality. In Canada, reference is frequently made to 'Charter values' but it is not entirely clear whether this refers to the 'rights' such as free speech (which, though not having general horizontal effect, influence the development of private law) or to the values that underlie them. In New Zealand, too, the courts refer to the values enshrined in the Bill of Rights Act when developing the common law.
4. International instruments forming part of the legal system (in particular the European Convention on Human Rights) in monist countries such as Denmark, France, Italy, Spain and, to a lesser extent, Germany.
5. International human rights treaties given effect by incorporation in domestic law and influencing the legislator or the courts in dualist systems such as England and Wales Ireland or New Zealand.
6. Unincorporated international instruments which influence the development of the law in dualist systems (such as India, which is a party to many international human rights instruments).

The private sphere protection of rights ranges from varying kinds and degrees of *direct effect* (as in France, Greece, India, Ireland, Italy, South Africa and Spain), through varying kinds and degrees of *indirect (horizontal) effect* (as in Denmark, England and Wales, France, Greece, Israel, Italy, New Zealand, Germany and, again, South Africa), to 'near zero' or *minimalist horizontal effect* (as in the United States and Canada). The jurisdictions in which rights have direct effect in the private sphere also tend to give indirect effect to rights. As we shall note in due course, however, jurisdictions differ as to the category into which techniques for securing private sphere protection fall (what is considered to be 'direct' effect in one jurisdiction may be categorised as 'indirect' effect in another) or as to the need to make distinctions between direct and indirect effect in the first place (as is the case, for instance, in Greece and South Africa). It seems as if these various approaches form a sliding scale with many intermediate shades of grey rather than a system of clearly defined categories, as traditional legal terminology would seem to suggest.

1. Self-executing constitutions

Some general points about constitutions and human rights protection emerge from our study. In countries whose legal systems are based on the common law, constitutional provisions give rise to rights that are directly enforceable in the courts, except where the constitution specifies otherwise, and subject to questions of legal certainty and what in English law is referred to as 'justiciability' (the question whether it is within the competence of the courts to determine certain highly 'political' or 'polycentric' matters). In these systems there is no need for implementing legislation to be on the statute books at the time of the introduction of the constitutional human rights provisions, or to be passed in order to implement the constitutional provisions at a later date, since constitutional provisions are 'self-executing'. Thus in the common law jurisdictions covered by our study where there are written constitutions (or equivalents) – see Canada, India, Ireland, Israel, South Africa (a 'hybrid' system with a strong common law element) and the United States – constitutional law, 'basic' laws or statutory provisions for the protection of human rights in the *public* sphere are, for example, directly enforceable in the courts even in the absence of implementing legislation. This is also true for Germany, a civil law system, where Article 1(3) of the Basic Law declares that the basic rights contained in the following provisions bind the legislature, the executive, and the judiciary as directly applicable law. But the relationship between constitutional human rights protections and subsequently enacted primary legislation in these countries depends on the hierarchy of laws in the system. It depends in particular whether and to what extent constitutional protections are procedurally entrenched or protected against repeal or amendment by laws passed subsequently and which authorise interference with rights. Thus, in Israel, where the Basic Laws of 1992 are not procedurally entrenched, the courts will give effect to primary legislation passed by the Knesset that is incompatible with a Basic Law. The Indian and German Constitutions are, by contrast, entrenched against amendment by ordinary legislation and require the courts to refuse to give effect to incompatible laws even if passed after these documents entered into force.

Whether constitutional human rights protections extend to the *private* sphere in jurisdictions such as these, with written constitutions having direct or self-executing effect, depends on the wording of the constitutional text and how the ordinary courts and/or constitutional or supreme courts have interpreted it. Thus, in the United States, the requirement of 'state action' as a precondition for establishing liability for a breach of human rights derives from the constitutional text itself, and has been taken by the Supreme Court to more or less preclude the development of 'pure' private sphere protection. This is not the case in Germany, Israel, India or Ireland.

As we shall see in the next section, the position as to the self-execution of constitutional provisions is different in most of the non-common law jurisdictions in our study. Much of the difference seems to revolve around the constitutional and political theories which influenced the development of the Napoleonic system in France, and from which many of these countries derive the basic structure of both their public and private law. In these systems the separation of powers is an important element in constitutional arrangements, more important than in many common law jurisdictions. It would be regarded as judicial trespass on the legislator's function in such countries for the judges to develop the law (public or private) on the basis of constitutional provisions rather than on implementing legislation or (as in Greece) a comprehensive codification of private law. The fact that human rights norms are often very general in character adds to these difficulties. Concerns that the direct application of widely phrased constitutional rights by judges could undermine legal certainty in many areas – beside democratic legitimacy the second important traditional justification for relying so heavily on legislation as the most important source of law – have thus emerged in most mainland Continental European systems. The common law, by contrast, has always involved flexible and incremental judicial development of the law. This is not something which causes too much concern in the legislatures of those jurisdictions, though executives may well be uncomfortable with judicial lawmaking. But to reverse the position and abolish the power of the courts to develop the law (and give direct effect to constitutional provisions) would be difficult in such jurisdictions, so entrenched is the common law method in the legal culture and so resistant is the political elite in many such countries to constitutional amendment. It should be noted, however, that the two approaches just described are today in ways converging, and that judges in civil law systems such as France and Germany have over the past decades assumed an increasingly important role in developing the law through interpretation and, even, barely disguised judicial law-making. This may not yet always be openly admitted but is especially evident in civil law systems which have introduced constitutional courts with the power to 'strike down' or 'invalidate' parliamentary legislation. Germany's Federal Constitutional Court in Karlsruhe is thus today as much an 'oracle of the law' as the democratically elected legislator in Berlin.

In some civil law jurisdictions, too, constitutional human rights provisions are directly enforceable in the public *and* the private spheres without the need for implementing legislation. Spain is such a system in our study, and even the German Basic Law – though understood as a document which becomes directly operational predominantly in vertical relationships between the state and its citizens – contains single provisions which expressly affect private disputes. The distinction between common law and civil law jurisdictions, despite the convergence of systems still a useful tool in analysing particular aspects of our topic, does therefore not strike us as being the decisive factor on which a wider theory of horizontal human rights protection could be grounded.

2. *Non-self-executing constitutions*

In some countries, constitutional human rights protections may not be relied upon in the ordinary courts unless either implementing legislation has been passed or other legislation – as, for instance, the Greek Civil Code – is regarded as providing a legal conduit through which constitutional rights can take effect in the private sphere. The point is illustrated as follows.

(a) Denmark

Denmark is a Nordic country in which the legal system broadly operates on the basis of a mixture of both common law and civil law techniques. The courts have not, however, relied on the text of the Danish Constitution – which does include constitutional rights – to justify the protection of individual interests, whether in the public or the private sphere. Traditionally, the protection of constitutional rights is rather considered a matter for the political process in Denmark, and the Constitution does not therefore have immediate direct legal effect. Human rights protection rests on the Incorporation Act 1991, which incorporates the European Convention into Danish law, and on the duty of all public authorities to interpret the law compatibly with international obligations. Human rights protection in Denmark is largely due to 'the development of judicial practice' – a technique similar to that of common law jurisdictions.

(b) France

In France, a civil law country, the text of the Constitution does not include human rights, but the Declaration of the Rights of Man and the Citizen of 1789 and the Preamble to the 1946 Constitution are mentioned in the Preamble to the 1958 Constitution. This reference was the starting point for the development of a fairly extensive human rights jurisprudence by the Conseil constitutionel. Both the Conseil constitutionel and the Conseil d'etat have made these rights operational in the public sphere, but this protection does not extend to private relationships. For reasons which will be outlined below, the Cour de cassation and the other civil courts which would have jurisdiction to deal with claims for private sphere protection do not rely on the Constitution or those documents as the basis for private sphere protection of rights. Instead, the civil courts rely directly on the European Convention, as required to do under (the monist) Article 55 of the Constitution.

(c) Germany

As briefly explained above, human rights are directly effective in vertical relationships and, in certain cases, even in private law disputes in Germany. Parliamentary legislation, however, remains by far the most important vehicle for human rights protection in the private sphere. Any law can be subject to judicial scrutiny by the Federal Constitutional Court if its compatibility with human rights is in doubt. The Court can be approached by lower courts on any level of the system by means of a preliminary reference procedure or, once all other available legal remedies are exhausted, by the parties themselves. In practical terms, general provisions contained in the German Civil Code have provided the most important link between the private legal order and the Basic Law, but the so-called 'radiating effect' of constitutional rights has also influenced the interpretation of many more specific laws. The borderline between 'indirect' effect through constitutional interpretation of legislation and a more 'direct' effect through the judicial development of the law beyond the limits of a statutory regime as envisaged by the legislator is thus often blurred. As seen in early cases of the Federal Labour Court, 'direct' effect limited by considerations of proportionality may, moreover, lead to very similar (if not identical) outcomes as the thory of 'radiating' constitutional values which has been endorsed by the Federal Constitutional Court over the past four decades.

(d) Italy

The Italian Constitution includes provisions for the protection of human rights, but is silent as to their horizontal effect. For the most part these rights may not be enforced directly in the ordinary courts, but those courts interpret legislation so far as possible compatibly with constitutional rights and with rights contained in international treaties ratified by Italy, both in private sphere and public sphere cases. As in Germany, the Italian Constitutional Court may determine the constitutionality of legislation on reference from lower courts. There have, however, been some cases where – if there is a lacuna in ordinary legislation – the courts will give direct effect to constitutional rights in the private sphere in the absence of implementing legislation.

(e) Greece

In Greece there is express constitutional provision for private sphere protection, but this is not self-executing. No specific implementing legislation has been passed. The courts have, however, relied on particular clauses in the Greek Civil Code to develop private sphere protection, using the Code as a conduit for transferring the constitutional rights to the private sphere. There is, moreover, a self-executing provision in the Greek Constitution, Article 119(3), which prohibits the use of certain evidence which interferes with privacy. A further exception to the general requirement for implementing legislation has been the courts' 'law-creative' development of direct effect of private sphere rights where the Civil Code is considered to be silent on the matter so that it cannot provide the necessary conduit. But this jurisdiction is narrow and subject to criticism in Greece for being in breach of the separation of powers principle.

(f) Spain

In Spain, also a civil law country, there are different categories of rights in the Constitution. 'Fundamental' rights enjoy stronger procedural protection against repeal or amendment than 'constitutional' rights. Neither set of rights requires implementing legislation. In this respect Spain is unique among the non-common law countries in our study (with the exception of the narrow jurisdiction of the courts to fill gaps left by the Civil Code in Greece and the limited instances of direct effect in Germany mentioned above). However, only the Spanish Constitutional Court, to which such issues may be referred, may invalidate a law that is contrary to the Constitution. Apart from that, ordinary courts have jurisdiction to hear challenges to decisions and actions in cases involving constitutional rights and to grant remedies. Appeal lies from the ordinary courts to the Constitutional Court in its *recurso de amparo* jurisdiction in both vertical and private sphere human rights cases.

3. Similar responses despite local differences?

As will become apparent in the further course of this analysis, the reasons why systems have opted for one or the other approach to the protection of human rights in the private sphere is strongly influenced by local factors – historical experience, legal tradition, court structures, the constitutional landscape, or the importance given to international law. This first brief overview thus shows that a significant part of the constitutional background against which private sphere rights protection does or does not develop in any jurisdiction comes both from the general legal system – common law, Nordic law, or civil law in our study – and the express terms of a country's constitution (if any). Despite this complexity, two general observations can be made before we go into more detail. First, the emergence of human rights as a decisive guideline for state activity across the globe has also influenced legislators in the area of private law in all systems under review here. This has resulted in a considerable measure of horizontal protection for constitutionally acknowledged interests simply because the rules which regulate private interaction more often than not take human rights considerations into account. This is true both for systems which opt for a restrictive stance to a more direct horizontal application of human rights (such as the United States) and those which have accepted forms of direct effect (such as India or South Africa). The topic addressed in this study is thus in many jurisdictions one of limited practical importance in the sense that we are dealing with the more exceptional cases rather than the vast majority of 'regular' private disputes which are easily processed by all legal systems on a daily basis and without the need to invoke constitutional rights. Second, it seems interesting that the approaches adopted by systems as diverse as Germany, the United States, India, South Africa, Ireland or the United Kingdom often seem to be quite similar as far as both the practical outcome of private legal disputes and their basic moral justification is concerned. The protection of the weaker party, by whatever technical device, is thus the central theme. This consideration, together with the emergence of ever more powerful private entities in most modern societes, seems to work against a polarisation of legal responses in this field of law. The rule of the thumb formulated by Konrad Zweigert and Hein Kötz – that '[D]ifferent legal systems give the same or very similar solutions, even as to detail, to the same problems of life, despite great differences in their historical development, conceptual structure, and style of operation'[1] – thus also holds true for this study.

---

[1] K. Zweigert and H. Kötz, *An Introduction to Comparative Law* (3rd edn, 1998), p 39.

B. Horizontal human rights protection: direct or indirect effect and the 'state action' doctrine

In this section we consider the ways in which human rights are given effect, directly or indirectly, in the private sphere, and the barriers to any kind of effect that are posed by the 'state action' doctrine in the United States and Canada. Our analysis will consider, first, how constitutionally and internationally protected human rights are given direct effect. We shall then consider their indirect effect, which can take various forms. Constitutional or internationally protected rights may thus be given indirect effect by compatible interpretation or through the judicial development of ordinary domestic laws. Finally, we will consider how the 'state action' doctrine in two of the jurisdictions in our study, the United States and Canada, tends to operate against any private sphere effect for human rights.

1. Direct effect in the private sphere: constitutional and international rights

Of the jurisdictions in our study, France, Greece, India, Ireland, Spain and South Africa purport to give 'direct' private sphere protection or 'horizontal' effect (or equivalent conceptualisations used in the countries concerned) to civil and political rights. In Italy, direct effect is exceptional, and given only where there is a lack of legislation implementing the particular right in question. The German Bill of Rights, though predominantly 'indirectly' effective in private disputes, also contains an exception (the right to form associations aimed at safeguarding and improving working conditions and, more generally, the economic environment of the country).[2] In some jurisdictions, the rights which are given direct effect are those set out in the country's national constitution; in others, the focus is on rights contained in international instruments, including the European Convention for the Protection of Human Rights and Fundamental Freedoms, an instrument of the Council of Europe.

(a) Direct effect of constitutional and international rights: India

India is perhaps the clearest example of direct private sphere protection in our study since there the doctrine of 'non-state action'

[2] See Article 9(3) BL.

means that many of the normal civil and political rights that are set out in the form of 'fundamental rights' (FRs) in the Indian Constitution are given effect by the courts 'horizontally' if the text of the Constitution so allows. The state is regarded as being under a duty to secure the protection of FRs against private as well as public bodies. If protection has not been provided for by specific legislation applying to the private sphere, the courts will develop it, not only giving remedies against private bodies which have breached rights, but going so far as to make recommendations and even give directions as to how private bodies and the state should act in future in order to protect the rights of those they deal with. These recommendations and directions will be treated by the courts as sources of obligations for the state or the private body concerned until appropriate legislation is passed to deal with the problem. This is an unusual constitutional arrangement in terms of division of powers. Courts with the competence to review legislative activity will generally only be able to invalidate unconstitutional laws rather than prescribe a particular legislative course of action, though the borderline between striking down (a form of 'negative' legislation) and giving indications of what might pass constitutional muster in a future case (a form of judicial 'lawmaking') will often be a difficult one to draw.[3]

Indian courts also give private sphere protection to the rights set out in international instruments, unless they are incompatible with Indian legislation. In a country such as India, where many areas of private sphere activity are regulated by the common law (and not by statute), which does not – as in South Africa – fall within the scope of 'legislation', this leaves considerable room for the direct judicial incorporation of international human rights – despite the fact that the country is avowedly dualist. Here we have an example of the fluidity of dualist systems, where perhaps the rhetoric of dualism is important for political reasons but where the reality is very close to the monist end of the spectrum.

(b) Direct effect of European Convention rights only: France

In France, too, some human rights have direct private sphere protection. This effect is not, however, given to the (few) rights set out

[3] The *Abortion* decision of the *Bundesverfassungsgericht*, referred to in Chapter 4 on Germany, probably comes close to what the Indian courts are doing on a more

in the Constitution, itself, or 'discovered' by the Conseil constitutionnel in the Preamble's brief reference to the Declaration of the Rights of Man and the Citizen or the Preamble to the Constitution of 1946 (both important constitutional documents) but rather to the rights set out in the (international) European Convention on Human Rights. The reasons why constitutional rights are not directly applicable in France are linked to the limited role of the Conseil constitutionnel, the traditions of the Cour de cassation, and adherence to the public/private law divide. The French position on private sphere protection of *constitutional* rights is thus quite the opposite of that in India or Ireland (discussed below), a point which highlights the different approaches to the role of the courts in these respectively civil law and common law countries.

Article 55 of the Constitution (the monist article) allows direct application of international treaties by French courts subject to reciprocal enforcement by the other party.[4] This has led to the direct horizontal effect of European Convention rights in France, giving rise to what has become known as the 'conventionalisation' of private law. The jurisprudence of the European Court of Human Rights in Strasbourg and the positive obligation of states to protect their citizens against the violation of their rights by private parties have led French courts to apply Strasbourg case law directly (and also to develop the horizontal application indirectly, through the interpretation of French legislation). The Cour de cassation may set aside French legislation that is incompatible with an international treaty, including the European Convention. There remains, however, a certain measure of discomfort regarding judge-made law in France.

(c) Direct effect of constitutional rights and the 'constitutional tort': Ireland

The Irish version of direct effect is found in the Supreme Court's creation of a 'constitutional tort' giving rise to the award of damages for breach of the rights set out in the Irish Constitution. This cause of

---

regular basis. The German court was heavily criticised for transgressing the limits of its powers in this instance.

4 The provision declares: 'Treaties or agreements duly ratified or approved shall, upon publication, prevail over Acts of Parliament, subject, in regard to each agreement or treaty, to its application by the other party.'

action is based on the view that the Constitution is the foundational legal norm to which all other norms, including those regulating the private sphere, must conform. The courts interpret the Constitution so as to provide direct protection in private relationships: it is the duty of the courts to do so in order to provide protection. However, due to concerns about the implications of direct horizontal effect that have emerged since the creation of the constitutional tort in the 1970s, the tort may only be relied upon in limited circumstances, in particular if ordinary law provides plainly inadequate protection for the right or is manifestly deficient; unless that is the case, the constitutional tort cannot be relied on to shape existing torts or adjust adjectival law, for instance on the burden of proof. There is thus resistance in Ireland to indirect horizontal effect. It is interesting to note that the German system set off from the same starting point (no rule of private law may conflict with the objective values established by the Basic Law) but went down what is called an 'indirect' route, requiring that all rules of law must be construed in accordance with the spirit of the Constitution.[5] This has, inter alia, led to important modifications of German tort law (e.g., the award of damages for the infringement of personality rights contrary to the express provisions of the German Civil Code).[6] The Irish courts thus went further in their initial move towards a broad constitutional tort but seem to have backtracked later on (reducing the tool to an ultima ratio device), while their civil law counterparts in Germany have embarked on a continuous exchange between ordinary law and constitutional values. This difference may reflect a greater confidence of German judges in the ability of codified private law to maintain its coherence and predictability despite constitutional interference, though concerns about the erosion of the private legal system have been voiced in both countries.

It is unclear whether Ireland's constitutional tort is actionable per se or only on proof of damage, whether liability is strict, whether all constitutional rights are actionable in the private sphere (e.g., the equality clause), and how the balancing process works in the resolution of private disputes where conflicting rights and interests are at stake.

---

[5] See the *Lüth* decision of the *Bundesverfassungsgericht*, BVerfGE 7, 198 ff of 15 January 1958.

[6] See the *Soraya* decision of the *Bundesverfassungsgericht*, BVerfGE 34, 269 ff of 14 February 1973.

Modifications to direct horizontal effect via the constitutional tort in recent case law reflect not only concern at emerging issues regarding the development of the tort, but also a shift from natural law theory to a liberal democratic approach to human rights. It is worth noting at this point the contrast to the position in Israel, where there has been reluctance to develop a judge-made 'constitutional law of torts' alongside the existing legislative tort law because of the generality of the provisions contained in the two Basic Laws dealing with human rights protection. Israeli courts would thus have to develop a new set of doctrines dealing with causation, vicarious liability, multiplicity of liabilities, and the law of remedies and defences if such a tort were ever to be developed. Such development in Israeli law could create problems of overlap and conflict between the new and the old law of torts, and therefore erode and undermine the latter, for example by circumventing existing limits on the scope of liability.

(d) Direct effect of constitutional rights: Spain

The Spanish Constitution establishes freedom, justice and equality as superior values, includes many of the usual civil and political rights, and provides that citizens and public authorities are all subject to the Constitution. This has resulted in the ordinary courts having jurisdiction to apply constitutional human rights in the private sphere so that private parties are under negative obligations, i.e. not to interfere with the rights of others. This approach is referred to as 'direct' horizontal effect in Spain. The courts must also interpret the rights set out in the Constitution compatibly with the international instruments to which Spain is a party, but a right recognised only in a treaty and not in the Spanish Constitution is not remediable. The system therefore includes elements of indirect effect when it comes to international obligations. Spain's system is the opposite to that in France, a fellow civil law country, in that the human rights set out in the Spanish constitution have direct effect, but rights in international treaties do not.

Only the Spanish Constitutional Court, to which such issues may be referred, has the power to invalidate a law that is contrary to the Constitution. Apart from that, the ordinary courts have jurisdiction to hear challenges to decisions and actions in rights cases, and appeal lies from them to the *recurso de amparo*, a special jurisdiction of the Constitutional Court, in human rights cases with both vertical and horizontal effect. Thus in Spain direct horizontal effect exists for constitutional and not necessarily international human rights provisions, and is to a greater extent subject to rather complex rules about the jurisdiction of the courts than in other, especially common law, jurisdictions. The last point may result from the existence of a constitutional court, which only exercises a limited (specialised) jurisdiction but ranks above all other courts if this jurisdiction is engaged in a particular case. Conflicts are thereby especially likely to arise in the context of human rights protection, which cuts across all other areas of the law. We encounter the same phenomenon in Germany, while France, which also operates a specialised system of courts, avoids these difficulties since each of the three highest courts of the land (Conseil constitutionnel, Conseil d'etat and Cour de cassation) exercises final authority within its respective jurisdiction.

(e) The 'law-creative' direct effect of constitutional rights: Greece

In Greece, direct effect is given to constitutional rights only where the situation is 'beyond the law', meaning beyond the ordinary law, namely in relation to the prohibition on the admissibility of unlawfully obtained evidence established by the Greek Constitution. The courts have decided in particular cases whether such evidence should be admitted on the basis of a range of constitutional rights including dignity, privacy and freedom of communication, and have balanced these values against the search for truth in trials and the right of defence. There has been no recourse to private law norms in such cases, which is seen as a form of direct effect. In this particular situation, the courts in effect develop the law, but unlike the development of the common law by their counterparts in England and Wales, which is considered to be a kind of indirect effect, in Greece the development is seen as direct. Interestingly, the development of the law by judges in Germany, expressly endorsed by the Federal Constitutional Court in the *Soraya* case of 1973 (which confirmed the award of damages for infringements of human dignity and constitutionally protected personality rights by private parties), is also regarded as indirect effect. Local terminology thus seems to be a precarious tool in the comparative analysis of different approaches. As in Spain and Germany, there is, however, more concern about the difficulties in the legal development and application that flow from the abstract and general nature of constitutional principles than there is in England and Wales.

(f) Direct effect of constitutional rights where there is a gap in legislation: Italy

For the most part the rights set out in the Italian Constitution have been implemented by legislation, which the courts will interpret compatibly with the Constitution. Where, however, a constitutional right has – exceptionally – not been so implemented, the ordinary courts will attempt to base their decision directly upon a provision in the Constitution, thus giving it direct effect.

(g) Direct effect as the constitutional exception: Germany

As will be seen below, Germany falls into the group of systems which give indirect effect to constitutional rights. This was a judicial decision; the Basic Law itself does not contain a clear provision which limits the effect of human rights to vertical relationships, and for some time at least one important court, the Federal Labour Court, argued in favour of (limited) direct effect. Article 9(3) BL, however, establishes one exception with respect to the activities of associations aimed at safeguarding and improving working conditions (employers' associations and trade unions). Human dignity, too, is regarded by some as an overarching value which directly affects private relationships, though in practice it has been made operational only through the interpretation of the law.

(h) Direct effect in theory but indirect effect in practice: South Africa

The effect of constitutional rights in the private sphere was a matter of much debate in South Africa. The multi-party negotiations leading up to the so-called 'Interim' Constitution of 1993 ended in an ambiguous constitutional compromise, which could be interpreted both ways – horizontal or strictly vertical effect of human rights. The South African Constitutional Court, confronted with the question in 1995, came out in favour of indirect effect along the lines of the German model. The Constitutional Assembly reversed this decision in the 'Final' Constitution of 1996, introducing a clear provision in favour of direct horizontal effect – constitutional rights thus bind a natural or a juristic person if, and to the extent that, they are applicable, taking into account the nature of the right in question and the nature of any duty imposed by the right. In order to give effect to a provision in the Bill of Rights, courts must apply – or if necessary develop – the common law to the extent that legislation does not give effect to that right, and may develop rules of the common law to limit the right, provided that the limitation is in accordance with the general limitation clause.[7] The 1996 Constitution, however, also acknowledges indirect effect. Section 39(2) declares that every court, tribunal or forum must, when interpreting any legislation, and when developing the common law or customary law, promote the spirit, purport and objects of the Bill of Rights. In legal practice, the latter approach has prevailed. Courts have thus far interpreted and developed existing law (whether legislation or rules of common or customary law) in the light of constitutional values rather than allowing private actions based directly on constitutional rights to go forward. The Constitutional Court indicated recently that closer adherence to the principle of direct effect would be preferable, but the implications of the judgment are not at all clear at this point. Direct effect thus exists only in theory while courts in fact rely on indirect effect.

2. *Indirect effect of constitutional rights in the private sphere*

We turn now to jurisdictions in which human rights have indirect effect in the private sphere, bearing in mind that in some jurisdictions the courts may give either direct or indirect effect to rights, depending upon the state of the ordinary law. Indirect effect can take two main forms: (1) the *interpretation of domestic legislation* in a way that is compatible with human rights provisions, whether in the constitution, a special charter or other document equivalent to a bill of rights, or in international instruments such as the European Convention; and (2) the *judicial development of private law* so as to secure that it is compatible either with the constitution,

[7] Section 8 of the Republic of South Africa Constitution Act 1996.

a domestic charter of rights, international instruments to which the state in question is a party to, or (exceptionally) international instruments to which it is not a party. Each of these forms has variations as between jurisdictions, including a weaker or stronger indirect effect. Clear distinctions are, as pointed out above and confirmed by the discussions in Germany and South Africa, often difficult to draw. In the next three sections we focus on the interpretive approach to, respectively, constitutional and international rights. The following section considers indirect effect and the developmental approach.

(a) Indirect effect through interpretation of domestic legislation and constitutional rights

An obligation on the courts to interpret domestic legislation compatibly with a constitution or a national bill of rights exists to greater or lesser degrees in a number of the jurisdictions in our study.

(i) Constitutional rights and the civil code: Greece

In Greece, the civil courts have taken the constitutional provision declaring that human rights 'apply to the relations between individuals to which they are appropriate' to authorise the interpretation and/or enforcement of certain specific norms contained in the Greek Civil Code according to principles deriving from constitutional rights. This is known as a 'constitutionally-orientated interpretation of private law norms'. The process involves balancing private law norms and constitutional principles, thus enabling the judge to avoid judicial review of private law norms and protect the (presumedly constitutional) intentions of the legislator in the area of private law.

Together with Germany, where the same is done without express constitutional authorisation, Greece thus stands out in the jurisdictions covered by this study for its judicial *praxis* in developing the application of the Civil Code so as to give effect to rights in the private sphere. There is some ambiguity about whether such development amounts to direct or indirect effect (again a similarity with Germany). Where the judges exercise a 'law-creative' function, as they do in relation to private sphere protection under the Greek Civil Code, this is regarded as 'direct' effect – unlike the position in common law jurisdictions where the term 'indirect' tends to be applied to such judicial activity. In order to provide private sphere protection, Greek courts have relied on certain clauses in the Civil

Code to legitimise the development of codified law. The Code's protection against the abuse of rights, for instance, enables judges to balance conflicting constitutional rights and interests (e.g., those of employers and employees), and the right to personality, again established by the Code, provides protection for the constitutional rights to respect for the environment and culture, and also gives courts an opportunity to apply the Code so as to protect the constitutional right of children to the recognition of their parentage.

(ii) Interpretation and development of private law in the light of constitutional values: Germany

The situation in Germany is very similar to that in Greece. As indicated above, indirect effect of constitutional values – first construed as an 'objective value system' by the German Constitutional Court in 1958 – becomes operational in Germany mainly through the interpretation of existing legislation by judges in all areas of private law. Not surprisingly, many cases thus involve provisions of the German Civil Code as it provides the most important source of law in private disputes. The German approach to *Drittwirkung* is not, however, restricted to interpretation. Ever since the issue first arose in a series of cases dealing with equality between man and woman, German judges have also developed the law. This reflects a significant change in the role they perform today. While John Henry Merryman described the judicial function in civil law systems as 'narrow, mechanical, and uncreative' in 1969,[8] senior judges such as Günter Hirsch, the current President of the Federal Supreme Court, and Paul Kirchhof, former judge of the Federal Constitutional Court, see the judge as a pianist who both interprets the melody composed by the legislature *and* fills any gaps found in the score.[9] This is also true for the area of *Drittwirkung*. There is, however, still some measure of discomfort with the approach, mainly for two reasons. First, the formula developed by the Federal Constitutional Court in the *Lüth* case nearly five decades ago has never been fleshed out in greater detail and remains today an often repeated but, for many academic commentators, insufficient justification of the influence constitutional values exert on private law. Critics thus feel that the theory of state duties, also found, inter alia, in the

---

[8] J. H. Merryman, *The Civil Law Tradition* (2nd edn, 1985, 2003 reprint), p 38.

[9] See 'Akteure der Rechtspolitik' (ZRP-Rechtsgespräch) [2006] *Zeitschrift für Rechtspolitik* 269 at 270.

jurisprudence of the European Court of Human Rights and the European Court of Justice,[10] would provide a more precise and workable formula to identify the situations in which private parties should be able to invoke the Basic Law. As in Spain, the German system is, second, confronted with the problem of distinguishing the specialised constitutional jurisdiction of the *Bundesverfassungsgericht* from that of other, equally specialised, federal courts. This is not merely a procedural question. The power of the ordinary and labour courts to interpret and develop the law in their respective areas of competence to some extent runs parallel to the traditional notion of a private sphere which should essentially be kept free from state (i.e. constitutional) interference. The criticism concerning the role of the Federal Constitutional Court in enforcing human rights considerations in many areas over the past decades is also fuelled by concerns that the influence of constitutional rights could result in an incoherent development of the law and legal uncertainty. The ordinary courts are felt to be better placed to fine tune the law to the values established by the German Constitution. That said, it should be noted that the number of cases which involve constitutional interpretation and development of ordinary laws by lower courts by far exceeds the few (but, of course, more prominent) ones which eventually reach the *Bundesverfassungsgericht*, and that only a very limited number of the roughly 2 million new private law cases that reach German courts each year will actually involve questions of constitutional relevance.

(iii) The Basic Laws and private law concepts – public policy, unlawfulness and good faith in Israel

The common view in Israel is that human rights have indirect effect in the private sphere, as a result of the influence of Basic Laws leading to rights-sympathetic interpretation of legislative terms such as 'public policy', 'unlawfulness', and 'good faith'.

(iv) The indirect effect of human rights on legislation, common law and customary law: South Africa

As explained above, the text of the 1996 South African Constitution actually prescribes direct effect of the Bill of Rights in private disputes, but indirect effect has until now prevailed in practice.

---

10 See ECJ Case C-265/95 of 9 December 1997.

This resistance to change may be due to three closely interrelated factors. First, the introduction of a new constitutional settlement in 1993 has had a profound effect on all parts of the legal system, and judges have obviously become well accustomed to taking constitutional values into account when interpreting and developing the law. The approach seems to have produced reasonable results, and pressure for further change was thus limited. The Constitutional Assembly, which finalised the text of the 1996 Constitution only months after the Court had handed down its seminal decision in *Du Plessis* earlier that year, could not have foreseen this development and may have been a little too anxious to dispel the fear of 'privatised apartheid' by prescribing direct effect. The 1996 Constitution, moreover, also provides a basis for indirect effect.[11]

Secondly, other systems offered a fair amount of guidance as far as the 'radiating' or 'indirect' influence of constitutional values on the private sphere is concerned. Direct effect is, by contrast, a less explored terrain (if not terra incognita). The preference of common law judges for incremental developments may thus have won the day.

Finally, court structures were again a contributing factor. Judges Kentridge, Ackermann and Sachs emphasised in *Du Plessis* that the newly established Constitutional Court should be careful not to interfere in the development of ordinary law.[12] Division of powers considerations come into play at this point. Besides exercising a specialised constitutional jurisdiction and lacking the expertise and experience of the ordinary courts in non-constitutional matters, decisions of the Constitutional Court have a binding effect on all branches of government. This includes the legislature, which may otherwise overturn judicial developments of the law. This special status of the Constitutional Court, under the 1993 Constitution the only court with the power to adjudicate constitutional issues,[13] was an important argument in limiting the influence of constitutional principles on private law. These procedural concerns do not play such a role in other common law systems which do not have the equivalent of a constitutional court.

11 Section 39(2) of the Republic of South Africa Act 1996.

12 1996 (3) SA 850 at pp 883 f (Kentridge), 906 (Ackermann) and 931 f (Sachs).

13 Under s 168(3) of the 1996 Constitution, the Supreme Court of Appeal may decide appeals in *any* matter, though the Constitutional Court remains the court of final instance when it comes to constitutional questions.

(v) Constitutional rights and exceptions to the interpretive obligation

There are, however, major exceptions to the interpretive obligation in relation to constitutional rights. In Canada and the United States, discussed below, the 'state action' requirements in both constitutions seem to preclude even a rights-compatible interpretation of statutes in private sphere disputes. Restrictions also exist in Denmark, France and Ireland.

In Denmark, despite the existence of human rights protection provisions in the Danish Constitution, the courts do not indulge in interpretive approaches to those rights since the protection of constitutional rights is considered to be the responsibility of the political process.

In France, the interpretive obligation in respect of the Constitution of 1958 is weak in relation to the private sphere: the Constitution of the Fifth Republic does not itself include human rights provisions but the 1789 Declaration of the Rights of Man and the Citizen and the Preamble to the 1946 Constitution are treated as sources for 'vertical' human rights protection. The Conseil constitutionnel, to which *projets de loi* (Bills) may be referred before promulgation, does not generally consider the private sphere implications of Bills. This may have to do with the fact that the Conseil performs an abstract review of draft legislation instead of deciding concrete cases (many issues highlighted in this book are, after all, problems which the legislator did not anticipate), and is usually under strong time constraints. The Cour de cassation, the highest civil court which does concern itself with human rights, does not do so by reference to these constitutional sources because of the tradition of not citing case law in its decisions and not referring to the French Constitution, and the effect of a strong public/private law divide in France – the Constitution being viewed as belonging exclusively to the realm of public law. The same inhibitions do not apply, however, in relation to the European Convention (as explained in the section on direct effect, above).

In Ireland, the principal technique for providing private sphere protection for the rights set out explicitly and implicitly (unenumerated rights) in the Constitution and not protected by the ordinary law is recourse to the so-called 'constitutional tort' (discussed above), which gives direct effect to the constitutional right. There is resistance to giving indirect effect to these rights through constitutionally compatible interpretation of legislation, but there is case law in which an interpretive approach has been taken. The Irish European Convention on Human Rights Act 2003 is not as strong as the UK Human Rights Act 1998 in requiring the courts to engage in compatible interpretation.

(b) Indirect effect, interpretation and internationally protected rights

We now turn to the interpretive approach to legislation where international instruments become relevant. An obligation to interpret legislation compatibly with international human rights instruments exists in most of the countries in our study, though where such rights have direct effect the (indirect) interpretive obligation is less significant. Jurisdictions may be divided into those where there are express legislative duties of compatible interpretation of legislation, and those where compatible interpretation is the result of judicial practice, including common law development.

(i) Express duties of ECHR-compatible interpretation: Denmark, England and Wales, and Spain

In Denmark, human rights protection rests on two express legal sources: the Incorporation Act 1991, which incorporated the European Convention into domestic law; and the general constitutional duty of all public authorities, including the courts, to interpret Danish law compatibly with the country's international obligations. The interpretive approach is regarded as meaning that international human rights have 'domestic applicability' – an example of the operation of a 'dualist' system which finds its place close to the monist end of the monist-dualist spectrum.

In England and Wales, under the Human Rights Act 1998, the courts and other public authorities are to interpret domestic legislation 'so far as possible' compatibly with the Convention rights (i.e. most of the substantive articles in the European Convention), regardless of Parliament's intention when passing domestic legislation. If, however, compatible interpretation turns out to be impossible, incompatible domestic legislation prevails, though the relevant minister may use a power to present amending legislation by order to Parliament to remove the incompatibility.

In Ireland, legislation must be interpreted compatibly with international obligations, particularly the European Convention under the European Convention on Human Rights Act 2003.

In Spain, the courts must, according to their interpretation of the Spanish Constitution, interpret constitutional rights compatibly with the international instruments to which Spain is a party, but a right recognised only in a treaty and not set out in the Spanish Constitution is not remediable.

(ii) Judicial practice and duties of international rights-compatible interpretation: France, Germany, and England and Wales

In France, as we have seen, the principal technique for giving private sphere protection to human rights is the *direct* application of the European Convention, but French courts have also used interpretive techniques to give effect to the decisions of the European Court on Human Rights in French law. This is quite similar to the position in Germany. The European Convention, which ranks below the Basic Law, is given indirect effect on the interpretation of both ordinary law and the German Constitution.[14] Decisions of the European Court on Human Rights are given special consideration.[15]

In the United Kingdom, the courts have developed the principle that domestic legislation should be interpreted so as to be compatible with the country's international obligations. The underlying assumption is that Parliament, when it legislates, does not intend to breach the United Kingdom's international obligations. But if legislation cannot be interpreted compatibly with the treaty obligation, the latter will be overridden.

(c) Indirect effect and the developmental approach

An obligation to develop the law compatibly with various domestically recognised human rights provisions and/or the values that underlie them exists in a number of the common law jurisdictions in our study, namely Canada (under the Charter as interpreted by the

---

[14] H. Jarass, *Grundgesetz für die Bundesrepublic Deutschland* (8th edn, 2006), Art 25, no. 10.

[15] BVerfGE 111, 307 at p 319.

courts), England and Wales (under the Human Rights Act), Israel (under the Basic Law), New Zealand (at common law and under the Bill of Rights Act 1990), and South Africa (under the 1993 and 1996 Constitutions). In the United Kingdom, Israel and South Africa, the human rights legislation itself requires the courts in effect so to develop the common law. In others – Canada in our examples – the courts have decided to do so, holding that an obligation to develop the common law is implicit in the Constitution. Here the boundary between rights compatible interpretation and common law development is blurred, since principles of interpretation are themselves often derived from the common law. Thus in Ireland, of the common law jurisdictions covered by our study, there is no express obligation under the European Convention on Human Rights Act 2003 of rights-compatible common law development, but well before that Act came into being the courts had already developed the 'constitutional tort' based on their interpretation of the requirements of the Irish Constitution. However, as noted earlier, they have been reluctant to develop the ordinary law of torts to protect human rights, and they allow 'constitutional tort' claims only where the ordinary law is plainly inadequate. Their presumption is that the ordinary law generally provides appropriate private sphere protection.

This is not so different in some civil law jurisdictions. Constitutional rights contained in the German Basic Law thus operate predominantly in *vertical* relationships between citizens and the state; there is *no* express provision in the Constitution which would require the courts to develop the law in a rights-compatible way; judges are traditionally *not* regarded as oracles of the law; and the notion of indirect *Drittwirkung* will in most cases utilise *existing legislation* as a conduit to interpret the law in the light of constitutional values. The borderline between the interpretation of an existing provision and the development of the law is, however, often extremely fluid; and it is not surprising that the Federal Constitutional Court has in many cases been seen (and criticised) as performing a quasi-legislative role. But even the more recent approaches to the question of *Drittwirkung*, which tend to focus on the duty of the state to protect weaker parties through appropriate legislative intervention in private sphere autonomy, accept the (subsidiary) obligation of the courts to fill by judicial development of the law any gaps left by legislative inactivity.

Developments in New Zealand are different again. Generally, the common law is taken to provide appropriate protection for human rights. As in Germany, the Bill of Rights Act 1990 (or BORA) does not specifically require judges to develop the common law so as to protect rights, but the courts have nevertheless done so in order to fill private sphere protection lacunae in the law. Thus a new tort of unreasonable invasion of privacy has been developed: this is seen by many as a necessary step in order to fulfil New Zealand's obligations under the ICCPR, or because privacy (though not specified in the Bill of Rights Act) is a BORA value which should 'inform' the common law and be given 'appropriate weight'. Courts in New Zealand have also developed a defence of 'reasonable error' in defamation cases in order to provide protection for a media defendant's freedom of expression. Where private rights clash, the law of remedies (e.g., the discretionary award of injunctions) has been developed so as to take account of the defendant's rights and public interests, for instance in the openness of court proceedings. As far as the balancing of rights – e.g., privacy against freedom of speech – is concerned, judges have relied on section 5 of the Bill of Rights Act, which permits only 'reasonable limits' to rights, and on a principle that the common law should not develop so as to infringe rights, which include of course the rights of defendants in private sphere cases. In developing the common law in these ways, courts in New Zealand have engaged in classic common law reasoning, finding some of the vocabulary for development in the BORA but many of the actual values and substantive justifications for development in the common law itself.

3. *'State action' – denial of private sphere protection?*

The United States and Canada are the countries in our study whose legal systems have most strongly resisted explicit recognition of a horizontal effect of, respectively, the Constitutional Amendments and the Charter of Rights. Both require 'state action' as a precondition for human rights protection. The approach of the two countries differs in some respects, but it is remarkable that they appear to be out of line with the other jurisdictions we have considered and, we assume, with many Western democracies. However, all is not as it seems at first sight.

The US Constitution expressly proscribes only 'state action' that breaches constitutional rights. It is noteworthy that American courts, both at federal and state level, have not done much to develop the common law in private situations so as to give what we would regard as *indirect* effect (whether via interpretation or development of the common law) to the rights that are protected in the Constitution or, indeed, in international instruments to which the United States is a party. Save in relation to discrimination and free speech, noted below, they have not been creative in this respect. Why this is so is not entirely clear. It may be that ordinary state legislation (and the common law in each common law state) provides full protection for private sphere rights, so that no issues arise. We may draw a parallel here with the fact that there has been very little litigation on private sphere common law protection of rights in England and Wales (except again in relation to conflicts between rights of privacy and press freedom), or in New Zealand. The position in India, however, provides a sharp contrast, since there the ordinary law has not provided sufficient protection and there has been very considerable judicial creativity in private sphere protection through the development of the common law in that jurisdiction.

Both in the United States and Canada we find complex case law on what amounts to 'state action', and in particular what bodies count as state bodies and what functions or activities fall within the scope of the concept. For reasons of space our focus here is on 'pure' private sphere activity, and in what follows we shall not go into this fascinating field beyond noting the position of the courts, which differs as between the United States and Canada.

(a) The United States

The explanation for the unwillingness to give private sphere protection to human rights as such appears to lie partly in the background against which the American Bill of Rights was adopted, namely the focus on the need to protect citizens against abuse of state power. But this has also been the background to provisions for human rights protection in many other jurisdictions which, as we have seen, do, nonetheless, give some horizontal effect to their domestic human rights provisions. Some of these countries – in our study Denmark, the United Kingdom, France, Greece, Ireland, Spain and Germany – are also parties to the European Convention, which imposes positive obligations to secure the protection of Convention rights in the private sphere, thus stimulating the development of such protection. The United States, not being a party to any comparable international instrument to which enforcement powers of an international court are attached, has not been under the same international pressures to extend rights protection to the private sphere as have many European countries. Another explanation of the absence of horizontal protection of rights lies in the reluctance of the Federal Supreme Court to interfere in the laws of the states.

Part of the explanation of approaches to private sphere protection in the United States, as indeed in most jurisdictions, may lie in the general culture. The United States, essentially a capitalist, free enterprise country, may be influenced by a *laissez faire* liberal approach, which resists imposing limitations on the powers of the economically influential in order to protect the weaker or more vulnerable members of society. This is reflected in the fact that there appears to be relatively little consciousness of or concern about the potential for abuse of private power in that system, and where such concerns do surface, abuses are dealt with by specific legislation (e.g., in labour relations) rather than by resort to the Constitution and private sphere common law development. A sharp contrast may be drawn here, again, with the position at the other end of our spectrum of jurisdictions – India – where the primary concern is with abuses of private power rather than of state power and, interestingly, the phrase 'liability for non-state action' is used to describe the approach, as if to highlight the contrast with the United States.

Yet the 'state action' doctrine often cloaks what to foreign eyes looks very much like private sphere protection is some areas of law. The notion that legislation and common law rules and/or the involvement of a state court in a dispute between private parties constitutes 'state action' is an odd one (though it reappears in procedural guise in Germany, where private parties can raise a constitutional complaint against a final court decision, which is regarded as state action). On this basis all jurisdictions in which there are laws or norms about the protection of rights in the private sphere and which permit judicial private sphere protection are employing a 'state action' approach or filter, even if those jurisdictions claim to be giving horizontal effect to rights. Cases such as *Shelley v Kraemer* (1948) (a restrictive covenant preventing the sale of private property to blacks was held to be a breach of the constitutional equal protection right and 'state action' because enforcement was by the state courts) and *New York Times v Sullivan* (1964) (court enforcement of state libel laws that inhibited free speech contrary to the free speech provision in the Constitution was held to be 'state action' and the court decision was quashed) would be regarded as private sphere cases in most of the jurisdictions which accept some horizontal effect of human rights. In effect both cases give strong horizontal protection to rights. This has been 'direct' in the sense that the Supreme Court has held the decisions of the state courts to be in breach of the Constitution. But such decisions also give 'indirect' effect to the Bill of Rights in that state courts will need to develop the common law in order to remove the incompatibility with the constitutional requirements. As we see in our discussion of other jurisdictions, the rhetoric of the courts or commentators when discussing private sphere protection often fails to accord with the reality as viewed from the more detached – or at least different – perspectives of other jurisdictions.

(b) Canada

Canada is another jurisdiction which adopts a 'state action' (otherwise known in Canada as 'governmental action') doctrine. The approach limits private sphere protection of Charter rights. In Canada, too, there is interesting case law on the extent of governmental action (or, to use the language of the Charter, 'government'), but save in respect of court decisions this falls outside the scope of this project. In the *Dolphin Delivery* case (1961), the Canadian Supreme Court held that since the Charter in terms bound only the legislatures and governments of Canada, it did not directly bind the courts. Here the parallel with the country's southern neighbour is strong. However, in *Hill v Church of Scientology of Toronto and Manning* (1995), a purely private sphere case, the Supreme Court held that the common law should not be applied if a party shows that it is unjustifiably inconsistent with Charter values. The implication is that in such a case the common law should be developed so as not to breach Charter values. The Charter thus does have some, albeit weak, indirect effect in Canada in relation to the development of the common law. This effect is weaker than that in the United States in relation to the decisions of state courts, or in England and Wales or New Zealand, where the courts have been developing the common law compatibly with, respectively, ECHR and international or BORA rights, and have been willing to change the common law quite radically so as to bring it into line with those requirements.

Individuals must respect Canadian Charter rights when acting on the basis of powers conferred by legislation or delegated legislation.

This includes the Civil Code in Quebec (here a similarity with the position in Germany and Greece may be noted, where civil codes also provide a conduit through which constitutional rights are introduced to the private sphere). This provision gives considerable horizontal effect to human rights, but the effect differs as between Quebec (where most powers are conferred by legislation or delegated legislation) and the other – common law – provinces, since much private activity is lawful at common law but the powers exercised are not conferred by legislation. As we have noted, a remedy will be available to a claimant in the private sphere only if the common law is so inconsistent with a Charter right that it can no longer be justified. The horizontal effect of Charter rights in Canada will thus depend on the happenstance whether activity is regulated by the common law or by legislation. Private sphere protection is therefore highly asymmetric in this system.

C. Some general points of comparison

We move now from consideration of the direct and indirect nature of private sphere protection to other cross-cutting general themes that emerge from the jurisdiction-based chapters in this collection.

1. Monist and dualist systems

It is plain from our jurisdiction-based chapters that there is a fairly wide range or spectrum of versions of monist and dualist systems when it comes to human rights protection. The distinction between the monist and dualist approaches to the enforceability or applicability of international treaties in domestic law is not at all clear-cut. The position of countries as to the legal status of international treaties and the extent to which unincorporated international instruments can give rise to rights that will be enforceable in domestic courts would be better represented on a spectrum of monist and dualist *tendencies*, rather than as dichotomous *opposites*.

India, for example, is – or at least claims to be – a dualist system. And yet the courts will give direct effect to human rights provisions in international treaties to which India is a party, and even to some treaties to which it is *not* a party, as long as they are not inconsistent with Indian legislation. In Ireland, also a dualist system, an interpretive approach is adopted; primary legislation and common law will be, respectively, interpreted and applied so as to be compatible with the international obligations of the country. In New Zealand, one reason for the development of the tort of unreasonable invasion of privacy has been the requirements of the ICCPR, but this international instrument is given effect in New Zealand under the Bill of Rights Act 1990, thus piercing what could otherwise form a barrier to private sphere protection in a dualist system. Canada and the United States, on the other hand, appear to be strongly dualist as far as private sphere protection is concerned.

There is also a variety of versions of the monist system in our study. In France, the European Convention is given direct horizontal effect under a system that involves the 'conventionalisation of private law', as required by Article 55 of the French Constitution. In Denmark, also a monist system, international human rights provisions are, by contrast, said to have 'domestic applicability'. This takes the form of the duty of the courts to interpret Danish law compatibly with the international obligations of the country, which is a kind of indirect effect. In Italy, the legislature has to authorise the ratification of treaties, and once ratified they can, if self-executing, be applied directly by the courts. In Spain, again a monist system which claims to give direct effect to the rights guaranteed by the Spanish Constitution, the courts must also interpret constitutional rights compatibly with the international instruments to which Spain is a party. This is a form of 'double' or 'indirect indirect' effect. A right recognised only in a treaty and not in the Spanish Constitution is not remediable unless specific implementing legislation has been passed.

The United States and Canada appear to be strict dualist systems as far as the horizontal effect of constitutional rights is concerned, and there is no reference in the chapter on those jurisdictions to case law on the duties of the courts in relation to international treaties in this field. It should be noted that the track record of the United States in enforcing international treaties within the country – especially in the area of human rights protection – is currently subject to much criticism, and that any indirect effect of such treaties on private relationships would indeed be surprising.

Both in Germany and South Africa, finally, international human rights are taken into account on a regular basis when courts interpret and develop either constitutional or ordinary cases involving human rights issues. The general rules of international law automatically rank as federal law in Germany,[16] but the country is dualist as far as specific international treaties such as the European Convention on Human Rights are concerned. This treaty, too, has been incorporated by federal law[17] and is used to interpret both the Basic Law (which remains superior in status) and ordinary law. The situation in South Africa is different as any court, tribunal and legal forum is under an express constitutional duty to consider international law when interpreting the 1996 Bill of Rights.[18]

2. *Conceptualisations of private sphere protection*

Where there is private sphere protection for human rights in a legal system, it is conceptualised in a range of ways. In many of the jurisdictions in this study it is referred to as 'horizontal effect' (which may be direct or indirect), a term borrowed from European Union law, where the phrase refers to the effect of Community provisions between private parties. This term is thus commonly used by the courts and academic commentators in Denmark, England and Wales, Greece, Ireland and Spain, but also in New Zealand and South Africa.

In France, the term 'conventionalisation' is also found, which emphasises the fact that the private sphere effect derives from the European Convention on Human Rights rather than from the French Constitution of 1958.

In Germany and Italy, the terms used are *mittelbare* (indirect) or *unmittelbare* (direct) *Drittwirking* (which may be rendered into English as 'third party effect'). Another image employed by the German Federal Constitutional Court is that of human rights protection 'radiating' into all other parts of the legal system (so-called *Ausstrahlungswirkung*). In Greece, *Drittwirkung* is also used, but the term is criticised for categorising those claiming private sphere protection as 'third parties' and thus not as citizens and parties to a normal private dispute within the country. The terms 'horizontal' or 'interpersonal' effect are usually preferred. This is different in

16 See Article 25 of the Basic Law.

17 This has been confirmed by several decisions of the Federal Constitutional Court; see, e.g., BVerfGE 74, 358 (at p 370), 80, 106 (at p 115) and 111, 307 (at p 317/318).

18 Section 39(1)(b) of the Republic of South Africa Constitution Act 1996.

South Africa, where *Drittwirkung* is used fairly frequently, revealing both the influence of German legal doctrine on constitutional developments after 1992/1993 and the close linguistic relationship between Afrikaans, the compound language of the country's white minority, and German.

In India, the favoured expression is 'liability for non-state action' – a stark contrast with the requirement for 'state action' found in the United States.

Ireland refers to the 'constitutional tort' while the same phenomenon is known as the 'constitutionalisation of private law' in Israel (an expression also used by some authors to describe the influence of the Basic Law on private law in Germany).

This plethora of slightly nuanced vocabulary seems to us more a question of local preference than an expression of fundamental differences; in many cases, the use of one or the other term might even have been influenced by legal translation as the idea of constitutional protection against the activities of private parties spread around the globe. One particular facet of the picture, however, deserves emphasis. '*Drittwirkung*' and 'horizontal effect' indicate to us in principle a wider and more fundamental approach to the influence of constitutional values on other parts of a legal system (an idea also captured by the phrases 'constitutionalisation of private law' or 'radiating effect of human rights'), while notions such as 'liability for non-state action' or 'constitutional tort' seem to place more emphasis on the delictual aspect of the phenomenon – the infringement of constitutionally protected interests by a private tortfeasor and the award of financial compensation to an equally private victim. That said, it has also become quite clear in the course of this study that a great number of cases in all systems do, in fact, involve tortious acts (particularly in the area of journalism).

3. *Attitudes to the courts and their jurisdiction in private sphere cases*

In most of our jurisdictions, there is no particular problem about which courts have jurisdiction to deal with cases involving allegations of a breach of human rights in the private sphere. Particularly in systems with a specialised form of constitutional review, however, problems have arisen.

In common law countries, the ordinary courts will generally have jurisdiction to deal with such cases. In private sphere human rights cases in the United Kingdom, all courts and tribunals have jurisdiction to deal with points raised with respect to the Human Rights Act 1998 in cases before them, although only courts starting from the level of the High Court may make formal declarations of incompatibility of English statutory provisions with European Convention rights. In South Africa, similarly, every court, tribunal or forum must promote the spirit, purport and objects of the 1996 Bill of Rights when interpreting any legislation, and when developing the common law or customary law. The situation is different from the United Kingdom, however, as far as unconstitutional *legislation* is concerned. When deciding a matter within its power, a South African court must thus declare that any law or conduct that is inconsistent with the 1996 Constitution is invalid to the extent of its inconsistency. The final verdict concerning an Act of Parliament or a provincial Act is then left to the Constitutional Court, which must confirm any order of invalidity made by the Supreme Court of Appeal, a High Court, or a court of similar status, before that order has any force. The Constitutional Court has, however, indicated that the development of common law and customary law should preferably remain in the hands of the Supreme Court, and at least some judges felt that a direct effect of constitutional rights could jeopardise this goal. German experience with indirect effect indicates that the number of cases which are made subject to constitutional scrutiny may indeed be lower, maintaining to some extent the balance between legislator and Constitutional Court in this area of the law. In India, all of the ordinary courts have power to entertain claims for breach of constitutional or international human rights that fall within their jurisdiction. In Ireland, finally, the ordinary courts have jurisdiction whether a claim is based on the ordinary law as developed to take account of human rights or on a 'constitutional tort'.

In civil law countries, too, the jurisdictional position is relatively simple, unless a challenge is made to a constitutional provision or legislation. The French civil and criminal courts may deal with points concerning the European Convention on Human Rights in the course of litigation. In civil litigation, only the Cour de cassation may set aside French legislation that is incompatible with Convention rights. All Spanish courts may deal with direct horizontal effect issues in cases within their jurisdiction, and the Spanish Constitutional Court has a supervisory jurisdiction where it is alleged that a lower court has failed to protect human rights in a case, including a private sphere one. In Greece, the civil courts deal with horizontal effect cases as they develop the application of the Greek Civil Code. In Italy, too, the civil courts may deal with these issues, though if a question arises as to the constitutionality of a law that might infringe the Italian Constitution only the Constitutional Court may determine the issue. The only civil law jurisdiction covered by our study in which procedural questions seem to have caused major discussions is thus Germany. The reason for this lies in the specialised court structure of the system rather than in division of powers concerns. Germany (in contrast to South Africa) relies on separate courts for administrative, social, tax, labour, criminal, and ordinary private law cases. Five federal courts exercise final jurisdiction over these matters unless cases involve decisive questions of a constitutional nature. While all courts are bound by the Basic Law and the theory of *Drittwirkung*, final jurisdiction in *constitutional* matters is exercised by the Federal Constitutional Court. The final judgment of any other German court is thereby regarded as state action, which will allow the losing party to challenge the decision on constitutional grounds if it violates the human rights enshrined in the Basic Law. A second route to the *Bundesverfassungsgericht* – involving the review of legislation – is a preliminary reference from the lower court. This procedural structure has two consequences. The Federal Constitutional Court is, first, fairly accessible to private parties (the Court has dealt with approximately 140,000 individual constitutional complaints since its creation, though usually through screening panels composed of three judges). More importantly, its judgments have, second, often influenced the development of non-constitutional law – despite the fact that the Court's jurisdiction is, in theory, limited to the constitutional aspect of a case. Criticism has focused on the latter phenomenon; many academic commentators feel that the specialised courts are in a better position to interpret and develop, in particular, private law.

4. Reference to the 'values' underlying human rights provisions

We have seen that the values underlying human rights provisions – particularly dignity, equality and autonomy – are often expressed in national constitutions. The Constitutions of India and Ireland thus contain rights to equality; the German, Indian and Italian

Constitutions and the Israeli Basic Laws include rights to dignity; and the Greek Constitution contains a reference to the principle of human dignity. In other jurisdictions, these values are articulated in other legislation or case law rather than explicitly in constitutional documents. Thus in the United Kingdom and Ireland, the courts have emphasised the importance of dignity and autonomy; in France, dignity is protected by the Code Civil.

These values, where they are recognised to form part of the legal system, help to legitimise and guide the courts in their development or application of the law in a way that promotes and protects private sphere protection. Given that this judicial function may well be exercised in controversial situations and that the judicial creativity apparent in most jurisdictions where private sphere protection is available does not, in any event, fit easily alongside the separation of powers principle, legitimising devices and rhetoric such as reference to 'widely respected' values can provide a lubricant capable of reducing at least some of the tensions which many cases will produce between the courts, the legislator, and the executive.

5. *Rationales and reasons for private sphere protection*

India is exceptional in the jurisdictions considered in this collection, since private sphere protection is consistent with the historical development of Indian law and India's social experience (except for the period of British rule), where threats to the rights and dignity of individuals have emanated from powerful *private* bodies rather than the state. In other jurisdictions, too, a focus on inequalities of power and the vulnerability of individuals in inferior positions has been influential in the development of private sphere protection in a number of private relationships. This has been a factor in England and Wales, France, Israel, and Germany as well as in India. It has been considered in some detail in academic literature in Greece, where the lacunae that such an approach occasionally leaves in the protection of the private sphere – such as the failure to provide constitutional safeguards in equal relationships – has led to the rejection of power inequalities as the justification for private sphere protection. Greek courts have instead approached the matter in a more pragmatic and non-doctrinaire way.

The Bill of Rights in the US Constitution was introduced for the protection of citizen against state action, which is specified in the constitutional text. Generally, the creation of constitutional rights protection in most of our jurisdictions initially followed this model, having been introduced with the threats posed by state bodies in mind. This was particularly the case with the European Convention on Human Rights, introduced in the aftermath of the Nazi experience in Europe, and (for obvious reasons) the German Basic Law of 1949.

Hence private sphere protection, where it has developed, has done so for a variety of reasons: awareness of the increasing imbalances of power between many private individuals and powerful bodies, and the potential for abuse of such private power; in response to 'state responsibility' and the 'positive obligations' identified both by the European Court of Human Rights in Strasbourg in countries which are parties to the European Convention (which has itself resulted in part from increased private power) and the European Court of Justice for the Member States of the EU; and partly as cultural tolerance towards the abuse of rights by private parties (i.e. in the family context) has waned in the societies under review. This latter factor may reflect changing and interrelated political, social and economic realities – notably the democratisation of political systems, giving voices and influence to individuals whose rights and liberties may be abused by other private parties.

The growth of private sphere protection suggests a change in the nature of the liberal and other theories that underlie human rights protection. In Ireland, for instance, natural law theory has given way to social liberal theory. Economic liberal theory emphasises the importance of the market and capitalism, and resists regulation; the dominance of this approach in the United States and Canada, at least at the time that the US Bill of Rights and the Canadian Charter of Rights were introduced, may have been a factor in the reluctance of those jurisdictions to embrace private sphere human rights protection. Social liberal theory, by contrast, emphasises the importance of freedom and rights of all – both the powerful and the vulnerable – and seeks to strike a balance between them when rights conflict; this approach may be implicit, for instance, in the jurisprudence of the European Court on Human Rights, and, through the influence of the European Convention, in the case law of other European countries. The jurisprudence of the European Court of Justice, too, seems to have been based in social liberal theory. The importance of rights as social values is, finally, expressly recognised in Israeli case law.

6. Objections to and concerns about private sphere protection

Of the jurisdictions covered by our study, only India and France appear to have wholeheartedly embraced direct horizontal effect of, respectively, constitutional and European Convention rights. In some jurisdictions, direct horizontal effect – if it exists – is of very limited application or subject to a range of exceptions and/or modifications (as in Greece and Ireland). The South African Constitution of 1996 offers both direct and indirect effect, though the latter has prevailed in practice. In the rest of the countries represented in this study, private sphere effect is indirect.

Beside arguments arising from the specific constitutional language of the various national constitutions involved, a range of more material concerns about giving full direct horizontal effect to human rights in the private sphere emerges from our study. These include:

1. concerns about legal uncertainty in Denmark;
2. attachment to the public-private law divide, the limited role of the *Conseil constitutionnel*, cultural concerns about a *gouvernement des juges*, and the fear of undermining the stability and legal certainty in contract law in France;
3. fear of the overarching jurisdiction of a constitutional court, combined with concerns about legal certainty and the protection of private autonomy, both in Germany and South Africa;
4. concerns about the separation of powers, i.e. the need to avoid the 'law creative power' of judges or limitations on the power of the legislator to regulate interpersonal relations, in Greece;
5. concerns about the implications of developing a new 'constitutional' tort rather than the ordinary law of tort in India, since doing the former would raise many new problems, i.e. in the development of appropriate remedies;
6. concerns about legal certainty and unresolved problems about the balancing of conflicting rights in Ireland;
7. concerns about balancing conflicting rights in New Zealand, as only 'reasonable limits' may be placed on private sphere rights; and
8. a reluctance to go beyond imposing negative duties on private parties in Spain (rights under international instruments are only protected if they are also constitutionally protected).

It is particularly notable that some of these reasons for limiting private sphere protection are diametrically opposed to one another. The concern that the legislator's power should *not* be restricted in Greece is thus at odds with the aim to do just that in India, and the fairly high readiness of courts in Canada, England and Wales, Greece, India, Israel, Italy, New Zealand, Germany or South Africa to develop the rules of ordinary private law in the light of constitutional values contrasts with the strong resistance to similar trends in France, where objections to a *gouvernement des juges* has historical roots (which oddly do not seem to apply if judges are developing the law in line with the European Convention simply because it is an international treaty which the country has entered into). In Ireland it is feared that judicial development of the constitutional tort might undermine ordinary tort law.

7. Effectiveness of private sphere protection

This study has been largely concerned with *legal* approach to the protection of human rights in the private sphere. It does not, of course, follow from the fact that a country's laws provide for the protection of rights, if this is indeed the case, that those rights will *in practice* be respected, and that interferences with them will actually be remedied. The evolution of the 'state responsibility' and 'positive obligation' doctrines by the European Court of Human Rights, motivated by the desire to achieve the *practical* and *effective* protection of human rights, acknowledges this. The actual degree of protection achieved by the various legal instruments will thus depend upon matters such as:

1. whether constitutional human rights provisions require implementing legislation in a particular legal system, as is the case in Denmark, and (if so) whether such legislation has been passed;
2. the efficiency of policing and criminal justice systems, which has been a concern of the European Court of Human Rights in a number of cases;
3. access to courts where claimants themselves wish to seek civil redress, which may be limited by jurisdictional rules (as in Spain, where only the Constitutional Court may invalidate a law that is contrary to the Spanish Constitution), or by the lack of education and financial resources of potential claimants (a problem dealt with in India by very liberal Public Interest Litigation rules);

4. the vulnerability of claimants to persecution by defendants;
5. the availability of legal assistance; and
6. adjectival law such as procedural rules, rules of evidence, and appropriate remedies (in England and Wales, for instance, no court may invalidate a statutory provision that is incompatible with the Human Rights Act).

The European Court of Human Rights has been exerting considerable pressure on states who are parties to the European Convention on Human Rights to secure effectiveness in these matters. In some countries, pressure also emanates from non-governmental organisations (such as Liberty in England and Wales), political parties, or public-spirited practitioners (as is frequently the case in India).

It is also worthwhile noting that remedies for breach of rights in the private sphere go much further in India than in most other jurisdictions covered by this study. To secure the effective protection of constitutional rights, the Indian Supreme Court may thus (and does) make recommendations and give directions to both the private defendant and the government as to how obligations to promote human rights should be fulfilled in practice; these rulings are binding until appropriate legislation is passed to give effect to them.

8. *Balancing conflicting rights – proportionality and 'reasonable limits'*

In some jurisdictions, there is not much in the way of express constitutional or legislative provision for, or case law dealing explicitly with, the balancing of competing constitutional rights and interests or conflicts between private rights and public interests in private sphere cases, despite the fact that such balancing is necessary in all legal systems that give any horizontal effect to rights. The jurisdictions in our study tackle these problems in various ways, as outlined below.

(a) The restriction of private sphere protection

The difficulties resulting from a conflict of constitutionally protected rights are largely avoided in the United States and Canada by the 'state action' doctrine, which places substantial restrictions on the level of protection offered in horizontal situations. In Ireland, where provision is made for direct horizontal effect through the 'constitutional tort', the balancing of competing private rights is acknowledged to be a potentially difficult issue, and the need for it has been reduced by the trend in recent years to restrict the availability of the mechanism to instances where the ordinary law (in particular contract and tort) does not resolve the issues. Problems of balancing rights have arisen in Ireland mainly in relation to the conflicting rights of an unborn child and its mother rather than the balancing of private rights and public interests.

(b) The rejection of private sphere claims where the balancing exercise would have negative effects for legal certainty

In Denmark, a great deal of attention has been paid to the problem of balancing interests, the main concerns being about legal certainty, unanticipated limitations of the rights of the defendant for the sake of private sphere protection of the claimant, and practical difficulties in distinguishing between individual and societal interests and between horizontal and vertical effect. These concerns have been reflected in the reliance on judicial practice and incremental development of indirect horizontal protection. The courts may, for instance, not recognise the need for a balancing process at all (as, for example, between the right of a journalist not to disclose sources and an alleged public interest in the detection of crime – in a case on that point, the journalist was held not to be obliged to disclose sources). Conflicts appear to be resolved on a case-by-case basis.

(c) Developing a proportionality test

In England and Wales, France, Greece, Germany and South Africa, the balancing process used to resolve conflicting private rights is acknowledged to involve a proportionality analysis.

In England and Wales, there is as yet little case law on horizontal effect, and the balancing of competing rights has not attracted much attention from the courts save in cases where privacy rights of individuals conflict with the rights of the Press. But the test is recognised to be one of proportionality, in which public interests such as the importance of a free press for democracy may also be taken into account. The balance is achieved on a case by case basis, with matters of public interest and private health being put in the scales, and generally decided in favour of the individual whose privacy has been invaded. In Israel, by contrast, in cases involving a clash between reputation (an aspect of privacy) and freedom of the press, the balance is likely to come down in favour of the press for democratic reasons. In France, two proportionality tests have been developed, depending on whether the issue at hand concerns a positive obligation of the state to protect the right in question or the direct effect of the European Convention in French law. In Greece, too, it is widely acknowledged that the balancing of constitutional rights in private sphere cases brought under the Greek Civil Code involves a proportionality analysis. In some cases, the necessary balance may have to be struck between conflicting private rights, but it may also be between private law norms and constitutional principles (which can include matters of public policy) where the two conflict. It is also recognised that some rights have both civil (individual) and social dimensions; this is, for example, true for the right to respect for the natural and cultural environment.

In Israel, although the term proportionality is not used, it is recognised that the balancing of human rights against collective interests in the public sphere is significantly different from the balancing exercise in the private sphere (where one human right is often balanced against another human right). This accounts for the preference in Israel for the judicial development of indirect horizontal affect rather than giving direct effect to human rights, whether expressed in the Basic Laws or recognised by the courts. Ordinary tort law, developed over many years, is considered to have achieved an appropriate and satisfactory balance between private rights and social interests, giving indirect effect to rights without the need for direct effect. Since the passage of the two Basic Laws of 1992, the values underlying rights are put into the scales to help strike the necessary balance in tort cases. The constitutionalisation of the right to dignity has thus increased the relative weight attached to this right in the balancing process and, as a result, different emanations of this right (such as autonomy) have gained stronger and even novel forms of protection in recent years. The impact on the balancing process is most significant in the area of negligence law, where it determines whether a given activity is negligent and whether a duty of care should be recognised. But if, in a situation of competing rights, both sides rely on basic law values such as dignity, the tort law balance will be the same as it would have been before 1992.

In New Zealand, rights under the Bill of Rights Act are subject to 'reasonable limits prescribed by law' that are 'demonstrably justified in a free and democratic society'. This version of proportionality in fact mirrors the approach commonly adopted in common law reasoning. It has been particularly important in the development of a new common law tort of invasion of privacy and involves giving 'appropriate weight' to each conflicting right. It does not, however, give further guidance as to what weight is actually to be considered appropriate.

South Africa and Germany, finally, apply more or less the same proportionality analysis in both 'vertical' and 'horizontal' disputes. When applying a provision of the 1996 Bill of Rights to a natural or juristic person, courts in South Africa may thus develop rules of the common law to limit a right subject to the principles set out in the general limitation clause.[19] Limitations must be reasonable and justifiable in an open and democratic society based on human dignity, equality and freedom, and take into account, beside all other relevant factors, the nature of the right, the importance of the limitation, the nature and extent of the limitation, the relation between the limitation and its purpose, and any less restrictive means to achieve the purpose. Very similar considerations influence the balancing process in Germany, where the principle of proportionality (*Verhältnismäßigkeit*) is regarded as a (substantive) part of the rule of law. Some concerns have, however, been voiced in regard to the application of the same proportionality analysis in both vertical state–citizen disputes and horizontal conflicts between private parties. This critique is valid to the extent that these relationships are different simply because the state, itself, is not able to invoke human rights considerations (here, the public interest comes into play instead), whereas both private parties can. The differences do not, however, strike us as crucial. In many cases, legislation tested by the Federal Constitutional Court involves the balancing not only of human rights and public interests; opposing constitutional rights will very often also play a role, and the question then is whether the legislative solution indeed represents an appropriate compromise with regard to the competing private interests. Public interests, such as the existence of a free press in privacy cases, will, on the other hand, also play a considerable role in seemingly purely 'private'

[19] Section 36 of the Republic of South Africa Constitution Act 1996.

disputes. The borderline between the two cannot be clearly drawn, and a case by case approach to the balancing exercise – as taken by the German courts over the decades – seems quite appropriate. A gradual shift in the justification for constitutional intervention in private relationships (from the rather nebulous notion of an overarching 'objective system of values' to the identification of specific state duties to protect particularly vulnerable private parties) may, however, lead to a more restrictive application of the test in the future. On the upside, this could foster legal certainty.

(d) Pragmatic approaches

In other countries, balancing issues arise but tend to be resolved on a case by case basis rather than resorting to any wider theory or explicit test. In Greece, private sphere protection has thus been developed by judicial *praxis* in a pragmatic way aimed at achieving the outcomes required by the revised Article 25 of the Greek Constitution. In India, judges balancing the privacy right of an HIV-positive bridegroom against his bride's right to information (in support of her autonomy) came out in favour of the latter; the bride's right to a healthy life and public interests in marriage and morality prevailed.

9. Examples and case studies in private sphere protection

It would be inappropriate to generalise too much from the examples and case studies in the jurisdictions covered by our study. Our contributors have selected just a few from what may be large numbers of areas of law in a jurisdiction in which private sphere protection is given. The examples all illustrate situations in which allegations of a breach of constitutional rights in the private sphere were made, and/or where the courts had to balance competing private rights or interests, or conflicts between private rights or interests and public interests. The fact that in some jurisdictions particular conflicts have been conceptualised as raising private sphere rights protection whereas in other jurisdictions such an approach would seem out of place serves to bring out how our perceptions of these issues tend to be coloured by a large number of preconceptions. In Denmark, for example, issues involving the compellability of witnesses raise private sphere protection issues which, at first sight, seem (to us at least) rather anomalous. In Canada, problems concerning the assurance of fair trials in criminal cases by the banning of pre-trial broadcasts are regarded as raising 'state action' issues requiring the balancing of rights to free speech against the importance of fair trials.

Many jurisdictions recognise that the protection of constitutional rights serves public or societal interests and promotes societal values, as well as the interests of the individuals who may claim them. Private sphere protection was thus required in Greece under the 2001 revision of the Greek Constitution, and this is also taken to represent a decision about where the public interest lies. In India, the transformative potential of rights if extended to the private sphere is considered an important justification for them (the protection of women against rape and exploitation thus promotes a public interest in equality, and freedom of the Press safeguards democratic debate and accountability). The following sections draw on some of the examples provided by the jurisdiction-based chapters of our study.

(a) Differences in private power

The case law of countries where imbalances of private power have formed part of the rationale for private sphere protection illustrates the range of relationships that have attracted attention from the courts, and how they may be resolved:

1. The right against self-incrimination of board members of a bankrupt company is fundamental and may prevail over the debtors' property rights (Denmark).
2. An employer's management rights do not entitle him or her to dictate where an employee shall live with his family (France).
3. A landlord who did not know of his tenant's religious objection to using digital keys is not acting in breach of the tenant's right to practise his or her religion (France).
4. A landlord must tolerate the use of television antennae by foreign tenants who have no other way of receiving media coverage from the home country (Germany).
5. A child's right to know who his biological father is forms part of the right to personality and prevails over the private law provision that the child is presumed to be the offspring of his mother's husband (Greece).

6. A bridegroom's right to privacy is subject to his bride's right to know if he is HIV-positive for the protection of her health (India).
7. Protection of 'untouchables' does not involve unlawful interference with freedom of religion (India).
8. A strike to force the dismissal of female employees breaches their right to earn a livelihood (Ireland).
9. A patient's right to information forms part of the right to dignity and may give rise to an award of damages against a doctor (Israel).
10. The freedom of religion of Catholic church authorities entitles them to approve or not approve the appointment of teachers or their dismissal at private colleges despite the interference with individual freedom that this involves (Italy).
11. Members of ideologically oriented associations are free to withdraw from these despite internal rules to the contrary (Italy).
12. Employees may enforce the constitutional right to a weekly day of rest and annual paid holidays against private employers (Italy).
13. Employers must protect their employees from bullying ('mobbing') and compensate them by virtue of their constitutional right to dignity (Italy).
14. The state is under a positive obligation to ensure that a parent is not deprived of contact with children by the other parent (Germany).
15. The personal securities which banks demand from their customers or third parties must respect the principle of personal autonomy (Germany).

Where relationships are at issue, they have been based on *contract*, as in many employment, landlord–tenant, and membership (notably trade union) situations, *consent* (as in marriage cases and cases concerning consensual non-marital relationships, whether same sex or heterosexual), or *status*, as in cases of the European Court of Human Rights involving the relationship between children, parents and other relatives. As we have noted above, concerns about imbalances of power in such relationships have been made explicit by the courts in England and Wales, France and Israel. The rationales for protection within relationships are, however, not always put in terms of power imbalance. In Greece, India, Ireland and Spain, there is thus case law protecting the rights of employees with no particular emphasis on the inequality between the parties; the same is true in English and French cases involving the landlord and tenant relationship.

(b) Arm's-length rights infringements

Situations where private sphere protection for rights is sought are, of course, not all based on contractual, consensual or status-based relationships. In Greece, in academic debates before the revision of the Greek Constitution confirming private sphere protection, the anomalies that would be produced by limiting private sphere protection to unequal relationships were recognised and formed part of the background for the rejection of such a criterion as definitive.

Cases – and there have been many – where the allegation is that members of the press have invaded the privacy of the claimant commonly do not involve prior relationships (a factor which has influenced the development of the law of confidentiality in England and Wales so that the, earlier, equitable requirement of a relationship on which a duty of confidentiality could be based has been dropped). Cases on freedom of speech may raise issues about the right to silence and protection of another individual's freedom from self-incrimination. The Danish chapter also gives a number of examples of how the rights of one party to property may clash with another party's freedom from self-incrimination, of freedom of speech outside prior relationships, of how one person's right to respect for family life may collide with another person's right to a fair trial, and of how rights to property may clash with freedom of religion, or freedom of speech with freedom of conscience. The balance in such cases will normally be highly dependent on the circumstances of each case (unless a 'fundamental' right is involved that cannot be 'trumped' by a competing right – as with the right against self-incrimination).

The position in respect of non-relational private sphere protection can be illustrated by the following examples:

1. A witness's right against self-incrimination is a fundamental right and prevails over the defendant's right to a fair trial (Denmark).
2. Peaceful demonstrators should not be subject to violent anti-protest (European Court of Human Rights).

3. Commercial property is not covered by the right to a family home (France).
4. The right to respect for one's cultural and social environment may prevail over the right to free speech (Greece).
5. Environmental pollution may be a threat to the right to life (India).
6. Prohibition of discrimination against non-adherents is not a breach of religious rights (India).
7. Unfair proselytising may be in breach of freedom of conscience (India).
8. Pre-contractual discrimination may be a breach of the right to dignity (Israel).
9. Sexual harassment and discrimination are breaches of the right to dignity (Israel).
10. The constitutional right to good health gives rise to awards of compensation for interference with that right which are not formerly provided for under statutory legislation (Italy).
11. Owners of a private shopping centre must permit political campaigners to distribute leaflets in the common areas (Italy).
12. Unreasonable invasion of privacy is a tort as required by the ICCPR and the Bill of Rights Act (New Zealand).
13. 'Reasonable error' is a defence in defamation as a value under the Bill of Rights Act (New Zealand).

D. Concluding observations

The chapters in Part II of this volume have each summarised some of the historical, constitutional, political, theoretical and international backgrounds against which the law relating to the protection of human rights in the private sphere has developed. Our understanding of this issue can be enhanced if viewed from these perspectives.

In some countries there may be a social preference for upholding the position of those in authority in relationships such as employment and marriage, and concern to protect the operation of the market, perhaps coupled with a cultural lack of concern about or awareness of the possibilities that private bodies have to abuse human rights. In such countries, constitutional law and political theory will be pitted strongly against private sphere protection. The United States and Canada stand out in this respect. In both systems, the extension of human rights protection to the private sphere is hampered by the 'state action' doctrine and apparent broad judicial support for it, as well, of course, as being proscribed by the terms of the constitutional arrangements.

In India, which seems to lie at the other end of the international spectrum when it comes to the protection of constitutional rights in the private sphere, history is taken to show that serious threats are posed to individual rights and interests by powerful private bodies, and there is a culture (at least in the courts and parts of the legal profession) in favour of the development of private sphere protection as a natural step which is not seen as raising difficulties about authority in society or the economy. Abuse of rights by private parties is seen, in Indian legal circles at least, as a reflection on the state, implying either connivance at abuse or culpable failure to protect the vulnerable.

In between these two extremes a range of doctrines and devices have been adopted by the courts to provide at least some private sphere protection. State duties to protect weaker parties in private disputes are clearly the most important justification.

In only a few of these jurisdictions (South Africa, Greece and, to a very limited extent, Germany) have the national constitutions expressly provided for private sphere protection. The South African Consititution of 1996 is particularly interesting in this respect, as it expressly opens the way for both direct and indirect effect; legal practice has, however, preferred the indirect route developed under the previous Constitution of 1993.

The next nearest express private sphere provisions not contained in written Constitutions are, first, the provision in section 6 of the United Kingdom Human Rights Act 1998 that it is unlawful for public authorities, including the courts, to act incompatibly with Convention rights, thus authorising the courts to develop the common law so far as they feel able to do so in order to protect those rights in the private sphere; and, secondly, the requirement in section 3 of the same Act that legislation should be interpreted, so far as is practicable, compatibly with Convention rights. In Denmark, the Incorporation Act of 1991 requires public bodies to interpret Danish law compatibly with *international* obligations (which generally do require states to provide private as well as public sphere protection). This provision in the Danish Act is a rough parallel to the section 3 of the Human Rights Act in the United Kingdom, and it has enabled the Danish courts to develop private sphere protection despite the fact that the Danish Constitution, itself, is not regarded as creating judicially enforceable rights.

The development of private sphere protection has lain largely in the hands of the judges – both in the national courts of the countries covered by our study and the European Court of Justice and the European Court of Human Rights. With the exception of Greece and India, in each of those jurisdictions the starting point has broadly been that protection is primarily required against state activity (this is also true for South Africa) – and 'state' may be quite widely interpreted – but the courts have responded to claims about private sphere abuse by adopting interpretive principles when referring to their national constitutions, fundamental laws or international instruments. In states that are parties to the European Convention on Human Rights, the jurisprudence of the Strasbourg court has provided justifications and thus legitimacy for the judicial development of private sphere protection, and guidance as to the form it should take. This jurisprudence may provide a technique for the courts to circumvent the provisions in their constitutions or in the prevailing constitutional orthodoxy against judicial law-making as being contrary to the separation of powers and democratic principles.

In some jurisdictions, the courts have found ways round constitutional obstacles to the extension of protection into the private sphere, as in France, where the source of such rights is the European Convention rather than the French Constitution of 1958. In others, the national constitution itself has been broadly interpreted so as to permit the extension of private sphere protection by the courts. Constitutional interpretation may produce direct effect, as it has – to varying extents – in India, Ireland, Israel, Italy and Spain. Or it may produce indirect effect of various kinds, as in Denmark, France, Greece, India, Ireland, Israel, Italy, Spain, Germany and South Africa. The constitutional text may be taken to justify creative rights-compatible development of the ordinary law, as in some common law jurisdictions – here Canada, England and Wales, Israel, South Africa and New Zealand feature prominently in our study, with the United States being a notable exception – and in Germany and Greece.

All jurisdictions in our study except the United States and Canada turn out to have strong similarities as far as the effects and outcomes are concerned in areas in which there has been litigation. As pointed out earlier in this chapter, our impression is that systems are converging towards forms of indirect effect, which seem to form a large centre ground; even if a more direct route is chosen, as in Ireland ('constitutional tort') or – for a limited period of time – by the German Federal Labour Court, it will tend to be limited in its scope and practical effect. It is worth noting at this point, however, that in some of our jurisdictions there seems to have been relatively little case law on private sphere protection. This does not come as a surprise, bearing in mind the effect that human rights thinking has had on legislative activity in most countries around the world. In most systems, 'rights' enjoy explicit though not 'constitutional' private sphere legislative protection – examples are, for instance, the fairly extensive requirements for non-discrimination established by European Union law or domestic legislation concerning employment, health and safety at work, family relationships, conflicts between landlord and tenant, or trade union law (to take the subject areas of many of the examples and case studies presented in the essays in Part II). The principal source of human rights protection in the private sphere may thus well be the ordinary legislator – regardless of specific obligations which national constitutions may or may not impose. This prompts two further observations. First, ordinary legislation may be the more effective mechanism to provide private sphere human rights protection in practice. This was recently acknowledged by the German legislator in an explanatory memorandum to newly introduced anti-discrimination laws in the wake of European Union obligations. Indirect effect of the equality clause in the Basic Law, so the verdict went, had in decades of legal practice not proven an adequate tool to safeguard individuals in the private sphere; more immediate instruments are needed. Second, we may well be looking at an 'interim' phase in the development of this topic. The past 60 years since the end of the Second World War have brought significant changes in human rights thinking, which are starting to affect ever wider areas of the law. As the private law of most systems increasingly absorbs these ideas, the number of cases which require recourse to a set of higher (quasi)constitutional rules and values will inevitably decrease. The United States and Canada remain special cases in this respect. It was not within the scope of the chapter on these two systems to indicate whether the private sphere 'rights' which are protected as '(quasi) constitutional rights' in other jurisdictions are protected by ordinary legislation in those countries. To the extent that they are so protected in the United States and Canada, this may reflect a cultural preference not to use constitutional law for such purposes and to defer on these matters to the states and provinces of which the two federations are formed. Similar outcomes may be achieved there without conceptualising measures as providing private sphere protection – which would be yet another interesting cultural difference.

So while our study brings out strong common features between most of our jurisdictions and some measure of contrast between the United States and Canada as against the other countries covered, it also illuminates the very striking differences in history, political tradition and theory, economic development, social relationships, and legal reasoning. This is indeed a very rich tapestry.

Country by Country Chart

Canada

Written Constitution 1982. Human rights are set out in the Charter of Rights and Freedoms 1982. Dualist system. All provinces are common law based except Quebec (civil law system). At federal level the law is based on the Constitution and legislation plus case law.

Private sphere effect?

- **The text of the Constitution is explicit that it is binding only on government and legislatures. This 'governmental action' doctrine resembles in some respects the US 'state action' doctrine**. This does not normally include the courts, though some case law and dicta suggest that the fact that a court decides a private or criminal matter involves state action.
- **The common law should be developed in line with Charter values if it is inconsistent with them**. Thus there is some **indirect horizontal effect in the common law** but in principle private sphere protection should be left to the legislatures and an alternative tort system should not be developed.

- **If state responsibilities have been delegated to or assumed by private bodies**, or if there **was state involvement** in private action, Charter rights will apply.
- If **private sphere activity is regulated by statute**, e.g. where the common law has been codified, or there **statutory authority** for or approval of infringements, **Charter rights apply**.
- **In Quebec the civil code is statutory**, the Charter applies, and so there is **stronger private sphere protection** in that province than elsewhere.

Examples from case law

- **Freedom of speech** – a trade union engaging in secondary picketing of a private company that was unlawful at common law claimed a right to freedom of speech under the Charter. Held that there being no governmental action based in the common law the free speech guarantee was not breached. An injunction against the union was granted (*Dolphin Delivery*).
- **Freedom of speech** – court ban on broadcasting of fictional material that might prejudice a trial held not to be in line with the need to develop the common law in line with the Charter values. Bans only to be made where necessary to prevent substantial risk to a fair trial (*Dagenais case*).
- Burden is on the claimant to show that the **common law** is so inconsistent with a Charter right that it can no longer be justified (*Hill v Church of Scientology*).
- **'Government'** does not include universities (*Guelph* case). But a body, e.g. a private hospital, may be part of government if it is implementing a specific governmental policy or programme. Repeal of protective legislation may be 'government action' and attract government liability (*Dunmore case*).

Denmark

Written Constitution 1849, amended 1953. Human rights included in the Constitution. The ECHR was incorporated into Danish law in 1991. A dualist Nordic law system – a mix between a civil law system (codes and legislation) and a common law system (much law the result of judicial practice/case law).

Private sphere effect?

- Despite the fact that there is human rights protection in the Constitution, the courts have not relied on this to justify protection of human rights in the private sphere. Traditionally, the **protection of constitutional rights is considered a matter for politics**, and protection of **international human rights has been primarily a foreign policy matter.**
- Human rights protection rests on the Incorporation Act 1991 and the duty of all public authorities to interpret the law compatibly with international obligations.
- **Human rights protection in Denmark is largely due to legislation and the development of judicial practice.**
- The prevailing view is that human rights have **indirect rather than direct horizontal effect**.
- The interpretive approach is regarded as meaning that **international human rights have domestic applicability**.
- **Human rights are well protected by ordinary law**, in the public and private spheres, and horizontal effect of ordinary legislation has not been considered problematic.
- **All courts have jurisdiction** to deal with human rights issues. There is no public law private law divide.
- In many cases it is **difficult to distinguish horizontal from vertical effect. The main feature of a horizontal case is that A's interests or rights are affected by the implementation of B's human rights.**
- In balancing conflicting rights the courts are particularly concerned about **legal certainty**, i.e. the **foreseeability** of limitations of A's rights for the sake of B's rights and the question **whether the limits on either's right are prescribed by law**. Individual rights and interests may also coincide or clash with **public interests, thus making it difficult to distinguish horizontal from vertical effect**.

Examples from case law

The interaction between judicial and legislative implementation of international human rights: duties to provide information, the right to silence

- **A witness's right to silence** under Danish legislation to avoid self-incrimination prevails over a **claim by defendants in a criminal trial to hear the witness's evidence**, and this does not breach Article 6 ECHR. To the extent that this situation involves balancing conflicting interests it has a horizontal aspect.
- In **bankruptcy proceedings** the board members' **rights against self-incrimination prevail over their duty in Danish legislation to provide information** to the trustee to protect the property rights of creditors. **The right to silence was a fundamental right** in Danish law and the ECHR Article 6.
- In **competition law proceedings a physical or legal person's right to remain silent will not necessarily prevail over European law requirements that it provide information** in order to protect the rights of the competitors and the public interest.
- Implementation of the EU Enforcement Directive in Denmark provides for **the right to silence of alleged infringers of IP rights to prevail over the owner's property rights**.
- **Children may be compelled to give evidence against their mother** in a criminal trial in which she was charged with assaulting another child, and this was not regarded as a breach of ECHR **Article 8 or of the Convention on the Rights of the Child**.
- **Child victims** of crime may have their evidence videotaped, but the defence lawyer is entitled under Danish legislation to see the video and ask questions of the witness through the interviewer. If these rules are breached the use of the video as evidence will be restricted and a conviction based in part on the video may be quashed. **The fair trial right of the defendant is balanced, through legislation, with the child victim's rights**.
- **Resolution of indirect horizontal effect issues is fact-sensitive in each particular case**. In each such situation the balance is achieved pragmatically.

England and Wales

No written constitution. Human Rights Act 1998 – not entrenched. Dualist common law system.

Private sphere effect?

- **Most human rights are protected in ordinary law** by a combination of statutes and common law and equity developments.
- Additional protection is provided under the Human Rights Act 1998 which imposes an interpretive obligation and an obligation to develop the common law, both obligations creating **forms of indirect horizontal effect of rights under the ECHR**.
- Development of horizontal effect is largely the **responsibility of all courts** under the Human Rights Act. Practitioners rarely take horizontal effect points.
- Explicit reference is made in the (rather sparse) case law to the **ECHR** and to **values underlying human rights** such as dignity and autonomy.
- In the absence of a traditional public private divide the courts have been able to develop private sphere protection through development of the common law, importing concepts from 'public' law.

Examples from case law

Private life/freedom of the press

- Since the HRA **the tort of breach of confidence** has developed into a **right to the protection of private information**, through the development of the common law, but without giving direct horizontal effect to ECHR Article 8.
- **Balance of privacy and free speech** involves 'parallel analysis' in which neither trumps the other. But the weight given to **individual interests in health and psychological wellbeing and respect has tended to outbalance press freedom** unless the court is satisfied that a public interest in publication outweighs it.
- **A proportionality test**, weighing the interests of the two sides and public interests, is applied to achieve the balance.

Private life/right to a home/non-discrimination

- **Same-sex relationships and right to respect for private life and home** have been given recognition and status **through Convention compatible interpretation** of legislation regulating the landlord and tenant relationship, **thus implementing the positive obligation of the UK to secure the ECHR Article 8 right** to respect for private life and the **Article 14 right** not to be discriminated against.

France

Fifth Republic Constitution 1958. No bill of rights in the Constitution, but the 1789 Declaration of the Rights of Man and the Citizen and the Preamble to the 1946 Constitution are treated as sources for human rights protection. Monist, civil law system.

Private sphere effect?

- **Constitutional human rights protections have not been given direct horizontal effect** (save possibly in one Cour de cassation case) because of the limited role of the Conseil constitutionnel, the reluctance of the Cour de cassation to cite case law or refer to the Constitution in its decisions, and the tradition of a public/private law divide in France.
- Article 55 of the Constitution (the monist article) allows direct application of international treaties by French courts: this has led to the **direct horizontal effect of ECHR rights in France**, giving rise to the '**conventionalisation**' of private law. The jurisprudence of the Strasbourg court and the positive obligation of states to protect against violation of rights by private parties have led **French courts to apply the case law of the Strasbourg court directly**, and to **develop horizontal application indirectly (through interpretation) as well**. The Cour de cassation may set aside French legislation that is incompatible with a Treaty, including the ECHR. There remains, however, a fear of judge-made law.
- The focus in direct horizontal effect cases has been on **relationships where there are power inequalities**, for instance employer/employee, landlord/tenant, press/individual.

Examples from case law

Employment

- In unequal relationships such as employer/employee the stronger party may only restrict the weaker party's rights, e.g. to **decide where his family home shall be**, if he can show that this is necessary to protect the employer's legitimate interests and is proportionate. This raises issues as to the place of **proportionality** in such cases. If the court is founding its decision on the positive obligation of the state to protect rights in the private sphere (indirect horizontal effect), then the question is whether the state, or court, obligation is proportionate. If the decision is based on the direct horizontal effect of Convention rights, the question is one of balancing conflicting rights – a different form of proportionality. This approach also raises issues to do with the making and performance of contracts.

Landlord/tenant

- **A term in a tenancy agreement limiting the tenant's right to have family members living with him or her** is a breach of Article 8. However, the position of the landlord was not considered or balanced against the tenant in this case and no proportionality test was applied.

Property rights

- **A court order to a divorced wife to let out commercial premises to her husband** was quashed as a breach of her constitutionally protected property right. This may be seen as an example of indirect horizontal effect of a constitutional right. The real issue, however, was the divorce judge's misinterpretation of Article 285-1 of the Civil Code, which only protects the family home and not, as he had held, other adjacent land to which, the divorced husband claimed, Article 285-1 applied.

Privacy vs freedom of speech

- **An employer had breached an employee's privacy right when he accessed his private emails and then dismissed him for misconduct**. No proportionality test was applied, perhaps because of the employer's impropriety towards the employee.

- **Press invasion of privacy**. Before the ECHR the emphasis was on the right to privacy and the issue was whether the 'victim' of press intrusion had consented. Under the influence of the ECHR more importance than hitherto is given to the right of the Press and **the two rights under Articles 8 and 10 need to be balanced by a proportionality test**.

Dignity

- **Dignity is recognised as a constitutional principle which may also apply in the private sphere**: it limits the right of the press to photograph and report on accident victims. Contracts for dwarf throwings are unenforceable as infringing dignity, even if the parties agree to the terms. Dignity is a value that pervades the legal system. Article 6 of the Civil Code on 'ordre public' justifies limitations on freedom of contract in the name of the protection of dignity.

Freedom of conscience/religion

- **Jewish tenants complained that the electrical digicode installed by their landlord to control access to the premises** infringed their freedom of religion and of movement, as they were not permitted to use them on the Sabbath. They claimed the landlord had a positive obligation not to interfere with these rights. The Cour de cassation overruled the Court of appeal decision in favour of the tenants, holding that **such considerations cannot impose positive duties on the landlord** if they are not specified in the contract.

Germany

Basic Law (BL) 1949 includes Bill of Rights with usual civil and political rights plus equality of the sexes and protection against discrimination. It also provides for human dignity as a core constitutional value. The *Bundesverfassungsgericht* (BVG) or Constitutional Court has power to set aside legislation that is incompatible with the BL, which prevails over all other law, both pre- and post-1949, including the Civil Code of 1900 and the ECHR. Individuals have direct access to the BVG.

Private sphere effect?

- Rights bind the legislature, executive and judiciary. **No express provision for private sphere effect** except in relation to certain exercises of freedom of association and an exceptional right to resist attempts to abolish the constitutional order. These receive direct effect protection – *unmittelbare Drittwirkung*. The extent of this form of protection is limited because of concern to protect the autonomy of civil society.
- The BVG has also developed some indirect effect – *mittelbare Drittwirkung*. It has held that the **BL has a 'radiating effect'** and embodies a **'fundamental and objective system of values'.** The BL places the state under an obligation to protect human dignity and this justifies extending human rights protection to the private sphere. This is done through a form of indirect horizontal effect (*mittelbare Drittwirkung*). Law, including the Civil Code, must be interpreted compatibly with the BL. A law which breaches BL rights will be invalidated by the BVG.
- In order to protect the autonomy of civil society, there has to be a **balancing of the rights of both parties in a private dispute. The BVG will only exercise its protective jurisdiction if the infringement is substantial** and affects an important right, if damage is very likely and if the balance between the parties so indicates. Thus private sphere effect of human rights does not affect the normal operation of private law save in extreme circumstances, unless specifically provided for by a law. This is because of **concern about legal certainty**, since constitutional rights are imprecisely drafted and the judges may not be well equipped to extend rights protection into the private sphere.

- Academic commentary justifies private sphere effect on the ground that the state is under a **positive constitutional duty to protect human rights,** but is critical of interference with freedom of contract.

Examples from case law

- An employer dismissed an employee for distributing political pamphlets during working hours. The dismissal was upheld by the Federal Labour Court, but it was *held* that **the BL prohibition of discrimination on grounds of political views and the freedom of expression provision in the BL could place limits on the employer's rights under labour law**, in order to prevent very unreasonable exercise of private power. The decision thus acknowledges some **direct horizontal effect of BL rights**.
- Where an author criticised another for his involvement in the Nazi regime, he should not be restrained by the courts from future criticism to protect the financial interests of those he criticised. The **author's constitutional right to human personality and dignity**, which lie at the heart of the BL, should be protected via *mittelbare Drittwirkung*: *Luth* (1958).
- Publishing house A called for the boycotting of publishing house B's publications and threatened to end commercial relationships with newsagents who stocked B's publications. The BVG *held* that the **balance need not be in favour of A's free speech as against B's commercial interests, and indeed B's free speech rights entitled B to a remedy** which the lower courts had a positive obligation to provide: *Blinkfuer*.
- **Abortion**: when the rights of a pregnant woman and unborn child conflicted, the **state should protect the unborn child's right to life** except where the burden on the mother of continuing the pregnancy would be intolerable. The BVG set out a detailed scheme for constitutionally acceptable legislation which the legislature in due course complied with.

Greece

Written Constitution, most recently revised 2001. Contains many human rights provisions. Monist civil law system.

Private sphere effect?

- **Constitutional and other, e.g. international, human rights** expressly **'apply to the relations between individuals to which they are appropriate'** since the 2001 constitutional revision (Article 25(1) and section 3). However, the abstract nature of constitutional principles (they are not self-executing) is not adequate to found claims and remedies: **a link with private law is required to provide a conduit for the transfer of constitutional rights to the private sphere** since Article 25(1). In the absence of express provision Article 25(1) does not give judges the power to apply Constitutional rights horizontally and directly.
- The Article 25(1) principle is seen as an **objective (public policy) justification for private sphere protection, permeating the whole legal order**. Before this article was included in the Constitution, theoretical discussion centred around a number of themes: **'*Drittwirkung*', suggesting 'third party' effect, was rejected as implying that the individual in the private sphere was an outcast of the state-citizen relationship;** 'horizontal effect' or 'interpersonal effect' were preferred terms.
- **The addition of Article 25(1) has put an end to earlier theoretical discussion about the basis for human rights protection – whether it was or should be direct or indirect '*Drittwirkung*'**. In the theoretical debate, horizontal effect would be 'direct' if constitutional rights were enforced independently of existing private law so that the effect was 'law creative'. This would have been unacceptable: it would have been in breach of the separation of powers as understood in Greece, since it would have given the judge a legislative power and it would have undermined the power of the legislator to regulate interpersonal relations through private law.
- **An 'indirect' horizontal approach seemed more suited to the Greek legal system, involving the 'co-application' of constitutional rights and private law norms through a 'dialogue' between constitutional and private**

law. The courts have developed this approach through case law or *praxis*. This has produced a pragmatic and effective set of outcomes with elements of both direct and indirect horizontal effect.

- Links between constitutional norms and private law have been sought, through the **constitutional principles of human dignity** (Article 2(1)), the right to free development of **personality** (Article 5(1)) in the Constitution, and the **duty of the state to guarantee** protection of constitutional rights, as an expression of the rule of law (Article 25(1), section 1). The private sphere principle functions as a mediator facilitating the transfer of constitutional rights to private law. The courts do this in four ways:

  Article 281 of the Civil Code. The code includes **general clauses** of private law, e.g. the prohibition of the 'exercise of a right if it exceeds the limits of good faith or good usages or the social or economic scope of the right' (Article 281). This is seen as a reflection of constitutional principles and values, transferring them into the private law system. The courts give concrete effect to such clauses in line with constitutional rights, which thus enable them to develop private law (a law-creative or developmental function) so as to give private sphere protection to those rights. They enable the courts to balance situations where one individual's exercise of autonomy suppresses another's.

  Article 57 of the Civil Code. The code also includes rights such as the right to **personality** which have an interesting interrelationship with constitutional rights. Personality does not clearly protect privacy, data protection and protection of one's image. The courts have **developed** the Article 57 right by linking it to constitutional rights, e.g to respect for the environment, so as to include these elements in the right to personality. In such cases the issue is not whether protection of constitutional rights is direct or indirect but achieving a balance between the rights of the parties in a private sphere dispute and deciding whether both can be enjoyed equally or one should be preferred over the other.

  The Civil Code includes specific norms of private law. The courts **interpret** and/or **enforce** these norms according to principles deriving from constitutional rights (constitutionally orientated interpretation of private law norms). Unlike (a) and (b) above this process does not involve balancing of conflicting rights and interests, but **balancing private law norms and constitutional principles**, thus enabling the judge to avoid judicially reviewing private law norms and protecting the (presumedly constitutional) intentions of the legislator of private law. It is interpretive and/or developmental but if the latter it would be regarded as a form of 'direct' effect.

Constitutional rights 'beyond the law'. In the case of the constitutional prohibition on the **admissibility of unlawfully obtained evidence, the courts have decided in particular cases whether such evidence should be admitted, on the basis of a range of constitutional rights, including dignity,** privacy and freedom of communication as against the search for truth in trials and the right of defence. There has been no recourse to private law norms. **This is seen as a form of direct effect.** However, difficulties flow from the abstract and general nature of constitutional principles.

- These four approaches provide concrete effects for constitutional rights in private law instead of what would otherwise be abstract application. **They combine 'law creative' effect (which is regarded as direct) and hermeneutic or interpretive effect (which would be indirect) but avoiding the need to characterise the effect specifically in either category.**
- **The role of the judge is considered to be to act as 'mediator' of constitutional rights in private law.** This is part of his role in the separation of powers and not a breach of it, and of his duties of equal respect for the legislator and the Constitution and to give judicial protection to individuals. He must take into account the constitutional positions of parties, and justify in his decisions a refusal to protect their constitutional rights. He need not specify whether he is giving direct or indirect effect to them.

Examples from case law

Article 281 of the Civil Code

- **Employers' autonomy right** involves a right to 'manage' the enterprise, including dismissing employees. The civil courts have invoked the Article 281 (abusive enforcement of rights) to hold that the **employer's autonomy right is constrained by fundamental constitutional principles protecting personality and dignity** so that the employer must justify dismissal to the courts in terms of financial reasons or the need to preserve the viability of the enterprise or proportionality. Employees have rights, derived from the constitutional protection of personality, against unjustified decisions by employers. **Thus the courts have prevented dismissal on personal or political grounds**, or when they have been disproportionate to the management right. **This is not an example of 'indirect' effect but of the development of constitutional rights in private sphere disputes and a balancing process.**

Article 57 of the Civil Code

- **The protection of the cultural and natural environment,** protected as both a social and a civil right by Article 24(1) of the Constitution, can be an element of the **private right to personality** under the Civil Code. A monastic community at Meteora complained when a famous singer sang, danced and filmed inside the monastery in the presence of the monks and made and marketed a video to promote her CD. It was *held* the private law right to personality included respect for their natural and cultural environment. The courts found in favour of the monks **and prohibited the singer to use the photographic or videotaped material.** The case shows how **a collective constitutional interest such as the environment can acquire an individualistic dimension when combined with a private law right**.

Constitutional rights and specific private law norms – renunciation of paternity

- In the early 1980s the Civil Code was taken to mean that a **child born in wedlock was automatically recognised as the child of the mother's husband** and could not renounce the relationship if they were not in fact blood relations; only the legally acknowledged father could renounce the relationship under Articles 1471 and 1475 of the Civil Code. **More recently, the courts have decided that the constitutional protection of dignity, the constitutional and Civil Code right to personality and the constitutional protection of the family taken together mean that a child has the right to discover its true identity** as part of the right to personality. This approach is regarded in some

Greek theoretical literature as a form of 'direct' *Drittwirkung*, because it is seen to be law-creative, filling vacuums in the law, rather than interpretive. If this is the case it is a breach of the separation of powers as understood in Greece.

Use of unlawfully obtained evidence

- By Article 19(3) of the 2001 Constitutional revision, **use of some unlawfully obtained evidence is prohibited**. This includes evidence concerning the private sphere of the individual. This provision causes conflicts between constitutional principles outside private law – dignity, privacy, freedom of communication versus the search for truth in trials and the right of the individual to present evidence in support of their case to the court. Before the 2001 constitutional revision, the courts were balancing freely between constitutional provisions concerning the private sphere of the individual and the importance of the use of evidence for the search of truth permitting in general the use and submission of such evidence. After the constitutional revision of 2001, Article 19(3) has limited the way courts appreciate such cases in the opposite direction, thus in favouring the private sphere. Thereby, this article is interpreted in two ways: when it is applied to the criminal trial it is subject to limited exceptions, e.g., the interest in the protection of life and the presumption of innocence. On the other hand, when it is applied in the civil trial it is considered to protect the private sphere of the individual in an absolute manner. In those cases the **civil courts have brought into the balance the protection of dignity, the private sphere as providing a foundation for the enjoyment of freedom of communication between individuals.** This transforms a procedural issue about the admissibility of evidence into a substantive issue to do with rights. It is regarded as direct effect as it is independent of any private law norm and rests on Article 19(3) of the Constitution.

India

Written Constitution came into effect 1950. Contains many human rights provisions. Dualist *sui generis* variant of common law system.

Private sphere effect?

- **Fundamental human rights** (mostly civil and political rights) as set out in the Constitution and some of those set out in international treaties are **binding not only on the state but, depending on the text of the Constitution and its interpretation by the courts, also against private parties.**
- This is conceptualised as **liability for non-state action**, i.e. liability of non-state actors, the justification for this liability being that the state has failed to take steps to protect individuals from abuse or has connived at abuse, in which case the court may impose liability on the non-state actor.
- The Constitution contains judicially enforceable **fundamental rights**, as well as **Directive Principles of State Policy** and **Fundamental Duties.** The latter entail the idea that citizens should respect the rights of others.
- The history of India suggests **that serious threats to individuals' rights come from private parties more than from the state.** The spirit of the constitution is to promote the welfare of all and the courts have adopted this spirit in developing the effect of rights in the private sphere.
- **All courts have jurisdiction** to enforce the fundamental rights against all bodies, public or private.
- The Constitution's express provision for state liability for breach of some fundamental rights includes **a very broad definition of 'the state'**, which the courts have extended to include many bodies that would be regarded as private in other jurisdictions: bodies that are agents of the state including corporations, societies and other bodies: e.g., educational and research institutes, co-operative banks, electricity boards and private educational institutions (bound to respect a right to equality). But the **Board of Cricket Control has been held not to be an agency of the state**. **Courts are not, however, included in 'the state'** and the remedy for a judge's failure in judicial decisions to respect rights is the appeal.

- **The duty of the state to protect rights gives rise to liability of private parties, developed by the courts, for breaches of fundamental rights.**
- **In the Indian version of dualism and in support of the rule of law,** human rights protections in international instruments to which India is party, and in others, **can be enforced without legislative support as long as they are not inconsistent with Indian law.** Other treaty provisions do not have direct effect.
- There is **no public law/private law dichotomy** in India except in relation to the remedy of judicial review. Human rights theory in India requires the state to bring forward legislation to remove inequalities and indignities in the private as well as the public sphere.
- **Liberal Public Interest Litigation (PIL) rules** enable the rights of the poor to be judicially enforced against private bodies.
- **The Supreme Court may, and does, make recommendations and give directions to government as to how obligations to promote human rights should be fulfilled.**

Examples from case law

Equality

- Unreasonable **contractual clauses may be struck down** as infringing equality.
- **Sexual harassment** in the workplace is a breach of the right to gender equality and liberty, and a breach of international human rights norms. In PIL the court issued directions for both public and private employers as to how to protect the women's rights which would be binding until Parliament legislated on the matter.

Employment

- **Rights against forced labour and child labour** are enforced against private employers (and responsible state bodies) as being contrary to the right to dignity. Here directive principles may be enforced if they are recognised as falling within fundamental rights.

The right to life

- This includes **a right to health against private polluters** and distributors of injurious drugs or chemicals. In some cases the court directs the state to take measures to protect the rights.

Privacy, marriage, autonomy

- Where a person who is HIV (+) finds a planned marriage is called off because a hospital has disclosed his condition to his **bride, the right of the bride and the bridegroom have to be balanced.** The disclosure was not an unlawful breach of his privacy.

Environmental protection

- **Freedom from pollution** is part of the right to life and a leaseholder who had caused pollution had his lease cancelled by the court.

Untouchability and freedom of religion

- **Protection of untouchables** does not involve an unlawful interference with freedom of religion.
- Unfair **proselytising by Christians is a violation of freedom of conscience**.

Ireland

Written Constitution 1937. Human rights included in the Constitution and the European Court of Human Rights Act 2003 (the latter not entrenched). Dualist common law based system.

Private sphere effect?

- **Most rights are protected in ordinary law** by a combination of statutes and common law and equity.
- **Additional protection is provided under the Constitution,** including **express and implied (unenumerated) rights.** Express protection for personal rights such as equality, fair trial, liberty etc. and, since 1983, by constitutional amendment 'right to life of the unborn child'. Unenumerated personal rights include livelihood and privacy to communicate.
- The **European Court of Human Rights Act** 2003 provides additional protections via a **duty of compatible interpretation.** But there is **no duty on the courts to develop the common law** compatibly with the ECHR. There is as yet little case law on this.
- **Legal recognition is given to underlying constitutional values**, e.g. human dignity.
- Private sphere protection is conceptualised as **direct horizontal effect of Constitutional rights**, developed by the Supreme Court through awards of damages for the **'constitutional tort'.** This is based on the view that the Constitution is the foundational legal norm to which all other norms must conform. It is the courts' duty to provide protection.
- **No general distinction is made between public and private bodies.**
- Human rights issues may be raised before **all courts.**
- But the original **doctrine of direct horizontal effect is now subject to modifications**: it only applies if ordinary law provides plainly inadequate protection for the right or is manifestly deficient; unless that is the case it cannot be relied on to shape existing torts or adjust adjectival law, e.g. re the burden of proof; there is thus **resistance to indirect horizontal effect.** There is, however, case law where the courts have interpreted legislation so as to be compatible with constitutional rights, for instance trade union legislation.

- **Unclear** whether the **constitutional tort** is actionable per se or only on proof of damage, whether liability is strict, whether all constitutional rights are **actionable in the private sphere** (e.g., the equality clause), how the **balancing process** works in the private sphere where conflicting rights and interests are at stake.
- Modifications to direct horizontal effect in more recent case law reflect **a shift from natural law theory to a democratic approach**.
- **Ad hoc liberal judicial approach produces legal uncertainty** and untheorised and unresolved difficulties, e.g., in the anti-abortion cases, which seek to protect the right to life of the unborn child but impose liability on private actors who could not know they were acting unlawfully and were exercising freedoms to disseminate information etc. or also seek to balance the rights to life of the unborn child and the mother.

Examples from case law

- **Trade unions** – Strike in support of closed shop held to be contrary to express constitutional right to freedom of association: statute to the contrary disapplied and injunction granted.
- **Strike to force dismissal of female employees contrary to implied constitution right to earn a livelihood.** The legislation was **interpreted** so as to be compatible with the Constitution.
- Dismissal of employees refusing to sign new employment contracts **requiring union membership is a constitutional tort**.
- Trade union activity which closes down schools is a **breach of the pupils' right to education**.
- **Natural justice** requirements in private decision making.
- **Abortion** would be in breach of the unborn child's express constitutional right to life, and thus dissemination of information about abortion is restrainable. *The suicidal mother's right to life should be balanced against the unborn child's right.* The balance was in favour of the mother.

Israel

No written constitution, but a series of Basic Laws perceived as chapters in the future constitution. At present the 'Bill of Rights' is composed of two Basic Laws enacted in 1992: Human Dignity and Liberty, Freedom of Occupation. The former explicitly protects life, bodily integrity, dignity, property, personal liberty, movement and privacy. Freedom of speech, association, religion and conscience and equality are not explicitly included but courts tend to treat these rights as derivatives of human dignity. Courts claim jurisdiction to review primary legislation for compatibility with these Basic Laws.

Private sphere effect?

- Until recently, the **assumption, inspired by the liberal tradition, was that human rights only bound the state and other administrative authorities.**
- **Basic Laws protect many rights and this has affected the private sphere.**
- **Ordinary tort law has always been seen as protecting the most basic rights** – note concept of 'right' as not necessarily implying a specially protected status. Tort law is based on legislation but is inspired by common law tradition.
- **The tradition of an unwritten constitution as developed by the courts has long protected many of the usual rights, but until the enactment of the Basic Laws of 1992 the courts have not asserted a right to invalidate acts of the Parliament (Knesset). The two human rights Basic Laws were interpreted by the Supreme Court as empowering the courts to carry out judicial review of primary legislation.**
- The values implicit and explicit in the Basic Laws provide the framework for the development of the common law protection of human rights.
- **The effect of human rights in the private sphere is conceptualised as the constitutionalisation of private law** and the **constitutionalisation of human rights. For example, it affects the balancing process in tort law by increasing the weight given to constitutional rights in the balance.**

- **The common view is that human rights have indirect effect in the private sphere** as a result of the influence of Basic Laws leading to **rights-sympathetic interpretation of legislative terms** such as 'public policy', 'unlawfulness' and 'good faith', **development of the common law in line with the values in Basic Laws, and the balancing process** where rights conflict.
- Some judicial statements suggest **possible direct application of basic law** in some cases, e.g. where the right to life is at stake, but the development of **a separate 'constitutional law of torts' has been rejected so far because of concerns of overlap and conflict with ordinary tort law and the need to develop a new set of general doctrines such as causation, vicarious liability, remedies etc.**
- Courts refer to **values such as dignity, equality and non-discrimination in developing the law.**
- Care taken **by courts to balance conflicting private rights**, and rights and public interests.
- **Recognition of power of private actors** grew with privatisation – but the courts do not use this as a justification for effects in private law.
- **Development of judge-made, common law principles such as equality** inform judicial reasoning.
- **The courts are explicit about importance of rights for 'social values'** such as sex equality and not just to individuals.

Examples from case law

- **Contract** – The principle of public policy has enabled the courts to protect freedom of occupation, dignity, freedom to organise, access to courts, non-discrimination from contractual infringements.

- **Pre-contract** – arbitrary individual preferences permitted in the name of contractual autonomy. Group discrimination in pre-contract may be considered unlawful bad faith or even a tortious breach of the Basic Law right to human dignity, but there is no case law of the Supreme Court on this matter.
- Some statutory provisions prohibit **discrimination** and imply a tortious right not to be discriminated against. These are especially laws on employment and access to public services. Basic Law: Human Dignity and Liberty has inspired the legislation of some of these specific laws (for example regarding sexual harassment).
- **Tort** – traditionally, tort law has been perceived as protecting many human rights.
- The basic laws have indirectly influenced the development of tort law, for instance the courts refer to the importance of autonomy, but not through direct effect in the private sphere – **basic laws are probably too vague to give rise to a 'constitutional law of torts'** and direct effect would create problems in clashes between individual rights and social values. But the basic laws may provide residual basis for liability.
- The **Basic Law Human: Dignity and Liberty** has inspired the development of tortious liability for sexual harassment and unlawful discrimination.
- Tort of breach of statutory duty – **basic law right to dignity has not been applied so far as a basis for this cause of action. This may result also from the vagueness and generality of the duty implied by the Basic Law.**
- **Rights to damages for 'pure' losses** e.g. pecuniary and non-pecuniary losses, have been extended to provide **remedies for breach of right to dignity**.
- Rights have been developed to damages for loss of autonomy and dignity when **information has been withheld from a patient** making a decision.
- **Right to reputation is seen as an aspect of dignity but it does not trump free speech, even though free speech is not expressly protected in a Basic Law.**
- **Awards of compensation** for interference with dignity, autonomy and equality in tort law **have increased**.

Italy

Written Constitution 1948, as amended. Bill or Rights included in the Constitution. Monist civil law system.

Private sphere effect?

- The Constitution includes references to **values** and **principles** such as **dignity**, and **rights and freedoms, and lists most of the usual civil and political rights** (health, reputation, freedom of thought etc). The **Constitutional Court has elaborated on these and recognises constitutionally protected interests**. Inviolable rights do not include economic freedoms and the balance may fall in favour of social rights.
- The supremacy of the legislator is regarded as a **safeguard against judicial subjectivity**.
- The Constitution, since 2001, provides for the supremacy and direct application of **international conventions** once ratified. Before, subsequently enacted Italian laws were apt to impliedly repeal such provisions; this should not be the case any more, although scholars share different opinions and the Constitutional Court has not shed any light on this issue as yet. On the other hand, in most instances **courts will seek to interpret Italian law compatibly with international treaties.**
- **The Constitution makes no express provision for private sphere effect but the courts have developed it**. There is, however, not much case law and it is not a big issue since the ordinary law generally provides rights protection in accordance with the Constitution.
- All **courts may refer issues to the Constitutional Court** which decides upon the constitutionality of laws or their interpretation, rather than of particular decisions or acts. Ordinary courts may also interpret and apply laws in conformity with the Constitution.
- In private sphere cases the **courts normally seek to interpret laws compatibly with the Constitution – *mittelbare Drittwirking* or indirect effect** - but if there is a **lacuna in the law or they consider it necessary they may apply Constitutional rights directly – *unmittelbare Drittwirkung*.** The courts may also refer to **international treaties and the jurisprudence of international courts** in aid of their interpretation of ordinary law.

- Development of private sphere effect has been influenced by **judicial awareness of inequalities between private parties.**
- **Conflicts of rights cases have been seen by the ordinary courts to involve questions as to which right trumps another right, and these courts do not consider proportionality issues, which are the concern of the Constitutional Court.**

Examples from case law

Employment

- Non-unionised employees may rely **on the right to fair pay** under the Constitution in their claims to the benefit of terms and conditions agreed with employers by trade unions.
- Employees may enforce the Constitutional right to a **weekly day of rest and annual paid holidays** against private employers.
- Employers must protect their employees from bullying ('mobbing') and compensate them by virtue of the right to dignity under art. 2 of the Constitution.

Contract and tort law

- The courts have **developed new heads of non-economic loss or compensation for non-pecuniary damages** in both contract and tort law and may grant **injunctions** through interpretation of the Constitution and constitutionally compatible interpretation of the civil code: hence the **constitutional right to good health has given rise to awards of compensation** for interference with that right which was not formerly provided under the civil code as originally interpreted.

Freedom of political expression vs property rights

- Owners of a private shopping centre were ordered to permit political campaigners to distribute leaflets in the common areas, an example of ***unmittelbare Drittwirkung*** **– the free speech right trumping the property right.**

Freedom of expression vs religious freedom of association

- **Catholic church authorities' freedom of religion** entitles them to approve or not approve the appointment of teachers or their dismissal at private colleges despite the interference with their freedom that this involves.
- **Members of ideologically oriented associations are free to withdraw** from the association despite rules to the contrary of that association.

New Zealand

Unwritten constitution, but several important (unentrenched) constitutional statutes including Constitution Act 1986, Electoral Act 1993, New Zealand Bill of Rights Act 1990. Dualist common law system.

Private sphere effect?

- **The ordinary common law provides protection for most civil and political rights** and debate is in areas where there are **lacunae in protection.** Some of these lacunae have been filled by legislation, notably on discrimination.
- **The Bill of Rights Act 1990 (BORA) affirms but does not create rights**. It implements most rights in the ICCPR and other **human rights treaties**. It applies to acts done by 'the legislative, executive, or judicial branches …' and in respect of public functions.
- There **is no power in the courts to set aside rights incompatible legislation,** but a power to make declarations of inconsistency has been asserted. Judges are to **interpret statutes compatibly with the BORA.**
- Not much litigation so far but under the influence of the BORA and the international human rights treaties to which New Zealand is a party **some judicial re-evaluation of rights-reflecting balances is taking place.**
- **The BORA informs the common law: courts resolve cases in a BORA-consistent manner – referred to as 'indirect horizontality'** which is intrinsic to the legal system. Development takes place according to classic **common law reasoning which is taken itself to legitimate development. The BORA provides the language for debate** about whether development of the common law is necessary or possible, and the extent of any such development.
- Existing rights-limiting doctrines must pass the **reasonable limits test** in section 5 BORA, which has been treated as a version of proportionality.
- The courts **have taken international rights treaties into account** in developing the common law.
- **The legislature has taken the lead by passing 'rights promoting' legislation** for the private sphere in many areas. Employment law is infused with public law values, for instance.

- There is debate about **whether the BORA compels rights-consistent common law** or whether judges should only **apply the values of the BORA**; in practice the values approach seems to apply, **but there may be no practical difference in the outcome of either approach.**

Examples from case law

- **A common law tort of unreasonable invasion of privacy to fill a lacuna in the common law** has been developed on the basis (a) that it is required by international conventions, e.g. the ICCPR, but the limit on freedom of speech that this involves must be no more than a reasonable limit demonstrably justified in a free and democratic society and (b) that privacy is a BORA value which should inform the development of the common law and be given 'appropriate weight'. The common law should not develop so as to infringe rights. This is a form of **developmental indirect effect**.
- **The law of defamation has been developed to protect the freedom of speech of the press through a 'reasonable error' defence,** relying on substantive common law reasoning leading to the conclusion that such judicial development was appropriate rather than on the BORA to legitimate the development.
- In several cases **confidentiality of information has been recognised but decisions about the award of remedies have taken into account the defendant's freedom of expression** and public interests in the openness of court proceedings. Thus an injunction preventing the broadcast of a (private) confession to murder by a person acquitted of the offence was refused on the ground of 'legitimate public concern'.

South Africa

Written 'Final Constitution' 1996 includes an extensive Bill of Rights, protecting civil, political and socio-economic rights. Mixed system with common law, Roman Dutch law and customary law.

Private sphere effect?

- The Final Constitution (FC) 1996 makes express provision **for the direct horizontal effect of rights where applicable (section 8(2)(3) FC) and for indirect effect through interpretation of legislation and the development of common and customary law (section 39(2) FC).** In both cases the principle of proportionality will be taken into account.
- **The Constitution is the supreme law of the land and all law or conduct inconsistent with it is invalid**.
- All **court decisions are subject to human rights considerations**.
- The Constitutional Court has thus far left it to the Supreme Court **and other civil courts to develop and interpret private, including common, law so as to protect human rights in the private sphere, subject to a balancing, proportionality test.**
- **The judge is perceived as being a legitimate source of law**, a characteristic of common law systems.
- There has been **disagreement as to whether direct or indirect horizontal effect should be preferred** but in practice the outcomes of each approach are seen to be the same. The Constitutional Court has recently veered towards direct effect.

Examples from the case law

- In a **defamation case against a newspaper** the Constitutional Court held that the defendant could rely on the constitutional right to free speech: human rights had **indirect horizontal effect** via the duty of the courts under the interpretive rule in the Interim Constitution and their duty to develop the common law compatibly with human rights; some direct effect might also apply: *Du Plessis v Du Klerk* (a case under the Interim Constitution 1993).
- **Indirect effect is normally relied upon, but direct horizontal effect under the Final Constitution** has been invoked in a number of cases, including defamation and the freedom not to attend religious observance in private schools. In *Khumalo v Holomisa*, a defamation case, the Constitutional Court has applied human rights considerations directly.

Spain

Written Constitution 1978. Bill of Rights in Title I of the Constitution, especially Articles 14–38. Monist system, but treaty rights are not remediable unless also protected in the Constitution. Civil law system.

Private sphere effect?

- **Human rights are both objective and subjective rights.**
- **Although there is no express provision for horizontal effect in the Constitution, it establishes freedom, justice and equality as superior legal values.**
- The Constitution also provides that **citizens and public authorities are all subject to the Constitution**.
- **The Constitutional Court must guarantee respect for the constitution, including fundamental rights by, inter alia, private parties.** The public or private **nature of the alleged violator of a right is immaterial.** The jurisdiction of the Constitutional Court under the *recurso de amparo* to hear cases involving horizontal effect rests on the allegation that the *ordinario* court failed to fulfil its role in protecting rights: it is a supervisory jurisdiction. But this is not regarded as making the horizontal effect 'indirect', unlike the position in Germany.
- The effect of human rights in the private sphere is conceptualised as **direct horizontal application**.
- But there are differences between obligations on public authorities and private parties. E.g. **public authorities have positive obligations to respect the Constitution, while private parties have negative duties to abstain from violating the Constitution.**
- **Some rights apply equally in both private relationships and relationships with public bodies** (e.g. the right to strike), others only apply vertically, e.g. the right to a fair trial. When private rights clash they have to be balanced.
- The courts must interpret the rights set out in the Constitution compatibly with the international instruments to which Spain is party, but **a right recognised only in a treaty and not in the Spanish Constitution as interpreted by the Constitutional Court is not remediable.**

- **There are different categories of rights in the Constitution. 'Fundamental' rights** enjoy stronger procedural protection against repeal or amendment than **'constitutional' rights**. Much importance is attached to fact that neither set of rights requires implementing legislation, and to **the differences between the jurisdiction of the *ordinario* courts and the *recurso de amparo* in relation to rights.**
- **Only the Constitutional Court, to which such issues may be referred, may invalidate a law that is contrary to the Constitution.** Apart from that the *ordinario* courts have jurisdiction to hear challenges to decisions and actions in rights cases, and appeal lies from them to the *recurso de amparo*, in both vertical and horizontal effect human rights cases.
- **All courts must interpret laws so as to be compatible with the rights set out in the Constitution.** There are no separate specialised courts dealing with constitutional issues. This is different from the position in Germany where issues of human rights in the private sphere may not be referred to the Constitutional Court/*Bundesverfassungsgeright*.

Examples from case law

- **Employment law** – dismissal of a **worker for publicly criticising his employer** involved a balancing of the employee's constitutional right to freedom of expression against the employer's interests. The employee must act in good faith but was not subject to a generic duty of loyalty. His rights were only to be modified to the extent strictly necessary for the correct and efficient development of the employer's productive activity.
- Dismissal for legal exercise of a fundamental right would be unfair and unlawful.
- The burden lies on the employer to justify the restriction of an employee's right.

United States

Written Constitution 1787. Bill of Rights added to the Constitution by Constitutional Amendments 1791. Dualist system. All states have a common law system except Louisiana (civil law). Federal law is based on the text of the Constitution, statutes.

Private sphere effect?

- **The Constitution only proscribes 'state action' that breaches constitutional rights**. Individuals are not directly bound to honour constitutional rights. Some case law suggests that the fact that a court enforces a private right involves state action.
- **Some indirect horizontal effect or impact of constitutional rights on private persons does exist; e.g. if state responsibilities have been delegated to or assumed by private bodies,** if there was state involvement in private action, or statutory authority for or approval of infringements.
- There is **some strong indirect horizontal effect on the common law.**
- **The text of the Constitution is explicit that it is binding only on government and public authorities**. Individuals are not directly bound to honour constitutional rights as such.
- Complex and confusing area of law with strong dissents in some cases where state action was not found. **Strong resistance to horizontal effect** of constitutional rights in the absence of state action. But **some very artificial or strained**

reasoning trying to reconcile state action requirement with protection of constitutional rights in private relationships in, e.g., *Shelley v Kraemer* and *NYT v Sullivan*.

Examples from case law

- **A company town** may not ban the distribution of religious literature on its pavements (*Marsh v Alabama*).
- A **privately owned shopping mall** may forbid meetings and leafleting on its premises (*Hudgens v NLRB*).
- **Court enforcement of a breach of constitutional rights, e.g. a discriminatory restrictive covenant, may count as state action** thus giving rise to rights protection. (*Shelley v Kraemer*).
- **State common law or statutory rules, e.g. re libel laws, may be regarded as state action which** brings in the protection of constitutional rights. This approach has surfaced in **free speech** cases. It is strong indirect horizontal effect (*NYT v Sullivan*).
- Sale of goods under a lien does not amount to a breach of **due process** rights, even if there is statutory provision which could have, but did not, provide protection for the owner (*Flagg Bros v Brooks*).
- **Failure by social services to protect a child** from violence by a parent does not amount to state action (*DeShaney v Winnebago*).

European Convention on Human Rights

Private sphere effect?

- Procedures: By **Article 34** ECHR complaints may only be made to the ECHR about violations by the Contracting Parties, and not therefore by private parties – **state action doctrine**. But direct state responsibility extends to breaches by private parties in some instances, for instance if the body is exercising a public function.
- Even if the conduct complained of as a violation of a Convention right emanates from a purely private body, the state may be under a **positive obligation** under Article 1 to secure the claimant's rights, e.g. by a change in the law and/or compensation.
- The **'positive obligations'** doctrine developed by the European Court of Human Rights introduced **indirect horizontal effect** to the substantive provisions in the ECHR in the Contracting States. It recognises that **not only do states have negative obligations** not to interfere with rights, **but also obligations to secure that rights are effectively protected even against interference by private parties**.
- **The proportionality test is concerned with whether the state has been guilty of excessive inaction in failing to protect the right** in question, and is designed to achieve **a fair balance** between competing rights and public interests; the second para in Articles 8–11 will be relevant. States enjoy a **wide margin of appreciation here.**
- **The ECHR** has laid down principles for **balancing competing rights and public interests which in effect transpose the vertical process to the horizontal sphere**.
- The ECHR requires the courts of Contracting States to **interpret private law instruments (e.g. wills) compatibly with the Convention, which is a living instrument the interpretation of which may change over time.**
- The following **Convention rights have been extended to the private sphere: freedom of assembly and association, private and family life, right to property, and the unqualified rights to life, freedom from torture and expulsion, prohibition of slavery and forced labour, protection from unlawful detention.**

- In each instance **the state may be under obligations to provide protections against private interference, for instance by the provision of protective legislation and criminal and civil law enforcement measures.**

Examples from case law

Right to property/positive obligation

- **Houses destroyed by a landslide** caused by an explosion in a rubbish tip. The domestic court refused compensation. *Held* that the state should take positive measures of protection where there is a direct link between the measures which an applicant may legitimately expect from the authorities and his effective enjoyment of his possessions.

Private life/compatible interpretation of private law instruments

- A will provided that property could only be inherited by a son of a legitimate and canonical marriage. The domestic court held that this disqualified an adopted child. *Held*, the **will should be interpreted compatibly with Article 8.** An issue of interference with private and family life could only arise under the Convention if **the national courts' assessment of the facts or domestic law were manifestly unreasonable or arbitrary or blatantly inconsistent with the fundamental principles of the Convention.** There was nothing in the relevant will suggesting that the word '*son*' indicated only biological sons or that the testator intended to exclude adopted grandchildren from inheriting her property. In exercising its **European supervisory role, the Court could not remain passive where a national court's interpretation of a legal act appeared unreasonable, arbitrary or, as in the applicants' case, blatantly inconsistent with the prohibition of discrimination established by Article 14** and more broadly with the principles underlying the Convention. The domestic court's interpretation amounted to the judicial deprivation of an adopted child's inheritance rights. (But this approach interferes with the testator's rights, a point that led one judge to a dissenting opinion.)

Competing rights to privacy and free speech/balancing process

- *Von Hannover:* The press published photos of a public figure in an everyday situation. The domestic court refused an injunction for invasion of privacy on the ground that the public had a legitimate interest in the life of a public figure. *Held* that the respondent state did not fulfil its **obligation to secure the applicant's right to respect for her private life** and correspondence. There had consequently been a violation of Article 8. The domestic court **had not struck a fair balance** between the competing rights and the public interest. Photographs were a particularly objectionable intrusion into private life. The balancing of the two competing rights required consideration also of the **contribution that the published photographs and articles made to a debate of general interest, in this case none**. If there had been a **legitimate public interest in the information, it should yield to the claimant's right to privacy since she exercised no public function. She had a 'legitimate expectation' that her privacy would be protected by law.**
- *Craxi:* On the reporting of private conversations of public figures the Court *held* that **even public figures have the right to respect for their private lives** and conversations of a purely private nature should not have been published. **Publication by the press did not correspond to a pressing social need.** Therefore, the interference with the applicant's rights under Article 8 § 1 of the Convention **was not proportionate to the legitimate aims** which could have been pursued and was consequently **not 'necessary in a democratic society'.**

Right to protest vs property right/the balance

- *Appleby:* owner of **a private shopping mall** refused to allow the applicant to set up a stall and canvas political views. *Held*, freedom of expression was not unlimited. The property rights of the owner of the shopping centre also had to be taken into consideration. **If a bar on access to property were to result in the lack of any effective exercise of freedom of expression a positive obligation could arise for the state to protect the enjoyment of Convention rights by regulating property rights.** But the applicants had alternative means of communicating their views to the public. The Court did not find that the government had failed to comply with any positive obligation to protect the applicants' freedom of expression.

Positive obligations and qualified rights

Freedom of association and assembly

- **Where domestic legislation authorises interference with employees' freedom of association by employers, as in closed shop legislation, state responsibility is engaged.**
- The principle of positive obligations imposes a requirement on **state authorities to ensure that the participants in a peaceful demonstration are not subjected to physical violence by counter-demonstrators.**

Respect for family life

- The state will be under a positive obligation to **ensure that a parent is not deprived of contact with children by the other parent**.
- Where family life is disrupted by privately generated night time noise pollution, the **state may be liable for not enforcing noise reduction laws to protect the family.**

Positive obligations and unqualified rights

Right to life

- In addition to the obligation to implement preventive measures to ensure the protection of life within a state's jurisdiction, there is an additional **obligation to conduct an effective investigation into losses of life and punish private individuals** and other non-state actors that are found responsible.
- The ECHR imposes a duty on a state to **secure the right to life by putting in place effective criminal law provisions** to deter the commission of offences, backed up by law enforcement machinery for the prevention, suppression and punishment of breaches of such provisions.

Further Reading

Canada

Hogg, P., *Constitutional Law of Canada* (4th edn, Carswell, Toronto, 1997) ch 34.2

Sharpe, R. and Roach, K., *The Charter of Rights and Freedoms* (3rd edn, Irwin Law, Toronto, 2005) ch 6

Reichman, A., 'A *Charter*-Free Domain: In Defence of *Dolphin Delivery*' (2002) 35 *University of British Columbia Law Rev* 329 ff

Slattery, B., 'The *Charter's* Relevance to Private Litigation: Does *Dolphin Deliver?*' (1987) 32 *McGill Law Journal* 905 ff

Weinrib, L. and Weinrib, E., 'Constitutional Values and Private Law in Canada' in D. Friedmann and D. Barak-Erez (eds), *Human Rights in Private Law* (Hart, Oxford, 2001), pp 43 ff

Denmark

Dahl, B., Melchior, T. and Tamm, D. (eds), *Danish Law in a European Perspective* (GadJura, Copenhagen, 2002)

Gulmann, C., 'The position of international law within the Danish legal order' (1983) 52(3–4) *Nordisk tidskrift for international ret (Acta scandinavia juris gentium)* 45–52

Jensen, A., 'Incorporation of the European Convention Seen From a Danish Point of View' in L. A. Rehof and C. Gulmann (eds), *Human Rights in Domestic Law and Development Assistance Policies of the Nordic Countries* (Kluwer, Dordrecht, 1989), pp 161–70

Stenderup Jensen, S., *The European Convention on Human Rights in Scandinavian Law – A Case Law Study* (Jurist- og Økonomforbundets Forlag, Copenhagen, 1992) [Ph.d.-thesis describing Danish law prior to incorporation]

Commission Report No. 1220/1991 on the Incorporation of the European Convention for the Protection of Human Rights and Fundamental Freedoms in Danish Law [with a summary in English]

Commission Report No. 1407/2001 on the Incorporation of the Human Rights Conventions in Danish Law [with a summary in English]

England and wales

Bradley, A.W. and Ewing, K.D., *Constitutional and Administrative Law* (14th edn, Harlow, Pearson, 2006)

Feldman, D., *Civil Liberties and Human Rights in England and Wales* (2nd edn, Oxford, OUP, 2002)

Hunt, M., 'The "horizontal effect" of the Human Rights Act' [1998] *Public Law* 423 ff

Moreham, N.A., 'Privacy in the common law: A doctrinal and theoretical analysis' (2005) 121 *Law Quarterly Review* 629 ff

Phillipson, G., 'Transforming Breach of Confidence? Towards a Common Law Right of Privacy under the Human Rights Act' (2003) 66 *Modern Law Review* 726 ff

Tugendhat, M. and Christie, I., *The Law of Privacy and the Media* (Oxford, OUP, 2002)

France

Alkema, E.A., 'The Third Party Applicability or Drittwirkung of the European Convention on Human Rights in protecting Human Rights: the European Dimension' in F. Matscher and H. Petzold (eds), *Protecting Human Rights: The European Dimension* (*Studies in Honour of Gerard J. Wiarda*) (Cologne, Carl Heymanns Verlag, 1988), pp 33–45

Beardesley, J.-E., 'The Constitutional Council and Constitutional Liberties in France' (1972) *American Journal of Comparative Law* 431–52

Millns, S., 'Dwarf-throwing and Human Dignity: A French Perspective' (1996) 18(3) *Journal of Social Welfare and Family Law* 375 ff

Picard, E., 'The Right to Privacy in French Law' in B. Markesinis (ed.), *Protecting Privacy, The Clifford Chance Lectures, vol. 4* (Oxford, OUP, 1999), pp 49–79

Germany

Brinktrine, R., 'The Horizontal Effect of Human Rights in German Constitutional Law' (2001) 6 *European Human Rights Law Review* 421 ff

Currie, D., *The Constitution of the Federal Republic of Germany* (Chicago, University of Chicago Press, 1994)

Gardbaum, S., 'The "Horizontal Effect" of Constitutional Rights', (2003) 102(3) *Michigan Law Review* 387 ff

Lewan, K.M., 'The Significance of Constitutional Rights for Private Law: Theory and Practice in West Germany' (1968) 17 *International and Comparative Law Quarterly* 571 ff

Kommers, D.P., 'Germany: Balancing Rights and Duties' in J. Goldsworthy (ed.), *Interpreting Constitutions* (Oxford, OUP, 2006), pp 161 ff

Markesinis, B. and Unberath, H., *The German Law of Torts* (4th edn, Oxford, Hart, 2002), pp 406–7

Taylor, G., 'The Horizontal Effect of Human Rights, the German Model and its Applicability to Common Law Jurisdictions' (2002) 13 *King's College Law Journal* 187 ff

Quint, P.E., 'Free Speech and Private Law in German Constitutional Theory' (1989) 48 *Modern Law Review* 247 ff

Greece

Alivizatos, N. and Eleftheriadis, P., 'The Greek Constitutional Amendments of 2001' (2002) *South European Society & Politics* 63 ff

Anthopoulos, Ch., 'The "third party effect" (Drittwirkung) as constitutional Principle. An analysis of Art. 25 § 1 c of the Greek Constitution' (2005) *Revue Hellénique Des Droits De l' Homme* 707 ff

Eleftheriadis, P., 'Constitutional Reform and the Rule of Law in Greece' (2005) *West European Politics* 317 ff

Greek Constitutional Law and Practice (special issue) (1999) *Journal of Modern Greek Studies*

Ηλιοπούλου-Στράγγα Τ., 'Η θεωρία τηζ 'Τριτενέργειαζ' των ατομικών και κοινωνικών δικαιωμάτων' [Iliopoulou-Stragga, J., 'The 'Drittwirkung' of Individual and Social Right' (2001) *Greek Justice* 1527 ff]

Μανιτάκη Α., 'Η τριτενέργεια μια περιττή για την ελληνική έννομη τάξη έννοια' [Manitakis A., 'Drittwirkung, a concept needless for the Greek legal system] in J. Iliopoulou-Stragga (ed.), *Annals of Marangopoulos Human Rights Foundation* (Athens, Ant. N. Sakkoulas Publishers, 1991), pp 289 ff

Pollis, A., 'The State, the Law and Human Rights in Greece' (1987) *Human Rights Quarterly* 587 ff

Skouris, W., 'Constitutional Disputes and Judicial Review in Greece' in Chr. Landfried (ed.), *Constitutional Review and Legislation. An International Comparison* (Baden-Baden, Nomos, 1988), pp 177 ff

Tassopoulos, I.A., 'New trends in Greek contemporary constitutional theory: A comment on the interplay between reason and will' (2000) *Duke Journal of Comparative and International Law* 223 ff

India

Anand, A.S., 'Protection of human rights – Judicial obligation or judicial activism?' (1997) 11 (J.) 7 *Supreme Court Cases*

Austin, G., *The Indian Constitution: Cornerstone of a nation* (New Delhi, OUP, 1966)

Austin, G., *Working a democratic constitution. The Indian experience* (New Delhi, OUP, 1999)

Baxi, U., 'Taking suffering seriously: social action litigation in the Supreme Court of India' (1979–80) 8-9 *Delhi Law Review* 91 ff

Baxi, U., 'The Avtars of Indian judicial activism: exploration in the geographies of (in)justice' in S.K. Verma and Kusum (eds), *Fifty years of the Supreme Court of India: Its grasp and reach* (New Delhi, OUP, 2003), pp 156 ff

Chugh, A., 'Fundamental rights – vertical or horizontal?' (2005) 9 (J.) 7 *Supreme Court Cases*

Cunningham, C.D., 'Public interest litigation in the Indian Supreme Court: A study in the light of the American experience' (1987) 29 *Journal of Indian Law Institute* 494 ff

Jain, M.P., *Indian Constitutional Law* (5th edn, Nagpur, Wadhwa & Co, 2003)

Krishnaswamy, S., 'Horizontal Application of Fundamental Rights and State Action in India' in C. Raj Kumar and K. Chokalingam (eds), *Human Rights, Criminal Justice and Constitutional Empowerment* (New Delhi, OUP, 2006)

Rai, A.K., *Concept of State and Fundamental Rights* (Deep and Deep Publications, 1996)

Seervai, H.M., *Constitutional Law of India* (4th edn, Bombay, N.M. Tripathi, 1991/1996)
Sathe, S.P., *Judicial Activism in India* (New Delhi, OUP, 2002)
Singh, M.P., *V. N. Shukla's Constitution of India* (11th edn, Lucknow, Eastern Book Co, 2006)
Singh, M.P., 'Fundamental rights, state action and cricket in India' (2005) 13 *Asia Pacific Law Review* 203 ff
Singh, M.P., 'Human rights protection through public interest litigation in India' (1999) XLV *Indian Journal of Public Administration* 731 ff

Ireland

Binchy, W., 'Some Unanswered Questions in Irish Defamation Law', in J. Sarkin and W. Binchy (eds), *Human Rights, the Citizen and the State* (Dublin, Round Hall, 2001), pp 243–63
Butler, A.S., 'Constitutional Rights in Private Litigation: A Critique and Comparative Analysis' (1993) 22 *Anglo-American Law Review* 1 ff.
Forde, M., 'Who Can Remedy Human Rights Abuses? The "State Action" Question' in K.D. Ewing, C.A. Gearty and B.A. Hepple (eds), *Human Rights and Labour Law: Essays for Paul O'Higgins* (London, Mansell, 1994), pp 221–39
McMahon, B. and Binchy, W., *Law of Torts* (3rd edn, Dublin, Butterworths, 2000)
Murphy, R., 'The Incorporation of the ECHR into Irish Domestic Law' (2001) 6 *European Human Rights Law Review* 640 ff.
O'Cinneide, C., 'Taking Horizontal Effect Seriously: Private Law, Constitutional Rights and The European Convention on Human Rights' [2003] 4 *Hibernian Law Journal* 77–108
O'Dell, E., 'Does Defamation Value Free Expression? The Possible Influence of *New York Times v Sullivan* on Irish Law' (1990) 12 *Dublin University Law Journal* 50 ff.
Temple Lang, J., 'Private Law Aspects of the Irish Constitution' (1971) 6 *Irish Jurist* (n.s.) 237, 244–9

Israel

Barak, A., 'Constitutional Human Rights and Private Law' in D. Friedmann and D. Barak-Erez (eds), *Human Rights in Private Law* (Oxford, Hart, 2001), pp 13 ff

Barak-Erez, D., 'From an Unwritten to a Written Constitution: The Israeli Challenge in American Perspective' (1995) 26 *Columbia Human Rights Law Review* 309 ff

Gilead, I., 'Israeli Tort Law' in *International Encyclopedia of Laws* (The Hague, Kluwer, 2003), pp 19–28 and 37–9

Gilead, I., 'Constitutionalization of Tort Law? – an Israeli Perspective' in H. Koziol and J. Spier (eds), *Liber Amicorum Pierre Widmer* (Berlin, Springer, 2003), pp 99 ff

Gross, A.M., 'The Politics of Rights in Israeli Constitutional Law' (1998) 3 *Israel Studies* 80 ff

Raday, F., 'Privatising Human Rights and the Abuse of Power' (2000) 13 *Canadian Journal of Law and Jurisprudence* 103 ff

Italy

Blackburn, R. and Polakiewicz, J., *Fundamental Rights in Europe – The European Convention on Human Rights and its Member States, 1950–2000* (Oxford, OUP, 2001)

Cartabia, M., 'The multilevel protection of fundamental rights in Europe: the European pluralism and the need for a judicial dialogue' in C. Casonato (ed.), *The Protection of Fundamental Rights in Europe: Lessons from Canada* (Trento, Università degli studi di Trento, 2004)

Comandé, G. (ed.), *Diritto privato europeo e diritti fondamentali: saggi e ricerche* (Torino, Giappichelli, 2004), pp 7–14

Conforti, B., 'Community law and European Convention on Human Rights: a quest for coordination' in L.C. Vohrah et al. (eds), *Man's Inhumanity to Man* (The Hague, Kluwer, 2003)

Conforti, B. and Francioni, F., *Enforcing International Human Rights in Domestic Courts* (The Hague, Martinus Nijhoff, 1997)

Drzemczewski, A.Z., *European Human Rights Convention in Domestic Law: A Comparative Study* (Oxford, OUP, 1997)

Scovazzi, T., 'The Application by Italian Courts of Human Rights Treaty Law in Enforcing International Human Rights in Domestic Courts' in B. Conforti and F. Francioni, *Enforcing International Human Rights in Domestic Courts* (The Hague, Martinus Nijhoff, 1997).

Stone, A.S., *The Reception of the ECHR in the Member States: Guidelines for Project Participants* (www.rwi.unizh.ch/keller)

Valabrega, P.V., 'Invoking the European Convention on Human Rights in the Italian Supreme Criminal Court' (1995) *Finnish Yearbook of International Law* 279 ff

New Zealand

Butler, A.S., 'The New Zealand Bill of Rights and Private Common Law Litigation' [1991] *New Zealand Law Journal* 265 ff

Butler, A. and Butler, P., *The New Zealand Bill of Rights: A Commentary* (Wellington, Lexis Nexis, 2005)

Rishworth, P., Huscroft, G., Optican, S. and Mahoney, R., *The New Zealand Bill of Rights* (Oxford, OUP, 2003)

Geddis, A., 'The Horizontal Effects of the New Zealand Bill of Rights Act, as Applied in *Hosking v Runting*' [2004] *New Zealand Law Rev* 681 ff

South Africa

Currie, I. and Erasmus, G., *The Bill of Rights Handbook* (5th edn, Kenwyn, Juta and Co Ltd, 2005)

Davis, D., *Democracy and Deliberation* (1999)

De Waal, J., 'A Comparative Analysis of the Provisions of German Origin in the Interim Bill of Rights' (1995) *South African Journal on Human Rights* 1 ff

Gardbaum, S., 'The "Horizontal Effect" of Constitutional Rights' (2003) 102 *Michigan Law Review* 387 ff

Motala, Z. and Ramaphosa, C., *Constitutional Law* (Oxford, OUP, 2002)

Rautenbach, I.M. and Malherbe, E.F.J., *Constitutional Law* (4th edn, Durban, Butterworths, 2004)

Woolman, S., 'Limitations' in M. Chaskalson et al. (eds), *Constitutional Law of South Africa* (2nd edn, Original Service: 02-05)

Van Aswegen, A., 'The Implications of a Bill of Rights for the Law of Contract and Delict' (1995) *South African Journal on Human Rights* 50 ff

Van Aswegen, A., 'Policy considerations in the law of delict' (1993) *Tydskrif vir Hedendaagse Romeins-Holland Reg* 171 ff

Van der Vyver, J.D., 'The private sphere in constitutional litigation' (1994) *Tydskrif vir Hedendaagse Romeins-Holland Reg* 378 ff

Visser, P.J., 'The Relevance of the Bill of Rights in the Field of Delict' (1998) *Tydskrif vir die Suid-Afrikaanse Reg* 530 ff

Spain

(There is no literature in English on the topic in Spain.)

Bilbao Ubillos, J.M., *La eficacia de los derechos fundamentales frente a particulares: Análisis de la Jurisprudencia del Tribunal Constitutional*, Boletín Oficial del Estado y Centro de Estudios Constitucionales, Madrid, 1997

De la Quadra Salcedo y Fernández Castillo, T., *El recurso de amparo y los derechos fundamentales en las relaciones entre particulares,* Cívitas, Madrid, 1981

De Vega Garcia, P., 'Dificultades y problemas para la construcción de un constitucionalismo de la igualdad (El caso de la eficacia horizontal de los Derechos Fundamentales)', *Estudios de Derecho Constitucional y de Ciencia Politica Homenaje al Profesor Rodrigo Fernandez-Carvajal*, AA.VV. vol. I, Universidad de Murcia, Murcia, 1997, pp 729–45

Diez-Picazo, L.M., *Sistema de Derechos Fundamentales,* Thomson-Civitas, Madrid, 2005

Pérez Tremps, P., *El Recurso de Amparo,* Tirant Lo Blanch, Valencia, 2004

Pérez Tremps, P. (Coordinator), *La Reforma del Recurso de Amparo,* Tirant Lo Blanch, Valencia, 2004

García Torres, J. and Jimenez-Blanco, A., *Derechos fundamentales y relaciones entre particulares. La Drittwirkung en la jursiprudencia del Tribunal Constitucional,* Civitas, Madrid, 1996

Gutiérrez, I., 'Criterios de eficacia de los derecho fundamentales en las relaciones entre particulares' Teoria y reailded Constitutional no. 3 (1999) pp 193–211

Mijangos y Gonzales, J., *La vigencia de los derechos fundamentales en las relaciones entre particulares,* Porrúa, México, 2004

Naranjo de la Cruz, R., *Los límites de los derechos fundamentales en las relaciones entre particulares: la buena fe*, Boletín Oficial del Estado y Centro de Estudios Políticos y Constitucionales, Madrid, 2000

Pabón de Acuna, J.M., 'La llamada "Drittwirkung" de los derechos fundamentales', AA.VV.: *Poder Judicial*, vol. III, Instituto de Estudios Fiscales, Madrid, 1983, pp 2205–35

Venegas Grau, M., *Derechos fundamentales y Derecho Privado: Los derechos fundamentales en las relaciones entre particulares y el principi o de antonomia privada,* Marcial Pons, Madrid, 2004

United States

Black, C., '"State Action", Equal Protection, and California's Proposition 14' (1967) 81 *Harvard Law Review* 69 ff

Chemerinsky, E., 'Rethinking State Action' (1986) 80 *Northwestern University Law Review* 503 ff

Choper, J., 'Thoughts on State Action: The "Government Function" and "Power Theory" Approaches' [1979] *Washington University Law Quarterly* 757 ff

Gardbaum, S., 'The "Horizontal Effect" of Constitutional Rights' (2003) 102 *Michigan Law Review* 387 ff

Henkin, L., '*Shelley v Kraemer*: Notes for a Revised Opinion' (1962) 110 *University of Pennsylvania Law Review* 473 ff

Kay, R., 'The State Action Doctrine, The Public–Private Distinction, and the Independence of Constitutional Law' (1993) 10 *Constitutional Commentary* 329 ff

Marshall, W., 'Diluting Constitutional Rights: Rethinking "Rethinking State Action"' (1986) 80 *Northwestern University Law Review* 558 ff

Tribe, L.H., 'Refocusing the "State Action" Inquiry: Separating State Acts from State Actors' in *Constitutional Choices* (Cambridge, MA, Harvard University Press, 1985), pp 246 ff

European Convention

Alkema, E.A., 'The Third-Party Applicability or "Drittwirkung" of the ECHR' in F. Matscher and H. Petzold (eds), *Protecting Human Rights. The European Dimension (Studies in Honour of G.J. Wiarda)* (Cologne, Carl Heymans Verlag, 1988), pp 33 ff

Clapham, A., *Human Rights in the Private Sphere* (Oxford, Clarendon Press, 1993)

Clapham, A., 'The "*Drittwirkung*" of the Convention' in R. St. J. Macdonald et al. (eds), *The European System for the Protection of Human Rights* (Dordrecht, Martinus Nijhoff Publishers, 1993), pp 163 ff

Clapham, A., *Human Rights Obligations of Non-State Actors* (Oxford, OUP, 2006)

Drzemczewski, A., 'The European Human Rights Convention and Relations between Private Parties' (1979) 2 *Netherlands International Law Review* 168 ff

Garlicki, L., 'Relations between Private Actors and the European Convention on Human Rights' in A. Sajo and R. Utiz (eds), *The Constitution in Private Relations: Expanding Constitutionalism* (2005), pp 129 ff

Mowbray, A.R., *The Development of Positive Obligations under the European Convention on Human Rights by the European Court of Human Rights* (Oxford, Hart, 2004)

Starmer, K., 'Positive Obligations Under the Convention' in *Understanding Human Rights Principles* (Oxford/Portland, Oregon, Hart Publishing, 2001), pp 139 ff

General

Friedmann, D. and Barak-Erez, D., *Human Rights in Private Law* (Oxford, Hart, 2001)

Clapham, A., *Human Rights in the Private Sphere* (Oxford, OUP, 1993)

Clapham, A., *Human Rights Obligations of Non-State Actors* (Oxford, OUP, 2006)

The Authors of this Book

Christina Akrivopoulou (Greece)
PhD Candidate in Constitutional Law at the Aristotle University of Thessaloniki

Daphne Barak-Erez (Israel)
Professor of Law, Faculty of Law, Tel-Aviv University

Eric Barendt (United States and Canada)
Goodman Professor of Media Law, University College London

Jonas Christoffersen (Denmark)
Assistant Professor, University of Copenhagen

Chiara Favilli (Italy)
Lecturer in European Law, University of Florence

Jörg Fedtke (Germany and South Africa)
Reader in Comparative Law, University College London

Carlo Fusaro (Italy)
Professor in Public and Public Comparative Law, University of Florence

Israel Gilead (Israel)
Bora Laskin Professor of Law, Faculty of Law, Hebrew University of Jerusalem

Myriam Hunter-Henin (France)
Lecturer in French Law, University College London

Andrea Rodríguez Liboreiro (Spain)
Universidad Carlos III de Madrid

Colm O'Cinneide (Ireland)
Senior Lecturer, University College London

Dawn Oliver (England and Wales)
Professor of Public Law, University College London

Paul Rishworth (New Zealand)
Professor, Faculty of Law, University of Auckland

Mahendra P. Singh (India)
Vice-Chancellor, The W.B. National University of Juridical Sciences, Kolkata, India; formerly Professor of Law, University of Delhi, India.

Dean Spielmann (European Convention on Human Rights)
Judge of the European Court of Human Rights

Index

B

Balancing 18–19, 28, 51, 79, 90–91, 94, 96, 107–108, 111, 119, 133, 145–146, 149, 159, 160–161, 165, 172–173, 175, 177, 223, 255–257, 266–267, 273, 283, 306–307, 310–311, 359, 372, 375, 391, 417, 428, 433, 435, 440–443, 446, 464, 480, 485, 493, 505, 507–512, 522–523, 527, 529, 532, 534, 535, 540–542, 549, 551, 554, 556, 560

bodily integrity 237–238, 253–254, 266, 327–328, 541

C

Charter of Fundamental Rights of the European Union 57, 287

common law 11, 13, 20, 22, 24, 28, 63–64, 66–68, 70, 73–74, 77, 80, 82–83, 88–89, 91, 93–96, 162, 180, 184, 187, 189, 213, 216–218, 222–223, 236–243, 246, 249–251, 307, 314–317, 319, 321–325, 336–344, 346–350, 353, 355–356, 358–359, 361–370, 372, 373–377, 399, 401, 412, 415–421, 425–426, 468–470, 479, 482, 484–485, 487–488, 490–498, 500–501, 510, 516–17, 520–521, 542, 547–549, 552–553, 559–560, 564

Community law 63, 67, 70, 134, 154, 295, 303, 563

Comparative Analysis
- constitutional rights 467, 468, 472–474, 476, 479, 480, 482, 489, 491–493, 497, 498, 501, 504, 507, 509–510, 516, 518
- economic liberal theory 504
- governmental action doctrine 496
- *Hill v. Church of Scientology of Toronto and Manning* 496
- law of remedies 481, 493
- monist article 473, 479
- natural law theory 481, 504
- negative legislation 478
- reciprocal enforcement 479
- right to form associations 477
- social liberal theory 504
- *Soraya* case 482
- striking down 478
- tortfeasor 500

constitutional freedoms 101, 363

constitutional protection of rights 29

constitutional rights 6, 8, 14, 19, 29–30, 47, 68, 70, 102–103, 116, 128–130, 143, 146, 148–179, 213–231, 243–245, 256, 252, 259, 282–284, 286, 297, 299, 301–302, 308–311, 352, 356–360, 362, 365–368,

constitutional rights (*continued*) 371–373, 376, 381–383, 388, 391, 394, 395, 399, 400–405, 407–408, 411, 413, 414, 416–417, 425–426, 467, 468, 472–476, 479–487, 489, 491–493, 497–498, 501, 504, 507, 509–512, 516, 518, 522, 529, 531–534, 539–541, 551–553, 560, 562, 564, 566
constitutionalism 12, 181, 279, 287, 321–322, 360, 370, 429, 567
Convention against Torture and Other Cruel, Inhuman or Degrading Treatment or Punishment 288
Convention on the Elimination of all forms of Discrimination against Women 184, 200, 288
Convention on the Elimination of all forms of Racial Discrimination 288, 330
Convention on the Rights of the Child 69, 184, 203, 288, 331, 359, 523
criminal law 4, 31, 49, 51, 59, 100, 131–132, 138, 142–143, 303, 328, 332, 342, 455–458, 461–462, 557

D
Declaration of the Rights of Man and the Citizen of 1789 473
Denmark
  access to work 29
  Act on Chartered Accountants 53
  Act on Contracts 41
  Act on Parental Authority and Access 40
  Administration of Justice Act 40, 47, 53–54, 56, 58, 60
  agents 54
  arbitration clauses 49
  bankruptcy 54
  Bankruptcy Act 54
  closed shop agreement 34, 51
  collective bargaining agreement 51
  conflicting individual rights 28, 47, 62
  constitutional protection of property 30
  contract law 33, 40
  creditor 48, 54
  criminal and civil liability 47
  criminal procedural law 53
  debtor 48
  defamation 47
  defamatory statements 50
  diplomatic immunity 49
  distribution channels 58
  doctrine of non-recognition of direct horizontal effect 44
  domestic peace 50
  duty of interpretation 37
  duty of professional secrecy 51
  duty to give a witness statement 53
  duty to provide information 52, 54–56
  duty to provide information to the trustee of a bankrupt estate 54
  economic crime 53
  employees' place of prayer 50
  enforcement directive 56–58
  foreseeability 36–38, 45, 62
  fraud 54
  freedom of assembly 29–31
  freedom of association 29, 34–35, 49, 51
  freedom of expression 29–30, 34, 45–46, 48–50
  freedom of home and correspondence 29
  freedom of religion 29
  fundamental right 54, 57
  German border guards 46
  Incorporation Act 35–36, 38–39, 40–41, 44, 61
  incorporation of the ECHR 34–35

indecent exposure 60
independence of judges 29
indirect horizontal effect 34, 39, 40–41, 45, 60–61
intellectual property rights 56, 57–58
internal Danish law 32
interpretation of national law 35
judicial implementation of international obligations 33
judicial practice 27–28, 32, 40, 42, 48, 50, 53, 60
judicial restraint 28, 30
legal certainty 36–38, 39, 46, 55, 62
legislative implementation 32, 52, 61
municipal courts 32
national competition law 55
negative freedom of association 34, 49, 51
negative obligations 33, 45, 46, 61
non-discrimination 29
non-incorporated treaties 31, 49
non-press freedom of expression 50
parental access 49
parental authority 40–41
parliamentary committees 32
parliamentary scrutiny 32
paternity 40, 50
protection against self-incrimination 52–55, 58
protection in the internal market 56–57
protection of property 29, 30, 54, 57
public authority 45
public care of children 35
public figure 45
public interests 45, 47
public law regulation 48
public prosecutor 47
public-private law divide 33, 61
quasi-constitutional status 35
racially discriminatory speech 48
reasonable time requirement 42
reasonableness clause 41
retroactive affect 36
right of access to court 49
right of access to occupation 29
right to a public trial 29–30
right to custody 49
right to education 29
right to erect an antenna in open land 50
right to examine witnesses 53
right to personal liberty 29
right to personal life 51
right to remain silent 53–58
right to renounce membership of a trade union 51
right to wear religiously motivated headdress 50
seizure or provision of unedited tapes 51
special judicial review 50
spousal rape 47
Supreme Court 30, 32, 34–36, 49, 53–55, 58–60
temporal effect 60
tenants' right to mount satellite dishes in apartment buildings 50
trade union 50
trademark legislation 51
transfer of custody 50
vertical and horizontal obligations 52
violation of the ECHR 42
von Hannover case 45
Young, James and Webster v. the United Kingdom 34
direct effect 14–15, 27, 31, 38–41, 46, 61–62, 98, 103, 115, 127, 131, 139, 141–145, 152–153, 155–156, 159–160, 165–166, 169, 238, 242, 245,

direct effect (*continued*)
249–250, 256, 271, 275, 294, 301, 351–353, 357, 358–361, 363–368, 371–376, 388, 393, 464, 470, 472, 477–479, 481–491, 494, 496–498, 501, 505, 509, 516–518, 529, 532–535, 537, 542–544, 548–549
direct horizontal effect 34, 39, 40–41, 44–45, 60–61, 69, 71, 74, 76, 80, 88–89, 94–96, 213–215, 218–219, 223–224, 227, 229, 230–234, 236, 238–241, 243–247, 249, 251, 335, 352, 366, 388, 399, 400, 411, 421, 425, 428, 436, 479, 480–482, 484, 498, 501, 505, 508, 520, 522–527, 529–530, 532, 539– 540, 549, 552–554
doctrine of positive obligations 34, 104, 107, 435
dualism 184, 478, 537

E
environmental protection 206, 451, 538
environmental rights 4, 8
equality 7, 21, 123, 131–132, 138, 140, 151, 177, 182, 194, 198–200, 202, 209, 216, 230, 260–261, 563, 268, 273–275, 282, 298, 302–305, 333–334, 336, 349–350, 355, 360, 379, 382, 389, 392, 417, 421–422, 424, 469, 480–481, 486, 502, 512, 514, 518, 529, 537, 539, 540–543, 550
EU Charter of Fundamental Rights and Freedoms 19
European Community 24, 63, 67, 79
European Convention on Human Rights (ECHR)
A. v. United Kingdom 458, 459
Abdulaziz, Cabales and Balkandali 435
adopted child's inheritance rights 438
Ahmed v. Austria 460
Allard v. Sweden 451–452
Andorran High Court of Justice 437
Appleby case 445
Article 1 428, 430–434, 436–439, 441, 445, 447–448, 451, 453, 457, 459, 463
Article 3 428, 429, 458–461, 463
Article 4 461
Article 5 461–464
Article 8 433–435, 437, 439, 441, 443–446, 449, 450–451, 459, 463–464
Article 10 433, 441, 445
Article 13 432, 457
Article 17 432
Article 34 428–429, 430
Article 1 of Protocol No. 1 436–437, 439, 447, 451
Belgian Linguistics case 434
Calvelli and Ciglio 458
Caroline von Hannover 440, 442
corporal punishment 458, 459
Costello-Roberts v. the United Kingdom 463
Craxi (n° 2) 433
Cyprus v. Turkey 431
doctrine of positive obligations 433
duty to prevent unlawful interferences with the convention rights 436
duty to provide information and advice 436
duty to provide resources to individuals to ensure respect for their rights 436
duty to rescue 452, 457
duty to respond to breaches of Convention rights 436
expulsion 460
Florin Mihailescu v. Romania 429

forced labour 460
Fotopoulou v. Greece 452
freedom from torture or inhuman and degrading treatment 448, 458–459
freedom from slavery 460–461
rights to liberty and security 462
respect for private and family life 437
freedom of expression 427, 440–442, 446
freedom of assembly and association 447–448
freedom from discrimination 438
freedom of association 436, 447–449
gross negligence 453
HLR v. France 460
indirect third-party effect 439
inheritance 437–440
injunction 441
Karad ic v. Croatia 450
L.C.B. v. the United Kingdom 455, 463
M.C. v. Bulgaria 458, 461
Mahmut Kaya v. Turkey 453, 457
Marckx v. Belgium 434, 439
Menson 454
Moreno Gómez v. Spain 450–451
murder 453
Oneryildiz v. Turkey 436–437
Osman v. the United Kingdom 446
parental neglect 458
physical abuse 458
Pla and Puncernau v. Andorra 437–438
positive obligations doctrine 428, 433–434
Powell and Rayner 435
public figure 441–443
public function 430
public interest 433, 436, 440, 442–443, 445–446, 464
rape 458
reasonable chastisement 459
Rees v. the United Kingdom 445
right to education 434
rights to peaceful enjoyment of possessions 437
right to education 434
right to life 444, 452–453, 457–458
right to protection from unlawful detention 437
right to the peaceful enjoyment of possessions 437
rights of entry to private property 446
sexual assault 449
Sibson v. The United Kingdom 448
Siliadin v. France 460
slavery 460–461
Sørensen and Rasmussen v. Denmark 448
Sovtransavto Holding v. Ukraine 440, 447
Storck v. Germany 462
strict liability 431
Stubbings and Others v. the United Kingdom 459
third-party effect 428, 439
torture 444, 458, 459
ultra vires 431
Verliere case 446
Vermeire v. Belgium 439
von Hannover v. Germany 440–441
Worm v. Austria 443
Wos v. Poland 429
X and Y v. the Netherlands 459, 463
Young, James and Webster v. the United Kingdom 430, 447–448
European Convention on Human Rights and Fundamental Freedoms (ECHR) 7, 10, 14, 15, 24, 25, 29, 31, 32, 68, 69,

Freedoms (ECHR) (*continued*) 98, 104, 106, 112, 115, 123, 213, 215, 244, 245, 249, 286–288, 292, 431, 433, 435, 437, 439, 441, 443, 445, 447, 449, 451, 453, 455, 457, 459, 461, 463, 467, 469, 479, 490–492, 499, 501, 504, 507, 517, 554, 558, 559, 562–564, 567, 569
European Court of Human Rights 10, 14, 18, 22, 24, 36, 66, 70, 73, 75, 77, 81–82, 85–86, 90–91, 97, 104, 137, 177, 224, 250, 292, 296, 427, 439, 443, 451, 457, 479, 487, 504, 506–507, 513–514, 554, 567, 569
European Court of Justice (ECJ) 54

F
France
17 July 1970 Act 118
1946 Constitution 99
1958 Constitution 105
Act of 19 July 1881 on Freedom of the Press 118
administrative case law 113
Amar 121, 122
Buckley v. UK 111
censorship 105
Civil Code 101, 108, 115–118, 120–121
Code of Civil Procedure 101, 117
Conseil Constitutionnel 99, 100–105, 110, 119–120
Conseil d'Etat 102, 110, 119–120
consent 118
conventionalisation 103, 105
Cour de Cassation 100–111, 113–117, 119–120, 122
divorce 115
doctrine of frustration 124
European Convention 98, 103–106, 110, 112, 115, 117–119, 123
family interests 106
family status 113
foreseeability 122
good faith 108, 121
horizontal application of human rights 98–100, 103, 105, 107, 116, 120, 122, 123–124
immigration 113
insolvency 113
Jacques Vabre 105
landlord-tenant relationships 111
Labour Code 108, 110, 117
le respect de l'Autre 109
Mel Yedei 112–115
Nikon 117, 118
nuisance 113
Plon 119
positive duties 107, 122–123
pre-promulgation 99, 102
privacy and family life 106
privacy in the workplace 117
privacy rights 119
private individuals 98
private litigation 99, 101–103, 120, 123
property rights 114–116, 124
proportionality 106–108, 110, 113–115, 118–119
public action 98
public order 120
right to stay in commercial premises 116
social rights 99
Spileers 106, 110–111, 114
termination of the tenancy 112
family 78, 20, 23, 46, 65, 71, 72, 76, 77, 79, 83, 88, 106, 108–113, 115–117, 121, 123, 125, 129, 132, 133, 134, 138, 150, 159, 168, 173–175, 216, 235, 259, 327, 330–331, 412, 434, 437–438, 441, 443, 447, 449, 457, 462, 504, 512, 514–515, 518, 526, 527, 534, 554–555, 557, 559

freedom of assembly and association 8, 355, 447, 554
freedom of association 8, 12, 29, 34, 35, 49, 51, 127, 128, 216, 217, 221, 236, 257, 308, 311, 392, 423–424, 426, 436, 447–449, 529, 540, 546, 557
freedom of conscience 121, 208, 210, 286, 514–515, 528, 538
freedom of contract 19, 20, 120–124, 150, 154, 275, 418, 528, 530
freedom of expression 7, 8, 30, 34, 45–46, 48, 50, 74, 80, 81, 85, 86, 90–91, 119, 127, 131, 133, 139, 140, 161, 210, 259, 306–309, 326, 333–335, 337–339, 341, 350, 355, 362, 375, 392, 399, 416, 418–421, 425, 427, 440–442, 446, 493, 530, 546, 548, 556
freedom of religion 216, 257, 354
freedom of speech 13, 85, 95, 117–119, 123, 210, 257, 267, 273, 358, 400, 403, 405, 410–412, 415, 419, 421, 425, 493, 514, 521, 527, 541, 548
freedom of the press 18, 20, 80, 91, 94, 117–118, 120, 146, 450, 509, 512, 525
fundamental rights 19, 57, 98, 115, 125, 127, 135, 181–183, 195–196, 198–200, 202, 207, 211, 213–215, 218, 222, 226–227, 229, 241–245, 284, 286–287, 289, 295, 303–304, 357–358, 360–361, 364, 368, 370–371, 379, 388–391, 393–399, 433, 440, 475, 478, 536–537, 550–551, 561–563

G
Germany
  Adolf Süsterhenn 127
  advertisement 147, 152
  anti-discrimination 155
  banking 125, 134
  Blinkfüer 141, 145–146, 151
  bones mores 143
  Bundesgerichtshof 132
  Bundesverfassungsgericht 126, 132–137, 144–150, 152–153, 155–156; *see* Federal Constitutional Court
  burden of proof 154
  Bürgerliches Gesetzbuch 131
  Caroline von Monaco 147, 152
  Civil Code 131–132, 143, 147
  Constitution of Weimar 127, 151
  constitutional amendment 126–127
  constitutional control of state legislation 156
  constitutional council 127
  constitutional court 126, 129–131, 134–136, 143–146, 148–150, 152–153
  constitutional duty to protect the unborn child 146
  constitutional review 133, 148, 152
  constitutionalisation 153
  creditors 150
  criminal investigations 138
  criminal law 131–132, 138, 142–143
  direct effect 127, 131, 139, 142–143, 145, 152–153, 155–156
  division of powers 133, 150, 152–153
  Drittwirkung 125–128, 130–131, 133–134, 136, 139, 142, 146, 148, 152–153, 156
  duty of the state to protect individual private interests 150
  Dürig, Günter 143
  employment relationships 125, 128, 154
  equal treatment 154
  essential private interests 149

Germany (*continued*)
family law 125, 132, 134
Federal Constitutional Court 126, 129, 130–131, 133–136, 143–146, 148–150, 152–153, 173, 359, 441, 472, 474, 482, 486–487, 492, 499, 502, 510; *see* Bundesverfassungsgericht
Federal Labour Court 139–141, 155–156
freedom of expression 127, 131, 139–140
freedom of movement 138
fundamental values 140, 153
general law 144
good faith 143
horizontal interference 128
indirect effect 131, 141–143, 145, 153, 155–156
indirect application of human rights 128
individual constitutional complaint 135
injunction 142–145, 154
insurance contracts 154
invalidation of laws 152
inviolability of the home 138
judicial intervention 150–151
judicial restraint 146
judicial review 131
judicial scrutiny of legislation 152
labour law 131, 134–135, 139, 141–142, 149, 151–153
Lüth 129, 133, 139, 141
minimum level of protection 149–150, 152
natural and legal persons 127
Nipperdey, Hans Carl 139
objective value order 152
pain and suffering 154
personal financial security contracts 150
personality right 125, 131, 147
privacy of correspondence and telecommunications 138
private actors 127, 138
private autonomy 129, 131, 144–145
proportionality 130, 140, 142, 144, 149, 156
protection of economic activity 138
protective duty of the state 146
public authority 126–127, 129, 134–135, 138, 140–141, 143, 155
radiating effect of human rights 128, 141, 143, 147
restrictive interpretation 152
review powers 146
right to form associations 126
right to individual self-determination 131
right to participate in general, direct, free, equal, and secret elections 138
right to resist attempts to abolish the constitutional order 138
scrutiny of legislation 152
social justice 140
societal goods 150
Solange decisions 136
specialised constitutional review 133
supreme constitutional values 156
theory of protective duties 153
third party effect 158–159
Third Reich 128
Treaty of Maastricht decision 136
unconstitutional legislation 132, 135
undue limitation 145
Greece
abortion 179
abusive enforcement of rights 166, 168
admission of evidence 176
autonomy 167, 172, 175
bioethics 179

Caroline of Monaco decision 177
civil code166–169, 173
civil trials 175
constitutional amendment of 2001 175
constitutional charter 158
Constitutional Court 173, 179
constitutional norms 158, 167, 177
constitutional protection of the family and child 174
constitutional values 174
criminal acts 178
criminal proceedings 175
criminal trials 166, 175
direct and indirect Drittwirkung 157, 159, 163, 165
direct application of constitutional rights 162–163, 172, 177
discretion of the judge 164
division of powers 177
erga omnes effect of constitutional rights 162
European Convention of Human Rights 163 176
euthanasia 179
extortion 178
fair trial 175, 178
free development of personality 168, 174
freedom of communication 176
human dignity 158, 168, 170, 174, 176
innocence 175
interpersonal effect 158, 162–163, 165–166, 178–179
judicial protection 164, 165, 179
judicial review 160, 173
labour relations 160
legal ability of the child to renounce his father 173
legally acknowledged father 173
natural descendants 173
non-applicable rights 161
normative liberal constitution 167
paternity 166
power relationships 160–161
protection of personal data 170, 178
protection of the image 170
public figures 177
right of a child 174
right of personality 161, 169–171
right of the employer to manage his enterprise 167
right of the individual to present evidence 176
right to express the last will 178
right to personality 158, 166, 168, 170–171
secrecy of communication 175, 178
separation of powers 160, 164, 174
state-citizen relationship 158, 160
Supreme Administrative Court 176, 178
third party effect 158, 163
unlawfully obtained evidence 175, 178
wedlock 173

H
Harare Declaration of Human Rights 7
health 8–9, 18, 20, 67–68, 85, 88, 90, 95, 170, 204–206, 208, 233, 282, 298, 300–301, 319, 331, 355, 426, 449, 458, 468, 509, 511, 513, 515, 518, 538, 544, 545
healthy environment 8, 206, 355
horizontal effect 21, 27–34, 36–41, 43–49, 52–54, 58, 60–62, 65, 69–71, 74, 76–80, 87, 89, 94–96, 98, 158,

horizontal effect (*continued*) 162–163, 165, 213–219, 223–224, 227, 229, 230–236, 238–241, 243–247, 249, 250–251, 278, 335, 337, 352, 363–364, 366, 368, 376, 387–388, 391, 399, 400, 402, 411, 421, 425, 427–428, 430, 436, 440, 467, 469, 470, 474, 477, 479–480, 499, 500–502, 505, 507–508, 520, 522–527, 529–532, 539–540, 549, 550–554, 559–560, 562, 564, 566
human dignity 7, 13, 20, 119–123, 127–128, 131, 137, 140–141, 143, 158, 168, 170, 174, 176, 188, 202–203, 206, 208, 212, 221, 231, 253, 256–257, 259, 262, 264, 267–268, 272–273, 298, 354, 375, 469, 482–483, 503, 529, 532, 539, 541, 543, 559

I

India
- affirmative action 188, 200
- agency 190, 193–195
- *Ajay Hasia* v *Khalid Mujib* 193, 194, 199
- alienation of property 199
- *Apparel Export Promotion Council v. AK Chopra* 200
- *Ashok v Union of India* 204
- *Bandhua Mukti Morcha v Union of India* 186, 198, 203
- beggar 201
- bigamy 206
- *Bodhisattwa Gautam v Subhra Chakraborty* 207
- bona fide 198
- bonded labour 201, 203, 205
- Bonded Labour System (Abolition) Act 201, 204
- *Chairman Railway Board v Chandrima Das* 208
- checks and balances 181
- Child Labour (Prohibition and Regulation) Act 1986 203
- Chinnappa Reddy 197
- civil and political rights 181, 184, 211
- *Common Cause v Union of India* 205
- constitutional amendment 185
- constitutionalism 181
- corporation 193–194
- Delhi Development Authority (DDA) 201–202
- directive principles of state policy 181, 203
- equal protection 198, 200
- Equal Remuneration Act 1976 201–202
- executive act 185, 196
- forced labour 201, 202
- functions test 195
- fundamental right to gender equality 200
- hostile audience 210
- Immoral Traffic (Prevention) Act 201
- Industrial Disputes Act 1947 204
- International Labour Organisation 184
- J & K Registration of Societies Act 193
- judicial and non-judicial functions of the judiciary 195
- judicial enforcement 182
- judicial order 196
- judicial redress 198
- judicial review 185, 186, 196
- *Kahaosan Thangkhul v Simirei Shailei* 201
- kidnapping 208
- labour laws 201–203
- League of Nations 184
- liberalization 191–192
- Major Port Trust Act 194
- *MC Mehta Mehta v Union of India* 186, 194, 203–204, 207
- *MC Mehta v. Kamal Nath* 207
- Minimum Wages Act 201–202

N Adithyan v Travancore Devaswom Board 209
National Human Rights Commission 208
NHRC v State of Arunachal Pradesh 208
non-government companies 194
non-judicial determinations of the judiciary 197
non-state actors 188, 191
Parmanand Katara v Union of India 204
People's Union for Democratic Rights v. Union of India 201
Pradeep Kumar Biswas v. Indian Institute of Chemical Biology 195
private parties 183
privatization 191–192
Protection of Civil Rights Act 1955 209
public authorities 185, 210
public functions 193
public interest litigation 197, 199
public limited company 204
Ram Pal v. Maishi Lal Raj Kumar 203
rape 199, 207–208
reasonableness 199, 206
Regional Rural Banks Act 194
restitution of conjugal rights 206
Right to Information Act 2005 210
right to propagate one's religion 210
right to property 182, 189
right to safety 208
right to strike 204
Rural Banks Act 194
S. *Rangrajan v. P. Jagjivan Ram* 210
Sarla Mudgal v Union of India 206
sexual harassment 199–200, 208
slave trade 202
social action litigation 198
social and economic rights 181
state inaction 202
suffrage 211
supreme court 181–183, 185–186, 189, 192, 196–198, 200, 206, 208–209
Surya Narayan Choudhary v State 209
T. Sreetha v. T. Venkata Subbaiah 206
Tarun Bora v. State of Assam 208
temple entry laws 209
Town Planning Act 194
traffic in human beings 201–202
tribunals of limited jurisdiction 196
undue restriction 199
Union of India 183, 186, 190–191, 194–1196, 198–208, 211
universal adult franchise 181
Universal Declaration of Human Responsibilities 181
Vincent v Union of India 204
Vishaka v. State of Rajasthan 185, 199
writ proceedings 196
X v Hospital Z 205
Zee Telefilms Ltd v. Union of India 195
indirect effect 14–15, 27, 38–41, 46, 62, 115, 131–133, 145, 153, 155–156, 164–166, 169, 242, 249–250, 256, 271, 275, 352, 357, 359, 360, 363–364, 366–368, 372, 373, 375–376, 388, 470, 474, 477, 481–488, 469, 490–491, 494, 496, 498, 501, 505, 509, 516–518, 529, 533–534, 542, 548–549
indirect horizontal effect 34, 39, 40–41, 45, 60–61, 71, 74, 76, 80, 88, 94–96, 241, 243, 245,

indirect horizontal effect (*continued*)
247, 249, 335, 366, 400, 411, 421, 425, 428, 436, 480, 520, 523–524, 527, 529, 532, 539, 549, 552–554
International Convention on the Elimination of all forms of Racial Discrimination 184
International Convention on the Prevention and Punishment of the Crime of Genocide 184
International Covenant on Civil and Political Rights (ICCPR) 7 181
International Covenant on Economic Social and Political Rights 380
Ireland
abortion 215, 226, 232–236, 244
administration of justice 221
advisory group on defamation 242
annexation of state power 236
Attorney General (Society of the Protection of Unborn Children) v Open Door 226 Counselling and Dublin Well Woman Centre 226
Attorney General v Open Door Counselling 232
Attorney General v X 234
Byrne v Ireland 217
Carna Foods Ltd. v Eagle Star Insurance Co. Ltd. (Ireland) Ltd 236
catholic natural law theory 221
closed shop arrangement 217
Constitution Review Group 230, 241, 247
constitutional duty 218, 239, 241
constitutional entitlements 245
constitutional guarantees 221, 247
constitutional tort 214–215, 219–220, 222–224, 226–230, 232, 238–245, 249
contracting out 245
Conway v INTO 225
corporations 214
Crowley v Ireland 225
defamation 237, 242–243
discrimination 218, 223, 226–229, 232
Doyle v Croke 226
duty of care 238
education 216–217, 220, 222, 224–225
Educational Co. of Ireland v Fitzpatrick (No. 2) 217
European Court of Human Rights Act 2003 250
exemplary damages 225
fair trial 216, 221
Glover v BLN Ltd 219–220
habeas corpus *216*
Hanrahan v Merck Shape and Dohme 236
Hayes v Ireland 225
Hosford v John Murphy & Sons Ltd 239
Hunter v Blom–Cooper 243
Icon Clinical Research Ltd. v Tsourova 226
injunction 217–218, 226, 231, 233–234, 244
judicial activism 221
judicial interpretation 221
Kennedy v Ireland 232
legislative dereliction of duty 241
lex superior 228, 246
liberal democratic theory 248
liberal norms 248
liberal state theory 222
limited companies 221
locus standi 233, 244
Lovett v Grogan 226, 231
McDonnell v Ireland 239
McGee v Ireland 232

McGrath and O'Rourke v Trustees of Maynooth College 227
Meskell v CIE 219, 237
Murtagh Properties Ltd. v Cleary 216, 218, 222
natural justice 226
natural law 221–222, 247–248
negligence 237–238
nuisance 237
objective norms 217
organs of state 250
Constitution of 1922 215
personal rights 216, 218, 231, 233
plain inadequacy 238, 241–242
private individuals 214–215, 218–219, 226, 230, 244, 249
private law remedies 215, 242–244
public authorities 213, 219, 229, 245
public–private partnerships 245
rape 234
referendum 226, 233
religious discrimination 226
right to bodily integrity 238
right to communicate 216
right to disassociate 220
right to earn a livelihood 216, 218, 231
right to education 225
right to life of the unborn child 216, 226, 233–235
Rodgers v ITGWU 221, 226
royal prerogative 217, 223
rule of law 250
Ryan v Attorney General 216
S.P.U.C. (Ireland) Ltd. v Grogan (No. 1) 233
Schlegel v Corcoran 223
separation of powers 215, 231, 232, 248
Society for the Protection of the Unborn Child (S.P.U.C.) 233
state immunity 217
statute of limitations 239
subjective rights 217
supremacy of constitutional norms and values 223, 241
Supreme Court 217, 218–239, 242, 248
third–party violation of fundamental rights 244
tort liability 225
Trade Disputes Act 1904 225
Trade Disputes Act 1906 217
trespass to person or property 237
unenumerated constitutional rights 221
vertical state action 227
W v Ireland (No. 2) 238
X v Attorney General 226
X v Flynn and others 231
Israel
absolute and strict liability 254
AES case 258
alimony 260
assault 254, 272, 277
autonomy 259, 261, 266–267, 271–275
basic law: freedom of occupation 253, 256
basic baw: buman dignity and liberty. 253, 256, 266–267, 272–273
basic laws 252–253, 255–258, 262, 264–266, 269–271, 275
Beit Yules case 261
bill of rights 253
bodily integrity 253–254, 266
breach of statutory duty 254–264, 269, 270, 272–273
carelessness 264
causation 265
Civil Wrongs Ordinance [New Version] 254
Civil Wrongs Ordinance 254, 264, 269
collective bargaining 260–261
constitutionalization of private law 255

Israel (*continued*)
contract law 254–255, 257, 261, 263–264, 274–275
contractual autonomy 261
criminal harassment 274
criminal liability 268
criminal offenders 267
Da'aka case 265, 272, 274
damage 254, 264, 266–270, 272, 274
deceit 270
defamation 254–255, 264, 267, 270, 273
Defamation (Prohibition) Law 1965 255, 267
dependents 274
discrimination 260–263, 268
duty of a husband not to divorce his wife without consent 270
economic discrimination 262
employment law 263
exclusionary rules 270
false imprisonment 270
Frumer case 258
gender discrimination 268
good faith 256, 258, 261
Horn case 259
indecent acts 268
informed consent 271, 274
Israeli National Labor Court 258
Israeli Supreme Court 252, 255, 257–258, 261, 262, 264–265, 273
judicial presumption 274
judicial review 253
Kastenbaum case 256, 259
law of compensation 265, 266
law of remedies and defenses 265
legislative sovereignty 253
Levin case 260
loss of ability to become a parent 271
lost earnings 274
malicious prosecution 270
marital relations 273
mental anguish 254, 273–274
minor 257, 261, 274
multiplicity of liabilities 265
Na'amne case 262, 269
negligence 254, 264, 266–267, 270, 271–273
negligent misrepresentation 270
negligent prosecution and imprisonment 270
passing off 254
Patient's Rights Law 1996 270, 272
pre-contractual discrimination 262–263
private actors 255–256, 262, 266–267, 275
private nuisance 270
privatization 255
Prohibition of Discrimination in Products, Services and Entrance to Areas of
Entertainment and Public Areas Law 2000 263
Protection of Privacy Law 1981 254
protection of reputation 255, 272
public authorities 265, 267, 271
public figure 255, 272–273
public nuisance 254
public policy 254, 256, 260, 273
pure economic loss 270
pure losses – pecuniary and non-pecuniary 270
pure mental anguish 254
reasonable patient test 272
reputation 254–255, 264, 267, 272–273
rescission 262
right to engage in any occupation, profession or trade 253
right to free access to the courts 260

right to freely enter and leave the country 253
right to good reputation 267, 272
right to personal liberty 253
right to strike 260
separation of powers 265
sexual blackmail 268
Sexual Harassment Prevention Law 1998 268
Shamsian case 262
tender 261
Tenenbaum case 266
tort law 254, 257, 263, 265–267, 269–271, 273–275
tort liability 268–270, 273
tortfeasor 274
trade secrets 258
trespass 254, 264
ubi ius ibi remedium 266
uninformed consent 271
unmarried partners 274
vicarious liability 265
workers' right to organize 259
Yaniv case 259

Italy
absolute right 298
ad hoc law 289
administrative courts 279
allocation of powers 293
bill of rights 277, 283, 309
Charter of Fundamental Rights of the European Union 287
Charter of the Employees' Rights (*Statuto dei lavoratori*) 286
civil code 280–281, 298–301, 306, 309
civil law system 283
civil tribunals 297
Community law 284, 286–287, 293–295, 303
constitutional amendment 284, 289
Constitutional Assembly 292
Constitutional Court 276–278, 280–281, 283–284, 286, 289–298, 300–303, 307–311
constitutional entrenchment for international conventions 291
constitutional law 3/2001 292
constitutionalisation of international conventions 291
constitutionalism 279, 287
contractual freedom 299
Convention on Refugee Status (1951) 288
Council of State 300
Court of Auditors 279
criminal intent 302
criminal offence 300–301
direct application of international treaties and conventions 279
discrimination in labour relationships 298
ecclesiastical tribunals 308
ECJ Case 106/77 of 9 March 1978 – *Simmenthal* 295
ECJ Case 283/81 of 6 Oct. 1982 – *Cilfit* 295
ECJ Case 6/64 of 15 July 1964 – *Costa* 295
economic freedom 305, 310
employer's liability 398
employer-employee relationships 281
equality between men and women 298
erga omnes effect 307
European Convention on Human Rights 286–288, 292, 294–296, 300
European Social Charter 288
execution order 289, 292
executive agreements 293
financial compensation 299
free exercise of political rights 306
freedom of association 308, 311
freedom of correspondence 283

Italy (*continued*)
freedom of expression 306–309
ILO 288
individual constitutional complaint 278
international customary law 288– 289
inviolable rights 282–285, 301, 311
Italian Criminal Code 292
Italian Magistrates Association (ANM) 282
judicial review 276
judicial subjectivism 278
labour relations 281, 297–299, 302–303
Law 13 Oct. 1975 no. 654 on racial discrimination 303
Law 40/1998 (Legislative Decree 286/1998) 303
Law 903/1977 298
Law of 20 May 1970 no. 300 298
law of contract 282
legal persons 278
legislative decrees 304
liability clauses 300
minors 281, 298
multi-leveled constitutionalism 287
non-discrimination principle 305–306
non-economic loss 299, 302
non-pecuniary damages 299
ombudsman 279
parliamentary powers 293
personal domicile 283
personal freedom 283
political rights 284, 288, 292, 306
positivist approach 278
private parties 278, 282
private property 282, 305–307, 311
proportionality 282, 283
Protocol of 1967 288
race 283, 302, 304
reasonableness 283
religious freedom 308
reputation 285, 300, 302
right of a member to withdraw from an association 309
right of all associations to organise freely 309
right of doctors and nurses 286
right of religious denominations 308
right of workers 297
right to be heard in court and to have a fair trial 308
right to emigrate 285
right to enjoy a full sexual life 301
right to freely establish schools and educational institutions 308
right to good health 282, 292, 301
right to have a home 285
right to inform 283
right to one's name 285
right to one's own identity 285
right to one's reputation 285
right to sexual freedom 285, 301
rights of autonomous organisations 309
Second Optional Protocol to the Civil and Political Rights aiming at the Abolition of the Death Penalty (1989) 288
social security 297
spoiled holidays 302
stare decisis 307
sub-national (autonomous) jurisdictions 285
supremacy 279–280, 294, 301
Supreme Court of Cassation 280
theory of subjective public rights 280
third party effects 280, 282
UNESCO 288

United Nations 288
workers' rights 281
wrongful life 302

J
judge-made law 105, 106, 111, 264, 279, 361, 472, 517, 526, 542
judicial activity 5, 143, 149, 372, 485

L
legislative inactivity 492
liberal economic theory 9, 17
liberty 4, 8, 17, 29, 190, 192, 199–200, 208, 216, 242, 253, 256, 262, 266–270, 272–273, 317, 327, 334, 336, 349, 350, 385, 393, 401, 403, 413–414, 462–464, 507, 537, 539, 541, 543
life 4, 7–8, 20, 29, 45–46, 51–52, 58, 64, 71, 76, 81, 85, 88–89, 91–93, 106, 108, 110, 117, 123–124, 137, 140, 142, 146–147, 154, 158, 161, 168, 175, 177, 188, 190, 198–200, 203–208, 211, 216, 226, 233–235, 254, 266, 285, 301–302, 326, 328–329, 354, 359, 367, 389, 391, 401, 404, 413–414, 434, 436–438, 440–444, 447, 449–454, 456–458, 461, 464, 476, 511, 515, 525, 530, 535, 538–539, 540–542, 554–557

M
majoritarian theory of democracy 17
marriage 49, 65, 71–72, 77, 113, 138, 141, 173, 205–206, 331–332, 437, 511, 513, 515, 538, 555

N
natural person 283, 299
negative obligations 33, 45, 61, 107, 434, 435, 481, 554
New Zealand
acquittal 332, 344
administrative challenges 314
administrative decisions 347
age 312–350
anti-discrimination principle 331
apartheid 312, 321
arbitrary detention 315
assault 332
Attorney-General for England and Wales v Television New Zealand Ltd 344
autochthonous constitution 319
autonomy 314, 317, 327, 329, 336, 341
Bill of Rights 313–328, 331, 328–350
Canadian Charter of Rights and Freedoms 324, 327, 345
Carmichele v Minister of Safety and Security 340
censorship law 333–334
Civil Union Act 2004 331
Code of Patients Rights 331
commercial decisions 315
confession 343–344
Constitution Act 1986 318–319
constitutionalism 321–322
corporatisation 313
Crimes Act 1961 332
criminal and tort law 328
declarations of incompatibility 321–322, 326
defamation 328, 345
direct horizontality 314, 322, 340, 349
disability 330–331
discrimination 315, 326, 329, 330–331, 333–336
Duff v Communicado Ltd 342
education statutes 328
Electoral Act 1993 318
employment 319, 329, 330, 332–334, 336
Employment Relations Act 2000 332

New Zealand (*continued*)
 Equal Opportunities Tribunal 330
 fair play 333
 fair trial 326
 family law 331
 family status 330
 Films, Videos and Publications Classification Act 1993 333
 forced association 336
 freedom of expression 341–344, 347–348, 350
 good faith 313, 323, 333
 hate speech 334
 health and disability commissioner 331
 Hosking v Runting 313, 337, 347
 Human Rights Act 321, 326, 329–330, 334–335
 Human Rights Commission Act 1977 330
 Human Rights Committee 327, 329
 ICCPR Optional Protocol 327
 imperial statutes 318–319
 incompatibility 321–322, 326
 inconsistency 321, 326, 346–347
 incorporation 326
 indigenous issues 317
 indigenous jurisprudence 346
 indirect horizontality 314, 322, 340, 349
 information privacy 319
 injunctions 343
 intellectual property 343
 judicial branch 314, 316, 318, 322–325, 335, 338, 349
 judicial review 213, 315, 321, 322, 342
 Lange v Atkinson 335, 339, 345
 law of confidence 343
 legitimate public concern 344, 348
 liberty 317, 327, 334, 336, 341, 349–350
 limitations clauses 345
 Little Sisters Book and Art Emporium v Canada 344
 Living Word Distributors Ltd v Human Rights Action Group 334–335
 Maori institutional autonomy 317
 marital status 330
 Moonen v Film and Literature Board of Review 346
 natural and juristic persons 340
 natural justice 327, 332–334
 negative rights 329
 New York Times v Sullivan 339
 New Zealand Bill of Rights Act 1990 313–315, 318–320, 324, 335, 344
 New Zealand Constitution Act 1852 318
 New Zealand Constitution Amendment Act 1973 318
 non-adjudicative acts 325
 non-governmental bodies 313, 322
 Official Information Act 1982 331
 possession and enjoyment of property 327
 prior restraint 334, 344
 Privacy Act 1993 331
 privacy commissioner 331
 privatisation 313
 proceedings commissioner 330
 proportionality 346
 public functions 313, 316, 322, 335
 public interest 312–313, 346, 348
 public obligations 314
 public-private boundary 315
 Race Relations Act 1971 330
 reasonable limits clause 316, 327
 reputation 327–328

right to life 329
rights to education 328
rights-compliant common law 324, 366
same-sex couples 331, 349
search and seizure 335, 338
sexual orientation 330, 332, 334
Shelley v Kraemer 323, 341
sovereign legislative power 318
speech-restricting injunctions 343
Television New Zealand Ltd v Rogers 343
test of reasonable limits 346
Treaty of Waitangi 317
United Nations 326, 329
unwritten constitution 320
non–state bodies 16, 22, 215, 223

P
physical integrity 137, 146, 170, 285, 298, 391
political rights 3–4, 7, 8–10, 13, 15, 17, 29, 64–69, 138, 161, 181, 211, 284, 288, 292, 306, 325–326, 330, 355, 380, 368, 477, 478, 481, 529, 536, 544, 547
positive constitutional duties 148
positive obligations 14, 22, 33, 34, 37, 45, 52, 61, 69, 70, 73, 81, 104, 107, 210, 428, 431–436, 445–450, 457, 461, 464, 494, 504, 509, 527, 550, 554, 557, 567
principle of equality 151, 198, 259, 260, 261, 298, 302–304, 392
privacy 4, 7, 18–19, 64–65, 70, 72, 74, 76, 80–94, 96, 106, 117–119, 123, 138, 160, 170, 172, 175–178, 205–206, 216, 231–233, 253, 254, 329, 331, 337–338, 341, 344–345, 347–350, 354, 401, 415, 420, 427, 440, 443, 475, 482, 493–494, 498, 508–511, 513–515, 525, 527–528, 532, 535, 538–539, 541, 548, 556, 559
private law, constitutionalisation 22, 59, 153, 255, 267, 272, 291, 500, 509, 541
property 4–5, 19–20, 23, 28–30, 54, 56–58, 64–65, 71, 76–78, 114–116, 124, 138, 150–151, 169, 281–282, 305–307, 311, 327, 331, 343, 355, 381, 401, 407–409, 411–412, 433, 436–439, 445–446, 451–452, 468, 495, 512, 514–515, 523, 527, 541, 546, 554 556
proportionality 10, 12, 18, 79, 82, 91–92, 95, 106–108, 110, 113–115, 118–119, 130, 140, 142, 144, 149, 156, 168–169, 282–283, 346, 373, 474, 507–510, 525, 527–528, 533, 545, 549, 554
protection of the environment 170–171, 451
public law 11, 13, 21, 43, 48, 65, 70, 74, 100–103, 114, 139, 144, 185–186, 213–214, 218, 245–246, 255, 311, 314, 321, 332, 360, 489, 523–524, 537, 547, 559, 569

R
religious freedom 137, 206, 209, 308
right to a home 112, 114–117, 525
freedom of religion 29, 121, 123, 182, 208, 223, 257, 299, 335, 354, 403, 415, 513–514, 528, 546
Rome Statute on the International Criminal Court (1998) 288

S
separation of powers 20, 160, 164, 174, 215, 231–232, 248, 265, 471, 475, 503, 505, 517, 531, 533, 535

South Africa
access to courts 355
access to information 355, 374
African National Congress 351
anti-discrimination clauses 355
anti-discrimination laws 362
anti-horizontalists 352
apartheid 351, 352, 355, 361, 371
autonomy 361
Bank of British Columbia v *Canadian Broadcasting Corporation* 367
boni mores 367, 372
Certification Judgement 376
childrens' rights 355
classical liberal rights 354
Constitution of 1996 351, 371
right to just administrative action 355
Constitutional Assembly 352, 371–372
Constitutional Court 351–355, 359, 362–371, 373–376
customary law 356, 359, 366, 368, 370, 376
De Klerk and Another v Du Plessis and Others 362
death penalty 352, 368
defamation 352, 364, 366, 374–375
Democratic Party 357
direct horizontal effect 352, 366
division of powers 366
Dolphin Delivery 369
Du Plessis decision 352, 356, 364
European Convention on Human Rights 353
fairness 360, 367
Final Constitution of 1996 351, 371
freedom and security of the person 354
Gardener v Whitaker 363, 370
good faith 360, 365
health care 355
Holomisa v Argus Newspapers Limited 364
hybrid system 355
Interim Constitution of 1993 351, 356
interpretation clause 359
just administrative action 355, 374
Khumalo v Holomisa 375
Lüth decision 359
Multi-Party Negotiation Process 352
National Party 352, 371
natural or juristic persons 352
parliamentary sovereignty 354
right of access to information held by another person 374
right to a fair trial 372
right to basic education 355
right to citizenship 374
right to fair labour practices 355
right to just administrative action 355
rights of arrested, detained and accused persons 374
rights to housing 355
socio-economic rights 355
South African Communist Party 352, 358
South African Department of Foreign Affairs 365
South African Law Commission 359
Technical Committee on Fundamental Rights 352, 356–357
United Democratic Movement 375
Spain
abstract review 386
citizenship rights 381
Congress of Deputies 383
Constitutional Court 379–380, 382, 384–390, 393–394, 396–397

Crown Prosecution Service 387
declaration of unconstitutionality 394
deprivation of liberty 385
doctrine of direct effect 393
duty of loyalty 392
duty to respect fundamental
 rights 396
European Social Charter 380
Franco 378–379
freedom of establishment
 392–393
freedom to belong to a trade
 union 391
good faith 392
inter privatos relationships
 388, 397–398
interception of
 communications 385
majoritarianism 384
Ministerio Fiscal 387
multi-directional rights 391
natural or legal person 387
ordinario courts 382,
 387–388, 395
recourse of unconstitutionality
 384
recurso de amparo 382, 384,
 386–387, 390–391, 396–398
recurso de inconstitucionalidad
 387
right to be a conscientious
 objector 391
right to collective bargaining
 and freedom of enterprise 381
right to obtain a fair hearing
 391
right to one's image 393
right to petition 379
right to strike 391
right to use the Castilian
 language 379
right to work 381
rights affiliated to the principle
 of legality 391
rights to life and to physical
 integrity 391
social and economic policy
 381, 383
Spanish Constitution of 1978
 379
summary and preferential
 proceedings 395
state action 9, 14, 95, 107, 180,
 183, 187–188, 190, 195, 199,
 204, 206, 213–214, 217, 223,
 227, 235, 245, 247–248,
 322–323, 399, 400–412, 439,
 467–468, 471, 477, 489,
 493–496, 500, 502, 505, 507,
 512, 516, 536, 552–554,
 561–562, 566

T
Treaty Establishing a
 Constitution for Europe 287
Treaty on European Union of
 1993 287

U
UN Convention on the Rights of
 Children 40
United Kingdom
 A v. B and others 87, 90
 anti–discrimination 71
 assured tenancy 76–77
 autonomy 65–67, 74, 85,
 95–96
 balance of convenience 86
 balancing exercise 79, 91
 Bellinger v. Bellinger 71–72, 79
 best interests of the child 66
 breach of confidence 81–82,
 86–87
 *Campbell v. Mirror Group
 Newspapers Ltd* 89
 children's legislation 65
 civil and political rights 64–65,
 67–69
 commercial confidence 87
 common law 63–70, 73–74, 77,
 80, 82–83, 88–89, 91, 93–96
 compatible interpretation 68,
 72–73, 78, 94–95

United Kingdom (*continued*)
consent 66, 75, 83
constitutional statutes 67–68
constitutionalisation 69
consumer credit 71
convention rights 68–70, 72–75, 82, 87–89, 93, 97
conventionalization 69
damages 82, 86–88, 90–91, 94–95
declaration of incompatibility 71–72, 75
defamation 82, 84
defamatory publication 82
defences to breaches of privacy 82
developmental indirect horizontal effect 74
dignity 65–67, 74, 85, 90, 95–96
discretionary remedy 82
discrimination on grounds of sexual orientation 64, 78
dissemination of information 85
divorce 65
Douglas v. Hello! Ltd 64, 66, 70, 74, 85
duty of compatible interpretation 72
employment 65–67
equitable jurisdiction 82
equitable tort 83–84
equity 63, 65–66, 74, 83, 96
European Communities Act 1972 67
European Convention on Human Rights 63, 65–66, 68–69, 74, 83, 96
family law 65
family rights 77
First Protocol to the ECHR 71, 78
Fitzpatrick v. Sterling Housing Association Ltd 77
freedom 63, 64, 66, 74, 76, 80–81, 85–86, 88, 90–91, 93–96
freedom from inhuman and degrading treatment 89
fundamental constitutional rights 68
Ghaidan v Godin- Mendoza 73, 77
Gillick v. West Norfolk and Wisbech Area Health Authority 66
Human Rights Act 1998 64, 68–79, 80, 82–89, 91, 94–95
HRH The Princess of Wales v. MGN Newspapers Ltd 84
imbalance of power 67
implied repeal 67–68
inductive reasoning 96
injunctions 24, 85–86, 88–89
International Convention on the Rights of the Child 69
International Labour Organisation 68
Joint Committee on Human Rights 75
judicial declaration of incompatibility 71–72, 75
judicial development of the common law 74
Kaye v. Robertson 83–84, 94
landlord and tenant 71, 94
law of confidentiality 81, 92
law of persons 65
legitimate expectation 87, 92
legitimate interest 81, 85, 87, 92
liberties 63, 64–66, 83
life 64, 71, 76, 81, 83, 89, 91–93
malicious falsehood 84
marital rape exemption 66
marriage 65, 71–72, 77, 79
Matrimonial Causes Act 1973 72
McKennitt v. Ash 81, 83, 85, 91
non-constitutional statutes 68
nuisance 82
occupiers of land 82

parental rights 66
parliamentary sovereignty 64, 67, 69, 75
passing off 84
perjury 93
personal security 65
perverting the course of justice 93
policy considerations 95
possession 76–77, 84
Press Complaints Commission 80, 86
presumption of parity 82
Prince Albert v. Strange 83–84
principle of compatible interpretation 68, 95
privacy 64–65, 70, 72, 74, 76, 80–96
private bodies 64, 67, 69, 70, 80
privatisation of human rights 69
proportionality 79, 82, 91–92, 95
public authorities 69, 70–71
public interest groups 74
R. (on the application of Heather) v. Leonard Cheshire Foundation 73
R. v. R 66
rape 66
reasonable expectation 87–88, 90, 92–94
Rent Act 1977 71, 76–77
residual liberties 63
right to respect for the home 76
right to health and psychological welfare 85
right to own property 65
right to respect for private and family life, home and correspondence 76
right to the esteem and respect of other people 85
rights to life and security 88
same-sex partner 77–78
special status protection 64
spouse 76–79
statutory interpretation 65, 96
statutory tenant 76
supremacy of Parliament 63
Supreme Court 66
tenure 76, 78
Thoburn case 68
tortious rights 82
trespass 82, 84
trivial information 93
UK Gender Recognition Act 2004 72
Venables v. News Group Newspapers 85, 88
von Hannover v. Germany 70, 81, 86
Wilkinson. v. Kitzinger 71, 79
United Nations Convention on the Rights of the Child 459
United Nations Declaration of Human Rights of 1948 329
United States and Canada
14th Amendment 400–404, 406–407, 413, 425–426
15th Amendment 405
actual malice rule 420
bailor 412
Bell v Maryland 408
breach of contract 408
Burton v Wilmington Park Authority 406
Canadian Supreme Court 410, 420–421, 425–426
charitable trusts 409
Charter of Rights and Freedoms (1982) 399
Civil Rights Act of 1875 401
Civil Rights Act of 1964 415
civil war 399, 401
Claiborne Hardware case 411
Columbia Broadcasting System (CBS) v Democratic National Committee 406
commerce clause 415
company town 405
conspiracy 411

United States and Canada (*continued*)
- Constitution Act 1982 399, 416
- Constitution of California 407
- creditor 412
- criminal trespass 408
- cruel and unusual treatment or punishment 419
- *Dagenais v Canadian Broadcasting Corporation* (CBC) 418
- debtor 412
- declaratory judgement 408
- defamation 420
- defences of justification, fair comment and privilege 420
- *DeShaney v Winnebago Department* 413
- due process 400–401, 403–404, 406, 412–415, 426
- *Dunmore v Attorney General for Ontario* 423
- equal protection 401–404, 408–409, 415, 425
- equality rights 417, 421–422, 424
- *Evans v Abney* 409
- Federal Communications Commission (FCC) 406
- federalism 404
- freedom of association 423–424, 426
- freedom of contract 418
- *Hill v Church of Scientology of Toronto and Manning* 420
- interpretation of wills 409
- inter-state commerce 415
- Labour Relations Act 1995 423
- libel 410–411, 420–421, 425
- *Lugar v Edmondson Oil Co* 402
- malicious interference with business 411
- *McKinney v University of Guelph* 418, 421
- New York Commercial Code 412
- *New York Times v Sullivan* 402, 410, 420, 421
- privileges or immunities 401
- public function 405, 409, 412, 422, 426
- Quebec 418
- racial discrimination 401, 404, 406, 408
- racially discriminatory covenants 407
- *Reitman v Mulkey* 407
- *Retail, Wholesale and Development Store Union v Dolphin Delivery* 416, 419–420, 423
- right against self-incrimination 400
- right to a speedy and public trial 400
- right to a fair trial 399
- right to decline to sell or lease his property 407
- rights to reputati 412
- *Shelley v Kraemer* 402, 404, 408, 410, 417, 419
- state action doctrine 407, 414–415
- statutory lien 412
- Supreme Court 400–402, 405–406, 408–412, 414–422, 425–426
- testamentary freedom 409
- US Bill of Rights 418
- US Constitution 399, 402, 415, 425
- US First Amendment 419
- voting rights 405

Printed in the United States
200490BV00011B/1/A